CHINA IN THE SIXTEENTH CENTURY:

The Journals of Matthew Ricci: 1583-1610

Louis J. Gallagher S.J.

Copper engraving of the XVIIth Century. (*The Bettmann Archive*)

Left: Matthew Ricci, S. J. (1552-1610) Founder of the first Christian missions in China.

Right: Li Paul, Mandarin Colao, prominent convert and champion of the faith.

CHINA IN THE SIXTEENTH CENTURY: The Journals of Matthew Ricci: 1583-1610

Translated from the Latin by
LOUIS J. GALLAGHER, S.J.

With a Foreword by
RICHARD J. CUSHING, D.D., LL.D.
Archbishop of Boston

 Random House · New York

IMPRIMI POTEST: William E. FitzGerald, S.J., Provincial, Province of New England.

NIHIL OBSTAT: John J. Consodine, Diocesan Censor.

IMPRIMATUR: ✠ Richard J. Cushing, Archbishop of Boston.

May 5th, 1953.

CONTENTS

Book Three

Book Four

Book Five

FOREWORD

WHEN AN ASTRONOMER discovers a new star, he reveals new light of age-old existence, hitherto probably observed by others but not recognized as a new and a valuable contribution to the science of astronomy and to the knowledge of the world. A similar satisfaction must follow for the archivist who reveals a document previously known to exist but unrecognized for the light it sheds upon past experience and into future research; light of which a large portion of the reading world had been deprived for centuries. The Ricci Diary is just such a document. One of the world's greatest missionary records, it now appears for the first time to the English reading world, disclosing startling historic and geographic revelations, a reliable directive not only for missionary methods but also for the proper manner of treating with the Chinese people. Its appearance is also very timely, coming as it does at the beginning of a crucial period of international relations, as well as of missionary history.

Both China and Japan have experienced a founding of Christianity which was all but eradicated on several occasions by anti-Christian persecutions, following war and revolution, and subsequent to international conflict for control of Far Eastern trade. Shortly after the Portuguese were permitted to establish their first trading-post with the Chinese at Macao, in 1557, the first Chinese converts were taught the Portuguese language, given Portuguese names and instructed to conform to the way of living of the foreign colonists. It was not until the arrival of a Visitor General of the Society of Jesus, Father Alexander Valignano, known as another Xavier and called The Father of the Missions of the Far East, that the Jesuits decided to turn Chinese rather than attempt to convert the Celestial Kingdom by changing its millions into Portuguese and Italians. Father Valignano established a Chinese parish at Macao and then sent to India for three Jesuits who were known to have a reputation for acquiring Eastern languages as well as for zealous and untiring labor. Father Francesco Pasio took over the temporal and administrative affairs of the mission. Fathers Michael Ruggieri and Matthew Ricci became masters of the Chinese language, and together with Father Valignano were the first universally known Jesuit missionaries in China.

The Ricci method of converting the pagan is reminiscent of Christ among the Doctors in the temple and of Paul in the midst of the learned Greeks on the Acropolis. What Xavier experienced in Japan Ricci encountered in China, though the ultimate results of opposition to their labors were far more drastic in the island kingdom than on the continent. After several futile attempts to enter the secluded kingdom, Ricci finally gained a foothold on the forbidden soil, and his influence on the educated classes of China, over a period of twenty-seven years, resulted in a permanent foundation of Christianity. How he and his pioneering companions overcame the seemingly insurmountable material and intellectual barriers separating them from the imperial court, from the mental attitude of the Chinese philosophers, and from the interest and devotion of the Chinese people, is described in graphic detail in Trigault's narrative of the Ricci Diary.

The destruction of Catholic Missions during the two great world wars was nowhere more keenly felt than in Japan and China. With this destruction, however, the dominance of an enlightened paganism may well be fading into oblivion before the rising of a new day of Christian splendor. The dawn of this day means the beginning of a new missionary era. The material foundations of the Chinese Christian Missions may be piled up in the waste of war, in the rubble of revolution and in the clutter of Communism, but the indestructible spiritual basis of the Christian way of life, to which the Chinese took so readily, was too solidly set by Ricci and his companions to be eradicated by the seismic disturbances of human instability. The doctrine they taught is founded upon the irremovable rock of Peter on which the enduring stability of Christianity in China and elsewhere must inevitably rest.

Ricci's great rediscovered document should serve as a source of enlightenment for the mission minded. It will also reveal to the world in general more than a few of the secrets of the Chinese mind which render this great people so amenable to the grace of God.

Richard J. Cushing, DD., LL.D.
Archbishop of Boston

TRIGAULT, TO THE READER

My dear genial reader:

I have not taken up this book, which appeared after the death of Father Matthew Ricci, with any intention of claiming that it is an original work of mine, but rather to acquaint you with its true and original author. The following discourse is made up almost entirely of his activities, and of the manner in which he, more than any other, courageously executed the original design of this expedition, and labored with determination to develop it, to the very end of his days.

Father Matthew Ricci was born in Macerata, in the March of Ancona, Italy, in 1552, on the 16th of October. Here, too, he began his studies under Father Niccolo Benivegni, a secular priest who afterwards entered the Society of Jesus. Later on he pursued higher studies with distinction, at the Jesuit College of that district. At the age of seventeen, his father sent him to Rome, to continue his education. He studied law for three years, and though occupied during this time, by order of his father, with studies not too intimately connected with a religious vocation, he continued in Rome to cultivate the spirit he had absorbed, and to favor the inclination he had developed, during his acquaintance with Fathers at Macerata. It was there that he became a member of the Sodality of the Blessed Virgin, and regulated his life according to its rules, under the direction of its reverend prefect. Harkening to the call of a religious vocation, he asked for admittance into the Society of Jesus, toward which he had felt an inclination from the days of his youth. He was received into the Society in Rome, by Father Giovanni Polanco, who was taking the place of the General of the Society, Father Francis Borgia, then on visitation in Spain. Ricci entered the Society on the feast of the Assumption, August 15th, 1571, and knowing that his father had other designs in mind for him, he sent home a letter, asking for his father's approval of the step he had taken. This letter so surprised his parent, that he immediately set out for Rome, with the avowed intention of withdrawing his son from the Jesuit novitiate. En route to Rome, he fell sick at Tolentino, on the first day of his journey, and being persuaded that his illness was a visitation from heaven, he returned to his home and sent his son a letter, stating that the resolution he had taken was quite reasonable, and evidently in keeping with the holy will of God.

Matthew Ricci's Novice-Master was Father Alexander Valignano, who was afterwards to become famous for his masterly direction of the Society of Jesus in India, in Japan and in China. Until 1577, Ricci pursued his studies in Philosophy and Theology at the Jesuit College in Rome. During that year Father Martino a Sylva, Procurator of the East India Mission, arrived at Rome from India, and with his assistance Matthew and several of his Jesuit colleagues obtained permission from Father Everardo Mercuriano, Fourth General of the Society, to join the India Mission. On his way from Rome to Genoa, to take passage for Spain, he could not be persuaded to visit his people at Macerata, nor even to make a detour to that town, to visit the famous church of Our Lady of Loretto. He and his companions received the blessing of Pope Gregory the Thirteenth, and then left straightway for Portugal. They spent the greater part of that year at Coimbra, after discovering that the India trading ships had already departed, and during the following year they went to Lisbon, to embark for India.

Let us here insert what Ricci often recounted, with great satisfaction, about Sebastian, the King of Portugal, who was so solicitous about his charges. When they went to visit him, to pay their respects, the Father Procurator told him that all of those who had come with him from Italy were noblemen, some of them from very distinguished families, and all desirous to convert the Indies and to promote the cause of Portugal. Among them was Rudolph Aquaviva, of distinguished birth but more celebrated, later, as a martyr, Nicola Spinola, Francesco Pasio, Michele Ruggieri, and Matthew Ricci, of whom we are now writing; each of them celebrated for holiness of life and for the offices he held in the Society of Jesus. They say the King replied to the Father Procurator, "How can I ever be sufficiently grateful to the Father General of the Order, for so much help for the Indies?" The good prince knew well that the Society was made up of subjects of different nationalities, united under the banner of Christ.

They left Portugal in a ship named after Saint Louis, and arrived in Goa, in India, on the 13th day of September, 1578. Ricci remained in India for four years, completing his course in Theology, acting as

Professor of Rhetoric, at Goa and at Cochin, and preparing for greater undertakings. He was assigned to the China Mission by the official Visitor of the Society of Jesus. After almost thirty years of labor and of successful government of the China Mission, realizing that his time was coming to an end, he undertook to record the beginnings of this Mission in an orderly commentary, and thus to furnish some future writer with material prepared for the Mission annals. There were many incidents for recording which no one, other than he himself, could have recovered from the obscurity of early pioneering, because he was the only one involved in them. He had almost completed his commentaries a few months, or rather a few days, before his death, leaving some lacunae to be filled from the records of the various Mission centers, which were to be sent to him. His manuscript was found in his desk after his demise, together with other papers pertaining to the administration of the Mission.

Ricci's commentaries were intended for Europe, and for fear that the record of the labor of so great a man might be lost amid the perils of such a long journey, and the dangers of overland travel on pack animals, it was decided to translate them into Portuguese, and to retain a copy of what he had written in Italian. Father Ricci had written his diary, believing that it would not be read before it was seen and approved by the Father General of the Society of Jesus. Such was the modesty of this man, in view of the fact that what he had written was nothing more than an account of what he had accomplished.

The status of the Christian Mission to China at that time demanded that a Procurator be sent to Europe to promote the mission interests, and being selected for this office, my first thought was to read the manuscript of Father Matthew Ricci's commentaries and translate them into Latin. My reasons for thinking so were, first, because I realized that this task could not be done by anyone who was not well acquainted with the affairs of the Mission, or with the various parts of the country that are mentioned, and secondly, as we have already said, because it was necessary to fill in various parts that were left unfinished, also to add certain items and to amplify others, which our good Father, in his modesty, had either omitted entirely, or only touched upon in passing. And so, although the sea voyage was long, the weather clear, and the sea calm, the work of translation was no small undertaking, and I realized that I had endeavored to accomplish something that demanded more leisure and more quiet than was customary among a crew of noisy sailors. Despite all this, however, I believe I would have come to the end of the book before coming to the end of the voyage, if I had continued on the regular course by sea. Instead, and for very good reasons, I went from India to the Persian Gulf by sea and then took an overland route, crossing Persia and the Arabian desert and a part of Turkey, and finally arrived at Heliopolis (near Cairo). From there I crossed the Mediterranean to Cyprus, Crete, Jacynthe (Zante) and finally under God's guidance, to Hydruntum (Otranto). My writing was only occasional on the latter part of the journey and was continually interrupted until arriving at Rome, where I managed, at night, to steal some hours from my other affairs. Here too there were many intermissions, leaving little time for writing, because of the illness that overtook me, but we did endeavor to continue the task, following the requests of friends and the advice of superiors.

You must understand, gentle reader, that we are more interested in offering you the truth of facts than the pleasure of literary style. Relative to the veracity of what is contained in the commentaries, in so far as it was humanly possible to attain to the truth, there is little if any room left for doubt. Father Ricci was too virtuous to deceive and too experienced to be deceived. As for myself, I can assure you that what I have added, I have seen with my own eyes, or have obtained it from the true report of other Fathers, who either witnessed it themselves, or approved of it for the annals of the Mission. I have not only visited China but have traversed six of its principal provinces, seen all the Mission Centers and, as I believe, garnered a thorough knowledge of the affairs of the Mission in general. We thought it best to inform you of all this, even at length, lest you be led into doubt by the contrary opinions appearing in the various writings thus far edited concerning the Kingdom of China.

Up to the present there are two kinds of authors who have written about China; those who have imagined much, and those who have heard much and have published the same without due consideration. From this latter class I can hardly except certain of our own Fathers, who placed their credence in Chinese merchants, without realizing that it is a common custom with them to exaggerate about everything and to report as true what never really happened. When our Fathers were first permitted to penetrate into the interior of China, it was remarked that they were taking much on faith, and for the first few years after they were allowed to enter the kingdom, it is quite probable that much went out in letters to Europe, that was not wholly reliable. No one, as is evident, could be expected to acquire a thorough understanding of European life without long years of contact. So too in China, in order to obtain a complete knowledge of this country and its people, one must consume years in traveling through the different provinces, learning to speak the native language and to read their books. All this we have done, and so it is only reasonable to believe that this most recent account of ours should supersede those that appeared before it, and that what it records should be taken for the truth, with due allowance, of course, for human errors, which if brought to our attention will be gratefully corrected and replaced in favor of more recent observation.

And so, kind reader, enjoy our present offering, until such time as we may be able to prepare a more ample and a more detailed history. If by God's grace, after so many deviating peregrinations, I shall be permitted to return to my former post, and if I am granted an extension of years, I shall give you a volume of commentary concerning the customs and the habits of the Chinese, together with a compendium of Chinese annals, dating back over four thousand years and arranged, without interruption, according to successive centuries. It will also include, in Latin, the Code of Chinese Ethics, so that one may understand how well adapted is the spirit of this people for the reception of the Christian faith, seeing that they argue so aptly on questions of morality.

In the meantime, you must rest contented with this effort, as a sort of apéritif. I am asking your pardon for its brevity, due to my numerous occupations, occasioned by the small number of Fathers engaged in mission work. May I also ask you to take in good part the lack of elegance in the literary style of our discourse. Having for so long abandoned the art of writing, in an endeavor to learn foreign languages, it may well be that the crudity of our composition is dissonant to the subtle appreciation of your experienced ear.

Farewell.

Rome, January 14, 1615.

TRANSLATOR'S PREFACE

FATHER MATTHEW RICCI'S DIARY, found among his papers after his demise, was originally written in Italian, and very probably with no thought of publication. Ricci died in 1610. The manuscript of his Diary was brought from Macao to Rome in 1614 by Father Nicola Trigault, who translated it into Latin and published it in 1615, together with an account of Ricci's death and burial. Ricci's Diary, as presented by Trigault, is a narrative account of the China Mission from the first Jesuit settlement at Macao in 1565 to the time of Ricci's death.

In our book title we use Journals rather than Diary because Trigault draws from Ricci sources other than the Diary, such as the Annual Mission Letters, Ricci documents to other missionaries, and personal narrative which Trigault says was omitted by Ricci because of his modesty.

The appearance of Trigault's book in 1615 took Europe by surprise. It reopened the door to China, which was first opened by Marco Polo, three centuries before, and then closed behind him by an incredulous public, who received the greater part of his fabulous narrative as the beguiling tales of a capricious traveler. Four Latin editions followed the first, in 1616, 1617, 1623 and 1648. It appeared in three French editions, in 1616, 1617 and 1618, in German, in 1617, in Spanish, in 1621, in Italian, in 1621, and excerpts from it are found in English in "Purchas His Pilgrims," in 1625. In so far as we can ascertain, no complete translation of Trigault's work was ever published in English before this present edition.

On the three hundredth anniversary of Ricci's death, Father Tacchi Venturi, S.J., published the original Diary in Italian, under title of "The Historical Works of Matthew Ricci." In 1942 the first volume of "Fonti Ricciane," a monumental opus by Father Pasquale D'Elia, S.J., appeared, and the second volume in 1949. The third volume of this great work is a three hundred and seventy-two page Index of volumes

I and II. This extraordinary publication of Ricci's edited and un-
edited writings, a prodigious undertaking of research, must remain as a
veritable mine of information for sinologues. The critique and commentary, the exhaustive footnotes, the volume of indices and the
Chinese character equivalents in the text and in the copious notes,
leave nothing in Ricci's works unidentified or unexplained.

In the introduction to his edition of Ricci's Diary, Father Venturi
remarks that his purpose in publishing his book is to honor an illustrious son of Italy and to rescue his name from historic oblivion. In the
critical commentary on "The Christian Expedition into China," Father
D'Elia reminds us that Ricci's Diary was given to the world as a book
in which Trigault seems to be the chief protagonist. Judging from
Trigault's wording of the first short chapter of Book I, the reader might
readily conclude that Trigault was the author of this first book, whereas
Book I is part of the original Ricci Diary, save for Trigault's interjection here of his purpose in translating the Diary from Italian into Latin.
In the very beginning of his book Trigault informs his reader that he
lays no claim to the authorship of the work, which, as he says, belongs
entirely to Ricci.

The Abbé Christian Dehaines, in his biography of Nicola Trigault,
states that the reason for writing his book was to give due credit to his
fellow citizen of Douai, as a scholar, historian and missionary, and as a
distinguished son of Belgium.

If, indeed, there were any call to rescue such illustrious names as
Ricci and Trigault from historic oblivion, or to restore them a balance
of credit, we are convinced that both the leader and the historian of
"The Christian Expedition into China" would be solicitous to share
the glory of their renown with the pioneer laborers who took part in the
titanic task involved in their common undertaking.

With due regard for the original author, Matthew Ricci, the co-
founder, with Father Alexander Valignano, of the China Mission, and
the prime mover in its development, and with equal regard for the
scholarly historian, Nicola Trigault, who first revealed to Europe who
the Chinese were and how they lived, we have chosen to entitle our
translation of Trigault's work, "China in the Sixteenth Century: The
Journals of Matthew Ricci: 1583-1610." Our purpose is, therefore, to
offer an English translation of Trigault's 1615 Latin version of the
Ricci commentaries.

We dare say that from the first appearance of Trigault's book, over
three centuries ago, not a single sinologue of any nation has failed to

mention Ricci, and few historians of China have failed to quote from Trigault's work, which opened a new era of Chinese-European relations and gave us one of the greatest, if not the greatest, missionary document in the world. Our further interest in presenting this book is to fill a long-lasting lacuna in English-written Jesuit Relations, and to offer the English-reading public a chapter in Jesuit history, to which they formerly had access only through quotations and excerpts.

Save to sinologues and to students of Chinese history, Trigault's book has been known to comparatively few, and yet it probably had more effect on the literary and scientific, the philosophical and the religious, phases of life in Europe than any other historical volume of the seventeenth century. It introduced Confucius to Europe and Copernicus and Euclid to China. It opened a new world, revealed a new race of people, and introduced into the family of nations a problem member which still remains a problem after three hundred years of acquaintance. The general theme of this work is the sixteenth-century discovery of China by the Jesuits.

Our present work might easily be augmented by a volume of footnotes more ample than the Diary itself, but all this has been done, and thoroughly done, by Father D'Elia in his "Fonti Ricciane." Book I of the Diary is in itself, as Trigault says, a book of footnotes to the following text, and as such it is quite sufficient to answer the purpose for which the Diary is now being presented.

Perhaps the most significant historical item in the Diary is the revelation that Cathay was another name for China, and not a separate kingdom, as Europe had believed since the time of Marco Polo. This discovery was the result of the famous overland Odyssey of the Jesuit Lay Brother, Bento Goës, from Agra in India, over the Hindu Kush to the China border, as related in the fifth book of the Diary. In Vol. 2 of the 1866 publication of the Hakluyt Society, entitled "Cathay and the Way Thither," as taken from Trigault, Henry Yule says, "It is a meagre record of a journey so interesting and so important. Had Benedict's diary, which he is stated to have kept in full detail, been spared, it would probably have been to this day by far the most valuable geographical record in any European language, on the subject of the countries through which he traveled." Why Bento's diary was destroyed by the Saracens is told in the Ricci story of the Goës expedition. The Goës undertaking, in turn, is intimately connected with the Christian Expedition into China, inasmuch as it opened the mysterious king-

dom to an overland entrance from the west, twenty years after Ricci
had entered it by sea from the east.

Ricci's design upon entering China was to win over the people by
first gaining the favor and the following of the lettered or educated
classes, and this he planned to do by teaching the sciences as they were
known in Europe. Educated at the Roman College under Clavius, he
was numbered among the most erudite scientists and mathematicians
of his time.

After tedious acquisition of the Chinese language, and once received
into the upper caste of philosophers, who virtually ruled the country,
Ricci adopted the costume of the bonzes or Chinese monks, and his
house became a rendezvous for civil and military authorities, afterwards known in Europe as mandarins. This was an ideal setting for his
purpose, because all officers, military as well as civil, were selected by
law from the literati or educated classes. He wore the costume of the
bonzes for six years before changing to that of the philosophers, the
highest intellectual caste in the kingdom.

Shut off from the rest of the world, of their own accord, as they were,
and self-satisfied that they alone were possessed of all knowledge of philosophy and the sciences, the Chinese Solons must have
looked upon Ricci's sudden appearance in their midst as a veritable
revelation. Supplied from Europe, by way of Macao, with a collection
of clocks and watches and with various other kinds of scientific apparatus, unknown in China, he would first thoroughly explain and
demonstrate the new devices and then give them as presents to his
distinguished visitors. He was an expert at making sundials, maps,
geographic and celestial globes, hour-glasses for sand and water, and
other such scientific equipment, most of which the Chinese had never
seen. These were welcome gifts to curious scholars and served for the
establishment of future beneficial relations. In collaboration with
Father Ruggieri, he composed, in Chinese, an exposition of the Christian faith, in the form of a dialogue between an educated Chinese and
a European Catholic priest. This was the first of a numerous series of
such tracts, which were in great demand among the upper classes, and
some of which were still in circulation a century after Ricci's death.

The marvels that Ricci wrought in Nankin and in Pekin are tempting
enough to lead us into long repetition, but these belong to his diary.
Three years after his first and futile visit to Nankin, we find him
securely installed there, where he founded a mission center that
flourished until the persecution of 1616. He set out for Pekin in the

year 1600, and after several months as a prisoner in Tientsin, the Emperor sent for him and he lived in the northern capital until his death in 1610. For the last fourteen years of his life he was Superior of the entire China Mission which was officially separated from Macao in 1596.

The author of numerous works on science and religion, written in Chinese, Ricci was well known to the educated classes of China as a prominent professor of physics, mathematics and geography, as a learned philosopher of Chinese and of extraneous doctrine, as a prominent commentator on Confucius, and particularly as an eminent teacher of the Christian religion. Some of his Chinese compositions, which he accomplished alone, together with those of later Jesuit missionaries, done with the assistance of Christian mandarins, are included in the official index of the best Chinese writings of all time.

The Ricci Diary is a detailed introduction to the history of European influence on China from 1615 to the suppression of the Society of Jesus in 1773. His first Chinese mappamondi stood as a model for European cartographers for a century after its publication; and earned him the title, The Ptolemy of China. His corrections of the Chinese calendars were a preface to a century and a half of scientific advancement in China. His solution of the China-Cathay problem instituted a new geographic era and opened five different overland routes into China, which lasted as standard but hazardous highways until the Flying Tigers flattened the Himalayas, three centuries later.

Missionary literature recounts the hazardous and, all too frequently, the fatal voyaging in Asiatic seas of Portuguese, Italian, French and German Jesuits, in their Society's effort to develop the China Mission. The success attained, during the century and a half that followed the pioneering period, was the direct result of the effect produced upon the Chinese people by the first Jesuits to enter the Celestial Kingdom. Nowhere are the missionary methods of these forerunners of the faith more graphically described or more intimately detailed than in Trigault's narrative rendition of the Ricci Diary.

Whatever design of civilization and culture may develop subsequent to the chaotic conditions existing in China since the collapse of the monarchy in 1911, China's ancient mode of living must always be reckoned with, in the establishment of any stable form of government. An ancient civilization may be coming to a definite end, but whatever form of government is established in China, or imposed upon it, the fundamental characteristics of the race will remain unchanged. The nobility of character of the Chinese people, their love of liberty, of order, and of learning, their devout tendency toward religion, and their keen sense of justice and of ethical interpretation, were never more clearly revealed than when set forth in what Ricci calls his summary study of the customs, laws, institutes and government of the Chinese people. Despite contrary opinions, he vehemently maintained that though deeply devoted to their parents in life, and for years publicly expressive of their grief for parents departed, they were never ancestor worshippers, in the religious sense of the term.

The benign and peaceful attitude of this people toward all other nations is clearly outlined in Ricci's lucid explanation of the Chinese form of government of his time. The value they set on national character is explained in the same chapter, when he says, "It must be said of the Chinese that they would prefer to die an honorable death rather than swear allegiance to a usurping monarch."

Chinese life of the future will be modeled, to a considerable extent, upon their own unique and original pattern of the past. Without a knowledge of that, there is no understanding and hence no appreciation of their singular genius. We know of no better literary portrayal of that particular pattern than the verbal picture of it done by Matthew Ricci.

We wish to acknowledge our indebtedness and to offer our thanks to Rev. Russell M. Sullivan, S.J., for his collaboration on the manuscript, to Rev. George T. Eberle, S.J., for his critique of our English version, to Rev. Joseph Sebes, S.J., and Professor Lien-Sheng Yang of Harvard University for the Chinese index, and to Mr. Vincent P. Roberts and Mr. Bernard Goldfine, as Sponsors of the present edition.

Louis J. Gallagher, S.J.,

Saint Robert's Hall,
Pomfret Center, Connecticut,
Feast of Saint Robert Bellarmine,
May 13, 1953.

BOOK ONE

1. Concerning the Mission to China Undertaken by the Society of Jesus

Reasons for this First Book and Its Method

~~~~~~

IT NOT INFREQUENTLY happens that the beginnings of vast expeditions and mighty undertakings which have matured in the course of ages are all but a closed book to those who live long after these events. After frequently pondering over the reasons for this fact, I came to the conclusion that the beginnings of all events, even of those which later took on vast proportions, were so very small and meager at the outset that they seemed to give no promise whatever of developing later into anything of importance. This would account for the fact that those who brought up these events from their infancy, so to speak, put themselves to no pains to commit to memory the facts which at that time seemed to have but little significance. Perhaps, too, it might be preferred to explain this fact by saying that the beginnings of such undertakings were beset with so many and such great difficulties, that we would be warranted in assuming that the authors of these happenings, who were straining every nerve to accomplish their tasks, found but little time and had but little energy left for keeping records of what was happening.

Such is the opening paragraph of the Ricci Diary, after which Father Trigault remarks, in the first person, that he is endeavoring to write an historical account of facts gathered from the posthumous papers of Father Matthew Ricci, facts which were set down in his Diary for the benefit of posterity. The Diary is then continued, with Ricci writing, in the first person.

It is, therefore, by keeping such records that I hope to rescue from oblivion the story of the entrance of our Society into the vast

3

dominion of China, whose borders have been closed for so many ages, and likewise of the first fruits of Christianity gathered from this noble race. There is another reason also which strongly urges me to undertake this work; namely, that if perchance it should sooner or later please the Divine Goodness to garner into the granaries of the Catholic Church a rich harvest from this initial sowing of the gospel seed, the faithful of later days may know to whose instrumentality to attribute the admirable work undertaken for God in past years for the conversion of this estimable people. If, on the other hand, it should happen, because of the hidden judgments of God, that the expected harvest should not come to fruition, then at least posterity will know how much our least Society of Jesus has labored and suffered to dispel the deep shadows of infidelity, and with what zeal and industry they labored with high hope of cultivating this new soil. Furthermore, who can doubt that this whole expedition of which we are now writing is divinely directed, since it is entirely devoted to bringing the light of the gospel to souls? Since we look upon it as such, we shall endeavor to present it to the reader rather with the frankness of truthful statements than in flattering words. Now I have no intention whatsoever in this account of belittling our annals or the private letters of our companions, provided these have the solidity of truth, based on authority, which of right they should possess, unless perchance there be a contradiction between them. Moreover, I do not propose to give every detail in a history of this kind or to exhaust the matter treated therein, for indeed there might well have been many other happenings fully worthy of recording.

China and Europe differ as much in manners and customs as they do in geographical position, and because this entire narration is intended for Europeans, I have thought it necessary before entering upon my chief task of recording our experience in China, to give a brief account of the position of this kingdom, of its customs, its laws, and of other like topics. My purpose in so doing is to save the reader the distasteful task of repeatedly breaking the thread of the diary story by frequently encountering explanatory passages that would otherwise have to be inserted. Concerning the matters treated, however, I shall adhere to the practice of touching only upon such things as are at variance with our own customs and manners, in so far as this will reveal something historically new. Although many books are circulating through Europe concerning these same topics, I am of the opinion that it will not bore anyone to hear these same things from our companions. We have been living here in China for well-nigh thirty years and have traveled through its most important provinces. Moreover, we have lived in friendly intercourse with the nobles, the supreme magistrates, and the most distinguished men of letters in the kingdom. We speak the native language of the country, have set ourselves to the study of their customs and laws and finally, what is of the highest importance, we have devoted ourselves day and night to the perusal of their literature. These advantages were, of course, entirely lacking to writers who never at any time penetrated into this alien world. Consequently they were writing about China, not as eyewitnesses but from hearsay and depending upon the trustworthiness of others. In truth, we ourselves have restricted the discussion of the topics mentioned to the somewhat limited compass of a few chapters in a single book, whereas each of the subjects could be deservedly expanded into a separate book, if its relative importance were taken into consideration.

2. Concerning the Name, Location, and the Extent of the Chinese Empire

THIS MOST DISTANT empire of the Far East has been known to Europeans under various names. The most ancient of these appellations is Sina, by which it was known in the time of Ptolemy. In later days it was called Cathay by Marco Polo, the Venetian traveler who first made Europeans fairly well acquainted with the empire. The most widely known name, however, China, was given by the Portuguese who reached this kingdom after vast maritime explorations and who even today carry on their trade in the southeastern province of Canton. The name, China, was slightly modified by the Italians and by some other European nations, due to their lack of familiarity with the Spanish pronunciation which differs somewhat from the Latin. China is pronounced by all Spaniards in the same way in which the Italians pronounce Cina.

In my judgment there can be little doubt that this is the country which is called the land of the Hippophagi, the horse eaters, for even to this very day, in this vast empire, the flesh of horse is eaten much in the same way as we eat the flesh of oxen. Nor again have I any doubt that this is the country referred to as the Land of Silk (Serica regio), for nowhere in the Far East except in China is silk found in such abundance that it is not only worn by all the inhabitants of the country, the poor as well as the rich, but it is also exported in great quantities to the most distant parts of the earth. There is no other staple of commerce with which the Portuguese prefer to lade their ships than Chinese silk, which they carry to Japan and India where it finds a ready market. The Spaniards, too, who dwell in the Philippine Islands, freight their trading vessels with Chinese silks for exportation to New Spain and other parts of the world. In the annals of the Chinese Empire, I find mention of the art of silk weaving as far back as the year 2636 before Christ, and it appears that the knowledge of this art was carried to the rest of Asia, to Europe, and even to Africa from the Chinese Empire.

It does not appear strange to us that the Chinese should never have heard of the variety of names given to their country by outsiders and that they should be entirely unaware of their existence. No vestige of these names is to be found among them nor is there any cause to explain the multiplicity of names. The Chinese themselves in the past have given many different names to their country and perhaps will impose others in the future. It is a custom of immemorial age in this country, that as often as the right to govern passes from one family to another, the country itself must be given a new name by the sovereign whose rule is about to begin. This the new ruler does by imposing some appropriate name according to his own good pleasure. Thus we read that the country was at one time called Than, meaning broad; at another time Yu, or quiet; and again Hia, equivalent to our word great. In later days it was called Sciam, which signifies splendid. Then it was known as Cheu, that is to say, perfect; and Han, which means the Milky Way, and through the ages it was known by many other names. From the time of the ascendency of the present reigning family which bears the name of Ciu, the empire was called Min, meaning brightness, and at present the syllable Ta is prefixed to Min, so that today the empire is called Ta-Min, that is to say, great brilliance. Among the nations bordering China, few are aware of this variety of names, whence it happens that China is called now by one name and now by another by the people beyond its confines. Today the people of Cochin and the Siamese as well, from whom the Portuguese learned to call the empire China, call this country Cin. The Japanese know it as Than. The Tartars know it as Han, and the Saracens, who live to the west, speak of it as Cathay. Among the Chinese themselves, and the Latin writers most frequently call them Chinese, after Ptolemy,[1] besides the name assumed with the coming of the new sovereign, the country also has a title which has come down through the ages and sometimes other names are joined to this title. Today we usually call this country Ciumquo or Ciumhoa, the first word signifying kingdom, and the second, garden. When put together the words are translated, "To be at the center." I have heard that this title is due to the fact that the Chinese look upon the heavens as spherical and imagine that the world is flat and that China is situated in the middle of this flat plain. Due to this idea, when they first saw our geographical maps, they were somewhat puzzled to find their empire placed not in the center of the map but at its extreme eastern border. When Father Matthew Ricci[2] drafted a map of the world for them and inscribed it with Chinese characters, out of deference to their ideas, he so arranged it that the empire of China occupied more or less of a central position. Now, however, the Chinese, for the most part, acknowledge their former error and make it a source of no little mirth.

He whose authority extends over this immense kingdom is called Lord of the Universe, because the Chinese are of the opinion that the extent of their vast dominion is to all intents and purposes coterminous with the borders of the universe. The few kingdoms contiguous to their state, of which they had any knowledge before they learned of the existence of Europe, were, in their estimation, hardly worthy of consideration. If this idea of assumed jurisdiction should seem strange to a European, let him consider that it would have seemed equally strange to the Chinese, if they had known that so many of our own rulers applied this same title to themselves, without at the same time having any jurisdiction over the vast expanse of China. So much then for the name of the kingdom known as China.

Relative to the extent of China, it is not without good reason that the writers of all times have added the prefix great to its name. Con-

---

[1] Claudius Ptolemy, Alexandrian geographer, astronomer, and mathematician of the second century.

[2] Here, as throughout Books 2 to 5, Trigault, the narrator, as he signs himself at the end of Book 5, uses the name of Matthew Ricci where the original manuscript has P. Matteo, il Padre or some other indefinite form.

sidering its vast stretches and the boundaries of its lands, it would at present surpass all the kingdoms of the earth, taken as one, and as far as I am aware, it has surpassed them during all previous ages. To the south, China is bounded by the 19° north latitude and terminates in the island which they call Hainam, which word signifies, the south sea. Thence it extends to the 42° north latitude, to the great northern wall, which the Chinese built to divide their territory from Tartary and which serves as a defense against the incursions of those peoples. To the west, China's frontier lies along the 112° longitude,[3] measured from the Fortunate Islands, in the province which they call Yunam, and from this point it extends eastward until it terminates at the 132° longitude in the sea of the rising sun. We ourselves have determined the positions of these boundaries, in those parts of the empire wherein we happened to travel, by means of the astrolabe and of such other instruments as are used by mathematicians. We have also checked our findings by consulting the data of eclipses found in Chinese records in which the new and full moons are accurately described and especially by the study of cosmographical maps. It appears to me that nothing further can be added concerning the length of the country from north to south, as our companions have labored industriously in both extremes. The same, however, cannot be said regarding the measurements of longitude spanned by this country. If it shall please divine providence that some of our companions should later on carry the light of the gospel further west, and that in the course of these travels they should make more accurate observations concerning the breadth of this country, differing from the figures I have assigned, I feel certain that the difference will be very small. In such case, however, I shall most readily yield to their authority in the matter, knowing that more recent observations will very probably be more accurate.

From what has been said, it will be seen that the extensive dominions of this great empire lie for the most part within the temperate zone and are favored with a mild climate. Taken as a whole, however, the country possesses all those gradations of climate which one might experience in passing from the Island of Meroe to a point as far north as Rome. Vast as the dimensions of this country are in reality, its length from north to south falls far short by almost one third of the distance commonly attributed to it by the writers of our time, who as a rule place the northern boundary slightly above the 53rd parallel of

---

[3] In the edition of 1615, Trigault writes *centesimo duodecimo* evidently for *centesimo secundo*. Yunnan lies between 98° and 104° longitude.

north latitude. Now lest one should imagine that this great expanse is for the most part made up of uncultivated desert land, let me insert here the testimony of eyewitnesses as I find it recorded in a Chinese book, entitled, A Description of the Chinese Empire, written in 1579. The passage, exactly translated, runs as follows: "In the Chinese Empire, there are two regal provinces—Nankin, the southern kingdom, and Pekin, the northern kingdom. Besides these two there are thirteen other provinces. These fifteen provinces"—which might very well be called kingdoms—"are further divided into one hundred and fifty-eight departments or small provinces," which the Chinese call Fu and most of which contain twelve to fifteen large cities, besides smaller towns, fortresses, villages, and farms. "In these regions two hundred and forty-seven large cities are designated by the title, Cheu, although for the most part these are differentiated from other large cities by their dignity and importance rather than by their size. Then there are eleven hundred and fifty-two common cities which are called Hien." At the time when the book I have just mentioned was printed, the adult population, of which every member was subject to royal taxes, numbered 58,550,801. This number does not include the women of the country, nor does it include the men who are exempt from taxation, such as soldiers, eunuchs, the relatives of the King, magistrates, scholars, and many others.

Notwithstanding the fact that apart from Tartar raids peace has now prevailed for a very long time, more than a million soldiers are retained in service, at the expense of the government. This number will not seem to be exaggerated if we recall that of the three provinces in the north, one of which is called Leatum, nearly half of the entire population is constantly under arms in the service of the King. The author of the book just quoted enumerates three countries to the east, more than fifty-three countries to the west, more than fifty-five to the south, and three to the north, all of which pay tribute to the empire. I have observed, however, that today very few of these countries are paying the stipulated tribute. Indeed, those who do continue to pay it, when they come into the country to fulfill their obligation, carry away with them from China more money than they bring in as tribute, so that the Chinese authorities have become quite indifferent as to whether or not the tribute is ever paid.

Referring again to the enormous extent and renown of this empire, it should be observed that it is quite well protected on all sides, by defenses supplied by both nature and science. To the south and the east it is washed by the sea, and the coast is dotted with so many small islands that it would be difficult for a hostile fleet to approach the mainland. To the north the country is defended against hostile Tartar raids by precipitous hills, which are joined into an unbroken line of defense with a tremendous wall four hundred and five miles long. To the northwest it is flanked by a great desert of many days' march, which either deters an advancing army from attacking the Chinese border or becomes the burial place of those who attempt the attack. Beyond the mountain range which hems in the kingdom to the west, there exist only impoverished countries to which the Chinese pay little or no attention, as they neither fear them nor consider them worth while annexing.

3. The Fertility and the Products of the Chinese Empire

DUE TO THE GREAT extent of this country north and south as well as east and west, it can be safely asserted that nowhere else in the world is found such a variety of plant and animal life within the confines of a single kingdom. The wide range of climatic conditions in China gives rise to a great diversity of vegetable products, some of which are most readily grown in tropical countries, others in arctic, and others again in the temperate zones. The Chinese themselves, in their geographies, give us detailed accounts of the fertility of the various provinces and of the variety of their products. It hardly falls within the scope of my present treatise to enter into a comprehensive discussion of these matters. Generally speaking, it may be said with truth that all of these writers are correct when they say that everything which the people need for their well-being and sustenance, whether it be for food or clothing or even delicacies and superfluities, is abundantly produced within the borders of the kingdom and not imported from foreign climes. I would even venture to say that practically everything which is grown in Europe is likewise found in China.

If not, then what is missing here is abundantly supplied by various other products unknown to Europeans. To begin with, the soil of China supplies its people with every species of grain—barley, millet, winter wheat, and similar grains.

Rice, which is the staple article of Chinese diet, is produced here in far greater abundance than in Europe. Vegetables, especially beans, and the like, all of which are used not only as food for the people but also as fodder for cattle and beasts of burden, are grown in unlimited variety. The Chinese harvest two and sometimes three crops of such plants every year, owing not only to the fertility of the soil and the mildness of the climate but in great measure to the industry of the people. With the exception of olives and almonds, all the principal fruits known in Europe grow also in China, while the real fig tree, which, by the way, our Fathers introduced into China, yields in nothing to its European progenitors. The Chinese, moreover, possess a variety of fruits unknown in Europe which are found exclusively in the province of Canton and in the southern parts of China. These fruits are called licya and longana by the natives and for the most part they are very pleasing to the taste. The Indian nut-bearing palm tree and other Indian fruits are found here, and there is a species of fruit called the Chinese fig, a very sweet and appetizing fruit which the Portuguese call sucusina. This particular fruit can be eaten only after it is dried, hence the Portuguese call it a fig. It has nothing in common with the real fig, however, since it resembles a large Persian apple,[1] only it is red, and lacks the soft down and the pit. Here, too, we find oranges and other citrus fruits and every kind of fruit that grows on thornbushes, in a larger variety and possessing a finer flavor than the same fruits grown in other countries.

Much the same can be said of the variety and quality of table vegetables and the cultivation of garden herbs, all of which the Chinese use in far greater quantities than is common among the people of Europe. In fact, there are many among the common folk who live entirely upon a vegetable diet through the whole course of their lives, either because they are forced to do so by reason of poverty or because they embrace this course of life for some religious motive. The profusion of flowering plants really leaves nothing to be desired, as the Chinese have many species unknown to us which make a deep appeal to the aesthetic sense and show forth the lavish bounty of the Creator. The Chinese seem to take more delight in the shape and color of flowers than in their odors;

---

[1] Probably the peach.

and the science of distilling essential oils from flowers and plants was practically unknown to them until they began trade relations with the Europeans. In the four southern provinces we find the splendid plant which the Indians call betre, and the tree which they call arequeiram is also very common. The Indians derive great pleasure from constant chewing of the leaf of the betre, mixed with lime, and they claim that the warmth produced by the chewing is quite beneficial to the stomach.

The Chinese have several substitutes for our olive oil, both for food and for the filling of lamps. Chief among these is an oil which has a pleasing odor and is obtained from the sesame, which grows everywhere in abundance. Their wines are inferior to our European products although they try to persuade themselves of the opposite. Grapes are not common and those that are obtainable are not of very good quality. Hence they do not manufacture wine from grapes but obtain it by fermenting rice and other grain seeds, which accounts for the fact that it is everywhere used plentifully. This rice-wine is very much to their taste and of a truth it is not at all unpleasant, though it does not produce the same feeling of warmth as our wines of Europe.

The meat most in vogue with the common people is pork but other meats are also plentiful. Beef, lamb, and goat mutton are not scarce. Hens, ducks, and geese are to be found everywhere in large flocks. Yet in spite of this plentiful supply of meat, the flesh of horses, mules, asses, and dogs finds equally as much favor as other meats, and this equine and canine meat is exposed for sale in all the markets. In some districts oxen and gazelles are not slaughtered because of some superstition or because of the needs of agriculture. The flesh of game animals, especially that of deer, hares, and other small animals is common and may be had cheaply.

Neither horses nor other beasts of burden are the equal of those in Europe, in stature or in form, but in numbers, in cheapness of price, and in carrying power, they excel our own and are used as pack carriers in those parts where one does not meet the rivers. This country is so thoroughly covered by an intersecting network of rivers and canals that it is possible to travel almost anywhere by water. Hence, an almost incredible number of boats of every variety pass hither and thither. Indeed there are so many of them that one of the writers of our day does not hesitate to affirm that there are as many people living on the water as there are dwellers on land. This may sound like an exaggeration and yet it all but expresses the truth, as it would seem, if one were to travel here only by water. In my opinion it might be said with greater truth and without fear of exaggeration, that there are as many boats in this kingdom as can be counted up in all the rest of the world.

This statement is true if we restrict our count to the number of boats sailing on fresh water. As to their ships that pass out into the sea, they are very few and not to be compared with ours either in number or in structure. Let us return for a moment to their horses. The Chinese know little about the taming or training of horses. Those which they make use of in daily life are all geldings and consequently quiet and good tempered. They have countless horses in the service of the army, but these are so degenerate and lacking in martial spirit that they are put to rout even by the neighing of the Tartars' steeds and so they are practically useless in battle. Moreover, since their hoofs are not shod and are very tender they cannot endure long journeys over flinty and rocky ground.

The sea which lies to the east and southeast of China is literally alive with fishes. The rivers, too, which in some places widen out into what might be called small seas, also yield a great quantity of fish. Stocked fishpounds are almost as common here as in Europe, and they are fished every day for private consumption and for market, and yet the fish are so numerous that a fisherman never casts a line without making a catch.

There are no lions in the forests in China, but tigers, bears, wolves, and foxes exist in large numbers. A great many elephants are reared in Pekin to lend color to the court pageantry, but the elephant is an importation and is to be seen nowhere else within the confines of the kingdom. The Chinese have no knowledge of linen, but the common people weave a cloth from cotton which is used for clothing.

Cotton seed was introduced to this country only forty years ago, and it thrives so well, because of the fertility of the soil, that enough cotton could be grown in China to supply the whole world. Silk is manufactured on so large a scale that it can readily compete with the European product, though perhaps the latter may be of a higher quality. From silk, too, they also weave a Damascene cloth having an admixture of cotton, and in imitation of European products they now weave a cloth made entirely of silk. Their other woven fabrics also find a ready market in Europe, and the price they receive for them is about one-third or one-fourth of what we pay for a similar product in the West. For summer use they make a rough cloth from the fiber of hemp and certain other plants.

The Chinese drink only the milk of cows and do not use the milk of goats either for making cheese or as a beverage. They shear sheep, but in the use of sheep's wool they are not nearly as adept as the people in Europe, and though they place a high value on imported woolen cloth they do not know how to weave wool into cloth for clothing. True, they do weave a woolen cloth of light weight for summer use which is much in demand by the poorer classes for hats and for the carpets which they use as sleeping mats. These carpets are also used in the performance of their social rites of which we shall speak later. Woolen cloth is more in demand in the northern parts of China where the cold is almost as biting as it is in the northern parts of Europe, despite the fact that the northern confines of China are much farther distant from the pole. In fact, it is not quite clear as yet why the great rivers and lakes of north China should freeze thick in the winter, unless it be their proximity to the snow-capped mountains of Tartary, on whose rugged slopes the natives gather the skins of foxes and of Scythian weasels, which they make into garments to ward off the rigorous frosts.

All of the known metals without exception are to be found in China. Besides brass and ordinary copper alloys, the Chinese manufacture another metal which is an imitation silver but which costs no more than yellow brass. From molten iron they fashion many more articles than we do, for example, cauldrons, pots, bells, gongs, mortars, gratings, furnaces, martial weapons, instruments of torture, and a great number of other things, all but equal in workmanship to our own metalcraft. Gold is considered to be a precious metal, but they do not appraise it as highly as we do. Silver is used as a currency and, whether by weight or in stamped coins, is used as legal tender in all commercial transactions. This, of course, gives rise to difficulties, such as the fluctuating value of silver, which must always be taken into account when paying bills, and the ease of counterfeiting which is not at all infrequent. In many places a small brass coin, which is struck off in a public mint, is used for smaller purchases. Silver vessels, and, among the very rich, even vessels of gold are used, but rather more sparingly than in Europe. Here, as elsewhere, much silver and gold is used to fashion headdresses and ornaments for womenfolk. The ordinary tableware of the Chinese is clay pottery. It is not quite clear to me why it is called porcelain in the West. There is nothing like it in European pottery either from the standpoint of the material itself or its thin and fragile construction. The finest specimens of porcelain are made from clay found in the province of Kiam, and these are shipped not only to every part of China but even to the remotest corners of Europe where they are highly prized by those who appreciate elegance at their banquets rather than pompous display. This porcelain, too, will bear the heat of hot foods without cracking and, what is more to be wondered at, if it is broken and sewed with a brass wire it will hold liquids without any leakage. These people have also acquired the art of glass blowing but their workmanship here falls far short of what we see at home.

Common dwellings are built of wood, but royal palaces are built with walls of brick, though the roofs are done in wood and are supported by wooden columns. Judging from this and from what we have already remarked about the existence of so many boats, one can easily understand how great is the quantity of lumber and how vast are the forests in which practically every species of wood known in Europe is to be found. Oak is not common, but the Chinese have a kind of wood which far excels oak for durability. It is a hard and imperishable wood, in color similar to iron, hence the name ironwood given to it by the Portuguese. The cedar, which is common enough, is considered by the Chinese to be a tree of mourning. It is used for making the caskets of the dead, and their tombs are so respected that the Chinese who can afford it think nothing of spending more than a thousand gold pieces[2] in constructing such a burial place. A common species of reed grows here, which the Portuguese call bamboo, cylindrical in form and almost as hard as iron. When fully grown it can hardly be spanned by both of a man's hands, and though it is hollow and formed like pieces joined together, its nodes and joints give it such strength that it is commonly used as the posts of small buildings. The slender sticks make excellent lances, and bamboo is used for a hundred and one different purposes, a catalogue of which would serve only to weary one in the reading. Bamboo grows only in the southern provinces, but it grows there so plentifully that the supply satisfies the demand of the whole country and probably no other wood is used so extensively.

Wood, reeds, and straw are burned in the hearth fires, and a kind of coal similar to that which is mined in the diocese of Leodienses in Belgium also is used. They call it Mui and use it for all purposes for which we use coal and it burns without giving off noisome smoke. Nature is more propitious to the man in the north, where this coal is found in plenty and of better quality. It is mined from the earth and widely distributed through the country at a low price, indicating its

---

[2] The value of the gold piece is nowhere given in the original manuscript.

abundance and making it possible for even the poorest to use it in their kitchens and in heating the bath.

China is rich in medicinal herbs which are known elsewhere only as importations. Rhubarb and musk were first brought in from the West by the Saracens, and after spreading through the whole of Asia, they were exported to Europe at an almost unbelievable profit. Here you can buy a pound of rhubarb for ten cents, which in Europe would cost six or seven times as many gold pieces. Here too, you find that famous remedy for many diseases, called Chinese Wood by the Portuguese and Sacred Wood by others. It grows freely in barren parts and without cultivation, and may be obtained for the price of the labor necessary to collect it, but it is exported at a high price. Salt is plentiful in the maritime provinces and may also be obtained from some inland lakes the water of which is easily crystallized. In fact, salt is found everywhere in large quantities, and with all its varied uses and so many people employed in its production and distribution, the taxes derived from it are a source of great wealth for the royal treasury. Sugar is much more commonly used among the Chinese than honey, although both are abundant in the country. Besides the wax obtained from bees, they have another and a better kind which is clearer and not so sticky and burns with a much brighter flame. This wax is obtained from a species of small worm which they breed in the trees for this purpose. They also have a third kind of wax, made from the fruit of a certain tree, which is as clear as the second but its flame has far less power of illumination.

The use of paper is much more common in China than elsewhere, and its methods of production more diversified. Yet the best variety produced here is inferior to many of our own brands. It cannot be printed or written upon on both sides, so that one of our sheets is equivalent to two of theirs. Moreover, it tears easily and does not stand up well against time. Sometimes they make paper in square sheets measuring one or two paces, and the kind they manufacture from cotton fiber is as white as the best paper found in the West.

We must, of necessity, forgo the discussion of many things such as variegated marbles, bronzes, precious stones, gems, various coloring materials for paints, scented woods, bitumens, and numerous other things indicating civilization and culture. However, two or three things are entirely unknown to Europeans of which I must give a brief account. First, there is a certain bush from the leaves of which is decocted that celebrated drink, known to the Chinese, the Japanese, and to their neighbors as Cia.[3] Its use cannot be of long duration among the Chinese, as no ideography in their old books designates this particular drink and their writing characters are all ancient. Indeed it might be that this same plant can be found in our own fields. Here they gather its leaves in the springtime and place them in a shady place to dry, and from the dried leaves they brew a drink which they use at meals and which is served to friends when they come to visit. On such occasions it is served continually as long as they remain together engaged in conversation. This beverage is sipped rather than drunk and it is always taken hot. It is not unpleasant to the taste, being somewhat bitter, and it is usually considered to be wholesome even if taken frequently.

The leaves of this shrub are of different grades and a pound of them will bring one, two, or even three gold pieces according to their quality. In Japan the best grades sell for ten or even twelve gold pieces a pound. The Japanese brew their drink from these leaves in a slightly different way from the Chinese. They reduce them to powder and then place two or three tablespoonfuls of the powder in a pot of boiling water and drink the resulting beverage. The Chinese place some of the dried leaves in a pot of boiling water and when the water has extracted the virtue from the leaves, they strain off the leaves and drink what is left.

Another thing worthy of detailed recording is a peculiar kind of pitch, pressed from the trunk of a certain tree. It has the appearance of milk but the consistency of glue. From this the Chinese prepare a kind of sandarac or coloring matter which they call Cie and which is known to the Portuguese as Ciaco. It is commonly used for staining wood in building houses and ships and in the manufacture of furniture. Woods finished with this stain can be made to hold varying shades of color and a gloss like that of a mirror, dazzling the eye with its luster and appealing to the touch by reason of its smoothness. This finish also is durable, and will wear for a long time. With an application of this polish any kind of wood can be easily imitated in color and in grain, and this is the finish that gives to the houses of China and Japan their rich and attractive appearance.

It is customary with the Chinese, more so than with other people who use this polish, not to spread their dining table with a cloth when they sit down to eat. If the table loses any of its luster or becomes soiled by particles of food falling upon it, the gloss can be

---

[3] Tea.

readily restored by washing with water and polishing with a cloth, because this thin but hard finish prevents any permanent stains. The export of the product of this particular tree might well be the beginning of a profitable enterprise, but up to the present it seems that no one has given any thought to such a possibility. Besides the particular kind of pitch just mentioned, another variety is obtained from the fruit of a different tree, quite similar to the former and used for much the same purposes. This second kind cannot be as highly polished as the first, but it has the advantage of being much more plentiful.

Here, too, we find a great variety of aromatic substances, both native and imported. Cinnamon and ginger are indigenous to the country and plentiful. Ginger, especially, is very prolific and of finer quality than can be found anywhere else in the world. Pepper, nuts, aloes, and other such products, which are imported from the neighboring islands of Molucca or from states bordering on China, are becoming less appreciated and are falling off in price as the supply increases.

Finally we should say something about the saltpeter, which is quite plentiful but which is not used extensively in the preparation of gunpowder, because the Chinese are not expert in the use of guns and artillery and make but little use of these in warfare. Saltpeter, however, is used in lavish quantities in making fireworks for display at public games and on festival days. The Chinese take great pleasure in such exhibitions and make them the chief attraction of all their festivities. Their skill in the manufacture of fireworks is really extraordinary, and there is scarcely anything which they cannot cleverly imitate with them. They are especially adept in reproducing battles and in making rotating spheres of fire, fiery trees, fruit, and the like, and they seem to have no regard for expense where fireworks are concerned. When I was in Nankin I witnessed a pyrotechnic display for the celebration of the first month of the year, which is their great festival, and on this occasion I calculated that they consumed enough powder to carry on a sizable war for a number of years.

4. Concerning the
Mechanical Arts Among the Chinese

IT IS A MATTER of common knowledge, borne out by our own experience, that the Chinese are a most industrious people, and it may be logically concluded from the foregoing chapter that most of the mechanical arts flourish among them. They have all sorts of raw material and they are endowed by nature with a talent for trading, both of which are potent factors in bringing about a high development of the mechanical arts. It will suffice to illustrate the versatility of this people by touching upon those phases only, of the arts in question, in which the practice of the Chinese seems to differ most widely from that of our own artisans. It should be noted that because these people are accustomed to live sparingly, the Chinese craftsman does not strive to reach a perfection of workmanship in the object he creates, with a view to obtaining a higher price for it. His labor is guided rather by the demand of the purchaser who is usually satisfied with a less finished object. Consequently they frequently sacrifice quality in their productions, and rest content with a super- ficial finish intended to catch the eye of the purchaser. This seems to be particularly noticeable when they toil for the magistrates who pay the craftsmen according to their own whims without any regard to the real value of what they buy. At times, too, they compel the artisans to design things for which they have no genius or aptitude.

Chinese architecture is in every way inferior to that of Europe with respect to the style and the durability of their buildings. In fact, it is dubious just which of these two qualities is the weaker. When they set about building, they seem to gauge things by the span of human life, building for themselves rather than for posterity. Whereas, Euro- peans in accordance with the urge of their civilization seem to strive for the eternal. This trait of theirs makes it impossible for them to appreciate the magnificence of our architecture as it appears in public and in private buildings, or even to give credence to what we tell

19

them about it. They seem to be utterly at a loss for expression when we tell them that many of our buildings have withstood the elements for the space of a hundred years and some even for one or two thousand years. When they question this and we tell them that the reason for this durability is the depth and massiveness of the foundations which are able to carry the superstructure unshaken for such an extent of time, they merely stare at us in blank amazement. This, however, is not to be wondered at, because they themselves do not dig into the ground to build up foundations but merely place large stones on an unbroken surface of the ground; or, if they do dig foundations, these do not go deeper than a yard or two even though the walls or towers are to be built up to a great height. The result is that their buildings and fortifications cannot even weather the storms of a century without the need of frequent repairs. We have stated already, as one will recall, that most of their buildings are constructed of wood, or if made in masonry they are covered in by roofs supported on wooden columns. The advantage of this latter method of construction is that the walls can be renovated at any time, while the rest of the building remains intact, since the roof is supported by the columns and is not carried by the walls.

The art of printing was practiced in China at a date somewhat earlier than that assigned to the beginning of printing in Europe, which was about 1405. It is quite certain that the Chinese knew the art of printing at least five centuries ago, and some of them assert that printing was known to their people before the beginning of the Christian era, about 50 B.C. Their method of printing differs widely from that employed in Europe, and our method would be quite impracticable for them because of the exceedingly large number of Chinese characters and symbols. At present they cut their characters in a reverse position and in a simplified form, on a comparatively small tablet made for the most part from the wood of the pear tree or the apple tree, although at times the wood of the jujube tree is also used for this purpose.

Their method of making printed books is quite ingenious. The text is written in ink, with a brush made of very fine hair, on a sheet of paper which is inverted and pasted on a wooden tablet. When the paper has become thoroughly dry, its surface is scraped off quickly and with great skill, until nothing but a fine tissue bearing the characters remains on the wooden tablet. Then, with a steel graver, the workman cuts away the surface following the outlines of the characters until these alone stand out in low relief. From such a block a skilled printer can make copies with incredible speed, turning out as many as fifteen hundred copies in a single day. Chinese printers are so skilled in engraving these blocks, that no more time is consumed in making one of them than would be required by one of our printers in setting up a form of type and making the necessary corrections. This scheme of engraving wooden blocks is well adapted for the large and complex nature of the Chinese characters, but I do not think it would lend itself very aptly to our European type which could hardly be engraved upon wood because of its small dimensions.

Their method of printing has one decided advantage, namely, that once these tablets are made, they can be preserved and used for making changes in the text as often as one wishes. Additions and subtractions can also be made as the tablets can be readily patched. Again, with this method, the printer and the author are not obliged to produce here and now an excessively large edition of a book, but are able to print a book in smaller or larger lots sufficient to meet the demand at the time. We have derived great benefit from this method of Chinese printing, as we employ the domestic help in our homes to strike off copies of the books on religious and scientific subjects which we translate into Chinese from the languages in which they were written originally. In truth, the whole method is so simple that one is tempted to try it for himself after once having watched the process. The simplicity of Chinese printing is what accounts for the exceedingly large numbers of books in circulation here and the ridiculously low prices at which they are sold. Such facts as these would scarcely be believed by one who had not witnessed them.

They have another odd method of reproducing reliefs which have been cut into marble or wood. An epitaph, for example, or a picture set out in low relief on marble or on wood, is covered with a piece of moist paper which in turn is overlaid with several pieces of cloth. Then the entire surface is beaten with a small mallet until all the lineaments of the relief are impressed upon the paper. When the paper dries, ink or some other coloring substance is applied with a light touch, after which only the impression of the relief stands out on the original whiteness of the paper. This method cannot be employed when the relief is shallow or made in delicate lines.

The Chinese use pictures extensively, even in the crafts, but in the production of these and especially in the making of statuary and cast images they have not at all acquired the skill of Europeans. They decorate their magnificent arches with the figures of men and beasts, and enrich their temples with the images of gods and with brass bells. Indeed, if my deductions have been rightly made, it seems to me that the Chinese, who in other respects are so ingenious, and by nature in no way inferior to any other people on earth, are very primitive in the use of these latter arts, because they have never come into intimate contact with the nations beyond their borders. Such intercourse would undoubtedly have been most helpful to them in making progress in this respect. They know nothing of the art of painting in oil or of the use of perspective in their pictures, with the result that their productions are likely to resemble the dead rather than the living. It seems also that they have not been very successful in the production of statuary, in which they follow rules of symmetry determined by the eye only. This, of course, frequently results in illusions and causes glaring defects in their works of larger proportions. Yet this does not prevent them from fashioning huge, ugly monsters in marble and brass and clay. Their bells are made of brass and sounded with wooden mallets. They cannot tolerate bells sounded with iron tongues on hammers, and consequently their bells do not compare with ours in quality of tone.

Musical instruments are quite common and of many varieties, but the use of the organ and the clavichord is unknown, and the Chinese possess no instrument of the keyboard type. On all of their stringed instruments the strings are made of twisted cotton, and they seem to be ignorant of the fact that the guts of animals can be used for this purpose. Their practice agrees fairly well with ours in the use of instruments to be played in concert. The whole art of Chinese music seems to consist in producing a monotonous rhythmic beat as they know nothing of the variations and harmony that can be produced by combining different musical notes. However, they themselves are highly flattered by their own music which to the ear of a stranger represents nothing but a discordant jangle. Despite the fact that they claim the first rank in the field of harmonious concert music, they have expressed themselves pleased with organ music and with all our musical instruments which they have heard thus far. Perhaps they will judge in like manner of our vocal harmony and orchestration when they have heard it. Up to the present they have not had this opportunity in our churches, as our modest beginnings here have not yet reached that stage of development.

All our initial efforts are necessarily quiet. I am of the opinion that the Chinese possess the ingenuous trait of preferring that which comes from without to that which they possess themselves, once they realize the superior quality of the foreign product. Their pride, it would seem, arises from an ignorance of the existence of higher things and from the fact that they find themselves far superior to the barbarous nations by which they are surrounded.

This land possesses few instruments for measuring time and in those instruments which they have, it is measured either by water or by fire. The instruments run by water are fashioned like huge waterpots. In those which are operated by fire, time is measured by an odoriferous ash, somewhat in imitation of our reversible grates through which ashes are filtered. A few instruments are made with wheels and are operated by a kind of bucket wheel in which sand is employed instead of water, but all of them fall far short of the perfection of our instruments, are subject to many errors, and are inaccurate in the measurement of time. Concerning sundials, they know that these take their name from the equator but they have not learned how to set them up with relation to the variations of latitude.

I believe this people is too much interested in dramatic representations and shows. At least they certainly surpass us in this respect. An exceedingly large number of the youth of the land is devoted to this activity. Some of them form traveling troupes which journey everywhere throughout the length and breadth of the country, while other groups reside permanently in the large centers and are in great demand for private as well as for public performances. Without question this is a curse in the empire, and so much so that it would be difficult to discover any other activity which is more prone to vice. Sometimes the leaders of the troupes of actors purchase young children and force them, almost from infancy, to take part in the choruses, to lead the dance, and to share in the acting and mimicry. Nearly all of their plays are of ancient origin, based upon history or fiction, and nowadays few new plays are being produced. These groups of actors are employed at all imposing banquets, and when they are called they come prepared to enact any of the ordinary plays. The host at the banquet is usually presented with a volume of plays and he selects the one or several he may like. The guests, between eating and drinking, follow the plays with so much satisfaction that the banquet at times may last for ten hours, and as one play leads to another the dramatic performance may last as long again as did the banquet. The text of these plays is generally sung, and it rarely happens that anything is enunciated in an ordinary tone of voice.

The use of seals for stamping objects is well known and very common here. Not only letters are safeguarded with a seal but they are affixed to private writings, poems, pictures, and many other things. Such seals are engraved with nothing but the name and the surname. Authors, however, do not limit themselves to a single seal but possess many of them, bearing their degrees and titles, and they are used indifferently at the beginning and end of their works. The result of this custom is that writers of the upper classes have their desks furnished with a cabinet filled with seals, engraved with their various titles and names, for the Chinese as a rule have more than one name by which they are addressed. These seals are not impressed in wax or any similar material, but are stamped in with a red coloring substance. As a rule, they are made of some more or less precious material, such as rare wood, marble, ivory, brass, crystal or red coral, or perhaps of some semiprecious stone. Many skilled workmen are engaged in making these seals and they are regarded as artists rather than as artisans, because the characters engraved upon the seals are very old forms, not in common use, and high esteem is always accorded to those who display any knowledge of antiquity.

Quite different from the art of making seals is that of making ink for writing. They prepare this by fashioning thin pads from the heavy residue of oil. The Chinese, perhaps more than any other people, are accustomed to pay close attention to elegance in the formation of their script, and writers who have gained proficiency in this art are held in high honor and esteem. So, too, those who prepare the ink for writing are usually classified as artists. The fluid ink is dipped from a thin marble disk or palette, which is moistened with a few drops of water and then rubbed with the ink pad. Thus the palette is stained and the ink is dipped from it with a small brush made from the fur of hares. The preparation of these palettes is also a common industry, and at times they are fashioned with great beauty from the more precious stones and sell for a high price. In general, implements used in the art of writing are likely to be highly ornate and also much prized, because they are used by men of rank, in an occupation which of its very nature lends dignity to those who are engaged in it.

One particular trade here is far more universal than elsewhere, namely, that of making fans. Ordinarily these fans are used to temper the breezes during the season of greater heat, and they are carried by every class and by both sexes. It would be considered a lack of taste to appear in public without a fan, even though the weather should prompt one to ward off breezes rather than to stir them up. Perhaps the reason for this particular custom is that fans are used more for ornamental display than for any necessity. There is a great variety of fashion in Chinese fans and in the material from which they are made. Ordinarily they consist of ribs of reed, wood, ivory, or ebony, covered with paper or perhaps with cotton and at times even with a sweet-scented straw. Some are round, some oval, and some square. Those used by the upper classes are generally made of bright paper decorated with a design, beautifully traced in gold, and they are carried either spread out or folded up. Sometimes, too, these fans are inscribed with certain maxims or even with whole poems. The gift most frequently exchanged as a sign of friendship and esteem is a fan. We have at our house a box full of these gift fans which have been given to us by our friends as a mark of esteem and which we in turn give to others as a proof of friendship. It is easy to imagine the number of artisans everywhere employed in the manufacture of these fans. It has always seemed to me that the use of the fan among the Chinese is like our own use of gloves. Although, the chief purpose of each seems to be quite opposite, one being used to ward off heat and the other to protect against cold; yet, both alike seem to be employed much more frequently either as a matter of display or as a small gift token of friendship.

In the practice of the arts and the crafts we have mentioned, the Chinese are certainly different from all other people, but for the most part their practice of the other arts and sciences is quite the same as our own, despite the great distance that separates them from our civilization. In fact, the similarity of customs is rather remarkable when we consider their methods of eating and sitting and sleeping, in which they alone of all nations outside of Europe are quite in accord with the West. Their use of tables, chairs, and beds is wholly unknown to any of the peoples of the states that border on China, all of whom place straw mats on the ground or floor and use them in place of chair, bed, or table. This difference of custom is quite remarkable, and I am somewhat at a loss to explain it, but I shall proceed no further with this matter lest it weary the patience of the reader. One may gather from what has been said that there are numerous points of advantageous contact between ourselves and the Chinese people.

5. Concerning the Liberal Arts, the Sciences, and the Use of Academic Degrees Among the Chinese

BEFORE DISCUSSING the question of the government of this wonderful empire, it will be helpful to give an outline of the progress the Chinese have made in literature and in the sciences, and of the nature of the academic degrees which they are accustomed to confer. The whole nature of the Chinese government is intimately bound up with these particular factors, and this government differs in form from that of any other in the world. While it is quite true to say that the literary class, known as the Philosophers, do not govern the empire, it must be admitted that they exercise a wide influence over its rulers.

First, a few words about Chinese writing in general, in which they employ ideographs resembling the hieroglyphic figures of the ancient Egyptians. In style and composition their written language differs widely from the language used in ordinary conversation, and no book is ever written in the colloquial idiom. A writer who would approach very close to the colloquial style in a book would be considered as placing himself and his book on a level with the ordinary people. Strange to say, however, that in spite of the difference that exists between the elegant language which is employed in writing and the ordinary idiom used in everyday life, the words employed are common to both languages. The difference between the two forms is therefore entirely a matter of composition and of style. All Chinese words, without exception, are monosyllabic. I have never encountered a dissyllabic or a polysyllabic word, although a number of words may have two or even three vowel sounds, some of which may be diphthongs.

When I speak of diphthongs I have in mind our European nomenclature. The Chinese are not accustomed to speak of vowels and consonants because every word, just as every object, is represented by its own ideograph, or symbol, used to represent a thought. The number of ideographs is, therefore, equal to the number of words, and the unit of diction is not the word but the syllable. Now, in this very work, the reader will encounter Chinese words consisting of more than one syllable, but it should be remembered that in Chinese each syllable constitutes a separate word, and since the syllables used are intended to signify the same object, we have followed the European method of compounding these into a word of several syllables.

Although every object has its own appropriate symbol, the symbols do not number more than seventy or eighty thousand in all because of the manner in which many of them are compounded. When one has acquired a knowledge of about ten thousand of these symbols, he has reached the point in his education where he is ready to begin to write. This is about the least number required for intelligent writing. There probably is no one in the entire kingdom who has mastered all the symbols or has what might be styled a complete ideographic knowledge of the Chinese language. Many of the symbols have the same sound in pronunciation, though they may differ much in written form and also in their signification. Hence it results that the Chinese is probably the most equivocal of all languages.

One could not write a book in Chinese from dictation nor could an audience understand the contents of a book being read to them unless each listener had a copy of the book before his eyes. The meanings of different written symbols having the same sound cannot be determined by the ear, but the forms of the symbols and consequently their meaning can be differentiated by the eye. In fact, it happens not infrequently that those who are conversing together do not fully and accurately understand one another's ideas even though they enunciate very clearly and concisely. At times they have to repeat what they have said, and more than once, or even to write it. If no writing material is at hand, they will trace the symbol on something with water, or perhaps write it with the finger in the air or even on the palm of the listener's hand. This, too, would happen more frequently in the conversation of the more cultured and elegant classes because their spoken language is purer and more ornate and approaches more nearly the written language.

The use of accents and tones serves to lessen what I might call the difficulty of equivocation or doubtful meaning. In all there are five different tones or inflections, very elusive, and differing so slightly that they are not easily apprehended. By these different tones and inflections they make up for their scarcity of distinct sounds or notes, so that a single syllable, which with us would have a definite significance, will with them have at least five different meanings, which may differ as widely as the poles because of the different tones in which they are uttered. The exact meaning of every spoken word is determined by its tone quality which, of course, increases the difficulties in learning to speak and in understanding the spoken language. I would venture to say that no other language is as difficult for a foreigner to learn as the Chinese. By the grace of God, however, and by unremitting labor, the members of our Society who have devoted themselves to missionary work among this people have learned to speak their language. Those who have been here from the beginning of our mission can read and write it as well as speak it with fluency. I am of the opinion that the equivocal nature of the Chinese language is due to the fact that, from time immemorial, they have devoted most of their attention to the development of the written language and did not concern themselves overmuch with the spoken tongue. Even up to the present all their eloquence is to be found in their writings rather than in the spoken word, in which they resemble Isocrates who had a reputation among the Greeks for the eloquence of his writings. Hence it happens that friends, even when they live close together in the same city, send messages to one another in writing rather than meeting for conversation.

While this method of writing, in which a definite symbol is employed to indicate each separate object, throws a heavy burden on the memory, it also possesses a singular advantage to which we had never previously adverted. Nations which differ widely from one another with respect to their spoken language, but have a written language in common, will eventually come into contact through the exchange of books and letters, which contact could never be made through their spoken vernacular.

For instance, the Japanese, the Koreans, the people of Cochin, and the Leuhians have books which are common to all, but they differ so widely in their spoken tongue that no one of them can understand the others. They all understand the written word in the same sense but each people speaks its own particular dialect. Even in the various provinces of China the spoken language differs so widely that their speech has little in common. Yet the common writing forms a thorough basis for contact. Besides the various dialects of the different provinces, the province vernacular so to speak, there is also a spoken language common to the whole Empire, known as the Quonhoa, an official language for civil and forensic use. This national tongue probably resulted from the fact that all the magistrates, as we shall explain later on, are strangers in the provinces which they govern, and to avoid the necessity of obliging them to learn the dialects of the provinces, a common speech was introduced for transacting official government business. The Quonhoa dialect is now in vogue among the cultured classes, and is used between strangers and the inhabitants of the province they may visit. With a knowledge of this common language, there really is no necessity for the members of our Society to learn the dialects of the provinces in which they work. A province dialect would not be used in polite society, although the more cultured classes might use it in their home province as a sign of neighborliness, or perhaps outside of the province from a sense of patriotism. This national, official tongue is so commonly used that even the women and children understand it.

I have heard that over and above the symbols which they have received from the Chinese, the Japanese also have an alphabet and certain elements similar to our own, which enables them to write their own vernacular without using the endless series of Chinese ideographs. This same practice may also exist among the nations bordering on China which we have enumerated. It is quite certain, however, that no such alphabet is in use among the Chinese, nor any trace of such. Those who make a profession of letters in this country are engaged in the study of their symbols from early childhood even to old age. In such a pursuit, no doubt, a great deal of the time is consumed that might have been spent in the acquisition of more profitable knowledge. However, even this kind of distraction may have its advantages, in as much as it lessens the danger of youthful licentiousness to which all are subject, especially those who have much leisure time at their disposal. This method of writing by drawing symbols instead of forming letters gives rise to a distinct mode of expression by which one is able, not only with a few phrases but with a few words, to set forth ideas with great clearness, which in our writing would have to be expressed in roundabout circumlocutions and perhaps with far less clarity. While we are on the topic of ideographs or symbols, we must not omit to remark that the position and order of Chinese writing is diametrically opposed to our own. They place their characters in columns running from the top of the page to the bottom and across the page from right to left, while we go across the page in lines from left to right and from top to bottom.

The only one of the higher philosophical sciences with which the Chinese have become acquainted is that of moral philosophy, and in this they seem to have obscured matters by the introduction of error rather than enlightened them. They have no conception of the rules of logic, and consequently treat the precepts of the science of ethics without any regard to the intrinsic co-ordination of the various divisions of this subject. The science of ethics with them is a series of confused maxims and deductions at which they have arrived under guidance of the light of reason. The most renowned of all Chinese philosophers was named Confucius. This great and learned man was born five hundred and fifty-one years before the beginning of the Christian era, lived more than seventy years, and spurred on his people to the pursuit of virtue not less by his own example than by his writings and conferences. His self-mastery and abstemious ways of life have led his countrymen to assert that he surpassed in holiness all those who in times past, in the various parts of the world, were considered to have excelled in virtue. Indeed, if we critically examine his actions and sayings as they are recorded in history, we shall be forced to admit that he was the equal of the pagan philosophers and superior to most of them. He is held in such high esteem by the learned Chinese that they do not dare to call into question any pronouncement of his and are ready to give full recognition to an oath sworn in his name, as in that of a common master.

Not only is this true of the philosophers as a class, but even the rulers, during the past ages, have paid him the highest homage due to a mortal. He was never venerated with religious rites, however, as they venerate a god. They gratefully acknowledge their indebtedness to him for the doctrines he bequeathed to them, and even today, after so long a lapse of time, his descendants are held in high esteem by all. Rulers have honored the heads of their families with dignities carrying the right of hereditary succession and entitling them to special immunities.

The Chinese have not only made considerable progress in moral philosophy but in astronomy and in many branches of mathematics as well. At one time they were quite proficient in arithmetic and geometry, but in the study and teaching of these branches of learning they labored with more or less confusion. They divide the heavens into constellations in a manner somewhat different from that which we employ. Their count of the stars outnumbers the calculations of our astronomers by fully four hundred, because they include in it many of the fainter stars which are not always visible. And yet with all this, the Chinese astronomers take no pains whatever to reduce the phenomena of celestial bodies to the discipline of mathematics. Much of their time is spent in determining the moment of eclipses and the mass of the planets and the stars, but here, too, their deductions are spoiled by innumerable errors. Finally they center their whole attention on that phase of astronomy which our scientists term astrology, which may be accounted for by the fact that they believe that everything happening on this terrestrial globe of ours depends upon the stars.

Some knowledge of the science of mathematics was given to the Chinese by the Saracens who penetrated into their country from the West, but very little of this knowledge was based upon definite mathematical proofs. What the Saracens left them, for the most part, consisted of certain tables of rules by which the Chinese regulated their calendar and to which they reduced their calculations of planets and the movements of the heavenly bodies in general. The founder of the family which at present regulates the study of astrology prohibited anyone from indulging in the study of this science unless he were chosen for it by hereditary right. The prohibition was founded upon fear, lest he who should acquire a knowledge of the stars might become capable of disrupting the order of the empire and seek an opportunity to do so.

The present Emperor supports two separate schools of mathematics at a very great expense, and those attending these royal academies are retained, either in the palace as eunuchs, or outside of it, as royal magistrates, two of whom are in the royal tribunal in Pekin. One of these schools follows the method of the Chinese who claim to possess the knowledge of determining the calendars and the eclipses. The other follows the system of the Saracens, reducing the same facts to the tables which have been introduced from abroad. The results arrived at by each school or tribunal are always compared so that one may be aided and corrected by the other for a final decision. Each school has a separate area leveled off on the top of a hill, where they have set up their mathematical instruments, which are of unusual size, cast in brass, and bearing undoubted signs of antiquity. Some member of the school is always kept on night watch to discover any strange or unaccustomed phenomenon of the heavens relative to stars or comets. If any such thing should occur they send a full account of it to the emperor on the following day, and indicate the portent of the event, whether it be for weal or for woe.

The observatory of the Nankin mathematicians is built on a mound within the confines of the city, and the instruments here surpass those of Pekin in size and in elegance, because the Royal Court was situated in that city at the time the instruments were set up. The astronomers of Pekin, however, have the exclusive right for the whole empire of predicting the eclipses of the sun and the moon. When they issue a proclamation announcing an eclipse, the magistrates and the priests of the idols are ordered to assemble in a given place, dressed in the robes of their particular offices, to assist the planet which they believe to be in travail. The assistance they render is made up of the clashing of innumerable cymbals and sometimes in a kneeling position, and the din is continued throughout the entire duration of the eclipse. I am told that, during an eclipse, they fear lest the planet will be devoured by a dragon; just what kind of a dragon, I do not know.

The practice of the art of medicine in China differs very much from what we are accustomed to. Their method of taking the pulse is the same as ours and they are quite successful in bringing about cures. In general, they make use of very simple remedies, such as herbs, roots, and other such things. In fact, the whole art of Chinese medicine is practically contained in the rules we ourselves follow for the use of herbs. There are no public schools for the teaching of medicine. Each aspirant is taught by someone skilled in the art. In both kingdoms (Pekin and Nankin) examinations may be taken for degrees in medicine. This, however, is a mere formality as there is no advantage attached to it. A man with a degree in medicine enjoys no more authority or esteem than one without it, because no one is prohibited from attempting to cure the sick, whether he be skilled in medicine or not.

It is evident to everyone here that no one will labor to attain proficiency in mathematics or in medicine who has any hope of becoming prominent in the field of philosophy. The result is that scarcely anyone devotes himself to these studies, unless he is deterred from the pursuit of what are considered to be the higher studies, either by reason of family affairs or by mediocrity of talent. The study of mathematics and that of medicine are held in low esteem, because they are not fostered by honors as is the study of philosophy, to which students are attracted by the hope of the glory and the rewards attached to it. This may be readily seen in the interest taken in the study of moral philosophy. The man who is promoted to the higher degrees in this field, prides himself on the fact that he has in truth attained to the pinnacle of Chinese happiness.

I think it will be as interesting as it is new to the reader to treat somewhat more fully of this phase of their studies. Confucius, called the Prince of Chinese Philosophers, compiled four volumes of the works of more ancient philosophers and wrote five books of his own. These five he entitled "The Doctrines," and they contain the ethical principles of right living, precepts governing the conduct of political life, customs, and examples of the ancients, their rites and sacrifices, and even samples of their poetry and other subjects of this nature. Besides these five books there is another one composed of the precepts of the great philosopher and of his disciples and compiled without particular arrangement. These are chiefly directions for proper moral proceedings, in the light of human reason, with a view to virtuous conduct on the part of the individual, of the family and of the kingdom in general. This volume, being a summary in excerpts from the four books mentioned, is called the Tetrabiblion. The nine books of Confucius, making up the most ancient of Chinese libraries, of which all others are a development, are written mostly in hieroglyphic characters, and present a collection of moral precepts for the future good and development of the kingdom.

There is a law in the land, handed down from ancient kings and confirmed by the custom of centuries, stating that he who wishes to be learned, and to be known as such, must draw his fundamental doctrine from these same books. In addition to this it is not sufficient for him to follow the general sense of the text, but what is far more difficult, he must be able to write aptly and exactly of every particular doctrine contained in these books. To this end he must commit the entire Tetrabiblion to memory, so as to be a recognized authority thereon. Contrary to what has been stated by some of our writers, there are no schools or public academies in which these books are taught or explained by masters. Each student selects his own master by whom he is instructed in his own home and at his personal expense.

The number of such private teachers, of course, is great, partly because it would be hard for one master to teach many at a time, owing to the difficulty of handling the Chinese characters, and partly because it is an old custom here for each home to have a private school for its own children. At times it happens that tutors, other than the one regularly employed, may be called in, as it would seem, to prevent the custom of bidding for the position from interfering with the interest of their profession.

In the field of philosophy there are three degrees, conferred upon those who pass the written examinations assigned for each degree. The first degree is awarded in the larger cities and in a public academy, by some prominent scholar, appointed by the emperor for that purpose. In virtue of his office this dignitary is known as Tihio, and the first degree, corresponding to our baccalaureate, is called Lieucai. The Tihio visits the various cities of his province in which the degree is to be conferred and for which a triple examination is required. Upon the arrival of this chancellor, as we would call him, the candidates assemble for the examinations. The preliminary examination is conducted by the local teachers who have attained to the baccalaureate and are preparing for a higher degree, and they are paid from the royal treasury for these particular examinations. Anyone may be admitted to the preliminary examinations, and sometimes four or five thousand from a single district will take them. Those who pass the first test are recommended by the teachers to the four city prefects, who are themselves learned men, otherwise they would not be in office. The prefects then select the candidates who are to be presented to the chancellor. Not more than two hundred may be thus presented, and these are chosen for the excellence of their written composition.

The third examination is conducted by the chancellor, himself, and is far more rigid than those preceding it. Of the two hundred admitted to this examination, the twenty or thirty obtaining the highest grades are granted the degree, depending upon the size of the district from which the candidates are drawn. They are then known as academic bachelors, a distinguished class representing the advanced citizenry of their particular town, and their company is cultivated by all who hope to attain to the same dignity. Their particular insignia is an ankle-long gown, a cap, and leggings, which no class other than their own is permitted to wear. They are given seats of honor at the conventions of the magistrates, and with them they may employ the more intimate rites of address which the common people are never permitted to use. In their home cities they enjoy a great many civil privileges and are looked upon as inferior to none, save the chancellor and the four city prefects, nor is it easy for other magistrates to pass judgment upon the cases they present or on charges made against them.

The duty of the chancellor is not confined to the class of new bachelors. He is also responsible for the conduct of those who attained to the degree in former years, weighing in a strict balance what progress they have made and what laxity they have suffered.

To this end he institutes five different grades or classes, which are adjudged according to the caliber of their writings. Those who are listed in the first category are awarded with a public office, but not one of superior grade. The second class is also awarded but with lesser honors. The third class is held as indifferent, with neither reward nor punishment. Class number four is considered as negligent and must pay a penalty for their shortcomings. Finally, if a bachelor is unfortunate enough to fall into the fifth or last class, he is stripped of his bachelor's insignia and reduced to the ranks of an ordinary citizen. This is done to prevent those who become bachelors from losing interest and forgetting in a life of ease what they have labored so hard to acquire.

The second degree of the Chinese literati is called Kiugin and may be compared to our licentiate. This degree is conferred with considerable solemnity in each metropolitan province but only every third year and at the eighth moon. This degree is not open to all who may aspire to it. Only those of the highest ranking are selected for it and their number depends upon the dignity or celebrity of the province. In the districts of Nankin and Pekin one hundred and fifty bachelors are called for the licentiate. From Cequin (Chekiang), Quiamsi (Kiangsi), and Fuquiam (Fu-kien), ninety-five are called and fewer in other provinces, according to the standing of the province and of the number of degrees already granted in the province. As has been stated, only the bachelors are called for this second degree, and not all of these. The selection is made by the chancellor of bachelors, who summons thirty or at most forty from each city or study center of the province, and this choice is made by written tests. Yet, despite this strict selection, in some of the larger provinces the number of those aspiring to the licentiate is frequently in excess of four thousand.

When the year comes for this triennial examination, as happened in 1609, and is to come again in 1612, a few days before the eighth moon, which frequently occurs in September, the magistrates of Pekin send to the King the credentials of the one hundred most distinguished philosophers of the realm. From this list, the King names thirty, or two for each province, to preside over the public discussions for the degree of licentiate. One of these judges must be chosen from the Royal College, called Hanlin, the faculty of which is supposed to be made up of the most celebrated scholars of the kingdom. Now these presiding officials are not named by the

King until there is just sufficient time left for them to get to the province in which the examination is to take place, and numerous inspectors are appointed to see that they do not speak to anyone in that province before the licentiates are called. In this examination, the more celebrated scholars or philosophers of the province are summoned by the Magistrates, to assist the two province examiners appointed by the royal court in a preliminary discussion of the writings submitted by the candidates.

There is an immense palace built especially for this examination in every metropolitan city, closed in by a great wall. In it there are a number of suites, secluded from all distraction, which are assigned to the examiners just mentioned, while they are discussing the submitted manuscripts. In the center of this palace there are more than four thousand small cells, just large enough to contain a small table and a seat for one person. The cells are so constructed that the occupant cannot converse with the one in the next compartment, or even see him. When the district examiner and the royal examiners arrive in the city, they are immediately conducted to the palace and to their places therein before being allowed to converse with anyone. Indeed, they are not even permitted to talk with one another during the time that the manuscripts are being examined. During that particular time, both night and day, a guard of magistrates and of military sentinels is in continual circulation to prevent all contact by word or by writing between those who are engaged in the palace and those outside.

The same three days are set aside for this examination throughout the kingdom, namely—the ninth, the twelfth, and fifteenth of the eighth moon. Those taking part in the examinations are permitted to write from dawn to sunset, behind locked doors, and they are served with light meals, prepared the day before at public expense. When the candidate bachelors are admitted to the palace, they are carefully searched to see that they have no book or written matter in their possession. Entering the examination, they are allowed to have several brushes for writing, the writer's palette, and also ink and paper. Their clothes and even the brushes and palettes are carefully examined lest they should contain anything deceitful, and if fraud of any kind is discovered they are not only excluded from the examination but are severely punished as well.

When the bachelor candidates are admitted to the palace and the doors closed and sealed on the outside with a public seal, each of the two presiding officers, appointed by the King, explains in public three passages selected at will from the Tetrabiblion. He then presents these passages as the general subject matter, and a separate paper must be written on the selection made by each examiner. Then four passages are selected from any one of the five Books of Doctrines and assigned for additional matter for examination. Each one being examined may select subjects drawn from the doctrine which he professes. These seven written papers must show evidence not only of a proper use of words but also of a proper appreciation of the ideas contained in the doctrines and a strict observance of the rules of Chinese rhetoric. No dissertation should exceed five hundred characters, corresponding to as many words in our usage.

On the second day of examination, after two days of rest, and behind closed doors as formerly, topics are offered for examination relative to things that have happened in the past, to the annals of the ancients, and to events which may be expected to happen in the near future. These papers are written in triplex, in the form of an advisory document, addressed to the King, as to what would seem to be the best course to follow for the good of the empire in certain eventualities.

On the third day three difficulties or arguments are offered for examination, which are drawn from possibilities that might arise in planning the direction of public administration. Again, papers are written in triple copy, and each one explains the judgment he wishes to offer in settlement of the argument he has chosen to discuss. When each of the candidates has selected his argument for discussion and committed it to memory, he enters into the room assigned him by the one in charge and does his writing in silence. Each one must also recopy his manuscript into a copybook prepared for that purpose and at the end of the dissertation, in addition to his own name, he signs the names of his parents, grandparents, and his great-grandparents. Then the book is so sealed that it can be opened only by the Deputies. Each one does this with as many copybooks as he may have used, and he presents them personally to the Deputy. These books are again recopied by the librarians or by amanuenses appointed for that purpose. To prevent any partiality, the books are marked with a particular character in red, before they are presented to the examiners, and the autographs are omitted. These manuscripts, without autographs, are the ones that are submitted to the examiners for rating. The autographed copies are numbered to correspond with the markings on the manuscript presented. This method is followed to prevent recognition of the manuscripts and to conceal the author's identity and his handwriting in the formation of the script characters.

The first set of examiners is chosen from the local magistrates, who go through the papers and reject the poorer ones. This is done in such a way that the number of papers coming up to the regal examiners will not be more than double the number of candidates for the licentiate degree. For example, if one hundred and fifty degrees are to be granted, three hundred manuscripts are chosen and sent to the office of the regal examiners for second examination. Then the best of these are selected up to the number of degrees to be awarded. When the papers are examined, they are arranged in first, second, and third classes and placed in order in the classes. Then the examiners compare the accepted manuscripts and the autographs with the numbers corresponding to each, in order to discover the names of the authors. Toward the end of the eighth moon, there is a general convention of the magistrates, and the names of the successful candidates are posted in public, in large letters, on an immense signboard. This ceremony is an occasion of great delight and rejoicing on the part of the relatives and associates of the fortunate contestants.

The degree of licentiate is far superior to that of bachelor and carries with it more dignity and more notable privileges. He who holds a licentiate degree is supposed to continue his studies and to go on to the doctorate, and if he declines to do so he is ineligible for even an inferior public office. When the examinations are over and the ceremonies described at an end, the royal examiners publish a book which is distributed throughout the whole empire, containing the results of the examinations, the names of the new licentiates, and the outstanding manuscripts on the various subjects treated in the examinations. The place of honor in this publication is assigned to the one who received the highest ranking, and he is honored with the title Quiayuen. This book is published as a de luxe edition, and several copies of it are presented to the Emperor and to the palatines.

Ordinarily, bachelors from outside are not admitted to the licentiate examinations. Some few, however, are accepted by special privilege in the capital districts of Pekin and Nankin. If they were admitted to study in the district, they became associated to it, and after obtaining the bachelor's degree, they could be received into the college of that district upon payment of a certain sum of gold to the district treasury.

The third literary degree among the Chinese is called Cin-su and is equivalent to our doctorate. This degree is also conferred every third year but only in the province of Pekin. The year for doctorate is always the one next following that for licentiate. No more than three hundred degrees are conferred at a time, for the entire country. Those holding licentiate degrees from any province are free to take this examination as often as they wish. It is held on the days mentioned, during the second phase of the moon, and in exactly the same manner as described for the former degree save, perhaps because of the great dignity of this degree, with more precaution against fraud or favoritism. The presiding examiners in this instance are chosen from among the strictest of the royal Magistrates, called the Colai, of whom we shall say more later on.

When this examination is over, the results are announced in the same manner and in the same place as already described. The only added feature is that the new doctors all adjourn to the royal palace and here, in presence of the Chief Magistrates of the court and at times of the Emperor also, they write a treatise on a given subject. The results of this contest determine to which of the three grades of the magistracy the doctors will be assigned. This is a celebrated examination, and it consists entirely of a rather brief written dissertation. The one who has already been awarded first place in the regular doctorate examination is assured of at least third place in this final, and those who receive first and second places in this are marked for signal honors and have the assurance of holding high public office for the rest of their lives. The position they hold would correspond to that of duke or marquis in our country, but the title to it is not bequeathed by hereditary right.

The new doctors immediately adorn their special garb and particular hat and leggings, with the other insignia of the magistrate, and are promoted to the richer and more elevated benefices of the magistracy. From that time on they belong to a social order superseding that of the licentiates, and are counted among the ranking citizens of the kingdom. It is difficult for a stranger to appreciate how superior their rank is to that of their colleagues of the day before, who always cede them the place of honor and greet them with the most flattering titles and courtesy.

If those who failed in the examinations for the doctor's degree give up hope of obtaining it in the future, they may be admitted to public office above the lower grades, but not in the category of offices held by the doctors. If, however, they wish to take the examination again, they continue to study for the next three years, and then return to try their luck again, and they may do this as often as they please.

Despite misfortune and with undying hope, some have been known to have made as many as ten attempts to gain this honor, and on the principle of all or nothing to have used up their whole lives in unsuccessful endeavor.

Here again, as in the case of the inferior order, the results are published in the form of a private volume, arranged by each of the examiners and containing the names of the successful candidates and the more distinguished dissertations. Each year, also, a book is published listing all the doctors of philosophy, giving their address, the names of their parents, the different offices they have held, and the places in which they held them. This is a sort of directory from which one may learn what offices each of the doctors has held from the year of his doctorate to the present, or to the time of his death. Besides this, a list of his promotions or demotions is given, either of which may be of daily occurrence among the Chinese, depending upon the reputation of the officeholder.

In this acquiring of degrees there really is something worthy of admiration in the relationship that grows up between candidates of the same year. Those whom fortune has brought together in attaining a higher degree look upon one another as brothers for the rest of their lives. There is mutual agreement and sympathy among them, and they help each other and one another's relatives as well, in every possible way. The friendship they enjoy with their examiners is like that of a son and father, or of a disciple and his master, and they continue to show them respect and deference though it might happen at times that the pupil is raised to even higher honors than are enjoyed by his former preceptor.

The same three grades which we have been discussing are also conferred with similar titles in military circles. These degrees are granted in the same year, but in the following month and in the same place as the former. They are conferred, however, with much less ceremony, due to the fact that military science is not highly cultivated or esteemed in this country. In fact, so few among the military aspire to these degrees that they are considered to be of little importance. Examinations for military degrees are divided into three parts. In the first part, nine arrows are shot by the soldier while he is coursing at full gallop on his charger. In the second, as many more are discharged on foot, standing still. Those who fix four arrows within the allotted space from horseback and two from afoot are admitted to the third part of the examination. In this they must answer in writing to certain questions pertaining to military tactics. The deciding judges announce the results and also the number of military licentiate degrees awarded in each province, amounting to about fifty in all. In the year in which the doctors of philosophy are named in Pekin, about a hundred doctors, chosen from the military licentiates of the entire kingdom, are also named, after completing a necessary triple examination. The soldiers holding doctor's degrees are given preference over those of the licentiate grade for appointment as military prefects, but they have to make payment for the office. When one has merited the title of doctor, either in the philosophic or in the military order, his title is inscribed in large letters over the door of his home, for the prestige of his family and as an indication of the honor he has acquired.

In concluding this account of degrees awarded among the Chinese, the following should not be omitted, which to Europeans might seem to be a rather strange and perhaps a somewhat inefficient method. The judges and the proctors of all examinations, whether they be in military science, in mathematics, or in medicine, and particularly so with examinations in philosophy, are always chosen from the senate of philosophy, nor is ever a military expert, a mathematician, or a medical doctor added to their number. The wisdom of those who excel in the profession of ethics is held in such high esteem that they would seem to be competent to express a proper judgment on any subject, though it be far afield from their own particular profession.

6. The Administrations of the Chinese Commonwealth

WE SHALL TOUCH upon this subject only in so far as it has to do with the purpose of our narrative. It would require a number of chapters, if not of whole books, to treat this matter in full detail. From time immemorial the monarchical government was the only one approved by the Chinese people. Aristocracy, democracy, plutarchy, or any other such form was not even known by name.

In their early history, titles corresponding to duke, marquis, count, and the like were numerous and dependent upon one supreme monarch, but these titles and the jurisdiction they carried have been obsolete for sóme eighteen hundred years. Before this change took place or perhaps because of it, though civil uprisings and war were common as far back as can be learned, and the great kingdom was divided into lesser subservient kingdoms, as we have heard is the custom in Japan, the first recorded conquest of the whole country by a foreign people did not occur until the year 1206.[1] At this time a certain Tartar leader, a conqueror of whole nations, marched a victorious army through this entire land. Some of our historians, and it seems to me with good reason, think it was Tamerlane[2] or one of his successors. The Chinese call him Tiemon, and their historians relate that he first conquered Persia and Tartary and then turned his attention to the conquest of China. Whoever he may have been, we shall just call him the Tartar. With his vast army it took him but a short time to subjugate this people, and his descendants held sway in the immense kingdom until 1368. At that time, when the Tartar power was waning, the rulers of the various districts succeeded in throwing off the yoke of the foreigners, and the Chinese were not again brought under barbaric rule or external direction. The hero who succeeded, either by genius or by guile, in dominating the other war lords was a scion of the family of Ciu, whom the Chinese later styled Humvu, Illustrious Commander, which is more exactly translated as "The Deluge of War." By winning over the rival forces of various other leaders, he was able in a brief period of time to build up a military power from these heterogeneous armies and to drive out not only the Tartar element but the native rival leaders who had been weakened by Tartar dominance. By no less a stroke of fortune, he also succeeded in quieting the remaining rebel elements and then consolidated an empire in China over which his descendants are still reigning. Hence the illustrious name Ta-min, which belongs to this dynasty and the glory of which we have already had occasion to mention.

Chinese imperial power passes on from father to son, or to other royal kin, as does our own. Two or three of the more ancient kings are known to have bequeathed the throne to successors without royal relationship rather than to their sons, whom they judged to be unfitted to rule. More than once, however, it has happened that the people,

---

[1] The date 1602 in the Latin version is a misprint.

[2] No mention of Tamerlane is made in the 1616 Latin edition.

growing weary of an inept ruler, have stripped him of his authority and replaced him with someone pre-eminent for character and courage whom they henceforth recognized as their legitimate King. It may be said in praise of the Chinese that ordinarily they would prefer to die an honorable death rather than swear allegiance to a usurping monarch. In fact, there is a proverb extant among their philosophers, which reads: "No woman is moral who has two husbands, nor any vassal faithful to two lords."

There are no ancient laws in China under which the republic is governed in perpetuum, such as our laws of the twelve tables and the Code of Caesar. Whoever succeeds in getting possession of the throne, regardless of his ancestry, makes new laws according to his own way of thinking. His successors on the throne are obliged to enforce the laws which he promulgated as founder of the dynasty, and these laws cannot be changed without good reason. The laws by which the Chinese are governed today are not older than Humvu, all of which he either formulated himself or accepted from his predecessors. His evident plan was to institute a code of comprehensive scope, admirably suited to insure the peace of the realm and its long duration for himself and his descendants.

The extent of their kingdom is so vast, its borders so distant, and their utter lack of knowledge of a transmaritime world is so complete that the Chinese imagine the whole world as included in their kingdom. Even now, as from time beyond recording, they call their Emperor, Thiencu, the Son of Heaven, and because they worship Heaven as the Supreme Being, the Son of Heaven and the Son of God are one and the same. In ordinary speech, he is referred to as Hoamsi, meaning supreme ruler or monarch, while other and subordinate rulers are called by the much inferior title of Guam.

This Humovus (Humvu), whom we have mentioned, was evidently distinguished for his inherent genius of sagacious diplomacy as well as for his warring valor. The many laws and statutes by which he stabilized the republic are sufficient proof of that. We shall touch upon a few of the more important of these, with a mind to necessary brevity in doing so. Because, as appears in the annals, the families and relatives of former rulers had been stripped of their royal prerogatives by long-drawn-out factions in the realm, and because the control of government had undergone considerable change, he decreed that, henceforth, no one of royal blood should be appointed to public office, either civil or military. To such leaders as had assisted him in freeing the country from Tartar tyranny, he granted the rule of a province with hereditary right. In order that the royalty of the minor kingdoms might not feel that they had been rendered wholly powerless by being excluded from all public service, the sons of kings were granted the title of rulers and called Guam, and were assigned a liberal annuity. This income was not to be derived from estates or from farm lands, lest they should accumulate clients, but was delivered in annual payments, drawn from the royal treasury by special administrators. He decreed also that everyone should respect these administrators, though they were to have no authority over anyone. The sons and nephews of rulers were to have honorary titles, which were to lose their significance with time, depending upon the antiquity of their royal descent. When they reached a certain age, the royal treasury allowed them an endowment sufficient to enable them to live comfortably and respectably without having to work or to engage in business.

Provision was also made for the daughters of royalty according to their rank and relationship, and they were permitted the use of high-sounding and flattering titles. To the sympathic leaders and liberators of the kingdom, honorary titles and annuities were granted. They were appointed military prefects, with generous salaries, but like all others they were to be subject to the civil magistrates. Among the numerous immunities granted by Humvu to his adjutants, certain privileges were accorded to an eldest son, which are quite unheard of among our people. For instance, the illustrious deeds wrought by the head of the family under the leadership of Humvu in the liberation of the kingdom, are pictured on iron disks, shaped like a saucer. This disk may be presented to the King three times for the pardon of any crime, not excepting one that might carry a sentence of death, and each time it is presented, the King has it marked with a secret mark indicating to him how often it has been used. The only exception to this regulation is the crime of treason, for which the penalty is, that those found guilty are immediately stripped of all authority and dignity, and this sentence passes on to all their descendants. Such honors and emoluments, which diminish with the lapse of time, were granted to the relatives of Kings and to their relatives-in-law and to certain others who were known to have distinguished themselves in the service of the country or of the individual state.

Only such as have earned a doctor's degree or that of licentiate are admitted to take part in the government of the kingdom, and due

to the interest of the magistrates and of the King himself there is
no lack of such candidates. Every public office is therefore fortified
with and dependent upon the attested science, prudence, and diplomacy of the person assigned to it, whether he be taking office for the
first time or is already experienced in the conduct of civil life. This
integrity of life is prescribed by the law of Humvu, and for the most
part it is lived up to, save in the case of such as are prone to violate
the dictates of justice from human weakness and from lack of religious
training among the gentiles. All magistrates, whether they belong to
the military or to the civil congress, are called Quon-fu, meaning
commander or president, though their honorary or unofficial title is
Lau-ye or Lau-sie, signifying lord or father. The Portuguese call the
Chinese magistrates, mandarins, probably from mandando, mando
mandare, to order or command, and they are now generally known
by this title in Europe.

Though we have already stated that the Chinese form of government is monarchical, it must be evident from what has been said, and
it will be made clearer by what is to come, that it is to some extent an
aristocracy. Although all legal statutes inaugurated by magistrates
must be confirmed by the King in writing on the written petition presented to him, the King himself makes no final decision in important
matters of state without consulting the magistrates or considering
their advice. If, perchance, a private citizen should present a request
to the King, which would rarely happen because all such documents
must be first examined by a magistrate before coming to the ruler,
and if he is pleased to give it his personal consideration, he signs the
request as follows: Let the tribunal interested in this particular matter
examine this petition and advise me as to the best method of procedure. I can assert the following as certain because I have made a
thorough investigation of it, namely: that the King has no power to
increase a monetary grant to anyone, or to confer a magistracy upon
anyone, or to increase the power thereof, except on request of one of
the magistrates. One should not conclude from this, however, that the
King of his own authority cannot make awards to those who are
connected with his household. This happens frequently. It is an ancient custom to favor one's friends from private income but such
awards may not be listed as public bequests. Gifts of this kind, made
by the King, are drawn from his private fortune and not from public
funds.

Tax returns, impost, and other tribute, which undoubtedly exceed a hundred and fifty million[3] a year, as is commonly said, do not go into the Imperial Exchequer, nor can the King dispose of this income as he pleases. The silver, which is the common currency, is placed in the public treasury, and the returns paid in rice are placed in the warehouses belonging to the government. The generous allowance made for the support of the royal family and their relatives, for the palace eunuchs and the royal household, is drawn from this national treasury. In keeping with the regal splendor and dignity of the crown, these annuities are large, but each individual account is determined and regulated by law. Civil and military accounts and the expenses of all government departments are paid out of this national treasury, and the size of the national budget is far in excess of what Europeans might imagine. Public buildings, the palaces of the King and of his relations, the upkeep of city prisons and fortresses, and the renewal of all kinds of war supplies must be met by the national treasury, and in a kingdom of such vast dimensions the program of building and of restoration is continuous. One would scarcely believe that at times even these enormous revenues are not sufficient to meet the expenses. When this happens, new taxes are imposed to balance the national budget.

Relative to the magistrates in general, there are two distinct orders or grades. The first and superior order is made up of the magistrates who govern the various courts of the royal palace, which is considered to be a model for the rule of the entire realm. The second order includes all provincial magistrates or governors who rule a province or a city. For each of these orders of magistrates, there are five or six large books containing the governmental roster of the entire country. These books are for sale throughout the kingdom. They are being continually revised, and the revision, which is dated twice a month in the royal city of Pekin, is not very difficult because of the singular typographical arrangement in which they are printed. The entire contents of these books consist of nothing other than the current lists of the names, addresses, and grades of the court officers of the entire government, and the frequent revision is necessary if the roster is to be kept up to date. In addition to the daily changes, occasioned by deaths, demotions, and dismissals in such an incredibly long list of names, there are the frequent departures of some to visit their homes at stated periods. We shall say more later on of this last instance, which is occasioned by the custom requiring every magistrate to

---

[3] No mention is made of a unit of currency.

lay aside his official duties and return to his home for three full years, on the death of his father or his mother. One result of these numerous changes is that there are always a great many in the city of Pekin awaiting the good fortune of being appointed to fill the vacancies thus created.

Of all the unlimited number of court offices, we shall touch upon those only which we judge to be necessary for a proper understanding of what is to follow. Any effort to describe the general military tribunal would take us far beyond our design of brevity. Let us first consider the bureaus of the Central Curia, and afterward those of the provinces. There are six courts of the Curia. The first is called the Li-pu; pu meaning court or tribunal, and Li-pu meaning the tribunal of the judges or magistrates. This is known as the Supreme Court because it is invested with the power of appointment of all the more influential magistrates belonging to what is called the philosophic order. These appointments are based chiefly upon the excellency of the written works of the candidates which are rated and judged solely and ultimately by the Supreme Court. All officials begin their careers in the lowest offices and are promoted on the honor system as prescribed by law on a rating of merit and character. Failure to attain a standard rating means either dismissal or demotion to a subordinate office. The possession of academic honors means that one is assured of continuous tenure of office with the right to promotion on merit to the very highest places in public service. It means, moreover, that the holder of such honors cannot be dismissed from office unless proven guilty of misdemeanor, but if once dismissed he may give up all hope of ever returning to the magistracy or of being reinstated in civil service.

The next bureau in order is called Hopu, corresponding to our Exchequer, or Department of the Treasury. This office handles the collection of taxes, the payment of public debts, the negotiation of loans, and other financial transactions. The third is called Lypu, which we shall designate as the Court of Rites, and to which belong the conduct of religious functions, the care of temples and shrines and of the services conducted therein. To this court also belong the supervision of priests, the arrangement of royal weddings, and the duty of inspection for the proper conduct of literary academies and examinations. It can suggest to the King the naming of certain days for festivals in celebration of extraordinary events. It confers titles upon those who merit them and has jurisdiction over medical doctors and over scientific schools, receives and dismisses official legations and regulates their procedure, negotiations, and correspondence. It would be considered wholly inconsistent with royal dignity for the sovereign to write a letter to anyone, no matter what might be his position, within or without the kingdom.

The fourth bureau is called Pimpu or the Military Court, which holds jurisdiction over all departments of national defense. It has power to punish the guilty and to reward the energetic, according to the magnitude of the crime committed or of the service rendered. This bureau also makes promotions and supervises military examinations.

The fifth court is called Cumpu and corresponds to our Commission of Public Works and Buildings, supervising the planning and construction of public institutions and edifices, such as the palaces of the King and of his relatives and the homes of magistrates. Naval construction, including bridges, the building of city walls, and the upkeep of all public construction are included in the scope of this particular bureau.

The sixth is the Criminal Court known as Himpu, established for both the detection and the punishment of crime. The police of the entire country come within its jurisdiction.

These six courts regulate the life of the whole empire. In every province and in every city there are stationed a special magistrate and notaries whose duty it is to keep the higher courts informed of the proceedings of the minor courts. This system results in the division and in the diminution of the tremendous amount of business to be handled by the upper courts, while the orderly arrangement and the great number of assistants tends to lessen the burden of the office of high magistrates. Each of the high courts is presided over by a single judge called Ciam-Ciu and he has two assistants entitled Cilam—the Assessor on the Right and the Assessor on the Left. In the capital city and throughout the land these three are numbered among the very highest of public dignitaries. To them belong the organization and the supervision of all the inferior courts, each of which has its associate judges, notaries, clerks, court assistants, caretakers, and numerous other help.

Besides these regular courts there is another kind of federal bureau, composed of three or four members, or at times of six. They are known as the Colao, and their particular obligation is the general safety of the kingdom; a secret service of the throne. As the King does not now take part, in a public way, in discussing the business of the realm with the Colao, as was formerly the custom, they remain in the palace during the whole day and answer the numerous petitions made to the King. Their answers are presented to the King himself by whom they are approved, or rejected, or changed as he sees fit, and his final decision, which he makes in writing, is put into execution as his direct command.

Besides the classes or orders of the magistrates already described and many others which we shall pass over because they differ but little from our own, there are two special orders never heard of among our people. These are the Choli and the Zauli, each consisting of sixty or more chosen philosophers, all prudent men and tried, who have already given exceptional proof of their fidelity to the King and to the realm. These two orders are reserved by the King for business of greater moment pertaining to the royal court or to the provinces, and by him they are entrusted with great responsibility, carrying with it both respect and authority. They correspond in some manner to what we would call keepers of the public conscience, inasmuch as they inform the King as often as they see fit, of any infraction of the law in any part of the entire kingdom. No one is spared from their scrutiny, even the highest magistrates, as they do not hesitate to speak, even though it concerns the King himself or his household. If they had the power of doing something more than talking, or rather of writing, and if they were not wholly dependent upon the King whom they admonish, their particular office would correspond to that of the Lacedemonian Ephors. And yet they do their duty so thoroughly that they are a source of wonder to outsiders and a good example for imitation. Neither King nor magistrates can escape their courage and frankness, and even when they arouse the royal wrath to such an extent that the King becomes severely angry with them, they will never desist from their admonitions and criticism until some remedy has been applied to the public evil against which they are inveighing. In fact, when the grievance is particularly acute, they are sure to put a sting into their complaints and to show no partiality where the crown or the courts are concerned. This same privilege of offering written criticism is also granted by law to any magistrate and even to a private citizen, but for the most part it is exercised only by those to whose particular office it pertains. Numerous copies are made of all such written documents submitted to the crown and of the answers made to them. In this way, what goes on in the royal headquarters is quickly communicated to every corner of the country. These documents are also compiled in book form, and whatever of their content is deemed worthy of handing down to posterity is transcribed into the annals of the King's regime.

Some few years ago, the present reigning monarch wanted to name his second son as crown prince instead of his first-born, because the younger boy was particularly dear to him and to the Queen. This change was contrary to the law of the land, and the number of written complaints the King received reprehending his action was so great that he flew into a passion and discharged or demoted more than a hundred officials. Nothing daunted by this, the admonitors refused to temper their attitude. On the contrary, those of the magistracy who still survived as such, arranged to visit the royal palace on a certain day, where they stripped themselves of all insignia of office, and sent a messenger to inform the King that, if he insisted upon violating the law in this way, they would relinquish all magisterial duties and retire to their homes as private citizens, leaving him free to entrust the care of the kingdom to whomsoever he wished. When this unusual proceeding was brought to his attention, the monarch made it known that he had changed his mind on the matter of his successor.

Only lately, when the chief Colao was delinquent in the performance of his duty, he was denounced to the King in nearly a hundred written complaints from the admonitors, within a space of two months, despite the fact that they knew he was a royal favorite. Shortly afterward he disappeared, and rumor has it that he was put out of the way with considerable torture.

Besides the regular magistrates there are in the royal palace various other organizations, instituted for particular purposes. The most exalted of these is what is known as the Han-lin-yuen, made up of selected doctors of philosophy and chosen by examination. Members of this cabinet have nothing to do with public administration but outrank all public officials in dignity of office. Ambition for a place in this select body means no end of labor and of sacrifice. These are the King's secretaries, who do both his writing and his composing. They edit and compile the royal annals and publish the laws and statutes of the land. The tutors of kings and princes are chosen from their number. They are entirely devoted to study and there are grades within the cabinet which are determined by the publications of its members. Hence, they are honored with the highest dignity within the regal court, but not beyond it. The Colao are appointed only from members of this cabinet. The income they receive from friends for whom they write inscriptions, epitaphs, and the like is considerable.

Such writings are continually in demand, and they are looked upon as the very choicest of their kind, if they were fashioned by or bear the name of one of the royal secretaries. These dignitaries also act as examiners and as proctors in all examinations for degrees of licentiate and doctorate, and they are afterward chosen as directors by the successful candidates, from whom they receive a salary.

All of the various bureaus of Pekin and the magistrates belonging to them, excepting the Colao, are duplicated in Nankin, but they are of less importance there because of the absence of the King. The change of royal residence from Nankin, the old capital, to Pekin, the new, they account for as follows: Under Humvu, the seat of royal residence was at Nankin. When he died, one of his nephews, a certain Yunlo, with his army, was protecting the boundaries of the kingdom in the northern provinces from inroads by the Tartars, who had recently been expelled. When Yunlo noticed that the heir of Humvu was weak and lacking in ambition, he decided to deprive him of the throne and to seize it for himself. The provinces of the north were easily won over. Then he marched upon Nankin, and by means of force, deceit, and bribes, succeeded in gaining over the other provinces and in expelling the authorities from Nankin. With no further opposition, he took over the entire kingdom. Having more forces as well as more confidence in the northern provinces, and because there was a possibility of the Tartars revolting to re-establish their government, he decided to remain in that vicinity and in the very city in which the Tartar king resided when the Chinese dethroned him. He then named the city Pekin, or Northern Court, just as the Southern Court had been called Nankin. Then, in order to placate the inhabitants of the former capital, when the change was made, he permitted them to retain the court and the privileges attached to it which they formerly enjoyed.

We now come to the public administration of the provinces. The special cities that belong to the legislatures of Pekin and Nankin are governed in the same manner as the other cities in these provinces, but their appeals are made to the particular legislature to whose jurisdiction they belong. The jurisdiction of the other thirteen provinces belongs to the two courts in each province, called the Pucinsu and the Naganzafu, the former being a general and the latter a criminal court. These courts are situated in the Metropolitan City of the province and are somewhat elaborate in procedure. Each court has a number of Associate Justices as well as the Chief Justice, called the Tauli. At times, the Tauli may be absent from the metropolis due to the fact that he has to preside in a number of cities, but it is understood that he will never withdraw very far from his jurisdiction.

The provinces, as we have remarked, are divided into different regions or districts called Fu, and each district has its own governor or Cifu. The districts in turn are subdivided into Ceu and Hien, which might be called cities and towns, corresponding to those of medium size in our own country. The prefects or mayors of these cities are called respectively Ciceu and Cihien; Ci in Chinese meaning, to govern. The governing officer in a district or in a city will have his assistants, such as the four assessors, who help as judges and advisers in deciding cases pertinent to their jurisdiction.

This would seem to be the proper place to note and to correct an error which has crept into certain writings on the matter now under consideration, namely: Because the governor and his Curia adopt the name of the city in which they are located, as for example, in the city of Nancian the entire district and the governor and his cabinet or council would be known as Nancian-fu, some writers have concluded that it is only to these cities to which the fu is attached, and that all other cities are known as Ceu and Hien, or towns and villages. This is quite a false idea, because the suffix fu is determined not from the size or the population of a city but from the method of its public administration. In fact, the city itself in which the ruler of a whole district lives is known as Hien, and it may have its own chief officer called the Cihien, who has his assistants, just as in other cities. The governor of the district would have no more authority in this particular city than he had in other parts of his district, but the law allows a first appeal to him when a case judged by the Ciceu or the Cihien is appealed to a superior. A second appeal, which is permitted in more serious cases, would be made to the higher magistrates of the metropolis: to the Pucinsu and the Naganzafu, or to their associates, depending upon the gravity of the case in question. The metropolitan cities likewise have their Cifu and Cihien just as the lesser or subordinate cities, and the jurisdiction of the courts, as well as the authority of the court officers, is well defined and admirably ordered throughout the entire system.

As the administration of the Commonwealth is dependent upon the capital city, besides the regular provincial magistrates, there are two more, ranking the local officials, who are delegated to each province from Pekin. One of these, the Tutam, resides in the province; the other, the Ciayuen, is sent from the capital to the province, once a year, for inspection. The authority of the former extends over all other magistrates and citizens, and he is a sort of plenipotentiary for military and for all other federal interests, similar to a regent. The office of the second would correspond to that of a commissioner or a royal investigator. Representing the King, as he does, he is responsible for the conduct of the entire province. He visits all cities and military centers, inspects the offices of all magistrates, and has power to punish and to demote those of minor rank. His reports go directly to the King, and having the power to impose capital punishment, he is naturally respected and feared by everyone. Besides those already mentioned, there are a great many other magistrates exercising various duties in cities, towns, and in country districts. There are also a great many military magistrates throughout the country, especially in maritime and in border cities, who have supervision over ports, walls, bridges, and forts. These officers are also in charge of recruiting and of military displays and games. These exhibitions are held daily and almost everywhere, giving one the impression that the country is actually at war, though the entire kingdom is enjoying the profoundest peace. Each of the two orders of magistrates, the philosophical and the military, is divided into nine classes.

The salaries of all magistrates are paid monthly by the government, either in money or in rice, and these salaries in either order are relatively small in comparison to the dignity of the offices held, in no case exceeding a thousand gold pieces[4] a year. Those holding corresponding office in philosophical and in military rank receive an equal amount of pay; the highest military commander receiving the same as the highest officer of literary ranking. This statement, however, is to be understood for each order as referring only to their official salaries, because they receive far more than their official pay from other than government sources. We make no mention here of what they receive from extra-official industry, by their business acumen, or from inheritance and gifts accruing from their particular positions, which at times may add up to a considerable fortune.

All magistrates, high or low and of either order, wear the same kind of black hat, which has two ovate wings just above the ears and so lightly attached to the hat that they fall off very easily. The reason for this particular arrangement, as they say, is to guarantee that the one wearing the hat will walk upright and modestly, without even slightly

---

[4] Here again the author assigns no definite or relative value to the gold piece mentioned.

bending the head, which would be unbecoming to magisterial dignity. They also wear the same kind of clothes and greaves, or leggings, specially designed in black polished leather. Their belt or girdle, about four inches wide with extended ends hanging at the side, is also of special pattern and ornamented with square and circular figures. The mantle or cope consists of two rectangular strips of fine texture worn back and front, and is elegantly embroidered in gold in Phrygian fashion. There is a great variety of these sashes and mantles indicating differences in dignity. One who knew how to distinguish them could immediately tell whether the magistrate belonged to the philosophical or to the military order, and what position he held in it, by the figures of beasts and birds and flowers that are wrought into the weaving of the cloth. The particular rank in either order is indicated by the decorative material on the sash, such as braided twigs or horn, perhaps of a unicorn, or it might be a design in highly scented reed wood, or of silver or gold. The very highest rank is indicated by a certain translucent stone like jasper, though it really is not jasper, having closer resemblance to a sapphire. They call it Yu-ce. It is brought from the kingdom of Cascar by merchants who trade with the Saracens of the west, and the Chinese look upon it as a precious stone of great value. We shall have occasion to say more about this later on.

The Chinese can distinguish between their magistrates by the parasols they use as protection against the sun when they go out in public. Some of these are blue and others yellow. Sometimes for effect they will have two or three of these sunshades, but only one if their rank does not permit of more. They may also be recognized by their mode of transportation in public. The lower ranks ride on horseback, the higher are carried about on the shoulders of their servants in gestatorial chairs. The number of carriers also has a significance of rank; some are allowed only four, others may have eight. There are other ways also of distinguishing the magistracy and the rank of dignity therein; by banners and pennants, chains and censer cups, and by the number of the guards who give orders to make way for the passage of the dignitary. The escort itself is held in such high esteem by the public that no one would question their orders. Even in a crowded city everyone gives way at the sound of their voices with a spontaneity that corresponds to the rank of the approaching celebrity.

Before closing this chapter on Chinese public administration, it would seem to be quite worth while recording a few more things in which this people differ from Europeans. To begin with, it seems to be quite remarkable when we stop to consider it, that in a kingdom of almost limitless expanse and innumerable population, and abounding in copious supplies of every description, though they have a well-equipped army and navy that could easily conquer the neighboring nations, neither the King nor his people ever think of waging a war of aggression. They are quite content with what they have and are not ambitious of conquest. In this respect they are much different from the people of Europe, who are frequently discontent with their own governments and covetous of what others enjoy. While the nations of the West seem to be entirely consumed with the idea of supreme domination, they cannot even preserve what their ancestors have bequeathed them, as the Chinese have done through a period of some thousands of years. This assertion seems to have some bearing upon what many of our writers maintain relative to the initial founding of the empire, when they assert that the Chinese not only subjugated the neighboring nations but extended their sway even as far as India. After diligent study of the history of China, covering a period of more than four thousand years, I must admit that I have never seen any mention of such conquest, nor have I ever heard of them extending the boundaries of their empire. On the contrary, in frequent inquiry among learned Chinese historians, relative to this assertion, their answer has always been the same; that it was not so and could not possibly be so. Not to question the reputation of the writers who have recorded the error, the mistake may have arisen from the fact that certain evidences of the presence of the Chinese have been discovered beyond the confines of the kingdom. For example, one might cite the Philippine Islands, to which they found their way in private enterprise rather than on any official commission by their government.

Another remarkable fact and quite worthy of note as marking a difference from the West, is that the entire kingdom is administered by the Order of the Learned, commonly known as The Philosophers. The responsibility for orderly management of the entire realm is wholly and completely committed to their charge and care. The army, both officers and soldiers, hold them in high respect and show them the promptest obedience and deference, and not infrequently the military are disciplined by them as a schoolboy might be punished by his master. Policies of war are formulated and military questions are decided by the Philosophers only, and their advice and counsel has more weight with the King than that of the military leaders. In fact very few of these, and only on rare occasions, are admitted to war consultations. Hence it follows that those who aspire to be cultured frown upon war and would prefer the lowest rank in the philosophical order to the highest in the military, realizing that the Philosophers far excel military leaders in the good will and the respect of the people and in opportunities of acquiring wealth. What is still more surprising to strangers is that these same Philosophers, as they are called, with respect to nobility of sentiment and in contempt of danger and death, where fidelity to King and country is concerned, surpass even those whose particular profession is the defense of the fatherland. Perhaps this sentiment has its origin in the fact that the mind of man is ennobled by the study of letters. Or again, it may have developed from the fact that from the beginning and foundation of this empire the study of letters was always more acceptable to the people than the profession of arms, as being more suitable to a people who had little or no interest in the extension of the empire.

The order and harmony that prevails among magistrates, both high and low, in the provinces and in the regal Curia is also worthy of admiration. Their attitude toward the King, in exact obedience and in external ceremony, is a cause of wonderment to a foreigner. The literati would never think of omitting certain customary formal visits to one another or the regular practice of freely offering gifts. In the courts and elsewhere, inferiors always bend the knee when speaking to a superior, and address him in the most dignified language. The same is true of the people toward their prefects and toward the mayor of the city, even though these officers may have arisen from the lowest state in life before attaining their literary degrees and admittance to the magistracy. The term of office of all the dignitaries we have been discussing is three years, unless one be confirmed in his position or promoted by order of the crown. Usually they are promoted but not for the same locality, lest they should develop friendships and become lenient in the administration of justice, or develop a following in the province in which they are so influential. The experience of past ages has taught them that a magistrate burdened with favors is likely to incline toward the introduction of novelties and away from the rigor of the law.

Every third year the ranking officials of all provinces, districts, and cities, namely, the Pu-cin-su, the Naganzafu, the Cifu, Ciceu, Cihien, and the like, must convene in Pekin to express their solemn fealty to the King. At that time a rigorous investigation is made concerning the magistrates of every province in the entire kingdom, including those present and those not called. The purpose of this inspection is to determine who shall be retained in public office, how many are to be removed, and the number to be promoted or demoted and punished, if need be. There is no respect for persons in this searching inquisition. I myself have observed that not even the King would dare to change a decision settled upon by the judges of this public investigation. Those who are punished are by no means few or of lower grade. After this general inquiry took place in 1607, we read that sentence was passed upon four thousand of the magistrates, and I say read because a list of the names of those concerned is published in a single volume and circulated throughout the land.

There are five classes of those who fall under a sentence. Class number one includes those who are condemned for venality in public office; who have enriched themselves from the fortunes of private individuals or from public appropriation. These are stripped of all insignia and immunities and are excluded from future appointment to public office. The second class is composed of those who were cruel in inflicting punishment upon the guilty. These are also shorn of all insignia and privileges of office and sent home as private citizens. Class number three is made up of the aged, the sick, and those who were remiss in inflicting punishment or in the conduct of their office. These are returned to private life but are permitted to wear the costume and to enjoy the immunities of the office they held, for the rest of their lives. Class four enumerates those who were too hasty or were lacking in consideration in passing sentence, and those lacking in reason or deliberation in the administration of public trust. Culprits in this class are demoted to offices of lower dignity, or transferred to a district in which the duties of public office are considered to be less difficult. Finally, in the last class we find those who are careless in regulating their own lives or the affairs of their family, and in general those who lead a life unbecoming to the dignity of their public office. Their punishment is likewise deprivation of office and of the privileges attached thereto. Officers of the royal court are also subject to a like investigation and liable to similar judgments, but their inspection is held only every fifth year. The same procedure is observed and with the same austerity in the quinquennial inspection of the federal prefects.

It is a general law that no judge may hold court in the province in which he was born unless he is a military prefect. This is a precaution against favoring relatives and friends and, in the case of the military, to foster a deeper love of country. When a judge is holding court, none of his children or domestics is permitted to leave home for fear he might be offered a bribe through them, but the usual deference shown to a magistrate in public by servants is always observed. When the judge himself leaves for court, the exits from his house, public and private, are sealed with a seal carrying a punishment for violation, in order to prevent his servants from going out without his knowledge.

The Chinese will not permit a foreigner to live at large within the confines of the kingdom if he has any intention of ever leaving it or if he has any communication with the outside world. Under no conditions will they permit a stranger to penetrate to the interior of the country. I have never heard of a law to this effect, but it seems quite clear that this custom has developed through the ages from an innate fear and distrust of outside nations. This suspicion exists not only of people who live overseas or at a great distance and are practically unknown to the Chinese. They are also suspicious of friendly as well as of enemy aliens, and even of those with whom they trade, such as the neighboring Koreans, who make use of Chinese laws. As long as I have been here, I have never seen a Korean in China, save one woman, a liberated slave, whom a Chinese general brought back with him after long residence in that country. If a foreigner should get into China secretly, he would not be put to death or kept in slavery, but he would be prevented from leaving China, lest he should stir up excitement outside to the detriment of the Chinese Government. Hence, the severest punishments are meted out to those who deal with outsiders without the direct consent of the sovereign.

When necessity demands that someone be sent beyond the borders, even though he will be supplied with the proper credentials and a mandate, it is difficult to get anyone to accept the commission. When such a legate is leaving, his whole family bewail his departure as though he were being sent to certain death. It is quite different, however, when he returns, because he is generally rewarded by being appointed to some kind of a judgeship.

No one is permitted to carry arms within city limits, not even soldiers or officers, military prefects or magistrates, unless one be en route to war or on the way to drill or to a military school. Certain of the higher magistrates, however, may be accompanied by an armed guard. Such is their dislike for arms that no one is allowed to have them in his home, except perhaps a metal dagger which might be needed on a journey as protection against robbers. Fighting and violence among the people are practically unheard of, save what might be concluded by hair pulling and scratching, and there is no requiting of injuries by wounds and death. On the contrary, one who will not fight and restrains himself from returning a blow is praised for his prudence and bravery.

When the King dies, in order to prevent the rise of factions over the lawful succession, no son or male relative of the King, other than the legitimate heir to the throne, is permitted to remain in the royal city. Moreover, these same relatives are prohibited under pain of death from wandering about separately from town to town. If disputes arise among them, they must be settled by the one of highest rank by whom they are governed. If a difficulty should arise between one of them and someone who is not a relative of the King, then they become subject to the proceedings and the penalties of the public courts, just as an ordinary citizen.

7. Concerning
Certain Chinese Customs

THE ANCIENT KINGDOM of China derived its name from the universal practice of urbanity and politeness, and this is one of the five cardinal virtues esteemed by them above all others and treated at length in their writings. With them, respect and deference and consideration in business transactions constitute the foundation of urbanity. Indeed they make so much of urbane ceremonies that a great part of their time is wasted in them. To one acquainted with their customs, it really is a source of regret that they do not rid themselves of this external show, in which they far surpass all Europeans.

We shall first treat of their manner of salutation and of the signs of mutual respect they employ on meeting. Afterward we shall say a word about some other polite customs and particularly of such as differ mostly from those of our own people. Taking off the hat has no meaning of respect among the Chinese, nor any motion of the feet, or embracing, or kissing one's hand, or any other such gesture. Their most common form of salutation is as follows: With their hands joined and hidden in the loose sleeves of the flowing toga they generally wear —and their hands will always be so concealed unless they are swaying a fan or are otherwise actually engaged—they face one another modestly elevating the hands still hidden in their sleeves; they then lower them slowly, at the same time repeating zin, zin, in a modulated undertone. This word zĭn has no particular meaning other than being an expression of respect. We might call it an interjection expressive of respect.

When one is paying an official visit and frequently when friends meet in the street, with hands concealed as mentioned, they bend the body, inclining the head toward the ground. This is the ordinary salutation performed by all simultaneously when they come together in a group. This custom is known as Zoye, and in it the one of superior rank stands on the right when there are only two, as does a visitor to the right of his host. In the northern provinces right and left are the reverse of what they are in the south. Frequently, too, when this ceremony of greeting is over they change places and pass to the opposite side so that he who ceded the place of honor may be returned to it. When the initial salutation is over they then face to the north, standing side by side, if they happen to be outside. If the meeting takes place indoors, they face toward the head of the room, opposite to the door of entrance, which would generally place them facing north. It seems as though it were an ancient custom with the Chinese to have their reception rooms in palaces and temples and other larger buildings, as well as in private homes, so designed that the entrance will be at the southern end of the room, so that those who sit opposite the door will be facing south. Hence, in the reception ceremony which is held in this hall, when they are facing the front or head of the room they are facing north. When they wish to express more profound veneration, as on an occasion of first meeting or after a long absence, or if congratulating each other on a solemn feast day or for any other special reason, after the bowing described above, they fall upon their knees and touch the forehead to the ground.

After the first kneeling they stand up, make another bow, and then genuflect again, and this may be done three or even four times. When parents or a superior, say a magistrate or some other dignitary, is being greeted, the one being honored will stand or sit at the head of the room and from there, with hands joined and hidden as described, will return each bow or genuflection with a slight inclination forward and a nod of the head. When the reception is less formal, the one being received takes his place at the east side of the room rather than at the north. This method of reception is precisely the same as the ceremony observed before an altar in the veneration of images, in a temple or in a private home. When servants greet a master, or one of a lower social class a superior, they fall upon their knees and touch the ground very lightly with the forehead three times, as they do before their images. In conversation with his master, a servant will stand a little to the side and accompany each response with a slight bend of the knee, just as a common citizen does when talking with a dignitary.

There are other customs also in their way of talking and writing in which they differ greatly from us, and these are increased in number by the difficulties involved in their language. When two are conversing they never use the grammatical second person, and different grammatical forms may be used in talking of those present and of those absent. The pronoun of the first person is not used when one is talking about himself, except perhaps when a master is addressing a servant or a superior an inferior. In conversation they have as many ways of avoiding self-praise as they have of lauding others, and perhaps the most modest of these is by using the proper name when referring to self, instead of saying I. If the conversation should fall upon parents, brothers, or children, or if reference is made to a part of the body, to the home, or the fatherland, to one's writing, or even to another's illness, a polite word of praise or of sympathy is always interjected. If, however, the topic has reference to the one speaking, a more reserved expression will be used. It will appear quite evident from this that one must be well acquainted with the different formulas for expressing his ideas if he is not to appear uncultured or ignorant and if he hopes to understand what is being said or written.

When relatives or friends pay a visit, the host is expected to return the visit, and a definite and detailed ceremony accompanies their custom of visiting. The one who is calling presents a little folder in which his name is written and which may contain a few words of address depending upon the rank of the visitor or of the host. This folder is presented by the door servant. If one person is calling upon more than one or if more than one are calling upon only one, then there will be as many calling cards in the form of folders as there are callers or recipients. These folders or booklets consist of about a dozen pages of white paper and are about a palm and a half in length, oblong in shape, with a two-inch strip of red paper down the middle of the cover. Usually this booklet is contained in a cardboard case with the same kind of red decoration. There is such a great variety of these calling tablets, and they are in such continual use, that one must have at least twenty different kinds on hand for different functions, marked with appropriate titles. It is a common custom with those who do much visiting to have the butler write into his memorandum the names and addresses of those who have called, lest the social obligation of returning a visit within three days should slip their memory. If those who are to be visited are not at home or for some reason or other cannot receive visitors, the caller may leave his or her folder at the door. Such a visit may be repaid in the same way, by merely leaving the booklet at the door, and then each one is satisfied that the obligation has been fulfilled. The more distinguished the visitor happens to be, the larger he will write his name in his visiting book. Sometimes the characters will be an inch high so that a single signing will take up a whole page of the book from top to bottom in which direction the Chinese write.

These same little books are used when they bring or send little gifts, which is a common custom among them, and these are generally answered by a gift of equal value. In this instance the folder is not only signed with the name of the donor but the gift is described in somewhat elegant terms. It is not considered to be a breach of etiquette, and the donor will take no offense at all, if the gifts are returned in whole or in part. When this happens, the gifts returned will be accompanied by a booklet expressing thanks and a polite refusal, or describing the presents that were retained and enumerating those that are offered in exchange. This exchanging of gifts is carried on continually and with such an extended ritual of social amenities that it would take altogether too long to describe it in full detail.

Another custom common among the Chinese but novel for us is that of giving money gifts, amounting to ten or five or fewer gold coins, which superiors might send to subordinates or sometimes vice versa. When a magistrate or one who has a literary degree is paying a visit, he wears a special visiting gown, which is quite different from his regular toga of daily attire. Even an important personage who has no title of honor will wear a specially designed gown when visiting, and it would be taken amiss if he should appear in his ordinary raiment. In keeping with this custom, so as to be able to attend the conventions and meetings of the leading dignitaries, we ourselves always dress, as need may be, according to the custom of the class in question. If perchance one should meet a person who is not wearing his top garment, which they call a courtesy vestment, he will not greet the other with the customary gestures until he puts it on. Usually when one goes out he has a servant with him who carries this ritual cape. However, when two friends meet, if one of them has on his visiting cloak and the other is without it, the one wearing the cloak will take it off. Then they salute each other in their everyday clothes with the ceremonies already described.

When a family is receiving at home, the one in charge takes a chair in both hands, and places it in the position of honor for the visitor. Then he dusts it off with his hand, though there will be no sign of dust on it at all. If there are several visitors, he arranges the chairs according to dignity of position in the reception room and then touches each of them with his hands, as it were, to see that they are properly aligned. This gesture is then repeated by all of those who are being visited. The next step in the ceremony is for the principal visitor to take the chair of the host and place it opposite his own, repeating the pretended gesture of dusting it off with his hand. This placing of chairs is then repeated by the other visitors, if there be more, in order of age or of dignity. While this is being done, the one to whom special honor is to be paid on the occasion stands a little aside, and with his hands joined and concealed in his sleeve continues to raise and to lower them slightly and slowly, while returning thanks and modestly refusing the proffered compliment. Undoubtedly they waste a lot of time in ceremonies connected with the proëdria or the principal seat of honor, concerning which definite regulations are to be observed. Age takes precedence among citizens of equal rank. In the courts, priority is determined by dignity of office. The place of honor is always granted to a welcome foreigner, and such visitors rank according to the greater distance from which they come. Under this formality we are given the first places in nearly every gathering, and it is not considered to be proper to refuse the honor or to excuse oneself because of modesty.

When the guests are seated, the best trained servant in the house, clad in a flowing robe reaching down to his ankles, sets out a decorated table on which there are as many saucers as there are people present. These saucers are filled with the drink called Cia, which we have had occasion to mention and in which there are small pieces of sweet fruits. This is considered to be a dessert and it is eaten with a silver spoon. The servant begins by serving the guest of honor first, then the others in order, and ends with the host, who occupies the last place at table. If the visit is extended, the servant makes the rounds again or even three or four times, and each time a different kind of dessert is served. When the visit is over, or the guests come to the threshold and are about to leave, they repeat the bowing ceremonies, and the host follows them to the door, returning the bows. Then he asks them if they are ready to take horse or to ascend the gestatorial chairs in which they came, but they answer that they will not do this until he has closed the door within. After that he turns toward the door and makes a bow and they repeat the gesture in the same direction. Finally, standing on the threshold, he makes a third bow and that, too, is returned by the departing guests. Then he disappears from their view behind the door to give them time to mount their horses or to take their places in the sedan chairs, and again reappears to salute them. This time he has his hands concealed in his sleeves, slowly raising them and letting them fall and repeating zin, zin, and the guests do the same as they disappear. After a little while he sends a servant after his guests to bid them good-by in his name, and they return the compliment through their servants to his.

A few words about Chinese banquets, which are both frequent and very ceremonious. With some, in fact, they are of almost daily occurrence, because the Chinese accompany nearly every function, social or religious, with a dinner and consider a banquet as the highest expression of friendship. After the fashion of the Greeks they speak of drink meetings rather than of banquets and not without reason, too, because, although their cups do not hold more wine than a nutshell, the frequency with which they fill them makes up for their moderate content. They do not use forks or spoons or knives for eating, but rather polished sticks, about a palm and a half long, with which they are very adept in lifting any kind of food to their mouths, without touching it with their fingers. The food is brought to the table already cut into small pieces, unless it be something that is soft, such as cooked eggs or fish and the like, which can be easily separated with the sticks. Their drinks, which may be wine or water or the drink called Cia, are always served warm, and this is so even in the hot summer. The idea behind this custom seems to be that it is more beneficial for the stomach and, generally speaking, the Chinese are longer-lived than Europeans and preserve their physical powers up to seventy or even eighty years of age. The custom might also account for the fact that they never suffer from gallstones, so common among the people of the West who are fond of cold drinks.

When one is to be invited to a formal dinner, on the day before the set date, or perhaps several days in advance, he will receive one of the booklets we have already described. In this, bearing the name of the host, there will be a brief set formula politely and elegantly expressing the fact that he has polished up the silverware and prepared a modest repast of herbs for a set day and hour. The dinners are usually held at night. The invitation continues, stating that the host would be pleased to hear his guest hold forth in the expression of his ideas, from which the company might hope to garner some jewels of wisdom, and requesting that he might not deprive them of so great a favor. On the longitudinal red strip running down the cover of the invitation booklet, as we have mentioned, the more honorable of the guests' names is inscribed, together with his various titles, in order. We say the more honorable of his names because, as stated before, the Chinese have a number of different names. This same kind of invitation is sent to each individual guest. On the morning of the day set for the dinner another invitation is sent to each one, in shorter form, urging him to be sure and be on time. Just before the time set for the dinner, a third invitation is sent, as they say, to meet the guests on the road.

On arriving at the house the usual salutations are exchanged, and the guests are invited to be seated in the antechamber to drink Cia before going to the dining room. This room will be very ornately decorated, not with carpets which they do not use at all, but with pictures and vases and flowers and antique furnishings. Each person is assigned a separate table, and sometimes two tables placed together are set before a single guest. These tables are several feet long and almost as wide, and are set with costly cloths, draped to the floor after the fashion of our altars. The chairs are highly polished with a bituminous stain and decorated with pictures, which are sometimes done in gold. Before the company sits down to dine, the host takes a bowl fashioned from gold or silver, or marble, or some other precious material and, filling it with wine, places it on a tray which he holds in both hands while gracefully saluting the principal guest with a profound bow. Then, going from the dining room into the courtyard, he faces to the south and pours out the wine on the ground, as an offering to the Lord of Heaven. After bowing again he returns to the dining room, puts another bowl on the salver, salutes the head guest from the customary position, and they both proceed to the table in the middle of the room where guest number one is to be seated. The head place among the Chinese is in the middle of the long side of the table, or of the tables arranged at length, and not, as among us, at the end. Here the host places the bowl in a dish, holding it in both hands, and, taking the eating sticks from a servant, arranges them very carefully for his principal visitor.

These sticks are made of ebony or of ivory or some other durable material that is not easily stained, and the ends which touch the food are usually burnished with gold or silver. When the host has finished setting the place at table for his guest, he places a chair for him, dusts it off with his sleeve, and returns to the center of the room, where he makes another ritual bow. This ceremony is repeated for each guest, placing the second on the right and the third on the left of the most important visitor. When all the chairs are placed, the principal guest receives a goblet on a tray from a servant. This is for the host, and ordering the servant to fill the cup with wine, together with all the guests, he makes the usual bow and places the tray with the cup on the host's table. This table is set at the end or the foot of the room, so that the host's back is to the door and to the south and he is facing the head table. The same guest of honor arranges the chair and the eating sticks for the host in the same manner in which the host arranged them for the guest. Finally, while the others are taking their places, right and left, all of which are set with chairs and eating sticks, the guest of honor stands by the side of the host, gracefully repeating the gesture of concealed hands and declining the proffered honor of first place at the banquet, while at the same time making a graceful curtsy of thanks as he accepts it.

The Chinese do not touch their food with the hands and so they do not wash their hands before going to table or after eating. At the conclusion of the foregoing ceremonies all the guests bow simultaneously to the host, then each guest to the others, and they take their places. They all drink at the same time, and when they do, the host lifts the tray or plate containing his cup, with both hands, lowers it slowly, and invites all to drink. This gesture is repeated by all at once as they turn toward the host and drink with him. Usually they drink very slowly, by sipping, and this ceremony may be repeated four or five times before a cup is emptied. This custom of sipping is their usual way of drinking, even when taking water. They never drink in a continued sequence of swallowing, as we do. The food is brought on in courses as soon as the first goblet has been emptied.

At the beginning of the meal there is a short ceremony with the eating sticks, in which they all follow the example of the host. The sticks are taken in each hand, slightly raised and slowly lowered so that everyone touches the food with them at the same time. After that they eat by selecting bits of food and lifting them to the mouth with the sticks. While they are eating they are careful not to replace the sticks on the table until the guest of honor does that first, which is a signal for the servants to refill his cup and then the cups of all the others. And so the ritual of eating and drinking is repeated again and again, but more time is consumed in drinking than in eating. During the whole time of the dinner they either talk on lighter or humorous subjects or watch the performance of a comedy. At times they may listen to a singer or a musician, as these entertainers frequently appear at a dinner, although not invited, hoping to be paid, as they usually are, by the invited guests.

The Chinese eat about everything that we do, and their food is well prepared. They do not give much attention to any one particular kind of food that might be served, as their dinners are rated by the variety rather than by the kind of courses offered. At times the table will be covered with dishes of food, large and small. They observe no particular order for courses of fish and meat as we do, but serve them indiscriminately. Once a dish is put on the table it is not removed until the end of the meal, and before the dinner is over the tables are creaking under the load, and dishes are piled up so high that you would think someone was building a miniature castle. No bread is served at a banquet or a special dinner, nor rice either, which takes the place of bread with the Chinese, except perhaps at less formal dinners and then at the end of the meal. If rice should be served, then no wine is taken before eating it. Even in their regular daily routine, the Chinese will never drink wine before eating rice. Sometimes, different games are introduced during the course of a banquet, in which the loser has to take an extra drink, at which the others applaud with great amusement. Toward the end of the meal the drinking cups are changed, and though each one is served the same number of times, no one is ever urged to drink beyond his rational capacity. This change of cups is merely a friendly invitation to continue drinking. The Chinese brew their wine as we brew beer and it is not very potent. A heavy drinker might get drunk on it but the aftereffects of the following day are not very distressing. In general, they are moderate eaters, and yet it might happen, say when one is leaving town for a long absence, that he will attend seven or eight dinners on the eve of his departure, so as not to slight any of his friends. These dinners, however, would be much less sumptuous than the regular banquets, which often last all night long and into the early dawn. What food is left over from a feast is generously distributed among the servants.

Perhaps the most striking of all Chinese ceremonies are those accorded to the King, and perhaps, too, there is no other individual on earth, lay or ecclesiastical, surrounded with such ritualistic formality. The first surprising fact is that no one ever speaks directly to the King, other than his children, or his relatives who live in his castle, or the eunuchs who serve there. We shall pass over the rites that are reserved for the King by his eunuchs, as they are of no interest to our narrative. However, different orders and grades are instituted for these particular servants, and the magistrates among them, who live outside of the royal palace, can address the King only by means of supplicatory folders or notebooks. These folders are strictly official and contain such a variety of formulas that only those who are trained in their composition, such as the secretaries of the royal palace, are capable of writing them. Not everyone, even of the literati, would know how to compose one.

On the first day of the Chinese New Year and the beginning of their season of spring, corresponding in our reckoning to the new moon just preceding or just following the nones or fifth of February, each province sends a legate to make an official call on the sovereign. This is like the more solemn triennial visit of allegiance which we have already noted. Moreover, on the first day of each new moon, all the magistrates convene in the chief cities, in which a throne is erected to the King and is decorated with the regal insignia of gilded carved dragons, and other ornate carvings. Before this they go through a ceremony of bowing and genuflecting, with other modest gestures, depending upon the customs of the district. In this way they express their veneration, and during it they are proclaiming the King and wishing him ten thousand years of life. This is the same custom that is everywhere observed on the King's birthday. On that day the magistrates of Pekin, the legates from the provinces, and relatives of the King living outside of the palace, and on whom he has bestowed titles of distinction, come together to congratulate the monarch and to assure him of their fidelity with costly gifts. Besides these, all who were named to the magistracy by this King and all who received any other distinction from him are ordered by law to be present at the regal palace before dawn to offer thanks for his generosity. Here, under the direction of the prefects and of the Instructors in Rites, they go through the special ceremonies reserved for the King alone, and they pay a penalty for the slightest mistake in observance, though the King himself is not present. For this ceremony they are clothed in a purple robe, like damask silk, and wear a triple crown of gilded silver. Each one also carries an ivory plaque, about six inches long, holding it in both hands, and if he has occasion to speak in the presence of the King he raises this plaque and touches it with his lips. Formerly, when the King came into his court, he first appeared at a large upper window, with a similar ivory plaque in his hand to conceal his countenance. On the crown he was wearing there was a thin ivory strip about a foot long and half as wide from which strings of precious stones were hung to hide his face on all sides from the gaze of those present.

The royal color, forbidden to all others, is yellow, and regal vestments are decorated with various designs of dragons either painted or wrought into the cloth in gold thread. Throughout the entire palace, one sees pictures of dragons on gold and silver vases, on the furniture, and in the draperies. The roof and tiling of the palace are also done in yellow and with various paintings of dragons. This has probably given rise to the story that the tiling of the palace is all of brass or gold. This I can assert to be a mere legend, because I have examined the painted tiles myself. They are yellow in color, somewhat larger than the kind we use, and are fixed to the roof with nails or spikes, the heads of which are gilded so that no color other than yellow will appear on the palace. If anyone other than the sovereign or a blood relation should presume to use this particular color or the dragons, he would be looked upon as a traitor.

Four entrances to the royal palace open to the four main points of the compass. Visitors to the palace must descend from their horses or from their palanquins, as the case may be, and proceed on foot from beyond the gates. This regulation must be observed by everyone, and those of higher grade observe it more exactly and walk from a greater distance. Strange to say, the same custom is also in vogue for the former royal palace at Nankin, although no ruler has been in residence there for many years. On the outside and on the inside entrances to the south, there are three doors, side by side, and the middle door is reserved for the King alone. Others enter on the right or on the left but the middle door is never opened except for the entrance or the exit of His Majesty.

The only point from which the Chinese reckon time, whether in published books or in printed documents, is the beginning of the reign of the present sovereign, just as we count in the Christian era, from the birth of Christ.

At times and for special reasons, the King will confer a title on the parents of a Supreme Magistrate, and this is presented in the form of a written document done by one of the Crown Philosophers, in the King's name. The Chinese look upon this as an extraordinary honor, and they will spare no expense to acquire it because it is handed down in the family as something sacred. Other titles also, expressed in two or three characters, are held in no less esteem, such as those conferred by the crown upon elderly widows who have lived through long years without remarrying, and upon those who have completed a hundred years of life or have become distinguished in some other manner. These title documents are affixed to the doorposts of the recipient's home. Sometimes, too, the magistrates themselves are empowered to confer these honors on their friends. A distinguished magistrate might even be honored with a public monument, built out of municipal funds, as we would erect a triumphal arch. Cities do the same for a citizen who has attained to exceptional honor, such as gaining first place in examinations for higher academic degrees or acquiring other distinctions, which are attended by great pomp and solemnity.

Whatever is considered to be rare or precious or very well made is sent to Pekin for the King, and every year he receives great quantities of such things from all parts of the country, at a heavy expense to the donors. Magistrates who are stationed in the capital city, appear in public in less ornate apparel. They go about on horseback rather than in a sedan chair, excepting those of the highest order, and even these will have only four carriers. Outside of court time the lesser magistrates will appear in the provinces with somewhat more display than in the metropolis. Their moderation in official dress at court is adopted out of respect for royalty and as ceding the better part to those who are nearest to the crown.

Every fourth year, and during each of the four seasons of that year, the Court Magistrates visit the tombs of the deceased kings and queens. These visits are accompanied with certain rites, and gifts are left at the graves. The Emperor Humvu, who restored the kingdom, is always the recipient of the most elaborate display. Several days are spent in preparation for these memorial rites, by remaining indoors in fasting and in mourning.

Next to the King, the people pay highest honors to their magistrates, in set formulas of address and in official visits, to which only those who hold public office, either here or abroad, can aspire to be admitted. When a citizen holding public office abroad returns to the country he is granted the same respect paid to a magistrate. This custom holds even though he may have forfeited his position through some fault of his own, at least in his home town, where he will be honored as a magistrate, paid the same official visits, and granted many privileges, especially if he is a holder of highest literary honors or of other public award.

The magistrates are also granted exceptional honors when they are about to leave the city over which they preside, for promotion or for other public award. When departing, they leave behind them, as a perpetual memorial of their service, their greaves or leg ornaments, which are the distinguishing sign of their particular office. These are then enclosed in a case decorated with laudatory inscriptions and verses and kept in a public museum. At times a distinguished citizen is honored with a marble shaft, erected in a public place and elegantly engraved with the record of his public service, as a reminder to posterity. Some may even be honored with memorial shrines, built at no little cost to the state, containing altars decorated with their statues bearing as close a likeness as their sculptors can attain. A yearly allowance is granted for these temples for incense and to pay servants for attending to perpetual lights. The large incense bowl, made of bronze, used in these shrines is similar to that employed for the same rite in veneration of the idols. The people in general seem to make no distinction between these memorial rites and the worship they pay their deities, as they call upon the deities during the rites. With the educated classes these are ceremonies conducted in recognition of benefits received, but there is little doubt that many of the lower classes confuse the practice with divine worship. The cities are full of these shrines, many of which have been erected to honor friends who had no claim to the honor. Certain times are set for visiting them, and the regular ceremonies of bowing and genuflecting and of leaving food offerings are always repeated.

Chinese books on morals are full of instructions relative to the respect that children should pay to parents and elders. Certainly if we look to an external display of filial piety, there is no people in the whole world who can compare with the Chinese, as witness the following illustrations. It is a solemn custom, and very strictly observed, that when children sit in the presence of their elders, they are seated to one side and somewhat to the rear, and so for pupils in presence of their teachers. Children are always taught to be respectful in conversation. Even the very poor will work hard to support their parents in plenty to the end of their days. There really is nothing in which these people are more religiously scrupulous than in their devotion to the details of parental funeral rites, in wearing mourning garments, which are white rather than black, and in furnishing a casket or a funeral bier of costly material. In general one would say that their obsequies are too pompous and frequently surpass their means. During the first few months of mourning for a parent, the sons wear a robe of rough hempen material quite out of keeping with their regular long tunic and with their hat and shoes. In fact at first glance they look rather shabby and miserable. During this time also they wear a rope cincture, somewhat like that worn by the Franciscan Fathers. Three years of mourning, from the day of the death of a father or mother, is the inviolable custom. The reason assigned for this, as one reads in their books, is to repay the three years of their childrens' infancy, when the parents carried them in their arms and worked so hard to rear them. For the death of other relatives the length of time of mourning is determined by the degree of consanguinity, varying from a year to three months. The regular period of mourning on the death of the King or Queen, which is common to the entire kingdom, has been changed by royal edict. Formerly it was three years, but days have been substituted for months and now the time of universal sorrow for departed royalty is only a month.

There is a special and a voluminous book of Chinese funeral rites, and when one dies, the survivors, who have charge of the funeral, consult this book to make certain that the proper ceremonies are observed and becoming display assured. This book contains not only the prescribed customs but also specific directions relative to the clothes, shoes, hats, waistbands, and other articles of costume to be worn by the bereaved. Within three or four days of the death of a prominent person, the son or the next of kin informs all relatives or friends in a written notice, couched in sad and solemn terms. In the meantime a casket is made and the deceased placed in it. The wake hall is all hung in white and the floor all covered with straw mats. In the middle of the room a platform is erected and the casket placed on it, together with a picture or a statue of the departed. For the next four or five days the friends and relatives clad in mourning clothes pay their visits of respect to the dead. They come in groups at stated hours, and place perfumes and two wax tapers on the platform. When they light the tapers they make four bows and four genuflections. First, however, they put a pinch of incense into the burning censer near the coffin. While they are going through this ceremony, the son or sons of the deceased stand to one side, dressed all in funereal white, tearfully but quietly lamenting their loss. The women servants of the household and at times a large group of them, also clad in white but concealed by a curtain, stand at the head of the casket and keep up a continuous chorus, weeping and wailing confusedly.

It is a custom also, in imitation of their minor sacrifices to the idols, to burn pieces of paper or of white silk. By doing this they imagine that they are offering a robe to the departed in memory of his kindness and generosity. Their caskets can be rendered absolutely airtight by sealing the seams with a certain kind of shiny pitch, and at times the Chinese have been known to keep the body of a parent in the house for three or four years. As long as the remains are kept they place food and drink before the coffin just as they might serve a living person, and during that time the children sit on low stools covered with white cloth rather than on regular chairs, and straw mats are placed upon the floor, beside the casket, to be used in place of beds. They eat neither meat nor seasoned food during the period of mourning, use very little wine, take no baths, attend no festivities, refrain from marital rights, and for some months they do not even appear in public. If necessity should require them to leave the house they travel in a palanquin covered with a white cloth.

Such are only some of the long list of customs connected with Chinese obsequies, but these austerities are gradually diminished as the three-year period of sorrow continues. At the time of the funeral, relatives and friends are again invited in writing and they come, all dressed in white, to add to the pomp of the occasion. The funeral procession itself is really a religious function, with a long line marching ahead of the bier and carrying little paper figures of men and women, or of elephants, tigers, or lions, in various colors or gilded over, all of which they burn at the grave. Following them on the road there will be a long file of the servants who minister to the idols in the temples and of cantors reciting prayers in common and accompanying the prayers on drums and reeds and cymbals and bells and other instruments. Next in order are men carrying on their shoulders the huge brass vessels for burning incense. Then comes the casket decorated in magnificent array, under a great canopy, hung with cotton curtains adorned with a variety of embroidery. This canopy and the casket will be carried by as many as forty or fifty pallbearers. The children walk behind the catafalque, carrying staffs and walking as though they were exhausted from grief. Then come the women of the family, who are carried in sedan chairs, shaded with white curtains so that they cannot be seen, and they are followed by the other women relatives in similar funeral palanquins. The tombs of the dead are always located beyond the limits of a city or town.

If any of the children are absent at the time of the death of a parent, the entire ceremony of obsequies is deferred for their return. If a prominent person is absent when his parent dies, he erects a cenotaph where he is and his friends visit to pay their respects. After that he returns home and arranges for the funeral, as described. It is a matter of strict law, admitting of no exception, for a son to return on such an occasion, no matter what public office he may hold. Even the presidents of tribunals, whom we mentioned as the Ciamciu, and likewise the Colao, must fill out the period of three years of mourning at home, and they will not be permitted to resume their official duties until it has been completed. This duty is imposed upon Magistrates, only for the death of a parent, not for that of other relatives, and Military Magistrates or military leaders are not bound by this particular law. If one should die beyond the national borders, he whose duty it is to arrange for the funeral is to leave no stone unturned and to spare no expense to bring the body home, so that it may find a last resting place in the family vault. Each family has a special tomb or vault which is generally located on a hillside just beyond town limits. They are usually built of marble and are quite spacious, and in front of them facing the grave, there are various statues of men and of animals. The marble fronts of these tombs are magnificently inscribed, commemorating the noble deeds of those who sleep within. Each year, and on days prescribed, the relatives gather at the grave to perform anniversary rites. Incense is burned, gifts are offered, and funeral meals are left there, the ceremonies varying according to the accepted customs which have been handed down through the centuries in the particular districts.

Rites and ceremonies of betrothal are also numerous. These people usually marry at an early age, and they do not favor a great difference in the ages of those being married. Marriage contracts are arranged by the parents of both parties but without the consent of those to be married, though at times they may be consulted. Those who belong to the upper social classes, marry within their class and equal family rating in the class is required for legitimate marriage. All men are free to have concubines, and class or fortune means nothing in their selection, as the only standard of preference is physical beauty. These concubines may be purchased for a hundred pieces of gold and at times for much less. Among the lower classes wives are bought and sold for silver and as often as a man may wish. The King and his sons select their wives for their beauty only, with no regard to nobility of race. The women of the aristocracy do not aspire to royal marriage because the wives of the King have no special standing in society and being confined to the palace they can never see their own people. Moreover since the selection for connubial consort from among the royal wives is left to certain magistrates appointed for that purpose, comparatively few are chosen from the many available.

The King really has only one legitimate wife or queen, though he and his heirs may have nine other wives and thirty-six others who are called wives. Besides these he has a great number of concubines who are called neither queen nor wife. Those who bear him male children are most in favor, and the first son born to him from any of his women is always the successor to the throne. This is an accepted fact, not only with the King and his household, but likewise with the entire kingdom. Only the first or recognized consort is permitted to sit at table with the sovereign. All the others, excepting those who may be related to him, are servants of the King and attendants of the Queen and always stand in their presence. All sons born to the King look upon the legitimate Queen as their mother and call her by that title, which belongs to her alone. Neither do they practice the customary three years of mourning for their real mothers when they die, but for the Queen only, for whom they also perform the stated funeral rites and relinquish whatever office they may be holding for that period.

Another custom religiously observed is, that no one shall marry a woman of the same family name as his own, even though there be no blood relation between them. Family names among the Chinese are fewer by far than ours, numbering scarcely a thousand in all. They are never permitted to take a new family name, save in the case of adoption, but must keep those that have come down to them through the centuries from the father's side, not from the mother's. Affinity and consanguinity are not taken into consideration in their marriages, the only condition required being a difference in the family names of the contracting parties. In fact they marry their children to the mother's relatives in almost any grade of relationship. No dowry is required of a bride. When she comes to her husband's house she brings along with her enough furniture and trappings to supply the home but all this has been paid for by the husband, who has given her money to purchase it some months in advance of the wedding.

The Chinese celebrate their birthdays with gifts and feasts and other signs of rejoicing. A special display is made on the fiftieth birthday because from that time on one is considered to be an old man, and on every tenth year following he is specially feted. On these occasions, if the family belongs to the literary class, the children get their friends to write poems and citations and other such testimonials, done in elaborate form, in praise of their parents. Sometimes they publish these in book form, and a common method of congratulating the person honored is to decorate the house with these written tributes.

Another day of rejoicing is that on which a boy becomes of age and is permitted to put on the virile cap, as Roman youths were accustomed to don the toga virilis. This will be his twentieth birthday and up to that time he has worn his hair loose and flowing.

The most important of all Chinese holidays, and the one celebrated throughout the whole country and by every sect, is their New Year's Day, which is celebrated at the time of the first new moon and again at the time of the first full moon. This is known as the feast of the lights because everyone illuminates his home with lanterns, curiously made of cardboard or glass or of cloth. At this time the markets are filled with samples of these lanterns, and each one purchases the design that strikes his fancy. One would think the houses were afire, so many lights are burning in every part of them. During this time, too, there is a great deal of night reveling. Long files of people parade through the streets, made up in sections like fiery dragons, cavorting like bacchantes and shooting off fireworks and festive lights, and the whole town presents a glaring spectacle of unusual brilliance.

8. Concerning Dress and Other Customs and Peculiarities

〰〰〰〰〰〰〰〰〰〰〰〰〰〰〰〰〰〰

THE CHINESE people are almost white, though some of them in the southern provinces are quite dark because of their proximity to the torrid zone. The men's beards are thin and meager and at times they have none at all. Their hair is rough and straight and the moustache late in showing, so that a man of thirty would compare with one of ours of twenty, in that respect. The beard and the head hair are universally black. Red hair they dislike. Their narrow, elliptical-shaped eyes are noticeably black. The nose is small and flat and their ears are of medium size. In some of the outlying districts the people's faces are almost square. In the Provinces of Canton and Quamsi there are peoples who have two nails on the little toe of each foot, and this is common with nearly all the inhabitants of Cocincina and that vicinity. It may be that at one time they had six toes on each foot. The women are all small in stature, and the smallness of their feet is considered to be a mark of beauty. In order to produce this effect their feet are tightly wrapped in bandages from infancy to prevent growth, and when they walk one would think that their feet had been partly cut off. These foot bandages are worn throughout the whole course of life. They look upon it as unbecoming for women to walk about the streets. Probably one of their sages hit upon this idea to keep them in the house. Both men and women let their hair grow long, but children up to the age of fifteen have their hair close cut, except for a tuft on the top of the head. After that age they allow it to grow long and to spread over the shoulders, until they are twenty, when the boys assume the cap of manhood, as already mentioned.

Most of those who act as priests for the sacrifices shave their faces and their heads every eighth day. Men sometimes cover their hair with a net, made of horsehair, or of human hair, or at times of steel wire. This is a caplike device, worn on the top of the head and the hair is drawn through it and tied into fancy knots. Women do not use this kind of hair net, but gather their hair into a large pug knot and decorate it with gold and silver ornaments or with flowers. They also wear earrings but do not wear rings on their fingers. Both men and women wear the ankle-long tunic. Men fold this garment over the chest, fastening the underfold with a clasp under the left arm and the overlap under the right arm. Women fasten the tunic in front. Loose long sleeves, Venetian style, are common to both, but women's sleeves are wide and open at the wrists, while the sleeve of a man's tunic will have just enough opening to protrude the hand. Men's caps are variously and elegantly made, the best of them being woven in horsehair. In cold weather, however, woolen or silk caps are worn. Perhaps the greatest divergence from our style of apparel is to be seen in Chinese shoes. Men's shoes are made of cotton or of silk and are even more highly decorated with embroidered flowers than the footwear of our ladies. They do not use leather even in the soles of their shoes, which are made of layers of tightly sewn cloth. Only the lowest classes wear leather footwear. Those belonging to the literary castes may wear square hats; all others are round. The usual morning hairdressing takes about half an hour, which would be quite a nuisance for our men. The common custom of wrapping long bandages about the feet and shins gives an appearance of loose-fitting stockings. They have no garment corresponding to our shirt; instead, they wear a loose-fitting tunic of white cloth against the skin and they bathe frequently. Part of their regular apparel, when walking out of doors, is a large umbrella for warding off the rays of the sun. If one can afford it, he will have a servant to carry the umbrella; if not, he himself will carry a smaller parasol.

The Chinese custom relative to proper names is very interesting and is quite unheard of in Europe. Each one inherits his ancient and unchangeable family name, as already related, but this is not so of surnames. These are invented with a significance somewhat related to the family name. The surname is ordinarily written with a single character and pronounced in a single syllable, which really amounts to the same thing. It may, however, consist of two syllables. The first of these names is given to a child by his parents. Girls and adult women have no name other than the family name. Instead of names they are given numbers, in sequence, according to order of birth. Men and boys are called by this first name only by their parents and older relatives. All others call them by a number, in order among brothers, just as their sisters are called. On their visiting or business cards, in letters and in other writing, they sign the first name, given them by their parents. If anyone other than a parent, whether he be an equal or a superior, should address one by this first name, or use it with reference to a man's parents or relatives, it would be considered not only a breach of etiquette but a positive insult. When a boy first goes to school, his teacher gives him a new name, called a play name, which is used only by the teacher and by school companions. When he reaches the age of the virile cap or when he gets married, he is honored with another name of dignity, which is conferred by some distinguished official and this is called his letter. Anyone may address him by this name, excepting his household servants. Finally when a man approaches middle age he is given what is known as his great or his big name, and this is conferred by highest ranking officials. Whether he be present or absent, anyone may refer to him by this name, though his parents and older relatives will always use his letter, once he has acquired it. If one should join some particular sect, the literary doctor who introduces him gives him still another name, known as his religious name. When men call upon one another in an official capacity, although the one calling signs his visiting card with his family name and his first given name, each one will ask for the more honorable name of the other, so as to avoid a faux pas in addressing him. Even we ourselves have to accept what is considered to be a bigger name than the one we received in baptism.

The Chinese have a great liking for antiques, though they have no very ancient statues. Tripods made of bell-metal bronze are considered to be precious because of their rusty iron color, which makes them look very old, and they like vases made of Cretan chalk and of the particular kind of marble which we have referred to as jasper. Pictures done by well-known artists are in great demand, despite the fact that Chinese pictures are only outlines, done in black rather than in varied colors. Character-writing manuscripts of prominent writers, generally written on paper or on cloth, are also sought for, but they must be protected against fraud by bearing the autograph of the author. Counterfeiters of antiques are numerous, and they are clever at cheating the unwary by selling them utterly worthless things, taking advantage of the fact that they are poorly posted in values.

Every magistrate has his own private seal of office, handed down from King Humvus himself, and all his juridical documents must be signed in red with this particular seal. The loss of this seal would mean not only loss of office but a severe penalty in addition. Consequently these seals are guarded with most scrupulous care. Whenever a magistrate leaves home he carries his official seal with him, locked in a case, which in turn is officially sealed and never left out of his sight. They say that magistrates sleep with their seals under their pillows.

Men of high station in life are never seen walking in the streets. They are carried about enclosed in sedan chairs and cannot be seen by passers-by, unless they leave the front curtain open. The magistrates, however, go about in open chairs. It is customary for women of society to have palanquins that are wholly closed but these are easily distinguished from a man's sedan by their shape and style. Carriages and wagons are prohibited by law.

Here one sees cities built in the middle of rivers and lakes, like Venice in the sea, with palatial boats plying between them. The whole country is divided up by rivers and canals. People here travel more by boat than we in the West, and their boats are more ornate and more commodious than ours. A magistrate's yacht, for instance, will be large enough to accommodate his whole family with as much liberty as they would have at home. These are run at public expense and fitted with kitchen, bedrooms, and sitting room, and are decorated to look more like a rich man's home than like a houseboat. Sometimes they give sumptuous dinners aboard their yachts and make a pleasure cruise of it on the lake or along the river. The interior of such a yacht is usually finished in different colors with a highly polished bituminous paint, which the Portuguese call Ciara, and the ornamentation is as pleasing to the eye as the various mixtures of incense are to the nose.

These people pay more respect to their teachers than we do, and if one man places himself under another for instruction, even for a day, he will call him master for the rest of his life. Not only that, but he will show him the deference of a pupil to his master, by sitting beside him at any public gathering and by honoring him with the titles and the rites that are due to a magistrate.

Dice throwing and card playing, which have found their way into this country, are considered to be plebeian and vulgar. The more serious minded play a game of chess for diversion and pastime and also for gambling, which in many respects is like our own game of the same name. The method of playing, however, is decidedly different. In their game, the kingpiece does not go beyond the four spaces contiguous to his original position and neither do the pieces corresponding to our bishops. There is no queenpiece. They have two rather novel pieces which they call gunpowder bowls or cartridges, which are placed before the knights and behind two pawns placed one space in advance of the regular line of pawns. This powder-bowl unit moves in about the same manner as our castle but does not seek to disturb the opposing king unless a piece belonging to the opposition is between it and the king in question. The kingpiece has three ways of avoiding a checkmate; by moving aside into the next space, by taking the piece holding him in check, or by sacrificing a protecting piece. The Chinese have several games of this kind, but the one they take most seriously is played on a hollowed gaming board of more than three hundred spaces and played with two hundred black and white pieces. The purpose in this game is to dominate a greater number of spaces. Each one endeavors to drive his opponent's pieces to the middle of the board and in so doing to win over spaces, and the one who accumulates the greater number of vacant places wins the game. The magistrates are very keen about this game and frequently use up the greater part of a day playing it. Sometimes it takes players an hour to play a single game. An expert at this particular play will always have a great following, and he is sure to be well known even though this may be his only accomplishment. In fact, some people select these experts as instructors and show them special favor in order to acquire an accurate knowledge of this intricate game.

With respect to the punishment of crime, one would say that in general Chinese authorities are rather remiss and particularly so in the case of a first theft. Capital punishment is never administered for this crime. On a second conviction for theft, the culprit is burned on the arm with a brand and marked with two letters in black ink to show he is a repeater. On third offense the same brand is burned into his face. If he insists on stealing after that, he is flogged every time he is apprehended, the severity of the beating depending on the nature of his crime, or he might be condemned to the triremes as a galley slave, for a length of time determined by the law. And yet, thieves are numerous everywhere, especially among the lower classes.

Thousands of night watchmen in the cities roam the streets sounding a gong at regular intervals. Yet, despite this, and the fact that the streets are closed with iron bars and locks, it frequently happens that houses are thoroughly ransacked by night marauders. This probably happens because the watchmen themselves are robbers or are in league with the robbers, and the result of frequent thieving is that others are engaged to watch the watchmen. It really amazes them to hear that in the most thickly populated cities in Europe, guards are employed not so much to prevent domestic stealing as to protect the citizenry against inroads from invaders. Here, even though they may be in the middle of the kingdom and enjoying the most profound peace, the city gates are locked every night and the keys delivered to the prefect.

9.Concerning Certain Rites, Superstitious and Otherwise

~~~~~~~~~~~~~~~~~~~~~~~~~~~~~~~~~~~~~~~

IN THIS CHAPTER we shall treat of the superstitious rites peculiar to certain sects, and shall touch upon such as may serve as a summary of them all.

First, however, I would request of the reader that he recognize in the two following chapters a reason for sympathizing with this people and for praying God for their salvation, rather than becoming impatient with them and losing all hope of a remedy for their misfortune. One should remember that they have been obscured in pagan darkness for some thousands of years, without ever, or scarcely ever, beholding a ray of the light of Christianity. Yet, through the goodness of God and by their own innate genius, they did have sufficient natural enlightenment to recognize and to admit their unfortunate plight, though up to the present they know of no means of escape from it.

No superstition is so common to the entire kingdom as that which pertains to the observance of certain days and hours as being good or bad, lucky or unlucky, in which to act or to refrain from acting, because the result of everything they do is supposed to depend upon a measurement of time. This imposture has assumed such a semblance of truth among them that two calendars are edited every year, written by the astrologers of the crown and published by public authority. These almanacs are sold in such great quantities that every house has a supply of them. They are produced in pamphlet form, and in them one finds directions as to what should be done and what should be left undone for each particular day, and at what precise time each and every thing should be done. In this manner the entire year is carefully mapped out in exact detail. Besides these regular calendars there are other books of this kind, more complex in their contents. Then, too, a horde of deceitful directors make a living by instructing those who consult them as to the correct day and hour for doing each particular thing in a day's routine. They charge but very little for their fraudulent advice so that no one will hesitate to have an adviser.

It happens not infrequently that if one is about to build he will put off the work for days and days, or those intending to go on a journey will defer their departure, so as not to be in the least at variance from the time prescribed for such things by the divining mountebanks. Even the elements cannot turn them aside from this superstition. If the appointed day should bring a downpour of rain, or contrary winds for a voyage, they would never be deterred from beginning an undertaking on the day and at the exact time designated beforehand as being propitious for a successful culmination. Relative to a journey and to building, if they take four steps they consider that their journey is begun, and if they turn two shovelfuls of dirt their building operation is started. In order to hold to the superstitions, they will do just that much at the time prescribed to begin such activities and then persuade themselves that the undertaking must be a success.

These people worry a great deal about judging their whole lives and fortunes as dependent upon the exact moment of birth, and so everyone makes an inquiry as to that precise moment and takes an accurate note of it. Masters in this kind of fortunetelling are numerous everywhere, as are also those who claim a knowledge of reading the stars and of manipulating certain superstitious numbers. Some of them also read one's life in his face or from his hands. Others again foretell from dreams or from certain little words which they elicit in conversation, or from the posture of the body when one is seated, and in various other ways. The strange part of it all is that they do all this with such assurance that they leave no room for doubt as to their conclusions in the minds of their unwitting victims. Fraud is so common and new methods of deceiving are of such daily occurrence that a simple and credulous people are easily led into error. These sooth-sayers frequently have confederates in a gathering who declare to a crowd that everything that was told them by the performer came to pass just as he had predicted it. Sometimes, too, when strangers are brought in as confederates and relate marvels of the past, the fol-lowers of the local impostor respond with loud applause. The result is that many, deceived by this trickery, have their own fortunes told and accept what is predicted for them as the certain truth.

There is another trick also which gives this deception a semblance of truth. Handwritten catalogues are common among the people, containing a description of each family of a town, arranged according to streets and houses. The fortunetellers transcribe these catalogues or buy them cheaply and then go into a town as strangers and tell anyone all about his family. After telling what has happened in the past they predict what will take place in the future, and then betake themselves to other parts, trusting that fortune will prove them right. Some of these poor people believe in such predictions out of sheer fear. If, for example, they are told that they will fall sick on a certain day, when that day comes they will actually persuade themselves that they are sick and will fight against the imaginary sickness in fear of im-pending death. Such happenings as this serve as good advertising for the charlatans and help not a little to build up their reputations.

It is a common practice also to consult the demons, the family spirits, as the Chinese call them, and there are many of them. In this, how-ever, they imagine that there is more of divination than anything dia-bolical, but in this, too, they are victims of fraud and deception. In such consultations, oracles are received through the voices of little children and from the sounds of brute beasts, revealing the past and the absent, as proof of the truth of what they foretell for the future. These oracles are always produced by fraud and trickery. Of course, we read that such superstitions are common to heathens in general, but the following sample is quite peculiar to the Chinese. In choosing a place to erect a public edifice or a private house, or in selecting a plot of ground in which to bury the dead, they study the location with ref-erence to the head and the tail and the feet of the particular dragons which are supposed to dwell beneath that spot. Upon these local dragons they believe that the good and bad fortune, not only of the family but also of the town and the province and of the entire king-dom, is wholly dependent. Many of their most distinguished men are interested in this recondite science and, when necessary, they are called in for consultation, even from a great distance. This might happen when some public building or a monument is to be erected and the machines used for that purpose are to be placed so that public misfortune might be avoided and good fortune attend the undertaking. Just as their astrologers read the stars, so their geologists reckon the fate or the fortune of a place from the relative position of mountains or rivers or fields, and their reckoning is just as deceitful as the reading of the stargazers. What could be more absurd than their imagining that the safety of a family, honors, and their entire existence must depend upon such trifles as a door being opened from one side or another, as rain falling into a courtyard from the right or from the left, a window opened here or there, or one roof being higher than another?

The streets and the taverns and all other public places abound in these astrologers and geologists, diviners and fortunetellers, or, to group them all in one class, in these impostors. Their business consists in making vain promises of prosperous fortunes at a given price. Some of them are blind men, others of low station in life, and at times, women of questionable character. According to the dictum of the Gospel, they really are, "The blind leading the blind," and their number is so great that they may be said to constitute a universal nuisance. In fact, this obnoxious class is a veritable pest in the capital cities and even in the court. Such is their means of livelihood, and not a few of them are able to support a large family in luxury and at times to accumulate considerable wealth. The high and the low, the noble and the plebeian, the educated and the illiterate are counted among their victims, as are the magistrates, the dignitaries of the realm, and even the King himself. One can readily judge from what has been said, of the auguries they read into the cackling of birds, how solicitous they are about first morning meetings and about shadows cast upon a roof by the rays of the sun. In a word, whatever misfortune befalls an individual, a city, a province, or the kingdom, they attribute it to adverse fortune, or to something wrong in the person or in the realm, as the case may be. They look upon such adversity as being a just visitation for their sins, which have called down a private or a public vindication from above.

We shall add here a few shocking practices which the Chinese look upon with indifference and which, God forbid, they even seem to consider as quite morally correct, and from these one can readily conclude to others of the same category. This people is really to be pitied rather than censured, and the deeper one finds them involved in the darkness of ignorance, the more earnest one should be in praying for their salvation.

Many of them, not being able to forgo the company of women, sell themselves to wealthy patrons, so as to find a wife among his women servants, and in so doing, subject their children to perpetual slavery. Others buy a wife when they can save money enough to do so, and when their family becomes too numerous to be supported, they sell their children into slavery for about the same price that one would pay for a pig or a cheap little donkey—about one crown or maybe one and a half. Sometimes this is done when there is really no necessity, and children are separated from their parents forever, becoming slaves to the purchaser, to be used for whatever purpose he pleases. The result of this practice is that the whole country is virtually filled with slaves; not such as are captured in war or brought in from abroad, but slaves born in the country and even in the same city or village in which they live. Many of them are also taken out of the country as slaves by the Portuguese and the Spaniards. These few at least have an opportunity of becoming Christian and of thus escaping the slavery of Satan. The only ameliorating feature in this traffic of children is the fact that it lessens the great multitude of the extremely poor who have to labor incessantly in the sweat of their brow to eke out a miserable living. One might add also that slavery among the Chinese is more bearable because less exacting than among any other people in the world. A Chinese slave can purchase his freedom for the same price that was paid for him, if he can manage to acquire that amount of money.

A far more serious evil here is the practice in some provinces of disposing of female infants by drowning them. The reason assigned for this is that their parents despair of being able to support them. At times this is also done by people who are not abjectly poor, for fear the time might come when they would not be able to care for these children and they would be forced to sell them to unknown or to cruel slave masters. Thus they become cruel in an effort to be considerate. This barbarism is probably rendered less atrocious by their belief in metempsychosis, or the transmigration of souls. Believing that souls are transferred from one body that ceases to exist into another that begins to exist, they cover up their frightful cruelty with a pretext of piety, thinking that they are doing the child a benefit by murdering it. According to their way of thinking, they are releasing the child from the poverty of the family into which it was born, so that it may be reborn into a family of better means. So it happens that this slaughter of the innocents is carried on not in secret but in the open and with general public knowledge.

Another more or less common custom, and still more barbarous than that aforementioned, is the practice of committing suicide in desperation of earning a living, or in utter despair because of misfortune, or still more foolishly and more cowardly, out of spite for an enemy. They say that thousands of people, women as well as men, take their own lives in the course of a year. This is frequently done by hanging or by choking oneself to death in a public place or perhaps before the home of an enemy. Jumping into rivers and swallowing poison are other common methods and they often commit suicide for very trivial reasons. If a magistrate should pass a severe sentence upon one who is accused by the parents of a suicide of having driven their son to despair, the accused will frequently see no other way out of the difficulty than by taking his own life. Many of the magistrates show great wisdom in this respect by making it a law unto themselves never to handle a case involving a suicide and they probably save many a life by doing so.

Yet another barbarity common in the northern provinces is that of castrating a great number of male children, so they may act as servants or as slaves to the King. This condition is demanded for service in the royal palace, so much so, indeed, that the King will have no others nor will he consult with or even speak to any other. Almost the whole administration of the entire kingdom is in the hands of this class of semimen, who number nearly ten thousand in the service of the royal palace alone. They are a meager-looking class, uneducated and brought up in perpetual slavery, a dull and stolid lot, as incapable of understanding an important order as they are inefficient in carrying it out.

The penal laws of the country do not seem to be too severe, but it seems that as many are illegally put to death by the magistrates as are legally executed. This is brought about by a fixed and ancient custom of the country permitting a magistrate, without any legal process or judgment, to subject a person to flogging when it might please him to do so. This punishment is administered in public. The victim, lying prone, face down to the ground, is beaten on the bare legs and buttocks with a tough reed, split down the middle, about an inch thick, four inches wide, and about a yard long. The executioners swing this flail with both hands and strike unmercifully. The regular number of blows is ten, with thirty as a limit, but the first blow usually breaks the skin and the flesh flies about in the subsequent beating, with the result that the victim frequently dies from the flogging. At times the accused will buy off his life by paying a high price to the magistrate, contrary to all law and justice.

So great is the lust for domination on the part of the magistrates that scarcely anyone can be said to possess his belongings in security, and everyone lives in continual fear of being deprived of what he has, by a false accusation. Just as this people is grossly subject to superstition, so, too, they have very little regard for the truth, acting always with great circumspection, and very cautious about trusting anyone. Subject to this same fear, the kings of modern times abandoned the custom of going out in public. Even formerly, when they did leave the royal enclosure, they would never dare to do so without a thousand preliminary precautions. On such occasions the whole court was placed under military guard. Secret-servicemen were placed along the route over which the King was to travel and on all roads leading into it. He was not only hidden from view, but the public never knew in which of the many palanquins of his cortege he was actually riding. One would think he was making a journey through enemy country rather than through multitudes of his own subjects and clients.

Those who are reputed to be of royal blood are supported at public expense. At present they are supposed to number somewhat over sixty thousand, and as they are continually increasing, one can readily imagine what a public burden they constitute. Removed, as they are, from all public office and administration, they have developed into a leisure class given to loose living and to insolence. The King guards himself against these people as he would against personal enemies, knowing full well that they have their own system of espionage. Everyone of them is obligated to live in a designated city which he is not permitted to leave without the King's consent, under heaviest penalty, and no one of them is ever allowed to live in the royal cities of Pekin and Nankin. It will not seem extraordinary to anyone, that a people who place no trust in their own citizens and relatives, should be suspicious of strangers, whether they come from the environs or from abroad. What knowledge they have of these is likely to be obscure or false as it is received from other strangers who come into their kingdom as fawning clients looking to benefit from their visit.

The Chinese look upon all foreigners as illiterate and barbarous, and refer to them in just these terms. They even disdain to learn anything from the books of outsiders because they believe that all true science and knowledge belongs to them alone. If perchance they have occasion to make mention of externs in their own writings, they treat them as though there was no room for doubt that they differ but little from the beasts of the field and the forest. Even the written characters by which they express the word foreigner are those that are applied to beasts, and scarcely ever do they give them a title more honorable than they would assign to their demons. One would scarcely believe how suspicious they are of a legate or an ambassador of a neighboring country, sent in to pay respect to the King, to settle a tributary tax, or to conduct any sort of business. The fact that China may have been on friendly terms with the kingdom of the visiting legates, from time immemorial, does not exempt the visiting dignitaries from being conducted along their entire route within the realm as captives or prisoners and permitted to see nothing in the course of their journey. During their whole sojourn they are lodged in buildings, constructed like cattle barns, within the limits of the palace grounds, to which they are confined under lock and key. They are never permitted to see the King, and their diplomatic or other business is carried on with selected magistrates. No one in the whole kingdom is ever permitted to do business with foreigners, excepting at certain times and in certain places, as on the peninsula of Macao where a trading mart was established with the Portuguese in 1557. Anyone carrying on foreign trade without official sanction would be subject to the severest punishment.

Soldiers doing guard duty are always watched by other sentinels for fear they might attempt a revolution or cause a disturbance, and for the same reason no one commander is ever placed over a great number of soldiers. The whole military is under the jurisdiction of the Philosophic Senate, which issues their pay as well as their military supplies and rations. In this way the soldiers themselves, and also their care and keep, are dependent upon authorities other than their military superiors in order to make more certain of their individual fidelity. There probably is no class of people in the country as degraded and as lazy as the soldiers. Everyone under arms necessarily leads a miserable life because he is following his calling not out of love for his country, nor from loyalty to the King, nor from any desire to acquire fame and honor, but solely as a subject laboring for an employer. The greater part of the army are bondsmen to the crown, and serve in slavery either for their own crimes or for those of their ancestors. When they are not actually engaged in military activities they are assigned to the lowest menial employments, such as carrying palanquins, tending pack animals, and other such servile occupations. Only the high officers and military prefects acquire any authority in the military sphere. The arms supplied to the army are practically worthless for an offensive against an enemy or even for self-defense. Except in actual war they carry only imitation arms, and they are given these so that they will not be totally disarmed in their sham battles. We have already portrayed how ridiculous these encounters are, in which both the soldiers and their officers are actually beaten like schoolboys by the magistrates, without any consideration for rank or dignity.

We shall terminate this chapter with an account of what are aptly styled two very foolish practices of the Chinese, common in every part of the land and especially so among the more influential classes. The first is an effort to produce silver from other metals, and the second, an attempt to escape death and to become immortal by rendering one's life indestructible. The story goes that directions for accomplishing these two desired results were discovered and handed down by certain celebrities who are now numbered among the blessed. It seems that having accomplished many signal and useful undertakings in life, when they finally grew weary of their worldly existence, they were taken up body and soul into heaven. A tremendous number of books is in circulation, treating of these two occult sciences, some printed and some in manuscript, but the manuscripts are more sought for as having more authority.

Relative to the first insane practice, it is best explained as an effort on the part of the avaricious alchemists who squander their entire fortunes in a vain effort to accomplish a foolish ambition. It is a daily and a public spectacle to see the wealthiest among them reduced to poverty after spending a great sum of money in attempting to verify this fraud. The more astute and clever of them in this particular science produce an imitation or adulterated silver which arouses the interest of the unsuspecting. Without any regard to education or truth, they labor in their laboratories night and day, to lead others into new errors or to fall into such themselves, performing experiments, transscribing books at great expense, and preparing various paraphernalia for further experimentation.

Many a Cyclops is engaged in this fraud of Vulcan's stithy, some of them cheating the truth beneath a veneer of refinement and culture and others cheating themselves and holding to their error under the sordid rags of a beggar. One and all in an unending quest, they are aglow with the hope of accumulating wealth and of inducing others to take up the search by the vain promises of this deceitful art. The madness of this vagabond horde develops from a preconceived idea that the thing can really be accomplished. Then they spend their last cent of savings in buying necessary apparatus to work and to fit up a workshop for research. Unfortunately, however, when success is just within their grasp, the harpy flies away, never to return, and they have nothing left but empty pockets and numerous debts to be paid to the usurers. Moreover the mental derangement that seems to accompany this particular kind of obsession is, that in spite of the fact that one again and again reduces himself to beggary in this fashion, he does not realize the evil of it, and cannot resist falling victim once more to similar promises of some other more cunning deceiver. The result of this mania, and a common one too, is that great numbers of them waste their whole lives in this vain hope, becoming dejected in their failures and falling sick under the strain. Yet, no persuasion of friend or relative or their own dire necessity can bring them to their right senses.

The second kind of insanity is frequently found in conjunction with the first. The question of immortality, of its very nature, calls for serious study, and so this blight has seized upon many of the intellectuals and even upon some holding the high office of magistrate. This upper class, after they have acquired an exalted position in life, and gathered in the honors and riches that go with it, get the idea that there is nothing to be added to their perfect beatitude but the means of rendering their present state unending and themselves immortal. Therefore, they devote themselves entirely to the study of discovering the necessary means to this vainly coveted end. Here in the province of Pekin, in which we are living, there are few, if any, of the magistrates, of the eunuchs, or of others of high station, who are not addicted to this foolish pursuit. Since there is no lack of rich disciples of this cult, the teachers of it are necessarily numerous. The more devoted the instructors are to this study of immortality and the more excited they become from its burning urge, so, too, and on that account, are they more eagerly sought for by their superiors. Once this malady has afflicted a victim it is quite as incurable as that described above. Despite the fact that these vendors of immortality are daily paying the penalty of being mortal, they cannot be dissuaded from this preposterous habit of study, believing that eventually fortune must favor them and that what is harmful for others may prove to be beneficial for them. In short, there seems to be no way whatever of persuading them that what they hope to realize is beyond the limit of human faculties and industry.

A story is told in the ancient Chinese annals of a certain king who was so given to this silly search for immortality that he did serious harm to his mortal life in striving to become immortal. Now this ancient monarch prepared for himself a secret potion, according to the prescription of certain impostors. The very fact of drinking it down was to render him immune from death, and when he was about to consume it, no sane counsel from his advisers could prevent him carrying out his avowed proposal. Suddenly, as he happened to look away from the goblet, one of his friends seized it, and in a single draught, drained it to the dregs. Whereupon the King became so angry on being robbed of his cup of immortality, that he drew a dagger to slay the culprit on the spot. "Hold," cried his friend, gallantly addressing his liege Lord, "how can you deprive me of life when I have just drunk of your nectar of unending life? If you can, then indeed I have committed no crime, nor have I robbed you of immortality but rather my Lord I have freed you from an insidious fraud." With these words the King regained his composure and praised the courage of his friend who had rescued him from his own enslaving imagination.

In conclusion it is only fair to say that the Chinese have never been lacking in wise men who have labored strenuously to wipe out this double affliction from the minds of their people, but they have never succeeded in doing it. On the contrary, these infections seem to be spreading, and at present they are more prevalent than ever before, universally widespread, and afflicting more and more victims with the contagion of their plague-laden pestilence.

10. Religious Sects Among the Chinese

OF ALL THE PAGAN sects known to Europe, I know of no people who fell into fewer errors in the early ages of their antiquity than did the Chinese. From the very beginning of their history it is recorded in their writings that they recognized and worshipped one supreme being whom they called the King of Heaven, or designated by some other name indicating his rule over heaven and earth. It would appear that the ancient Chinese considered heaven and earth to be animated things and that their common soul was worshipped as a supreme deity. As subject to this spirit, they also worshipped the different spirits of the mountains and rivers, and of the four corners of the earth. They also taught that the light of reason came from heaven and that the dictates of reason should be hearkened to in every human action. Nowhere do we read that the Chinese created monsters of vice out of this supreme being or from his ministering deities, such as the Romans, the Greeks, and the Egyptians evolved into gods or patrons of the vices.

One can confidently hope that in the mercy of God, many of the ancient Chinese found salvation in the natural law, assisted as they must have been by that special help which, as the theologians teach, is denied to no one who does what he can toward salvation, according to the light of his conscience. That they endeavored to do this is readily determined from their history of more than four thousand years, which really is a record of good deeds done on behalf of their country and for the common good. The same conclusion might also be drawn from the books of rare wisdom of their ancient philosophers. These books are still extant and are filled with most salutary advice on training men to be virtuous. In this particular respect, they seem to be quite the equals of our own most distinguished philosophers. Just as fallen human nature continues to degenerate without the help of divine grace, so, too, primitive ideas of religion become so obscure with the passing of time, that there are very few who do not descend to the worse error of atheism when they abandon the cult of inanimate gods.

In this chapter, we shall treat only of the triple cult of the Chinese as distinguished from all other pagan sects. The traces of Saracen, Judaic, and of Christian worship evident in China we shall leave for later consideration. Chinese books enumerate only three cults or systems of religious observance for the whole world and this people knows of no others. These are, the Literati, the Sciequia, and the Laucu. All Chinese and all people of the surrounding nations who make use of Chinese writing—the Japanese, the Koreans, the Leuquici or Formosans, and the Cochin Chinese—belong to one or other of these three sects.

The sect of the Literati is proper to China and is the most ancient in the kingdom. They rule the country, have an extensive literature, and are far more celebrated than the others. Individually, the Chinese do not choose this sect; they rather imbibe the doctrine of it in the study of letters. No one who attains honors in the study of letters or who even undertakes the study would belong to any other sect. Confucius is their Prince of Philosophers, and according to them, it was he who discovered the art of philosophy. They do not believe in idol worship. In fact they have no idols. They do, however, believe in one deity who preserves and governs all things on earth. Other spirits they admit, but these are of less restricted domination and receive only minor honors. The real Literati teach nothing relative to the time, the manner, or the author of the creation of the world. We use the word real, or true, because there are some of them, less celebrated, who interpret dreams, but not much faith is placed in them as they deal mostly with trifles and improbable things. Their law contains a doctrine of reward for good done and of punishment for evil, but they seem to limit it to the present life and to apply it to the evil-doer and to his descendants, according to their merits. The ancients scarcely seem to doubt about the immortality of the soul because, for a long time after a death, they make frequent reference to the departed as dwelling in heaven. They say nothing, however, about punishment for the wicked in hell. The more recent Literati teach that the soul ceases to exist when the body does, or a short time after it. They, therefore, make no mention of heaven or of hell. To some of them this seems to be rather a severe doctrine and so this school teaches that only the souls of the just survive. They say that the soul of a man is strengthened by virtue and solidified to endure, and since this is not true of the wicked, their souls vanish, like thin smoke, immediately after leaving the body.

The doctrine most commonly held among the Literati at present seems to me to have been taken from the sect of idols, as promulgated about five centuries ago. This doctrine asserts that the entire universe is composed of a common substance; that the creator of the universe is one in a continuous body, a corpus continuum as it were, together with heaven and earth, men and beasts, trees and plants, and the four elements, and that each individual thing is a member of this body. From this unity of substance they reason to the love that should unite the individual constituents and also that man can become like unto God because he is created one with God. This philosophy we endeavor to refute, not only from reason but also from the testimony of their own ancient philosophers to whom they are indebted for all the philosophy they have.

Although the Literati, as they are called, do recognize one supreme deity, they erect no temples in his honor. No special places are assigned for his worship, consequently no priests or ministers are designated to direct that worship. We do not find any special rites to be observed by all, or precepts to be followed, nor any supreme authority to explain or promulgate laws or to punish violations of laws pertaining to a supreme being. Neither are there any public or private prayers or hymns to be said or sung in honor of a supreme deity. The duty of sacrifice and the rites of worship for this supreme being belong to the imperial majesty alone. This is so true that if anyone else should offer such a sacrifice in usurpation of this right, he would be punished as an intruder upon the duty of the King and as a public enemy.

Two magnificent temples are reserved for the King; one in each of the capital cities, Pekin and Nankin. The sole purpose of these temples is for the King to offer homage to the supreme deity. One of these temples is dedicated to heaven and the other to earth. Formerly it was the custom for the sovereign only to offer any sacrifice in these temples, but now religious functions are conducted in them by the highest magistrates who sacrifice sheep and oxen in great numbers to the gods of heaven and earth. So, too, only ranking magistrates and the highest officers in the realm are permitted to sacrifice to the spirits of the mountains, or the rivers, or of the four sections of the universe. Such religious ceremonies are strictly forbidden to private individuals. The precepts of this law are contained in the Tetrabiblion and in the five books of doctrine. Other than these books, there are no legal codes, excepting certain commentaries on these same volumes.

The most common ceremony practiced by all the Literati, from the King down to the very lowest of them, is that of the annual funeral rites, which we have already described. As they themselves say, they consider this ceremony as an honor bestowed upon their departed ancestors, just as they might honor them if they were living. They do not really believe that the dead actually need the victuals which are placed upon their graves, but they say that they observe the custom of placing them there because it seems to be the best way of testifying their love for their dear departed. Indeed, it is asserted by many that this particular rite was first instituted for the benefit of the living rather than for that of the dead. In this way it was hoped that children, and unlearned adults as well, might learn how to respect and to support their parents who were living, when they saw that parents departed were so highly honored by those who were educated and prominent. This practice of placing food upon the graves of the dead seems to be beyond any charge of sacrilege and perhaps also free from any taint of superstition, because they do not in any respect consider their ancestors to be gods, nor do they petition them for anything or hope for anything from them. However, for those who have accepted the teachings of Christianity, it would seem much better to replace this custom with alms for the poor and for the salvation of souls.

The Temple of Confucius is really the cathedral of the upper lettered and exclusive class of the Literati. The law demands that a temple be built to the Prince of Chinese Philosophers in every city, and in that particular part of the city which has been described as the center of learning. These temples are sumptuously built and adjoining them is the palace of the magistrate who presides over those who have acquired their first literary degree. In the most conspicuous place in the temple there will be a statue of Confucius, or if not a statue, a plaque with his name carved in large letters of gold. Near to this are placed the statues of certain of his disciples whom the Chinese revere as saints, but of an inferior order.

With the coming of each new moon and also at the time of the full moon, the magistrates congregate in this temple, together with those of the baccalaureate order, to do honor to their great master. The ritual in this instance is made up of bowing and of bending the knees, of the lighting of candles, and the burning of incense. Each year on his birthday and at other times fixed by custom, they offer him dishes of food elaborately prepared and assert their thanks for the doctrines contained in his writings. This they do because by means of these doctrines they acquired their literary degrees, and the country acquired the excellent public civil authority invested in the magistracy. They do not recite prayers to Confucius nor do they ask favors of him or expect help from him. They honor him only in the manner mentioned of honoring their respected dead.

This same sect has other temples built to honor the titular spirits of the cities included in the jurisdiction of the local magistrate. Here the magistrate binds himself by solemn oath to do what is right and lawful and to live up to the obligations of his office. This is done by each judge as soon as he is appointed to office, or, as they say, when he is entrusted with the official seal. Viands are offered to these spirits of the cities and incense burned for them but not for the same purpose as this is done for Confucius or for ancestors. The difference is that in these spirits they do recognize the power of a deity who can punish the wicked and reward the good.

The ultimate purpose and the general intention of this sect, the Literati, is public peace and order in the kingdom. They likewise look toward the economic security of the family and the virtuous training of the individual. The precepts they formulate are certainly directive to such ends and quite in conformity with the light of conscience and with Christian truth. They make capital of five different combinations, making up the entire gamut of human relations; namely, the relations of father and son, husband and wife, master and servants, older and younger brothers, and finally, of companions and equals. According to their belief, they alone know how to respect these relationships, which are supposed to be wholly unknown to foreigners, or if known, wholly neglected. Celibacy is not approved of and polygamy is permitted. Their writings explain at length the second precept of charity: "Do not do unto others what you would not wish others to do unto you." It really is remarkable how highly they esteem the respect and obedience of children toward parents, the fidelity of servants to a master, and devotion of the young to their elders.

Because of the fact that they neither prohibit nor command anything relative to what should be believed regarding a future life, many who belong to this caste identify the other two cults with their own. They really believe that they are practicing a high form of religion if they are tolerant of falsehood and do not openly spurn or disapprove of an untruth. The Literati deny that they belong to a sect and claim that their class or society is rather an academy instituted for the proper government and general good of the kingdom. One might say in truth that the teachings of this academy, save in some few instances, are so far from being contrary to Christian principles, that such an institution could derive great benefit from Christianity and might be developed and perfected by it.

The second important sect among the Chinese is known as Sciequia or Omitose. The Japanese call it Sciacca and Amidabu, the sect being quite similar in character in both countries. The Japanese also call it the Lex Totoqui. This code of law was brought to China from the West, in the year sixty-five of the Christian era. It was imported from the region of Thiencio, also called Shinto, which was formerly two kingdoms but today is known by the single title of Hindustan, lying between the rivers Indus and Ganges. A written record is extant that the King of China sent legates to this country, after being enlightened in a dream to do so. These messengers brought back the books of the laws and also interpreters to translate them into Chinese. The founders of the sect had died before the doctrine found its way into China. From this it would appear quite evident that this doctrine passed from the Chinese to the Japanese, and it is not at all clear why the Japanese followers of this creed assert that the Sciacca or the Amidabu was introduced into Japan from the kingdom of Siam, where they say it had its origin. It is made quite evident in the books of the followers of this doctrine that Siam was too well known to the Chinese to be mistaken for the far-distant Thiencio in a matter of this kind.

It is historically clear that this doctrine was brought into China at the identical period in which the Apostles were preaching the doctrine of Christ. Bartholomew was preaching in upper India, namely in Hindustan and the surrounding countries, when Thomas was spreading the Gospel in lower India, to the south. It is not beyond the realm of possibility, therefore, that the Chinese, moved and interested by reports of the truths contained in the Christian Gospel, sought to contact it and to learn it from the West. Instead, however, either through error on the part of their legates, or perhaps through ill-will toward the Gospel on the part of the people they visited, the Chinese received a false importation in place of the truth they were seeking.

It would seem that the original authors of the teachings of this second sect had drawn certain of their ideas from our philosophers of the West. For example, they recognize only four elements, to which the Chinese, rather foolishly, add a fifth. According to the latter, the entire material world—men, beasts, plants, and mixed bodies—is composed of the elements of fire, water, earth, metal, and wood. With Democritus and his school, they believe in a multiplicity of worlds. Their doctrine of the transmigration of souls sounds like that of Pythagoras, except that they have added much commentary and produced something still more hazy and obscure. This philosophy seems not only to have borrowed from the West but to have actually caught a glimpse of light from the Christian Gospels. The doctrine of this second sect mentions a certain trinity in which three different gods are fused into one deity, and it teaches reward for the good in heaven and punishment for the wicked in hell. They make so much of celibacy that they seem to reject marriage entirely and it is a common custom with them to abandon their homes and families and to go on pilgrimage to beg alms. In some respects their profane rites resemble our own ecclesiastical ceremonies, as for instance their recitation in chant which hardly differs from our Gregorian. There are statues in their temples and the vestments worn by those offering a sacrifice are not unlike our copes. In reciting prayers they frequently repeat a certain name, which they pronounce Tolome but which they themselves do not understand. Again, it might possibly be that in doing this they wish to honor their cult with the authority of the Apostle Bartholomew.

Whatever ray of truth there may be in their doctrine is, however, unfortunately obscured by clouds of noisome mendacity. Heaven and earth are quite confused in their ideas, as are also a place of reward and one of punishment, in neither of which do they look for an eternity for souls departed. These souls are supposed to be reborn after a certain number of years in some one of the many worlds which they postulate. There they may do penance for their crimes if they wish to make amends for them. This is only one of the many nonsensical doctrines with which they have afflicted the unfortunate country.

Neither meat nor any living thing should be eaten, according to the doctrine of this sect, but very few of its adherents observe this regulation. This violation of a rule and other faults as well can be readily atoned for by almsgiving, and, more than that, they can redeem any soul at all from eternal punishment by means of prayers.

We read that this sect was very much in favor when it first appeared, chiefly because it preached the immortality of the soul and future happiness. On the other hand, the Chinese Literati of the time inform us that as rapidly as this sect outdistanced the others in its approach to truth, the unconscious spread of its vile pest of impostures was just as rapid. Nothing served to undermine the progress of this cult more than the reputation given to it by the Literati. It was their contention, that as a result of its teachings, the King and the princes who first embraced its doctrines perished miserably in a violent death. Every thing it had to do with, they claimed, went into decline and ruin. Instead of good fortune, which the Sciequia promised and boasted of, the Literati made it evident that the country experienced only misfortune and calamity. Despite such beginnings and down to the present time, this sect has increased and decreased according to the varying fervor of the years. The continual multiplication of its books, whether currently introduced from the West or made in China, which is more probable, is the fuel that keeps its ardor ablaze with a popularity that seems impossible to extinguish. The very number and variety of its writings has resulted in such a complicated mixture of doctrine and of nonsensical trifles that even those who profess to believe in it cannot riddle it out.

Traces of the antiquity of this sect are evident today in the great number of its temples, which are usually very ornate in decorations. In these temples one sees enormous and monstrous idols of brass and marble, of wood and of yellow clay. Adjoining the temples there are high towers, built of stone or of brick tile, in which huge bells and other ornaments of great value are preserved.

The sacrificing priests of this cult are called Osciami. Their faces and their heads are kept clean shaven, contrary to the custom of the country. Some of them are on a continual pilgrimage; others lead a very trying life in caves in the mountains. The greater part of them, numbering as one might figure about two or three millions, live in the numerous cloisters of the temples. These latter are supported by alms and by revenues formerly established for that purpose, though they also provide for their keep by personal labor. This special class of temple servants is considered to be, and in reality is, the lowest and most despised caste in the whole kingdom. They come from the very dregs of the populace, and in their youth are sold into slavery to the Osciami. From being servants they become disciples and afterward succeed to the positions and to the emoluments of their masters. This method of succession is accepted in order to preserve the office. Not a single one of them could ever have elected of his own will to join this vile class of cenobites as a means to leading a holy life. Being like unto their masters as to ignorance and inexperience, and with no inclination toward learning and good manners, their natural bent to evil becomes worse with the lapse of time. There may be some exceptions to this way of life but, if so, they constitute the very few among them who have a liking for learning and accomplish something by their own industry. Though not a marrying class, they are so given to sexual indulgence that only the heaviest penalties can deter them from promiscuous living.

The monasteries of the Osciami are graded according to size. Each grade or class is ruled over by a perpetual administrator, who is succeeded in office, according to hereditary law, by one of the disciples whom he has brought into service as a slave. Of these he educates as many as he cares to, or can. There are no superiors, as such, in the separate communities. Each member is permitted to build as many cells or rooms as he may wish to at the particular station to which he is assigned. This is a common practice throughout the land, and particularly so at the court, and these rooms are let out at a good price to strangers who come for instructions. The result of this custom is that these common dwellings, which are used as religious centers, look more like large and noisy hotels, where people convene to spend time in idol worship or in learning the doctrines of this iniquitous cult.

As vile and as abject as they are known to be, even that does not prevent many from calling them in to assist at funeral services. At times also they are summoned by members of their sect for other ceremonies, in which wild animals, birds and beasts and even fishes are set at liberty, on payment of a small fee. The more religiously inclined buy the living animals, and set them free in their native element, in the air or water or in the woods, believing that such an act is an omen of good fortune.

This second sect is acquiring a new impetus, even now in our own times, building many temples and restoring others. Its followers for the most part are women and eunuchs and the common horde, and particularly a certain class who claim to be the more religious followers of the cult, who call themselves Ciaicum, or the observers of the fast. They abstain at all times from meat and fish, and in their homes they venerate a whole collection of idols with frequent praying. So as not to be wholly lacking of some means of livelihood, they answer invitations to recite prayers in the homes of others. Women are not excluded from residence in these religious centers, but they live apart from the men, shave their heads, and do not get married. They are known to the Chinese as Nicu and are not nearly as numerous as the men.

The third religious sect is called Lauzu, and had its origin with a philosopher who was contemporaneous with Confucius. The period of gestation anticipating his birth is supposed to have lasted for eighty years and so he is called Lauzu, or the Old Man Philosopher. He left no writings of his doctrine, nor does it appear that he desired to institute a new or separate cult. After his death, however, certain sectaries, called the Taufu, named him as the head of their sect and compiled various books and commentaries from other religions, and these were written in rather elegant literary style. These enthusiasts, too, have their own religious houses and live as celibates. They buy in their disciples and are as low and dishonest a class as those already described. They do not cut their hair but rather wear it as do the people in general, but they are easily distinguished by the custom of wearing a wooden skullcap on the knot or cluster of hair worn on the top of the head. Some of the followers of this creed, who are married, profess a more religious observance in their homes, where they recite set prayers for themselves and for others. Among their many gods, the devotees of this faith claim that they worship the one lord of heaven, a corporeal being to whom, it would seem, many untoward things are continually happening.

Their books recount their ravings, which we would repeat here, were it not beside our purpose to do so. A single example will give one an idea of what the rest must be like. They tell a story of the present reigning lord of heaven, who is called Ciam and his predecessor Leu. One day Leu came to earth riding on a white dragon, and Ciam, who was a diviner of dreams, invited Leu to a banquet. While the heavenly guest was enjoying himself at table, his host jumped on the white dragon and was carried back to the celestial realm, where he took possession of the throne and still excludes Leu in his efforts to return. The unfortunate outcast did, however, obtain from the usurping King permission to preside over a certain mountain in his kingdom, where they say he now lives but entirely stripped of his former dignity. And so these poor people now admit that they are venerating a false lord, a usurper, and a tyrant.

In addition to the Supreme Deity, this sect has fashioned three other gods, one of whom is Lauzu, himself, the founder of the faith. Thus we have the two sects, each in its own way fashioning a trinity of gods, so that it would seem as if the original parent of falsehood, the father of lies, has not as yet put aside his ambitious desire of divine similitude. They also talk of places of punishment and of reward, but their ideas of such places differ not a little from those of the sectaries already mentioned. This group favors a paradise of body and of soul for its members, and in their temples they have pictures of those who have been taken bodily up into heaven. Certain exercises are prescribed in order to accomplish this phenomenon, such as definite sitting positions accompanied with particular prayers and medicines, by use of which they promise their followers the favor of the gods and eternal life in heaven, or at least a longer life on earth. From such nonsense as this one can easily conclude as to the deceit injected into their delirium.

The special duty of the ministers of this group is to drive demons from homes by means of incantations. This is done in two different ways; by covering the walls of the house with pictures of horrid monsters drawn in ink on yellow paper and by filling the house with a bedlam of uncanny yelling and screaming and in this manner making demons of themselves. Bringing down rain from heaven in time of drought, stopping it when rain is too abundant, and preventing public and private calamities in general are some of the powers they claim to possess. If what is promised really came to pass, then those who permit themselves to be attracted by the promises would have a reason for their interest. Since, however, these impostors are invariably wrong in everything they foretell, it is difficult to understand what excuse or pretext can be alleged for following them, by men who otherwise are sufficiently intelligent. Unless we include everything they say under the common designation of falsehood, it would seem that some of them had acquired the secret of a magic art.

The ministers of this sect live in the royal temples of heaven and earth, and it is part of their office to be present at all sacrifices made in these temples either by the King himself or by a magistrate representing him. This, of course, serves to increase their prestige and their authority. The orchestra for such occasions is also composed of the ministers. Every musical instrument known to the Chinese will be included in this assembly, but the music they produce sounds decidedly off key to European ears. These same musicians are frequently invited to funeral services which they attend in ornate vestments, playing upon flutes and other musical instruments. The consecration of new temples and the direction of public processions of supplicants through the streets also come within their jurisdiction. These processions are ordered by the civil authorities of the towns, at stated times, and at the expense of the local neighborhood.

This sect recognized Ciam as its original high priest, and he is supposed to have handed down his office and the dignity that accompanies it, by right of hereditary succession, through a thousand years to the present day. The office itself seems to have had its origin with a certain magician, who lived in a cave in the province of Quiamsi, where his descendants still live and where the secrets of his art are handed on to his children, if there be any truth in the story. Their present leader spends most of his time in Pekin. He is a recognized favorite of the King and is even admitted into the most secret chambers of the palace for ceremonies of exorcism, if perchance suspicion should arise that these places are infested with evil spirits. He is carried through the streets in an open palanquin, wears the paraphernalia of the highest magistrates, and receives a fat annual stipend from the crown. One of our neophytes informs us that the present-day prelates of this sect are so ignorant that they do not even know the unholy hymns and rites of their own order. They have no jurisdiction whatsoever over the people. Their authority is confined to the subministers, or the Tausus, of their cult and to their own religious residence, where their power is supreme. Like the sectaries already treated, a great number of their cenobites, in an effort to formulate precepts for a longer life, spend much time experimenting in alchemy, in imitation of their holy ones, who they say have handed down certain precepts of this double science.

These three sects embrace about all the capital superstitions of this pagan people, but the vanity of their human folly does not cease here. As time goes on, through the influence of their leaders, each of these sources of superstition gives rise to so many streams of deceit and deception, that under these three captions one could number nearer to three hundred different and disparate religious sects. The frequent innovations go from bad to worse by the daily augmentation of corrupt practices and rules, of which the members of the sects take advantage for loose and licentious living.

Humvu, the founder of the present reigning family, ordained that these three laws, namely the sects, should be preserved for the good of the kingdom. This he did in order to conciliate the followers of each sect. In legislating for their continuance, however, he made it of strict legal requirement that the cult of the Literati should have preference over the others, and that they alone should be entrusted with the administration of public affairs. Thus it happens that no sect is allowed to work for the extinction of another. The rulers make it a practice to cultivate the devotion of all three of them, using them in their own interest when need be, and conciliating each in turn by renovating their old temples or by building new ones. The wives of the King are usually more devoted to the sect of the idols, conferring alms upon the ministers and even supporting a whole institution of them, beyond the palace walls, in order to profit by their prayers.

The number of idols in evidence throughout the kingdom of China is simply incredible. Not only are they on exhibition in the temples, where a single temple might contain thousands of them, but in nearly every private dwelling. Idols are assigned a definite place in a private home, according to the custom of the locality. In public squares, in villages, on boats, and through the public buildings, this common abomination is the first thing to strike the attention of a spectator. Yet, it is quite certain that comparatively few of these people have any faith in this unnatural and hideous fiction of idol worship. The only thing they are persuaded of in this respect is, that if their external devotion to idols brings them no good, at least it can do them no harm.

In conclusion to our consideration of the religious sects, at the present time, the most commonly accepted opinion of those who are at all educated among the Chinese is, that these three laws or cults really coalesce into one creed and that all of them can and should be believed. In such a judgment, of course, they are leading themselves and others into the very distracting error of believing that the more different ways there are of talking about religious questions, the more beneficial it will be for the public good. In reality they finally end up by accomplishing something altogether different from what they expected. In believing that they can honor all three laws at the same time, they find themselves without any law at all, because they do not sincerely follow any one of them. Most of them openly admit that they have no religion, and so by deceiving themselves in pretending to believe, they generally fall into the deepest depths of utter atheism.

11. Signs of the Doctrines of the Saracens, the Jews, and of Christianity Among the Chinese

(Excerpts on Christianity taken from the Ricci Diary written by Trigault)

IN THE FOREGOING chapter we treated of the heathen sects and their ceremonies which are proper to the Chinese people, or which, at least, are supposed to be peculiar to them. We shall now consider what amount of knowledge, containing some cognizance of the true Divinity, has come to this people from externs and from intruders into their country. We shall deal first with the Saracens, then with the Jews, and finally with traces and evidences of Christianity, endeavoring to preserve the continuity between ancient times and the introduction of the light of the Gospel into China in our own days.

It seems quite evident that at various times many of the followers of Mohamet found their way into China from the West, from Persia, under which name I would include Mogores and other regions where the Persian language is spoken. This is particularly true of the period during which the Tartars held sway over the Chinese, when entrance to the kingdom from that approach was unrestricted. Even at present it is an annual occurrence for Persian merchants to make excursions into China, under the pretense of being official legations. These missions generally smuggle in other Saracens whom the Chinese Magistrates always endeavor to send back to their native land. We shall say more about this later, when we have occasion to mention an expedition made by a member of our Society into Cathay, that is, into the Kingdom of China.[1] Irrespective of how they came here, the

---

[1] The story is told in Book V, Chap. 11 sq. of Ricci's Diary. Cf. *The Month*, June, 1940, "Hunting for Cathay: An Episode of Mission History," by James Brodrick, S.J.

Saracens are everywhere in evidence, and except for some few of them, they are always looked upon as outsiders. Due to their rapid propagation, they have become so numerous that their thousands of families are scattered about in nearly every province and are to be found in nearly every sizable city. In the cities in which they are numerous they have their own temples, built at great expense, where their children are circumcised and in which they recite prayers at stated times and hold other religious functions.

So far as we have noted up to the present, the Saracens here make no effort to spread their doctrines among others. Save for the fact that they do not eat pork, they live according to Chinese law, are quite ignorant of their own ritual, and are looked down upon by the Chinese. At present they are treated as natives and are not held as suspects, like other strangers. In fact, they are admitted to literary studies and to public degrees without discrimination and even to the magistracy. Most Saracens who attain to a Chinese literary degree renounce the law of their ancestors, except the precept forbidding them to eat the flesh of swine. In this observance, however, they really abstain because of a natural abhorrence rather than from any religious motive.

The Jews came into China at an early period, as seems evident from the following narrative. Some few years after our Society had taken a fixed residence in Pekin, a man who was Jewish by race and by profession, learning of the reputation of Father Ricci, decided to pay him a visit. He had read about Ricci and his companions in a book about the Europeans, written by a Chinese scholar. The man's name was Ngai and he was born in Chaifamfu, the metropolitan city of the Province of Honan. At that time he was on his way to Pekin to take the examinations for the doctorate. He had already attained to the order of the licentiate. Being a Jew and having read in the book mentioned that our Fathers were not Saracens and that they believed in only one God of heaven and earth, he concluded that we must be believers in, and followers of, the Mosaic Law. On entering our home he seemed to be quite excited over the fact, as he expressed it, that he professed the same faith that we did. His whole external appearance, nose, eyes, and all his facial lineaments, were anything but Chinese. Father Ricci took him into the church and showed him a picture above the high altar, a painting of the Blessed Virgin and the child Jesus, with John the Precursor, praying on his knees before them. Being a Jew and believing that we were of the same religious belief, he thought the picture represented Rebecca and her two children, Jacob and Esau, and so made a humble curtsy before it. He could not refrain, as he remarked, from doing honor to the parents of his race, though it was not his custom to venerate images. This happened on the Feast of St. John The Baptist.

The pictures flanking the altar were those of the four Evangelists and the Jew asked if they were four of the twelve children of the one represented on the altar. Father Ricci, thinking that he had made reference to the Apostles, nodded in agreement. Actually, however, each one was mistaken as to what the other had in mind. When he brought the visitor back to the house and began to question him as to his identity, it gradually dawned upon him that he was talking with a believer in the ancient Jewish law. The man admitted that he was an Israelite, but he knew of no such word as Jew. It would seem from this that the dispersion of the ten tribes penetrated to the extreme confines of the East. Later on Ngai saw a royal edition of the Bible, printed by Plantin, and though he recognized the Hebrew characters he could not read the book. We heard from him also that there were ten or twelve families of Israelites in his home town and a magnificent synagogue, which only recently they had renovated at a cost of ten thousand gold pieces. In this same temple, as he related, the five books of Moses, namely the Pentateuch, had been preserved in the form of scrolls, and with great veneration, through a period of five or six hundred years. In Hamcheu, the capital city of the Province of Cequian, he claimed, there were a far greater number of families, with their own synagogue, and others scattered about, who had no place of worship because their numbers were almost extinct.

Our visitor was familiar with the history of the Old Testament, such as the stories of Abraham, Judith, Mardochai, and Esther. He pronounced the names somewhat differently from ourselves and perhaps he was closer to the ancient and original pronunciation: Jerusalem was Jerusoloim and our word Messiah he called Moscia. Some of his brethren, including his own brother, were quite expert in the Hebrew language. He himself had given all his time to Chinese literature from his early youth and consequently had neglected the study of Hebrew. It was no secret with him that in the judgment of the high priest of the synagogue, he himself, because of his Chinese studies, was considered to be almost unworthy to associate with his Hebrew brethren. This, however, made little difference to him, if he could acquire the doctor's degree. This was also a common practice with the Saracens, and they showed no fear of their native religious superiors in doing it. Father

Ricci was indebted to this same man for information relative to traces of Christianity, which we shall consider when we have finished our account of the Jews.

About three years later, and that was as soon as he could get around to it, Father Ricci sent a Jesuit Chinese Lay Brother to the metropolis mentioned, namely to Chaifamfu, to investigate the truth of what the visiting Israelite had told him. Everything, according to the Brother's report, was just as it had been narrated. Moreover, Father Ricci had the Brother copy out the beginnings and the ends of the books that were preserved in the synagogue, which were found to be identical with our own Pentateuch and written in the same characters, save for the points, which the ancients did not use. Ricci then sent the same brother on a second visit, this time to the ruler of the synagogue, with a letter, informing him that he had all the books of the Old Testament at his house in Pekin, together with a copy of the New Testament, containing the life and works of the Messiah, who he asserted had already appeared. The Archisynagogus took exception to this last remark and replied that the Messiah would not come for another ten thousand years. He added, however, that since they had heard so much of Ricci's reputation and learning, they would confer upon him the dignity of high priest of the Synagogue, if he would join their faith and abstain from eating pork.

Three other Jews came from that same city to Pekin later on, and as they were detained here for several days on business and were ready to receive the Christian faith, they decided to be baptized. One of these was a nephew of our first visitor, on the father's side. Our Fathers received them with hospitality and taught them a great deal about the Scriptures that was unknown to their Rabbis. When they learned that the Messiah had really come, they knelt down and prayed before his statue, as Christians do, and they were delighted with a compendium volume of the Christian faith, and with the other books on Christian doctrine, written in Chinese, which they brought back to their people.

These three made numerous inquiries about the Jewish religion, from which they had become entirely estranged because they were ignorant of the language of their ancestors. In brief, they were well on the way to becoming Saracens or heathen gentiles. They informed us that the ruler of the synagogue, whom we had known, had died of old age, and his son who had taken his place by right of hereditary law, was quite unlearned in matters pertaining to his faith. It seemed strange to them that there were no pictures or statues in their own luxurious temple or in the homes and private oratories of their people. A statue of Christ the Saviour in their temple, it seemed to them would do much to increase their zeal and devotion. One complaint they made against the religious requirements of their brethren was that they were forbidden to eat the flesh of animals that had not been slaughtered by their own hands. If they had been forced to observe that law on their present journey, they said they would have died from hunger. To their wives and their gentile relations, the practice of circumcising children on the eighth day after their birth seemed cruel and barbarous. With that part of the law omitted, there would be no difficulty about accepting the rest of it, because they really felt no objection to abstaining from the flesh of swine. This, in summary, is the gist of what we learned from firsthand evidence about the Jews in the Kingdom of China.

Now to offer some evidence of the traces of Christianity, which we do very willingly, believing it should be of special interest to our friends in Europe. The following testimony was in part received from the visitor we have already mentioned, and in part deduced from other indications observed in past years. When Father Ricci made certain that his friend, the Chinese licentiate, really was a believer in the ancient Hebrew law, he made up his mind to look for more definite evidences of Christianity in China than he had acquired up to that time. As long as he continued to call the Christians by that name he made no definite progress in his quest. Eventually, however, while he was describing the Christians and using various passages from the Old Testament in connection with the holy cross, he hit upon exactly what he was looking for. Now, the Chinese had no concept of such a thing as a cross. In fact there was no special word in their language to express the idea, and so our Fathers had to give them a Chinese word for it. In doing so they chose the Chinese character expressing the number ten, which is written in the form of a cross, thus ✝.

It probably was not without the guidance of divine providence that a Christian in our day, selecting a name for the cross for the Chinese, should hit upon the very word that their ancestors had invented because of a similar paucity of symbolic expressions. In each instance the word selected was Scie-cu, meaning, the tenth. In so doing they really were not far afield from the practice observed in sacred literature, in which the cross is expressed by the letter T,[2] which is even a more exact form than the one in question. When the conversation came

---

[2] The reference is to Ezekiel 9:4.

around to designating the cross by this particular symbol, our friend the Israelite remembered that in Chaifamfu, the capital of his district, and in Lincin, a trading post in the Province of Sciantum, there were certain strangers whose ancestors came from abroad and who observed the religious custom of venerating a cross. They were accustomed, he said, to make a gesture with the hand in the form of a cross over their food and drink. He had no realization of the significance of such a rite and assured us that neither had the people in question who were accustomed to use it.

This discovery seemed to fit in perfectly with what some of the Fathers had heard from different sources about a custom of making the sign of the cross, which was more or less common in various places. It was reported that in some regions they placed the sign of salvation on the foreheads of babies with ink as a protection against misfortune in their infancy. All of this seems to be quite in agreement with what Jerome Rufellus writes when treating of the Chinese in his commentary on the Cosmography of Ptolemy.

Since we are speaking of evidences of the cross among the Chinese, we probably should not omit the following incident, which is still another trace of its presence. One day one of our Fathers saw a beautifully cast bell, which was for sale by an itinerant antiquary. At the top of it, was an engraving representing a temple or a church and in front of this was a cross surrounded by an inscription, done in Greek letters. He wanted to buy the piece but he could not get the dealer to settle upon a suitable price. Later on he went looking for the man and the bell so as to translate the lettering but he never found him.

Some of the prayers which were recited by these adorers of the cross, as our Jewish narrator informed us, were identical with passages in the books of his own law, and evidently taken from them. He probably had reference to the Psalms of David. According to him also, these people were formerly very numerous in the northern provinces. It seems, however, that they became so flourishing in a literary way and so strongly armed, that the Chinese, who are naturally very suspicious, decided that they were revolutionaries. His own idea was that this suspicion was first aroused, some sixty years ago, by the Saracens, who are the avowed enemies of everything Christian wherever it be discovered. As a result of this distrust they were afraid that the magistrates might lay hands on them, and so they dispersed and scattered in all directions. Some of them afterward professed to be Saracens, others Jews, but most of them became worshippers of idols, to escape a penalty of death.

Their places of worship were converted into temples of the idols. One of their churches, which they called The Church of the Cross, they themselves have still referred to by that name, ever since it was taken over by the idol worshippers. From the time of their dispersion, they were so frightened that they kept nothing more secret than the fact that they once belonged to that particular group.

When our Lay Brother was sent into those parts, with the names of several families, furnished by the Israelite, to discover what signs of Christianity might be evident, it could only be expected from what had been related, that nobody would willingly admit his identity. Knowing that the Brother was Chinese, they naturally suspected that he was a spy in the service of the magistrates. Up to the present time, no European priest has been able to visit those districts because no one could be spared from the Mission, but the time will come when we shall have to establish a residence there and dispel the terrible fear by which these people are haunted. Please God that time will not be far distant.

The three sects first discussed, called barbarian sects by the Chinese, are all designated by one common term, and their followers are all known as Hoei-hoei. What the origin of that name may be is still a puzzle to us. The more learned Chinese generally distinguish them as follows: The Saracens are called Hoei because they abstain from pork. The Jews are Hoei also because they do not eat the portion of meat containing the thigh nerve. This custom was introduced by the Jews because Jacob was stricken in that nerve.[3] Those who venerate the cross are called Hoei because they do not eat of the flesh of animals with rounded hoofs. Although the Chinese and the Saracens and the Jews all partake of the flesh of horses, asses, and mules, this last class probably refrain from such meats in accordance with a custom peculiar to their race. The Chinese have other names also for this third class. In general they use the word Hoei with reference to those who follow the cult of the cross, while both Chinese and Jews say Hoei, referring to the Saracens. By this they mean that the Saracens belong to all three sects since they have adopted something of their belief from gentiles, Jews, and Christians. Besides the ordinary term Isai or Jesuini which the Saracens apply to all Christians, here in China the followers of the ancient cult of the cross are known to them as Terzai. The origin of this term is also uncertain, except that we have learned from a certain Armenian that in Persia the Armenians call the Christians by that same

---

[3] Reference to Genesis, Chap. 32.

name. It might be concluded from this, with some probability, that the devotees of the cross had their origin in Armenia, and at various times found their way into China from the West. This could have happened when the vast armies of the Tartars poured over China, about the time, as it would seem, when the Venetian Marco Polo found his way hither.

Such, for the most part, are the signs and vestiges we have observed here in China. We can, however, go back to a much earlier origin of Christianity in these parts by referring to what we have gathered from the Chaldean codices, from the region of Malabar, which even the most critical objector will hardly deny was evangelized by the Apostle Thomas. In these records it is clearly stated that Christianity was introduced into China by St. Thomas himself and that he actually built churches within the kingdom. To forestall any doubt about the reading of these documents, we shall give a translation of the Chaldean manuscripts which were literally rendered into Latin by Father John Maria Campori, a Jesuit who labored in that particular vineyard for many years and who was expert in the use of the Chaldean language. This translation was made at the request of the Very Reverend Archbishop Father Francis Roitz, pastor of the Jesuit church there. Father Campori himself, at the request of our Fathers, made a transcript of it, so that we might include it in these commentaries and thus prevent the loss of so valuable a document of antiquity.

In the Chaldean Breviary of the Malabar Church of St. Thomas, in one of the lessons of the second nocturn of the office recited on the Feast of St. Thomas, we find what is called the Gaza, or the thesaurus, which reads exactly as follows: "The error of idolatry was banished from India by St. Thomas. The Chinese and Ethiopians were converted to the truth by St. Thomas. From St. Thomas they received the sacrament of baptism and became children of adoption. Through St. Thomas they believed in and professed the Father, Son, and Holy Spirit. Through St. Thomas they preserved the faith in one God which they received from him. Through St. Thomas the splendor of a life-giving faith flourished through all of India. Through St. Thomas the Kingdom of Heaven took wings and sped its flight to the Chinese." Again in one of the antiphons we read: "The people of India, of China, of Persia and others on the islands, together with those of Syria, Armenia, Greece, and Roumania, venerate The Holy Name, in memory of St. Thomas."

In part second, subject six, chapter nineteen of the Summary of the Synodal Canons, under Regulations for Bishops and Metropolitans, we have the Canon of the Patriarch Theodore, which reads: "These six Metropolitan Sees and Capitals of Provinces, namely, Helan, Nziuin, Prath, Afsur, Bethgarmi, and Halah, which are deemed worthy of sharing the jurisdiction of the Patriarch, should be represented at the Patriarchal Convention, every fourth year. So likewise the Bishops of the great province, namely the remaining Metropolitans of China, India, Pase, Mauzai, Xam, of the Raziqui, Heriona (namely Cambaia), of Samarkand (namely Mogor), as they are far distant and cannot travel at will because of vast mountain ranges and turbulent seas, let them forward letters of compliance (that is communion) to the Patriarch, at least during each sixth year."

When the Portuguese arrived in Cochin, the Church of the Malabar Mountains was ruled over by Dom. James, who signed himself, Metropolitan of India and China. This is made quite clear in his codex manuscript of the New Testament, at the end of which we read, "This book written by James, the Metropolitan of India and China." In like manner, Joseph who succeeded James and who died in Rome, signed himself Dom. Joseph, Metropolitan of all India and China. This, in fact, is the most ancient title of that Church.

Let this suffice for the time being relative to the kingdom of China, until we can give the world a fuller and a more detailed volume on the same subject, which, God willing, shall some day be accomplished.

BOOK TWO

1. Blessed Francis Xavier Undertakes to Enter China, but Fails

~~~~~~

IN JUSTICE to the author and the prime mover of this Mission and to the expedition as well, our narrative must begin with the name of Francis Xavier. The original idea and the first efforts towards its accomplishment were his, and the circumstances surrounding his death and burial, which led to its final success, afford adequate proof of his title of author and founder. We confidently believe that when he opened the door of China to his brethren, he accomplished more from his place in heaven than his ardent zeal could effect during the course of his energetic life on earth. Xavier was the first of the Society of Jesus to realize the aptitude of the innumerable people of this vast empire for absorbing the truth of the Gospel, as he was also the first to entertain the hope of spreading the faith among them. Some of his biographers have already mentioned the series of events here narrated, relative to his attempt to enter China, but we think they should be repeated in some detail as being necessary to the fullness of our story. The repetition, which is limited to its pertinence to the present work, is taken from The History of the Society of Jesus, of which the first volume appeared only recently.

While Xavier was working among the idol-worshippers of Japan, he observed that whenever they were hard pressed in an argument, they always had recourse to the authority of the Chinese. This was quite in keeping with the fact that they also deferred to the wisdom of the Chinese in questions pertaining to religious worship and in matters of public administration. Whence it happened that they commonly asserted, that if the Christian religion was really the one true religion, it surely would have been known to the intelligent Chinese and also accepted by them. Whereupon Xavier decided that he must visit the Chinese as soon as possible and convert them from their superstitious beliefs. With that done, he could more easily win over the Japanese, with the Gospel brought to them from China. On his return voyage from Japan, along the coast of China to India, he stopped off at the Island of Sanchan, which at that time, before the founding of the City of Macao, was a trading post between the Chinese and the Portuguese. Here he was fortunate in meeting an old friend, one Diego Pereira, a wealthy and industrious trader and an experienced navigator, who was preparing to set sail for India in the near future. He told Pereira of his plan of going into China and visiting the Emperor, and outlined the manner in which he hoped to accomplish it. Since all foreigners were forbidden to enter the kingdom, excepting officially appointed legates, he planned to return to India and arrange for the Viceroy and the Bishop of Goa to organize an embassy to the Royal Court. He could then have himself attached to this embassy and once he had gained an entrance and visited the Emperor, he would announce the Gospel to the Chinese; publicly if allowed to and secretly if not.

Evidently the holy man was not as yet acquainted with the conditions prevailing in this country and was estimating the success of his undertaking from his knowledge of other lands. Pereira was enthusiastic for the venture and thought it would help if the legation were to bring along some gifts. He and his ship and his fortune were at Xavier's disposal, and as an earnest of his interest he offered him thirty thousand gold pieces and a man to accompany him to Goa. Here we would like to give an account of this man's celebrated voyages, but we shall have to pass them over as they do not pertain to the immediate interest of our story.

On his arrival at Goa, Xavier laid his plans before Alphonso Naronia, Viceroy of India, and Giovanni Albuquerque, the Bishop of Goa. With Pereira's help they were to organize an embassy to China, and as a member of such a legation Xavier himself would be able to effect an entrance into the kingdom which was firmly closed to all foreigners at every approach. The embassy was established as designed, and since Pereira was a man of considerable influence and in sympathy with Xavier's ideas, he was appointed as its official director. He was at Malacca at the time, where he had stopped off to prepare for a voyage to the Island of Sunda. In the meantime, while awaiting Xavier's return to Malacca, his representatives were sparing no expense in preparing what was necessary for the proposed expedition and in collecting presents that would be suitable for the occasion. Within a month Xavier had everything ready for his departure and naturally he was overjoyed with the prospects. Letters patent and letters of credence were secured from the Viceroy and from the Bishop, and gifts were procured for the Emperor. Then he turned his attention toward regulating the affairs of the Society and arranging for its proper government during his absence.

Xavier left Goa on the 14th of April, 1552, and his first thought upon arriving at Malacca was to visit his friend the Governor General, Alvares Taidio, to whom he was bringing the official appointment of Prefect of the Maritime Province, which Xavier had obtained for him from the Viceroy of Goa. And so, although there was no just cause for fear, yet he realized that if passion should stir up opposition in this man, he could injure the legation by delaying it. Realizing the importance of this mission and knowing that the Devil never sleeps, he was always somewhat timorous lest anything might happen to impede its auspicious beginning. He was continually exhorting his servants to pray fervently for its success and he was also very careful to be obliging to Taidio. Results were to prove that his fears were well founded and that his favors were tendered to no avail. From the very beginning he had sensed that if this honorable and important expedition were entrusted to the direction of Pereira, Taidio would be set against it. The Navigator had not as yet returned from Sunda, but when he did, Xavier earnestly advised him to assume an air of indifference and by no means to start an argument. The entire settlement of the question was to be left to Taidio, and if he had to be conciliated, the best way to do it was by a showing of calmness and courtesy. The Governor, who was no friend of Pereira's before that, was highly incensed at the new honors conferred upon Pereira, and immediately trumped up a story to the effect that the city was in danger of being besieged. He said he feared that there were not people enough in the place to defend it, and Pereira was forbidden to leave the city. His ship was to be detained in port; and to make sure that it was, he had the rudder removed and delivered to him in person.

Disturbed and worried by the gravity of the situation, because of the importance of the cause involved, Xavier sent some of their mutual friends, dignitaries of the city, to plead with Taidio in all humility not to obstruct the spread of the Gospel. They were instructed to beseech him in the name of Christ not to prevent Xavier from setting out for China in company with the legate, Pereira, who had been legally appointed to the position by the Viceroy of India. When his petitions were rejected, Xavier proceeded to inject a note of terror into his messages, explaining what serious harm Taidio was doing to his own interests. Francesco Suario, Parish Priest of Malacca and Vicar General of the diocese, went to the Governor with letters from the Bishop, seriously admonishing him to think twice over a matter of such grave importance. He was advised, moreover, not to bring down upon himself the anger of the King and the displeasure of Heaven as well, by resisting the order of the Bishop. However, neither the denunciation of the Vicar nor the letters of the Bishop produced any change in his attitude, save to render him more obdurate than he had been. Finally, Francesco Alvares, who at that time had not as yet handed over the prefecture to Taidio, went personally to the Governor with letters from the King of Portugal, in which the Sovereign asserted that when he sent Xavier to India his intention was that he should preach the Gospel to the entire Orient. Together with these letters he also produced the decree of the Viceroy, making it a crime against the Crown for anyone wilfully to impede the legation to China. When Taidio heard these documents read, in presence of a numerous gathering, he jumped up from his chair, stamped his foot in anger and exclaimed, "What interest have I in decrees of the Viceroy? I know it is for the King's best interests that this expedition should not be undertaken."

Up to this time Xavier had never acted in his official capacity of Apostolic Nuncio. Now, however, he felt obliged to forgo further modesty, in order to put the fear of God into the heart of this obdurate official. Unwilling as he was to do so, he finally made known the document, so long concealed, creating him Nuncio and empowering him to threaten with anathema anyone who persisted in obstructing his efforts to spread the faith. His purpose in making this revelation was not to inflict punishment but to offer an opportunity for avoiding it. The mission of threatened denunciation was entrusted to the Vicar General, Suarez, who went straightway to the Governor and, as a father rather than a judge, explained to him the full measure of the excommunication. Then he begged and pleaded with him in the name of Christ Crucified not to cast himself knowingly and deliberately into such dire and mortal misfortune, which must eventually lead to dishonor and disgrace. Finally, he besought him not to commit a crime, from which it would be so difficult to unburden his soul and for which he could hardly expect to escape the vengeance of Heaven. Neither the authority of the Pope nor the menace of disaster had any effect upon the pertinacious will of the Governor, and threatening only served to render him more adamant. Worse still, as one wrong defends itself by creating another, he endeavored to defame the character of Xavier by spreading about the report that under the guise of sanctity he had forged the apostolic letters in order to build up a reputation for discovering new countries.

The result of the whole controversy was that Xavier's whole plan, which seemed to have been inspired from above, came to naught through the jealousy of one perverted individual. Against such pride and audacity Xavier was forced to exercise his severity, in order to set an example for others who might be tempted to prevent the progress of the faith. This he did by informing the newly appointed Prefect of the Maritime Province that he, together with his abettors and satellites, were excommunicated, and placed under the interdict as to divine services. His purpose in adopting this extreme measure was not to add to their misery but to remind them of the evil they had done and to offer a means by which it might be remedied. Later on, he sent a letter from the island of Sanchan to Gaspar, Rector of the school at Goa, instructing him to have the excommunication published with the authority of the Bishop.

Of all the trials and disappointments that ever beset his laborious life nothing ever affected Xavier like the failure of this project. Filled with promise for the spread of the Christian religion, it was reduced to nothing by one from whom such treatment was least to be expected. But zeal for the glory of God and the salvation of souls does not lie dormant; rather it inflames and energizes the hearts it captivates, as Xavier was about to prove. His soul was saddened not because of his own misfortune but for the lot of the Prefect, whose crime had exposed him to impending punishment. Indeed, this was so evident to him that he openly declared that this man's avarice and ambition would soon succumb to a proper sanction, affecting his wealth, his character and his person as well. The prophecy was swift of realization. Alvares Taidio fell a victim of leprosy, was publicly accused of various crimes, and despising the jurisdiction of the Viceroy, as he had the authority of Xavier, was arrested, charged with treason, taken to Goa in chains and thence transported to Portugal for trial before the King. Sentenced to be deprived of his wealth and publicly disgraced, he really seemed to have been overtaken by the displeasure of Heaven, and died a victim of a dread disease and an outcast from society.

The sudden disappearance of such promising aid for the legation served only to increase Xavier's perseverance, as well as his conviction that where human help waned divine help was more to be sought for. So he set himself to studying new methods of getting into China. First he thought of cultivating or, if necessary, of purchasing the friendship of some Chinese merchant who would smuggle him into the mainland. The royal edict, threatening chains and imprisonment for foreigners who landed in China without official permission, was no obstacle to his zeal for souls. As a prisoner he could sow the seed of religion among his fellow prisoners and when they were released, they would spread it among the people. As for himself, if ever he were set free he would immediately begin to preach the knowledge of Christ and His law and doctrine. There was new hope and new courage in the idea of succeeding with the aid of a pagan where he had failed through the fault of a Christian, and with this thought in mind he left the city with a Chinese interpreter and one other companion to embark upon the venture. Before departing, he foretold that the city would suffer many a dire disaster and costly calamity.

Some of the city officials came to visit him when he was ready to leave, and the Vicar of the place modestly suggested that he pay a farewell visit to the Governor. As the Prelate explained, it would cause talk and he would appear to be leaving in anger, or as one who was being turned away, if he left without making an official call on the authorities. "What," replied Xavier, "am I supposed to pay homage to an excommunicate? I shall never see him again nor will he see me, either in this life or in the next, unless it be when I accuse him before Christ, the Judge, in the Valley of Josaphat." As he was saying this he turned to a nearby church, fell upon his knees, and with hands joined and tears in his eyes, he prayed for God's help, in touching words that were heard by those about him. Thus, in an attitude of prayer he remained for some time with his gaze fixed upon the earth. Then standing up, his face alight and with an air of majesty, in full view of the crowd that had gathered, he took off his shoes and proceeded to shake the dust from off them according to the directions of the Gospel. This gesture brought tears to the eyes of the bystanders and filled their souls with a sense of alarming fear. As their Superior, he ordered every member of the Society of Jesus to leave the City of Malacca. To Pereira he sent a letter of farewell from the ship on

which he was leaving. To have seen him personally would have increased their mutual grief, whereas his purpose was to lessen the
sorrow of his friend, and to this end he promised him in the letter
that the injury and loss he had recently suffered would soon be recom-
pensed by greater honor and profit. This promise was fulfilled by
Xavier himself through letters of recommendation to the King of
Portugal, which resulted in greater glory and fortune than Pereira
had ever dreamed of. Xavier sailed in July in Pereira's ship which
had been manned by a small crew of the trusted friends of Taidio and
dispatched in his name, while its owner was still detained in Malacca.
During a brief stop in the Strait of Singapore, Xavier sent another
letter of consolation to his friend Pereira. Running before favorable
winds, they were not many days out from Malacca when they sighted
the coast of China.

Sanchan is a barren and desert island about thirty leagues off the
coast of China. At that time it was the scene of a trading post between
the Portuguese and the Chinese; a mere cluster of huts rapidly thrown
together and built of branches and straw. When Xavier arrived here,
wholly preoccupied with the idea of his expedition, he immediately
went about among the merchants, both Portuguese and Chinese, inquiring what means he might adopt to get into the cities of China.
Every approach to the continent, as he was informed, was closed and
protected by vigilant guards. There was no possibility of a stranger
landing. In fact, there was a very severe edict against foreigners entering and against natives assisting them in the effort. Nothing daunted
by such threats, and since there was no other way of doing it, he
openly asserted his intention of using every means to make a clandes-
tine entrance and, once in, to go directly to the local Governor and
declare his mission. To the Portuguese this looked like too daring and
too dangerous an effort, and some of them tried every means at their
disposal to dissuade him from risking his life or falling into slavery.
His magnanimous reply to this was that his life was a cheap price for
the salvation of the Chinese people, about whose disposition and
talents he had heard so much. Chains and slavery and even a violent
death were not worth considering, when there was question of liberating souls from the danger of eternal death in everlasting servitude.

In the midst of all this trouble and anxiety he fell victim to a fever
which clung to him for a fortnight, but at first signs of recovery he was
back again with even more zeal to his search for a trader who would
consent to take him to China. Hoping to win over either an oriental

or a European, he would inform first one and then the other that he was entrusting him with a great secret and then try to persuade him to take part in such a praiseworthy undertaking. They would listen, but their ears were ringing with fear at the thought of such a risk of fortune and perhaps of life itself, and he found no one who would agree to share the dangers of the venture. Sickness was increasing among his companions, and things began to look really desperate when he realized that Antonio, his interpreter, a former pupil at the school in Goa, had already rendered himself practically useless by forgetting his native language, for lack of practice. Surrounded by so many difficulties that even hope seemed to be vanishing, he suddenly found new courage and acquired new life in prospects from an unsuspected quarter. A new interpreter, not only skilled in his own language but versed in its literature, offered himself gratis to undertake the proposed expedition. His next surprise was a trader of wavering decision whom he finally won over by promises, but principally by means of a gift of a quantity of pepper valued at more than two hundred gold pieces. This was his savings which the merchants had given him by way of alms. The trader agreed to land Xavier and his interpreter somewhere on the China coast, together with a small amount of baggage including a few books. In an effort to keep the project a secret and not wishing to entrust his life to his regular crew, the trader captain decided to take his own sons and his most trusted servants as oarsmen and to make the crossing on a stormy night. Moreover, he promised to conceal Xavier in his own home, after the landing, until such time as he could safely emerge, at his own risk, and make his way to the Governor of Canton to expose his mission.

This whole plan was so alarming that, once it became known, his friends were not slow in denouncing it. To them it was charged with a double danger. The Chinese trader, already in possession of his reward might cast his passengers into the sea to destroy all evidence of his contract, or he might leave them to perish on some uncharted rocky isle. Again, if a stranger were to enter China without proper credentials, the Governor might have him scourged or even put to death, or perhaps subject him to chains and perpetual slavery. There was nothing new in all this to Xavier. In fact, he had counted upon more serious dangers than were mentioned and had even written about them to his fellow Jesuits. His answer to his friends was that it might look like a loss of confidence in Divine Providence, if he were to withdraw, because of a sense of fear, from a commission which he had undertaken by divine guidance. How was he to interpret the Gospel declaration that, "He who loses his life for me shall find it"? Finally, he would have to deem himself unworthy of the Kingdom of Heaven if he turned back now, seeing that he had already put his hand to the plough.

New hope brought new energy, but it also brought new difficulties. Through the efforts of the Portuguese, or perhaps because of the threatened danger, the recently acquired interpreter suddenly changed his mind and lost all interest in the affair. That was just another disappointment for Xavier, who was adamant in his decision and decided to set out with his former interpreter, although this man was far less suited to the work. Then the Portuguese merchants, moved by their own interests more than by his, decided upon a deliberate intervention. First they begged him to consider the safety of others, if he thought nothing of his own. Then they reminded him that if he were to force an entrance into China, the native Governors, incensed by the daring of one foreigner, might avenge themselves by condemning them all. If he really had decided upon tempting such a dubious fortune, they requested him at least to put off the venture until they had time to set sail and thus escape the impending danger. To this he replied that they could put aside all fear for their personal safety and for their merchandise as well. He would not set out upon his voyage until they were far enough away to be wholly assured of their safety. Evidently he had made up his mind, and while they were preparing for a general exodus, he was getting ready for his own private Odyssey. Then, lo and behold, another and a seemingly insurmountable obstacle presented itself. His friends had told him so. The trader whom he had engaged and for whom he had been anxiously waiting failed to appear at the appointed time. The fear of detection and death, or perhaps suspicion of his enemies may have proved too much for him. Thus, the Ambassador of God was being abandoned by his aides, one by one, until all he had left was his own personal courage and his trust in Heaven. Faith waxed strong as human help was waning, until finally there was nothing left to rely upon save a ray of hope that appeared in a current rumor.

The King of Siam was supposed to be preparing a legation to be sent to the Royal Court of China. If the Canton trader did not put in an appearance within a certain time, Xavier decided that he would sail to Siam and use every possible means to secure a place in the retinue of the legate. The Portuguese ships had nearly all departed, and with them Xavier sent along his only fellow worker who had long been suffering from a lingering illness. India offered better climate for a sick man, and he could have given little or no help on the hazardous journey to be undertaken. This left him practically abandoned on the island of Sanchan. His only companions were his interpreter and one other Chinese youth, and yet his incredible ardor and his capacity for suffering for Christ were such that he continued his charitable ministrations to the indigent squatters of the place. In the meantime, he never ceased his vigilant watching for the trader with whom he had bargained and for whom he was still hopefully waiting.

It would seem, indeed, as though it had pleased God to reward his servant Francis for a work almost accomplished, rather than have him bring it to a successful end. Maybe this kingdom was not as yet ready for the sowing of the Gospel seed, and perhaps it was more suitable to reserve that for those who were to follow. Or was it better to reward the hero with an eternal crown in heaven for his gigantic labors accomplished, rather than open a road for another exhausting task? On the twentieth of November, after offering Mass for a soul departed, he was again seized with a fever. In spite of this, he made his way to a ship in the harbor to visit the sick, as was his daily custom. He had intended to stay there among the sick, but the rolling of the vessel forced him to return to the shore. Later on, one of the Portuguese found him lying in the open and burning up with the fever, and touched by his pitiable condition he had the victim removed to his cabin where he cared for him as well as his poverty would permit. The cabin was one of those tottering huts built on the shore and open to the wind on all sides. The Portuguese had been forbidden by the Chinese authorities to erect a solid structure of any kind, and what they did build, they left in ruins on their departure.

When his host asked to be allowed to open a vein of the patient to secure him some relief, Xavier, suffering as he was and knowing the lack of medical skill on the island, showed himself patiently obedient to whatever was suggested for his cure. The bleeding brought on convulsions and a spasm of his delicate frame, accompanied by a sickening nausea. There was no food at hand suitable for the sick. In fact, there was no food at all, save a few almond kernels brought in by a Portuguese sailor. Such a distaste for food had developed from the fever that for two whole days not a morsel passed his lips. Wracked by a consuming fever and destitute of all aid, with the malady increasing every hour, he bore it all with such patience and equanimity that he muttered no murmur of complaint and asked no help of anyone. The only thing that seemed to disappoint him, was that he was dying in bed, or rather stretched upon the earth, and was thus missing the longed-for crown of martyrdom which was, in a way, being snatched from him. Soon, however, he resigned himself to the will of God, as being unworthy of such an exalted distinction.

As a man's true character is frequently revealed in sickness, so Xavier in his agony showed the same exalted courage in the hour of death that had rendered him distinguished during the whole course of his noble life. With his eyes turned to Heaven and conversing with Christ, repeating familiar passages from the Psalms, or ejaculations, such as, Jesus Son of David, Have Mercy on Me, and Mother of God, remember me, he passed two full days wrapped in prayerful contemplation. As the hour for his eternal journey approached, he held up the Crucifix, sighing and moaning, as though trying to increase the fervor of his prayer. On the second day of December, 1552, at the age of fifty-five, continually praying, though his voice and his strength were exhausted, Xavier died in the eleventh year of his missionary peregrinations in the Orient, and in his last prayer still absorbed in contemplating the conversion of China. The wonders that followed upon his death, the story of his holy body remaining uncorrupted though buried in quick-lime, and the miracles wrought during the return of his remains to Goa, we shall leave for his biographers to narrate. Let us now proceed to the actual story of the expedition to China, the land which Xavier, in heaven, must have begged God to prepare and to throw open, by means of his fellow Jesuits, by whom it was accomplished.

2. The Chinese Expedition Is Again Attempted by the Jesuits

BOTH THE Franciscans and the Dominicans, men of piety and endowed with virtue and learning, endeavored to promote this Christian expedition into China after the death of Xavier. Some of them came from India with the Portuguese and others from farther west with the Spaniards, but despite their extraordinary zeal they met with no lasting success. Divine Providence probably found their labors more fruitful in other fields. We shall leave their story to others, it being our purpose to narrate what was accomplished by the members of the Society of Jesus who took over the task. With all aid lacking for the achievement of anything great, the brothers of Xavier never abandoned the heritage he bequeathed to them, and to which they had rightful claim, since his holy body was still entombed within its boundaries. Like an army laying siege to a strongly fortified castle, they garrisoned one position with everything necessary for action when the opportune moment should arrive. They opened a house on the very threshold of China and the place was so suitably accommodated to their purpose that it deserves a few words of description, so that those unacquainted with the position of the place may better appreciate its advantages.

In years past when the Portuguese had traversed the immeasurable stretches of ocean that brought them to the known extremities of the Orient, they finally stopped at the seaboard of China. To them the riches of this country were well known and they left no means unattempted to draw its people into trade and barter. This, however, was no easy task to accomplish because the Chinese, beyond all other people in the world, are suspicious of strangers. This is particularly true of them since the time they lost their entire empire and served under the yoke of the conquering Tartar, as is mentioned in the preceding book. The size of the Portuguese ships, their unusual rigging and the roar of their cannon served only to increase the innate fear of the Chinese, and the Mohammedans who were numerous in the Canton Province convinced them that their fears were well grounded.

The Portuguese first arrived off the southern coast of China and the inhabitants there called them Franks, the name given by the Saracens to all Europeans. But the Chinese having no liquid R in their language, and never using two consonant sounds without a vowel sound between, pronounced the word Falanci, as it is still pronounced in the Province of Canton. They afterwards gave the same name to our European instruments of war. They were persuaded that these Franks, robust warriors that they were and conquerors of nations, placed no boundaries to their empire save the ultimate confines of the world. They had heard of Malacca and of India, conquered by the Europeans under the pretext of trading. Their suspicions, not wholly void of reason, prevented the entrance of a Portuguese legation as soon as it was suggested, but their own desire for wealth was so great that they could not wholly restrain their urge for bargaining. The revenue for public funds, and the profit from private business derived from trading, was so great that the Magistrates were not long in putting aside their suspicions. They never entirely prohibited it. In fact they allowed it to increase, but not too rapidly, and always with the provision that when the time for trading was at an end the Portuguese would promptly return to India with all their belongings. This kind of trafficking went on for several years until the fears of the Chinese gradually vanished, and they granted the visiting merchants a trading post on the point of a nearby island. There was an idol erected there called Ama. It may be seen today and the place is called Macao, on the Bay of Ama. It is more of a protruding rock than a peninsula, but it soon became inhabited not only by the Portuguese, but by a motley gathering from the neighboring shores, eager to barter for all sorts of merchandise brought from Europe, India, and the Islands of the Moluccas. The prospects of quick fortunes were an enticement to the Chinese merchants to take up residence on the island, and in the course of a few years the trading post began to assume the appearance of a city. Numerous houses were built when the Portuguese and the Chinese began to intermarry, and before long the rock point was developed into a respectable port and a prominent market. The desire to travel by sea in search of fortune brought these mariner merchants to the very confines of the known world, but the Portuguese Empire could not spread further than the Christian religion. Members of religious orders, or secular priests, always accompanied the seafarers to preserve their faith and to bring Christ to the pagans they might encounter. To this end also the King of Portugal granted charters to this new city and, with Pontifical authority, had a Bishop appointed there to facilitate the administration of the sacraments and to lend the proper ecclesiastical dignity to divine services.

It was here at Macao that the Society of Jesus established a permanent residence and built a church in honor of the Mother of God. This was the first of many churches to follow. From the earliest days of the Society, our brethren had been laboring with others, gathering a harvest white for the reaping in eastern and western India. In this new settlement, centrally located to so many harbors, they saw an opening to new fields of apostolic labor that should not be neglected. To the north was China, more extensive than the broad stretches of the Moluccan Islands. To the east lay Japan and the Philippine Islands and to the west was Cochinchina, Camboia, Siam and several other kingdoms.

We shall pass over what had been accomplished by long excursions to other parts of the earth, and especially that tremendous undertaking which won over no small part of Japan to the faith. Our present interest is in this insignificant spot from which a little band of Christ's warriors, after considerable delay and effort, finally succeeded in carrying the banner of Christianity into the Kingdom of China. How it was done we shall endeavor to relate. The Jesuits, who had been stationed at Macao since the time the place was first inhabited, made several attempts to get into China but without success. They may have been prevented by the difficulties to be overcome in order to effect an entrance, but more probably they were too occupied with the mission in Japan, which was meeting with such great success, to give much attention to China. Thus the Kingdom of China, not as yet white unto harvest, was to remain so for many years to come. Finally, when it pleased God, who arranges all things according to His holy will, the thing so long desired and hoped for became a fact accomplished.

An Italian Jesuit, Alexander Valignano, appointed by the General of the Society of Jesus as Official Visitor to the whole India Mission, came from Europe and made his first inspection in the Cis-Ganges region, as it is called by the Europeans. Then he passed over to the Ultra-Ganges areas and from there he came to Macao, preparatory to continuing on to Japan. The laws of navigation prohibited his sailing for a time, and he remained at Macao for at least ten months. This gave him a good opportunity to make a thorough and detailed study of the China situation, which resulted in rekindling the dormant ardor for the Chinese expedition. The conclusions drawn from his observations were somewhat as follows. Judging from the immense expanse of this empire, from the nobility of character of its people and from the fact that they had lived in peace for centuries, surely the wisdom of their system of public administration and the well known prudence of their governing Magistrates would seem to favor the proposed expedition. One can easily believe that a clever and accomplished people, devoted to the study of the fine-arts, could be persuaded to accept a few strangers, who were also distinguished for their learning and virtue, to come and dwell among them, especially if their visitors were well versed in the Chinese language and literature. There seemed to be some hope also that this people would one day gladly accept the

Christian religion, seeing that it could serve as a help rather than as a detriment to their system of government. They might also be educated to replace their vanity with a spiritual concept of life and a desire for eternal happiness. The prospects arising from this line of thought were sufficient reason for appointing several men to study the Chinese language and literature, and to be ready to take advantage of any opportunity that might be presented for introducing the Gospel into this new world.

Some few who had had experience with the Chinese people said that any attempt to win them over was sheer waste of time, like trying to whiten an Ethiopian. Even Xavier with all his ardor and labor had not succeeded in getting into China and other religious, endeavoring to follow the example of his effort, had given it up in despair. Valignano, however, had made up his mind on the matter and it was not to be changed. When the occasion demands it, there are times when the minds of superiors seem to be divinely enlightened to go through with what they have decided upon.

There was no one at Macao who could be spared for the work, so he wrote to Rodrigo Vincens, the Provincial in India, to select at least one priest, whom he judged to be suitably adapted for the mission in question, and to send him to Macao as soon as possible. Then before leaving for Japan he left written instructions for the one who was to come, as to the manner he should prepare for his future work in China. Michele Ruggieri, an Italian from Naples, was selected for the position. He had arrived from Europe a year previous and was at that time preaching the Gospel in the fishing colonies. He came to Macao in July, 1579, and immediately applied himself to the work of preparation as outlined by the Visitor General. The first thing he had to do was to learn the Chinese language; the curial dialect of the language, as it was called, the particular dialect in universal use throughout the kingdom. Besides this court or curial dialect, as happens in other countries also, each province has its own local or provincial idiom. To acquire the language he had first to learn how to read and write the Chinese hieroglyphic characters.

Unlike the rest of the world the Chinese do not express their ideas in writing by means of an alphabet. They draw figures of the things signified by words, and use as many figures as they do words. If the acquisition of knowledge were measured solely by diligence of application, one could probably make considerable progress in this particular study in a shorter space of time. This, however, was not the case in the present instance, because the Chinese language, being the most difficult and most intricate ever heard of or read about, was made doubly difficult by the lack of teachers who could teach it. The Chinese who had become Christians at Macao and were living according to European customs, and those who visited the place from inland for commercial purposes, were all inexperienced in the use of the curial dialect and of Portuguese as well. The provincial traders all understood the curial idiom but spoke it very poorly, as they were accustomed to conversing in their own dialect. Even they did not know the universal written characters. The only writing they did was done to carry on their trade, and a Chinese teacher who fills in as a painter what he lacks in language is scarcely a model teacher for anyone. Frequently, when such a Chinese teacher can not express the meaning of a European word in a Chinese character he will have recourse to drawing a series of symbols. Nothing but incessant labor, passed unnoticed in his absorbing zeal for the work, could have enabled Father Ruggieri to overcome such stubborn difficulties.

The study of language was not the only means to be used in the solution of the Chinese problem. The Portuguese merchants had already instituted a custom of holding a public fair, twice a year, to dispose of what the ships from India brought in during January, and what arrived from Japan toward the end of June. These fairs were no longer held in the port of Macao or on the island, as formerly, but in the Metropolitan City itself. By special permission of the Magistrates, the Portuguese were allowed to make a two-day trip up the river to the magnificent capital city of the Province of Canton. Here they had to live aboard their ships at night, but during the day they were permitted to carry on trade in the streets of the town. This, however, was done with so many guards and precautions that it was quite evident that the people of the place were still subject to their inherited suspicion of foreigners. The time allotted to this public marketing was usually limited to two months but it was frequently extended. Our reason for recording these semiannual fairs is, that they afforded the first and only entrance for the heralds of the Gospel to penetrate into the interior of the country. We can give thanks for this to the industry, the good will and the religious spirit of the Portuguese, whose praises are heard and whose religious influence is felt wherever they appear.

It was with the Portuguese merchants that Michele Ruggieri decided to set out and to begin his own kind of commerce with the

Chinese. What he had especially in mind was that he might possibly meet one of the Governors who could be coaxed to allow him to take up residence in his province. His first efforts met with almost insurmountable difficulties because of a recent unfortunate event. It happened, only a short time previous, that one of the Fathers, who had accompanied the Portuguese merchants, to say Mass for them during the public fairs, converted a disciple of a native temple-priest and brought him back to Macao. The young man was quite willing to go along, but his exit had to be made in secrecy. When his absence was discovered, both his teacher and his parents complained bitterly to the courts, with the result that he was seized and returned by force, and not without considerable embarrassment to our reputation. The people were given to understand that we were seducing youth and stealing them away from their parents. This is a practice of frequent occurrence among the Cantonese, and because of its frequency it is one of the few offenses listed as a capital crime. Nothing but the ingenuity and the courteous manners of a Ruggieri could have succeeded in overcoming this difficulty and regaining their good graces. He selected certain of their prominent citizens for contact and in a short time they became very well disposed. Chief among them was the Grand Admiral or Hai-tao, under whose jurisdiction were all foreigners arriving in the Province of Canton, and also the particular business in which they were engaged.

Ruggieri's reputation for honesty and learning helped to develop this friendship, and it was further advanced by the fact that he was known among the Portuguese as a priest and an instructor who was continually absorbed in Chinese literature. Whenever he visited the Admiral in company with Portuguese companions, he was, at the host's command, placed to one side and exempted from the regulation of bending the knee. Moreover, he was granted the privilege of exception to the rule obliging foreigners to pass the night aboard their ships during the trading fairs. He was even given a place of residence in the palace assigned to the legation from Siam, when they came to pay their taxes due to the Royal Crown. This offered him an opportunity to begin the work of his sacred mission, and he spent whole nights delving into Chinese volumes. On Sundays and on feast days, the Portuguese came to him in his retreat to attend Mass, and to receive the sacraments. On other days when they were trading, he was left to himself and his studies, but when the time arrived for their departure he was obliged to go along with them. The military head of the

Province was also numbered among his friends, and it was to him that Ruggieri presented a watch; an instrument for measuring the hours by means of an adjusted series of little metal wheels. The Zumpin, or General, as this official was called, also showed him special attention when the Father had occasion to pay him a visit. These early friendships with the Magistrates were of no small value in developing a favorable attitude toward Christianity.

Not a few of the Chinese who came to Macao to sell food and other provisions did emerge from the darkness of paganism into the light of Christianity, and when the number of catechumens began to increase, donations from the pious Portuguese enabled the Fathers to erect a house for their instruction. It was built on a hill behind the church, and was called the Oratorio of Saint Martin. Here the zealous Ruggieri gave much of his time to instructing the natives without disturbing the order of the main residence, which was principally intended for the spiritual good of the Portuguese. This was also his study where, with the help of interpreters, he gave much time to Chinese books.

These modest beginnings were fast developing hope of a more abundant harvest, but there were two obstacles to the development of the soil, both arising from a scarcity of laborers. The duties of the Fathers caring for the needs of the Portuguese were so numerous that Father Michele had to take his share of them, and in so doing to sacrifice that much time from his study of Chinese. Again, when he left Macao for the sales-fairs in the Metropolis, the work he was doing at home was interrupted for lack of a substitute. This of course meant a considerable loss to the cause as the two lengthy fairs took up nearly half of the year. To these difficulties may be added the fact that the acquisition and the mastery of a new and a difficult language, within a limited time, needs continual application of both theory and practice, and should be a full-time occupation. All this time, the Father Visitor was in Japan, but he kept in close touch with all that was going on in Macao, and decided to call Father Matthew Ricci from India to take part in the work of the proposed mission to China. Ricci and Ruggieri were together before, on the voyage from Europe to India, but Ricci remained in Goa to complete his theological studies. When he arrived in Macao he immediately shared the work, and when his associate was absent he carried on the work which Ruggieri had begun. He had a decided advantage in undertaking this particular labor, inasmuch as the Official Visitor had strictly forbidden the assignment to any other work, of those who were appointed to the Chinese mission. To Ricci, more than to any of the others who labored so untiringly with him, we are obliged for the success of the Expedition to China.

3. Three Times in 1582 the Missionaries Are Admitted to China, but Fail to Establish a Residence

RETURNING FROM JAPAN in 1582, Father Valignano brought with him four native princes who were being sent to Rome by some of the Japanese Lords, as representatives of the Christian Faith, to acknowledge the submission of these same Lords to the Apostolic jurisdiction of the Holy See. This, as a matter of fact, they did and afterwards returned to their native land. En route to Rome they stopped at Macao to await an opportune time for sailing to India, and during their sojourn there Valignano lost no time in promoting the affairs of the Chinese Mission. He established a Sodality at the Jesuit residence, called the Sodality of the Holy Name of Jesus and governed by rules especially adapted for the spiritual advancement of the newly converted. In order to promote its progress, this society was maintained exclusively for Chinese and for Japanese, and for new converts of other nations, and its rapid advancement made it a great spiritual influence in the settlement. It was on his recommendation that this confraternity was placed in charge of one of the Fathers assigned to the China Mission, who was called Father of the Neophytes, because of his special care of converts and catechumens. In this capacity he had charge not only of their spiritual needs but also of their temporal advancement. Their meetings were held in the parish residence, until better provision could be made for their needs, and that was accomplished in a short time, as will be seen.

The Viceroy of the Province of Canton is looked upon as one of the influentials of his order. His province is situated on the confines of the realm, very far from the Royal City of Pekin and bounded by a long stretch of ocean. The result of its geographic position is, that its roads are infested with robbers and its sea-lanes with pirates, most of whom are Japanese. To remedy this situation he is given jurisdiction over the neighboring Province of Quam-si, which enables him, if need be, to draft a larger number of soldiers. Because of the difficulties involved, his seat of government is not in the capital city of his major province, as it is in other districts, but in Sciauquin, situated on the border of the two provinces over which he rules. At the time in question, the Magistrate or Governor was one Cinsui, a native of the Province of Fuquian. A cautious and a prudent administrator, he was also decidedly avaricious and took advantage of the settlement at Macao, as one might judge from the following subterfuge.

He asserted that he had been given to understand that the Bishop and the Mayor of Macao were the directors and the managers of the foreign merchants, and as such he sent them official notices to appear before him without delay. This command was somewhat of a surprise, and when it was taken up in conference it was decided that it would be a reflection on Portuguese dignity to comply with the order as made. However, since it would not do to belittle the authority of the Viceroy by appearing to despise his orders, it was agreed to send two others to represent those who were called. Valignano appointed Michele Ruggieri to represent the Bishop, hoping that he would be able to obtain permission for a permanent residence on the continent, and Mattia Penella, the City Auditor, was selected as a substitute for the Mayor. As a good-will offering to the Viceroy, for fear he might interrupt the trading, the City presented him with a gift from the people, made up of a collection of things which they knew were specially prized by the Chinese. There was cloth of pure silk, which the Chinese did not know how to make at that time, pleated garments, crystal mirrors and other such novelties, valued in all at more than a thousand gold pieces. The representatives were received by the Viceroy with a grandiose display intended to frighten them rather than to do them honor, but when he saw the gifts, which were intended for such an emergency, his supercilious mien immediately disappeared. Then he informed them with a smile that everything might continue at the settlement as formerly, subject, of course, to the rules of the Chinese Governors. This was only a customary formal announcement, because the Portuguese at Macao were governed by

Portuguese laws, and other nationalities there lived as they pleased. Even the Chinese, when they became Christians, put aside their Chinese clothes and dressed as Europeans. The other Chinese were subject to the officials appointed there by the Canton Government.

To return to the Viceroy, or Governor; he insisted that he could take nothing for which he did not pay, and questioning the interpreter as to the price of each article, he ordered the total amount to be weighed out in silver in the presence of his attendants. This he did because in this province it was forbidden under severe penalty for any government official to receive such a gift. Later on, he secretly sent a messenger to his visitors to tell them that the silver he had given them was for the purchase of another allotment of their novelties, which were to be delivered to him in person and privately. Father Ruggieri did not forget the request to be made about a residence, which was the main reason for his coming, and though speaking through an interpreter, he reminded the Governor that he had already taken up the study of the Chinese language and literature. This seemed to please him and he did offer some hope that the request might be granted when the visitors returned later on. At the close of the audience and after the presentation of the silver, he gave them an abundance of different food supplies, and sent them back to their boat with great ceremony; parading through the streets of the city with a large retinue of soldiers and civil officials, amid a grand fanfare of trumpets and other noisy instruments. Such is the power over men of the dazzling hope of gain, wherever it shines forth.

The Portuguese argosies arrived at Macao during August, as is customary, and several members of the Society, destined for the local college or for the Mission of Japan, were among the passengers. With them also was Matthew Ricci who was called from India, to assist in a work, from which so much was to be hoped. The Father Provincial of India had given him a rather elaborate watch, as a gift to the China Mission. Now it happened just at that time that the Mayor of the City was sending back his Auditor with the novelties which the Governor had asked for. Unfortunately, or perhaps one should say fortunately, Father Ruggieri who was to accompany him was taken ill. So he asked the Auditor to tell the Governor that he regretted being detained by his illness, because he had intended to bring with him a certain beautiful little piece of mechanism made of brass that struck the hours without anyone touching it. Up to this time a watch was something unheard of by the Chinese, something new and to them quite mystifying. When the Auditor delivered the presents and then told about the Father's illness, the Governor seemed to be very sad, but when he heard about the watch, he became so interested that he ordered one of his secretaries to write a letter of invitation in his name, asking Ruggieri, by all means, to come and see him, as soon as he was well, and to bring along the wonderful gadget. When this document was examined at Macao it proved to be something more than a simple invitation. In fact, it was an official document granting the Fathers public authority to build a house and a church in the city of Canton. It can be readily imagined what rejoicing this caused, both in our religious community and outside of it. It was the attainment, at last, of a long desired hope. The only one who seemed to be suspicious about the whole affair was the Father Visitor himself, who was somewhat at a loss as to how to proceed after such an unexpected announcement. So very much depended upon the initial steps, that he doubted whether Father Ruggieri was sufficiently prepared to undertake such an exacting assignment. Indeed the opportunity might have been missed entirely, if the other Fathers had not entreated him to make the best of it.

Father Francesco Pasio was at Macao at the time. He had sailed from Europe to India en route to Japan in company with those who had been assigned to the Chinese Mission. Here was a man gifted with understanding, prudence and ingenuity, and of recognized executive ability. His mental endowments would make up for his lack of knowledge of the Chinese language. So he was placed in charge, with Ruggieri as his assistant, and Ricci was appointed to care for the school of catechumens in Macao, with orders to join the other two if they met with any success. By this time, the weather was favorable for a voyage to India, and the Father Visitor decided to set out with the Japanese princes. Before leaving, he gave instructions in writing that if for any unforeseen reason the attempt failed and the Fathers were forced to return from Canton, Father Pasio should go to Japan, as he was originally intended to, and the other two should await another favorable opportunity for carrying out the plan proposed.

When the two delegates came into the presence of the Viceroy of Sciauquin, they presented him with the watch and also with several pieces of triangular shaped glass in which objects were reflected in beautiful multi-colored tints. This was something new for the Chinese, and for a long time they believed that the glass was a kind of precious stone of wonderful value. It was surprising to note how pleased the

Viceroy-Governor was with the gifts and how cordially he received the visitors. He assigned them quite a commodious residence, connected with a suburban temple of idols called Thien-nin-su, to which at times he sent food and other provisions. On their official visits, he received them into his own palace. Thus they lived for four or five months, receiving visits from some of the Magistrates and other prominent citizens, and they were beginning to hope that the concession might develop into a permanent grant. They had already obtained permission from the Secretary of the Viceroy to send for Father Matthew Ricci and he in turn was making preparations for the journey, at the College at Macao. Then suddenly everything went into reverse and hope that was flourishing faded and died.

Just when it seemed that the Mission was making some progress, a message arrived from the palace to announce that for some unaccountable fault, the Viceroy himself had been relieved of his office, and realizing that their presence in the city of the seat of government might not be so pleasing to his successor, and might also increase his own punishment, he felt obliged to request them to withdraw. In sending them away, however, he provided them with documents admitting them to the Capital City of the province and instructing the ruling Magistrate there to provide them with a house and with ground on which to build a church. The Chinese call the Capital City Quamcheu but the Portuguese, misled by the name of the province, called it Canton. It was a sad blow to the Fathers to realize that they must abandon all hope of success in this particular effort, knowing as they did that such a document of an ex-Viceroy would have no authority whatsoever. Yet, in order to leave no possibility untried, they voyaged up the river to the Capital and encountered just what they had anticipated. The Admiral, or Maritime Commissioner, whom we have mentioned before as the Hai-tao, and to whom the document was addressed, happened to be absent and, even if he had been present, he would have regarded the document as worthless. The riparian guards would not even allow them to disembark. Under these circumstances, there was nothing left to do but to return in disappointment and in sorrow to the residence at Macao.

In accordance with the orders left by the official Visitor of the Society, Father Pasio went to Japan where he labored strenuously for several years and was appointed Provincial, governing both the Japanese and the Chinese Missions for a long time. When these two settlements became provinces of the Society of Jesus, Father Pasio was named official Visitor to both, and returned to Macao to reorganize the Chinese interests. Several months after his arrival he died and his loss was keenly felt and deeply regretted by all his brethren. From the very outset of his labors in the East, his desire to spread the faith in China increased with his experience, and he missed no opportunity to promote the interests of the Chinese Mission, even when he was absent in far-off Japan.

We shall now pass on to the third excursion made by the Jesuit Missionaries into the Kingdom of China, which also terminated without any appreciable results. It is a custom among the Chinese Magistrates to preserve a copy of all official documents in the state archives, with a memorandum attached, as to what had been effected by each particular document. These records are kept so that the authorities may know what was ordered and what resulted from the orders. When the successor to the deposed Viceroy arrived, and the records of letters patent were being examined in his presence, a copy of the letters issued to our Fathers was discovered, and since nothing had resulted from these letters there was no memorandum attached recording the result of their issue. Whereupon, the new incumbent immediately wrote to the Admiral, or Commissioner of Maritime Affairs, to whom the letters had been addressed. The Admiral, however, was absent when the letters were first issued, and, as the port of Macao was under his jurisdiction, he in turn wrote to the Mayor of the City of Ansam, as it is called by the Portuguese, Hiam-Xan in Chinese. But the Mayor knew nothing about the whole affair and he passed it on, by writing to the Military Guards of the Port of Macao, asking them to investigate the matter and to report as soon as possible. The first one to be interviewed was the Bishop who sent the Inspectors to our college, where they were shown the letters, duly signed and fortified with the public seal. Their first reaction was to insist upon the surrender of the letters, asserting that it was quite unbecoming that letters issued by a Viceroy should be retained by foreigners. In reply, it was decided that the question should be submitted to consultation. The official Visitor of the Society was absent at the time, but there were several prominent members of the Society present in the house. Among them was Melchior Carnero, Patriarch of Ethiopia, who was residing here after the interruption of the expedition to Ethiopia. He had governed the diocese during the absence of the Ordinary and was for some time Rector of the College of Macao. Father Francesco Caprale, Superior of the Chinese Mission, was present and Father Pietro Gomez, who had also been Rector of the College. All this took place before Father Pasio departed for Japan, and so he and several others who were waiting to go with him were present at this consultation. The unanimous decision arrived at relative to the letters was that they should by no means be entrusted to the Chinese Military Prefects. Instead, it was agreed that two of the Fathers should personally take the documents to the Admiral and request that they be put into execution as written.

Father Ruggieri and Father Ricci were elected for this commission. The military inspectors had no objection to the decision and, since they could scarcely do otherwise under the circumstances, they granted permission for the voyage by boat to the City of Ansam, with a promise that the Mayor of the City, the Ci-hiem, would send them on to the Capital. When they arrived at Ansam the delegates were granted an audience, at which the Mayor demanded the letters, in order to send them on to the Capital, and when the Fathers refused to hand them over, he flew into a rage, snatched the letters and threw them on the floor. "Do you hope to advance a cause with documents signed by a deposed Viceroy," he exclaimed. Then he refused them permission to go to the Capital City and ordered them back to their house at Macao. Thus the door of their mission was closed against them, just as they had come to its threshold, and they left the Mayor's residence saddened and in silence.

At their local dwelling in Ansam, however, they decided upon a rather hazardous adventure. There was a packboat, not a very large one, leaving this village for the Capital every day, on which a goodly number of people always traveled and with plenty of baggage. They decided to go aboard it without asking anyone's permission and, if possible, they would make the trip to the Metropolis without the Mayor knowing anything about it. At first the pilot was reluctant to receive strangers aboard his bark, but the interpreter for the Fathers, a young man and somewhat of a trickster, showed the pilot the letters of the former Viceroy and won him over to his confidence. They were on the boat, with their baggage installed, and just about to sail, when the episode was brought to a rather sudden ending. The other passengers, suspicious of the strangers, remonstrated with the captain and frightened him into throwing off the baggage of the Fathers onto the river bank, and thus forcing them to disembark. There was nothing left to do but return to their lodgings.

Now it happened just at that time that the Mayor of the City received the sad news of the death of his father which, according to Chinese custom, forced him to retire from public life and to return to his home as a private citizen, for a period of three years of filial mourning. This created an occasion for the Fathers to remain for some time in the city, since there was no one with authority to expel them, and they set about seeking further means of getting to the Capital. Finally, by means of the presentation of a small sum to the substitute Mayor they were granted the necessary permission. However, in order to prevent any evil aftereffects, the permission was secured through a lawyer who arranged to have it officially granted, not for a remuneration but in advancement of the public interest. Thus the delegates were sent on to Province headquarters, but in their own innocence and ignorance they were really being dispatched as prisoners. The notice sent on before them informed the authorities that these foreign priests were picked up at Ansam because, for some unknown reason, they had letters patent of the deposed Viceroy, addressed to the Admiral, to whom they were being sent.

Despite this notice they were received very cordially by the Admiral, who, without even opening the letters, asked them their reason for coming. Their answer was contained in their written request which explained that they were members of a religious order, who had left their native land over distant seas, attracted by the fame of the Chinese Empire. It continued: that they intended to remain here for the rest of their lives, and that all they wanted was a small plot of ground to build a house, and also a church in honor of the King of Heaven. It asserted that they would be a burden to no one, and that they would supply their own sustenance by way of offerings from their own people. Neither in this request nor in any other way was any mention made of Christianity at the outset of the mission for fear it might interfere with the one thing necessary, namely, to remain within the kingdom.

The Chinese are so self-opinionated that they cannot be made to believe that the day will ever come when they will learn anything from foreigners which is not already set down in their own books. Indeed, the preaching of a new law is their particular aversion, because they have already learned, from the experience of former times, that civil tumults and sedition have been caused by gathering a following of conspirators for rebellion and for the ruin of the country, under pretext of preaching a new law. The Admiral himself praised the design of the missionaries, but he repeatedly reminded them that the whole affair depended upon the decision of the Chief Magistrate, the Viceroy, and that only he or the Official Inspector of the Province, called the Ciai-yuen, could grant the permission they were asking. Persuaded that the Admiral was looking for an excuse, they asked that at least he might permit them to remain in the city, in the lodging of the Ambassadors of the King of Siam, where Father Ruggieri had lived during the general fairs, and that they be allowed to remain there until the Portuguese returned for the trading. In the meantime, they hoped to be able to persuade the Viceroy or the Inspector to agree to their permanent residence. This permission the Admiral actually granted to them in their presence, but on the same day he sent word to them retracting it. The Official Inspector was due to arrive in the province within a few days, and the Admiral said he was afraid it would turn the Inspector against him if he permitted them to remain in the city at a time when there was no fair going on. He also reminded them that as he himself was an appointed Magistrate, an Inspector's censure might result in very severe punishment. He therefore admonished them to return post-haste to Macao.

One can readily imagine what disappointment this unexpected message occasioned for the delegates. After exhausting every means at their disposal to prolong their sojourn they finally set out on the homeward journey. When they arrived at Ansam they discovered that conditions were worse than when they had left it. Affixed to the gates of the city was an edict, signed by the newly appointed Viceroy, the Co, and reading: "Besides various other matters relating to the general good of the Province, the following, which concerns us very intimately, is to be noted with reference to those residing at Macao. Serious complaints have been made that various crimes and abuses of the law have been perpetrated at Macao, which are attributed to the Chinese interpreters employed by the foreigners. These interpreters are soliciting the strangers and teaching them the ways of our people. Most serious of all, we are well informed that they have persuaded certain priests from abroad to learn the Chinese language and study Chinese letters, and that now these priests are demanding a residence at the Capital, in order to build a church and a private home. This we declare to be injurious to the realm, to which no benefit can accrue by admitting foreigners. The said interpreters will be put to a cruel death if they do not immediately desist from the practices mentioned."

In view of this decree and of what had happened to the delegates during the month following their departure from the Capital, and also considering the incredible repugnance the Chinese have to foreigners, the Fathers seemed to have lost all hope of establishing a residence in the interior of the kingdom. At least it seemed so during the incumbency of this particular Viceroy. It was not very likely that he would ever favor a project which he was then so vehemently denouncing.

4. The Missionaries Are Invited to Sciauquin, Where They Build a House and Open a Center

FROM THE VERY depths of discouragement there suddenly appeared a new ray of hope. Scarcely a week had passed since the return of the Fathers, when an officer of the Viceroy's Guard arrived at Macao from the town of Sciauquin. He was a messenger of the Ci-fu, as the Chinese call him, the local Governor of that district, and he had come to deliver a letter authorized by the Viceroy, inviting the Fathers of the Society of Jesus to Sciauquin, to take over a piece of property granted by the State for the erection of a church and a house. Such a sudden change as that must be attributed to the grace of God rather than to any human merit. Far be it from us to assert that it was our accomplishment. Indeed, it should serve as a lesson for the future to keep on hoping even after every human effort has failed, and never to give up hope of better things. Only lately the Viceroy himself had disapproved of our work in a public document and in no uncertain way, and the Governor of this district would not even see the Fathers. But there is no gainsaying the Lord, Who governs the time and the hour, and Who decreed from eternity that this people should receive of His light. By the hand of the Lord, and by His extended right arm, the gates of this kingdom, closed for ages against His gospel were to be thrown open for the reception of its messengers. Whatever may be set down in human records of the deeds accomplished by the missionaries in this great undertaking, they would all have come to naught, had they not been supported by the power that from nothing has produced all things that are.

It was related by the Fathers who had recently acted as delegates, that when they came to Sciauquin for the second time and were sent back to the Capital by the deposed Viceroy, there were several servants of the new Viceroy present, and that a certain sum of money was offered to whichever one of them would secure permission for their return. One of these was a soldier of lowest rank, a palace guard, and when he heard of the reward he immediately sent in a request to the Viceroy, in the name of our interpreters, asking for a residence in the city for the missionaries, and also for a place to build a house and a church. Strange as it may seem, the man who had found fault with the priests from abroad and had issued a cruel ukase against their interpreters, accepted the petition of an ordinary soldier and sent it to the Governor of the district, Guam-puon by name, from the Province of Cequian, to have it put into immediate effect. It was the same soldier, the palace guard, who was sent as a messenger to deliver the welcome letter.

The sense of joy created by such an announcement is more readily imagined than expressed, because in such cases the mental reaction depends upon the element of surprise. The less the hope the greater the surprise, and here hope had all but disappeared. It looked like the hand of God and a heavenly favor surpassing human power. And so the promoters of the expedition, already frequently named, set about preparing what they thought would be necessary for the undertaking. It was not an easy task, because the whole enterprise was dependent upon the liberality of their friends, many of whom had every reason to suspect that this attempt like the other three of the past few months would also peter out in failure. In addition, they had to take into consideration the many shipwrecks that had occurred during the past year and particularly the great loss, off the Isle of Formosa, of a rich cargo destined for trade in Japan, and constituting almost the entire present wealth of the town. This in itself was enough to tie the strings of purses that otherwise would have been opened with liberality. Here again, as formerly, Divine Providence came to their assistance.

There was a Portuguese merchant at Macao named Gaspar Viegas, as renowned for scattering money as for making it. He had been interested in the expedition from the very beginning and would not abandon it even with the colony in its direst straits. His donation was sufficient to care for all the necessary preparations. In justice to Viegas, while making formal mention of his connection with the expedition, it should be recorded that he also built the Novitiate at Goa and endowed it with an annuity. Shortly before his death he asked to be received into the Society of Jesus and his request was granted. There were other contributors to the China Mission also, and among the most liberal was Father Francesco Caprale, Rector of the College of Goa. The time for departure was at hand and the party set out in high hope that, at long last, the Christian invasion of China had finally been launched.

On their arrival in the Metropolitan City of Canton they met some Spaniards who had been there since the Fathers were dismissed from Sciauquin. Their ship had been wrecked on the island of Nan-tau, off the coast of the Canton Province, during a voyage from the Philippine Islands to New Spain. The entire crew succeeded in making the mainland and were being held by the Chinese until the Viceroy decided what to do with them, and three of them had been sent to Canton to explain their presence in China. There were also in the city eight or ten Franciscans who had voyaged from the Philippines to a kingdom contiguous to China, called Cochinchina. They had heard that the king of that country wanted to build a church like the Christian churches, but they were so badly treated there that they decided to return to their own country. It was on the return trip that their ship was aground on the Chinese island of Hainan, off the Canton coast, where they were captured by the Chinese navy and robbed of all they possessed. When the Jesuits arrived the Franciscans were being held to appear before the Magistrates as pirates. This meeting was a cause of mutual rejoicing as both groups of priests had a common reason for being present among the heathens. Since our Fathers were at liberty, they were permitted to treat the captives with kindness and courtesy, even arranging for some of them to celebrate Mass at the palace of the Ambassador of Siam, where the Jesuits were housed. This, of course, was a Heaven sent consolation, of which they had been long deprived and the happy meeting finally resulted in the deliverance of the whole party. It was made clear to the authorities that these men were members of a religious order, that one would never dream of accusing them of being pirates, and that they really should not be treated so harshly. Our Fathers promised that whatever was demanded of the prisoners would be paid with interest from Macao, and in a short time, after they distributed their belongings to the poor, the captives were dispatched to Macao. We tell their story here as a passing incident in our own experience.

The entrance party we are now considering left the College at Macao at the beginning of September, 1583, and, under the guard of the same soldier that brought them the welcome permission, arrived at Sciauquin on the tenth of the same month. They were politely received at the palace by the Governor, seated in his gubernatorial chair, and as they knelt before him, according to custom, he asked them who they were, whence they had come and why they were present. They answered through their interpreters somewhat as follows. We belong to an order of religious men who adore the King of Heaven as the one true God. We come from the very uttermost reaches of the west and it has taken us some three or four years to reach the Kingdom of China, to which we were attracted by the renown and glory of its name. They then explained that they were seeking permission to build a little house as a residence and also a little church for divine worship, somewhere apart from the noisy traffic of merchants and from the profane distractions which caused them so much trouble at Macao. This was their design and they desired to establish a residence and to remain there for the rest of their lives. They besought him very humbly not to reject their prayer, and explained that such a bequest would place them under obligation to him forever. Moreover, they promised to live within the law and without expense to anyone. Now, the Governor was a personage who seemed to be naturally predisposed to doing good, and with somewhat of a debonnaire manner about him. He was friendly with the Fathers from the beginning and favored them whenever opportunity allowed. At their final interview his reply amounted to this: that he had no doubt at all about their integrity and that he would take them under his protection. Yes, they could come into the city, look over all the available parcels of land and choose one to their own liking. He would see to it also that the Viceroy would place his sanction on the permit.

Just at that time, it happened that the District of Sciauquin levied a common tax on the eleven cities within its bounds to build a tower which, as their ancient superstition held, would bring good fortune to the entire province. The first story was already erected and there were nine more to go above it. It was situated on a very pleasant spot, on a large and navigable river which watered the properties of the

Viceroy and of the Governor, beyond the city wall. The tower was a little more than a mile distant from their estates and the intervening district, which was rather thickly inhabited, presented a pleasant spectacle of parks for recreation and of well arranged gardens. In the same field in which the tower was being erected, they also proposed to build a magnificent temple in which, according to the national custom, they were to place a statue of the Governor, who for six years in public office had well merited the praise of the educated classes and of the unlettered multitude as well. This location was pointed out to the Fathers by the soldier who had accompanied them on the journey, and by other friends whom they had acquired during the past few months of their residence, as presenting a desirable environment for their house. Their first view of the place was so pleasant that they decided then and there to make a request for part of the field in which the Flowery Tower was under construction. The name is derived from the variety of colored ornamentation. On the following day they made known their wish to the Governor, who seemed to be more pleased with it than anything else they could have thought of. The temple and the tower and the whole layout of the place were being designed with his authority, a tribute to him as a benefactor of his people, and he was as interested in it all as though it had been his own personal property. To him the whole development would only be made more honorable and more respectable by the addition of a suitable home for the priests from abroad, but to the Chinese people in general such a thing was hitherto unheard of. He was still in the same frame of mind when he dismissed them, with the assurance that he would present their request to the Viceroy and that they could rest assured that it would be granted.

Not far from another temple our Fathers had a dwelling under the former Viceroy, and in that vicinity there was a young man, of good character and of pleasant disposition, named Ciu-Ni-Co. He soon developed into a friendly neighbor, and before long he was sufficiently instructed in the Christian religion to be received into the Church, but he was unexpectedly called away and so could not carry out his design. At the time of their forced departure from the city they gave this young man the altar on which they were accustomed to offer daily Mass. There were no neophytes with whom it might be placed in keeping, and so they entrusted it to him as being the most Christian inhabitant of their acquaintance. They went to visit him on their return and were received by his family with great pleasure and rejoicing. The young man himself had set up the altar in a large room and above it, in large letters, placed a sign reading: Thien-ciu, To the God of Heaven. On the altar he always kept seven or eight vases in which he burned a sweet smelling incense. Here too he had developed the habit of praying at stated times and of offering his sacrifice, as he explained it, to the God of Whose existence he had some knowledge.

It was a source of no little consolation to the returning missionaries to find at least one who had prayed to the true God, after the long ages of spiritual darkness that had enveloped this great multitude of people. He was quite anxious to have the Fathers remain as his guests until the Governor sent them the reply of the Viceroy, and his invitation was quite acceptable, as it gave them an opportunity to use the altar and to say Mass for the success of their mission. They did not have to wait very long. On the Feast of the Exaltation of the Holy Cross, the Governor sent for them to inform them that the Viceroy was pleased to grant their request. He asked them also to go out on the following day to the place where the tower was being built, and to wait there until he assigned them a plot of ground on which they could build their church as soon as they wished. In thanking him for the favor conferred they knelt before him as was the custom, bending down three times and each time touching their foreheads to the floor. They returned to their residence thanking God for His many benefits, and adding a prayer of thanksgiving for what they considered to be an extraordinary grace, so long desired. Coming, as it did, after so many years of waiting, they felt that it would be for God's greater glory in the spacious Orient, and for the everlasting benefit of the Chinese Commonwealth.

On the following day the Fathers arrived at the place assigned and found the Governor waiting for them. He had brought along one of his Assessors and the Commissioner of Public Buildings, a man of the educated class who had served for some time in public life, and now, as a private citizen, was acting on the committee that had charge of building the tower. It seems that the plans of the Fathers were not very pleasing to this Committee, which had already informed the Governor that they were somewhat suspicious that the strangers might invite others from Macao, to the public detriment of the city. This prompted the Governor to warn the Fathers not to invite any of their compatriots to their house, and to observe the laws of the country very exactly, and the visitors replied that they would do just as he commanded. They were then assigned a corner of the field on which to build their church, but the lot was too small for both a church and a house. The interpreter explained this with difficulty, and they were told that the place assigned to them was intended for a dwelling-house only, and that later on they would be given ground for a magnificent temple. From this they concluded that the Governor was laboring under the impression that they were anxious to preside in a temple erected in his honor, and so they had to explain that they did not worship idols, and that God in Heaven was their only deity. This caused him some perplexity, as he probably believed that there was no way of worshipping other than that known to the Chinese. After a short consultation with his companions he finally said, "What difference does it make. Let us build the temple and they can put into it whatever gods they prefer." Whereupon, he decided to enlarge the size of the original grant.

This was all very new to the Chinese people, something as yet unheard of, and a tremendous crowd had gathered for the occasion. The field in which the Flowery Tower was being built was so crowded with a curious multitude, anxious to see the foreign priests, that the Governor and his guard, even with all his authority, could not pass through it. The people were astonished beyond words when they first saw the triangular prism of glass, intended for the former Governor, and they stared in surprise at a little statue of the Blessed Virgin. Those who saw the glass at close view simply stood in mute admiration. This was particularly true of the Magistrates who accompanied the Governor, and the more they praised it the more they aroused the curiosity of the multitude. Finally, our generous host asked that he might be permitted to take the novelties to his palace, to show them to his family. Later on, the Fathers sent him some more curios and requested him to accept them as tokens of friendship. This he would not do, and he sent back everything, even a delicately embroidered European handkerchief which one of his wives was very anxious to keep. From this, one might be inclined to conclude that it is not his conscience but his fear which prevents a Chinese official from openly accepting a gift in public. There was a danger here that the whole village, having seen these things, might accuse him of accepting the precious gifts as an inducement to receive foreign priests into the Kingdom of China and to allow them a permanent residence.

Once the Fathers were aware of the fact that there was some objection to their installation, they decided to hasten the building of

their house, for fear that further delay might present a reason for preventing them from ever getting started. First, they decided to lay
down the foundation of the building, and then to rent a small house
near the spot, to be close to the work and to hasten it along at every
opportunity. They put up an altar in the house and held divine service
there on feast days and on Sundays. Most of their time, however, was
spent in a shelter which they erected from the tiles to be used in the
upper structure of the house, and they used this as a temporary workshop. When the general work began, crowds of curious people from
all classes were attracted, sometimes from a great distance, evidently
moved by the stories told about the foreign priests. Rumors had spread
about, with the customary exaggeration of this country, about strangers
with peculiar faces and other European peculiarities, never before
seen in China. One had to be careful to satisfy their curiosity, and
being a people who were naturally hostile to strangers, the Fathers
showed them every courtesy and carried on their work in such a
way as to win their good will and friendship. The triangular glass
prism, which they called the priceless stone, was shown to everyone
that asked to see it, as were also the books, the statue of the Blessed
Virgin and other things of European make, which they considered
beautiful because of their novelty.

The Bachelors and others of the literary class, and particularly the
members of the commission supervising the building of the Flowery
Tower, did not approve at all of the strangers coming into their town,
and what displeased them most was that they had been allotted a place
on their particular field. Perhaps they were afraid that the strangers
were in a position to see what was going on. First, they spread a
rumor, which later caused open dissension, claiming that the foreigners
would do here what they had already done at Macao, where, as was
generally known, the first arrivals were only a few merchants. Each
year, however, the number of Europeans coming to Macao had in- ·
creased until, as they claimed, they became so numerous that it was
doubtful at present if they could be ejected. Finally, the malcontents
succeeded in having the Building Committee, called the Tan-siao-hu,
call upon the Fathers and inform them that they should not begin
their building project because, according to their calendar, the day
they had chosen to start the work was marked as an unlucky day.
Later on, as they were informed, they could choose a day of more
propitious omen to begin the work. The ruse was quite evident and
the reply to it was, that one day was just as lucky as another. How-

ever, it did pour rain on the day selected and the work had to be postponed, whether one liked it or not. That, too, may have been a special blessing rather than ill-luck, because it prevented possible trouble and the disagreement was peacefully settled shortly afterwards. In fact, they not only gave their consent but their willing assistance as well, and the work was successfully accomplished with more ease than had been expected. All this was the result of the fact that the Fathers had put aside all defense of their cause, and showed due respect for the wishes of those in authority.

Father Ruggieri, with his interpreter, had sought out the instigators of the dissatisfaction and explained the reasons for his plans. He made it clear that they had not come there to give offense to the state, or to the city that had treated them so well, and that they had no intention of doing anything that could be interpreted as being harmful. That was sufficient for an appeasement, and as the Commissioners could not reprove the Governor for having granted the permission, they agreed to settle the whole matter with a compromise. The Commission requested the Fathers to give up the place assigned to them, asserting that their house would turn the people against the place by spoiling the architectural scheme of their own buildings. In exchange they would be granted a lot nearer to the road, where the entrance to their house could be placed outside the enclosure of the field. This was exactly what the Fathers had wished for. They had already purchased several bungalows, and as they were to retain a portion of the field, they were glad to accept the compromise. Thus both parties were satisfied and arguments were brought to an end. In truth, the foreigners felt that they had profited in the bargain, because the tile-workers were not working at the time, and they presented the Fathers with several thousand tile-brick and a quantity of lumber to hasten the completion of the construction they had already begun. Their original intention was to build a small but imposing structure on European lines and two stories high, quite contrary to the Chinese custom of building only one-story dwellings. They had scarcely begun building when their program was held up by the common cause of delay, namely, poverty.

Hard times in Macao, caused by the recent losses, prevented any assistance from there, and the Father Rector of the College, who was also Superior of the Mission, thought it more prudent to give up the idea of a two-story edifice, for fear the people, naturally prone to suspicion, might think they were building some kind of a stronghold.

Finally, so as not to lose what was already done, they sold the triangular prism, for twenty gold pieces, enough to finish the section then under construction. That was sufficient to accommodate them until such time as their hoped-for relief should arrive from abroad. With that much done, the next step was to make sure that their residence was approved by the authority of the governing Magistrate, and that was effected by securing letters patent from the Viceroy, to be posted at the entrance to the house. This official document explained how our Fathers happened to come to China, praised their character and religious devotion and then revealed that they had been assigned a domicile by Viceroyal authority. They were to live at their own expense, and all persons were strictly prohibited under pain of severe punishment from molesting them in any manner whatsoever. A little later on, two more documents arrived under seal of the Governor's office; one confirming the donation of the land and a second permitting them to circulate in the Metropolis, to go to Macao, and to travel wherever they wished in the Kingdom.

The Governor made frequent visits to the Fathers and brought others of the high Magistrates with him. On these occasions he never missed an opportunity to sound their praises in most solemn tone. On the recurrence of the Feast of the New Moon, the Fathers went to the Governor's palace, to do him honor in the accustomed ceremonies, and he in turn received them with a great display of courtesy. No doubt, as they always asserted, they were greatly indebted to this Governor for the help he afforded them at the outset of their mission, and by way of souvenirs, in recognition of his good will, on different occasions, they presented him with divers little presents. His recognized authority and his reputation for honesty and frankness in the administration of public affairs were such, that no one thereafter dared to broach the question of expelling his friends. He not only openly favored and protected the missionaries, but his example induced others of the Magistrates to visit them with similar favorable results. The Viceroy himself was the only one who would not receive the Europeans in audience. When they called upon him, to thank him for the grant of their residence and to offer him several little souvenir gifts, he would neither receive the gifts nor permit them to enter. He merely sent word by messenger, that there was no need of calling on him, and not to bother about presents. He thought it would be quite enough if they would live quietly in the place assigned to them.

5. The Missionaries Begin to Preach Christianity to the Chinese

~~~~~~

IN ORDER THAT the appearance of a new religion might not arouse suspicion among the Chinese people, the Fathers did not speak openly about religious matters when they began to appear in public. What time was left to them, after paying their respects and civil compliments and courteously receiving their visitors, was spent in studying the language of the country, the methods of writing and the customs of the people. They did, however, endeavor to teach this pagan people in a more direct way, namely, by virtue of their example and by the sanctity of their lives. In this way they attempted to win the good will of the people and little by little, without affectation, to dispose their minds to receive what they could not be persuaded to accept by word of mouth, without endangering what had been thus far accomplished. The great difficulty in attempting to preach openly at that time lay in a lack of knowledge of the language and in the natural indisposition of the people. From the time of their entrance they wore the ordinary Chinese outer garment, which was somewhat similar to their own religious habits; a long robe reaching down to the heels and with very ample sleeves, which are much in favor with the Chinese.

The Mission House, as it was called, had two rooms on either side, with an open hall space between, which served as a chapel, with an altar in the center and above it a picture of the Madonna. In order to couple the idea of authority with the name of God, instead of saying God, the missionaries always used the title Thien-ciu, meaning, Lord of Heaven. They could hardly have chosen a more appropriate expression, because there is no consonant sound of D in the Chinese language, and to them there was something magnificent and a touch of the divine in this particular name. In fact, this title, first used at the beginning of our missionary work, is still in vogue today when God is mentioned in discourse and in writing, though several others have been introduced by way of amplification and for clearer understanding. Among the titles most commonly employed are, Sovereign Director of All Things, and First Cause of All Things. The Blessed Virgin is known as The Glorious Mother of God. When people came to visit the Fathers, Magistrates and other holders of literary degrees, the common people, and even those who offered sacrifice to idols, everyone in short, paid reverence to the Madonna in her picture above the altar, with the customary bows and kneeling and touching of the forehead to the floor. All of this was done with an air of real religious sentiment. They never ceased to admire the beauty and the elegance of this painting; the coloring, the very natural lines and the lifelike posture of the figure. Before long it became evident, and for several reasons, that it would be better to remove the picture of the Virgin Mother from above the altar and replace it with one of Christ the Saviour. First, so that they would not believe, as rumor had already announced, that we adored a woman as our God; and secondly, that they might more easily be taught the doctrine of the Word made Flesh.

Once the Mission was established, frequent visitors came uninvited to hear something of the principal articles of our faith. The Chinese are a thinking people who frequently entertain doubts, and not without reason, about the many absurdities contained in their own religious beliefs. Copies of the Commandments were printed in Chinese and given out to all who asked for them. Many who received them said they would live in the future according to these commandments, because as they claimed, they were in such perfect accord with the voice of conscience and with the natural law. Their reverence for the Christian law increased with their admiration for it. Some of them, without being asked or told of it, began to bring incense for the benedictions, others brought oil for the sanctuary lamp and a few made voluntary offerings for the support of the house.

If they had wished to accept the generosity of the Governor, the Fathers might have obtained a grant of land that was originally intended for a temple of idols, but they deemed it wiser not to compromise the newborn liberty of Christianity by subjecting it to the power of the governing Magistrates. Their refusal to accept the offer served to exempt Christianity from any suspicion of cupidity or avarice, and it became known among the people from the very beginning that the preachers of the divine law were not looking for material gain from their religion. This gave them an easy entrée to the palaces of the officials who knew that when the European priests came they were

not looking for favors, as was generally the case with those who cultivated the friendship of all civil rulers. Thus the method of mute
publication, substituting deeds for words, was more than a little ef-
fective in spreading the reputation of the newly arrived Christianity.
No doubt, many who came to see a Christian service were prompted
by curiosity, but many returned touched with admiration of the evidence of the divine. At times some of the more learned Chinese, who
were interested in the religious customs of the Christian world, requested that we discuss the whole question more openly and freely
and also the question of Chinese idols. These discussions were carried
on through interpreters and at times without them, but the latter
method was rather awkward because of a lack of knowledge of the
language, which forced the foreigners to say what they could, rather
than what they wanted to say. What the Fathers continually endeavored to emphasize in these talks was the fact that the Christian law
was in perfect accord with the innate light of conscience. It was, as
they maintained, by this same light of conscience that the most ancient
of the Chinese scholars had approached to this same doctrine of
Christianity in their writings, centuries before the appearance of the
idols. They explained, also, that they themselves were not abolishing
the natural law, rather they were adding to it what was lacking,
namely, the supernatural as taught by God who Himself had become
a man. All this seemed to have met with more applause than approval,
because the pride of the Chinese was not as yet reduced to such a
state that they could accept a new religion of foreigners, which none
of their race had ever embraced.

The first one in the Chinese Kingdom to make open profession of
the Christian faith was from the very lowest rank of the people. God
had evidently chosen the lesser things of earth to confound the greater.
This man was afflicted with an incurable disease, and when the doctors
held out no hope of betterment, his people, who could no longer support him, cruelly put him out of the house, and he was left lying
abandoned on a public road. When the Fathers heard of the case they
went out and found the man, told him there was no hope of curing his
bodily ailments, but that there was a means of taking care of his soul
and of leading him to salvation and eternal happiness. His reaction
was as joyful as it was courageous, and he answered that any law offering such sympathy and pity to its observers was quite acceptable
to him. They took him home and had their Chinese servants construct
a neat little rustic hut for him, close to the mission house, where they

took good care of him and taught him the fundamental truths of Christianity. When he was sufficiently prepared, he became the first one in the great empire to receive the sacrament of baptism. Indeed, it would seem that in order to preserve his innocence, God in His mercy took him to Himself in Heaven only a few days after his conversion. This was the first small beginning of the great work to follow. It was quite in keeping with the established tradition of the Church, and what followed immediately was also in keeping with the story of the spread of Christianity. For fear the servants of God might lose any of the merit attached to the performance of a holy deed, by the praise that might follow it, the Lord permitted this particular charitable act to become a subject of severe attack and slander. Rumor was spread about that the Europeans knew, from the shape of that man's face, that he had a precious stone concealed in his head, and that they took good care of him while he was alive so that they would have possession of his body, to extract the stone of great price when he died.

The high esteem acquired by the Christian religion, from its seemingly futile beginnings, was built up not only by the truth of its doctrine and the holy lives of its missionaries, but at times from little things which in themselves were quite insignificant. For example, among the many books in the mission library there were two large volumes of Canon Law, which were greatly admired by the learned Chinese for their exquisite printing and also for the excellent workmanship of the covers, which were ornamented in gold. The Chinese could neither read these books nor did they have any idea of what they treated, and yet they judged that the content of such volumes must be of major importance, when no expense was spared on their binding. Moreover, they concluded that letters and science must be held in high esteem in Europe, and that in this respect the Europeans, with such books, must surpass not only the other nations but even China itself. This indeed was an admission that they would never have made without seeing evidence of it with their own eyes. They noticed also that the Fathers, not satisfied with a knowledge of European science, were continually, day and night, delving into Chinese scientific tomes. In fact, they had hired a Chinese scholar of high reputation, and at good wages, to live at the house with them as an instructor, and their library was well stocked with Chinese books. There was no doubt among the educated Chinese that these Europeans had a reputation for doctrine and learning. It was this reputation that accounted for the fact that some of the highly lettered class requested a fuller explanation of the precepts of Christianity than was contained in a copy of the Commandments which they were accustomed to carry about with them.

Encouraged by their success and becoming a bit more enterprising, with the help of their domestic tutor, the Fathers composed a volume of Christian Doctrine in a style adapted to the capabilities of the people. In it some of the errors of the sects of idol worshippers were refuted, and the points of doctrine that were chiefly developed were such as could be readily accepted as evidence drawn only from the natural law. The rest was reserved for the particular instruction of the catechumens. The Fathers themselves were not as yet sufficiently adept in writing to treat of every subject, nor were they certain that the Chinese would approve of their style of writing Chinese characters. They published this first volume themselves and printed it on their own press, and the educated Chinese received it with great admiration. The Governor was particularly pleased with this book and a great number of copies were struck off and spread throughout the kingdom. Thus the law of Christianity was dispersed through the land and made an easy entrance into parts of the country to which the authors had not as yet penetrated after years of endeavor. In this way, the fundamentals of the Christian faith were more apt to become widespread by writing than by word of mouth, because the Chinese are curious to read books containing anything new, and also because Chinese writing, expressed in hieroglyphic characters, enjoys peculiar power and majesty of expression.

When the Governor discovered that the European priests were more advanced in learning and more cultured than he had imagined, he decided to confer upon them a certain favor which the Chinese held in high esteem. When a Magistrate wishes to make a public demonstration of his affection for his friends, he sends them a present of a tablet beautifully wrought and decorated in colors, and the presentation is made an occasion for considerable show and display. On the front of this tablet there are three or four large, engraved, characters expressing the praises of those being honored. To one side and below these characters is inscribed, in smaller forms, the name and the title of the Magistrate who is honoring his friends, and on the other side is inscribed the date of the presentation, which is reckoned from the beginning of the reign of the present Emperor. The Governor of Sciauquin took this particular way of honoring those whom he had undertaken to protect and to sponsor, because he deemed them worthy of it in view of what they had accomplished, and also to promote the respect and the friendship of the people, who he knew would follow his example with reference to his intimates. Two of these plaques were sent to the Mission House and with all the customary pomp and parade. One of them he wished to have placed at the entrance to the chapel, which also served as entrance to the house. The inscription on this one read "The House of the Saints of the Flower." The second one, he asked to have placed in the reception room where friendly guests were received, and the inscription on that one was, "A Holy People from the Occident." These tablets greatly increased the reputation of the Fathers among all classes of the people. The first one was read by everyone entering the outer door, and the second when they passed into the hall. So it happened that no one could leave the place unaware of the fact that the missionaries were held in very high esteem by the ranking Magistrate in the district. Here was a Governor whose reputation was supreme in his Province, not so much because of the office he held and of his literary attainment as for the dignity resulting from his personal virtue and his efficient administration of the affairs of state.

6. In the Absence of Father Ruggieri, Father Ricci Is Cleared of a Grave Charge. He Astounds the Chinese with His Knowledge of Mathematics

DUE TO THE FACT that they had received no help from Macao in a long time, the Missionaries, reduced to poverty and already in debt to several creditors, could no longer retain an interpreter or servants, and had to discontinue any building improvements. Their financial status was becoming worse every day, until finally Father Ruggieri decided to go to Macao to arouse the interest of the friends of the Mission, who had been rejoicing in the success of this long desired undertaking. He asked the Governor for a boat and received a really sumptuous one, such as the Magistrates rated at public expense, manned by more than thirty oarsmen. The friendship of the Governor was manifested in the promptitude and the good will with which he granted their request. He had heard that clocks were made in Macao and he asked that they have one made for him and he promised to pay well for it.

When Father Ruggieri arrived at Macao, he found that the town was actually desolate and passing through a period of hard times and financial reverses. The traders, upon whom the prosperity of the place was entirely dependent, had not returned from Japan. This caused him to defer his return for a whole year, fearing that if he went back empty-handed his creditors might conclude that there was no hope of ever being paid. The Portuguese were worried about the unusual delay of their argosies, and the College, which up to that time had had no regular annual income, was so financially reduced that it could not afford to buy the clock the Governor had asked for. As an alternate, they sent the clock-maker back to the Governor at Sciauquin. This man was from the Province of Goa in India, one of the so-called Canarii, of deep brown complexion which the Chinese admired as something unusual. When the boat returned with the artisan and the explanation of his arrival, the Governor expressed himself as pleased with his coming and also with the valuable little present, in the form of a European rarity, that was brought to him from the College at Macao. Immediately he sent for the two best craftsmen in the city, to assist the visiting jeweler in his work and the clock was made at the Mission House.

As might be expected under the circumstances, the friendship of the Magistrates was arousing the jealousy of the people. The inhabitants of Sciauquin had already turned against the Fathers and were growing troublesome. First, a word about the cause of their general dislike, and then about a particular calumny. We have frequently remarked that the Chinese fear and distrust all foreigners. Their suspicion seems to be innate, and their aversion has increased in strength and become a habit after centuries of strict prohibition against all dealings with outsiders. This feeling of ill-will which is common to all Chinese, and especially so to the common people, is particularly noticeable among the inhabitants of the Province of Canton, which is not as advanced in culture as the other provinces. In fact, the Province of Canton is an annexation to the Empire, and even today is numbered among the barbarian countries by the other provinces, which are far superior to it in cultural training, conferring many more literary degrees, and providing many more high ranking and ruling Magistrates. The adverse disposition of these people is only aggravated by the fact that their province is exposed to foreigners by land and by sea, and that they have suffered heavy and frequent losses from inland robbers and from marauding pirates. Of late they had become quite disturbed by the coming of the Portuguese, and particularly so because they can do nothing about it, due to the great profit reaped from Portuguese traders by the public treasury and by certain influential merchants. Without referring to the public treasury or to the merchants who come from every other province, they complain that the foreign commerce raises the price of all commodities and that outsiders are the only ones to profit from it. As an expression of their contempt for Europeans, when the Portuguese first arrived they were called foreign devils, and this name is still in common use among the Cantonese.

The citizens of Sciauquin have their own particular reasons for hating the strangers. They are afraid that the Portuguese merchants will get into the interior of the realm with the missionaries, and their fears are not without some foundation. The frequent visits of the Fathers to the town of Macao and their growing intimacy with the Governor have already aroused their antipathy. There is nothing that stirs them up like a wide-spreading slander, and they had a good one in the story that the tower which had been built at such great expense, and with so much labor, was erected at the request of the foreign priests. This probably had its origin in the fact that the tower was completed while the Fathers were building their mission houses. This false rumor had such an effect that the people called it the Tower of the Foreigners instead of The Flowery Tower, as it was named. As a result of the animosity which grew out of this incident, when they realized that they could not drive out the Mission, as they wanted to, they took to insulting the missionaries whenever an occasion occurred or they could trump up a reason for doing so. It was quite annoying and dangerous to be made a continual target for stones hurled from the tower, when people came there every day to play games, the purpose for which these towers are built. Not a stone was thrown at the Mission House from the high tower nearby that missed its roof as a target. These showers of stones were heaviest when they knew that there were only one or two of the servants at home. Another silly reason for their taking offense was that the doors of our house, which were kept open for inspection while it was being built, were now kept closed according to the rule of our Society. What they wanted to do was to use the house as they did their temples of idols, which are always left wide open and are often the scenes of uncouth frivolity.

It happened one day, when their insolence became really unbearable, that one of our servants ran out and seized a boy, who had been throwing stones at the house, and dragging him inside threatened to bring him to court. Attracted by the shrieking of the boy, several men, who were known in the neighborhood, ran into the house to intercede for the culprit, and Father Ricci ordered that he be allowed to depart without further ado. Here was a good pretext for a major calumny, and two of the neighbors who disliked the Fathers went into conference with a bogus relative of the boy, who knew something about court procedure. Then they trumped up a story that the boy had been seized by the Fathers and hidden in their house for three days, that he had been given a certain drug, well known to the Chinese, which prevented him from crying out, and that the purpose of it all was to smuggle him back to Macao, where they could sell him into slavery. The two men were to be called in as witnesses. They didn't have much trouble persuading the other to take the case, as he knew it would be favored by the townspeople who had become open enemies of the foreigners and were looking for a means of having them expelled. When the so-called lawyer had instructed the boy, whom he called his brother, as to what he should say, he took him along with him to the Governor's court. On their way thither, in order to increase the credulity of the people, they passed through the most thickly crowded parts of the town, and both of them with their hair unkempt and dishevelled, set up a piteous lamentation, passing from one street to another, and crying out to heaven and to the City Magistrates, to punish the wickedness of the foreign devils. In presence of the Governor, the accuser explained his case with astounding cunning, making it all look very plausible, especially when he said he had witnesses for every detail of it; men who were thoroughly trustworthy, because they were nearby neighbors with a reputation for veracity. What help or recourse could one look for in such a sudden surprise, save to betake oneself to prayer.

On the following day, while one of the Fathers was discussing the case with some of his friends and drawing up a brief in an effort to reveal the calumny, an officer of the Governor's staff made a sudden appearance in the house and took him off to the court in such haste that he hadn't even time to gather up his papers. Fortunately he was accompanied by a young man from India who spoke Chinese more fluently than the Father in question. At the opening of the case, the Governor spoke like one who had given a credulous ear to the accusation, bitterly lamenting the fact that the Fathers should act in this way toward him and toward the people, after they had been received into the kingdom and shown such favor on his part. The Indian interpreter, however, was very well posted as to the method of their procedure. He had filled his long and spacious sleeves with stones, and at these words of the Governor, he unfolded his arms and the stones went rolling all over the floor of the court, as a protest that he should not be obliged to give a better proof of the falsity of the calumny. Before the surprise was over, he called for an exact and thorough investigation into the source of the extraordinary story. Then he told how the Fathers had been stoned and how the boy had been caught in the act of throwing stones, but was immediately released. The court was crowded with a multitude of the curious who had no doubt of a conviction, and who were anxious to see what punishment would be meted out to the unholy foreigners for such a heinous crime.

After the Governor had heard the defense, it was as easy for him to recognize the truth of the affair as it had been to receive the story of the calumniator. He suddenly awoke to the fact that the accusation was a lie. Yet, since the accuser insisted and repeated that he could prove his case by reliable witnesses, the Governor, pretending to be in doubt, decided to get all the available information and to expose the impostor to the whole assembly. This would prevent the plaintiff from protesting that he was working under the disadvantage of the favors which everyone knew the Governor had shown to the Fathers. Finally, in order to save the Father present from any embarrassment, he declared him wholly innocent and placed whatever blame there was upon the Canarine jeweler who had been sent there to make the clock. This man was ordered back to Macao immediately and the Governor canceled his order for the clock. His next move was to summon the three members of the building commission, who were at the tower on the day the incident occurred, and the plaintiff requested that he call in the neighbors also, the real authors of the charge, who had a full knowledge of all its details. The Governor dismissed the multitude and, as he was leaving, he forbade the Father to leave the court. In the meantime, and in deep humiliation, the Father betook himself to prayer, commending his cause and its solution to God, to the Blessed Mother and to the Saints. The plaintiff, who was free to leave, went out with the officers of the court to find the members of the building commission, and when he found them he entreated them, and offered to pay them money, to testify on behalf of his client. He also insisted that the officers should bring in the two neighbors who had started the court proceedings, since they had been named by the Governor. There was no doubt in the mind of the accused that the Commissioners would agree to the charge. The coming of the Fathers and their presence had always displeased them, and it was thought that they would probably seize upon this occasion to have the missionaries put out of their house. What caused the most worry was that this affair might undo the work of years, and result in great damage to the spread of Christianity. The final result of the inquest proved quite the contrary, as it turned out to be more fortunate than was expected.

Three venerable old men, the Commissioners, were called to give witness. When the Governor ascended his seat of judgment, the trio were on bended knees, waiting to see which one would be questioned first and what would be asked of him. Addressing the most aged of them the judge asked whether or not the plaintiff was speaking the truth when he said the boy was taken from his father. "Quite the contrary," said the old man, who then attested that he had often seen this same boy throwing stones at the Mission House, that one of the servants on that occasion ran out and caught the boy and pushed him into the house, that several men who were passing were attracted by the boy's shrieking, and going into the house they asked the Father to pardon the boy and let him go. This, they asserted, he did very willingly. "And was the boy detained in the house for three days," the Governor inquired. The answer to this question, given in real Chinese style, was merely a smile of ridicule, with a response somewhat similar to our own expression when we say, for the time it would take to say the Apostles' Creed three times. That was enough to throw the Governor into a fit of anger against the accuser, whom he sentenced in harsh and threatening terms to a sound and thorough beating. The culprit was immediately stripped of his outer garments, placed face down to the ground and, according to the custom, cruelly beaten by the court attendants on the legs and buttocks, with sizable sticks of tough bamboo. It was all to no avail that the Father, kneeling before the Governor, continued bowing and touching his forehead to the floor in supplication for pardon and remission of the punishment. The answer given to his supplications was, that such a crime should not be pardoned, because it exposed the reputation of the innocent to infamy and even placed him in danger of capital punishment. Then he told the missionary and his interpreter and the three Commissioners that he had heard enough of this affair, and that they might return to their homes and their business.

The neighbors who had made up the charge escaped scot-free. They were not called to give evidence. In fact, the Governor did not know that they were present at the trial in disguise, but when things began to look bad for their representative, for fear of being detected, they made an early and quiet exit from the crowded court by crawling on their hands and knees. It need not be recorded that the Father was pleased with the verdict and that he thanked God for it. The people outside, those who could not get in because of the crowd, were somewhat astonished at the results. They asked the interpreter what had happened and, not long after he had explained the whole story, every street in the city was aware of the falsity of the charge that had been brought against the Mission.

On the following day the Governor sent a solemn document to be posted at the main entrance of the Mission House. This notice, after explaining that the foreigners were living here with permission of the Viceroy, stated that certain unprincipled persons, contrary to right and reason, were known to have molested the strangers living herein, wherefore: he, the Governor, strictly forbade under severest penalty that anyone from now on should dare to cause them further molestation. Moreover, as it stated, if anyone should transgress this edict, the interpreter of the Father was hereby empowered to summon him before the Governor's court, where exemplary punishment would be administered. Such a notice was quite sufficient to put a damper on their insolence. That was the end of the first great difficulty, but there were others still to come. Our purpose in recording such incidents is to show that with the grace of God, the result of surmounting such difficulties, created by our adversaries to dislodge us, was, that we became more and more firmly established in our undertaking. With this over, let us go to something more pleasant and agreeable.

Hanging on the wall of the reception room in the Mission House there was a cosmographical chart of the universe, done with European lettering. The more learned among the Chinese admired it very much and, when they were told that it was both a view and a description of the entire world, they became greatly interested in seeing the same thing done in Chinese. Of all the great nations, the Chinese have had the least commerce, indeed, one might say that they have had practically no contact whatever, with outside nations, and consequently they are grossly ignorant of what the world in general is like. True, they had charts somewhat similar to this one, that were supposed to represent the whole world, but their universe was limited to their own fifteen provinces, and in the sea painted around it they had placed a few little islands to which they gave the names of different kingdoms they had heard of. All of these islands put together would not be as large as the smallest of the Chinese provinces. With such a limited knowledge, it is evident why they boasted of their kingdom as being the whole world, and why they called it Thienhia, meaning, everything under the heavens. When they learned that China was only a part of the great east, they considered such an idea, so unlike their own, to be something utterly impossible, and they wanted to be able to read about it, in order to form a better judgment. So the Governor consulted with Father Matthew Ricci and asked him, as he expressed it, if he, with the help of his interpreter, would make his map speak Chinese, assuring him that such a work would bring him great credit and favor with everyone.

Ricci had had considerable training in mathematics, which he studied for several years at Rome under Father Christophoro Clavius, Doctor of Science and Prince of Mathematicians of his day. In answer to the Governor's request, he went to work immediately at this task, which was not at all out of keeping with his ideas of preaching the Gospel. According to the disposition of Divine Providence, various ways have been employed at different times, and with different races, to interest people in Christianity. In fact this very attraction was to draw many of the Chinese into the net of Peter. The new chart was made on a larger scale than the original, so as to give more room for the Chinese written characters which are somewhat larger than our own. New annotations were also added, more in keeping with the Chinese genius, and more appropriate also to the author's intentions. When there was question of describing the various religious rites of the different nations, he took occasion to insert a mention of the sacred mysteries of the Christian faith, hitherto unknown to Chinese. In this way he hoped to spread the name and the fame of Christianity through the whole of China in a brief space of time. We must mention here another discovery which helped to win the good will of the Chinese. To them the heavens are round but the earth is flat and square, and they firmly believe that their empire is right in the middle of it. They do not like the idea of our geographies pushing their China into one corner of the Orient. They could not comprehend the demonstrations proving that the earth is a globe, made up of land and water, and that a globe of its very nature has neither beginning nor end. The geographer was therefore obliged to change his design and, by omitting the first meridian of the Fortunate Islands, he left a margin on either side of the map, making the Kingdom of China to appear right in the center. This was more in keeping with their ideas and it gave them a great deal of pleasure and satisfaction. Really, at that time and in the particular circumstances, one could not have hit upon a discovery more appropriate for disposing this people for the reception of the faith. This statement might appear to many to be somewhat of a paradox, so I shall briefly state the reason for making it, something which afterwards was confirmed by experience.

Because of their ignorance of the size of the earth and the exaggerated opinion they have of themselves, the Chinese are of the opinion that only China among the nations is deserving of admiration. Relative to grandeur of empire, of public administration and of reputation for learning, they look upon all other people not only as barbarous but as unreasoning animals. To them there is no other place on earth that can boast of a king, of a dynasty, or of culture. The more their pride is inflated by this ignorance, the more humiliated they become when the truth is revealed. When they first saw our delineation of the universe, some of the uneducated laughed at it and made fun of it, but it was different with the better instructed, especially when they studied the placement of the parallels and meridians and of the equator, relative to the tropics of Cancer and of Capricorn. Again, when they learned of the symmetry of the five zones, and after reading of the customs of so many different people, and seeing the names of many places in perfect accord with those given by their own ancient writers, they admitted that the chart really did represent the size and figure of the world. From that time on, they had a much higher opinion of the European system of education. This, however, was not the only result. There was another, and of no less importance. When they saw on the map what an almost unlimited stretch of land and sea lay between Europe and the Kingdom of China, that realization seemed to diminish the fear our presence had occasioned. Why fear a people whom nature had placed so far away from them, and if this geographic fact of distance were generally known by all the

Chinese, the knowledge would serve to remove a great obstruction to the spread of the Gospel throughout the kingdom. Nothing has impeded our work more than clouds of suspicion. This geographic study, frequently revised and refined and often reprinted, found its way into the courts of the Governor and of the Viceroy, where it was greatly admired, and finally into the palace of the King, on his own request. We shall say more later, relative to the way in which that was brought about.

Now it happened that just at the time when the map was being completed, the finishing touches were also being put upon the clock, which the Governor had refused to accept at the court trial, and Ricci presented them both to him at the same time. He was delighted beyond measure with the gifts, and expressed his pleasure in most gracious terms, accompanied by several presents in return. He had more copies of the map made, at his personal expense, for distribution to his friends in the district, and gave orders for other copies to be sent to different provinces. After several months, during which time he could find no one in his household who could regulate the clock, he sent it back, to be used in the Mission House for the amusement of visiting friends.

Let us now return to Father Michele Ruggieri, during whose absence the events just related were taking place. The day finally arrived when the long expected merchant ships from Japan sailed into the port of Macao. That put an end to Father Ruggieri's want of money, which was liberally supplied, by way of alms, through the generosity of the Portuguese. The Government and others who were well disposed sent money and various presents to the Mission; enough in all to pay off the debts, to complete the building and to amply supply it with furniture. The house itself was small but it was quite presentable. The Chinese took great pleasure in just looking at it; a European structure, different from their own houses because of the extra story and the tile-work, and also because its graceful lines were emphasized by the even disposition of the windows. The site and the placement of the house also served to enhance its beauty. From here one could see all the buildings along the water front, a variety of all kinds of boats on the river, and beyond it the whole horizon of wooded mountains. It was known as the most beautiful spot in the district and being adorned with European novelties everyone was curious to see it. Visits from the ranking Magistrates were almost of daily occurrence, and not only of those from our own city but of officials who came from other provinces to interview the Viceroy. This, of course, did not hurt the reputation of the Mission and it helped the Chinese also by gradually building up their desire to know more about the Christian religion.

The geographic charts were such a huge success that Ricci took to making astronomical spheres and globes, out of copper and iron, illustrating the heavens and demonstrating the proper shape of the earth. At home he also painted sundials or engraved them on copper sheets, which he presented to friendly Magistrates, including the Viceroy. When these various devices were exhibited and their purpose explained, showing the position of the sun, the courses of the stars and the central position of the earth, their designer and artisan was looked upon as the world's great astronomer. This nation measures all others according to its own standards, and they are thoroughly convinced that what is unknown to them is unknown to the rest of the world.

7. The Spanish Embassy to the King of China

IT WAS A FORTUNATE occurrence for the Mission that the Governor, who was friendly, was promoted to the exalted position of 'Lin-si-tau, which gave him jurisdiction over several districts, and it was an added blessing that he did not change his residence from Sciauquin. The heathens in general, and particularly those in this quarter, are given to the practice of augury and foretelling the future, and the Governor was of the opinion that his friendship with the Mission not only did him no harm but was a sure sign of future prosperity. In fact he seemed to be quite pleased about his acquaintance with the Fathers. So much so indeed, that, thanks to Divine Providence, he made it quite evident by an expression of more than ordinary cordiality when they went, as was customary, to offer him a present, by way of congratulations, at the time of his promotion.

The good news of the happy beginning of the Mission, which meant the planting of Christianity in China, was soon spread far and wide, not only to Macao but even to Japan and farther still to the Philippine Islands. The Society and the world in general found it a cause of common joy, and particularly so because it was universally known that several attempts to enter the kingdom, made over a space of years, had come to naught, leaving the impression that it was an impossible undertaking.

It happened just at that time that the Viceroy of the Philippine Islands called a general council of the Archdiocese of Manila, and of the Senate, and decided to lend some assistance to our enterprise in China. The principal reason for this decision was the hope of opening commercial relations between the Spaniards and the Chinese, though they knew that such relations, up to that time, had been closed to all except to the Portuguese. Their idea was to get permission to trade through a new port in the Canton Province. Jean Baptiste Roman, Royal Procurator of the King of Spain, and a man of long and tried experience, was sent to Macao to open negotiations, and with him came the Spanish Jesuit Alphonso Sanchez. He had letters for the Rector of the College at Macao, and also for the Fathers at Sciauquin, the contents of which amounted to the following: Felicitations on our fortunate entrance to the Kingdom of China. This is something that the Catholic King of Spain and all the Christian world have been looking forward to for years. In view of the common religion which they shared, they were prompted to lend whatever aid they could to the advancement of the Mission. They were sending a donation of money and of other presents, by way of alms, among which was an elegant clock which measured time by the movement of wheels without the aid of weights. The letters also recalled the fact that in years past the Catholic King had sent costly presents for the King of China, which were known to have been misdirected to Mexico. Then came a request to the Fathers to obtain permission from the Viceroy of Canton for a diplomatic embassy to the Royal Court of China. This would afford them an opportunity to get to the capital city and perhaps in that way they could secure permission from the King to publish the Christian religion to the entire realm. The expenses of the entire expedition were to be defrayed by the Procurator of the King of Spain. Such was the tenor of the letters, and the Philippine Procurator and Father Alphonso requested that permission be obtained for them to see the King personally, to treat of the embassy in question.

Father Francesco Caprale, Rector of the College of Macao at the time, wrote to the Fathers at Sciauquin, advising them to handle this affair in such a manner that their own mission would not be endangered. This they did according to directions, as the China Mission up to that time was under the jurisdiction of the College of Macao. With the assistance of a certain courtier from the palace of the Viceroy, they composed a letter of request to which they did not sign their names nor the name of anyone connected with their house. Before sending this letter to the Viceroy they brought it to their recently promoted Protector, the Governor, to find out what he thought of the venture, which to them seemed somewhat perilous and decidedly dubious. Strange to say, he was more pleased with it than they had expected. He approved of the request, and, on his suggestion, it was signed by his own interpreter. Then the Governor himself set out in his palanquin chair to find the magistrate whose duty it was either to present such requests to the Viceroy or to reject them as he saw fit. The Governor presented him with the letter and ordered him to have it brought to the Viceroy without delay, stating that it contained a message as advantageous to the Chinese Kingdom as it was truly honorable. Wonderful to relate, it was not at all displeasing to the Viceroy and he sent it, as was the custom, to the Grand Admiral, at the capital city of the district, the Hai-tau, as we have called him, with orders to make an inquiry into the request and to return the findings.

We have already mentioned that all foreign affairs come under the jurisdiction of the Grand Admiral. When a petition has advanced to this point, it is a sign that it has met with the approval of the Viceroy, unless something untoward appears in the Admiral's inquiry. If the request had been rejected by the Viceroy, it would have been suppressed without ceremony and without answer, and never permitted to go beyond his court. The Fathers had already advanced the project to this particular point when new orders, quite contrary to those first received, arrived from Macao. While the cause was being advanced in Sciauquin, the civil authorities at Macao concluded that the prime reason for presenting a Spanish embassy was to open trade with the Chinese in the same province in which they themselves were already operating. This would mean the certain ruin of their commerce and of their settlement. There was a great quantity of silver in the Philippine Islands, which had been sent thither yearly from New Spain and from the Province of Peru, and the Portuguese calculated that if this money were spent to purchase Chinese goods in the Province of Canton, it would ruin the trading market. In the future, the Portuguese would have to purchase these goods at a higher price and be obliged to sell them abroad at a lower price.

The Fathers were therefore advised, in a public notice, to make no further advance of the project in question, because it meant disaster to the settlement, to which they themselves were obliged for numerous benefits. The notice recalled that the people of Macao were certain that the Missionaries did not want to be the cause of their misfortune, and, as they said, it was not at all becoming that the Spaniards should be honored by an embassy to the King of China. That honor should go to the Portuguese, to whom China trade was adjudicated a long time ago by Pope Alexander the Sixth, when the question arose for decision between the Kings of Spain and of Portugal. Although these two kingdoms were now under one crown, it was the will of the Catholic King that each nation should carry on its own affairs, and it was forbidden for one to interfere with the rights or the former privileges of the other. Such was the content of the public notice.

As for the presents that were sent some time before, to advance the proposed embassy, it was well known that they had been distributed in various places, and that it would be next to impossible to recover any of them. Evidently it had been decided that since the entry to the Chinese realm had failed as often as it was attempted, it was taken for granted that this embassy would also fail, and the material prepared for it was dispersed by those who had charge of it. This information was given to the Fathers by the Mayor of Macao, and it was by his authority that the Rector of the College gave orders not to pursue the project any further. This incident created a difficult situation at the Mission, because the affair had advanced so far that it was not easy to find a way of entirely disposing of it. At any rate, it was decided to have nothing more to do with it. Perhaps the whole thing would die out of itself if no further interest were taken in it, and that was exactly what happened.

When the Grand Admiral of Canton received the request, together with the orders of the Viceroy, he delayed a few days, awaiting the arrival of the author of the request. As we noted, the request was signed by the interpreter, who failed to make an appearance, because we ourselves had dropped all interest in the matter. So the Admiral wrote to the Mayor of the town of Ansam, who had jurisdiction over the port of Macao, to inquire if an ambassador who claimed to be bringing presents to the King of China had arrived at that port. The Mayor then sent a commission to Macao to ascertain the facts. This delegation was cordially received and presented with gifts by the Procurator from the Philippine Islands, and then made a favorable report on its inquest, including the fact that the request was really genuine. But the Mayor of Macao also sent in a report to the Governor, informing him of the difficulty that existed, and asserting quite the contrary to what the commission had reported. He made it clear also that those who were promoting this venture were not Portuguese, and that it would not be at all expedient to receive a legation from the people concerned, because of the difficulties that might result between the two foreign powers. These objections were brought to the Admiral from different quarters, and he immediately published a notice which he ordered to be placed on a large sign at the gates of the capital city of the province. The following summary will afford us an idea of the contents of the notice.

He, the Admiral, being fully informed relative to the origin and the progress of the request, enumerates the objections to it, presented to him from various sources. Then follows a bitter complaint against the interpreter because he had failed to present himself in the court. Finally, he pronounces sentence on the whole affair in this fashion. If the embassy which is being prepared is from a people who have never been invited to send a legation to China, they had better not bother their heads any more about it, because no one would give them permission for such an innovation, whether they were or were not of the same nationality as the foreigners at Macao. However, if there were documents, such as letters patent, formerly in circulation relative to an embassy, then the legation would be given consideration. In conclusion, he warns the Mayor of Ansam not to permit the people interested to approach the Viceroy with these petitions, adding that he will inflict severe punishment on anyone that attempts to. And so the whole affair came to an end, without harm to the Mission, which might easily have resulted, since the Fathers had unwittingly involved themselves with other foreigners in an affair that was contrary to the law of the Empire.

With this fear removed, Father Francesco Caprale, Rector of the College of Macao, and Superior of the Chinese Mission, decided to visit the settlement at Sciauquin, in order to report firsthand information to the Official Visitor of the Society in India, and also to the General of the Society at Rome. The necessary permission for his visit was easily obtained through the favor of the Lin-si-tau. He was a frequent visitor at our house, and when he was asked about it, he said there would be no difficulty if the Father were coming to pay a visit but not to remain. On his arrival, Father Caprale went to see the Lin-si-tau, offered him some gifts and received some in return. With permission to move about freely in the city and outside of it, he learned that the Mission was much better off than he imagined. It was Father Caprale who baptized the first converts received into the Church, with solemn ceremony. There were two baptized at the time; one, who took the name of Paul, was of the lettered or cultured class from the Province of Fuquian. He was afterwards engaged by the Fathers as an instructor in the Chinese language. The other was the young man we have already mentioned, who kept the altar when the Fathers were expelled, and lodged them in his house when they returned. He took the name Giovanni. The baptismal ceremony was held in public and was taken in good part by the Chinese. In fact, they congratulated the Fathers on receiving new disciples, and many others followed the example of the first two and were received for instruction. The visit of the Superior proved to be a great help to the Mission, as both the Official Visitor and the Father General became greatly interested in supplying the help it needed to confirm its stability.

8. Two More Missionaries Are Admitted to China. Cequian Visited

FATHER ALEXANDER VALIGNANO was always very solicitous about this expedition to China, which he himself had organized. When he was appointed Provincial of India, and had to abandon his trip to Europe with the Japanese Legates, he devoted himself to the consolidation of the Chinese Mission. His long experience as a religious superior enabled him to handle the situation and to control it by means of orders and precepts that were quite suitable for the occasion. When he learned of the fortunate beginning, namely: the successful entrance, the permanent residence, the new house and the great prestige gained by the Gospel, and by those who were preaching it, his first impulse was to give thanks to God, the source of all grace, and then to arrange for the future stability of the Mission.

His first move was to appoint Father Eduardo Sande, a Portuguese, as Superior of the Mission, a man of outstanding prudence and of other notable qualities. He then withdrew the China Mission from the jurisdiction of the College of Macao, making it subject only to his own authority and to that of the Provincial of Japan. At that time Father Sande had been in the Society for some years. He had arrived in India from Portugal, together with those who had been working on the China Mission up to the present. His assistant, Father Antonio Almeida, also Portuguese, who had arrived in India from Europe during the past year, was a younger man, gifted with talent and virtue, pious and zealous for the salvation of souls. Through Eduardo Meneses, the Viceroy of India, Father Valignano secured an annual grant, given in the name of the Catholic King, for the support of the China Mission. It was also arranged that this pension should be paid through the Bank of Malacca, the nearest available to China. When he was sending these two Fathers to China from India, Father Valignano wrote to those in Sciauquin asking them to arrange for the entrance of the new-comers, but to do so with all care and caution, avoiding anything that might jeopardize the general welfare of the Mission. During the time the two Fathers had to wait at Macao for an opportunity to enter China, they were to procure whatever was needed for those in Sciauquin, so as not to increase the suspicion of the Chinese by making frequent trips to Macao. Fathers Sande and Almeida arrived at Macao toward the end of July in 1585. Directions relative to employment were sent on from India by the Father Visitor, who retained his interest, and held to his plan in the future, as is seen in his frequent letters and instructions, manifesting his affection for the Fathers, and encouraging them to zeal and devotion in the arduous task to which they had been assigned. All this correspondence is preserved in the archives for future reference. Its repetition here would be too lengthy and not wholly in keeping with the purpose of the present narrative.

When the Fathers at the Mission received the Father Visitor's letters, they asked permission of their protector, the Lin-si-tau, for one of the new men to live at their house. He, however, had some misgivings, because of the presence of the Viceroy, and said they could both come for a visit but they must return to Macao after a few days.

It happened rather fortunately that the Viceroy himself had just received a message from the royal court, ordering him to purchase some elegant plumes from the merchants at Macao and to send them to the King as soon as possible. So the Governor sent Father Michele Ruggieri to Macao in rather a large boat, to make the purchase for the Viceroy, and on his return trip he brought Father Sande with him. The first thing for the new arrival to do, in order to win the good grace of the Governor, was to pay him a visit and offer him a present of European rarities. What pleased him most was one of the glass prisms we have already mentioned, something he had wanted for a long time. When the Governor asked him when he intended to return to Macao, he answered that he would like to stay there with his companions if it pleased his Excellency, if not, he would return whenever he was told to. "Why don't you make the request of the Viceroy?" the Governor said. "He will send it back to me for approval and then I can grant your wish." The request was forwarded as directed. However, it was not returned to the Mission House and there was no way of finding out whether it had been held by the Magistrate whose duty it was to present such requests, or presented to the Viceroy and then suppressed. When the Governor heard this he granted permission for Father Sande to remain on condition that there would be no further additions to the household community. The merchandise which the Viceroy had called for had to be purchased at a price higher than the merchants at Macao had agreed to, and the Governor reimbursed the Fathers with several ounces of silver to make up for their trouble.

The only thing lacking to complete the joy of the missionaries on their recent success was the presence of Father Antonio Almeida who was still at Macao, longing for the post to which he had been assigned. Then, thanks to Divine Providence, his entrance to China was brought about more easily than anyone had hoped for. We have already noted that the first Governor of our acquaintance was promoted to a higher position. It so happened that the official appointed to take his place was a co-citizen of our great protector from Cequian, and that at that time he was planning his official triennial visit to Pekin, to pay homage to the King, as his office required. One day he was present in our house for the celebration of a solemn festival. That in itself was not extraordinary, as the Magistrates frequently came to visit, but during the dinner he informed the Fathers that he had intended to have one of them accompany him to Pekin, were it not for the fact that some of his own people remonstrated that it probably would not be safe to bring a foreigner to the capital city, when the most influential officials were assembled there from all parts of the realm. So he had to change his mind about that, but, as he added, there was nothing to prevent them. from going as far as his native province of Cequian, if they wished to. That was just what they were waiting for, as they had been ordered by the Official Visitor of the Society to open a new house if possible, so that less suspicion would be aroused if more of our missionaries were introduced into the Kingdom. Then if anything happened that might force us to close one house, it would not put an end to the whole mission. It had already cost a prolonged struggle to establish a foot-hold in China and it would probably cost a greater effort if we were ever forced to repeat the task. The invitation of the new Governor was gladly accepted.

The Superior named Father Ruggieri to make the journey and Father Almeida was assigned as his companion. By order of the Governor, the Fourth Assessor, who was locum tenens during his absence, sent letters patent to Father Ruggieri authorizing him to travel in the provinces of Cequian and Huquam, and in the neighboring districts. The first move for Father Ruggieri was to go to Canton to purchase whatever was necessary for the voyage, which was to last for two months, and also to contact his traveling companion who happened to be there at the time. Fortunately, the great fairs were in progress when the Portuguese merchants were permitted to enter Canton, and Father Almeida, whose patience had come to an end, came along with them to see if he could find some means of arranging for a stay in China. One can readily imagine his excitement and his joy when he heard that he was selected, not only to stay but to go further into the Kingdom to open a new residence. In addition to that, he was also assured of making the journey in safety and at very little or no expense. This latter phase of the journey was brought about by the merest chance. The brother of our old friend, the Lin-si-tau, had come to the fair at Canton with a large stock of silk and other varieties of cloth which are produced in great quantities in the Province of Cequian. He had intended to sell the cloth and return to his home without delay, but not being able to get the price he had set upon it, he was forced to remain in Canton longer than he had planned. Finally, it was through our Fathers that the Portuguese merchants bought his merchandise at the price he was asking. We might say here, in passing, that the Portuguese never hesitated to spend their money or to reduce their gains when their doing so was a help to the cause of religion. In grateful acknowledgment of the favor, and because of our friendship with his brother, the Chinese industrialist took the Fathers aboard his boat and conducted them without mishap through the Province of Cequian, to his native village of Sciauhin, the birthplace of our first and also our present Governor. The name of this place is quite similar to that of our first residence, but among the Chinese a slight difference of intonation in pronunciation often indicates a considerable difference of meaning.

Among the various arrangements that had to be made before the Fathers separated, there was one thing in particular that should be recorded here since this was the first time it was adopted as a general practice. As we have mentioned in our first book, the Chinese have several names, but their real or proper name is never used except by a superior or when one names himself or signs his signature. In fact, a violation of this propriety would be an injury to the one addressed. Hence each one is honored with an added and a more honorable name by which he is addressed or named by others. Up to this time, the Fathers had always used their own names and were so called by their servants and domestics. To the Chinese this was, to put it mildly, quite unrefined. Therefore, in order to make themselves all things to all persons, for the winning of souls to Christ, they adopted the custom of taking an honor-name, as it is called, and this really was a necessary gesture if they were to maintain their authority among an infidel people who have no idea of Christian humility. From that time on, all of our missionaries going into the Kingdom took an honor name before entering, so as to make it appear that they always had it.

On arrival at the village of Sciauhin, in the Province of Cequian, they were received by the family of the Lin-si-tau, and given lodging in an annex to the family home, the part called the temple, which made a very suitable residence. There was only one entrance, common to the home and to the temple, which proved to be a convenient arrangement for excluding those of all classes who came to see the foreigners, and who did not belong to the higher or the literary orders of society.

This town, though not a metropolitan city, is always numbered among the principal centers of the province. It is distinguished for its commerce and also for its unique situation on an island in the middle of a fresh water lake. In this respect it reminds one of Venice. It is also renowned for its scholars and as the dwelling place of a great number of the educated class. During the receptions which took place in this house, frequent mention was made of the Christian religion, but without much effect, because one of the Fathers, knowing nothing of the Chinese language could only listen in silence, and the other, who could only struggle with it and spoke in a faltering and hesitant manner, had only an inexperienced old man as an interpreter. The white-haired father of the Lin-si-tau was baptized and received into the Church, and two or three dying infants were laved in the saving waters of baptism and sent to heaven, unconscious of it all. The whole town seemed to be quite pleased with the presence of the Fathers and particularly so the Governor of the district, who developed a close friendship with Father Ruggieri. It was a source of no little joy to have the Lin-si-tau here publicly proclaim his admiration for the visitors, as it led them to believe that they were already assured of a second settlement of the Society, and this one in the interior of the Kingdom of China.

9. The Fathers Lose Their New Abode. Father Ruggieri Makes a Tour of the Province of Quamsi

THE NEWS OF the Christian expedition to China had recently passed from India to Europe and to the whole Christian world, and was received with those sentiments of joy that Christian piety is accustomed to manifest on such occasions. The Holy Father, Sixtus the Fifth, granted a highly privileged jubilee to the Society of Jesus, with instructions that all should pray for the success of the missions in Japan and China. The Society in turn was prompt in publishing the salutary jubilee to be celebrated under the requisite conditions. Father Claudio Aquaviva, General of the Society of Jesus, sent letters to the missions, as an evidence of his paternal affection and interest. In these letters he besought his subjects to persevere in the Lord in the tasks they had undertaken, and not to be frightened or overcome by the difficult nature of the enterprise. For his part, he promised every possible help, first, by prayers, for which he called upon the entire Society, and then of men, who were afterwards appointed to the Mission. He also sent certain gifts that were very helpful in the mission work, among which was a painting of Christ, done by a well known artist in Rome, and four time-pieces, well wrought and artistically designed. Three of these were watches, made to be worn on a cord about the neck, so that the subtle workmanship of the machinery could be readily seen. The fourth, considerably larger, was a clock, designed for a table. It was more valuable than the watches because of its intricate works, without weights, and because it not only kept good time and struck the hours, but also sounded the half hours and the quarters in triple chimes. This timepiece became the talk and the admiration of the entire Kingdom of China, and with God's blessing it was destined to produce results that are still evident at the present time.

From Japan, Father Gaspare Coehlo, the Provincial, sent a larger painting of Christ, a real work of art, done by Father Giovanni Nichola, the first master under whom both the Japanese and the Chinese learned to paint in European style, to the great benefit of both national churches. A priest of a religious order in the Philippine Islands sent a beautiful painting of the Blessed Mother holding the Infant Jesus in her arms, with John the Baptist kneeling before them in devout adoration. This piece, painted in Spain, was beautifully done and pleasant to gaze at, because of the skillful blending of natural colors and the lifelike expressions of the figures portrayed. It was presented to the China Mission by the Rector of the College of Macao. Many other gifts were also received from people in various parts, proofs of their spontaneous liberality and interest. This happy beginning and fortunate progress aroused the interest of other religious Orders: of the Augustinians, the Dominicans and the Franciscans, but, as they were not permitted to enter the Kingdom of China, they had to remain in Macao, where they opened houses as centers, from which they carried on a very useful work, similar to their work of instructing converts in the Philippine Islands.

Once the house at Sciauquin was properly established, the missionaries devoted themselves more freely to the conversion of the gentiles. Certain days were appointed for preaching and some who were won over from their superstition and idolatry were duly baptized. The congregation was increasing with every feastday. What time was left over from their work was gainfully employed by the Fathers in laboring over Chinese books, with the help of an interpreter. In this way they increased their prestige among the Chinese, who have great respect for men of letters, and this respect increased under the force of their preaching and example.

The new undertaking at Cequian, however, was destined for a different fate. The relatives of the Lin-si-tau, fearing that the great number of visitors coming to see the Fathers might result in trouble, wrote a spurious letter directing the Fathers to return to their companions at Canton, and asserting that they were in danger with Father Ruggieri away. The fraud was quite evident, and so they remained where they were until our friend, the Governor of Sciauquin, who was misinformed on this occasion, rather reluctantly commanded them to withdraw. This order they had to obey, and Father Ruggieri returned from his journey and joined them at Sciauquin. The result of this event and of the letter of his relatives, was that the Lin-si-tau, who had been our ardent protector, gradually withdrew his friendship and finally dropped it altogether. He even notified the Fathers not to pay him the customary visit at the festivals of the New Moons, and ordered them to remove his name from the honorary tablets he had sent them for the door and for the reception-room of their residence, and also from the geographic map made by Ricci, which he had signed. Finally, when he met one of them in public, he replaced his usual courteous greeting with a scowl, but he made no move or reference affecting their residence. Beset by this unexpected calm, and with the wind gone from their sails, so to speak, they were forced to make what progress they could with their oars. Taking every possible precaution, they still feared that this mission would collapse under pressure of a storm of persecution. Hence, the present emergency prompted them to be alert for an occasion to open another residence in some other province.

The Lin-si-tau was a close friend of one Tan-siao hu, of Sciauquin, the Commissioner who had built the city tower, and this man made the most of his friendship, as the Chinese are wont to do. Having made up his mind to take advantage of the presence of the Mission, he came one day to talk about a certain mountain in the Province of Huquam, which the inhabitants call Vu-Tan, where great crowds were said to gather on pilgrimage. He asked Father Ruggieri why he had not visited the place and the answer was that he did not think the Magistrate would grant the necessary permission. The visitor assured him that he would take care of that, so far as the Lin-si-tau was concerned. From what he had said previously, the journey did not seem to be any too safe in the making nor did it promise much for the future. However, with permission of his Superior, Father Ruggieri decided to undertake it, in company with a very cautious interpreter, so that no means of rendering the Mission more secure might be left unattempted. In the course of his travels he came to the metropolitan city of the Province of Quamsi. This city is contiguous to the Province of Canton, and he decided to enter it. There was a relative of the King living here who was forbidden by royal edict from holding public office of any kind. Father Ruggieri made every effort to see this scion of royalty, thinking that his favor might further the Mission plans.

Evidently our Fathers were not as yet acquainted with the laws of the Chinese Republic and were judging things according to European custom. Father Ruggieri was not received by the Prince. Instead, he was sent away with directions to go first to the Viceroy and then to the other Magistrates, to get permission for the visit. The Viceroy lived in the same city and Father Ruggieri, rather boldly it would seem for a foreign priest without an introduction, followed the directions and called upon the Viceroy and the other Magistrates. He was received by each one in turn with little or no welcome, and, though he received no injury, he was advised by each one of them to continue on his journey, and to make no stop in that particular city. Still holding to some hope of success, before leaving, he again asked for an audience with the royal citizen, but the presents he sent before him were returned, and he was asked to leave the Metropolis without delay. This he did, and his departure was somewhat hastened by an edict published throughout the city against his presence, which placed the police of that quarter of the city where he dwelt, in jeopardy, for permitting a foreigner to enter the city without leave of the governing Magistrates. Finally, as though the safety of the town depended upon getting them out, the travelers had no rest until they were well beyond its enclosure. Fortunately, however, they did meet someone, and he, a member of the household of the royal personage, who showed considerably more sympathy for the misfortune of a foreign priest. One of the Prince's chief eunuchs, offended at the lack of hospitality on the part of the Viceroy, offered some words of consolation and presented Father Ruggieri with a letter to the Procurator of a village in the Province of Huquam, adjoining the Province of Quamsi. The village was called Pa-Sciui, and the letter was a grant for the Father to live at the home of the Procurator as long as he wished. This letter was equivalent to an order, because the Procurator himself was a subject of the Prince. In addition to this, he was promised that on the departure of the Viceroy, it would be arranged for him to return to the Metropolitan City from which he was now being unceremoniously ejected by the Magistrates. When Father Sande, the Superior, was informed by letters of all that was happening on the journey, he recalled Father Ruggieri to Sciauquin. There seemed to be little if any hope of effecting what they had set out to accomplish, namely, the founding of a new residence, and there was more than a possibility that this effort might endanger the work already in progress, but as yet lacking any guarantee of permanence.

10. The Superior Returns to Macao. The Harassed Missionaries Are Cleared of Another Serious Charge

~~~~~~

WHEN FATHER RUGGIERI returned to Sciauquin, the Lin-si-tau, learning what had happened on the journey, realized that the publicity given to it would be a source of further embarrassment for him. It was reported that someone from this province had written to him, telling him that Father Ruggieri had not been received by the Viceroy, had been spoken to very harshly by an Army General, and had barely escaped being thrown into chains. In addition to all this, there was the fear aroused at Cequian and the suspicion of the Magistrates of Canton. The whole affair was being looked upon in Canton as a presage of some great evil to the Empire, because of the presence of foreign priests from Macao, who were associated with and trading with the inhabitants of the city. The poor Governor was at his wits' end to find some means for getting out from under the accumulating burden of trouble, and issued an order for the Fathers to return at once to Macao. This order seemed to be timed to the moment. With it came the public announcement that the Viceroy of Canton was to be elevated to a higher position in the Royal City of Nankin, and that the Viceroy of Quamsi, who was said to have ignominiously ejected Father Ruggieri, was to take his place. Seizing upon this as a pretext, the Governor sent orders to the Fathers that they were all to return to Macao, whence they had come. In explanation, he said he feared lest the new Viceroy might take it amiss that foreign priests had a residence in the city in which he presided. He promised to refund what it had cost to build the mission houses, and that later on, if it were agreeable to the Viceroy, he would recall them as soon as possible. This unexpected order was more than a surprise to the Fathers who were filled with fear at the realization of the impending dissolution of a mission, the fame of which had already spread with great approval throughout the Christian world. Nor did it seem at all probable that there would ever be any recalling, once they were definitely dismissed. Immediately, the two Fathers, the first two to come here, betook themselves to the Governor's court, in sorrow and dejection, to present a final request.

Relating at length how they had traversed the great wastes of ocean before coming to China, how they had lived here for a period of years at great expense, and doing no harm to anyone, they asserted that they could not settle at Macao, and that it was out of the question for them to return to their home across the sea. Then they reminded the Governor of the sympathy and favor he had shown them when they first came. As to the Viceroy, they promised to explain their presence to him without involving the interests of anyone else. If his objection was, that there were more present now than at the beginning of the mission, would he not send away one or two and permit those to remain who had been formerly received by the Viceroy himself. To all of this his response was very courteous; saying, that he personally had always had a very high opinion of the Fathers, and that he had no reason for turning against them, but time and again he had received letters from the Magistrates of Canton, asserting their fear that the presence of the Mission would bring some great calamity upon the country. Added to this, there was the hatred of the people who took it ill that the praise for building the tower, which was their work, was falsely attributed to the foreigners, while they had borne the brunt of the labor and of the expense as well.

Moreover, he complained of Father Ruggieri having entered the Capital of Quamsi, where, as it was reported, he had been rebuffed and harshly treated by the Magistrates. The two Fathers explained all these difficulties as best they could, with the result that the Governor said he would take more time, and consider the whole affair. Their petition was then forwarded to Tansiaohu, the Building Commissioner, whom the Governor took into consultation on nearly all matters concerning the Mission. He did this so that he might benefit from the favor asked. These two were hand in hand. The Commissioner was the liaison man. The Governor was evidently holding out for a purpose, as he did when the Fathers first got permission to settle here. He had not forgotten that he was presented with twenty gold-pieces and numerous small gifts, as promised after the second request for a residence. In order to hasten the termination of the whole difficulty, it was thought best that Father Sande, the Superior, should go back to Macao of his own volition, before he was sent back. There he could await the final issue, and there too he was greatly needed because the merchant ship from India had not arrived, and no mail or assistance had come from the Father Visitor. This was sufficient reason to give a timely appearance to his departure.

Shortly afterwards, the Governor issued an edict relative to the affairs of the Fathers, which he ordered to be posted in the town in which they were living. The content of the document was substantially this: The Mission House had been built at the expense and by the labor of the foreign priests, but the tower was erected by the Court of Sciauquin, at public expense, to insure the happiness and prosperity of the Province. The foreigners made no contribution whatsoever to its building. Some of them had been received by the Viceroy, and they in turn brought in others to live with them. For that reason, and in keeping with the duty of his office, he had ordered them all to depart. Then, the edict continued, they presented themselves before him, weeping and wailing, protesting that they were an immense distance away from their fatherland, and mentioning the money they had spent. They asserted that they had been received by the Viceroy, had done no harm to anyone, had never violated a single law of the realm, and added other such claims in their own defense. Admitting, as he did in the edict, that he found all this to be quite true, and moved by compassion for their lot, seeing that they were religious men and given to the practice of virtue, he said he granted permission for one or two of them to remain at the house allotted to them by the Viceroys. All the others were ordered to depart and those remaining were warned not to bring in any more. If they did, they

too would be expelled post-haste and without ceremony. To disobey
this order would be only a proof that they were plotting a conspiracy
for the ruin of the Empire. To this edict was added a special order
to the police, commanding them in no gentle terms, to see that the
foreign priests carried out the requirements imposed upon them, and
to keep the Magistrates informed of everything that happened. This
proclamation afforded the Fathers a temporary breathing space, but
that was about all. The end of one difficulty seemed to be only the
beginning of another. Besides being robbed several times by night
intruders, and subjected to continual annoyance, the missionaries
were charged with a serious accusation from which, by the grace of
God, they were finally liberated.

A certain new convert named Martin, unworthy of the faith and of
the name, was received into the Church at Macao and proved to be
both a burden and a menace to the Mission. He had come to our house
at Sciauquin from Canton to see the Fathers or rather to defraud
them. Father Ruggieri made much of him, appointing him to various
little offices and duties, fearing that, because of his indifferent practice
of the Christian religion, he would have to dismiss him from the small
number of converts. His familiarity with the Fathers enabled him to
take advantage of several other converts of Sciauquin.

As we have noted elsewhere, there are many among the Chinese
who are so steeped in the practice of alchemy that it almost drives
them insane. They believe that mercury can be changed into silver
by the application of a certain herb which is found only in foreign
countries. Being the only foreigners here, word was spread about
that we had brought this herb with us and that we knew the secret
of its application. They endeavored to prove this by referring to the
Portuguese who, as they say, purchase great quantities of mercury
from the Chinese at exorbitant prices, and take it to Japan; whence
they return to their own country laden down with silver coins. From
this they concluded that the Fathers did the same thing, since they
saw them living honestly, asking alms of no one, and engaging in
no business, whence it must follow that they had plenty of silver made
with the mysterious herb. They find it difficult to believe that anyone
could be so honest as to bring silver to China from afar, and they do
not dream that anyone could be charitable to the extent of wanting
to teach others without being paid for it. Although no one has ever
discovered the secret in question, there is no lack of impostors who
spend their entire lives in pursuit of it, using every imaginable artifice in
the quest, and never yet has one of them been cured of the vice.

Among the new Christians at Sciauquin there were two, a father and a son, who before their conversion had burned up their whole fortune in the furnace of alchemy, and were not as yet wholly separated from it. These two came to the impostor Martin and asked him if it really were true that the Fathers knew the secret of making silver. To deceive them, he assured them that they did, and that Father Ruggieri had promised to teach him the formula, on condition that he would never communicate it to anyone else. The poor unfortunates took him at his word and immediately began to cultivate his friendship. Martin himself was poor and in need. They had a new coat made for him, took him to live in their home and gave him the best of things to eat and drink. More than that, they even bought a wife for him, as is customary among the common people, and all this to make him more beholden to them and finally to get his secret. At last, and with reluctance, he promised to reveal it to them but only on the same condition with which he himself was to receive it. Above all else they were to be cautious not to give the Fathers any cause for suspicion, as they might retract their promise if they thought he had mentioned it to anyone. This deceit and intrigue went on for three or four months, and finally when it could not be carried on any longer, he set a definite day on which Father Ruggieri was to make the revelation, and promised to pass it on to them soon after. When the day in question arrived, he stole the glass prism from the Mission House and fled to Canton, believing that he had secured a precious stone of great value. When his convert hosts heard of his flight, they came to the Mission House, bitterly complaining about the fraud of the impostor, and they revealed that he had robbed them of considerable money that was loaned to him, or paid for his bills, and asked for the Fathers' advice. Father Ruggieri made two trips to Canton before he discovered that Martin was somewhere in the City and that he had the triangular glass. That was news enough for his other victims. They tricked him into giving them the glass by sending him a letter, pretending that it was written by the Lin-si-tau, and stating that the Fathers would pay the money which Martin owed to his former hosts, provided they got back the precious jewel.

One day, while all this was going on, the Governor and several other Magistrates came to the Mission House for a short visit by way of recreation. In the course of the conversation he asked for the glass prism to look through it at the mountains, the rivers, and the boats in the harbor. The theft could no longer be concealed and he was told that Martin had stolen the glass. Incensed at the news, he immediately wrote a letter, gave it to an officer and dispatched him to the Capital with orders to arrest the thief and bring him back at once. The Fathers explained that the glass was really not as valuable as was commonly thought, and that they did not wish to press the matter any further, but their wishes were of no avail. In reply the Governor said he was not thinking of the Fathers but of the Magistrates of the City who came here from time to time for the pleasure of using the prism. One of the gendarmes, who knew Martin as a fellow citizen, was sent to Canton. He easily found out that Martin was in hiding, arrested his brother and threatened to put him in prison if he did not reveal where Martin was hiding, or at least restore the glass to him, which he said was worth more than all their belongings. With that, in order to save himself, the frightened brother delivered up the culprit to the law, and Martin was brought back to Sciauquin in chains.

By that time the impostor had succeeded in piling up a series of calumnies, even going so far as to spread leaflets through the streets accusing one of the Fathers of misconduct with a certain woman. The husband of the woman, who was a party to the calumny, presented the case to the Lin-si-tau, asserting that when he returned to the city from somewhere or other, he saw the leaflets scattered about, and going to his home he had to beat his wife to get her to tell him what had happened. Then he petitioned that the guilty party be brought to justice and punished accordingly. Martin was held as a prisoner. The alleged scandal was taken to the courts, but it was not difficult for the accused to dispose of the charge. On the day upon which the crime was supposed to have been committed, Father Ruggieri, the one in question, was absent in the Province of Quamsi on a two months' journey and that fact was well known to the judges. Finally it was revealed that the whole story had been concocted by Martin, and that the husband himself was very poor and expected a bribe to keep him quiet. In fact, the Fathers had been approached with that proposition, but they refused to listen to it, for fear that the stain of this calumny would remain, if it got abroad that they had cast a bone into the gullet of a noisy canine to end his yelping.

Fearing that he might end up with a total loss rather than an ill-gotten gain, the husband took to flight, and when the case was called into court, the judge was informed that the man's house was vacant and that he and his wife had disappeared. By decision of the court the Father was declared totally innocent and Martin was found guilty of the calumny. He was then ordered to be brought before the Governor and, in the presence of Father Ruggieri, he was cruelly beaten with twenty blows of a bamboo cane, sentenced to make amends to his debtors and ordered to the galleys. After the sentence was passed he was sent back to the Overlord, the Lin-si-tau, so that he who had handed on his case to the Governor might approve of the sentence. This was the utter undoing of the unfortunate fellow; for when the Lin-si-tau was told the whole truth he ordered sixty more blows with the bamboo cane, as vicious as the first. After that, the victim was thrown into irons and reduced to such extremities that he was deserted by all his friends and relatives. Only the Fathers, who were his victims, were left to take care of him, which they did, aiding him in every way they could until he died of his wounds, a few days after his punishment. This case served as a terrible example to other offenders. The other convert who had received the prism from Martin, hearing that he was in chains, returned it to the Mission of his own accord. He was afraid that if the Court heard that the glass prism was in his house, he too would be arrested and accused of the theft. Thus, by the grace of God, the Fathers were delivered from a perilous position and freed from an ugly calumny.

11.Father Ruggieri Is Detained at Macao. Father Sande Returns to Sciauquin. Another Outbreak

ACCORDING TO THE CUSTOM of promoting Magistrates, the Lin-si-tau should have been elevated to higher public office before this time, but no news of his advancement was forthcoming from the high court. He was becoming doubtful and sad, fearing that he had been passed over because of his friendship with the foreigners. Finally, Heaven lifted his doubt, as well as the fear of others and the impending danger to the Mission, all at once. He was informed that he had been selected for a position of great dignity in the province of Huquam; to the governorship of the Pu-cin-su, and his former happy disposition reappeared. We have already mentioned that the district of Sciauquin had dedicated a hall of sacrifice, a temple, to him in the atrium of the tower, as to a holy man who for so many years had merited well of the Kingdom. There was a statue of him on an altar in this temple, with a large urn before it for burning incense, placed between elaborately wrought candelabra. In preparation for his departure, the townspeople gathered in the temple to congratulate him on his newly acquired honors, with an unusual ceremony, unknown to Europeans but quite common among the Chinese. At his farewell reception a Magistrate removes the boots he is wearing and puts on a new pair. Then the old ones are placed in a decorated box which is sealed and kept in a public place as a souvenir in perpetual memory of a local public benefactor. This general custom is a civil ceremony, implying no superstition. It is customary in this way to testify to the virtue of a man who has merited well of the people.

The new Viceroy from the Province of Quamsi was presented at this reception, and the Fathers went to visit him, but with considerable misgiving. However, he granted them an official reception, with more courtesy than they had expected. He recognized Father Ruggieri from their former meeting and remarked that he knew him. The Viceroy was not to enjoy his dignity much longer. He was already very old, weakening with age, and died a few months later. The man who took the place of the departing Lin-si-tau was well known to the Fathers. He was brought from a nearby district to take this position, and formerly, when he came on official visits to the Viceroy, he would pay a friendly visit to the Mission House. All was quiet and peaceful at the time, with everything so disposed that we were looking forward to a period of relaxation. Father Ruggieri left for Macao on business; principally, to arrange for the return of Father Sande, the Superior. At Macao they thought it would be best for Father Ruggieri to remain there and await the return of Father Alexander Valignano, the Official Visitor of the Society to the entire Orient, who was en route to Japan with the Japanese legates on their return voyage from Europe. In the meantime, Father Matthew Ricci obtained permission for Father Sande to return to Sciauquin, which he did, to offer some comfort to his afflicted brethren in this time of quiet and also some advice for the development of the Mission.

New storms were brewing and the winds of persecution were rising from diverse points. The two converts, who had lost their money when the unfortunate Martin died, were resentful toward the Mission and set themselves to planning various schemes for causing trouble, though the Fathers knew nothing whatsoever about their dealings with the deceased. They began by spreading leaflets in the streets insinuating that Father Sande had been brought back to Sciauquin contrary to the edicts of the Magistrates. They threatened that if he did not depart, within a certain time, all the student Bachelors would convene and present a complaint to the courts. There was an admixture of other charges in the leaflets also, which made it difficult to decide definitely which course to take in such circumstances. But this was only the beginning of the trouble. The next incident shook the house to its very foundation.

The village of Sciauquin is built upon the bank of a well-known river flowing through the Province of Quamsi, a two or three days' sail from the Capital City to the sea. During the past year, this river overflowed its banks and the force of the flood did much damage in the towns and villages. The levees built to restrain it were either broken or submerged. Our house, although built in the flooded fields, stood firm, though the levee admitted the waters to all the lower spaces. When the flood abated, and the river was confined to its bed, a great horde of men was summoned to rebuild the dikes. This year the flood was more destructive than the last; so much so indeed, that it washed out the new embankments in no time. In order to stem the tide of the flood and to secure material for repairing the protections, the City Government granted permission for anyone to cut down trees whereever they might be, provided they were not fruitbearing. Taking advantage of this permit, bands of vagabonds entered neighboring gardens and destroyed everything in sight and no one could restrain their insolence, armed as they were with public authority.

When a frenzied crowd rushed into our yard they came face to face with an Ethiopian guard, a black African, such as one meets on the voyage from Europe after passing the Cape of Good Hope. The Portuguese call them Cafres. They are big and robust by nature and utterly fearless. This one chased away the whole mob, single-handed. I believe the Chinese are the most easily frightened people in the world, and they feel a certain horror at the very sight of a black man, as though he were a devil or an opaque ghost. At first, the crowd took to flight, and then realizing their cowardice they reassembled and from a distance showered the house with stones. We could easily have driven them off by force, because nearly all of our domestics were from India and almost as dark as the Ethiopian. The house was high and strongly built and would have served as a good bulwark for protection. But we had to be careful not to offer them another pretext for calumny, and in these circumstances it was thought better to be restrained. At first, they were throwing the stones with an air of fear, but when they saw that there was no opposition, and that the Fathers were taking it very patiently, one excited crowd gathered into a thickly packed group and rushed into the house with such violence that in a few minutes they smashed windows, doors, furniture, and even the roof. Finally, when the entrance-walk was somewhat cleared, they broke down the wall between the yard and the street. Father Sande and his interpreter went out by a side door to inform the police. Father Ricci remonstrated with them and pleaded with them to take whatever they wanted from the house without ruining everything, but when he exposed himself, to talk to them, he was showered with a rain of stones that really endangered his life. Moved by some sudden impulse, he gathered up a bundle of bamboo sticks, about all that was left of the garden hedge, put them on his shoulder, and pushing his way into the thickest of the crowd, told them very humbly, to take this bundle, and more if they wished, to repair the broken levees, and to cease destroying the house in their mad fury. The poor heathens were so affected by this gesture that they ceased throwing stones and went away, taking nothing with them save some wood that was scattered about the yard. As they were leaving, they raised a tumultuous din of rejoicing; sounding cymbals as a sign of victory and congratulating each other on the successful attack. With night approaching they disbanded and disappeared into their homes.

Early in the evening, one of the assembled magistrates was sent to offer aid and, being moved with sympathy at the ruinous state of the house, he called some soldiers and ordered them to stand guard at the entrances during the night, for fear some of the frenzied mob or other robbers might get into the ruins and carry off what was left, or perhaps do even worse. On the following day, this same Magistrate, who probably was bribed, reported everything to his superiors just as he pleased. Father Ricci received word of the garbled report and went straightway to the Governor, to whom he complained of the indignity contained in the injury done. Then he asked that no further inquiry be made into the whole matter, because it was a confused question of mob violence which is always very difficult to punish. Any punishment that might be meted out, as he explained, would only result in further trouble for the foreigners. It would be quite enough if the Governor would issue another edict threatening anyone who molested them in the future. This sounded like very good counsel, accompanied as it was with calm and patience. So the Governor issued the edict and that was the end of the incident. Father Sande, realizing his presence there would be of no great advantage, returned to Macao and reported the whole story to the Visitor General in order to get his counsel.

12. Father Ruggieri Goes to Rome to Arrange for an Embassy from the Pope. Father Antonio Almeida Goes to Sciauquin. New Difficulties Here Originate in Canton

WHEN THE VISITOR GENERAL learned from eye-witnesses of the turbulent state of affairs through which our Fathers were passing at the Mission, he gave all his attention to discovering some new means by which they could acquire more prestige in the Kingdom of China. He deemed this to be so necessary, for the missionaries to carry on their work, that without it he saw little hope of any further progress. The work would be well grounded if their residence was established with the permission of the Crown, without which it seemed to be neither certain nor enduring. After long deliberation on the various ways of going about this undertaking, the most appropriate method seemed to be for one of the Fathers to arrange an Apostolic Delegation to the King of China. By means of such an embassy, equipped with gifts and authorized by letters from the Pope, they could probably guarantee a permanent station in China. Father Ruggieri was the pioneer of the Mission. He had seen it develop from the beginning, and so he was selected for the task proposed.

By order of the Visitor General of the Society, Father Matthew

Ricci, with the assistance of a Chinese scholar, was to write the letters which were to be addressed by the Pope to the King of China, also a letter to the Viceroy of Canton and letters patent which the Pope was to give to his Ambassador. These letters, all written in Chinese, were to be sent from Europe, and when elegantly done in large characters, the Chinese undoubtedly would be greatly pleased to receive them. The Visitor himself wrote several letters: to the Holy Father, to the Catholic King, to the General of the Society, and to others who, as he thought, could advance the cause. He also sent some novelties from China to be presented to them or to be placed on exhibition for the public to view. One of these specimens was a descriptive painting of the entire Kingdom set in a distinctively oriental framework. These frames are delicate screens of most exquisite workmanship, that fold in one upon the other and when opened are beautiful to look at, standing upright without supports and sometimes filling a whole room. In the native language they are called Guer-Pim. They say the Pope and the Catholic King were greatly pleased with the screen paintings they received. Samples of the crown and of the costumes of the King of China, and the distinguishing insignia of the different grades of Magistrates, were some of the other souvenirs sent to Europe.

On his journey to Rome, Father Ruggieri was shipwrecked coming in to port at the islands known as Tercerae. He saved what he could of his luggage, and disembarking at Lisbon, with what he had left, went directly to Madrid to visit Philip II, King of Spain, who received him with more cordiality than is customary to Royalty. The King took it upon himself to use his authority to promote the embassy with the Pope, and agreed to contribute his own timely assistance to the China cause. At Rome the whole undertaking was greatly retarded by the successive deaths of two or three Popes, with the result that Father Ruggieri, worn out from his many labors, retired to Salerno in the Kingdom of Naples, where he spent the rest of his days.

In the meantime, Father Ricci lived at the Mission House alone, where he received an unusual number of visitors from the Chinese of all classes. These visits were probably incited by the novelty of a collection of European curios. What the visitors marveled at most was the clock he had set up for the house and for the neighborhood. It not only told the time of day to those passing by but to people at a distance, by sounding the hour on a large bell, and they could never quite make out how it could ring of itself, without anyone touching it.

Taking advantage of the present tranquility, the Father Visitor sent Father Antonio Almeida to the Mission as a companion to Father Ricci. He had already been designated for this position and it was decided to send him in without even asking a government permit to do so. He had hardly arrived at his post when news came from the Metropolitan City that a serious accusation had been presented against the Fathers to the Province Inspector, called the Ciai-yuen. It came about in this way. There are among the Chinese a certain class of Venerables, so-called, not so much because of advanced years, but because of the reputation they have acquired for good living, which chiefly consists in the fact that they have never personally summoned anyone to court and have never been summoned themselves. Once a year the Magistrates give a solemn banquet in their honor, at public expense, and they enjoy certain privileges, such as a special mode of attire, admitting them to all court hearings. The reason assigned for these distinctions is, that they make a profession of protecting the public weal, without demanding any recompense. These Venerables were disturbed by rumors from Canton which were persistently spread against the foreigners, who were said to have built the tower at Sciauquin. They concluded that the cost of the tower, amounting to four or five thousand gold pieces, was defrayed by the Portuguese of Macao, by whom the Mission was supported, and the only purpose they could see in it was the creation of some great misfortune to the Country. Surely it was something that must not escape the Official Government Inspector. The accusation, very skillfully drawn up in writing, and properly worded to carry persuasion according to the precepts of Chinese eloquence, is well deserving of repetition. We shall therefore render it word for word in so far as we are capable, though we believe that it must necessarily lose some of its force and natural grace, being arrayed in the strange garb of a foreign language. Here is the letter of accusation sent to the Inspector.

In view of the fact that it is permitted by the laws of the realm for every subject to advise his superiors of whatever he may judge to be harmful to the public good, we, the Ancients of the City of Canton, having observed certain irregularities, are of the opinion that they should be communicated to you, as Official Inspector of the District, so that by your intervention, suitable remedies may be applied. First, you should be informed that certain foreigners, now dwelling in the Metropolitan City of the Province of Sciauquin, have come here from outside nations to establish residences within the Chinese

Kingdom. There is grave reason to suspect that their presence indicates more than is evident, namely, that some great misfortune is in store for the country. Evidence of this is plainly apparent, as is amply illustrated in what we have hitherto revealed. A great gathering of foreigners from the barbarous countries beyond our confines has come ashore at the port of Macao, of the City of Ansan. Now that they are preparing an embassy to the Crown, it would seem that under this pretext they hope to open an entrance for themselves into our country, to trade with our people in staple products, for mutual profit. Although they asked for no grant or permission for such proceedings, and have not as yet succeeded in establishing the embassy, nevertheless, they continue to mill about the port, and for some years past have been coming inland and trading with the natives, despite the prohibition against strangers entering the country. When the annual fairs close, they then set sail and return to their own country. Recently they have begun to build two-story houses in which they are gathering like bees or ants.

There is not a person in the Province, who is aware of all this, whose hair does not stand on end, whose heart does not tremble at the thought of it, and especially so as it is known that these foreigners, who are adept at deceit and trickery, are every day attempting something new. They supplied enough money to build a tower as a means of getting into the town of Sciauquin, and of bringing in others, wicked men who are continually coming and going by boat. Indeed, we have grave cause to fear that they are spies of other countries seeking to discover our secrets. Moreover, we fear that after long acquaintance with our people, who are naturally curious about novelties, they might induce some of our folks to find their way across the distant seas, as do the fish and the whales. This in itself would be a public calamity. It would, in fact, be the verification of an epigram contained in our books: "Sow a fertile field with thorns and nettles and you are bringing serpents and dragons into your home." The dangerous condition at Macao is like an ulcer on the hand or the foot. It can be cured if cared for in time. The difficulty at Sciauquin is within, like an ulcer pressing on the lungs and the heart, and reason itself demands that it be given immediate attention. This, Honorable Inspector, is our reason for judging that you should issue orders to the Magistrates of Sciauquin to get rid of these intruders as soon as possible; to send them back to Macao, which in turn you can also relieve of its impending danger with the lapse of time and at the opportune hour. If you do this, you will save the life of the whole Province which will publicly admit that from your action it received the greatest possible blessing. The end of the letter of the Ancients.

The Official Inspector of the Province at that time, called Ciai, took great pride in the reputation he had acquired for vigorous enforcement of the law; hence he was universally feared and commanded the respect of everyone. He decided that this whole affair should be carefully examined, and then committed the investigation to the Grand Admiral of the Sea, of the Province of Canton. This position is officially known as Haitu because it handles all foreign affairs of the Province. The Admiral in turn handed it over to the Governor of the District of Canton, who sent letters patent signed by the Inspector, to the Governor of the District of Sciauquin, ordering him to open a judicial inquest and to return his findings to Canton. This order was known to several notaries, and Father Ricci was warned two days in advance that he would be summoned to court. From these same notaries he also received copies of the accusation drawn up by the Ancients and of the letters patent. Just at that time the Governor was absent from Sciauquin, having left for Pekin to take part in the solemn ceremonies of obedience, which are held every third year according to general custom. His Lieutenant, the Governor's Assessor, named Phan, a man of kindly nature and of a pleasant disposition, was an intimate friend of the Fathers. He sent for Father Ricci and informed him that the Inspector had a case against him and his companions. Knowing what it was all about beforehand, Ricci vehemently objected to the accusation as a whole, admitting some things and denying many more, and asserting that the item relative to the expense of the tower was a flagrant calumny, which the whole village would reject, if called upon to do so. The Assessor replied that the experience of several years was sufficient to convince him of the character and of the innocence of the Fathers. In fact, he was indignant at the idea that these importunate old men should meddle in the affairs of others, involving the interests of Sciauquin, about which they knew next to nothing. Then he advised Ricci to clear himself and his associates by suing his accusers for libel, saying that he himself would guard their interests and carefully submit to the Visitor what truth and reason revealed. Finally, he dismissed him, advising him to keep up his courage.

On the following day, the Lin-si-tau, having terminated his outside concerns, returned to the city, knowing nothing whatsoever about the new accusation. To pay him the customary respect that their position required, Fathers Ricci and Almeida went to visit him, where he was sitting in court. By way of rendering him benevolent in their present trouble, Ricci gave him the triangular glass prism, which he liked to look through and which he was very anxious to possess. He seemed to be pleased with the gift and especially so, when he learned on inquiry that it would cost very little in Europe. He doubted that assertion, and suspected they were lowering its value so that he would more readily accept it. Such a novelty as that, he assured them, would bring a high price anywhere, and in order to avoid a possible accusation of accepting a gift of any kind, he said he would rather buy it than accept it as a present. Then he called for two gold pieces which he paid for the glass and which, under the circumstances, it would have been an uncivil gesture to refuse. So it is, that Chinese Magistrates live in continual fear of the charge of venality in public office. As a result of this visit they were confirmed in the good graces of one of the highest Magistrates, and the permission for Father Almeida to remain was accordingly sanctioned.

It was on this visit that Ricci took occasion to redress the injury contained in the accusation of the Ancients. He explained that it was eight years ago that he and his companions, attracted by the glory of the Chinese Empire, had come from Europe over a vast expanse of twenty thousand miles of ocean. He explained that he himself was a man devoted to religion and vowed to poverty, and that his only profession was to serve the Supreme Deity. During all that time he had, as he insisted, been scrupulously careful to do no harm to anyone and to observe to the letter the laws and regulations of the Kingdom. This, he asserted, is the point upon which the extraordinary assertion in the accusation is chiefly centered, and it would be a cause of great worry and disturbance if the judge appointed to sit upon the case were not a man who was universally known to be a stickler for the law and a strict defender of justice. He claimed that in a court of strict justice it would be a foregone conclusion that he and his associates would easily be vindicated of the charges hurled at them. He then asked that a rigorous investigation be made of the indictment and that the results be duly forwarded to the Inspector. This request was passed on to the Governor's Lieutenant who immediately opened the judicial process, in the course of which he was always on the alert to protect the innocence of the accused, and particularly so, as he had already discovered that the whole complaint was contrary to the truth. The full proceedings of the trial were referred to the Lin-si-tau, so that the judgment might carry more authority. Just as all had hoped, he approved of everything, but more than any had expected, he added a high encomium of the Fathers. At the end of the documents of the process he attached an ordinance, to the effect that the petition of the Fathers and the full details of the trial be returned, not to the Governor of Canton, from whom the written accusation was received, but directly to the Official Inspector. That proved to be a benevolent gesture which, once and for all, put a felicitous end to this particular and decidedly dangerous incident.

From the very beginning of the case, Father Valignano had been kept informed of what was going on, and he was having Masses said and prayers offered for deliverance from the impending danger. When he received the letter announcing the happy termination of it all, he thanked God for the great grace bestowed upon the Mission and told the others how happy he was at the success attained. Then, as it were to spite the Devil, who seemed to be set upon chasing the Fathers out of China, he appointed another Father to the Mission, Father Francesco de Petris. Let us here insert what looks like a signal proof of this man's vocation to the China Mission. He had only recently arrived from Rome with the Japanese legates, returning home from their visit to the Pope. His original appointment was to Japan, though his heart was set on China, but he would not express his desire to Superiors, feeling, as he did, that his wish would be granted if it pleased God so to arrange it. He rejoiced at his new assignment as coming directly from Heaven, and with the assistance of Father Sande he immediately took up the study of the Chinese language and characters at Macao. He was a man of sterling qualities and particularly adept in the handling of men, but the Chinese got only a glimpse of him. He accomplished much in the short time allotted to him, as we shall see later on.

13. A Future Fruitful Harvest Is Planted at Sciauquin

OUR HOUSE at Sciauquin was appropriately situated for the purpose for which it was erected. It was not within the enclosure of the city, where surrounding noises and the clamor of the multitude are a hindrance to the proper conduct of Christian ceremonies. Neither was it so far distant from the town as to be lost beyond the suburbs, or in a desert place exposed to robbers. It was just below the town to the west and conveniently situated on the bank of a large river which almost washed the doorsteps. The river was usually covered with a flotilla of barges, and it was easy for us to make the semiannual trip to Canton, where we had to go twice a year to get the financial allowance made to the Mission by the College at Macao. This voyage was made when the Portuguese traders were permitted to bring in their merchandise for the fairs. At the same time they brought mail and presents from distant parts of Europe. If at times we were called to the College at Macao, on business, we could make an easy journey on the same river. Our House was also favorably situated for missionary excursions among the pagan villages on the opposite bank of the river, which in some places is a third of a mile wide, a very pleasing sight to look upon.

The fame of the temple built in the vicinity, attracted large crowds of people including the high city officials. The Magistrates used the temple as an excuse when they wanted to visit us, because visiting ordinary citizens, and especially foreigners, was considered to be below the dignity of their office. Here in this town also there were frequent assemblies of the state officers from the Viceregal courts of two provinces. These gatherings are customary when candidates are first admitted to the magistracy, when they are elevated to higher positions, or when a solemn ceremony, like the birthday of the King, requires them to assemble as an act of fealty. Besides these there were many other events that called for numerous gatherings. The first reports of our arrival and of the presence of the wonderful things brought from Europe attracted many to the house, and many more came rather to see our house than to visit the Viceroy. The big clock facing the road was an object of wonder to some and the smaller clocks, to others. The European pictures and statues, the mathematical computations and the geographic relief maps also drew much attention. Our books, although printed in a language unknown to the Chinese, were greatly admired because of their unusual bindings and the splendor of the gilt work which was something altogether new in China. These people are delighted and amazed when you show them books containing descriptive maps, or specimens of building architecture illustrated in diagrams or designs. They simply marvel at the idea that whole countries can be viewed in one book, with cities, towns, palaces, lofty towers, arches and bridges and majestic temples. They are curiously interested in the thought of witnessing the grandeur of these things so widespread and distant from each other, and of seeing it all right at home in their own houses. The same may be said about their admiration of our musical instruments which they like for their soft tones and for their novelty of design. The effect of all this and of the conversation and discourses of the Fathers, which are always well adapted, seems to be that they have gradually formed a better opinion of Europe in general. They realize that fundamentally our sciences are more solid than their own and that the Chinese in general, and especially the educated classes, have had a wrong idea of foreigners up to the present, placing them all in the same category and calling them all barbarians. And so they have finally begun to make clear the real differences which exist between nations.

The Fathers have made an effort to merit a reputation for learning, not as a matter of vain-glory but with a view to the end for which they came here, namely, to further the cause of Christianity, which on all occasions they purposely weave into their conversations. The leaders among the Chinese do not easily pass over to a new religion, but most of them admire the truth, and do not hesitate to publish it, once it is known. Moreover, they say that truth does not come to light of itself, rather it is made known in the religious life of those who preach it, and the Chinese are not only zealous searchers for the truth, they are also ardent admirers of sanctity. Whenever they come to visit the Fathers they always pay their respects with the regular ceremonies, and their visits are made more impressive by offering presents. This is not at all a general custom when the educated class are visiting priests, except perhaps when the priests are foreigners. These favors are generally repaid with European gifts which they accept with grateful thanks, considering them as more precious than their own, because the novelty of such gifts increases their value.

Not infrequently the Mission House was full of visitors, who were attracted not out of curiosity for the novelties, but for something more useful, the salvation of souls. The streets about the house were frequently crowded with palanquins, and the river with gondolas and with the larger boats of the Magistrates, which are rendered very imposing by their size and very attractive by their ornate decorations. These visits of the Magistrates and of the Literati soon spread the reputation of our faith and of our missionaries beyond the confines of Sciauquin, and even over the boundaries of the Provinces of Canton and of Quamsi, until it was beginning to be known throughout the whole Kingdom. The governing Magistrates were continually being summoned to this central seat from other provinces to consult on public affairs, and as they are changed about every three years, it soon happened that those who had some knowledge of our teaching carried it far and wide, wherever they were officiating. Thus the paths were opened gradually but imperceptibly for those who were later to preach the gospel in other parts of the realm.

It was here, while he was Military Commander, or Pimpithau, that we made the acquaintance of Sciutagim, who afterwards held the high position of Scilan in the Royal Palace of Nankin. It was here too that we became acquainted with Theno, who was elevated from the office of Pucimsu in this city to that of Viceroy at Nankin, and also with another dignitary who became Viceroy of the Province of Hoiceu. Then there was our friend Sciutaiso, frequently mentioned in our annals, whom God rewarded with the gift of faith for his many benefits bestowed upon the Society of Jesus and upon the Church in general. Here I should also mention our close friend and benefactor, Ignatius, the name he took in Baptism. There would be no end to the list if we were to enumerate all those of the Province of Canton who finally became Magistrates and were afterwards instrumental in the progress of Christianity. As yet, of course, all this was only potential fruit, still hidden in the seed, to develop into a fruitful tree, affording the blessing of its restful shade.

Neither the hope of the first years nor the fruits already garnered were to limit the progress of this Mission. Day by day the harvest was becoming more and more mature. The number of new converts was in-

creasing with every solemn feast until the chapel was crowded to
the altar rail and becoming too small for the attendance. When the
sacrifice of the Mass was over, a sermon was preached on the fundamentals of the faith, and on one occasion at the conclusion of the instruction on baptism, eighteen were baptized. At times it seemed as
though God enlightened the souls of the people by extraordinary
happenings.

On the opposite bank of the river, there lived a man who, seized by
some kind of terrifying panic or perhaps by the Devil, wandered
around among the tombs at night. He certainly acted like a demoniac.
His parents called in the priest of the idols to deliver him from this
evil and importunate spirit, whereupon the idol-worshipping priests
left nothing undone of profane exorcisms, and filled the house with
monstrous pictures of demons, as was their customary ritual. But
one devil could not be chased by another and that perhaps was so
ordained to spread the light of Christianity. The man's father was told
by one of the neophytes that the law preached by the European
priests was very powerful against such spirits. He called one of the
Fathers and asked him to do something for his son whose cure seemed
to be beyond all remedy. The Father who was summoned was slow to
believe that the victim was really possessed of a devil, and so he did
not perform an ecclesiastical exorcism. Instead, he ordered them to
take down all the horrible pictures of monsters attached to the walls
and to burn them. Then he recited some prayers and suspended a little
reliquary, containing a holy relic, about the neck of the afflicted and
went away. No sooner had he left the house than the man seemed to
have shaken off his torment and was perfectly well. Later on, his father
brought him to the chapel where he received instructions and became
a Christian, as did his whole family, and the father went about the
streets telling everyone that his son had been delivered from a devil
by the God of the Christians. Another man named Leam, a minor
official, with no children after several years of married life, but desirous of having a family, was told by one of the Fathers to make this
a subject of fervent prayer to God. In time his prayer was heard and
he became the father of twin boys. He was so pleased with the event
that he himself became a Christian and presented the children to
God by having them cleansed of original sin in the saving waters of
baptism.

It was indeed a source of relief and of rejoicing to us, who had encountered so much adversity, to realize that we were no longer merely

hoping for results but actually witnessing them. Besides the neophytes who were daily becoming better acquainted with the precepts of Christianity, many infants were baptized and entered heaven to become intercessors for their nation before the throne of God. The Mission at Sciauquin was also a great help to Macao. The Portuguese who came from there to treat with the Viceroy were frequently assisted by the Fathers in the transaction of their businesses. More than once we were instrumental in delivering shipwrecked Europeans who had met disaster on the treacherous sands of the Sea of Canton and were led captives to the court of the Viceroy. The Mission was also conveniently situated to render assistance to fugitive slaves from the City of Macao. Every year some of them succeeded in shaking off the yoke of servitude and sought liberty among the Chinese, where they seldom found it. These fugitives were generally apprehended by the Military Prefects, a body of men more courageous and more skilful at arms than the regular soldiers, because of their association with the Portuguese. For the most part they are Japanese, the terror of the Chinese Kingdom, or African Ethiopians, called Kafirs, or perhaps from the greater or lesser of the Java Islands, or other such, whose fierce and barbarous nature makes them more warlike than the Chinese. When the fugitives are brought before the Viceroy by the military police, if they are Christians, he admonishes them to be mindful of that fact, grants them pardon and advises them to return to their masters. Ordinarily it is not difficult to get them to return, because they realize that submission to the Prefects is even more drastic than servitude to the Portuguese. Both parties profit by this proceeding; the servant returns to where he can practice his religion, and the Portuguese family recovers a servant whose labor is very valuable.

Several times during this period, when the Ambassadors from the Kingdom of Cochinchina were making their triennial visit to the Chinese Imperial Court, to which their country is tributary, they took occasion to visit the Mission House, on their way to see the Viceroy who was to send them on to the King. If one were to judge from the demonstration they made, they were evidently greatly pleased with their visits. We presented them with several books treating of the Christian religion, the best of which was a catechism printed in Chinese characters, which they read in common with the Chinese, though their spoken languages are as far apart as the poles. Our purpose in giving them these books was based on the hope that some day, if we succeeded in gaining an entrance to their country, these books might have rendered them well disposed. Such an entrance is always possible if there are laborers to make it, and the means are not lacking.

14. Last Efforts at Sciauquin and Expulsion of the Missionaries

EVIDENTLY THE ENEMY of the human race was envious of the great progress being made by Christianity at Sciauquin, and of the certain hope of a more abundant harvest to be reaped in the future. He was certainly interrupting this new work by new schemes and new tricks, which we cannot relate in detail and which would not be worth relating, if we could. What he could not do himself, he left to the care of his emissaries to be accomplished in detail. These he discovered among the inhabitants of Sciauquin, some of whom, from the educated classes, were well suited to his purpose. These men were particularly envious of our familiarity with the civil authorities because of the prestige and the reputation it afforded us. Hence they took advantage of the arrival of a new Viceroy, to endeavor to oust us from our residence.

By order of the King the place of the lately deceased official was filled by the Viceroy of the neighboring province of Quamsi, a native of the Province of Nankin, named Leu. This man's timidity was so increased by superstition, that he would not take over the palace of his predecessor until the building was razed to its foundations and a new structure erected at enormous cost to the viceroyal treasury. He was afraid that a house in mourning would bring him only bad luck, and so he retired for the time being to a nearby village on the boundary of the Province of Canton. Hither came all the civil authorities to pay him the customary visit on his arrival. Among them was the head City Prefect of Sciauquin, named Than-Siarihiu, whom we found it difficult to place in either category of friend or enemy. The new Viceroy was told about the tower that was recently erected and the temple in it, dedicated to a well deserving Magistrate. All this had taken place very recently, and since it was done in favor of a deceased Viceroy, promoted from the magistracy, the new incumbent, ambitious for public honors, thought he might also be a candidate for such a memorial in Sciauquin. In fact, being a friendly enemy of ours, it seemed quite probable that he might decide to have his memorial temple in our residence; at least this seemed to be his reason for caus- ing us such trouble, at the instigation of the people, and what followed on his arrival could readily warrant that conclusion.

In a letter to the Lin-si-tau, the new Viceroy asserted that for some time past he had known that there were certain foreign religious from Macao in the town, who were communicating to the Portuguese a knowledge of everything that happened in China. They were, as he said, continually inventing new devices and methods for attracting the simple people, using their discourses and books for that purpose, and they even had a metal clock on public exhibition which struck the hours without anyone touching it. Knowing all this, as he did, according to his letter, after legal investigation, he informed the Lin- si-tau that he would either send them back to their own people at Macao as soon as possible, or that the local authorities could have them confined within the limits of the town of Xaucea, where they could lodge in the temple of Nansoa. At that time, as he added, there were more than a thousand pagan priests connected with that particu- lar temple. When the Lin-si-tau received this letter, he ordered the Lieutenant Governor to advise the Fathers, on his behalf, to go to the temple as ordered, and that he would see to it that they would be restored to their present residence when the Viceroy had completed his term of office. In reply, they requested that he institute an ex- amination of the objections made against them and then report every- thing truthfully to the Viceroy. His answer to this was, that he was fully aware of their innocence and that he was just as anxious to defend them now as he was formerly, in the case of the Ancients of Canton, but he was equally aware of the determined will of the new Viceroy, and that opposing it could only result in more harm than good.

Father Ricci sent a messenger post-haste to Macao, to the Visitor General of the Jesuit Province, who, though not sharing directly in the trouble, was sympathetic with those who did. Ricci's opinion was, that for the time being, it was necessary to follow the orders as issued; to change their domicile either to the temple named or to some place, as directed by the Viceroy. Thus they would not irritate the Viceroy, and if they had not entirely fallen from his favor, there would still be hope left of obtaining a suitable residence elsewhere for the present. This, at least, would afford occasions for returning to instruct the neophytes and, perhaps too, there would be some remaining hope of recovering their own residence later on. The Reverend Visitor General, however, held quite an opposite opinion and directed that on no condition whatever should they accept another residence, and by no means should they ask for one. They were to make every possible effort to retain their present home, and if they finally failed in that, they were to return to Macao. He said there were fields of labor elsewhere in which they could expend their efforts with more liberty and with greater hope of a harvest. In obedience to the orders of his Superiors, Ricci took up the defense of the cause by drawing up a series of requests. The Civil Magistrates were wholly in sympathy with the Fathers' complaint about the injury done by the Viceroy, but there was no one who dared to resist the will of so potent an adversary. Scarcely had this man taken office, a victim of avarice as he was, when he began to make trouble for everyone from whom he could extort anything, among whom were the Chinese merchants of Canton who were trading with the Portuguese. One of his prospective victims was a certain pirate Captain who had obtained a pardon some years before from the Superior Court, and was now living as a retired and a respectable citizen, doing no harm to anyone. Fearing, as he did, that the new Viceroy might institute another process against him, in desperation rather than from ennui, he gathered together his band of buccaneers and returned to his former trade of freebooting and of pearl fishing, off the island of Hainan to the south, in direct contradiction to the orders of the Crown.

Ricci decided to go personally and to visit the Viceroy who was still living in the frontier village, but the Viceroy had heard that a pirate was causing trouble along the coast and had gone to Canton to make preparations for war upon the corsairs. When he stopped off on his journey to Sciauquin, several of the City Magistrates recommended the case of the Fathers in a friendly way, and while he answered in a manner that would lead one to believe that he had nothing against them, yet he could not be persuaded to permit them to retain their residence. His mind was too preoccupied with the idea of a temple to be won away from it, consumed as he was with a burning ambition for popularity.

In this whole affair it would be difficult to determine the assistance contributed by the joint efforts of the Magistrates as a body. Just at that time, several of them stationed at the Royal Court of Pekin wrote to the Lin-si-tau, asking him to purchase some purple draperies from the Portuguese merchants and to send them on to Pekin. Not wishing to miss an opportunity that might assist the Fathers in gaining the favor of the Viceroy, the local Magistrates selected Father Ricci, rather than the Chinese merchants, to handle the purchase with the Portuguese traders, by whom he was well liked, and among whom he had considerable authority. The Viceroy himself arranged for Ricci to make the journey in a large boat with many rowers, and accompanied by a military Captain and several courtiers. There was a demonstration of welcome on his arrival in Macao, knowing, as the people did, what he and his companions had accomplished and the laborious trials they had endured. This journey offered an opportunity for solving several difficulties which could scarcely be treated safely in a mute exchange of letters. One important decision was reversed, namely, permission was granted to endeavor to set up a dwelling somewhere else, if the Fathers did not succeed in retaining the one at Sciauquin. This alone meant new strength and new encouragement for further undertakings, and Ricci hastened back to his station as soon as he could complete the commission entrusted to him by the civil authorities. On his return they gave him a friendly reception and, rendered more benign by the favor he had done them, they sought new means of defending his cause.

By this time the new palace of the Viceroy was ready for occupancy but before he came to live in it, he repeated his order to the local officials to dismiss the Fathers from the town. The officials in turn, still hoping for a better solution of the problem, decided to await his arrival before taking action. Finally, he did arrive at Sciauquin, still determined to get rid of the foreigners. The Magistrates then reminded him that these strangers had spent more than six hundred gold pieces in erecting their buildings, which was a considerable sum of money among the Chinese. They said that this statement rendered him somewhat dubious as to how he should act. He did not want to be accused of doing an injury to an innocent party, against whom there was no legal charge, as the courts agreed, and yet he could not return that much money to the foreigners. The sum was more than enough to build a good temple. He finally decided that they should be allowed fifty, or at most sixty gold pieces, and then be sent back to Macao.

When the Lieutenant Governor offered Ricci this money, he said that
he could not sell a house dedicated to the service of God, and that he
did not wish to appear to his own people to have so dissipated the
Mission property, because they might justly say that he had squandered it to no avail. Moreover, it would be a foolish bargain, as he
insisted, to exchange six hundred gold pieces for fifty. And so, as if
directed by Providence, in an exchange of dwellings, he concluded to
accept nothing from the Viceroy and he did this, not because of the
price offered, but in order to retain a right of action to recover
the residence at some future date. The events that followed proved the
wisdom of this decision for the preservation, or rather for the restoration, of the entire undertaking.

For a third time, Ricci went to the court of the Viceroy to refute,
viva voce, and in the officials' presence as well as in writing, the numerous calumnies in circulation, and to ask for an explanation of the
order which the Viceroy was said to have issued. Each time he came,
he was dismissed without ceremony, and with the same reply, namely:
that anyone who refuses the gifts of the Viceroy is unworthy to see
him. That put an end to all hope of saving the house at Sciauquin. The
last effort to be made was to change the tenor of the request, by soliciting the Magistrates to use their influence to prevent an outright
expulsion from the Kingdom, and to secure a permit to open another
residence anywhere it could be arranged for. The Province of Quamsi would be suitable, or even the Province of Chiansi, or any place the
authorities saw fit. By this time the Viceroy had become enraged, and
he issued a peremptory order for the foreigners to be sent back to
Macao, adding that he wanted to hear no more about these aliens or
about their affairs.

According to Chinese custom, when the Official Inspectors for the
Crown have completed their examination of the state affairs of a Province, and of the reputation of its civil authorities, before returning to
Pekin to make a report to the King, they pay a farewell visit to the
Viceroy of the Province just visited. This official call is generally attended with great pomp and display and made with considerable
retinue. The Viceroy of Sciauquin, probably suspecting the kind of
report that would be turned in about him, decided to make an impression on the occasion by accompanying the Inspector for a distance
up the river, at the time of his departure. With him, he took all the
governing Magistrates, the Literati, and the military police of the city.
The whole river was covered with boats and skiffs and its banks were

crowded with spectators. The sound of their various musical instruments was as displeasing to the ear as the general spectacle was pleasing to the eye. The Fathers and a few of their friends were watching the great display from the windows of the Mission House. Just after it passed the house, to their great surprise, and to that of the crowd of onlookers, who were utterly at a loss to understand the movement, the boats all turned and headed down the stream. Then, lo and behold, they stopped at our landing and the dignitaries came ashore. The Fathers, aghast at the gesture, made a hurried exit to receive them with the usual social and urbane rites of hospitality. The official party came in and examined everything in the house; pictures, clocks, pieces of glass-ware and whatever else was a novelty to them. What pleased them most was Ricci's museum and particularly its wealth of European and Chinese books. When they had seen the interior of the house, they passed out to the veranda overlooking the river. During the course of their call they asked all kinds of questions about things European, which we answered obligingly, and the visit terminated, seemingly at least, to the full satisfaction of both parties concerned.

From here the Crown Inspector returned to the Metropolitan City and the Viceroy to his palace. The favor of such an exceptional visitation prompted our friends, and our enemies as well, to conclude that the decree of expulsion had been revoked, and the feeling of fear in the house gave way to an impression of security. Indeed, the Magistrates even sent their congratulations and advised us to make no move until the final decision of the Viceroy was promulgated. It seemed as though peace had been finally restored.

At the beginning of August, like a bolt from the blue, the Viceroy, emboldened by the departure of the Inspector, issued a judgment, based on his own ideas rather than on equity or justice, which he wrote out to put an end to the whole matter. This was a mandatory order to the Civil Magistrates to expel the foreigners from the city as soon as possible and send them back to their own country, and in doing so, to give them as the price of their house, sixty gold pieces to defray the expenses of their voyage. It was left to the Lieutenant Governor to carry out the sentence, and he, in his sympathy with the Fathers and not wishing to make the sad announcement, kept putting it off as long as he dared. One day, when he happened to be with the Viceroy, he was asked if he had carried out the orders given him relative to the aliens. When he answered, "Not yet," his superior burst into a fit of anger. Whereupon, the Lieutenant called two of his attendant Prefects, and, according to legal procedure, had an edict copied on to a large tablet. With this done, the Magistrates had no choice but to announce the sentence to those against whom it was directed, and we were given three days to get beyond the confines of the Province of Sciauquin.

Quite overcome by this bolt, Ricci went to the Governor's Court, where the Lieutenant Governor very kindly handed over to him for inspection an account of the whole proceeding, written out in full detail. It contained the petitions made by the Fathers and the answers given by the Magistrates, all of which were surprisingly favorable to Ricci himself, and attached to it was the final sentence of dismissal, reading somewhat as follows: Although Matthew Ricci entered the Kingdom of China with no sinister motive, and, as due investigation has shown, he has violated none of its laws while here, it is not becoming to him that he should be wholly forgetful of his own native land. He must know that one can lead a religious life anywhere he chooses. Nor is it proper for strangers to remain too long in this Province. Therefore, there is no injustice or incivility done in sending him back to his own country. As to the amount of money he spent in building his Mission House, I do not deny that it was considerable, but since that money was collected as alms it did not in reality belong to him. Therefore, of the amount allotted to him by the Magistrates for expenses on his return journey, namely, sixty gold pieces, let fifty of it be taken from my personal account, and with that let him take his departure.

In reply to this, Ricci answered that so far as the money was concerned he was very thankful but he did not need it to get back to his people, nor did he wish to accept any amount for the Mission House. The Lieutenant Governor in turn was not insistent upon that particular point. Then he asked if it might not be possible to send him off to some other Province, and to leave his companion at Sciauquin with their belongings. This request the Lieutenant Governor granted more readily than he had a right to, and so, cheered by the hope of doing this, the house furniture was divided up; some to be left at Sciauquin and some to be taken on the voyage, but that was just so much labor lost. The local Prefects ordered everything out of the house and informed the departing Missionaries that the boats assigned for their voyage by the Magistrates were going to Canton only and not beyond it. Again Ricci went back to the Lieutenant Governor who informed him that the order of the Viceroy had to stand as given, and that he could make no change in it. This meant that he and his companion must return to Macao.

As pastors of souls, nothing grieved the Fathers more than being forced to abandon to the ravening wolves about them, the flock they had rescued and nourished with so much labor and care. The crowd of neophytes that gathered about them weeping and wailing like children at the funeral of a parent, only served to increase the sadness of their departure. And they too wept to think that they were leaving their spiritual children without a teacher to instruct them in the truths of their faith, and without a pastor to serve them the spiritual nourishment of the sacraments. Without comfort to themselves, but concealing their grief, they sought to enliven hope in these poor souls by exhorting them to preserve the Christian faith in the midst of a pagan nation, and to remember what it had taken them seven whole years to learn. They promised to return before long, when peace was restored, and again take over the mission they were leaving behind.

In the meantime, the converts were to take a statue of Christ the Saviour and place it in the house of one of the neophytes, where they were to gather for religious services on the holy days. In order to assist them in recalling these days, Father Ricci had arranged a catalogue of the Church feasts, with reference to the Chinese feasts which follow the phases of the moon. They were reminded that in these gatherings they should pray in common, talk of the divine mysteries, and conduct other such pious Christian exercises. Then exhorting them to be courageous and to remember that such was the lot of the new-born Church, which developed through trouble and trials, they were sent off to a certain spot on the banks of the river, where they could wave a final farewell to their departing friends.

In this sad departure the Fathers were careful about one thing in particular, namely, that since they were not abandoning hope of returning, they must leave on the best of terms with everyone and without giving offense to anyone. They must not only make no threat or complaint but rather ask pardon of all, if perchance they had unwittingly given offense to anyone. And yet perhaps a few threats would not have been altogether out of place. Even the most considerate among the Chinese would entertain a fear that foreigners who had acquired so much knowledge about the kingdom and who were being so inconsiderately expelled, might use that knowledge to the detriment or even to the destruction of their country. In truth, even our enemies rather mercifully turned to sympathy and admiration, when they saw us leaving in a placid state of mind, after suffering so much injustice.

The only ones to seize upon things of value in the house were the Prefects of the local Police, and when Ricci took these things away from them and threatened to inform the court of what they were doing, they became frightened and put an end to their depredations. The neophytes were given presents of pieces of furniture, which they took with reluctance, and the rest of it was given to others, to be placed in storage. With the baggage placed aboard and the Fathers embarked, the boats proceeded to the place assigned for the neophytes to meet them just beyond the city. Here Ricci ordered a stop and presenting himself to the Lieutenant Governor handed over to him a large bunch of keys, and at the same time thanked him profusely for the assistance he had offered them, assuring him that his kindness would never be forgotten. Again he was offered the money and again it was refused. The Lieutenant Governor asked if they would sign a document attesting that the money was offered and refused. This was done, and to the document there was added a message of thanks to the Viceroy and a request that he would not permit the Mission House to be used for any profane or unworthy purpose, because it had been dedicated to religious service. Then in turn, Ricci asked the Lieutenant Governor if he would place his seal on a document, to the effect that they were not being expelled from China for any crime committed, and that during their sojourn they had lived a life of religious quiet. The effect of this document was to remove the dishonor of proscription from the minds of those who needed to know the truth. This he did very willingly, and added a high encomium of the two who were departing. Of his own accord also he wrote out a letter forbidding anyone from interfering with them or treating them in any but a civil and a cordial manner during the course of their journey. In closing he issued orders to the Mayor of the City of Canton, in the name of the Viceroy, to supply them with transportation and with a military guard as far as Macao. With all that at an end, Ricci returned to the place where his companion and the converts awaited him. Here in the sorrow of thwarted desires, they consoled the neophytes with a brief and appropriate farewell talk, and took their departure, and with it the good wishes and the blessing of all assembled.

It happened providentially that when they arrived at the Metropolitan City, the Prefect of the Admiralty happened to be away. He was to return in a day or two, and during that time they took occasion to purchase some cloth, the kind from which their cassocks were made. This delay also afforded Ricci time to write to the Visitor General of the Society at Macao and to the others there, saying that the Mission had been expelled from Sciauquin by the Viceroy, and that he and his companion would arrive in two or three days to tell the whole story in detail.

BOOK THREE

1.The Mission Is Restored. New Residence at Xaucea

~~~~~~

IT WAS WITH such Tantalian labors that the small band of Jesuits built up the mission to the heights we have described. Thus far, it was like rolling a great stone up the side of a high mountain and having it slip out of one's control just as he was about to reach the top and then roll back to where he started. The result, of course, was sorrow and grief for the one who had perspired in the effort. However, so strong was the hope of success of the two who had undertaken this mission, that when they were able to turn their thoughts and direct their efforts to their original design, they decided to forget about the past and to begin all over again. With that decided upon, they gave thanks to God and girded themselves for the task.

While they were still living aboard the barge that had brought them from Sciauquin to Canton, awaiting the arrival of the Admiral, on the second day of their sojourn, a brigantine appeared, advancing under fast moving oars and steering directly at their boat. At first they were surprised and perplexed, and particularly so when they were asked on behalf of the Viceroy to return straightway to Sciauquin. There was no one aboard the other boat who could tell, or who even knew, why they had been recalled. The order sounded favorable and they immediately took advantage of the occasion, realizing, as was very probable, that once they had reached the Island of Macao, it would not be an easy matter to get back into the Kingdom of China. Humanly speaking, the fear of the foreigner had so permeated the soul of the Chinese that once they had departed, it would have been impossible to obtain per-

mission to return. It was with this in mind that they gladly decided to
return to Sciauquin immediately with those who were sent after them.
Even before their arrival, their reputation had given rise to various
rumors concerning their return. It was reported that the wife of the
Viceroy, who was given to the superstitious adoration of idols, had had
a strange dream which influenced her husband to recall the foreign
priests. Others said that the Viceroy himself was troubled in conscience, fearing that the aliens who were unjustly treated might endeavor, with the help of the Portuguese, to avenge the wrong they had
suffered.

Whatever may have been the reason for the recall, when Father
Ricci went to the Lieutenant Governor, he learned that the Viceroy
had been informed of their departure the day after they left Sciauquin.
This meant that the Lieutenant Governor had carried out the order for
their expulsion, but he had also informed his Superior that he could
not by any means induce the Europeans to accept the money they were
offered. This was proven in Father Matthew's own hand-writing. The
Viceroy was astounded at this and his anger was evident on his countenance. He had already planned to make a temple out of their residence, dedicated to himself, and he had reason for being fearful of
being blamed for injustice. It looked as if he had trumped up a pretext
for taking over their house by pretending to be doing something for
the public good, in chasing out the foreigners, whom several other
Viceroys before him had received very courteously and treated very
respectfully. It seems as if Heaven had so arranged matters, that the
Viceroy commanded the Lieutenant Governor to man a fast frigate,
with plenty of rowers, and to set out with all haste to overtake the
journeying strangers, and when they had returned, to make every
effort to have them accept the sixty gold pieces* that had been offered
to them. He wanted to have a marble inscription engraved, which he
afterwards did, to place in front of the Mission House, stating that he
had paid for its purchase. The Lieutenant Governor exhorted and admonished the Father by all means to accept the money, reminding him
that a show of stubbornness could result in serious harm, but the
money was again refused for the reason often stated, namely, that since
it was utterly unbecoming to accept that money, it would not be unbecoming to keep refusing it, if this were not done in disdain. Then he
was informed that he would have to appear before the Viceroy. This

---

* Trigault writes 'aureos.' Nowhere in the Journals is the value of the gold piece
determined, though it is frequently mentioned. cf. D'Elia. TRANSLATOR.

rather pleased him, though he did harbor some misgivings about the
results which might follow from his visit.

When Father Ricci entered, the Viceroy was seated in his chair of
judgment whence he radiated a sense of fear for most people because
of his show of majesty. There was a Chinese interpreter with the
Father, but he knew very little Portuguese. He was brought along as
a companion, and for show, because the Father needed no interpreter.
As he was making a double genuflection, at some distance, as was the
rule before a sovereign magistrate, the Viceroy asked him to come
closer to his throne. With a gracious smile and a pleasant voice, he
asked him why he had not accepted the money, offered to him in good
faith, to pay the expense of his voyage. That it was being offered in
good faith was quite evident, as he claimed, from the fact that he had
recalled him to offer it with his own hand, not wishing him to leave
without receiving some kind of gift. To all of this Father Ricci replied
that he was very thankful indeed, but that he really had no need of
money, because he was returning to his own country and to his own
people, and he was certain to meet friends and companions on the
way who would take good care of his needs and wants. To which the
Viceroy answered, "Be that as it may, you must realize that it is still a
discourtesy to refuse a gift from a Viceroy." To which Ricci in turn replied, "Since you put me out of my house, where I lived for so many
years without harming anyone, and sent me off as a malefactor, it did
not seem to be unreasonable, nor did I consider it to be an act of incivility, to refuse the present you offered." At that the Viceroy became
really angry and rising to his feet, he began to speak somewhat inco-
herently. "Can it be," he shouted, "that the Viceroy gives a command
and is not obeyed!" Whereupon he turned toward the interpreter and
continued, "The cause of all this trouble is this villian here who told
this other man what to do," and in his excitement he ordered his court
officers to bring out an iron chain and fasten it around the interpreter's
neck. At these words, the poor man, in consternation, tried to remove
the blame from himself by declaring his innocence and asserting that
Father Ricci, being hurt by the loss of his house, had become stubborn
in this matter of the money. Ricci agreed to this, freeing the interpreter
from all fault and taking the full blame upon himself. He then boldly
advised the Viceroy not to become angry without sufficient reason,
assuring him that if he really was as friendly as he pretended to be,
instead of becoming upset over a few pieces of money, he should rather
be considering the terrible perils to which Ricci himself was being ex-

posed in having to sail the great expanses of the ocean, without a seeming reason. After all, if he did not want him to remain in the viceregal
village, why not send him somewhere else? Any place at all would be
quite acceptable. At first, the Viceroy did not fully understand what
Ricci had said, but a Captain standing at his side, bent his knee and
made clear to him just what the Father did say. Finally, his excitement
subsided, and he replied with a feeling of pity that he had not intended
from the beginning to expel the Fathers from the kingdom, but to send
them to some other city. With that, Ricci asked to be allowed to go to
the Province of Quamsi or to that of Quiamsi, but that was something
that could not be granted, because these provinces were not within
the jurisdiction of the Viceroy. He was then told that any city within
the Province of Canton was open for choice, excepting Sciauquin, the
viceregal seat, and Canton, the capital city, in either of which the prolonged presence of foreigners would not be tolerated. So, Ricci selected
Nanhium, a frontier village in the Province of Quiamsi. That was
agreed upon, but the Viceroy advised him to go first to the cloister of
Nanhoa, which has already been mentioned, and from there to the City
of Xaucea, and if neither of these places appealed to him, he could
then settle down in the village of Nanhium.

Evidently, the Viceroy had been won over and was pleased with the
interview, for when Father Matthew thanked him in true Chinese
fashion, by bending down and touching his forehead to the floor, the
high Magistrate produced a package of books, which he presented as
a token of his friendship. These books contained a history of the wars
against the pirates, and of other seditious outbreaks, which had been
put down by the Viceroy. Fortunately, on this particular occasion, the
Assessor of the Governor of the district of Xaucea happened to be
present. He had come to pay his respects to the Viceroy, who took occasion to inform him that the Fathers were going there to live, and
recommended them to his protection, because he was sending them
there.

The Lieutenant Governor of Sciauquin, happy at the success of the
interview, and rejoicing over the fact that the Mission was to remain
in China and to settle at Xaucea, very kindly placed the Fathers on the
boat, fortified them with diplomatic documents, and sent them off to
Xaucea. He recommended the Fathers to the acting Lieutenant Governor of Xaucea, the Assessor, who happened to be at Sciauquin, and
went with them to pay him a visit. When Ricci came into his presence,
this official was somewhat bewildered and remained for some time

without saying a word. On recovering his composure, he said to the Lieutenant Governor of Sciauquin, "What does all this mean? Only last night, in a dream, I saw several strange gods, such as we are not accustomed to see in our temples. I have no doubt but that these foreign priests are the persons I saw in my dreams." Turning then to Father Ricci, he spoke to him very respectfully, and from that time on, whenever occasion occurred, he was always very considerate in handling their affairs at Xaucea. Besides other favors, whenever they went to visit his court, and that was not seldom, he sent them a daily allowance of food from his own house. He also offered to take them from Sciauquin to Xaucea in his own boat, but since they had to wait for a day to accept the sixty pieces of gold and the letters of credence, and he himself could not defer his departure, he went on ahead and arrived a day or two before them.

When Ricci settled up his affairs in Sciauquin, he took time to call on all the Magistrates, and finally on the Viceroy himself, to thank him for his newly bestowed favors. This time he was received very graciously and assured that they might depart contented, because he had recommended them highly to the Governor of Xaucea, asking him to give them a suitable dwelling and to see to it that they were in no way molested.

We have already noted that at the time of departure, some of the furniture of the Mission House had been left in the custody of the Christian converts. It was these same converts who were first to congratulate the Fathers on the new decision made by the Viceroy. The missionaries had no sooner left the place the first time than some of the trouble makers accused the converts of having stolen what they were only keeping in custody. This difficulty, however, had been forestalled by the Lieutenant Governor who called for a written inventory of all the furniture and kept the list in his archives so that nothing would be lost and the converts would be protected against this very calumny. Later on every piece was restored intact.

They left Sciauquin on the feast of the Assumption, 1589. Directing their course toward the City of Xaucea, they arrived at a place called Sanceui, the Three Waters, where the Xaucea River, coming from the north, empties into a much larger stream. Here one has to change to boats that are built to navigate against the current, and during the delay occasioned by this change, they sent letters to the official Father Visitor, who was still at Macao, informing him of all that had happened.

On this particular journey they experienced no trouble from anyone, though they were in continual fear of a military brigantine that sailed beside them day and night, without ever getting very far away. There was a general suspicion that it might be a pirate bark, but on arrival at Xaucea it was learned that the Admiral had sent the boat along from Canton, with orders from the Viceroy to furnish the Fathers with a safe convoy until they were disembarked. For eight days they sailed directly west and came to a place from which, by a short overland route, they could reach the Temple of Nanhoa. At this stop, the servant of the Governor of Xaucea was awaiting their arrival, with orders to take them to the Temple and to provide a suitable place therein for their furniture. Now, they had no desire whatever to live in this place, at a distance from the village, preferring rather to dwell in the village proper, where they could preach the Gospel. So they decided to leave their furniture aboard the boat until they could see the Lieutenant Governor, explaining at the same time that they would be pleased to visit the famous temple.

This cloister was situated on a beautiful plateau, surrounded on all sides by pleasant hills on which, in addition to their natural beauty, an artistic arrangement of fruit orchards gave them an appearance of surpassing charm. Because of its mild climate and even temperature, this place never feels the rigors of winter, and these hills are never despoiled of their foliage. The plain is fertile in rice and in other vegetables, and is especially blessed with a permanent stream which runs through the middle of the plain and irrigates the area. The temple itself, magnificent in its grandeur, is built upon the most beautiful of all the hills and is copiously supplied with fresh water from a large fountain, graciously designed and wonderfully built. On the plateau and contiguous to the temple is the cloister, the dwelling, as they say, of a thousand priests of the idols. They are the lords of this demesne, inherited as a benefice from the impious piety of their ancestors. This institution had its origin with a man named Lusu, some eight hundred years ago. They say that he lived on this very spot and that he acquired a great reputation for sanctity because of his unusually austere manner of living. He wore iron chains against his flesh, and he was continually sifting rice and lightly pounding it, the way they do. In a single day he would prepare enough of it for a thousand temple dwellers, or conventuals. His flesh became so torn and mutilated by the iron chains that it was actually putrified and running with maggots, and if one of them fell off he would replace it and say, "Can you find nothing to gnaw? Why are you thinking of deserting me?" His body is enshrined in this magnificent temple, which was built in his honor, and the people, who venerate his memory and whatever belonged to him, come here on pilgrimage from all corners of the realm.

These idol-worshipping emissaries of Satan are divided into twelve lodges, each with its own chief, and there is a supreme ruler over all, who governs with absolute power. These pagan monks had already heard of Ricci and when they learned, on his arrival, that he had been sent by the Viceroy, they came to the conclusion that he had been named Superior of the place to reform their abandoned morals according to the rules of regular temple dwellers. Some of them lived dissolute lives and had many children, and many of them carried on a brigandage that made the roads unsafe to travel.

Throughout the entire kingdom, all those who sacrifice to idols in the temples are subject to the Magistrates, as are the common people. For this reason, perhaps, the upper or educated class do not adore idols and do not recognize the temple priests as their religious ministers.

On this occasion, in a council of the superiors, it was agreed not to show Ricci any place that might be suitable for a lodging, and yet, with the cunning of the Chinese, dressed in the full pomp of their sacrificial robes and pretending to be greatly pleased with his coming, they went out to meet him and showed him about the place. In their very politest way, they offered him the whole temple and assured him that everything connected with it was at his disposal. At the palace, he was received in the particular quarters reserved for the reception of the highest Magistrates. On the day of his arrival he was tendered a sumptuous banquet and afterwards shown the chief attractions of the temple.

This whole edifice was practically filled with idols fashioned from copper and other metals or from wood enriched with gilded decorations. There were more than five hundred of these idols in a single hall. The temple had numerous towers containing copper bells, one of which was so peculiarly cast that neither Ricci nor his companions had ever seen anything like it in Europe. The temple ministers also showed them the body of Lusu, enveloped in that peculiar shiny bituminous substance, known only to the Chinese. Many say that it is not his body, but the people believe that it is and they hold it in great veneration. In the middle of the temple there is an elevated section to which one climbs on an elegantly decorated ladder, and in this upper part there are about fifty hanging lamps which are lighted only on certain designated days. While the visitors were viewing all this, they too were being scrutinized. To the temple dwellers nothing seemed stranger than the fact that they paid no homage to their idols, for although the Chinese place no faith in idols, they do not disapprove of them nor do they think it an unholy practice to bow before them.

The ideas of the Fathers were perfectly in accord with those of the Superiors of the place, who expressed their fears that the beauty of their temple was not exactly what was being looked for. They had come there perfectly resolved to refuse anything they were offered by way of a lodging. The village at the foot of the hill was a densely crowded settlement and, on their arrival there they assured their host that, if they were to remain in this district, they would prefer the village to the temple as a place of residence.

At last they were under way for the village of Xaucea. Father Almeida had reloaded the baggage on a boat and went aboard to make the trip by water, but Father Ricci took the overland route which was much shorter. With him went the Lieutenant Governor's servant and the Grand Master of the Temple and two of his companions. He had decided to go along either to lend the honor of his company or to find out from the Lieutenant Governor what orders had been given by the Viceroy. The first one to be visited upon arrival was the Lieutenant Governor, to whom Father Matthew reported that the Temple seemed to be anything but an appropriate place for them to live in. It was too far from the town and too far away from the educated classes and the Magistrates, among whom, as among their equals, they were accustomed to live. He explained that these temple dwellers had an unsavory reputation, that one could not live with them in safety, and that his law and the books pertaining to it were altogether different from theirs. Then he added, "We do not adore idols; we adore only the one true God of Heaven and earth." The only reply to this was mute astonishment, because the Lieutenant Governor firmly believed that there was no law other than their own, and that there were no other written characters in all the world besides those known to the Chinese. He was so determined in defense of this belief that no amount of persuasion could turn him from it, until Father Ricci drew his breviary from his sleeve and showed it to him, remarking, "These are our prayers and this is how they are printed." With that, he admitted he was overcome.

The Grand Master of the Temple was looking on at all this and said it was all very true, because, only the other day, Ricci had visited the shrines of the idols and had paid no homage to any of them, even to

Lusu himself. In conclusion the Lieutenant Governor agreed with Father Ricci that the ancient Chinese really did not adore idols, and that this custom was introduced in later times. To this the Grand Master, instead of entering an objection, added a further explanation, namely, that idols as such were not worthy of any honor, but the wise men of the past, realizing that religion could not be preserved among the ordinary people without some kind of images, invented these figures for that very purpose. This declaration by the Grand Master was perfectly timed for the occasion, with the result that the Lieutenant Governor decided that they must find a place in the village where the Fathers could reside. When they heard this, they thought it would be wiser to put an end to the doubtful issue at once by accepting the present favor, rather than open the question of a residence in Nanhium. At the Lieutenant Governor's request, they then visited the Magistrates of the place, who proved to be very courteous, even more so than those at Sciauquin. Their friendly reception may have been due to the fact that the Magistrates knew that the Fathers had come on invitation from the Lieutenant Governor, or because they knew that they were well trained in Chinese ceremonies and in the Chinese language, better, in fact, than they themselves. While they were looking about for a place to build a house, they were told to take all their baggage and move it into another temple called Quamhiao, on the opposite side of the river, to the west.

The town of Xaucea is situated between two navigable rivers, which come together at this point. One river flows east of the City of Nanhium and the other, coming from the Province of Uquam, runs west of it. The walled-in village, with its many dwellings, is built on the plain between the two rivers. Being so placed, the village proper can not expand, so they cross the river in both directions to enlarge the settlement. The west bank is more thickly populated, and there is a boat-bridge connecting it with the island settlement. There were about five thousand families in this town. The rich earth about it is fertile in rice and fruit trees and there is an abundance of meat and fish and also good vegetables, but the climate is unhealthy and the weather generally bad. Every year, from mid-October to December, about a third or a fourth of the population suffer from a tertiary fever, so violent that to many it proves fatal. Those who recover from it remain pale and gaunt, indicating its malignant nature. This climate is even more dangerous to foreigners than to the natives, and some who have come here for trading have succumbed to it in a few days.

Right beside the temple just mentioned, there was a large vacant field, suitable for all the mission needs, and the court officers of the Lieutenant Governor advised the Fathers to ask him for it, as it belonged to the temple and hence came under the jurisdiction of the Magistrates. On the following day he came to the temple to pay the Fathers a visit, and to talk over a place of residence. They pointed out the field in question, and he thought it was an excellent choice. The Superiors of the temple and those who lived in it offered various reasons why they should not be deprived of their land. They did not like the idea of having strangers, who preached a law different from their own, living so close to them. The Lieutenant Governor paid little attention to their objections. Instead, he informed the Viceroy in writing that the foreign priests did not wish to live in the temple of Nanhoa and were asking for a vacant field near the Temple of Xaucea, outside of the village on the west bank of the river. In the meantime, while waiting for a reply, and not wishing to do anyone an injustice, the Lieutenant Governor advised the missioners to buy the field at a price asked by the land commissioners of the district. The Commission had already been bribed by the Superiors of the temple, for part of the price to be received, which was to be equally divided among them, and the venal commissioners asked eighty and more gold pieces for the property, which was really worth eight or ten.

The reputation of the European priests attracted all the dignitaries in the district surrounding the village, and here again the officials were found to be far more polite and considerate than their fellow notables at Sciauquin. Many of them developed into intimate friends. Unfortunately, perhaps because of the excitement caused by too many visitors, or maybe because of the difficulties they had passed through, the Fathers fell on evil days. Both of them came down with an almost fatal malady, and were left without provisions and without anyone to administer the assistance necessary for their recovery. They were both prepared for death, with their thoughts fixed upon the cause and purpose of their work, when behold, all unexpectedly, and for the preservation of the Christian expedition to China, by God's holy will and with no remedy whatsoever, save what came from Heaven, they were both restored to health. This happened simultaneously with the arrival of the Viceroy's ordinance granting them possession of the field. The Lieutenant Governor then authorized the acquisition, by granting the necessary letters patent. Shortly afterwards, with the recovery of some of the strength they had lost in their illness, they set about building a residence. The temple priests were paid nothing for the land, because it was decided by the authorities that they had exceeded all bounds of justice and of reason in demanding such an exorbitant price.

2. Father Valignano Stabilizes the Mission

IN THE LETTERS sent from the Capital city by Father Matthew to the Fathers at the College of Macao, they were informed that Ricci and his companion had been expelled from Sciauquin and expected to arrive at Macao in a very short time. Day by day their arrival was expected, and realizing the difficulties they had encountered and the labor they had endured, rooms and beds had been made ready for their repose, for a period of retirement and religious quiet. Father Fernando Martinez, a Portuguese, was at the college at the time. He was regarded as a holy man, was particularly devoted to the advancement of the faith in China, and never missed an opportunity to forward assistance to the Fathers working in that vineyard of the Lord. Whatever the others judged or said about the expulsion, he insisted and repeated that it could not happen and that they would not return to Macao. When Father Francesco Caprale asked why he was so sure of it, he replied, "Are you too as incredulous as the others? Rest assured you will not see Matthew Ricci at Macao in the near future." This answer was so surprising to the inquirer that he had no doubt that God had revealed something to Father Martinez.

In order to clear up the dubious situation, the Superior sent in a domestic with letters; one who had formerly worked for them at Sciauquin. First he went to Canton and then to Sciauquin, but he could find out nothing about the Fathers, save that they had been put out by the Viceroy and had set sail for Canton. Inquiries were made all along the road but no further information was discovered and the servant returned to Macao without accomplishing anything. That was enough to increase the suspense and to arouse suspicion that their companions had met with some evil, either by design or by accident. A second messenger was then dispatched, more able than the first, with orders not to return without certain news of the Fathers, or in their company. At Sciauquin he heard only the same story; so he went about inquiring everywhere and of everybody until finally by chance, or rather by the grace of God, he came upon the captain of the boat that had taken them to Canton and back again to Sciauquin, and after that to Xaucea. This man not only supplied the desired information but gave the messenger letters entrusted to him and destined for Macao. With these in his possession, the servant hastened back, his errand completed.

The news that they had settled in a new residence caused the community at Macao to rejoice in heart and in soul, and to offer prayers of thanksgiving to God. The Visitor General of the Society sent in a messenger with letters full of paternal sympathy which inflamed their zeal for their new undertaking. He advised them to exert every effort to establish a new center and not to interrupt a work, the fame of which had already reached Europe, the Holy See, the King of Spain and the rest of the Christian world, whose expectations must be fulfilled, if at all possible. It seemed to the Father Visitor that in the ordinary course of Heaven's design, after the labors and the failure at Sciauquin, the future must hold a promise of a more abundant and a less troublesome harvest.

After a short time and much to their pleasure, the Father Visitor sent them two young men who had been brought up and instructed in the school at Macao. One of these, Sebastiano Ferdinando, is still alive and active at the present time of writing. Of the other, Francesco Martinez, who died piously and, in a way, for his faith, we shall say more later on. Not long after their arrival these two entered the Society of Jesus and made their noviceship at Xaucea. They were the first Chinese to be received into the Society and they proved to be a great help to the Fathers who overcame many a difficult obstacle with their invaluable assistance, as this history will reveal. The Father Visitor also called two Portuguese priests from India, who studied Chinese characters and writing at Macao while waiting for the movement of the waters, an expression used for a favorable opportunity sent by divine clemency to advance the progress of the Christian religion in China. These two Fathers, whom we shall name at a more appropriate time, after several years of preparation, became valiant workers in the mission field.

So liberal was the Father Visitor in the care of the mission that in a short time, nothing was lacking for the continuation of the work. In the meantime, they continued the building of the Mission House and hurried the work as much as possible because of the inconveniences they were experiencing in the temple. In order to avoid hostile comment, and also to prevent the Magistrates from holding their banquets in the house, as they do in cloistered places, the house was designed in Chinese style and built only one story high. With this completed, the next interest was a large and a well built church, close by, as they were looking forward to a great number of neophytes in the near future. It was decided also not to lodge the interpreters in the house because they were not trustworthy. They had a habit of putting a wrong interpretation upon what they saw, and then reporting everything that was done in the house to the whole outside world. Experience had taught that they generally turned out to be trouble makers.

Keenly aware of what this and similar experiences of the past had taught them, they made sufficient advancement in a short time to conclude that they had lost nothing in leaving Sciauquin. In truth, they were rejoicing in the realization that they had profited by the change. It seemed that God had permitted the labor and troubles of the past for the greater glory of His name and for the greater good of the Christian Mission.

It was at this time that the Father Visitor was getting ready to return from Macao to Japan, with the Japanese legates who had returned from Europe. At this same time also his presence was really necessary in Japan, where the Christian Church was in a turmoil, because of a persecution launched by the Emperor Cambaco, as he was called. He had become enraged against Christianity in general, and against the Jesuits in particular, whom he was harassing in a furious persecution; banishing them all from the country, confiscating their houses and destroying their churches. Hence the hurried departure of the Visitor General of the Society. Before leaving he appointed Father Sande Rector of the College of Macao, because he was well acquainted with the affairs of the China mission, which, at that time, was under the jurisdiction of the Superior at Macao. Moreover, he seemed to be the most suitable for government and for the proper provision and advancement of the Chinese enterprise.

3. Chiutaiso

CHIUTAISO, whom we shall have occasion to mention frequently, was the son of a noble of the second order of Magistrates, called the Sciansciu, a native of the village of Sciceu and a well educated member of the lettered class. His father was well known for the dignity of the office he held, but still more distinguished because of the fact that he was first in a class of three hundred examined for the degree of Doctor of Letters. These examinations are held every third year, and in China this degree carries not only great honor but considerable authority in public affairs.

This particular Magistrate acquired a great reputation for his intellectual attainments, as well as for his integrity of life, and his books were everywhere read and admired. His son was the genius of the family, and if he had continued his studies, he would without doubt have acquired the highest honors. Instead, he turned out to be an ingenuous black sheep. He shook off the yoke of parental obedience in his youth and when his father died he went from bad to worse, keeping evil company and running headlong into all kinds of vice, including the mania that took possession of him when he became an alchemist. His paternal heritage, which must have been great, was burned up in the furnace of alchemy in an endeavor to create unlimited wealth. Reduced to poverty, which he could not endure in his own district, he took to continual traveling about the kingdom, with his wife and his servants, visiting his father's friends and taking advantage of their friendship by collecting presents in his memory. Many others gave him gifts in order to have him speak in their favor to the Magistrates whom he knew, and his shameless poverty prompted him to accept them. There are some among the Chinese who live and flourish by this latter practice, with little or no regard for justice or the law. He came to Sciauquin to visit the Viceroy and the Lin-si-tau, both sovereign Magistrates; the one his friend and the other his co-citizen, but in each case he received a very cool reception. It was here that the Jesuits made his acquaintance, but it was just at the time that they were being put out; so they saw very little of him then. When he heard that the Fathers were at Xaucea he came to visit them while they were at the temple, and through the Lieutenant Governor he secured a room in the cloister hall where they were lodged, in order to be near at hand for consultation. One day he came to visit, arrayed in the customary formal apparel and bringing costly gifts, as is the custom when a student petitions a master to become his teacher. His request was for Ricci to accept him as a pupil, and on the following day he invited his teacher to dinner in his apartment and presented him with a gift of silk cloth. Their giving of gifts is a regular custom and one cannot very well refuse them, but with the Fathers they were always balanced by return presents of European novelties, so as not to leave the impression that they were teaching for a recompense.

At the beginning of their acquaintance, Chiutaiso kept it a secret that his chief interest was dabbling in alchemy. The rumors and the belief that the Fathers were making silver in this way were still alive, but as a result of their daily company, he gave up the evil practice and applied his genius to more serious and more elevated science. He began with the study of arithmetic which with Europeans is simpler and more methodical than with the Chinese. They do their figuring on wooden frames, on which round pellets are slid along wires and changed from place to place to indicate numbers. This method, though exact, is quite susceptible to error and decidedly limited in its scientific application. He next took up the study of the globe of Christopher Clavius and the elements, or the first book, of Euclid. Then he learned to draw various designs of sundials, indicating the hours exactly, and to measure the height of objects by geometric rule. We have already remarked that he was intellectual and experienced in writing. The knowledge he acquired was reduced to a series of elegantly written commentaries, and when these were presented to his friends, the lettered Magistrates, both he and his teachers, to whom he gave the credit, acquired a widespread and an enviable reputation. The novelty of what he had been taught was a puzzle to the Chinese, and they concluded that he could not have acquired it of his own research. Night and day he applied himself to his work, and decorated his manuscripts with illustrations equal to the best of European artistry. He also made his own scientific apparatus, such as globes, astrolabes, quadrants, magnetic-boxes, sundials and other such paraphernalia, all of which were skilfully wrought and artistically decorated. The material in which he worked was as varied as his handicraft. Not satisfied with wood and copper, some of his instruments were designed in silver. Experience proved that the Fathers were not wasting their time on this man. It became a matter of general knowledge that this nobleman, who was so ambitious to excel, was a pupil of one of the European priests. European law and science were continually the subject of his conversation and his praise. In Xaucea and wherever his wanderings brought him, there was no end to his comment and his praise of things European.

The Christian religion, our principal interest, was part of this man's daily discourse, and in order to give it more time for consideration, he occasionally requested that his profane studies in which he was so constantly occupied ex professo, be put aside for a few days. One can gather how serious the educated Chinese are about religion, when we say that he was surprisingly exact and methodical in the manner in which he noted down objections to Christian teaching that occurred to him during discussions. He would leave vacant spaces in his notes to fill in the answers and explanations, and he was so exact about all this that Father Matthew was very rightly astounded, especially during religious discussions which touched upon difficult theological questions. If the missioners were surprised at his interest, he too was surprised by the solutions offered to his difficulties, which he took to be unanswerable. At times it was difficult to discern whether he was more puzzled by the solution of a difficulty or by the ease and facility with which the explanation was made acceptable. In due time he became convinced of the truth and expressed his desire to accept it, but he could not be received into the Church, because since the death of his wife, who left him no family, he was living with a concubine from whom he would not separate, and whom he would not marry because she was not of his social rank. Despite the fact that he had received both the light to know and the desire to accept the faith, there was no question of his baptism. Finally, after a few years, being more interested in a family than in social distinction, when their second child was born, he made the woman his legitimate wife and became a Christian. It was through his work that the Fathers formed an intimate friendship with one of the Army Chiefs, called the Pimpithau, and also with his townsman, the newly arrived Governor of Xaucea. Other local friendships followed with the Mayor of the city and with his Assessors, and further away, with the Governor of Nankin who was formerly the domestic tutor of their prodigy.

With these dignitaries as patrons, the progress of affairs increased and difficulties diminished. The Mayor of one of the district cities, called Inte, was particularly anxious to become acquainted with the Europeans. Whenever he had occasion to visit the metropolitan city of the Province, he would call upon them, always arrayed in the full panoply of a Magistrate, with a numerous guard of honor. Again and again he politely invited them to visit his seat of government, a journey of three or four days, but they repeatedly declined, explaining that they were not in favor with the Viceroy, who had ordered them moved to Xaucea, and therefore it did not seem prudent to them to enter that Province while he was in power. Finally, his importunity won them over, when he added to it what they judged to be a real necessity. This time he was even more courteous than usual, and he begged them not to refuse to come and instruct his father, who was seventy-two years old. In order to make his story more persuasive he added a rather astonishing detail, which would seem to be an instance of divine guidance. It was this: when his father was still young a certain soothsayer told him that he would marry a second time when he was sixty years old, and when he was seventy-two he would meet a stranger upon whom all his future happiness would depend. When his first and only wife died, he remarried in his sixtieth year. He came to these parts when his son was appointed to govern the city of Inte, namely, in his seventy-second year. Here he heard so much about a certain foreign priest, that he had no doubt at all that this was the man whom the soothsayer had indicated to determine his good fortune. It was this that prompted him to urge his son to make every effort to have the foreign priest come to see him. He, himself, could not go to the priest because of his age, and also because of the law which obliged him to remain within the limits of the palace estate, as long as his son was in office as Mayor of the town. After hearing such a story, they felt that they should not make further resistance, and they were quite pleased with the idea that a visit might be the occasion of the old man's conversion. Once the visit was agreed upon, the Mayor thought he should go on before, so as not to prolong the suspense of his father who was waiting for a reply. He then arranged for a special and an ornate boat for the Fathers' journey, such as Magistrates travel in, and equipped it with everything necessary for the trip.

Father Matthew took one of the other Fathers with him on this voyage and also Chiutaiso, so as not to interrupt his studies. They were received in apartments prepared for them in the Temple of the Idols, and nearly the entire town gathered just to look at them. The

Mayor came to pay a visit, with more show than he exhibited at Xaucea, which was not his proper seat of government, and he afterwards prepared a banquet for his visitors. On the following day Ricci paid his respects by visiting the Mayor's palace, where he met the amiable old gentleman who received him as though he were a messenger from heaven, come to complete his happiness. His first request was that they should all remain for three days. During the sojourn there, when they got around to talking about the soothsayer, Ricci remarked that it would seem indeed, that if what was foretold really happened as he predicted it, one could readily believe that reference was made, by divine inspiration, to the Christian religion, which he himself had come from the other side of the world to explain. He then added that the greatest happiness that could be imagined for his host would be for him to accept that religion. Then the old gentleman wanted to know all about it and, when Ricci began to explain it, the old man was so delighted with the explanation of the Christian law and mysteries, that he would have been baptized then and there, if one could have acceded to his desire. He never did receive what could not be granted to him at the time. He died in the Province of Nankin, among his own people at the age of eighty, without being baptized. They say he passed away calling upon the name of God, and holding a small copper medal over his heart, a medal of Christ the Saviour, which Ricci had given him. May it please God that he profited at that moment from what he had formerly learned.

A few days after their arrival at Inte the Mayor invited them, by way of recreation, to visit a certain beautiful cave in the village called Pelotum, a place of great renown and very rightly so. The cave was a natural formation, about a mile from the river, filled with clear water from mountain springs and abundantly stocked with fish. Here they met the former Second Assessor of the City of Nankin. He had been promoted to a more honorable position and was now a Government Inspector, making his rounds in this section with the authority of an official investigator. In keeping with their custom the Mayor entertained him at a banquet, at which there was music, dancing and a theatrical comedy which lasted into the early hours of the morning. On the following day they returned to Xaucea with the Inspector, who received them aboard his official barge. Due to the friendship of the Magistrates, the work progressed in leaps and bounds, and the officials of Sciauquin always called in when they came this way. It caused some comment among the people when the fifth son of the

Viceroy and the Viceroy's nephew were seen among the guests at the Mission House. They were passing this place, and after their official reception by the local authorities, they neglected to pay a courtesy visit to the Magistrates; yet they did come ashore with a whole suite of courtiers in full equipage, to visit the Fathers and to present them with gifts. The principal result of their visit was that the people of Xaucea concluded that the Fathers had been transferred from Sciau-quin, rather than expelled, and this was only a natural conclusion, in view of the fact that not only the Magistrates but the family of the Viceroy were so respectful and so pleased to pay them the customary social calls.

4. First Efforts in Xaucea

THANKS TO THE good will of the new Governor, the affairs of the Mission at Xaucea were progressing peaceably. At the instance of our friend Chiutaiso, he wrote out a strict edict and had it posted at the entrance to the Mission House, declaring himself as the defender and protector of the settlement. It was not in the plan of Divine Providence, however, for this peace and quietude to continue. It seemed rather that this nascent Church would sink deeper roots, if it were tried and troubled by a series of difficulties. Just at that time Father Almeida came down with a dangerous malady, so threatening indeed that Ricci decided to send him to Macao, in care of the Coadjutor Brothers. It was hoped that European medicines and food there, which was lacking here, might bring him more speedy relief. When Father Almeida departed, Father Ricci wanted to get the consent of the Governor for someone else to come in to replace him as a companion. This would give the sick man more time to recover his strength, and it would also mean a third member of the Society in the Empire. For some time past their design was to open another house in a different district, in order to make their position more secure. This would be an added assurance of remaining in China, and the success of the entire undertaking would not be dependent upon a single settlement. It was left to their friend and pupil to speak to the Governor about a third member coming to Xaucea, when he found it timely and apropos.

The patient had scarcely left the place when Xaucea staged an uprising against the Mission. In an ardent desire to spread the fire which Christ had come to kindle upon earth, Ricci decided to show the people something new during the festival of the New Year of the Chinese Calendar. He had a beautiful statue which was sent to him from New Spain; the one we have previously mentioned. Up to the present it had been kept in the house chapel and had never been seen by the public. The church was already decorated with statues, lamps and candles, and in order to increase the piety and devotion of the people, it was decided to place this statue on the altar in the church, where they could see it in full view. When the populace heard about it they came from all directions to admire it, but those dwelling in the neighborhood were not at all pleased with the expression of this particular spirit, on the occasion of the festival. When night fell they showered the house with a continual hail of stones. Then they hid along the roadside and remained under cover until the inmates went out to prevent further injury. They saw no one, but just as they re-entered the house, the interrupted stoning became more violent than before. Once the attackers revealed their hiding places, the domestics rushed out to put them to flight, but they were surrounded and pushed into the middle of the crowd, who treated them very roughly and tore off their clothes. Attracted by their cries for help the Fathers rushed to their assistance and, by a quick flight, got back just in time to escape serious injury themselves.

Chiutaiso was of the opinion that they should immediately inform the Governor of what had taken place, but since they wanted to bring in a companion from Macao, it did not seem advisable to present two petitions at once, for fear the granting of one might mean the refusal of the other. Chiutaiso held to his idea that the offense should be punished, reasoning as he did, that impunity in this case would only provoke further trouble, which would become more serious as time went on, and so he had his way. On the following day he went to see the Governor and in order to induce him to come to the Mission House, where they could talk over both matters more conveniently, he informed the Governor that he was living there with the Fathers. His idea was successful and in a few days the Governor came to call on

him. In the course of their conversation, the Governor asked how the
Mission was getting along, and Chiutaiso, exaggerating the injury done,
told him in detail of the attack on the house, adding that Father Ricci
was disturbed about it all, but did not wish to report the affair, as it
seemed better to exercise patience and pass it over in silence. For a
little while after this the Governor was utterly speechless. He was
more furious against the authors of the crime than one would believe.
Then he asked to have all the servants called in and when he saw their
condition, his anger became even greater. He immediately issued an
order to have all the leaders of the local Road Guards brought before
him, and demanded that they reveal the instigators of this serious offense against foreigners, whom they knew to be under his protection.
When they said they knew nothing about it, they barely escaped a
severe lashing, then and there. Instead, he threatened them severely,
had iron chains placed about their necks, as was customary in such
cases, and sent them out to find the perpetrators of the crime, with
orders to have them appear in his court without delay, to receive the
punishment that was their due. With that done, he asked if Father
Almeida had recovered from his illness, and Chiutaiso took advantage
of the inquiry to talk about another Father coming to the Mission. He
explained that the sick man had left to secure better medical attention,
and that Father Ricci was feeling the effects of being left here alone.
He really was anxious to have another Father with him, but his respect
for authority prevented him from asking for the necessary permission
for a companion. This proposal was received with favor and the Governor said he would be pleased to have Ricci call in an assistant.

To return to the Guardians of the local roads, who were involved in
no end of trouble because of the Governor's order, they knew very
well that the stone throwing had been done by the sons of some of
the leading citizens on the other side of the river, who had already
threatened to take vengeance upon them if their sons were accused. On
the other hand they stood in great fear of the Governor, knowing
for certain that they themselves would receive punishment for the
crime if they did not reveal the culprits.

Just at that time, two of the Mission servants, who had left the
house unknown to the Fathers, were waiting, for some reason or other,
on the bank of the river, near the bridge, when along came two of
the young men who like to throw stones at night. The servants seized
them and handed them over to the worried Road Guards, to be
brought to the Governor. Whereupon, the guards felt happier than

the parents, because they would thus escape the odium of making the arrest, while the parents knew that their sons were sure to be punished, and moreover, the rigor of the punishment would force the prisoners to reveal the names of their companions. With no other avenue of escape open to them, that same night, the fathers of the two boys came to Ricci and in all humility begged him to pardon their sons, alleging their youth as an excuse, and imploring him not to carry the matter any further. After calmly explaining the harm that had been done, he told them that he had no desire whatever to accuse anyone or to have anyone punished. He then assured them that the affair had come to the notice of the Governor through another channel, that he did not know at the time that his servants had left the house, and did not discover until afterwards who had taken the boys at the bridge and handed them over to the police. So far as he was concerned, as he explained, they themselves were the ones to have the matter suppressed. He personally would push it no further and, if necessary, he would even intercede for the release of their sons.

With that they departed with humble thanks, and then proceeded to persuade the guards to return to the court and say that, on the night of the attack, the assailants had so concealed themselves in the darkness that they could not be recognized. That was too much for the Governor, who became so angry that he ordered one of the guards to be cruelly beaten and another sent to jail until he revealed the names of the guilty persons. Finally, they broke under the punishment and named the two who were the ringleaders. The other culprits then took to flight, hither and yon, in search of safety. In the meantime the fathers of the two boys, on the verge of desperation, made frequent visits to the Mission with importunate pleadings for Ricci to come to their assistance. This he did very willingly as a religious, and also to show this heathen people, who are very susceptible to such lessons, that the Christian does not return evil for evil, and that his law teaches him, if need be, to help and to aid even those who do him an injury. Chiutaiso wrote a request to the Governor in Ricci's name, and Ricci himself went several times to the court to ask for pardon, which was finally granted, but only with reluctance. As a result of the whole affair the Governor published an edict, more stringent than the former, in which, after noting the outcome of this particular case, he prohibited under severest punishment, that anyone should take advantage of the clemency he exercised, in order to escape the penalty due for future crime. If anyone hereafter were to attempt an outrage similar to the one just pardoned, let him be assured, as the edict affirmed, that no amount of intercession on the part of others of any rank or station would save him.

With the arrival at Macao of the news that another Father could go into the realm, the Father Rector was anxious to take advantage of the occasion for himself, not to remain there as a companion to Father Ricci but to go in as an official Visitor of the Mission. This he did without any hindrance, to the satisfaction of all and with considerable advantage to the Christian cause.

Father Almeida was still in poor condition when the Rector returned to Macao, but his zeal and his desire to return to his post were so great that he was granted permission, but with considerable hesitation, to return to the Mission. It was confidently hoped that the contentment and the happiness accompanying the granting of his wish would hasten the recovery of his strength and health.

Lest we forget it in passing, let us recount here what happened to the Father Rector on his return voyage. He had gotten as far as the village of Ansam, a day's journey from Macao, when it was reported to the Governor of that district that he was a foreigner who had entered the kingdom without the permission of the Magistrates. Whereupon, the Rector was arrested and held for several days, until those at Xaucea and at Macao were notified and came to his assistance. Father Ricci obtained a public attestation that the Rector had come to Xaucea with the knowledge of the Magistrates, that there was no charge made against him, and that there was nothing that should prevent him from returning to Macao. Before this document arrived, the Magistrates governing the Chinese population of Macao had already confirmed the same assertions and obtained permission from the Governor for the Rector to return. As the Governor of the district of Ansam, who held jurisdiction over Macao, was by nature a violent individual and hated Europeans, he allowed only one of the Father's servants to go along with him, and had the other two thoroughly beaten in his presence and sent back to Xaucea under guard of an officer. It was only time lost trying to persuade him to permit them to go on to Macao.

5.Death of Father Almeida

~~~~~~

FATHER ANTONIO ALMEIDA, naturally of a frail physical constitution, failed to recover his strength and was again taken ill in October; so suddenly and so seriously that it was impossible to remove him to the College at Macao. He died on the 17th of October, after an illness of eight days. Let us pause in our sorrow at the loss of this great worker in the vineyard of the Lord, to give a brief account of his life. He was Portuguese by birth, from a place called Francosa, only thirty-five years old, and most of his life was spent in the Society of Jesus. An example of zeal and of virtue from the time of his novitiate, his reputation for sanctity was widespread wherever he was stationed. In order to satisfy his desire for work and for suffering, he asked to be sent to India, and on his arrival at Goa he petitioned to be appointed to one of the more difficult missions, remarking that he was too much at his ease in the schools, whose frugal simplicity he was wont to call a delicacy. His hopes were not disappointed. Superiors were aware of his fine mental qualities as well as of his ambition, and the Father Visitor sent him to the Great Hope, as the China Mission was rightly called. His first appointment was as Assistant to Father Eduardo Sande, then Superior of the College of Macao. He was so pleased with this assignment that he took occasion to express his delight on the subject in a nicely written letter to some of his religious brethren. There was one remarkable idea expressed in that letter, which really deserves to be recorded. When the members of the Society at Macao were planning ways of making an entry into the Kingdom of China, and such an entry was truly difficult at that time, because they knew practically nothing of the country, he suggested a way, somewhat extravagant no doubt, but probably prompted by his ardent zeal. He proposed that he offer himself as a slave to one of the Magistrates, and he was ready to do it if Superiors would grant him the necessary permission. Later on, during the inland voyage he made with Father Ruggieri in the Province of Cechian, when they could not accomplish what they had in view, it took considerable persuasion to get him to return. He requested, and with great insistence, that he be allowed to remain there alone, saying that he would find a way to live in safety. In fact, it took an order of holy obedience to get him to leave the place.

Father Almeida was so given to prayer, and to the chastisement of his feeble body, that Superiors had to be careful that he did not exceed the limits of prudence. One day his Superior asked him what vocal prayers he was accustomed to say, and it was discovered that besides the daily recitation of the divine office, he said nearly all the other prayers in the breviary. Considering the acts of piety that he performed every day, one wondered how much time he had left for study. He was advised to limit his reading of prayers to the regular office of the day, and to devote the rest of his reading time to study, but he succeeded, with a sort of pious insistence, in getting permission to continue at least the daily recitation of the Office of the Blessed Virgin, which he was in the habit of saying from the time of his early youth. His conversation was always of God and of things spiritual; so much so indeed, that he himself, no less than those who heard him, was deeply affected by it. He had great devotion to the Blessed Sacrament, and before ordination to the priesthood, not content with the days assigned by rule, he would seek permission for more frequent reception of Holy Communion. When stationed at the College of Macao, he spent much time in the chapel where the Blessed Sacrament was kept, and it was always a joy for him to serve Mass, and then to attend as many others as he could. This practice he held to, even during his stay in China. During his final illness this devotion was particularly evident. Whenever his feeble frame was dangerously shaken by the fatal malady which he had contracted, at the end of Mass he would say a tender good-bye to the Lord, as though he were never to say Mass again. In his last sudden seizure he was not to have the consolation of receiving the Blessed Sacrament, which was a source of deep regret. In his solicitude for this divine help on his last great journey, he asked for it frequently and ardently during that last night. However, at that time the Blessed Sacrament was not kept in our Church, and his request could not be granted until Mass was said. His whole mind was centered upon this one idea and, though he could hardly talk, his efforts were all requests for Holy Communion. He then remembered that on the authority of the theologians it was permitted to anticipate the dawn, so that Mass might finish with the break of day. But, truth to say, God saw fit to come to him to be seen as He is, rather than hidden in the species of the delicate host. He died before Mass could be said, too early in the night to partake of the divine repast. When he felt the end approaching he asked to be placed on the earthen floor and there, communing peacefully with Christ crucified, he passed into eternal life. They found some notes in his desk; a commentary written in his own hand, in which he had noted down whatever happened during the day, of good or of evil, affecting his soul, such as temptations from the Devil, and also religious suggestions and spiritual lights, all arranged, as if for his Superior or his confessor. Certainly it would be worth while, for the good of others, to recopy certain precepts of the religious life from these papers. They are an open evidence of the untiring effort with which the servant of God struggled toward perfection.

The death of Father Almeida was keenly felt by his religious brethren, who lost in him an excellent priest and a zealous laborer for the faith. Their sorrow was eased only by the assurance that the prosperity of the Mission and the advancement of the faith in China would benefit by his presence in heaven. The many Chinese friends he had made lamented his death according to their own custom, but they could not understand why his companions did not manifest their grief by wearing the garb of mourning for a long time, as they do. When it was explained to them that the Fathers, as religious, dedicated to the service of God, consider themselves to be dead to the world and pay no attention to temporal death, save as an entrance into a higher life, they were quick to comprehend, and the explanation seemed to be satisfactory.

During the period of the obsequies, the Mission servants were ordered to wear the usual white dress of mourning, until such time as the visits of the friends of the deceased were at an end. The Chinese honor their dead with an elaborate casket and so, everything had to be arranged in such a way that the people would not be offended by a lack of ornamentation, while at the same time religious moderation would be properly observed. Since it was not the practice to bury in the church which, according to Chinese custom, would prevent anyone from entering it thereafter, and because they did not want to follow the Chinese practice of burying on the side of a nearby hill, the casket was hermetically sealed and kept until the Rector of the College of Macao decided upon a place of burial.

Father Francesco de Petris was named to take the place of Father

Almeida, whom he resembled in some respects, save that he was stronger and more vigorous. Permission for his entry was neither asked for nor awaited. He arrived at the time when everyone in authority was preoccupied, and no one offered any resistance to his coming. The Viceroy, the same one who had formerly expelled them, was just then passing through Xaucea, on his way to the royal court to accept a higher position. Father Ricci took advantage of the occasion to pay him a visit and in doing so brought along his newly arrived associate. This was done openly and publicly, and the people concluded that Father de Petris must be well known to the Viceroy, since he received him in public audience. The reception was cordial and the Viceroy asked Ricci in a friendly way, why he did not want to take up residence in the famous temple of Nanhoa. He also presented him with some books he had written, and the presentation was made in public. All such occasions served in no small way for the advancement of Christianity, and for that same reason the Fathers lost no occasion to mention the friendship of the Magistrates.

This particular Viceroy, whom we have just mentioned, was being promoted to a higher position by means of bribes and gifts, and through the political scheming of his intimates. He was only half way on his journey to the capital when his many crimes were finally exposed by the Official Inspector of the Throne, who had heard of his malpractice and abuse of office. Then and there, he was stripped of all authority and fined forty thousand gold pieces, payable to the royal treasury for public larceny. What money he carried with him they seized and restored to the treasury, and he and his family were reduced to sheer poverty. Even here, retribution did not cease. It seemed as though the hand of Heaven were upon him. He fell victim to an ulcerous condition which his advancing age could not resist and in his last illness, struggling with death, he could not get even a drink of water from his children or his servants, who were occupied in carrying off the domestic furniture. He died, crying out in a loud voice and repeating the words: sorrow and labor and toil. By this kind of death Heaven seemed to punish, even in this life, the injuries he inflicted upon others, among whom the Mission Fathers could be counted. He had made a collection of statues of the demons, in the house he had taken away from the Mission and marked with an inscription in marble, indicating the origin of the house and the purpose for which he was using it. Not far away from this house he erected a temple in which, according to custom, he placed his own statue.

Reverting back to Sciauquin, we should here recount what rumor had spread about, relative to our banishment; a story that will probably last a long time before it is forgotten in these parts. It was reported and accepted as true wherever it was heard; that the European Missionaries were called before the Viceroy but could not be forced by threats of any kind to reveal the secrets and the formulae of the science of alchemy. In defense of their resistance they were said to have declared that a secret of such inestimable value could never be extorted by violence. Whereupon, the Viceroy in a fit of rage, expelled them from their houses. This was generally reported as an act of injustice, since the Fathers had not been accused of any particular crime. This story and similar falsehoods and unfounded rumors concerning the European priests, were not merely spread throughout the entire realm, as uncertain rumors, but were also preserved for future ages in printed books, and printed books generally carry so great a reputation for truth among this people, that when their contents are false, no one in after years would ever think of branding them as lies. Perhaps worries such as this should be wholly foreign to our profession, but it should be remembered that when writing in this way, the Chinese are not finding fault with the missionaries. On the contrary, the fact that the writers were recording the history of their own country, meant to the Chinese people that, as historians, they were admitting that the missionaries deserved to be remembered, and hence were equal to their own ancestors, whom they held in reverent and holy memory.

6.Converts in Nanhiun

THERE WAS A MERCHANT named Cosunhoa living in the village of Nanhiun who engaged about forty persons in the conduct of his business. He came from the town of Taicho, in the Province of Chiansi, and he was an ardent devotee of the cult of the dumb idols. His whole life was given to this cult, doing bodily penance by fasting in the Chinese manner, namely, by abstaining entirely from meat, fish, eggs and milk. He lived on an entirely vegetable diet of herbs and rice and a few small cakes made of flour. On this severe fasting he placed his hope of happiness in the world to come, because he could find no trace of a true religion among numerous Chinese sects. Somehow or other this man came into contact with our friend Chiutaiso, who frequently visited Nanhiun, where he kept his concubine.

One day when they were talking about religion, the merchant learned from Chiutaiso that there were foreign priests at Xaucea who had come from the Great Occident, as the Chinese are accustomed to call the whole of Europe. Chiutaiso told him that they could show him the true road to heaven and to eternal happiness, and advised him to go and see them, as he was now in his sixtieth year and should be thinking of going to heaven before long. When he was sufficiently informed of what the Fathers were really doing, he went to Xaucea and was given an affectionate welcome, both for his own sake and because of the friendship of the one who sent him. When he explained the purpose of his coming he was happily surprised to find more than he had expected. Touched by the grace of God, he seemed to listen with his soul, more than with his ears, and accepted instruction with a marvelous sentiment of piety. Whenever he heard a religious truth that was particularly pleasing to him, he would rise from his place, fall on his knees and, in Chinese fashion, bend forward and touch his forehead to the floor, in thanks to his instructor. Naturally of a quiet and gentle disposition and very friendly, he became a general favorite with all the domestic servants. After sufficient instruction he washed away the sins of his past life in the sacrament of baptism, and took the name of Giuseppe. Formerly, as a member of the cult of the idols, he was accustomed to practice the profane exercises they employ. Now, he inquired what sort of religious devotions were required by his newly found faith. In reply to this, Father Ricci put him through the meditations of the First Week of the Spiritual Exercises of Saint Ignatius, and he took to these so happily that in a short time he seemed to be more a formed religious than a student novice. He lived at the mission for a month and would have stayed longer had he not been called home to attend to business affairs. Quite well instructed as he was when he went away, he returned to Xaucea later on to renew the memory of all he had learned, and to receive new directions for a more detailed formation of his religious life.

In 1592, during the days for fasting, which occur at the time of the Chinese New Year, Father Ricci sent a present to his friend

Chiutaiso who was so pleased that he came to Xaucea to offer a return present in person. Profiting by his visit, Father Ricci took advantage of the occasion to return with him to Nanhiun. He had been contemplating this trip for some time and for several reasons; first, there was a branch of the bank of the Province of Canton in the Province of Chiansi; secondly, the Lieutenant Governor, who had favored the Fathers at Xaucea, was now Mayor of the town and would welcome the visit; and finally, Ricci was anxious to gather the rest of Giuseppe's family into the Church. Chiutaiso decided to go on ahead, to inform the Mayor and some others also who were anxious to see a foreign priest. Shortly afterwards, when Ricci's party was en route and as yet some distance from the city, Giuseppe and some of his friends came out to meet them on the road. He had already prepared a lodging for them in his home, but Chiutaiso decided that his house would be better, because the Magistrates and the lettered class would come there to visit more readily than to the home of a merchant. On arrival at the village, they went straight to the Lieutenant Governor, by whom they were courteously received in the palace, where they conversed for some time on a number of different subjects. On that same day he paid the Father a return visit, with all the usual ceremonies, and clad in all the apparel that Magistrates display, within their own jurisdiction, when visiting one of the educated class. Chiutaiso arranged a formal banquet for this reception. The Magistrates and the nobles of the place, scarcely anyone of them excepted, followed the example of the Lieutenant Governor. All their visits had to be repaid, and when Ricci went from place to place, not only the entire family but the whole neighborhood turned out to see what a European looked like. In fact, the crowds were so great that during the whole time of his visit, he had to travel in a palanquin, in order to make any headway. But even that was not sufficient to stem their curiosity, as some would pull aside the curtains to look in, and others would follow along to the end of the journey, when they could see him getting out of the chair.

Much against his wish, he continued these official visits and friendly entertainments for several days, but the novelty of it soon wore off, and when the crowds subsided, he left the home of Chiutaiso to take up lodging with Giuseppe. The stay here was more pleasant, and also more useful, because here, although the visitors were still great in number but less in dignity, they were present for a purpose, namely, to hear the Father discourse on the divine truths, on which he sometimes spent nearly the whole day, with scarcely time apart to take a meal or to read the divine office of the day. Even at night he continued to hold audience and sometimes into the early hours, so that the listeners had to remain in the house over night. In the part of the house assigned to him for living quarters, besides the living-room, there was a sort of hall where an altar had been set up, on which he said Mass every day at dawn. It was in this hall that the religious conferences were held, and at the beginning of each gathering, the listeners insisted upon rendering the courtesies which are accorded to one of their own high officials.

Giuseppe, the new convert, became a harbinger of the word of God and was already publishing various tracts recommending the Christian faith. Only six of the great number of listeners in attendance became sufficiently instructed to be received into the Church. Many others who gave evidence of their good will were placed in the class of catechumens and their reception deferred, among whom were the four sons of the family. This place gave promise of being a very fertile field, if one could have spared more time away from the Mission, and even the visit to it proved to be very useful in more ways than one. Later on, when the Fathers were passing into the interior of the country, these converts proved to be very helpful in assisting them to make the journey over the mountain that lies between the two rivers.

Now to get back to Xaucea. Here too, there was some fruit to be reaped and a few converts had already passed from the tyrannous reign of false gods into the camp of Christ. Some of these, who were permitted to live in the Mission House, showed extraordinary zeal in the service of the Lord. One of them was terribly beaten by his father because he became a Christian, but he could never be persuaded to pay homage to the ugly statues of demons he had formerly cultivated. Others of the converts stole into the temples and broke the hands and feet off the idols. When Father Ricci heard of this, he warned them to cease such practice, knowing that if ever it were discovered, a veritable tumult would follow, but even his warning was not enough to deter them.

The son of one of the domestic servants, a boy who had been lately baptized, stole an idol from a temple and brought it home. No one else knew of the theft, and fearing that he would be punished because of the warning just given, when everyone else had gone to bed, he threw it into the kitchen fireplace. It was made of scented wood and the odor it gave off soon revealed its whereabouts. One of the Lay Brothers, who was making the rounds of the house, traced the odor and discovered the false god burning on earth in a more delicate flame than would have consumed it below. The discovery was made known to Father Ricci and the little temple robber revealed, but he was not punished. The indulgent Father, pretending that the fault was due to youthful zeal, passed it over in silence. Another one of the servants, a catechumen, not yet converted, was walking with some friends on a mountain road, when they came by a temple in a deserted place. One of the Christians went in and dragged out an idol, saying to the catechumens, "Formerly this was one of your gods and you bowed down before it." Then he dug a hole and buried it for the worms to eat. There were other such instances but it would seem to no purpose to relate them here. One or two examples will suffice to show the zeal of the new Christians and the dislike they had for the false gods they were formerly accustomed to reverence.

7.Robbers in the Night

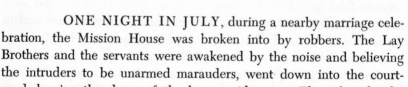

ONE NIGHT IN JULY, during a nearby marriage celebration, the Mission House was broken into by robbers. The Lay Brothers and the servants were awakened by the noise and believing the intruders to be unarmed marauders, went down into the courtyard, leaving the doors of the house wide open. They thought the intruders would take to flight as soon as they were detected. They were groping about in the darkness and believed they had come upon other servants, but instead, they found themselves right in the midst of the robbers, who were well armed and superior in number. Two or three of the servants were severely wounded and Father Francesco received a slight cut on the head from a hatchet. Father Ricci lighted the lamps, and realizing that his household was out-numbered, tried to withdraw them into the inner part of the residence, but the robbers prevented this by throwing their spears across the doors so they could not be closed. The house was so unprepared for defense that one could not find even a stick for protection. Defending the entrance to the inner house as best he could, by threats rather than with weapons, Father Ricci received a wound on the hand, but all finally managed to reach their rooms. The robbers got through and tried to force the doors of the rooms, but the doors were strong and well barred and held against their efforts. In the meantime a young man, a student who was living at the Mission, went up above and was throwing down tables and pieces of wood on the robbers in the court below, and Father Ricci, climbing out through a window into a little garden, turned his ankle so badly that he could not make his way to the road to call the police. He then began calling to the neighbors to come to his assistance, but the neighbors were in league with the robbers and had even instigated the attack. Finally, the call for help and the hail of wood falling on their heads was enough to frighten the bandits, and they withdrew without any booty to a nearby temple, whence they had very probably come.

This kind of treatment was, of course, intolerable, and on the following morning, the Fourth Assessor to the Governor, then acting as Mayor of the town, was informed of the attack. His indignation was aroused, principally at the thought that robbers should attempt such an outrage within the walls of the city during his administration. The result was an immediate investigation to discover the culprits. In as much as none of the neighbors had paid any attention to the outbreak, he concluded that the robbers belonged to the neighborhood, and he was afterwards proven to be right. He then summoned a few of the neighbors and, selecting the one who lived nearest the scene, he subjected him to punishment, while promising him immunity if he told the whole truth. First, he named himself and then all the others in order, including a gang of gamblers, among whom were some of the stone-throwers of the year before. This confession threw them and their parents into a state of fear and confusion, because some of them belonged to families of considerable influence. The Lieutenant Governor then ordered the Fathers to lodge a complaint against the accused in regular legal form, which they were forced to do but reluctantly. The accusation was worded mildly, making it clear that nothing had been stolen, and it concluded with a request to the Governor to pardon the guilty, and if that could not be done, to mitigate any punishment that might ensue. This was quite contrary to the manner in which the Chinese make such charges. Usually the plaintiff not only exaggerates the charges, but increases the amount that may have been stolen, in order to profit by the procedure. When the Lieutenant Governor read the complaint he was somewhat astonished, and though he approved of the leniency of the accusers, he was none the less incensed against the robbers, to think that they had attacked men who were so considerate. Whereupon he ordered all the culprits to be bound and brought into the court. The moderation of the charges brought against them and the promises the Fathers had made to their pleading parents had kept them from taking to flight, and as soon as they were submitted to torture, two or three of them made a full confession.

Now it happened that one of the culprits had lost his hat during the attack upon the house, and this hat was given to the Lieutenant Governor when the first complaint was made. During the trial, this hat was tried on the heads of each of the accused until it was found to be a perfect fit for one of them and undoubtedly his property. Chinese hats are made to fit the head of the wearer. Because of their close fit, it takes considerable pressing and arrangement to put them on, and they cannot be comfortably worn by anyone but the owner. So this particular criminal was identified from his hat. Other circumstantial evidence and their own confessions then brought out the whole story, and the following sentence was pronounced upon the guilty. The ringleader of the onslaught was condemned to death, and the others were sentenced either to the galleys or to servitude as slaves of the Emperor, according to the part they had taken in the crime. These sentences caused the Fathers no end of grief, realizing as they did that it was a great pity for foreigners to bring such punishment upon native citizens. Moreover, there was no little danger in making enemies of their families, nor was there any good done by creating the impression among the people on one side of the river, that those on the other side were robbers. In addition to this, it did not help the Mission for the Fathers to be going from one court to another with the accused.

The judgment passed by one Lieutenant Governor was not final. It had to be passed along to several other Magistrates to be examined and confirmed. What made this part of it worse was the fact that the wounds received by the Fathers in the attack were not as yet healed. This having to appear in the different courts did, however, have one advantage; it brought Father Ricci to Sciauquin, where the judgment passed at Xaucea had to be reviewed for approval in the viceroyal city by a Sovereign Magistrate. This review was easily made, since everything had already been confessed and clearly proven. The advantage attending the trip lay in the fact that it provided Father Matthew with an opportunity to visit the new converts, who had been left without spiritual guidance and instruction, and the visit proved to be very profitable. True, many of these converts had come to Xaucea to see the Fathers and others had gone to Macao and had grown stronger in their new faith, but others, and perhaps most of them, remaining without any instruction, had almost reverted to their former paganism. Several children of the new Christians were baptized on this visit, and the general result of it was that they were all encouraged to remain constant, and received an abundance of spiritual consolation.

While Ricci was at Sciauquin, a letter was received at the Mission from Macao, saying that the official Jesuit Visitor of the Society had returned from Japan. It has already been noted that the Emperor of Japan was banishing the Jesuits from his realm, and after the Father Visitor had gone there and restored some order he thought it best to leave Japan so as not to awaken the fury of the tyrant. This certainly would have happened, had he discovered that others were coming in while he was endeavoring to banish those who were there, and so the Father Visitor followed the advice of the Fathers there and returned to Macao.

When it was learned what had happened at Xaucea, Father Visitor wrote Father Ricci saying he would like to confer with him about several things pertaining to the Mission. He was anxious also to have the doctors at Macao examine Father Ricci's twisted ankle, which had not as yet fully healed, in order to prevent the possibility of his being rendered permanently lame. Whereupon, Ricci sent his companions back to Xaucea and set out by boat from Sciauquin, taking the shortest route to Macao.

Many important decisions were reached during this very profitable visit to Macao, but they decided not to meddle with the injured ankle, because Ricci was walking quite naturally and it gave him no trouble, save when he had to make a long journey on foot.

On his return to Xaucea he found the criminals in chains. Their relatives were still pleading their cause, and when Father Ricci got back, they never appeared in court and never even went to the courthouse, unless he accompanied them, believing, as they did, that they had no better advocate than the one who should have been contending against them.

Among the Chinese judges there is one whose title is derived from his special office of minimizing penalties. He exercises his duties in the name of the Queen, who among the Chinese is the mother of the King. In each province there is a Presidial, or Court of Judges, which passes sentence upon crime, and one of these judges is assigned to this special office of commiseration, in his respective province. In the course of his duty he visits the prisons, liberates some of the less culpable, and moderates sentences passed upon others. During his visitation he is specially honored and respected by the local judges in whose jurisdiction he happens to be operating.

The accused we have been considering placed all their hope in the arrival of this official in Xaucea, but they received no consideration, despite the fact that the Fathers interceded on their behalf. The last one who was to pass upon the sentence pronounced in this case, and possibly to revise it, was the official Inspector for the Throne, and his decision had not as yet been made. His coming to Xaucea naturally filled the accused with fear, because one could hardly hope that he would remit a punishment that had already been approved of by seven or eight judges.

At that time, in fear and almost in desperation of the outcome, the relatives of the prisoners, about fifty in number, convened for counsel, or rather for vengeance. In their despair they offered a sacrifice to the idols for their cause, in one of the temples, and then they took a common oath to secure the banishment of the Europeans from Xaucea. To this end they formulated a complaint, charging that the Fathers were in continual contact with outside nations, through Macao and Sciauquin, contrary to Chinese law. It was also alleged that they had built here a fort rather than a home, wherein they housed more than forty foreigners brought from Macao to make up a garrison. In addition, they had caused heavy punishment to be inflicted upon innocent natives, by the Magistrates; thus making themselves a menace to the realm in general and to this village in particular. Therefore, moved by a desire for the public good, as they claimed, they advised and requested that these foreigners be expelled.

In order to win the good will of the local Magistrates, they sent them a request to favor their petition, reminding them that the Official Inspector generally called for such requests for examination. Unfortunately for them, there was no one among the judges who would sponsor their petition. In fact, they were advised by some other citizens to lay aside such a complaint, with a warning that it might

prove to be harmful to themselves. The only official to interest himself in their design was the Second Assessor to the Governor and he
promised to advance it, only because he was at odds with the Lieutenant Governor whom he knew to be a friend of the Mission. It was
this same friend, indeed, who notified Father Ricci that the petition was
being presented, and who called several friends of the accused and
warned them to be careful, because the accused were not as yet out
of danger. He also advised them not to irritate those who were inter-
ceding for the culprits, since they too might appear before the Inspector as prosecutors. It was not to be supposed, he told them, that
those assailed were so blind that they could not recognize men who
attacked them with blazing torches. This warning so frightened the
relatives that they abandoned their enterprise, humbly asked for
pardon and then begged Father Ricci to act as their advocate with
the Inspector. This he did, and when called to give testimony, in an
effort to clear up the whole affair, he took occasion to be more favorable to their cause than they had asked or expected. He petitioned
the Inspector to lean toward clemency in a case that was probably
doubtful. On this request, and realizing that there was no one connected with the case who could bring it up against him later on, the
Inspector preferred to favor several of the city notables, whom the
relatives of the accused had called in to testify, rather than to insist
upon rigorous justice. In passing sentence he pronounced the culprits
to be marauders rather than robbers, and sentenced them each to receive twenty blows with a bamboo cane and then to be set at
liberty. The relatives were satisfied with this judgment and the men
themselves, though less happy, were more or less content to have
escaped the punishment they merited, and also the infamy of being
branded as robbers, a mark of enduring disgrace for them and for
their relatives. The Fathers were satisfied with the verdict because it
gave these pagan people an idea of Christian charity, which not only
did not seek vengeance, but rather, sought to avert it.

This particular instance of Christian piety, however, was to be
repaid with pagan impiety by the most unworthy ingrates that one
can well imagine. The very day after the prisoners were released,
with no fear of further punishment, the conspirators again took up
the accusation they had so recently laid aside. More than two hundred
of them, in a popular uprising, set up a tumultuous cry to the Inspector, who had crossed the river, to come back and listen to their
demands for the public safety. The Second Assessor to the Governor,

an enemy of the Mission, as well as of the Lieutenant Governor, was at their head, making it evident that he wanted to be known as the instigator and the ringleader of this insolent mob.

The Official Inspector either knew what the mutineers wanted, and did not wish to permit the perpetration of such an indignity, or he did not desire to take up a serious charge, especially when presented by a disorderly mob. At any rate, his reply to their clamoring was as follows: "Petitions concerning the public welfare should not be deferred until the time of my departure. They should be presented to me at the time of my arrival." With that he dismissed the whole affair and could not be persuaded to listen to their complaint. It followed, naturally, that the Fathers were as happy in their victory, as the ungrateful mob was shamed in being repulsed. Wholly dependent as they were upon the grace of God, on such occasions as this the Fathers always recommend their personal safety and the success of the Mission to His special protection. On this particular occasion the protecting care of Heaven seemed to be particularly evident, when the people of the country could make no headway with their own judges against utter strangers in the persons of two foreign priests.

At this same time the President of the Court of Ceremonies, of the second order of Magistrates, called Sciansciu, arrived at Xaucea from Pekin. He was on his way to his native island of Hainan, off the south coast of the Province of Canton, on a Royal Mission, and traveling in great pomp and splendor, together with his wife and children. From some source or other, difficult to determine, he had heard of the marvels accomplished by the foreign priests. It was never his custom to come ashore from the sumptuous barge in which he was traveling to return an official visit, yet he did come to see the Fathers at the Mission House. What was also exceptional, he remained conversing with them for nearly the whole day, and he was quite generous not only in his expression of friendship but also in his presentation of valuable gifts. Nothing seemed to please him more than the solutions offered for certain mathematical problems concerning which he had heard considerable in Pekin. Before leaving, he promised that on his return voyage, from his home district to Pekin, he would bring Father Matthew with him to the Royal City, to correct the errors in the Chinese calendars, which their own astronomers did not know how to remedy. He was of the opinion that it would enhance his own reputation to be known as the author of such an important undertaking.

By way of return compliment, Father Matthew decided to go aboard his large and beautiful boat, where he was received with even greater respect and courtesy than he had anticipated, and their conversation was continued until late in the evening. During this visit his host remarked that the Lieutenant Governor had informed him that the Fathers had been attacked by robbers at night and somewhat roughly handled. He was deeply impressed by the fact that instead of seeking vengeance for the affront, they had succeeded in liberating their assailants from a sentence to the galleys and from perpetual servitude, when they had already been sentenced to death. Such forbearance led him to believe that the Christian law was absolutely perfect beyond all comprehension, and he had no end of praise for it.

8.The Death of
Father Francesco de Petris

IT WAS JUST in the middle of the court case against the robbers, on the fifth of November, 1593, that Father Francesco de Petris was called to his eternal reward. A violent fever carried him off in a very few days. He was one of those men who accomplish years of labor in a short space of time. Father Francesco came from the abbey Parish of Forsa, a suburb of Rome. As a boy he was sent to study in the Jesuit College in Rome, where he lived a virtuous life, as a member of the Sodality of Our Lady. He was admitted to the Society of Jesus shortly after completing his course in philosophy, during which he gave a public defense of the entire course, which brought forth the general praise and approval of all who were present. He was highly esteemed by both friends and strangers for his spiritual demeanor and for his exercise of prudence in action. He came east, as has already been noted, with the Japanese Ambassadors, on their return from Rome. When he was appointed to this mission by the Father Visitor of the Society of Jesus, he set sail from Japan to China, with little concern for the riots at Sciauquin, or for the prospect of a meager harvest to be reaped. He had no misgivings about the intemperate climate of Xaucea or about the death of the missionary he was to replace. On the contrary, either belitting or concealing any fear of his appointment, he set out directly for the post to which he was named.

Father de Petris was humility in action. Some few days before his death, while he was talking with one of the Coadjutor Brothers about perseverance in one's vocation, he said he heard the voice of the Blessed Virgin saying to him, "Courage, continue to labor in the Society of my Son and persevere in your vocation," and when he turned to learn where the voice was coming from, he was looking directly at a statue of our Blessed Mother. He told this story himself and during his last illness, he asked to have a copy of a certain hymn to the Blessed Virgin placed on his bed, so he could read it frequently. There seems to be little doubt that Father Francesco felt the approach of death long before it arrived. One day a kind of salted meat was served at table, and when he saw it he said, in a somewhat serious tone, that his life would not last as long as that dish of meat. The conversation was light and jovial at the time, and those present took his remark as a joke. Sometime before he was taken ill, some one of the Fathers remarked to him that the meat had all been consumed, and that he was still alive. He corrected this and said there was still some of it left in the larder. In the meantime, Father Francesco fell violently ill and died, and the others noted that the meat in question was not as yet completely consumed.

They had no idea that his life was in danger when he first became ill, because of his robust constitution and his great physical strength. Sitting on the side of his bed, before he was in danger of death, he made a more detailed confession than usual to Father Matthew and then standing up he gave him a farewell embrace. Thinking that perhaps his mind was beginning to wander, Father Matthew told him to sit down and rest and to keep up his courage. To which Father de Petris replied with a tearful sigh, "I know what my sickness is and I know I am about to die of it." "Now please don't do that," Father Ricci said in turn, "because if you do you will be just doubling my trouble in transporting your body back to Macao and in finding someone to take your place." This remark had reference to the fact that the body of Father Almeida was still awaiting transportation, and the Fathers, not knowing what to do, were needlessly worrying about it. The sick man's rejoinder was offered very calmly, when he said, "You will have no trouble at all in disposing of what is left of me, nor in finding someone to take my place," and what he said turned out to be true.

They had just about heard of his death at Macao, as one of the Lay Brothers was sending a barge from the Metropolis to Xaucea, and on this boat both bodies were taken for burial in the cemetery of the College at Macao. Here a great crowd of people came from the city and assembled at the shore as the barge was approaching, and afterwards accompanied the religious community in funeral procession to the graves. Father Eduardo, the Rector of the College, preached the funeral oration, in which he exhorted the people to take part in the great mission on which the two Fathers had labored. In this way, he assured them, that the death of the missionaries could result in augmenting the Church Militant, which was sending two intercessors to plead the cause in the Church Triumphant in heaven.

These two Fathers died within a period of two years.* They had made such rapid progress in the study of Chinese philosophy, under the tutelage of Father Ricci, that they had time left over for writing, once the initial difficulties were overcome. And so, two almost fully developed laborers in the field were lost just when they were ready to reap the harvest. Perhaps God permitted this to happen because he was provoked by the crimes of this people.

Let us now introduce the Father who took up the work of the two whom the Mission had lost. Father Lazzaro Cattaneo had also come from Europe with the Japanese Ambassadors, but he was detained in India and appointed by the Father Rector to take over the mission frontier of the fishing coast. On the unexpected death of Father Francesco, he was dispatched to the China Mission. There were two others designated for this post but they were detained to complete their courses in theology. The presence of the new arrival added much to the pleasure and the serenity of the community. Thus the Fathers were working in comparative security, but the continued quiet that reigned was not without a constant feeling of fear, which in itself did no great harm.

The new Governor of the Province, the one who treated Father Francesco de Petris, as if he had been summoned by his predecessor, was now in his third year as a governing magistrate, in which he was obliged by custom to return to the seat of royalty, to renew his pledge of service and of loyalty to the king. During this Governor's

---

* Biennium evidently for triennium. TRANSLATOR.

absence, his office was to be taken over by his Second Assessor, an avowed enemy of the Mission, and the Fathers were convinced that he would not only be a constant menace to their work, but that he would make every effort to force their departure. They were convinced of this because of the recent disturbance mentioned, and also because of the threats he had frequently uttered against them. It would seem, however, that Heaven delivered them from both the fear and the danger in a rather extraordinary way. Within two or three days of the time when he was about to take over his new duties, on his way to his Assessor's Office, he fell prostrate on the road and was dead before they could carry him to his home. With his death, the temporary office of Governor fell to the Fourth Assessor, who was not only a friend to the Fathers but their special protector. The removal of this fear taught the Fathers, and others as well, that the preachers of His gospel are always laboring under God's protection, and that the troubles which beset them are either turned aside by God or, if not, are made to serve as benefits.

9. Father Ricci Reaches the Royal City of Nankin

WHEN THE FATHER VISITOR of the Society of Jesus returned to China from Japan, Father Matthew took advantage of his presence to establish the Mission on a solid basis and to render it more secure as well as more amply widespread, in keeping with the majesty of the Gospel they were preaching. He had already succeeded, at the Mission, in stopping the use of the belittling title of ministelli, or low grade ministers, as the Fathers were called. However, with the common people this was more difficult, because they were celibates, had a temple and recited prayers at stated hours. This name of itself was a hindrance to the accomplishment of anything of note. Again, the resemblance of some of the functions performed by the Fathers and by the priests of the Chinese temples caused the people to apply the same name to things that were altogether different. So Father Matthew told the Father Visitor that he thought it would be to the advantage of the Christian faith if they would let their beards grow and wear their hair longer, so they would not be taken for idol worshippers, or worse still for such as offer sacrifice to the idols. With these, as he explained, it was a set rule to be clean shaven and to wear the hair close cropped. He also asserted that experience had taught him that the Fathers should wear the same costume and ornaments as the highly educated Chinese, and that each of them should have a silk habit which he should wear when visiting a Magistrate, and without which, in the eyes of the Chinese, one was never considered to be the equal of a Magistrate or even of one of the educated class. Finally he persuaded the Father Visitor that he himself, Father Matthew, should endeavor to open another residence as soon as possible. The reasons offered for this were: first, the unhealthy climate of Xaucea, which had cost them the lives of two of the community within a short space of time, or, if that were not sufficient reason, there was the advantage of having a second residence. This would increase the security of the Mission, and the success of the whole enterprise would be in less danger, if a misfortune were to befall a single station. The Father Visitor considered these requests to be so reasonable that he granted permission for each and all of them, and took it upon himself to give a full report on each request to the Father General of the Society in Rome, and also to the Holy Father, the Pope.

The Fathers at Xaucea gradually accustomed themselves to this new mode of appearance, which proved to be quite pleasing to their friends, because according to their ritual they could now confer with the Fathers as equals and more at ease, which they could not do with their own priests who offered sacrifice to idols. The Magistrates and the upper class Chinese had always been very respectful to the Fathers because of the opinions they entertained of their learning and their virtue, both of which were noticeably lacking in the native clergy. The common people, on the other hand, who were too stupid to notice such things, thought that all priests were the same. So it was partly the fault of the Fathers that the upper classes could not treat them as their equals, for fear of overstepping the bounds of civility and of good taste by associating with those who dressed in a manner which was contrary to the custom of the country. When the missionaries went to the palace of the Magistrates, they observed the ceremonies of visiting intellectuals, which differed from those of the common people, and this in itself was an invitation to the Magistrates to do the same when visiting the Mission.

It might be opportune here to digress for a moment, to disabuse certain people in Europe of the idea that the Jesuit Fathers in China endeavor to acquire the academic degrees which are offered here. They are known here as Europeans, not as educated Chinese. The Chinese favor the universal idea that the class of the Literati, or the intellectuals, wherever they may live, should comport themselves as such, following the customs and wearing the clothes demanded by the customs of the country in which they reside. Unfortunately, in the Province of Canton, the Fathers had not been able to shake off the obnoxious title of sacrificers. Happily, and much to their benefit, from the time of their arrival in the other provinces, they were identified with the class of the learned.

As to the opening of another residence; in the month of May of the following year which was 1595, a fine opportunity for trying the experiment was presented, and Father Ricci, eager to take advantage of the occasion, set out for Nankin, without delay. Here is how it happened. The First Assessor of the Military Senate, which the Chinese call Scilan, was retiring from office. Many and high honors had been conferred upon him in the kingdom and he was held in great esteem by everyone in the Province of Quamsi. Just at this time it was reported that Cabacondono, the Prime Minister of Japan, had opened a military attack on Korea. This kingdom was both neighboring and tributary to China, and the King of China resolved to send an army of more than eighty thousand to its assistance. To do this he had to select leaders who were experienced and distinguished in warfare, and the First Assessor to the Military Senate, was reappointed to his former position, but this time in the Capital City. His position was superior to that of the Viceroys.

This man had a son, about twenty years old; who had fallen a victim of mental depression because he had failed to pass the examination offered for entrance into the highest class of the literati. The father left no effort untried to restore the boy to his normal disposition, but to no avail. So devoted was he to his son that he brought him along to the Royal Court, thinking that perhaps the mental health of the boy might be restored by the prayers and company of the Fathers who adore the one Lord of Heaven. So he summoned the Military Prefect and told him to have the Fathers brought to him in a special galleon, and the Magistrates present were astounded to see them received with such deference and respect. After an exchange of official salutations, he asked various questions about Europe and about the Christian religion. These subjects led to others and finally he spoke about his son and begged them, if they possibly could, to do something to remedy his illness. Father Matthew replied that this could not be hoped for in a short space of time, adding that he would like to take the boy with him on a voyage into the Province of Chian-si, where he hoped he might be restored to his normal self. This suggestion was quite acceptable to the boy's father, and he immediately ordered the Governor of Xaucea to make out letters patent for the journey, to be sealed with his official seal, and granting full faculties to Father Matthew to travel in the Province of Chian-si. He himself went on ahead and Father Ricci followed the next day, with two young men from Macao, who were novices of the Society of Jesus, and two domestic servants. The parties met in the first city of the Province of Chian-si, called Nangan. There were many Christian neophytes here from Nankin and they were a great help, with their hand-barrows, in assisting the party across the mountain pass.

Mount Muilin stands between two rivers and marks the boundary lines of two provinces. It takes a whole day to cross it and the route over it is, perhaps, the most celebrated mountain pass in the whole kingdom. From the southern base of the mountain, the Nanchiun River begins to be navigable, flowing from here through the Metropolitan City of Canton and thence south to the sea. On the other side of the mountain at the City of Nangan there is another big river which flows through the provinces of Chian-si and Nankin, passing through many other cities and descending eastward to the ocean. A tremendous amount of merchandise is brought here from many provinces to be carried over the mountain and sent south, and likewise, from the other side and over the mountain, to be sent in the opposite direction. Goods coming into Canton from foreign kingdoms are transferred over this same pass into the interior of the realm. Travelers cross on horseback or in palanquins and the merchandise is transported on beasts of burden or by carriers, who seem to be innumerable, and the procession is constant all day long and every day. The result of this continual flow of traffic is that the two cities on the opposite sides of the mountain are veritable bee-hives of industry, and yet the order is such that great numbers of people, with no end of baggage, are despatched in a short space of time.

The mountain is common to the two provinces, which are separated by a tremendous gate built into the precipitous rocks. Formerly this mountain was impassable but science and labor opened a highway. The entire journey over it is made through rocky country covered with forests, but the stopping places, wayside inns, are so frequent that one can pass either day or night in them in security and in comfort. The military guards and the continuous stream of travelers are protection against robbers, and the road is never flooded, even by a torrential downpour. At the top of the mountain there is a fountain of good drinking water, and here also there is a magnificent temple, protected by a military guard. From this spot one is afforded a magnificent view of the two adjacent provinces.

Having passed over the mountain, let us pause in this southern retreat, for such is the meaning of the word Nangan. Here Father Matthew encountered a great number of curious spectators who had come to see him because of the reputation he enjoyed in Xaucea. It had also been rumored about that the Sovereign Magistrate had invited him to travel on one of his boats as far as the City of Canceu.

During this voyage Father Ricci frequently went aboard the Magistrate's barge, where they held long conversations, much to their mutual satisfaction, concerning the customs and the scientific progress of Europe, and about the Christian law. He was always pleased with the Father's presence, and at times he invited him to the more familiar company of his table. So continuous was the stream of Magistrates and of other visitors who came to see the Father during the whole voyage, that he had scarcely any time to give to the afflicted son. In fact, that had been purposely deferred by the boy's father, with the result that an intimate friendship developed, not only with the parent but also with the other members of the family, which contributed greatly to the success of the voyage.

Here in this city of Canceu there is a viceroy who is superior in authority to the Viceroy of the Province. He is called the Viceroy of four provinces; namely, Chian-si, Fuchien, Canton and Uquam. He is so called, not because the entire four provinces are subject to his jurisdiction, but because he governs two regions, made up of minor sections of the four provinces named. There is a special reason for this arrangement, which is somewhat out of the ordinary. Formerly this district was infested with bandits, and when they fled from one province to another, it was not easy to capture them and to bring them to trial. The more officials there are concerned, the more difficult it is apt to be to reach an agreement. Hence, the bordering districts in each province, in which the bandits always took refuge, were cut off and placed under a single authority. With a little clever planning and with his military police, the new Viceroy soon put an end to the banditry.

All of the Magistrates, to whom the military in general are subject, belong to the Central War Board of Pekin, and since the one with whom Father Ricci was traveling was an Assessor to the Central Board, he was received at Canceu with considerable demonstration. When he was yet a mile away from the city, he was met by three thousand soldiers, with flying flags, and all dressed in full uniform and carrying arms. The Captains who were leading them carried guns which they discharged in salute when he passed. Civilian parades were organized with great display and pomp on both sides of the river, which is not very wide at this particular place. As he entered the city, the local Viceroy and the Magistrates were present to pay their respects. They also presented him with gifts and a supply of provisions, and afterwards entertained him at a banquet with all the splendor at their command. At night, the military guard of his barge was reinforced. What took place here was repeated and enlarged upon wherever his party stopped. Such is the respect and the veneration which the Chinese people have for a Magistrate of high station.

From this city the river is crossed on a bridge, made up of a number of boats lashed together, and this bridge is opened only once a day for boats to pass in each direction, after the required toll has been paid. In order to pass the bridge more easily, Father Matthew got himself a small boat and followed the larger ones through.

After passing the city, you come to a place where a second river joins the one on which you are voyaging and increases its volume. From here, for a distance of about thirty miles, the river bed is strewn with sharp, protruding rocks. This stretch of river is considered to be a dangerous run, because of the number of shipwrecks that have occurred here. It is covered with numerous whirlpools, which travel so rapidly that if the pilots are not experienced the boats may be caught in a current and dashed on a rock, with the loss of baggage and perhaps of lives as well. This place is called Scie-pa-than, because of eighteen danger spots it contains. It really is something extraordinary, that right here in the middle of the continent, one should happen upon a stretch of river bed, so shallow in places and so overspread with protruding rocks that they have the appearance of being placed there by design.

At the head of this dangerous section of river, there is a temple of idols, where both the pilots and the travelers are accustomed to pray for a successful voyage. The General Scilan himself followed this custom, but not with much success. His own boat avoided the rocks because of the number of sailors he had aboard and of the diligence of his deck hands. His second boat, carrying his wife and children, crashed into one of the rocks, but no one was lost. The height of the boat was greater than the depth of the river and everyone aboard rushed to the upper deck. There were a number of women and children aboard and they set up a loud cry when the boat struck, though they were really in no serious danger. Father Ricci was the first one to hear their call, and racing to their rescue in his faster boat he took them all aboard and then got into a smaller craft to point out a safe course. The Magistrate was decidedly frightened by the accident and immediately sent word to the town of Canceu to send on a large boat for his wife and children. He did not forget to thank Father Matthew very heartily, and he asked him to go aboard his freight barge, until the other boat arrived from Canceu. This was not long in coming. It arrived the same day, but it was not until that night that they got the women and children aboard it.

With the first wreck, their misfortunes had only begun and Father Ricci was to have his share of them. It happened that his boat was sailing in deep water, at a safe distance from any rocks, when a strong gust of wind hit it broadside, too suddenly for his crew to shift a sail, and over it went, throwing them all into the river. Father Matthew was swept into the channel and, being a very poor swimmer, all he could do was to recommend his soul to God and to be resigned that his end should come in this particular way. He was under water when he felt his hand brushed by a rope. He seized it and pulled and pulled until his head was above water. The rope was attached to his boat, so he held on to it until he could climb on to a floating log, on which he paddled about until he came upon his own book-box, which was floating by, and he held on to that for dear life. The boat was built high and was still floating upside down. Finally, he and some others managed to climb up on it. His companion, John Barradas, one of the young men we have already mentioned, was not so fortunate. Once he was submerged, he did not appear again. He may have been caught and trapped in the channel. All the others, children and even infants in arms, were eventually saved. Father Matthew was so moved by the death of his companion, for whom he had looked forward to a brilliant future, that he fell into grave doubt as to whether or not he should continue the journey. However, summoning his courage and trusting in divine grace for better things to come, he decided to carry out the project. The Magistrate, himself, who had led the Father into a double shipwreck, lost nearly all of his own baggage. What parts of it the divers recovered from the stream were watersoaked and ruined beyond further use. Yet, in the midst of all his trouble he remembered to send a messenger to Father Ricci, to extend his sympathy for the death of his young companion, and to bring him sufficient money to defray the funeral expenses.

This river journey was continued as far as the City of Chiengan, a distinguished and a populous center. Here a night wind rose, of such violence that it scattered the boats, and here again there was imminent danger of shipwreck. The Chinese looked upon these accidents as omens of evil, and the Magistrate, frightened at the outlook, decided to abandon the water and continue the journey to Pekin by land. The expenses of this journey were paid from the royal coffers, and at certain stations the travelers were provided with horses and palanquins and baggage carriers, and supplies of whatever else was needed.

It was here at Canceu that the Magistrate got the idea that he should send Father Ricci back to Xaucea, lest he should be criticized for bringing a foreigner into the Capital City during the period of a war scare. The Father was perplexed when he heard what was about to happen, and calling two of the Magistrate's servants, he showed them, much to their delight, a glass prism, which reflected both sides of the river and the city itself in very brilliant colors. He said he had intended to give this glass to his hero, the General, but he was anxious beforehand to know whether or not the General was going to take him with him to Pekin, because he would not return to Xaucea without that glass. His purpose was to get them to find out by the next day what their master had determined. They knew that already, but thinking that the glass was a precious gem of great value, they decided to tell the General all about it. So it happened that on the day before they were to set out again, the General sent the same two servants to tell the Father that he was sending on part of his baggage and several servants by the river route, and that he might go along with them as far as Nankin, if he so desired. This, he said, he would be glad to do with the General's permission and the necessary letters patent. Father Matthew then went to visit the General and gave him the glass prism, which he hesitated to take until it was almost forced upon him, after which he said that the Fathers were very dear to him, and he was profuse in his thanks for all they had done for him.

Later on, while they were talking about the place where Father Ricci should land, he advised him to disembark at the capital city of the Province of Chiansi, where he had formerly held the office of Chief Magistrate and still had many friends. Father Matthew preferred to go to Nankin, and he continued very modestly to insist upon this until his wish was granted. Whereupon, the General commanded the Mayor of the City of Chiengan to give Father Matthew the necessary papers for this journey, which he did, and very luckily. These papers recorded the length of time that Father Ricci had been in China and the various parts of the country where he had lived, and granted him permission to visit the provinces of Nankin and Cechian, while at the same time warning all Magistrates that he was in no wise to be interfered with. With this for security, Ricci set out in high hope for Nankin. At times on the trip he had a guard of soldiers, because he was traveling with two of the Scilan's domestic servants, and whenever they stopped they were met by the Military Police, as it was generally believed that if the General himself were not on the boat, at least one of his sons must be aboard it. Father Ricci seldom went ashore during this voyage, for fear of running into some difficulty. Finally, at the Capital City of the above mentioned province, which is situated at its north extremity, about twenty-nine degrees latitude, he landed, as one of the Scilan's servants, but not knowing which way to turn to find the friends to whom he was carrying letters, he decided to go into a celebrated temple called, The Temple of the Iron Shaft.

The legend connected with this place relates that some centuries ago a certain individual, named Huiunsin, gave huge sums of money to the neighboring people, which he made by transforming quicksilver into silver of the very purest kind. Moreover, he was supposed, in some mysterious way, to have delivered the city from a ferocious dragon by covering it with earth and chaining it to the iron shaft, which one sees here. After that he and his whole family took their flight to heaven, and with them they took the house in which they lived. The size and the beauty of this temple are well worth beholding, and all around it there is an unbroken chain of public markets, where one can purchase almost anything he can think of. The ministers in this temple belong to the same class of idolatrous sacrificers, whom we have already mentioned as Thausu. They let their hair and their beards grow long. An inquisitive crowd gathered to look at Father Ricci, when he entered the temple. In fact the crowd started to grow as he was leaving the boat, and continued to grow until he reached the temple. It was very strange for them, something almost sacred, to see a foreigner in the city. They all thought he had been prompted by the reputation of the idol in the temple to come from a far country to see it. They were quick to notice that he paid no reverence to the idol, and some of them advised him not to neglect to honor it, because even the highest Magistrates did that. When they saw that he paid no attention to their suggestions, they tried to frighten him by warning him that some evil would befall him, if he insisted upon being stubborn. He was still deaf to their entreaties, and as they were about to drag him before the idol by sheer force, some unidentified person from the boat told the excited crowd that this foreigner did not adore idols. This seemed to pacify them, because the Chinese never resort to force or to restraint in the matter of religion, and particularly so with regard to a stranger. There is entire liberty permitted in this respect, or perhaps one should say, that religious liberty has grown out of the great confusion of religious sects among them, and in some ways this fact was no slight help to our purpose in being there. The continually growing multitude of gazing spectators was of no particular advantage to Father Ricci, so he retired to his boat, explaining very politely that he had come here with an Assessor of the Council of War, who was known to everyone in the city. On the following day, the General's servants went to visit their master's friends, who were all very kind to them, especially the Viceroy's doctor, who gave them various presents as they were leaving.

Passing just beyond the city, one comes to a lake, which is worth-while noting for its size and for other reasons as well. Around the entire extent of its shore, as far as one can see, there is an endless circle of towns, villages, hamlets and castles. From here one can pass by water into the Province of Fuchian and from there, eastward to the sea. One of these cities is Nancan, situated at the foot of a mountain called Liu, on which many anchorets dwell in separate caves and practice a very severe chastisement of the body. They say there are as many of these cells as there are days in the year, and, strange to say, although the sky above is always clear and beautiful, this mountain is always covered with clouds and fog and, although it is nearby, it can never be seen from the lake. The current of the river from here is quite favorable for those who are voyaging toward Nankin, and in this latitude it is so slow that you would scarcely advert to it, which makes for pleasant sailing anywhere on this vast expanse of water.

Just where you leave the lake, journeying toward Nankin, a large river, flowing down from the Province of Uquam, loses its name where its muddy waters join the one on which Father Ricci had been traveling. Because of its great width it is called Yamsu, meaning, Son of the Sea. In some places it is two or three Italian miles wide. In these places navigation is dangerous, and at times the Son of the Sea can be as violently tempestuous as his mother. The water of this river is so rough and agitated that even a strong swimmer could scarcely survive in it. The Chinese are slow to venture on it, and they often get wrecked when they dare it. Larger boats can ride it and smaller ones at times. Our galleons can come up this far from the open sea. Further on, its size is increased by several smaller inflowing rivers. They do not travel on this river at night, rather they put in to a haven, which is also done when a storm is threatening. With a full or with a new moon, the sea water will force its way up the river as far as this lake. At other times it is not noticeable and though one can always scent the sea in Nankin, the river water there is fresh and with no taste of salt.

When Father Ricci arrived in Nankin, he went to a lodging place in one of the suburbs, where the General's servants left him.

10. Father Ricci Is Expelled from Nankin

THIS METROPOLITAN CITY is called Nankin, but the Portuguese who know this wonderful city by reputation from the inhabitants of the Province of Fuquian, call the city Lankin, because in that province the letter N is generally replaced by an L. Being the residential seat of a district Governor, it has another name and is commonly called Intiensu. In the judgment of the Chinese this city surpasses all other cities in the world in beauty and in grandeur, and in this respect there are probably very few others superior or equal to it. It is literally filled with palaces and temples and towers and bridges, and these are scarcely surpassed by similar structures in Europe. In some respects, it surpasses our European cities. The climate is mild and the soil is fertile. There is a gaiety of spirit among the people, who are well mannered and nicely spoken, and the dense population is made up of all classes; of hoi-polloi, of the lettered aristocracy and the Magistrates. These latter are equal in number and in dignity to those of Pekin, but due to the fact that the king does not reside here, the local Magistrates are not rated as equal with those of the Capital City. Yet in the whole kingdom of China and in all bordering countries, Nankin is rated as the first city. It is surrounded by three circles of walls. The first and innermost of these, and also the most decorative, contains the palace of the king. The palace, in turn, is surrounded by a triple wall of arches, and of circling moats, filled with circulating water. This palace wall is about four or five Italian miles in length. Considering the whole structure, rather than any particular feature of it, there is probably no king in the world with a palace surpassing this one. The second wall, encircling the inner one, which contains the king's palace, encloses the greater and the more important part of the city. It has twelve gates, which are covered with iron plates and fortified by cannon from within. This high wall is almost eighteen Italian miles in circumference. The third and exterior wall is not continuous. At places that were judged to be danger spots, they scientifically added to natural fortifications. It is difficult to determine the full length of the circuit of this particular wall. The natives here tell a story of two men who started from opposite sides of the city, riding on horses toward each other, and it took a whole day before they came together.

This will afford some idea of the prodigious expanse of this city, and being circular in form, it contains more space within it than if it were of any other design. Inside of this wall there are expansive parks, mountains and forests interspersed with lakes, and yet the inhabited section of the city is by far the largest part of it. One would scarcely believe it, had he not seen it, but the military guard of the city alone is forty thousand soldiers. This place is situated about thirty-two degrees longitude and figuring its latitude mathematically, it stands almost in the center of the kingdom. The river mentioned flows along the west side of the city. One might doubt whether its commercial value is more of an asset to the city than its beauty is an ornament. It washes the city bank and at certain places flows into the town, forming canals on which large boats may enter. These canals were dug by the ancestors of the present inhabitants, in hard and long enduring labor.

This city was once the capital of the entire realm and the ancient abode of kings through many centuries, and though the king changed his residence to Pekin, in the north, for reasons already mentioned, Nankin lost none of its splendor or of its reputation. Or if perchance it did, that fact would only prove that it was formerly more wonderful than it is at present.

Father Matthew disembarked at one of the suburbs, outside of the triple walls of Nankin, at a place large enough and sufficiently populated to be called a large city. Here he happened to meet a certain doctor, a friend of the sons of the Viceroy, who had expelled the Fathers from Sciauquin. The doctor knew that Father Matthew was a friend of Quintus Leu, Quintus meaning that he was the fifth son of the Viceroy, whose cognomen was Leu. Shortly after he took over a little house, Father Matthew sent a messenger to the doctor to find out if Quintus Leu was living in Nankin, hoping that he might help him to carry out his plans. Quintus was there and Father Matthew went to see him, much to the delight of both of them, and especially so to Ricci, because he was introduced to several prominent people who afterwards invited him to dinner on various occasions, and showed him great respect and deference. From that time on he made frequent visits to the city, but always in a covered palanquin, so as not to create talk, and also to protect the reputation for respectability which is recognized among this people. The distance to the homes of some of his friends would have demanded a robust constitution to walk it.

His next undertaking, with the help of some of his friends, was to open a mission center in the city proper. He informed them that he had heard so much about this famous place during his long stay in the Province of Canton, that he was prompted to take up residence here, where he could quietly spend the rest of his days. Relative to coming to Nankin, or for that matter, relative to going anywhere in China, for the purpose of spreading the Gospel, he always had to conceal his intention, on first acquaintance. So far as his friends were concerned they were as enthusiastic as he was, and offered no objection whatever to his staying. In fact, they promised him all the help they could offer of themselves or solicit through their acquaintances.

In the meantime, while he was thinking over the various ways of safely opening a residence, Father Matthew was informed that a friend of his from the Province of Canton was stationed in Nankin. This was the Magistrate Sciutagim, a man of considerable influence. Now it so happened that when this man was an inferior Magistrate, Father Matthew once presented him with a celestial globe and with an hourglass; things which even to this time the Chinese consider to be very valuable. In return, and on several occasions, the Magistrate gave him assistance, when he really needed it. About two years before, when this man stopped in Xaucea, on his way to take over his present position, he wanted to take Father Ricci with him to Nankin, but conditions were such in Xaucea that he could not accept the invitation. The news that Sciutagim was in Nankin delighted him beyond measure and he hastened to tell it to the son of the Viceroy. He felt as if God had granted him the favor he had been praying for in his daily Mass, and hoping for over a long time. No time was lost before calling on the Magistrate, which he did, dressed in the full panoply of the literati and carrying presents with him, to which many of the Magistrates look forward on such occasions.

This particular Magistrate was so avaricious that he lived a very frugal life at home, almost that of a beggar. His one ambition in life was to climb from one high office to another, with the result that at this time he was holding the high position of Scilan, or Assessor of Nankin, meaning that he was Assessor to the presiding officer of the high court. At first sight of Father Matthew he seemed to be astonished at his unexpected appearance, but his desire to possess the attractive presents did away with his astonishment. So much so indeed, that he received his visitor gracefully, invited him in, asked him to sit down and then inquired how he was getting along and why he had come. By way of flattery, Ricci answered that he had been moved by a strong desire to see him, and to that end he had obtained the letters patent from the Assessor of the War Board to travel to Nankin, adding that he wished to establish a residence in the city under his particular protection. On hearing this, the poor man became so frightened that at first he took a deep breath and then broke forth in a high voice, telling his guest that he had been ill advised to come to this city. Nankin, he explained, is no place for a foreigner to establish a home, because his very presence might be sufficient to cause an uprising. Moreover, as he informed the Father, he was making a great mistake in coming to see him, because the other Magistrates could take occasion from this visit to accuse him of the crime of inviting a foreigner to Nankin. Father Ricci showed him the letters patent he had from the Assessor of Pekin, who outranked this man by many grades, but they had no effect in placating him. He did not want to be placated, so he sent Ricci away, alleging many reasons why he could not help him in any way, and advising him to leave Nankin as soon as possible and betake himself to other parts.

His next step after the interview was to summon the master of the

house in which Ricci was living, and when Father Matthew reached
the house he discovered that the officers of his so-called friend were
there before him. The whole household was perturbed and struck
with fear, because the officers, in search of a bribe, had frightened
them by asserting that their over-lord was incensed with the Father
because he had come to Nankin. Father Ricci also was more than a
little disturbed for fear that an innocent party might suffer on his
account. The master of the house, encouraged by Father Matthew
and concealing his uneasiness, yet hovering between hope and fear,
presented himself before the Magistrate. At his very appearance,
Sciutagim burst into a rage and accused him of negotiating with a
foreigner, which was equal to lèse-majesté among the Chinese. The
host on trial asserted that the Assessor of Pekin had brought this
foreigner to his house and that he was carrying letters patent. This
the Magistrate did not wish to believe, pretending that he did not
wish to offend the Assessor of Pekin, or at least pretending that such a
thing was incredible, thus making it evident that he wanted to press
the charge against the poor man. In this way, he thought that the
fear of punishment would force the accused to admit that he had been
in communication with someone from outside of the kingdom.

Previous to this scene, the Magistrate had summoned a notary to
his court, with whom he had undoubtedly conferred beforehand. He
asked the notary if he knew the foreigner who had come to see him a
short time before. This notary was from Sciauquin in the Province of
Canton, and he promptly answered that he knew him very well and
that he had been expelled by the Viceroy of Sciauquin some years
back for causing an uprising and creating considerable trouble for
the Chinese dynasty. Whereupon, the Magistrate, clever actor that he
was, began to talk excitedly, telling the accused that he was guilty of
capital punishment for receiving such an unknown person into his
house. He then threatened to make a thorough investigation of the
whole affair, at which the poor accused was so frightened that he was
trembling all over. Little by little the Magistrate quieted down. He had
made this display so that no one would get the idea that he himself
had invited the foreigner. He finally decided that the accused master
of the house should conduct the stranger, whom he had harbored,
back to Canton, and that he should get a public acknowledgment
from the Magistrates of the Province of Chiansi, through which he
would have to pass, testifying that the foreigner had been returned
to the Province of Canton. The poor victim declared that he could not
absent himself from his home for so long a time, and that he was too

poor to carry out such an order, and so his excuse was accepted. Instead, the Magistrate made him promise, that he would dismiss the foreigner from his house and put him aboard a barge destined for Canton, and the promise was to be made in writing and returned to him in person. This he did and returned the written promise, in proof of which he received a document from the officials in charge of departing barges.

All these untoward happenings affected Father Ricci more than one can imagine. His friends advised him to pay no attention to the orders of Sciutagim, and to settle down somewhere else in Nankin or in one of the suburbs, but he was afraid that worse things might happen if he were to act contrary to the decision of a judge sitting in court. In following such orders he felt that he was doing God's will, and that all these reverses could never have happened unless God had permitted them for a purpose. So he set sail for the Province of Chiansi, against his own will and against the contrary current of the river.

He was of the opinion that he would be able to clear up the Nankin affair from the capital city of Chiansi, which was not far distant. There he could take advantage of every opportunity to carry out his plan, by contacting the friends he had made in Nankin, who would advise him of what was going on there and recall him when the storm had passed. He had embarked upon a sad voyage, during which he mused over the perils and the labors he had endured, with so little resulting. All his desires seemed to be useless and all his efforts made in vain. A whole day had passed in wondering what he should do, and when he fell asleep, fatigued in body and mind, he was not far from the capital of Chiansi.

During his sleep he had a dream, in which he met a strange wayfaring man, who said to him, "Is this the way you wander about this vast kingdom, imagining that you can uproot an age-old religion and replace it with a new one?" Now, it so happened that from the time of his entrance into China he had always kept his ultimate design as an utter secret. So he answered, "You must be either the Devil or God himself, to know what I have never revealed to anyone," to which he heard the reply, "By no means the Devil, say rather God." It seemed as if he had at last found the one he had been seeking, and falling at the feet of the mysterious person, he implored him, all in tears: "Since you know my design, O Lord, why do you not lend me a helping hand in such a difficult undertaking?" and with this said he lay prostrate and weeping, saying more with his tears than with his words. A wave of consolation passed over him when he heard the assuring words, "I shall be propitious to you in both of the royal cities." That was about the same number of words in which God once promised to assist Saint Ignatius in Rome. Still in his dream, he seemed to be entering the royal capital, perfectly free and safe and with no one objecting to his coming. He awoke with tears in his eyes and related his dream for the consolation of his companion, who was as downhearted as himself, and also because he really thought that there was something of the divine in it. Be that as it may, the events that followed certainly corresponded to the prediction. Within the years that immediately followed, when he returned from Pekin, where he was making no progress, he entered the exact part of Nankin which he had seen in his dream. It was here too that he set up a residence with such freedom and enjoyed such success, that his dream could certainly be looked upon as a prophecy. We shall say nothing here of the mission he later so happily founded and so admirably conducted in Pekin, as it might be an encroachment upon the interest of what is to come.

During his river journey to Nancian he met a friend, a citizen of the metropolis, who showed him a house for rental, belonging to one of his relatives. He told Father Ricci that he could take over the house for a residence, and going ashore first, his friend went to the house and sent some carriers to bring on the Father's luggage. Later on he sent him a palanquin, to use when he wished to go out. On the following day Father Ricci said Mass in the house. That was on the Feast of Saints Peter and Paul, and the Mass was celebrated in thanksgiving of his deliverance and in petition to the Apostles to act as his guides and patrons in the project he had undertaken.

11.A Mission Is Opened in Nancian

THE METROPOLITAN CITY of the Province of Chiansi is Nancian. It is not one of the largest or most flourishing cities, but it is known throughout the entire kingdom for the great number of the class of the literati who go out from here to take over government positions of dignity. In extent of territory it is about as large as Canton, but far inferior to it commercially. The people here are thrifty and accustomed to living on little, and though they practice a false religion, very many of them are strict observers of the Chinese fast. The literati, or the educated class, are formed into a society and on appointed days, certain of the most learned of them hold discussions relative to the practice of the various virtues. If one were to judge from their external appearance, he must conclude that nothing could be added to their modest demeanor, but lacking the light of the true faith, they are wandering aimlessly along the path of virtue, stray sheep without a shepherd.

For several days after arriving here Father Ricci remained indoors, recommending his undertaking to God in prayer. The only one he could recall who might be of service to him was the doctor, already mentioned, so he decided to pay him a visit. This man was well known among the Magistrates as a medical doctor, and particularly so by the Viceroy with whom he was in great favor. Apart from the practice of his medical vocation, the doctor was also known for the grace and the pleasant manner he always evidenced in company. The Viceroy was quite pleased when he heard that a certain foreigner, who had arrived in company with his friend, the Assessor of Pekin, was coming to call on him. He was to be somewhat surprised, however, when he saw the visitor and noticed that his features were quite different from those of the Chinese, and even more surprised when he discovered that the stranger was well versed in Chinese rites and customs and learned in Chinese literature.

From his long experience with the Magistrates, the governing class in China, Father Matthew had learned that when coming into their company, there was little to be gained by neglecting the customary external requirements of such a visit. It was for this reason, when entering the city, that he decided to assume a modest elegance, by wearing the silk robe that was customary for official visits, and also the hat which was distinctive of the literary class. This hat was not unlike the one worn by Spanish priests, save that it was a little higher. When visiting, he always took along two servants, clad in woolen dress, and he traveled in a gestatorial chair, carried on the shoulders of porters, all of which was customary, even among the learned of lesser reputation. In fact, if these customs were neglected one would not be known as learned. So it was, that externals, once adopted as customary, had become identified with what they only represented. When we speak of the literati, the learned class, we do not, as some suppose, indicate the Magistrates only, who go about in public with more pomp and splendor. They, of course, all belong to the literati, but the literati are not all Magistrates.

Father Ricci decided to call on his friend the doctor, dressed in a costume that would prevent him from being called by the mocking title of sacrificer. The doctor had one of the European novelties which Ricci had given him some time before, and with it he aroused the curiosity of his friends, because of its oddity. The friends in turn had already spread a rumor through the village that a foreigner had arrived, whom everyone should see because of his unusual features. By way of returning a favor, the doctor invited Father Ricci to a solemn banquet, held with all the rites and ceremonies already described. Some of the upper class were invited and also certain guests who were related to the king. There is a great number of royal relatives in this town, of whom more will be said later on.

Everyone was pleased with the Father's appearance and with his company, and the fact that they were well disposed gave him an opportunity to insert into the conversation something about his present status. He assured them that he would be quite pleased to stay in this city, if the occasion warranted his remaining. The idea was well received by everyone present and the doctor became so excited over it that he could scarcely believe what he had heard, or that it was seriously said. The Chinese are accustomed to cover up a falsehood with a pretext of expediency, and so, in order to advance the cause in question, the doctor pretended that he had received certain letters from the Assessor of Pekin, highly recommending Father Matthew and requesting that he should arrange to keep the Father in the metropolis, because the Province of Canton was not favorable to his health.

Such meetings of the upper classes were not the only means used in the endeavor to open a new station. At times, in an effort to win over the many inhabitants of the place, who came to visit him, Ricci would explain to them certain mathematical problems, and this seemed to please them more than a little. Sometimes he would amuse them by putting together a sundial, and showing them how it counted the hours. Nothing, however, seemed to please them more than an exhibition of his extraordinary memory, which he had developed by a certain technique and practice. This was particularly interesting to the more learned among them, because the Chinese, more than any other people, labor incessantly to commit whole volumes to memory. In fact, one might say that the first years of their studies are given over entirely to this accomplishment. Sometimes they would paint out a considerable number of their Chinese written characters in no particular order, and Father Matthew would read them over once or twice and then, from memory, repeat them as written. That was surprising, but they were simply at a loss to understand it, when he immediately repeated the whole line again from memory, but backwards. Many of them were eager to learn how he did this, and he taught the art to some few of them but not without considerable difficulty. So it was, that he sought to make himself all things to all men, in order to win them all to Christ.

While all this was going on, Ricci happened to meet a distinguished person with whom he was on friendly terms when this gentleman was a noble Magistrate in Xaucea. Being well received, he thought of enlisting the help of this man in securing the permission to establish a permanent residence. His friend promised him that he would get one of the Chief Magistrates of the city to present the case to the Viceroy, but he could find no one who would take the risk of becoming involved in the business of a foreigner. In the meantime, his former acquaintance of Xaucea was called to a judgeship in the Province of Pekin, but before leaving he recommended Ricci to one of his upper-class friends. Ricci thought it better to place his confidence in this man rather than in his doctor friend, whose authority up to the present had resulted in little. The advice he received and immediately followed, was to pay no attention to the Magistrates and settle down in the city, not, however, in the middle of the city where he was then residing, but just outside the city wall, not far from where he himself was living.

By this time the foreign priest was well known within the city, and when he changed his residence he could not be found by the many who were accustomed to visit him. The result of this was that various rumors began to circulate among the people, and fear arose that the commonweal might suffer some evil because of this stranger. These common but trifling stories eventually found their way into the tribunals of the Magistrates, and even of the Viceroy, with the result that a thorough investigation was ordered, relative to the whereabouts of the foreigner; whence he had come and why he was here. How it happened is not known, but the Viceroy, whose name was Lo, had already received a sympathetic report on Father Ricci, and when he heard of the mysterious stranger, he concluded that it must be the same individual. With this in mind, he summoned the Military Prefect of the district in which the foreigner was supposed to be living, and ordered him to make an inquiry as to who the man was and whence he had come. He admonished the Prefect to treat him with courteous civility and to abstain from all disrespect, and to report his findings on the following day. According to the prevailing custom, the Military Prefect sent his visiting card to Father Ricci and asked him, through one of the domestic servants, to send a report on his letters patent to the Viceroy. He also announced that the Viceroy himself wished to visit the Father but was prevented by urgent business from doing so. Then he asked if Father Ricci would come to see the Viceroy at his convenience. This the Father was glad to do, and arrayed in the customary dress, he made the visit and presented in writing what the Viceroy asked for. He explained that for several years he had lived in the Province of Canton at Sciauquin and at Xaucea. About half a year ago, he had come here with the Assessor of the Military Tribunal, whom he named. It was with his permission that he continued his journey on the river as far as Nankin, and he had disembarked here to rest until he could arrange for a return voyage to the Province of Canton.

As soon as his new friend, and with him the owner of the house in which Ricci was living, heard that the Viceroy was investigating the Father, they were seized with fear, and straightway, with a lack of urbanity bordering on cruelty, they urged him to go away that very night. They practically used force, dragging out all his belongings into the street and preventing him from appealing to the chief of the guards, who was making the inquest. It even came to a point where he would have been rudely driven out, if Ricci's servants had not made it evident that they were ready to meet force with force.

At first sight of the document which Father Ricci had sent him the Viceroy realized that he was the man he had suspected him to be. The discovery made him happy and he ordered the Military Prefect to bring the stranger into his court. Ricci was really puzzled. On his way to the court he was doubtful as to what reason he should give for prolonging his stay in the city. He had no suspicion at all of what was to follow. When he came into the palatial court, the Viceroy met him half way in the spacious room, coming down from his dais to receive him. Ricci was preparing to fall on his knees to greet him, which was the usual rite for the Magistrate in this tribunal, but the Viceroy signaled for him not to do so, asked him to come forward, and he was the first one to open the conversation. "I have been waiting for a long time to see you," he began. "Your reputation has come before you. I have heard tell of your virtue and of your learning, and now I have no doubt about either, because I see it in your countenance and in your bearing. Words are not necessary, for virtue seems to radiate from your personality."

Such an unexpected reception, surpassing his fondest hope, was almost too much of a surprise. Though he knew that he was far from deserving such an encomium, he rejoiced at the thought that, at this particular time, a man in so high station should form such an exalted opinion of him. All of this he referred back to the providence of God, which is gentle but strong; at one time casting down, at another lifting up, so that all things may attain to their proper ends, according to the disposition of His infinite wisdom.

Father Ricci's response to the Viceroy was only in keeping with the Chinese formula, when he said, "And who am I, that I should be so honored?" As he kept repeating these words, his blushing served to confirm the Viceroy in his opinion. Afterwards, he inquired about some of the incidents of Ricci's voyage with the Assessor, and he found out that they were perfectly in accord with the long narrative he had heard about their many misfortunes. He also asked which of the Magistrates Ricci had met at Nankin, and when Father Matthew named only the one by whom he had been disgracefully expelled, the Viceroy remained silent. The one Ricci had named was a friend of his, and his only comment was, that he was glad Ricci had made the acquaintance of a man who was so well known for his honesty. And so they talked on, going from one subject to another for fully an hour. Toward the end of their conversation, he asked Ricci whither he intended to go from there, and when he learned that he intended to return to the Province of Canton, the Viceroy added, "And why not remain here, with us, in this most distinguished city?" "Certainly I would be quite pleased to stay here," Ricci answered, "if you were to grant me the necessary permission." "Then stay here, by all means. You have my permission." This ended the interview and Father Matthew came away rejoicing.

He had scarcely left the palace, when their mutual friend the doctor came to call on the Viceroy, as he frequently did, and when he began to talk about Father Ricci, the Viceroy became excitedly interested. The doctor told him that the Father had mathematical instruments which marked the hours of the day and the signs of the zodiac and many other things, without ever making an error. More than that too, he knew a certain art by means of which he could commit to memory a whole chapter of a book in almost a single reading. He also related the wonders of the triangular prism of glass, the marvels contained in European books and many other startling revelations. Hearing all this, the Viceroy thought he would like to have a clock made for himself, and he asked to have the rules for this artificial training of the memory translated into Chinese, so he could teach them to his children. He wanted to see the glass prism, and to have it shown to his family, but later on he could not be persuaded to accept it when Father Ricci offered it to him as a gift. Even when the doctor assured him that it was being offered as a present he refused to take it. Instead, he told a story taken from the Chinese annals and a very apt one for the occasion.

Once upon a time, as he related, there was a religious man who had a precious stone of great value, and when a very virtuous man of high station in life came to visit him, he gave him the stone. The visitor accepted it and immediately gave it back, remarking, "This stone will always be yours. Do not ever give it away, except to the man who admits that he is a man of virtue. If he really is such a man, then, of course, he will never accept it, and so it will always be yours. You and I, Matthew, are both following the same path of virtue."

After parting with the Viceroy on such friendly terms, he began a series of visits to the other Magistrates of the city. Among them he found several whom he had known in the Province of Canton, who recommended him to the others. The doctor, who was a close friend of the Viceroy, became so beholden to Father Ricci, because of the many presents he received from him, that he was continually talking about him to the Magistrates who came to his house. The result of all this was that when the friendship of the Viceroy for the Father became bruited about, it was no time before everyone of any prominence in the city thought he should make a friendly call on Father Matthew.

12. The Royal Relatives

~~~~~~

IN THIS METROPOLITAN CITY of Nancian there are many who are of royal blood, and who date their ancestry back beyond memory. Among them there are two in particular who maintain the title and the dignity of royalty. We have spoken of them before. These two, to pass over the lesser type, show no hesitation whatever in making a friend of a foreigner. One of them is called The Royal Chiengan, the other The Royal Longan. No one, even a Magistrate, rates a visit from either of these two, and yet each of them sent his majordomo, with precious gifts, to invite Father Ricci to his palace. And palaces they really were, worthy of royal majesty in size and in architecture, in the design and beauty of the gardens, and with regal attendants and furnishings.

Chiengan was first to send his invitation and he offered the more sympathetic reception, which was held in the royal aula, with the host arrayed in full royal panoply and wearing a crown. The guest was first asked to be seated and then given the customary drink of welcome, indicative among them of friendship and urbanity. This custom has already been described, so we shall pass it by at present, rather than interrupt the course of our narrative. The guest was first to make a presentation, consisting of European gifts which the Chinese esteem very highly. Among the presents there was a horizontal clock, made according to their way of reckoning, with the signs of the zodiac cut in black China marble. This clock also indicated the hour of the rising and the setting of the sun, and the length of days and nights of each month. The hours were also inscribed at the beginning and in the middle of each month. We mention the beginning and the middle, because the Chinese count twenty-four signs in the zodiac. This gift was the subject of great admiration. Nothing like it had ever been seen before in the kingdom. The only mathematical instrument they had ever known for measuring time was the one which is still called after the equator, and this one they could not use with any precision except at an elevation of thirty-six degrees of latitude. He also presented his host with a globe of the entire universe, marked with the celestial circles, in addition to a geographic sphere, statuettes, glass ware and other such European products. But the Regulus Chiengan was not to be outdone. He really surpassed the Father's generosity with gifts of silk cloth, with silver pieces of various weights and with a munificent supply of comestibles, all of which he presented with due pomp and with royal ritual. Of all the gifts which Chiengan received, nothing gave him as much pleasure as two books bound in European style and printed on Japanese paper, which is very thin and yet very durable, so much so, indeed, that it is difficult to say which is its more valuable quality. One of these books contained several geographical maps, nine drawings of the orbits of celestial bodies, combinations of the four elements, mathematical demonstrations and an explanation in Chinese of all the illustrations.

The second book was a brief tract on friendship, done in Chinese, in which, like Cicero in his Lelius, Father Matthew is being questioned by the King as to what the Europeans think about friendship. In this dialogue, which is not too lengthy, the author has gathered together from the Philosophers, the Fathers of the Church and other approved writers, what little could be found on this subject in our own literature. This book is still being read and wondered at and recommended by those who read it. Being written in both European and Chinese characters, it became even more popular on that account. Shortly after it came off the press, it was republished entirely in Chinese by the Mayor of one of the Cancian cities and it spread through various provinces, including Pekin and Cechian. Everywhere it met with the approval and the praise of the literary class, and it was frequently quoted in other works by writers of authority. In fact, in a surprisingly short time, this book was accepted as a standard work. This was the first of the books that Father Matthew wrote in Chinese. It brought him many friends and gained him a wide reputation, due in part to the effect it had upon the two quasi kings.

The friendship of Chiengan lasted the longer of the two, and continued until his death when he bequeathed it to his son. While the father was living, Father Matthew was a frequent guest at his house, and when he came to dinner, his host always paid the carriers of his palanquin and gave money gifts to his servants. It is by such gestures as these that they are accustomed to express their delight at the coming of a visitor.

No less, perhaps even more, was Ricci's reputation increased by familiar contact with another class of men. These were the Solons of the city, the literary Satraps, who were accustomed in their literary conferences to determine the proper interpretation of the laws. The leader of this society at the time was Ciam who was seventy years old. Both he and his confreres had heard much of Father Ricci from our friend Chiutaiso, who had lived here for some time. As a matter of fact, Chiutaiso had so highly praised the zeal of Father Matthew to this group that Ricci himself, and with reason, began to fear lest the Chinese might expect too much of him. The Solons, however, who generally looked down upon others, came in all humility to visit the stranger and were greatly pleased to hear him discourse so aptly on Chinese books, and then prove what he had said on Chinese authority.

During one of these conferences at Ricci's house, an incident occurred, trifling in itself, but which added no little to his reputation. Because of the great number of visitors who insisted upon seeing him and of the resulting activities, occasioned by their visits, Father Ricci became so fatigued that his health was becoming endangered. When he spoke about this to the leader of the Solons, he was told to instruct the porter to tell visitors that he was not at home. The answer to this was, that if one intended to be virtuous he must strictly avoid telling a lie. At this the pagan philosopher only laughed. Whereupon, Father Matthew explained to him the Christian doctrine prohibiting not only the lie that does harm to another, but also the untruth that is uttered by way of compliance or in jest. This law, he explained, holds for everyone in Europe, especially for religious and for those who would teach others, and he added that lying should be particularly abhorrent to men of prominent station in life. At first, his listener was surprised at the sanctity of such a law, and then he broke forth in praise of it. Highly educated as he was, and of subtle perception, from this one example he readily perceived the purity of the Christian faith. He told all this to others and, although of little importance in itself, he narrated, as something extraordinary, the fact that Father Matthew, both by prescribed law and by common understanding in his country, was unwilling to tell a lie. When this subject came up for discussion in the council meeting, the presiding officer of the Solons, who had heard the statement announced, gave it as his opinion that it would seem sufficient if one were ashamed of having told a lie. "I scarcely believe," he concluded, "that we could ever reach the ideal of never telling a lie."

13. A Permanent Foundation in Nancian

~~~~~~

REJOICING IN the prospect of founding a new residence, Father Matthew was glad to share his happiness with his brethren and particularly so with Father Eduardo Sande, the Rector of the College of Macao, and his immediate superior. He had already asked for assistance in men and in means. In answer to this call the Superior sent to Nancian a Portuguese Father, Giovanni Soeiro, and with him a Lay Brother, Francesco Martinez, destined for Xaucea. As for subsistence, due to a lack of income, he sent only as much as would purchase a residence and support it for that present year. In the meantime, Father Ricci had obtained letters patent from one of the Magistrates of Nancian, to call an assistant from the Province of Canton, and with that assurance the newcomers arrived at Nancian without difficulty. In passing over the mountain, which has already been described, they were assisted by the converts of the Nanhium district, whom they took occasion to visit en route. Their arrival added no little joy to the celebration of the Christmas Day of 1595. The coming of an assistant to Father Ricci caused some concern in the city. Naturally suspicious of foreigners, the people were apt to think or to say nearly anything. The strangers must be planning something sinister, some harm to the public welfare. Their friend the doctor was partial to them, as it was rumored, because they had taught him the abominable secrets of alchemy. Such stories were repeated but only quietly. There were no signs of any public disturbance.

Being a friend of the Viceroy, Father Matthew thought that the safety of the Mission could be secured through his authority. So he got together some gifts which he thought the Viceroy would like, such as he had given to the quasi kings, went to call on the Viceroy and asked him, in virtue of the letters which he had, for a document that would permit him to buy a house and to settle down in the city. The Viceroy gladly accepted the presents and made a generous return for them, but said he would have to consult the Governor about the document and would inform the Father later. The Governor, called Guam, was a good sort of man but overtimid, for fear he might get himself into trouble. He really did try to dispose of the question by endeavoring to get the Mission to accept a place in one of the suburbs, in a temple of the native priests. This, of course, was politely refused. The Fathers had no desire whatever to be again contaminated by a despised and sordid title that would serve to prevent the spread of the Gospel. Whereupon, the Governor lost all interest in the cause, and on several occasions later on, though frequently requested, always refused to issue a document of any kind. At that time he withdrew all privileges formerly granted to the city, and this nearly put an end to the Mission. Such is the power of example which the rulers have over the people, either to make or to unmake.

Through the intercession of friends, the Governor finally granted permission for the Fathers to dwell in the city, provided they would not look for documents to do so from his court. On the other hand, his friend and fellow citizen, the Viceroy, was easily satisfied with a promise instead of a document. Incidents such as this were not sufficient to dampen the interest or the zeal of Father Ricci. He immediately wrote out an explanation of his method for training the memory, by the suggestion of things and places, dedicated it to the children of the Viceroy, and then presented it to their father. This commentary afterwards spread throughout the entire kingdom and was put into common use. In addition, he also gave the Viceroy a night clock, set to the North Pole, an astrolabe. The Viceroy accepted these gifts with his usual urbanity and said he had taken up the matter of documents for the house, but as yet had not received them from the Governor. However, he assured them that he would have them in a few days because they were being prepared. As a matter of fact, he had taken up this question and discussed it seriously with the Governor who had told him that there was no need of documents, that a vocal promise was quite sufficient. His personal advice was to go ahead and buy whatever land and house he wanted, to forget about a written guarantee and to rest assured that no trouble would follow. Later on Father Ricci received the same answer from the Governor, with an added promise that he would act as his patron. Together with this promise there came a request for two sundials one of which he wanted to send home to his province of Cechian, and the other to keep for his own personal use. These were soon put together and dispatched, and in return there came a sum of silver far in excess of the cost of the instruments. According to the custom of the country this money could not be returned, because it is never permitted to return a gift received from a dignitary.

Once they had made their request of the Magistrate for the required permission to acquire a residence, it seemed best to the Fathers to let well enough alone. So they decided, and perhaps rightly so, that this was the safer way to proceed. They reasoned that if any trouble should arise in the future concerning the Mission, the one who had issued a document of security, becoming frightened, would be the most anxious of all to send the Mission away. His fear would be that the disturbance might be laid at his door for permitting the circumstances that gave rise to it. Besides, it was easier for Magistrates to favor the Mission when they issued no documents for it, as happened several times at Sciauquin. Moreover, if the Fathers were too insistent upon securing documents, they would be giving rise to suspicion which would eventually create a spirit of fear. In other respects also, after some years in the kingdom, it seemed safer to act trustingly, as natives, rather than as foreigners.

With this much accomplished, there were other tasks to be undertaken. It was not easy to rent a house, nor was there money enough on hand to purchase a suitable dwelling. Yet it seemed best to take advantage of the moment, lest the good will of the Magistrates should cool off, or some unexpected impediment arise. There was a good house for sale, suitable for their use for the time being, and properly located. It was not far from the Palace of the Governor and the price being asked was not exorbitant. It could be bought for sixty gold pieces. The Superior had forwarded fifty to rent a house; but it seemed better to buy one and to have a house of their own, even though it was somewhat small, rather than to live dependently by renting one for only a year. There was nothing to prevent them from looking about and buying a larger one later on. So they went through with the bargain and moved into the new residence.

They had to accommodate the house to their way of living, and for fear that some commotion might arise, they did the whole thing so secretly that they were in the house before the neighbors even knew that they wanted to come there. In this way they eliminated any time for trumping up stories against their coming. The Heads of the Street Department did complain to the Governor that certain strange individuals had come into their district, but the Governor soon placated them. He told them that he himself, on order from the Viceroy, had made a thorough investigation of their presence. He assured them also, with some exaggeration on his part, that Father Ricci had lived in the Province of Canton for over twenty years and that he had never disturbed anyone. He informed them also that he himself knew that Father Matthew was a good man and one who should not be sent away, especially after the Viceroy had given him permission to buy a house and to live there. With that, they went away satisfied and explained it all to the neighbors.

Once the house was bought, Father Matthew went to visit all the major Magistrates in the city, and gave them little presents from the things that had been sent to him from Macao. In distributing these gifts he was careful not to set a precedent of giving more than was becoming, or more than he might be able to give in the future.

Once they were settled here, the missionaries, who had grown wiser from experience, managed their station better and more to their purpose than they had done in the Province of Canton. It was about this time that Father Ricci revised his catechism, augmenting and arranging it in such a way that it appeared to have been composed by men of letters. No longer did its readers, as formerly, develop a distaste for the odious name of sacrificer, or for the religious cult set forth in this book. When the new edition appeared, the old printing forms were broken up and discarded.

14. More Trouble at Xaucea

WHILE ALL THIS was going on at Nancian, Father Cattaneo was studying Chinese at Xaucea. Following the example of Ricci and in order to promote the Christian cause, he dressed in the costume of the educated class. He wore this gown when he went to visit the Magistrates and it always produced the results he had looked forward to. At that time in Xaucea, Christianity seemed to be holding to the even tenor of its way. In a nearby town, however, there were some of the so-called minor literary class who seemed to be bent upon trouble. In this particular section of Xaucea there is an illiterate class, more barbarous than the rest of the Cantonese, who actually call this group barbarians, and this was the element that was disturbing the progress of the Mission.

One night, a crowd of ruffians, many of whom were half inebriated, wanted to come into the house and when they were refused entrance, they took to force and began throwing stones at the door and at the house in general. The servants went out and succeeded in driving them away from the house and into their small boats at the river bank. Here they gathered new forces of friends and fellow citizens and renewed the attack on the house. In the fracas that followed, the servants did not want to give in, but they were not numerous enough to repel the assailants. When the Father, with considerable difficulty, put an end to the affair, some of the wounded aggressors were received into the house for treatment and the rest retired, but not all unscathed.

On the following day, either because they were still angry, or because they did not want to be charged with the assault, the leaders of the mob hastened to the Governor's court to enter an accusation. Here a thickly crowded multitude, with great clamoring, were yelling that they had been insulted and wounded by those who were living at the Mission. In the same way, a roistering crowd went through the main streets of the town, stopping to call upon the Magistrates on the way. The judges of the first two courts they came to, refused to grant them a warrant for arrest, saying that they knew that these foreigners never molested anyone, and that if they themselves had been harmed there must have been a reason for it. There was a third judge, the Governor's Assessor and an enemy of the Mission, who did not hesitate to use his authority to avenge what he considered to be an insult offered to him by the Fathers. The insult was built up out of his complaint that they did not leave their astronomical clock in his house as long as he wanted it. He accepted the complaint of the mob, summoned two of the Mission domestics to his court and had them cruelly whipped in presence of their accusers.

Sebastian Fernandez, one of the Lay Brothers, followed them to the courthouse to see if he could have them released, either by argument or by supplication. He no sooner appeared in court than several of the junior element, realizing that the judge was favorable to their cause, seized the Brother and dragged him before the inhuman Assessor, shouting that he, more so than the others, was the one by whom they had been assaulted and injured. Again without hearing the accused, the judge did not hesitate to sentence the Brother to whipping and to the following still more ignominious punishment. They had a table there about a yard and a half square, with a hole in the middle of it, wide enough to close around one's neck. The table could be opened and closed, leaving the head protruding, with the hands beneath, so they could not be raised to the mouth, thus preventing one from taking food or drink, save what was given by others. The Brother was sentenced to stand a whole day in this instrument of torture, at the entrance to the court, with a sign attached to the table reading, that he had dared to strike the Baccalaureates. This kind of punishment is not unusual in this particular district, and with that done by way of satisfaction, the judge dispersed the crowd.

Father Cattaneo decided to remedy this evil situation. He was of the opinion that the church building had been taken as a pretext for such disturbances and so he decided to transform it into a private chapel. He did this, not only for the purpose mentioned but also to get rid of the odious name of sacrificers to which it had given rise. In addition to tearing down the church, he did something more, which proved to be very opportune. He removed from sight every ornament in the house in which visitors took a special delight; first, in order to keep the curious away, and secondly, as a sign of mourning for the injustice they had suffered. With that done, they lived more quietly but not wholly unmolested. Finally, he sent the Brother who had been arrested to Father Ricci, and asked him to send another Brother in exchange, which Father Matthew did.

All this happened opportunely because, a short time afterwards, several Magistrates arrived at Xaucea and said they wanted to see the Europeans and the things they had brought with them. What they saw was one building practically torn down and the interior of the house stripped of nearly everything. They were quite disappointed at all this and they did not hesitate to attribute it to the Assessor who had come along with them, saying that he had presided at the trial and that the whole affair was anything but just. This he did not deny. Instead, he openly confessed his fault complaining that he had been driven beyond the limits of justice by the mob of spurious literati. He humbly begged pardon of Father Cattaneo before all and then, in order to appease him, invited him to a formal banquet which he was giving for the visiting Magistrates in a nearby temple. At this banquet he really did make amends for the injury he had done, by the great praise he bestowed upon Father Cattaneo.

At about the same time a certain Magistrate, a member of the Pimpi-thau, who had authority over the entire district of Xaucea, arrived at the City of Xaucea, and came with considerable pomp and show to visit the Mission. When he entered, he asked Father Cattaneo to sit beside him, which on his first visit was considered to be quite an unusual courtesy, and went far toward wiping out any injury of the past. But let us not dismiss the Assessor as yet. Still frightened by the thought of the injury he had done by his inconsiderate action, he was very much afraid that he might acquire a reputation for cruelty, which would cost him his position. Hence, in order to amend matters, of his own volition, he issued an edict in which he included the full story of what had happened, and placed the entire blame on the so-called literati. In it he declared the Mission to be free of all blame [such is the force of truth], and he concluded with strong words, reminding everyone, again and again, to make no trouble for the Father or for any of his household, under penalty of severe punishment.

In this way Father Cattaneo labored on without the help of another priest until 1597. The one who had been named to be his companion was not physically strong and he remained at Macao, because it seemed somewhat dangerous to send an ailing man into the unhealthy climate of Xaucea. In addition to this, Father Valignano, by order of the General of the Society of Jesus, had ceased to govern the Mission of India. His authority then, under the title of Official Visitor, extended only to Japan and to the China Mission; hence he could not send missionaries here from India. Alone and overwhelmed with work, Father Cattaneo fell seriously ill, almost beyond recovery. He was finally forced to return to Macao, and Father Giovanni Aroccia, a Portuguese, himself in ill health at Macao, was sent to take his place, with instructions to remain indoors and to take care of the house as best he could. In the meantime, the Official Visitor of the Society of Jesus arrived from India and appointed Father Nicolo Longobardo as assistant to Father Cattaneo at the Xaucea Mission, to which they were to return together. Father Aroccia, who was still thought to be in poor health, was recalled to the College of Macao, to take up some less difficult work. Father Giovanni, however, was holding out well. In fact, his health was better at Xaucea than it had been at Macao. Disappointed and sorry at being withdrawn from what he called his first vocation, just at a time when he had completed his studies and was ready to apply them, he happily pleaded his own case with the Father Visitor and was permitted, to the great joy of all, to remain with the other two. By this time the two were en route for Xaucea and they joined him without further mishap.

BOOK FOUR

1.Back to Nankin

~~~~~~

WITH THE BURDEN of the charge of the India Mission
off his shoulders, Father Valignano, the Official Visitor, turned his
attention to putting the China Mission on a secure basis, before he
sailed for Japan. From his own experience, he already knew enough
about China to realize that an embassy to the King from the Pope or
from the Catholic King, as proposed several years past, was out of the
question. Nor did he think that such an embassy would be the best
method of promoting Christianity in China. He realized that the China
Mission was making more progress than had been hoped for and that
it was growing more prosperous from day to day. This he attributed
especially to the help of Heaven and also to the caution and the industry of those who were better acquainted with what was going on
in China. So, with the meager means he had at his disposal, he determined to augment its prestige.

To begin with, and for various reasons, he thought that the Mission
was laboring at a disadvantage in being governed by the Rector of
the College at Macao, who was not present on the Mission proper,
and consequently could not be expected to appreciate its difficulties.
It followed only naturally that, being separated by such distances,
present opportunities that demanded quick action for the benefit of
the Mission, were frequently lost. His conclusion was that the Superior
of the Mission should be a man who was living in the interior of China
and on the scene of action. Father Eduardo Sande, the Rector of the
College of Macao, was growing old and could not be asked to go into
the interior of the kingdom. Of those who were deep into the vineyard,

Father Matthew Ricci was the oldest and most experienced with the Chinese, because of his long sojourn among them. Father Ricci was, therefore, appointed Superior of the entire Mission, with full authority to conduct it as he judged to be for its greater good, and to open a new center where there was most hope of success. As Superior he had the same ecclesiastical faculties as the Father Visitor. What the Father Visitor particularly recommended to the new Superior was that he bend every effort to open a residence in Pekin, because it seemed to him, that there would never be any assurance of remaining permanently in China, unless someone should be favorably received by the King.

In order to promote the purpose he had in mind, the Father Visitor gathered together whatever he thought would help the cause and sent it to Nancian; a statue of the Blessed Virgin, sent on from Spain, a statue of Christ the Saviour, and a medium-sized clock with a mechanical arrangement of wheels cleverly built into its mechanism for striking the hours, the half hours and the quarters. This clock was sent to the Mission by Very Reverend Claudio Aquaviva, the General of the Society of Jesus, with the hope that the Mission might be advanced by the same means by which it was begun. An almost identically made clock was also sent to the Father Visitor for the China Mission by the Bishop of the Philippine Islands. In addition to these things he collected, in Macao, whatever he thought would be of service to the missionaries and sent it all in to Nancian.

At this time, those who were appointed to the interior China Mission were delayed at Macao, awaiting an opportune sailing, and the Father Visitor requested the Rector of the College to provide for them during the delay, as he had formerly done when they were under his jurisdiction. He also arranged that there should be one Procurator, or Treasurer, for both the Chinese and Japanese Missions. He was to handle the subsidy donated by the Catholic King and also the alms donated by others. The Portuguese of Macao gave frequent and generous donations to these two missions; something that we note in passing, that it may not be forgotten in the future.

Father Emanuele Dias, who had left Portugal years before and was several times Superior of the mission in India, was at this time living in Macao. Possessed of the necessary qualities for governing in the Society, and being particularly interested in China, the Father Visitor appointed him Rector of the College of Macao, which was considered to be the seminary of the two great missions of Japan and China. The ex-Rector, Father Sande, had governed the College during the years of great changes, and his holy life in religion came to an end shortly after his retirement. He had entered the Society of Jesus as a young man, and for many years, until he reached old age, his intellectual genius and his many other endowments marked him as a learned professor, as a brilliant preacher, and especially as a religious Superior who was beloved of everyone both at home and abroad.

Knowing the mind of the Father Visitor, Father Ricci left no stone unturned, nor any means neglected, in planning to enter the royal City of Pekin. First he thought of contacting his friend, Chiengan, the quasi-king and the nearest in blood relationship to the reigning monarch. He showed him the clock and the other gifts which he thought of giving to the King. On second thought, however, he decided that this method of approach would be quite useless. He was aware of the fact that the King not only kept his relatives out of public life, but actually protected himself against them, fearing that if occasion offered they would not hesitate to take over his throne. Such an approach appeared to him to be dangerous, in fact, it could result in the utter ruin of the entire Mission. Besides, he concluded, even if the so-called Regulus were not conscious of the King's fear, he would undoubtedly refuse to interest himself in such a project.

Ricci had heard that the Guam, with whom we are acquainted, had visited the Mission at Xaucea and had become quite familiar with the Fathers, during his trip from Pekin to his birthplace on the Island of Hainan, to the south. He had also heard that this man had been recalled to Nankin by the King, to preside over the First Tribunal, called the Li Pu. To the Chinese it is known as the Tribunal for Magistrates, being the court by which Magistrates are made. With this in mind, he told Father Cattaneo to contact the Guam on his return trip, because he had promised that when he returned to the Royal Court, he would take the Fathers with him to correct certain errors in the Chinese calendar relative to the constellations, and to explain certain other mathematical difficulties. The Guam came to Xaucea and Father Cattaneo went to see him. He asked for Father Matthew, and when he learned that he was at the Capital of the Province of Nancian, he was delighted and said he would join him there. Father Cattaneo offered to go along with him as far as Nancian, to talk over the matter with Father Ricci, and so it was agreed. In the interim, the residence was turned over to the care of Father Nicolo Longobardo and Father Cattaneo went along, to remain at Nancian. It so happened that the

Guam, now called the President of the Tribunal, had left two days in advance of the appointed time, and Father Cattaneo traveled day and night to overtake him. The fact that he took an early start was somewhat to the advantage of the Fathers, as it gave them time to talk over what was to be done and to arrange their baggage accordingly. They were both of the opinion that Father Cattaneo should accompany Father Ricci. When the Guam arrived, the Fathers of Nancian went to visit him and brought him some European presents, and he was particularly pleased with the triangular glass prism, which he had seen at Xaucea and which he thought was a precious stone of great value.

The President of the Tribunal was highly pleased with being recalled to his former Magistrature by the King, and also with the hope that this would serve as a stepping-stone to the corresponding office in Pekin, which would give him supreme authority in the Colao. At the first opportune moment during their visit, the Fathers began talking about their own affairs and said that they would like to go to Pekin and bring some presents to the King. The President asked to see the presents and was delighted with them. In order to make it easier, they assured him that they expected nothing from the King other than his good will, and they would pay the expenses of the trip, exercise the necessary care, and make all the necessary preparations. In reply, the President told them that he would be pleased, not only to have them accompany him to Nankin, but to Pekin also, and that he would have to go there in about a month to congratulate the King on his birthday. That would be on the seventeenth day of the eighth moon, or as we would say on the seventeenth of September. He thought that would be quite an opportune occasion on which to offer the King presents, such as he had never seen before. Here was an opportunity so favorable to their plans that they could not afford to neglect it. Ricci hired a boat for the trip, took along Father Cattaneo, whom he expected to be of considerable help, leaving the other two at Nancian, and set out post haste. Two of our Brothers also accompanied the Fathers. We call them our Brothers because shortly afterwards they entered the Society of Jesus as Lay Brothers. They were Sebastiano Fernandez and Emanuele Pereira, both Chinese but with Portuguese names, and natives of Macao. They were the sons of Chinese, who accepted the faith and at the same time Portuguese ways. They took Portuguese names when they were baptized, and by this time they seemed to be more Portuguese than Chinese. Their sponsor at baptism gave them a surname and a family name, and they used their Chinese family name only when speaking or writing Chinese. The Fathers call them by their Portuguese names, which are better known to Europeans.

Being pressed for time at their departure, they did not bid adieu to friends, nor did they say good-bye to the Magistrates, for fear they might make some objection. They didn't even trouble to secure letters patent for traveling, as was done on other occasions. The company of this particular Magistrate would be better assurance than letters, and the fact that they had made this trip would render the residence at Nancian more secure and strengthen the Mission in general. No Magistrate would think of opposing the ideas of the President of the Court of Magistrates. What happened was just what they had looked forward to; not a murmur was heard against them either at Xaucea or in Nancian.

They set sail from Nancian, the day after the Octave of the Feast of Saint John the Baptist in 1598. During the voyage to Nankin they became better acquainted with the President and won the friendship of his children and of his servants with suitable presents. It was their good fortune also to become acquainted with the one whom the President consulted in all his affairs, and who acted almost in the capacity of his director. This was his wife's brother, who was blessed with an abundance of good nature and who remained a friend of the Fathers as long as he lived.

During the voyage they discussed the ways and means of bringing this enterprise to a happy end. The President proposed that one of the clocks be given to the Superintendent of the King's palace, for presentation, and the other to a certain one of the palace eunuchs, whom the President had in mind to promote the presentation. Father Matthew in turn refused to give a clock to anyone, or to accept any sponsor, other than the President, himself. This seemed to please him no end, and they agreed upon that procedure. The promise was made, and he was given one of the clocks, which he learned to set and to regulate when that was necessary.

On their arrival at Nankin, they were surprised to discover that everyone there was living under a cloud of fear. The Japanese had marched beyond the border, in an armed invasion of Korea, which was tributary to China. It would cost a tremendous amount to defend Korea and there was little hope that the Japanese advance could be halted. As a result of this condition, no one was willing to receive the Father's party into his home; for a recent law had been passed strictly

forbidding anyone to harbor a person whose clothes or whose countenance might give rise to suspicion. Only a few days before, they had
arrested Japanese spies who were wandering about the city, observing
everything that was going on. With such a law in effect, no one dared
to take in the Fathers and they were left in their small boat, in
extremely hot weather and with scarcely any protection. Even the
President himself would not dare make use of his authority. On the
contrary, he was almost trembling, for fear that someone might accuse
him of having secretly brought in foreigners. Several times, Father
Ricci went into the city to see the President, but always in a curtained
palanquin, and he could not travel, even in this manner, unless the
Supreme Commander of the Military was notified of his coming. No
one knew about these secret visits until he told the other Fathers about
them several years later. He also recounted that on one occasion the
Supreme Commander sent a military guard to arrest him, but when he
informed them that he was on his way to the palace of the Viceroy,
they let him pass, either in fear of the President of the Magistrates, or
because they knew that there was nothing to be feared from one who
was honored with the friendship of such an exalted dignitary.

A council was held as to what should be done in such circumstances
and it was decided to send a request to the King from Nankin. This
had to be done through the office of the local Chancellor, the Magistrate whose duty it was to send such documents to the King from
Nankin. Father Ricci had this request prepared and written by one of
the better known literati, who was familiar with negotiations pertaining to the royal court. The petition was not very long and yet the scribe
charged just short of eight gold pieces for it, which will afford one
some idea of what the Chinese literati thought of their manuscript
productions. This whole idea went up in smoke. The Chancellor Magistrate was a good friend of the President of the Magistrates, but he
could never be persuaded to interest himself in a request to the King,
coming from a foreigner. In order to bolster up his refusal, he suggested that the President take the Fathers with him to Pekin, where
he could more easily present the request to the King, and perhaps with
better results. With this advice, or rather with this refusal, the
full charge of the Fathers in Nankin reverted to the President of
the Magistrates.

2.From Nankin to Pekin

∿∿∿∿∿∿∿∿∿∿∿∿∿∿∿∿∿∿∿∿∿∿∿

DESPAIRING OF not being able to carry out his plan at Nankin, and not wishing to break his promise after receiving so many gifts, the President of the Magistrates resolved to take the Fathers with him to Pekin. Once there, he thought he would be able to have their presents offered to the King by the court eunuchs, with whom he was on friendly terms. He himself had to make the trip by land in order to get there for the King's birthday and to congratulate him on behalf of the six councils he governed. His luggage was to go by river, in charge of two servants, and he invited the Fathers to take passage on the boat with them, as members of his household. This particular kind of boat had some resemblance to a trireme, and because of its speed the Chinese called it a cavalier. In order to have more freedom on the voyage, the Fathers preferred to hire a separate cabin, rather than to share one with the domestics. This also afforded them ample space for their luggage.

Among the presents which they were taking along for the King, there was a large tablet, on which was drawn a map of the world, which Father Matthew had decorated with brief commentaries in Chinese writing. The President took great pleasure in studying this tablet, wondering that he could see the great expanse of the world depicted on such a small surface, and that it contained the names of so many new kingdoms and a list of their customs. He would examine it over and over again and very attentively, in an effort to memorize this new idea of the world.

As soon as the President arrived in Nankin, all the high Magistrates, according to Chinese custom, made haste to visit him and to congratulate him on his new appointment, or rather on his return to his former office. Such visits are not made empty handed. The Viceroy of Nankin, who was a close friend of the President, lived in a little town about a day's journey from the larger city. He lived outside, rather than in Nankin, because, although he was local Viceroy, he was of lower rank than the President of the Magistrates and inferior in grade

301

to many of the City Judges. This was generally true of the Viceroys of Nankin, and so they preferred to reside in a district where there was no superior Magistrate.

Now it happened that this particular Viceroy had received from the Mayor of a certain town in the Province of Nankin, a map of the world, which Father Matthew had previously made at Sciauquin. He was so pleased with it that he had it copied on marble, in the town of Luceu, together with a beautifully carved inscription, in praise of the drawing. He himself had composed the inscription, but he made no mention in it of the author of the original map. Among the gifts which he gave the President there was a copy of this map, given as his own original work. The Chinese method of first engraving on marble and then making copies of the engraving has been explained in our first book. When the President saw that the map he had received was exactly like the one which, as he thought, Father Matthew had copied, he called him and said, "You see we also have these universal maps. Here is one I received from the Viceroy of Nankin, which is exactly like the one I got from you." It was patently evident to Ricci that he was looking at his own work. He said he had first published this map at Sciauquin and given copies to his friends, and that it had come this far. His host was glad to hear this, because it increased his satisfaction with the present, to realize that a man with such a nation-wide reputation as the Viceroy esteemed it so highly. In truth, at that time there were very few in public life with reputations equal to that of Sciau, as the Viceroy was called. His vivacious spirit and his excellent conduct of public affairs were everywhere highly praised, and this fame, constantly attributed to him for his conduct of public affairs, was really genuine and none of it invented, as fame so frequently is. Only a year later he was called from the high office he was holding to be Assessor of the chief Presidial at Pekin, called the Scilam. It happened that the people in the Province of Uquam were rising in sedition against the tyranny of one of the eunuchs of the King's palace. The King, without seeking advice from anyone appointed this man to quell the rebellion. This he did in a quiet way, but in an unguarded moment, being too confident that peace had been fully restored, they say he was murdered in the same province by the King's relatives.

To return to the thread of our narrative, the President wrote to the Viceroy to thank him for his gift, and told him that the man who made the map was staying at his house and was going with him to Pekin. Whereupon, the Viceroy sent a military captain of the guard with a letter begging the President to send him the author of the map as soon as possible, saying that he had been waiting for a long time to meet him, because of his wide-spread reputation. He also sent a covered palanquin and carriers to bring Father Ricci to his house, and other carriers with horses to bring along his luggage. At the time of the arrival of the Viceroy and his retinue at Nankin, Father Ricci and his companions, with all their baggage, were already aboard the cavalier galley, ready to set sail on the following day. The President advised them not to refuse the Viceroy the visit he had requested, and the Fathers were of the opinion that they should not forgo an opportunity for making a friend of a dignitary with so much authority. So it was agreed that Father Cattaneo should set out in advance, as the boat could be easily overtaken by horses, later on. Father Ricci remained behind and went to visit the Viceroy, in the covered chair that had been sent for him. He took two servants with him and was accompanied on the road by the same captain who had brought the letter of invitation.

After greeting the Viceroy in Chinese fashion, he presented him with some European gifts; things which were wholly new to him and which he accepted with great pleasure. It seemed that the presence of his guest made him happier than the gifts, and there was no end to his desire for conversation. During Ricci's stay they discussed mathematical problems and talked over Europe in general, in which the Viceroy was so deeply interested that he detained his guest there, almost by force, for ten whole days. Father Ricci brought along with him some of the gifts intended for the King, in order to introduce conversation relative to offering presents to the monarch. Among these gifts there was a very highly ornamented crucifix, contained in a transparent case of fluted glass. At first sight of it, in his living room where Ricci showed it to him, the Viceroy stood in silent admiration, then with both hands opening the two little glass doors of the case, he turned his face away from it. Father Matthew could not understand this gesture and thought that perhaps the man was horrified. "This image," he said to the Viceroy, "represents none other than the Lord of Heaven and earth." "You don't have to tell me," his host replied, "it speaks for itself. It surely is not the image of any merely mortal being, and this room is no fitting place to expose the image of the Lord of Heaven and earth."

At the top of the house there was a beautifully furnished room, open to the sky, a sort of chapel, where they went to worship the heavens,

according to the law of the philosophers. There were three entrances
to this chapel, on the north, east and west, and it was surrounded by
a gallery with balustrades, and beyond these there were little gardens,
made very attractive by various fruits and flowers. The Viceroy had
his servants build an altar in this chapel, on which he placed lighted
candles and burning incense, with the crucifix set in the middle.
Dressed in the full robes and ornaments of his official position, he
would approach the altar with great reverence, repeat the customary
salutation four times over, and ascend the altar to gaze leisurely at
the crucifix. His approach was always from one side, never directly
in front of the image, and he spent so much time in contemplating the
crucifix that it seemed as if he could not be drawn away from it. After
him, the domestic servants would go through a similar ceremony. This
ceremony of veneration became a daily practice with the household,
and one of the servants was commissioned by the master to keep a
thurible of incense perpetually burning on the altar. The Viceroy invited the dignitaries of the city to come and view the marvelous image,
and among those who came was the presiding officer of the Literary
Academy of Nankin, who afterwards became an intimate friend of
Father Matthew in Pekin, and was later appointed Viceroy of the
Province of Fuchian. Father Matthew spent much time in the chapel
mentioned, reading the divine office and saying other prayers, and
he thanked God that these honors were being paid to Him even by
pagans.

The Viceroy was anxious to have Father Ricci remain longer, to
make certain mathematical instruments, but knowing that his companion had already set out for Pekin, his host agreed to his departure.
Considering the poverty of the Mission, the large sum of money which
he gave the Father, to defray the expenses of his voyage, was really a
welcome alms, but the good advice he offered was probably more
valuable for their present undertaking. In no wise minimizing the
difficulty, he openly expressed his opinion that the project would not
meet with the success to which the Fathers were looking forward.

After Father Ricci left the house, the Viceroy called for a palanquin
and had himself taken to the river landing. There he went aboard the
cavalier galley with one of his attendants, whom he had chosen to accompany the Father until he rejoined his companions. They overtook
the others at the town of Chingan, from which the attendant returned
and made his report to the Viceroy. It was this same Viceroy who afterwards in Pekin used to boast to the other Magistrates that for some

days his palace had harbored the image of Christ the Saviour, which was to be presented to the King.

The Nankin River, which has already been alluded to as the Son of the Sea, is called Hiansu, in Chinese. As far as Nankin it flows north, then turns somewhat south and flows rapidly to the sea, forty miles beyond Nankin. In order to go by water from Nankin to the royal city of Pekin, the Chinese kings had a long canal constructed from this river to another, called the Yellow River, because of the color of its turbulent waters. The Yellow River is the second greatest river in China, both in size and in importance. Its source is beyond the border of the kingdom, to the west, on a mountain called Cunlun, which they say, is the same mountain, or at least is near the mountain, from which the Ganges takes its rise. At the source of the Yellow River there is a great lake called the Lake of the Constellations. From there it enters China on the west border of the Province of Scensi. From the north walls it turns back again into the country of the Tartars. It then swings south into the same province from which it came, thence into the Province of Sciansi and from here into the Province of Honan, whence it turns east and flows in that direction to the ocean, not far north of the river Hiansu, which we have called the Son of the Sea.

This Yellow River has no respect at all for Chinese law and order. It comes from a barbarous region and, as it were, seeking vengeance for the hatred the Chinese have for outsiders, it frequently ravages whole districts of the realm when it fills up with sand and changes its course at will. There are certain Magistrates who try to control it with religious rites, offered to the river, or to its spirits. The Chinese assign governing spirits to many things and they say that the waters of the Yellow River become clear only once in every thousand years. Hence the Chinese proverb to indicate something that very seldom happens, "When the Yellow River clears." Those who sail on this river watch the water for several days, until the mud and the sand settle in it. The general content of its water is not less than one third silt. Entrance to the City of Pekin from the river, and also an exit from it are made by means of canals, constructed for boats bringing cargoes into the city. They say there are ten thousand boats engaged in this commerce and these come only from the five provinces of Chiansi, Cechian, Nankin, Uquam and Sciantum. These are the provinces that provide the King with his annual tribute of rice and grain. The other ten provinces pay their taxes in silver money. Besides these tribute vessels, a great many more, belonging to the Magistrates, are continually coming and going, and still more plying private trade.

Private merchants coming in from the Hiansu River are not permitted to enter these canals, excepting those who live between the canals to the north. This law was passed in order to prevent the multitude of boats from clogging the traffic, and cargoes destined for the royal city from being spoiled. And yet, so great is the number of boats, that frequently many days are lost in transit by crowding each other, particularly when the water is low in the canals. To prevent this, the water is held back at stated places by wooden locks, which also serve as bridges. These locks are opened when the water rises to full height behind them, and the boats are carried along by the force of the stream produced. Going from one lock to another creates a difficult task for the sailors and occasions tedious delays on the journey. The work is increased also by the fact that there is seldom enough wind in the canals for sailing, and ropes are stretched from the banks to pull the boats along. At times it happens that the rush of water is so high and so strong, at the exit from one lock or at the entrance to another, that the boats are capsized and the whole crew is drowned. The boats of the Magistrates and of other Government dignitaries are drawn up stream, against the current, by wooden devices on the shore, and the expense for such hauling is paid by the Government. The cost of maintaining these canals, which consists chiefly in keeping them navigable, mounts to a million a year, as a mathematician would express it. All this may seem rather strange to Europeans, who may judge from maps that one could take a shorter and a less expensive route to Pekin by sea. This may be true enough, but the fear of the sea and the pirates who infest the seacoast has so penetrated the Chinese mind, that they believe the sea route would be far more hazardous for conveying provisions to the royal court.

Along the route from Nankin to Pekin, one passes a great number of well known cities, in the Provinces of Nankin, Sciantum and Pekin. Besides the cities there are along the river banks so many towns, villages and scattered homes that one might say that the entire route is inhabited. Nowhere along the whole journey is there any lack of provisions, such as rice, wheat, meat, fish, fruit, vegetables and wine, and the like, all of which are bought very cheaply. Through the canal and into the royal city they bring great quantities of wood for royal buildings; beams, columns and flat boards, especially after a royal palace has been burned down, and it is said that two out of three of them go up in fire. All along the voyage the Fathers saw huge rafts of beams lashed together and hauling other cargoes of wood, being drawn with great effort by thousands of men trudging along the banks. Some of them were making five or six miles a day. Rafts such as these from the very distant province of Suscuen are sometimes two or three years in transit to the capital. A single beam of some of these rafts may cost as much as three thousand ecus in gold, and some of the rafts were two miles long. The Chinese prefer brick to stone, and the bricks destined for use in the royal palaces may be transported in barges, a distance of fifteen hundred miles. There are many boats used for this purpose only, and they are kept moving day and night. Along this route one could see enough building material to construct not only a royal palace but a whole village in addition.

Each year the southern provinces provide the King with everything needed or wanted to live well in the unfertile Province of Pekin; fruit, fish, rice, silk cloth for garments, and six hundred other things, all of which must arrive on a fixed day, otherwise those who are paid to transport them are subject to a heavy fine.

The boats called cavaliers are commanded by palace eunuchs, and they always travel rapidly, in fleets of eight or ten. The canal is navigable only during the summer season, when the water is high, perhaps due to the melting of the snow on the mountains where the river takes its rise. During the hot summer season much of the food stuffs, which are perhaps a month or two in transportation, would spoil before reaching Pekin; so they are kept in ice, to preserve them. The ice gradually melts, and so great stores of it are kept at certain stops, and the boats are liberally supplied with enough of it to keep their cargoes fresh until arrival. The eunuchs sometimes let out the vacant cabins on their palace boats for hire, and keep the money.

The Chinese look upon it as unbecoming to send all their donations to the King in one boat. It seems to be more becoming to forward them in several different crafts, but the King himself winks at this practice for another reason. There are numberless boats coming to Pekin with provisions for royalty, and many of them not carrying their full tonnage. The merchants take advantage of this and hire space on the half empty boats at very low rates. This practice supplies more than the soil produces, and thus relieves want and lessens the need of charity. Hence it is said that nothing grows in Pekin, but there is nothing lacking there.

Although the Fathers were traveling on the same boat with the servants of the President of the Magistrates, and had private quarters of their own, they fell sick one after the other on their trip, because of an extended period of extremely hot weather. With Heaven's help, however, they were fully restored to health before arriving at Pekin. During the voyage, in the Province of Sciantum, they left one river and entered another which was man made rather than natural. This river, or canal, passed close to Pekin, near a fort called Tiensin, where another river from the Pekin Province, or more correctly from Tartary, flows along beside it until the two meet and flow in common for about a day to the sea, or rather to the gulf between Korea and China. In this fort at Tiensin there was a specially appointed Viceroy Extraordinary, due to the fact that the Japanese had already invaded Korea. Under his direction a numerous fleet was being prepared to go to the aid of the Koreans. The whole river was covered with ships of war, laden with troops, but the cavalier in which the Fathers were traveling, wedged its way between their prows without interruption.

Finally they disembarked, not at the port, but on the river bank about a day's journey from the city walls. There was a canal running from there into the city, but to prevent it from being clogged up with boats, only those conveying cargoes to the royal court were permitted to use it. All other consignments were carried into the city by wagons or pack-horses or porters. The day on which the Fathers entered the royal city was considered to be quite appropriate for their arrival, being the eve of the Feast of the Nativity of the Blessed Virgin. It really was a cause for rejoicing which we should not pass over in silence; to think that the Christian faith, from across many seas had finally entered this kingdom, closed to it for so long a time, and its messengers come into the royal capital.

The principal places along the course of this voyage were these: Iamcheu, in the Province of Nankin, 32 degrees of latitude, Hoaingan, 34 degrees, approximately, Siuceu 34½ degrees, amply measured— in the Province of Sciantum, Zinim 35¾ degrees—Lincin 37¾ degrees— in the Province of Pekin, Tiensin, 39½ degrees and Pekin, fully 40 degrees, thus correcting the error of some who, using only their imagination, place Pekin at 50 degrees of latitude.

The journey to Pekin from the metropolitan city of Canton, which is two days away from Macao, we shall measure in Chinese stadia, of which there are five to an Italian mile and fifteen to a league. The journey, which the Fathers made by river travel, was therefore, as follows: from Canton to Nanhium, 1170 stadia, thence to Nancian 1120, from here to Nankin 1440, and then to Pekin 3335, making in all 7065 stadia or 1413 miles.

3.Failure at Pekin

HAVING HAD a first view of Pekin, it would be unfair to the Royal Capital and perhaps to the curiosity of the reader to pass by without saying a few words about it. The seat of Chinese royalty is situated far north in the realm, about a hundred miles distant from the great wall erected against the approach of the Tartars. The size of the city, the planning of its houses, the structure of its public buildings and its fortifications are far inferior to those of Nankin, but in population, in the number of soldiers and of governing Magistrates, it is superior. It is closed in on the south by two high, thick walls, wide enough for twelve horses to run along the tops of them without interference. These walls are built mostly of brick. At the foundations they are sustained by stones of tremendous dimensions, and the interiors are filled with prepared earth. They are not higher than city walls seen in Europe. On the north, the city is protected by a single wall. At night, all these walls are guarded by a host of soldiers, as numerous as if a war were raging. During the day the city gates are guarded by the palace eunuchs, or at least they are supposed to be guarded, but these eunuchs are too busy taking tolls, something that is never done in other cities. The royal palace is built into the southern wall, like an entrance to the city, and it extends clear to the northern wall, the entire length of the city and right through the middle of it. The rest of the town is spread on either side of the palace. This royal residence is not as wide as the palace at Nankin, but the grace and beauty of its architecture are emphasized by its slender lines. Due to the absence of the kings, Nankin is gradually falling into decay, like a spiritless body, while Pekin is growing more and more attractive because of their presence.

Very few of the streets in Pekin are paved with brick or stone, and it is difficult to say which season of the year is more objectionable for walking. The mud in the winter and the dust in the summer are equally obnoxious and fatiguing. As it seldom rains in this province, the surface earth dissolves into a coating of dust, which even a slight wind raises, blowing it into the houses, where it covers and soils nearly everything. In order to overcome this dust nuisance, they have introduced a custom which is probably unknown anywhere else. During the dust season here, nobody of any class would think of going out, either on foot or in conveyance, without wearing a long veil, falling in front from the hat, and thus sheltering the face. The material of the veil is fine enough to see through but no dust can penetrate it. It has other advantages also, namely, that one is recognized only when he wishes to be. He is saved innumerable salutes and greetings and can travel in whatever style and at whatever price he pleases. The Chinese do not consider it extravagant to travel by horse conveyance in the city, and as it is expensive to travel by chair, one can forgo pomp and fashion in Pekin without embarrassment.

This custom of wearing a veil was quite opportune for the Fathers. It would have been somewhat of a risk for foreigners to walk the streets during the war years, but with the veil they went about wherever they pleased and traveled unmolested. Because of the dust and the mud, there is scarcely any other city where it is so common to travel on horse or on some other mount, and they are everywhere waiting for hire; at the crossroads, at the city gates, the palace bridges and the much frequented arches, and it costs very little to hire one for a whole day. The city streets are so crowded that the muleteers have to lead their beasts with a bridle to make a passage through the people. They know every street in the city and the dwellings of every prominent citizen. They also have directories in which every section, street and plaza of the city is listed. In addition to travel on horse-back, there is the ubiquitous gestatorial chair, in which Magistrates and other dignitaries are carried about, and it costs much more for such conveyance in Pekin than it does in Nankin, or anywhere else in China.

We have already noted that there is an abundance of everything in Pekin, most of which is brought into the city, but despite this fact, living in Pekin is difficult, save for such as are wealthy and do not have to retrench. Firewood is always lacking here, but this shortage is made up for by a bituminous substance, which for want of a better name, we shall call asphalt or mineral pitch. It is a sort of fossil tar, dug out of the earth, like that used by the Belgians, around Liége. The Chinese use it for cooking and also for heating their houses during the extreme cold of winter, which almost reaches the temperature of the polar regions. The abundance of this material makes up nicely for the lack of firewood. The beds here are built up with bricks, with a hollow space underneath, through which pipes from a fireplace are passed, creating a heat chamber beneath the bed. One does not have to keep the heat on during the night because the chamber stays hot for a long time. This kind of bed is in common use through all the northern provinces. The northern Chinese are more warlike and courageous than those from the south but less alert mentally. Such is the balance of human nature, that some are superior in one respect and some in another.

With their arrival in Pekin, the truth about something which they had suspected for a long time finally dawned upon them namely, that the Kingdom of China is one and identical with what some writers call the Great Cathay, and that Pekin is the seat of the Great Can, the present King of China. These same writers call the city Cambalu. If there seems to be any doubt about our conviction, we shall prove it and very definitely. What caused considerable doubt for so long a time concerning our opinion was, that the authors mentioned, writing about the far-spread Kingdom of Cathay and about other Chinese provinces, assert that somewhere in this region, this kingdom touched upon the eastern borders of Persia. Now, Persia as they knew it, must be taken as being more widespread than it is at present. In fact their Persia must be understood as including those vast and unmeasured stretches of Asia in which the Persian tongue was spoken, up to the outer limits of China. They say also that to the south it was in view of the Tartars. Having failed to discover anything about this vast empire of Cathay after frequent investigation concerning it within the realm of China, it seems quite improbable that a matter of such importance should be wholly unknown in a neighboring kingdom, and that no record of war or of commerce with such a great power should be left after so many centuries. We have also read that the river Chian from its source to its mouth, flows through this same Cathay. Chian, in Chinese, means the big river. Other rivers are called Cho. We think this is the same river which we have noted as being called Son of the Sea, and which is now called Ian-su-chian. We have also read that south of this river there are nine kingdoms, and north of it, in this unknown empire, what would correspond both in name and in fact, to the remainder of the fifteen Chinese provinces. These provinces are in reality as many kingdoms, fifteen in all, any one of them larger than Italy. Nine of them lie south of the river just mentioned, and the other six north of it.

Another and perhaps a clearer proof of our contention that Cathay meant China, is offered from an individual experience. About forty years ago, and we are now in the year 1608, two Arabian Turks, or Mohammedans, came into Pekin by an overland route. With them, as a present for the King of China, they brought a lion, an animal about which the Chinese had often heard, but which they had very seldom seen. They were cordially received by the King and they were each granted a Magistrature and an income from the royal treasury, to be made hereditary in their families, provided they took care of the lion, as long as he lived, and did not return to their own country to start a war against the Chinese. These two men were still living when the Fathers arrived in Pekin, and Father Matthew sent one of the Brothers to question them on the subject of Cathay. Afterwards, when the Fathers came to Pekin the second time, Father Matthew himself often met these two men and they made it clear to him that, then and there, they were actually living in the Great Cathay, and that Pekin was called Cambalu. They hadn't the slightest doubt about that, and they said that during their whole journey to Pekin they had neither seen nor heard about any other Cathay. The Fathers heard the same story over and over again from men who had come from Persia, without any variation on the subject of Cathay. The Chinese also, when questioned on this subject, said that the title Grand Cathay was known to their people. As applied to China, however, this name is used only by foreigners and the word itself is undoubtedly partly of Chinese and partly of Tartar origin. Whenever the Chinese mention the Tartars in their books, they write Lu and they call the northern region Pa, as well as Pe. Cam to the Tartars means great, and the Chinese know the same word.

At the time that the Tartars invaded China, the King of Tartary fixed his capital at Pekin and called it Campalu. Now the consonant P is often interchangeable with B, hence the Tartars began to call it Cambalu, but the Chinese, who seldom use the consonant B, still pronounce the name Campalu. It seems clear that the Venetian, Marco Polo, came into this kingdom during the Tartar occupation. He may even have come in with them, and from his commentaries, the Kingdom of China became known to Europe by the name used by the Tartars, who called it Catai, and the capital city Cambalu. If one should offer the objection that perhaps the confines of Cathay were even more extended by Marco Polo than those of present China, the objection might stand, but it would prove nothing. We have not examined that as yet, but granted that a common name were extended to nearby Tartar regions on the north, this is no proof that at that time there was a separate kingdom beyond the border of China, which was known as Catai.

Later on, the Portuguese spread the fame of this country through all of Europe, under the name of China, a word probably taken from the inhabitants of Siam. At the same time they called the capital city, Pekin, a name known to all the Chinese. Hence, it is not surprising that our geographers envisioned two distinct but contiguous kingdoms, being so confused by the discrepancy of names, which were not known to be identical. Father Ricci forwarded these seemingly certain conjectures to India and thence to Europe, but even then they were not given any satisfying assurance, until the fact that Cathay and China were one and the same country was later established beyond further doubt. Of this we shall have more to say later on.

Shortly after the missionaries came into Pekin, they went to the house of the President of the Magistrates, under whose protection they had come. He himself had arrived by an overland route, with considerable saving of time and of effort. He gave them commodious lodging in his palace because he enjoyed their company and wished to have them near him, and he immediately took up their petition with the eunuch of the royal palace, with whom he was acquainted. The eunuch in turn promised to make every effort to expedite so important an affair, and asked to see the Fathers and the gifts they had brought for the King. On an appointed day, both he and the President came to the Fathers' lodging to see the presents. He was particularly gracious to Father Ricci and greeted him with the special ceremonies, performed only when one meets, for the first time, some distinguished person whom he has long desired to see. Afterwards, they all dined together, at the same table, in familiar conversation. Father Matthew showed them the clock, the crucifix, a statue of the Virgin Mother, a clavichord, the like of which the Chinese had never even heard of, and two triangular glass prisms. When the statue of the Blessed Virgin was being lifted down to the floor, it fell out of the hands of the carriers and was broken into three pieces. That would have ruined its value in Europe, but served only to increase it in China. When the pieces were put together again, the statue took on an appearance of antiquity, which made it more valuable here than when it was whole.

The palace eunuch, and everyone else, was highly pleased with the presents. He had heard that the Fathers could turn quicksilver into genuine silver metal and this seemed to please him more than anything else. He said he knew that this also would be the King's first interest. There is no question of satisfying human cupidity for wealth, even for the fabulously wealthy King of China, and when his servant heard that the Fathers were possessed of no such magic power, he was done with their petition. He told them that for various reasons he could not speak to the King on behalf of foreigners, especially at that particular time, when war was raging at their very walls, when rumors of war from Korea were daily increasing, when many were dying in war, and the Japanese getting ready to invade China. He assured them also that the Chinese make no distinction between outsiders, considering them all alike, or almost alike, and that the Fathers would probably be taken to be Japanese. For this same reason, and on the advice of his friends, the President of the Magistrates also began to realize that it was dangerous business, getting himself entangled in the affairs of aliens, and despairing of his effort, he thought of taking the Fathers back to Nankin. To them, the project did not appear to be utterly hopeless, and lest so much labor and expense should be wasted, they remained in Pekin for a month after the President left, and hired a house for residence. The President had to leave, by law, before a certain day. All Magistrates who visit the royal court to offer congratulations to the sovereign, on special occasions, must leave the City of Pekin within a month and return to the duties of their particular posts.

Father Emanuele Dias, the Rector of the College of Macao, had forwarded money enough for this voyage, but fearing that they would need more in Pekin he sent on a promissory note for a certain sum, purchased from a merchant in Macao, which they were to exchange for an equal amount in Pekin. But it proved to be a forgery because they could find no one in Pekin who would honor the name signed to the note. This same thing had happened in other places, too. The money was recovered in Macao, but we mention this incident here to show why this way of doing business is frowned upon by Chinese tradesmen, and is not a common practice anywhere in the kingdom.

With their sponsor departed, the Fathers tried various means of carrying out their undertaking, but to no avail. None of their acquaintances, neither the friends of Father Matthew nor any of the Magistrates would even receive them into their homes for a simple visit. So great was the fear of entertaining a foreigner that even when they presented letters written by the President of the Magistrates, recommending their cause, the letters had no influence whatsoever. Finally, their efforts appeared to be hopeless. They concluded that the hour to illumine the City of Pekin with the light of the Gospel had not yet come. The whole plan was put aside and they decided to return to Nankin. It appeared better to put off the attempt until another time because, with the present war scare, they might suffer the misfortune of endangering the work already done, and perhaps erect a barrier to returning in the future. With that decided upon, they hired places on a boat, at a low price, for the return voyage. Empty boats returning took passengers for nearly nothing but in this instance the avarice of the captain made this boat most unsuitable to travel on, because it was unprotected for want of arms, as well as lacking sufficient crew.

It took a whole month to reach the town of Lincin. This may seem like a month of good time wasted, but it really was not. With the valuable aid of Brother Sebastian, who was adept in the use of the Chinese language, the Fathers used this time to put together a glossary of Chinese words. They also arranged other sets and tables of words from which our missionaries learned a great deal when studying the language. In their observations they noted that the whole Chinese language was made up of monosyllables only, and that certain tones and breathings were used by the Chinese to vary the meanings of words. Ignorance of these tones results in a confusion of speech, making conversation almost impossible, because without them the speaker can not be understood, nor can he understand another. To distinguish the tones used, they introduced five marks by which the student could determine the particular tone to give to each meaning, there being that many tones. Father Cattaneo contributed greatly to this work. He was an excellent musician, with a discriminating ear for delicate variations of sound, and he readily discerned the variety of tones. A good ear for music is a great help in learning this language. This method of writing with tonic accents, introduced by two of our first Jesuit missionaries, is still in use by those who followed in their footsteps. If one were to write as he pleased and without such guidance, confusion might result, and the writing would mean nothing to the one who tried to read it.

The Latin paraphrase of the Chinese Tetrabiblion, which Father Ricci wrote and augmented with his commentary, was also of great value to the other Fathers in their study of Chinese writings. We have already mentioned this Tetrabiblion in our first book, in the discussion of Chinese literary degrees.

4.Overland Journey to Nankin

ONCE WINTER sets in, all the rivers in northern China are frozen over so hard that navigation on them is impossible, and a wagon may pass over them. The Fathers had set out late and were traveling slowly, with the result that they became ice-bound and had to wait until springtime to continue their river journey.

Lincin is one of the larger cities, and is surpassed in commerce by very few others. Not only the merchandise of the province but a great deal from the entire kingdom is handled here. Hence there is always a multitude of transients passing through. The forced delay during the winter months caused the Fathers considerable anxiety because of the time lost and of the consequent postponement of the project for which the trip was undertaken. After talking over the situation, it was decided that Father Ricci, with two servants, should take an overland route to the south, to see if he could open a Mission at Nankin, or in some other center. His companion and the Brothers were to remain at Lincin, with the baggage, until the winter broke, and then continue on to Nankin after the ice had melted.

Since Chiutaiso, his friend and former disciple from Xaucea, had often asked Father Matthew, both in conversation and in letters, to come back to his home district and settle down there permanently, he decided to go there and with God's grace to attempt a settlement in the well known city of Suceu. He could think of no greater help in accomplishing this design than the friendship and the authority of the one who had thus far proven to be his greatest supporter. Traveling through the middle of the Province of Sciantum, he came into the renowned settlements of Suceu and Hamceu. The winter weather delayed his journey, increasing his difficulties, but he went on cheerfully, making rapid progress and meeting with no very serious obstructions. After he crossed the Hiamceu River he came into Cinchiamsu, the metropolitan seat of the district, through a long canal, which is really an artificial river, and on which one can sail to the famous port of Suceu and to the equally celebrated port of Hamceu, the first city in the Province of Cechiam. The canal is so far south that it never freezes over, but it is also so narrow and so crowded with boats that it is impossible to make much progress on it in either direction. Knowing this, Father Matthew took another mode of continuing his journey, a method of travel common in this country, as well as time saving and comfortable. They use a cart, built over a single wheel, on which one person sits astride in the center, as he would on a horse, with two others sitting, one on either side. This cart or wagon is pushed by a driver by means of two wooden shafts. It affords a safe and a speedy means of travel, and it was thus that Father Matthew arrived in Suceu. This is one of the two towns which the Chinese have put into the proverb: "What in heaven is called the seat of the blessed, on earth is Suceu and Hamceu." It is one of the most important cities of this region and is known for its splendor and wealth, for its numerous population and for about everything else that makes a city grand. It is situated on a calm river of fresh water, or one might more aptly say on a lake, swept by gentle winds.

People move about here on land and on water, as they do in Venice, but the water here is fresh and clear, unlike that in Venice, which is salty and brackish. Both the streets and the bridges rest upon wooden piles of pine, sunk deep into the river, after the European fashion. A great part of the merchandise from Portugal, by way of Macao, and from other foreign countries, passes through this river port. The merchants here carry on a heavy trade throughout the whole year with the other trading centers of the kingdom, with the result that there is scarcely anything that one cannot purchase at this mart. There is only one entrance to the city by land but various entrances by water. The city is all bridges, very old but beautifully built, and those over the narrow canal are constructed as single arches. Nowhere in China can one find more butter and milk products, nor better rice wine, which is exported to Pekin and to the realm in general. This center is about two days' journey from the sea, heavily fortified, and is the principal of the eight cities in the district.

When the Tartars were expelled and the kingdom taken over by the ancestor of the present reigning monarch, this city of Suceu was stubbornly defended by its chiefs, and up to the present day a tremendous tax is still levied upon it as a rebellion city. One half of what is grown in this province goes to the King. Hence it may happen in China that one province pays twice as much as another in taxes to the royal treasury. The whole province followed its capital city in opposition to the King, and even up to now it is heavily patrolled and guarded, as the fear of rebellion from this quarter is greater than from anywhere else in the kingdom.

Chiutaiso, his friend, was absent when Father Matthew arrived in Suceu, but he was not far away, having taken up residence in a nearby village called Tanian. He received the Father with an expression of friendly joy, such as one would seldom witness at the meeting of intimate friends in Europe. He was lodging at the time in a temple of idols and in somewhat narrow quarters. He offered to give up his bed to his friend but Father Matthew would not listen to this and arranged one for himself on the floor. He was worn out from labor and travel and he fell sick, almost unto death, but Chiutaiso took such good care of him that within a month of his falling ill, his health was so fully restored that he felt better after the siege than before it. In return for his kindness he gave Chiutaiso several presents among which was one of the famous triangular glass prisms. He had been looking about for one of these prisms in the Province of Canton, and was willing to pay a high price for it. Now that he had one, he was overjoyed with it, and in order to make it more attractive he put it in a silver case, with gold chains attached, terminating in knots. He even had the case decorated with an inscription, to the effect that this gem was a fragment of the material of which the sky is composed.

The gifts which Chiutaiso received aroused the interest of many, and on one occasion he was offered five hundred gold pieces for the triangular prism. Much as he needed the money, and though he wanted to do so, he refused to sell it at that time, because he knew that there was a similar prism included in the presents intended for the King, and he was afraid that the purchaser might send his prism to the King and thus lessen the novelty of the one he was to receive from Father Ricci. Later on, after the King had accepted the presents, Chiutaiso did sell his prism at a higher price than had been formerly offered. The money he received for it enabled him to pay off many of his debts; something which he never forgot and which strengthened his zeal for the Mission. Once he heard of the Father's design, he was eager to assist in it, and he promised to remain with him until a new residence was opened in that district. When he learned that his friend was thinking of settling in Suceu, he advised him to develop that plan and to remain right there where he himself was living. Plentiful supplies and the large population would favor this idea, in addition to the facts that it was his own home, that he was a friend of the Fathers, and that he had relatives in high station here from whom, by the law of friendship, he could hope for whatever one expects from friends.

After consultation with several of the more prudent Solons, Chiutaiso and Father Matthew agreed that a place at Nankin might be better, but that there was little hope of acquiring one. There were various reasons assigned for this conclusion, the strongest of which was the following. In a city with so many governing Magistrates as Nankin, it could scarcely be hoped that they would all take a friendly attitude toward the Mission. It could easily happen, that for some reason or other, one of them might turn against the Fathers and have them put out of their house and ignominiously sent away. They foresaw no such trouble at Suceu, and the first move they decided upon, to carry out their plan, was to go to Nankin and see the President of the first Presidial, who had lately made a voyage with the Fathers, and to get letters from him to the Magistrates of Suceu. Other letters could then be received from the Magistrate friends of Chiutaiso, all of which should facilitate the accomplishment of their design.

Just at that time the Chinese were celebrating their New Year, which made it inconvenient for carrying on any kind of business negotiations. Everyone was engaged paying visits, giving and receiving presents and arranging for banquets and other festivities. Better perhaps not to intrude upon their merrymaking, so Father Matthew and Chiutaiso embarked for Cinchiam, to see the great public demonstrations and display. Everybody in this town knew Chiutaiso, which meant that they also knew about Father Ricci, because wherever Chiutaiso went, he was always loud in praise of his friend. While there, they were continually surrounded by a gathering of Magistrates and of other notables. After the excitement of the public celebration had quieted down, they prepared to set out for Nankin. The Governor supplied a large boat for this trip, which was paid for at public expense, a privilege the Governor enjoyed. This mode of travel was an assurance of security and Father Matthew was glad to take advantage of it. They arrived at Nankin on the sixth of February, 1599, and walked to a place of lodging without having to exercise any of the precautions that were formerly so necessary. Their place of residence was called Cinghensu; a spacious temple-cloister that was crowded with guests, who preferred to live there because it was situated in the middle of the city. The whole city seemed to have changed for the better since their last visit. According to report, the Japanese had been driven out of

Korea and back to their own country with heavy losses. The Emperor Cambaco had died, the one who had terrified the unwarlike Chinese with his plan of conquering Korea and the whole vast Chinese empire. There was added cause for joy also, in the fact that the extraordinary taxes levied for the royal treasury had been canceled, because the army had been reduced in number by a hundred thousand. Father Ricci soon discovered that various rumors had been spread around about him, but they were all in his favor. It was said that his trip to Pekin had been sponsored by the President of the Magistrates. He had gone there to offer valuable presents to the King. Nothing had come of his visit, but that was due to the disturbance caused by the Korean War. If he had sought an audience at some other time, it would undoubtedly have been granted to him. Such was the comment.

Everybody was anxious to see the clocks that Ricci had brought with him. Their particular attraction was that they sounded the hours on bells. The current comment about the statues and especially about the clavichord, was not only exaggerated, it was almost ridiculous. Their old friends came to see them at the cloister lodging and after a few days they went to call on the President Magistrate. He was delighted to learn of their success; of how Father Matthew had traveled alone through the country without any mishap, and that he had finally found a place to live and was being visited by his friends. In his usual and voluble praise of the Father, Chiutaiso added his part by commenting upon the scientific knowledge that Father Ricci had brought to China, and how he had opened the eyes of the lettered class, which had been closed to so much before his coming. That was why he had become so popular, according to Chiutaiso, and why everyone wanted to see him and to have him stay with them, but, of course, he would make no move, either for himself or for his Mission, without the authority of the President of the Magistrates, whom he had chosen as his special sponsor. In response to all this, the President advised Father Matthew to buy a house in Nankin. It was the best place for him, for various reasons. The climate was favorable and he would like to have him living nearby, so he could protect him, and without waiting for an answer, he called two of his court officers, who knew the city, and told them to go out and find a house for hire that would suit the Father's needs. Ricci preferred to receive this decision in silence rather than object to it, though it seemed to be contrary to what he had already settled upon.

They had scarcely arrived back at their place of lodging, when the President Judge appeared, to repay their visit. He insisted upon doing this with all the customary ceremonies and to honor them by wearing the full costume demanded by his high office. They were just seated in the reception-hall when the Archimandrate of the Temple, the high priest of the sacrificers to the idols, made his appearance to offer them the cup of welcome. He did this by approaching each of the three on his knees, and then handing him the goblet; a ceremony which he had to perform in the presence of this particular judge, who was the Supreme Moderator of the temples.

With the visit over, the Judge invited Father Matthew to come and spend a few days with him in his palace. He said he was anxious to have him witness the wonderful display of fireworks that would be shown by his domestics at night, and the ingenious display of lanterns they had arranged for several nights, on the occasion of the first full moon of the year. Such unusual displays are common for public celebrations but there is no sign of superstition attached to them. The invitation was gladly accepted. It would have been impolite to refuse it. He was received most graciously by the domestics and the spectacle he witnessed surprised him beyond all expectation. Nankin surpasses the rest of the kingdom in the science of pyrotechnic display, and perhaps the rest of the world.

When the news got about that Father Matthew had been visited by the President, all the judges and the other high officials came to do him honor. It will suffice to name only three of them; the Presiding Judge of the Criminal Court, his Assessor and the Chief of the Royal Exchequer, the second ranking tribunal. These three, like the principal visitor, paid their respects in full official dress, with all the usual ceremonies and bringing gifts worthy of their high station. After them there came one who, several years later, was to hold the exalted post of Colao, in Pekin. Their general opinion was that Father Matthew should take up residence in Nankin, and they all promised to help in finding him a house. After that he went about the city freely and visited the palaces of the Magistrates without being questioned by anyone.

This unusual turn of events brought to Father Ricci's memory the night on which he was expelled from Nankin, after his first arrival there. As he entered the city this time, he recognized it as the place the Lord had shown him in his dream, in which he seemed to be walking about unmolested. Now he marveled at the streets and the palaces he had not seen before, except in the dream, and he felt that it must have been something more than a dream, a vision perhaps, such as one might experience when his whole heart is set upon a single desire. Realizing the great change in the attitude of the people toward him, which God had brought about, he decided that it was God's will also that he should settle in Nankin, and nowhere else, despite all human considerations. Chiutaiso was in full agreement with this and set aside his ideas relative to residence in Suceu.

At that time, in the city of Nankin, there was a celebrated scholar, from the Province of Chiansi, the son of a former Viceroy. He had been granted the degree of Licentiate on two different occasions, the degree having been nullified the first time because of some difficulty with his colleagues. He had built up considerable influence with the governing judges of Nankin by writing addresses for them, such as funeral orations, poems for formal occasions, or speeches for receptions or departure ceremonies, like our own orations or poems. From the bounty of the Magistrates and the income from his writings he had become a rich man. He was also engaged in teaching the children of the officials to read Chinese books, and they say he could discourse very learnedly about the three Chinese religious sects which we have already mentioned in our first book. This man had a son who was not so successful in his literary studies, and in order to build up a reputation for his son, he hit upon the following unusual plan. He went to a scientist who was skilled in mathematics and had him write a thick volume on that subject, which he then published, with his son's name inscribed as the author. Realizing that Chiutaiso's praise of Father Ricci, as a mathematician, might jeopardize his son's falsely acquired reputation, the sage thought it would be a good idea to introduce Father Matthew to his would-be scientific son. As he was walking along the street with Father Matthew and Chiutaiso, on the way to his house, he met some friends who knew the whole story and turning to them said, laughingly, "I have one sheep whom I have been trying to educate for years. Now I am going to turn him over to the good pleasure of someone else."

During the course of their conversation, Chiutaiso took occasion to inform his host that he had not come to Nankin to remain there, but merely as a companion to an old friend, to help him find a safe domicile in one of the suburbs, and with that done he intended to return home. Then he added, "Since there is nobody in the whole city of Nankin, to whom this project could be more safely recommended than yourself, I earnestly beg and entreat you to become the advocate and protector of my friend Father Matthew." The distinguished scholar was so pleased with this unexpected meeting and conversation that he could hardly restrain his emotion. With the return of his composure he promised to make every effort to favor the design, and his future effort was in keeping with his promise. Continuing their conversation he assured them that Nankin really was the proper place for Father Matthew to live, and that for various reasons. They both objected that the courts of Nankin were fearful and suspicious of foreigners, to which he replied, "In that you are mistaken," and he continued, "Suceu is a port, not far from the sea. The place is tax-ridden, and consequently inclined to be revolutionary. It may break out in rebellion at any time. On the contrary, in Nankin, the fear of war has been so allayed within the last few months, that general peace and quiet are assured." He insisted, moreover, that the great number of Magistrates in Nankin would be more of an advantage to their cause than a hindrance, because for one of them who might become adverse, there would be ten others who would be friendly. Whereas, outside of the Court City, every Magistrate is a little king, and it is easier for a few to conspire against an individual than for many. His last argument seemed to settle their final objection to Nankin and left them facing a dilemma, with no outlet on either side.

Perhaps the most solicitous of all for the cause of the Fathers was one of the King's advisers, who are called Coli. This man was named Cioselinus, and as it happened at that time that there were no other judges of this particular court of King's advisers present in Nankin, when there should have been eight or ten of them, Cioselinus was acting for all of them. He was very highly esteemed by everyone and was celebrated as a moral philosopher. Moreover, he was so well known as a writer of Chinese characters, and as a penman, an art more highly regarded in China than in Europe, that only a few lines of his sample writing sold in Nankin for a high price, equivalent to our Julian, one-tenth of a ducat. A few years later the value of this manuscript had greatly increased. He was an author also and his books exhorting the people to virtue were highly praised, and he lectured at the meetings of the literati. Through hearsay from the President Judge and from others, he became interested in Father Ricci. His admiration awakened a desire to see the Father, and the book that Father Matthew had written on friendship was the means of bringing them together. During a discussion at the meeting of a notable assembly, the question of Father Ricci's status was brought up and Cioselinus is said to have remarked that, since this man had lived for a long time in the Provinces of Canton and of Chiansi, we should have no objection to his living here in Nankin, where there are so many other foreigners. The reference to foreigners indicated the Saracens, who had been there since the time of the Tartars, and were considered to be natives.

Encouraged by the interest of so many in high stations, but only after a period of doubt, Ricci finally decided to cast his lot in Nankin. His first interest was to find a house for residence. With that done, he would lay the foundation for a central establishment, hoping that other houses, to be opened elsewhere, later on, would acquire publicity from this city, as from a central seat of the Christian faith. He did nothing toward acquiring a first house until the arrival of Father Cattaneo from Lincin.

The President Judge, who was acting as patron for the Fathers, hearing that his fellow judges were so well disposed toward Father Matthew, began to show more courage and resolution. Whereas some of the judges had been misleading others, relative to their attitude in this matter, now they were all of a mind to favor it. They knew that their President wanted a permanent station for the Fathers, and so in deference to him, they also approved of it. On his part, once the President was certain of the disposition of the others, he offered Father Ricci the palace of his Assessor, which was vacant at the time. This offer was refused, as being quite beyond all expectation, and as something that might give rise to resentment and probably spoil the whole project. Father Matthew then hired a less conspicuous but commodious dwelling, and at the President's request accepted some necessary furniture from the Assessor's palace, until such time as he could purchase what would be more suitable for his house. Visitors were not lacking at the new home. From day to day they continued to increase, both in numbers and with respect to rank and class.

Father Ricci wrote at length to his companions at Nancian, telling them all about what had taken place. They had had no letter since his departure, and their anxiety as to what they should do, was continually increasing with the length of his absence. From the house at Nancian, they forwarded everything necessary for the celebration of Mass, and whatever money their poverty would permit, to help pay for the new foundation.

5.Mathematics and Converts

～～～～～～～～～～～～～～～～～～～～～～～～～

IN THE COURSE of the centuries, God has shown more than one way of drawing men to Him. So it was not to be wondered at that the fishers of men employed their own particular ways of attracting souls into their nets. Whoever may think that ethics, physics and mathematics are not important in the work of the Church, is unacquainted with the taste of the Chinese, who are slow to take a salutary spiritual potion, unless it be seasoned with an intellectual flavoring. It was by means of a knowledge of European science, new to the Chinese, that Father Ricci amazed the entire philosophical world of China; proving the truth of its novelty by sound and logical reasoning. From him, after so many centuries, they first learned that the world was round. Formerly they had held an old axiom as a first principle, namely: "The heavens are round but the earth is flat." None of them knew that the earth attracts a weighty body or that the force of gravity draws a falling body to the earth. They didn't know that the whole surface of the world was inhabited or that men can live on the opposite side of it without falling off; something which they may have believed but which many of them could not picture to the imagination. Up to Ricci's time they did not realize that an eclipse of the moon was caused by the earth coming between the moon and the sun. Their absurd explanation of an eclipse added more darkness to their minds than to the moon itself. Some of their sages said that the moon came face to face with the sun and lost its light from sheer fright. Others said that there was a hole in the sun and when the moon passed in front of that hole, it could receive no light. It was new to them to learn that the sun was larger than the entire earth, but some were inclined to believe it, because it was written in the ancient books of their mathematicians that they had measured the sun with certain instruments and discovered that it was more than a thousand miles wide. To them it was a paradox to say that certain stars, which look so small to the human eye, were larger than the whole extent of the earth. They never knew, in fact they had never heard, that the skies are composed of solid substance, that the stars were fixed and not wandering around aimlessly, that there were ten celestial orbs, enveloping one another, and moved by contrary forces. Their primitive science of astronomy knew nothing of eccentric orbits and epicycles. They did not know that relative to the horizon, the altitude of the pole varied high and low according to the zones on the earth, or that the length of days and nights varied, beyond the equator.

Until Matthew Ricci arrived in China, the Chinese had never seen a geographical exposition of the entire surface of the earth, either in the form of a globe or as represented on the plane surface of a map, nor had they ever seen the earth's surface divided by meridians, parallels or degrees, and they knew nothing of an equator, of tropics, of either pole, or of a division of the earth into five zones. They had seen various celestial circles marked on their astronomical instruments, but they had never seen them transferred to the surface of the earth. They knew nothing about an astrolabe with superimposed plates that could be accommodated to various regions, and they did not visualize the earth as a sphere, or as a globe suspended in the air. They had no knowledge of two poles, one fixed and one movable, from which they might have learned much about the movements of the planets. They did not understand how a sundial could be used on the horizontal, or fixed to a wall, nor would they believe that these and innumerable other things were possible.

Nothing surprised them more than to see the signs of the Zodiac, which they numbered as twenty-four, aptly pictured on a sundial, so that the shadow of the index did not vary an iota from the line indicating the day marked in Chinese characters. They marveled that one could figure the height of a tower, the depth of a ditch or of a valley, or the length of a road by means of quadrants, and it seemed strange to them that arithmetic could be expressed in writing. They did their counting on the cumbersome instrument already described.

All of these seemingly incredible things were put to the test and proven to the most pertinacious among them, and when one thing was clearly demonstrated it was easier for them to accept the rest. Once this new knowledge became known to a few, it was not long before it found its way into the academies of the learned class. One can gather from this how the reputation of Europe was enhanced, and how they were slow to segregate it as being barbarous, and ashamed to call it such in the future.

Relative to their attitude toward Europe, here is what happened to one of the missionaries, some years later. He did not know the Chinese language when he arrived here from Europe, and so he employed an interpreter in conversation. He was staying for three weeks in the house of a learned doctor, who was a convert to Christianity. Desirous of learning, the Doctor spent much time in the company of the Father, discussing philosophical and theological questions, and exchanging opinions on various subjects. The Father usually gave satisfactory answers to his inquiries, and one day the Doctor said, "I really should feel ashamed in your presence," and when asked why, he answered, "Because it seems to me that you put all the Chinese, and particularly myself, in the same class, into which we Chinese formerly put the unbelieving Tartars and barbarians." When his guest assured him that he was wrong, he said, "It can hardly be otherwise, because where we left off intellectually, you are merely beginning." The Father noted also that the Chinese pay no attention to oratory until they are grown up, whereas Europeans are taught it from their childhood.

With no other foundation for their belief than antiquity, Chinese scholars taught that there were five different elements. None of them doubted this or ever thought of questioning it. These elements were: metal, wood, fire, water, and earth, and what is stranger still, they taught that these elements were derived from one another. They knew nothing about the air, as such, because they could not see it. To them, the space occupied by air was merely a void. Yet, when they reason falsely, they are not obstinate in holding to the false conclusion.

Father Matthew paid little or no attention to their devotion to the authority of antiquity. He told them that there were four elements, no more and no less, possessed of contradictory qualities, and he taught them where each element was found. They had no objections with reference to the three inferior elements but they found it difficult to believe that fire, found beneath the sky, should occupy a large portion of the elementary earth. They did not think that comets and falling stars burned with the same kind of fire as they saw on earth, and they counted the comets among the regular stars. Father Matthew wrote a commentary on this subject in Chinese, in which he did away with their five elements, as such, and established the four, to which he assigned locations, and of which he showed illustrations. This commentary was received with great interest. They had numerous copies of it made, which were everywhere accepted with the same high praise as his other writings.

Some of their scientists wanted to become Father Ricci's pupils. They were attracted by his learning and also by the solicitation of Chiutaiso, who had developed from being a scholar to becoming an instructor. The learned sage who feared that his son's reputation might be jeopardized by Father Ricci's fame as a mathematician, brought him two of his own pupils, who were skilled in Chinese astronomy. One of these was the real author of the volume, which the sage had published as being the work of his son. With these two there came a third, more intelligent than either of the others. This third pupil had been sent by his master, who was a distinguished philosopher of the faculty of the Royal College of Pekin, called Hanlin. This faculty is composed of the most brilliant of the highly educated of the realm, and it is considered to be a singular honor to be chosen for it.

The professor lived in a small town in the Province of Nankin, about four days' journey from the court city. After a long course of study, he failed to find anything like a definite system of Chinese mathematics, and having tried in vain to establish one as a methodical science, he finally gave up the effort. So he sent on his pupil, with a letter of recommendation to Father Ricci, requesting him to accept the boy, instead of himself, for instruction. The boy was inclined to be somewhat insolent, but in a short time he became very respectful and pleasant and took for a motto, a dictum from Pythagoras, "He himself, the Master, has spoken." He learned the first book of Euclid without a teacher. He was continually asking Father Matthew for geometry problems, and when his teacher told him that he could not take time for that from the other pupils, he went to work and printed his own text books in the Chinese language. In the course of his instructions Father Matthew made mention of promulgating the Christian law, and this particular student told him that arguing with the idol worshippers was only a waste of time, and that he thought it would be sufficient for his purpose to enlighten the Chinese by teaching them mathematics.

It is generally known that the unholy sect of bogus sages, called the Magistelli, who are famous for their absurd doctrines, want to be known, not only as theologians and philosophers but also as mathematicians. They say that at night they hide the sun under a mountain, named Siumi, which has its base twenty-four thousand miles under the sea. They explain eclipses by inventing an imaginary deity called Holochan, who produces an eclipse of the sun by hiding it with his right hand, and of the moon by covering it with his left. So it happened that not only this particular scholar, but many others like him, were awakened to the absurdity of idol-worshipping by the reasoning demanded in the study of mathematics.

With the assistance of his pupils, Father Matthew made sundials of various designs, which he distributed among them. Afterwards he had many of them cast from forms and placed in the homes of the Magistrates. Besides these he made spheres, marked with the celestial circles, globes showing the entire surface of the earth, and other scientific equipment.

There is a college of Chinese mathematicians in Pekin, and one in Nankin also, more distinguished for the proportions of its buildings, than for the learning of its astronomers, for they have little knowledge and less science. They do scarcely anything more than revise their calendars for feast days, and make a daily reckoning according to their ancient method of calculating. If perchance their reckoning happens to be wrong, they say that whatever did happen was in perfect accord with their calculations, and place the blame for the error on falling stars, calling it a warning from heaven of some event to happen on earth, which they then invent to cover up their mistake. At first they paid no attention to Father Ricci, for fear he might injure their reputation, but before long their fear was allayed and they came as friends to visit him and to learn what he could teach them. When he went to pay them a return visit, he saw something new; something far surpassing anything he had expected to find.

There is a high mountain on one side of the city and within its walls, and on one side of it, an open level space, perfectly suitable for observing the stars. Around the border of this area there are a number of magnificent houses, the homes of the college faculty. One of this staff is appointed each night to observe the heavens and to record celestial phenomena, such as comets or streaks of fire appearing in the sky, which are reported in detail to the King, with an explanation of what the phenomena predict. They had installed here certain astronomical instruments or machines, made of cast metal which, in size and in elegance of design, surpassed anything of the kind as yet ever seen or read about in Europe. These instruments had stood the test of rain and snow and change of weather for nearly two hundred and fifty years, with no detriment to their original splendor. There were four of the larger kind. Not wishing to arouse the curiosity of the reader without satisfying it, let us here insert what may be a pleasant digression about these instruments.

The first was a large globe. Three men with outstretched arms could scarcely encircle it. It was marked with meridians and parallels according to degrees, and it stood on an axis, set into a huge bronze cube in which there was a small door, for entrance, to turn the sphere. There was nothing engraved on the surface of this globe, neither stars nor zones. Hence it appeared to be an unfinished work, unless it were probably left that way, so that it might serve as both a celestial and a terrestrial globe.

The second instrument was also a large sphere, about the length of the outstretched arms in diameter, mathematically about five feet. It was marked for the poles and a horizontal, and instead of celestial circles it had pairs of ridges, with the spaces between the ridges representing the circles on our globes, and divided into three hundred and sixty-five degrees and some minutes. It was not a geographical globe, but through its middle it was pierced with a thin pipe, like a gun barrel, which could be turned in all directions and placed at any elevation or degree for observing any star; as we do with astronomical sights, a rather clever device.

. The third instrument was a dial, about twice the size of the foregoing in diameter, mounted on a long marble slab and pointed north. The slab, or table, was cut around on all sides with a groove; a canal for holding water to determine whether or not the table was at a level. The stylus or gnomon was perpendicular. This instrument was probably constructed to indicate the exact moment of the solstices and the equinoxes by reading the shadow it registered, because both the slab and the indicator were marked off in degrees.

The fourth and largest instrument was made of three or four huge astrolabes, placed in line, each one about a stretch of arms in diameter, and fitted with an alidade and a dioptra. One of the astrolabes was set for midday and pointed south. Another was set for midday and pointed north, forming a cross with the first. The whole machine seemed to be employed to indicate the exact moment of the midday, but it could be turned in any direction. A third astrolabe stood vertical, probably indicating the vertical circle, though this one also could be turned to indicate any vertical. The degrees were marked on all of them by metal knobs, so that they could be distinguished by touch at night, without a light. This whole machine, made up of astrolabes, was also set on a marble plane, with a crevice around its edge, for water.

On each of these instruments, the purpose of every part was indicated in Chinese characters, and each was marked with their twenty-four signs of the Zodiac, doubling our twelve. The one error in the whole display of instruments was that they were set for thirty-six degrees, longitude, whereas the City of Nankin is situated at thirty-two and one fourth degrees. It would seem that these instruments were made for some other locality and placed here by someone lacking in astronomical knowledge, or with no regard for location. Later on, Father Matthew saw similar instruments at Pekin, or rather duplicates of these, and undoubtedly cast by the same artisan. It seems certain that they were molded when the Tartars were in power in China, and this would indicate that they were designed by a foreigner, who had some knowledge of European astronomical science. So much for their astronomical instruments.

The ruling Magistrate of that time asked Father Ricci if he would revise the map of the world which he had made while he was in the Province of Canton, and add to it a more detailed commentary. He said he wanted to have a copy of it cut on tablets for his palace and set in a place where the public could view it. Father Matthew was glad to do this and he remodeled his map on a larger scale and in higher relief, for better observation. He added to it and corrected faults, and he was not at all reluctant to revising the entire work. His Magistrate friend was delighted with the new map. He hired expert sculptors, at public expense, to reproduce it in stone and had it inscribed with an introductory comment, in which he gave high praise to the world-map and to its author. This amended map surpassed the orignal Canton production in workmanship and in the number of copies of it that were made. Samples of it were sent from Nankin to various parts of China, to Macao and even to Japan and they say that other copies of it were made from these in different places. One copy came into the possession of a Provincial Viceroy at Cuiceu. He had known Father Matthew in the Province of Canton and out of compliment to him, he undertook to reproduce the whole work in the form of a book. By reducing the projection, every country on the map was shown with relation to its position in one of the five zones, and to each there was added an appropriate commentary, offering the reader a summary description of the country in general. In the preface of the book he inserted a profuse encomium of the map and of its author, stating that part of his reputation, which in the opinion of the literati was derived from the books he had written, was due to him as the creator of this map.

All this, namely, what we have recounted relative to a knowledge of science, served as seed for a future harvest, and also as a foundation for the nascent Church in China.

6. The Leaders at Nankin Solicit the Company of Father Ricci

~~~~~~

IT SEEMED quite evident that Divine Providence was laying down a solid foundation of hope for the conservation of this great kingdom. Hence, it is only becoming that we shoud recall some of the extraordinary means by which this was being accomplished. We shall mention in this chapter some of the prominent personalities who made friends with Father Ricci. However, so as not to transgress the limits of brevity in a matter of lesser importance, we shall merely touch upon this subject in passing.

Among the most prominent of Ricci's friends were the six presiding officers of the chief tribunals of Nankin, who conduct the affairs of the entire province, and who are outranked by the corresponding officials of Pekin only because the King resides there. There were also three other prominent characters whom we have not as yet seen.

Here in Nankin there are people known as Quocum, who enjoy certain hereditary privileges because they are descendants of the military leaders who expelled the Tartars from China. Their families are highly honored by the King and particularly so the oldest sons of these families. With the lapse of several centuries this class has become very numerous, but none of them is ever eligible for appointment to a public office, unless it be to a military command. They have considerable dignity and wealth, and correspond, in a sense, to the nobility of Europe. The head of one of these families in Nankin may be described as typical of his social class. When he had occasion to leave his palace, he was carried about in a palanquin on the shoulders of eight of his servants. His gardens, the palace and its furnishings, were regal in every respect.

One day, this man sent his uncle to invite Father Matthew to come to his home and on the Father's arrival he was received in the most magnificent garden in the whole city. Passing over much that was delightful to look upon in this garden, he saw a hill artificially constructed in vari-colored unpolished marble. This hill was wonderfully hollowed out into a cave with reception rooms and halls, stairways, fishponds, trees and numerous other attractions, and it was difficult to say whether art or luxury prevailed. This grotto was built as an escape from the summer heat, when one wished to study or to entertain. The design of the cave, which added to its charm, was a sort of labyrinth, not too extensive, though it took several hours to see it all before passing out through a hidden exit. The man in question was a young nobleman, who had heard about certain things brought from Europe and was curious to see some of them.

Another dignitary whom Father Matthew now counted among his friends was the Military Prefect of the City of Nankin, who also held another high civil office, the second highest in rank, called Heu. He frequently invited Father Matthew to meetings and banquets and his friendship was a source of security to the Mission. He was in command of the city. In fact, he was the same man who was about to have Father Matthew arrested on his first visit to Nankin, and hesitated to do so when he learned that the stranger in the city was a friend of the President of the Magistrates.

A third individual, and one of almost unlimited power, was the chief eunuch of the King's palace, who had command over the several thousand of his kind in the city. He was also in charge of the tolls at the city gates, and with the general just named arranged for all military celebrations. This man held various other public offices and always made considerable show and parade of his authority. He was old and somewhat decrepit, and like all the palace eunuchs, he was inclined to be snobbish, and he showed this disposition in his reception of Father Ricci. Some of his court staff had told the Father to greet him with a certain title, like, Your Exalted Highness; something rather novel and perhaps in need of explanation.

When greeting the King of China, it is customary to wish him ten thousand thousand years of life, which is expressed in three syllables: van, van, siu. To the queens and the children of the palace, being of inferior title, one wishes only a thousand years. The palace eunuchs are so arrogant, that they also want to be greeted with a bend of the knee and a wish of a thousand years. Father Ricci refused to tender such a greeting to the majordomo of the palace, because he did not wish to insult the highest Magistrates by showing more respect for the eunuch than he did for them, and yet, as we shall see, he was cordially received. Father Matthew had learned from experience not to omit certain reasonable formalities, when dealing with the Chinese and with other oriental pagans, and so on this occasion he was careful to observe the usual introductory ceremony. The chief eunuch was hard of hearing and employed an assistant, who spoke close to his ear and was supposed to repeat the Father's part of the conversation. At the first greeting, and of his own accord, he wished his master the customary thousand years and the old man was so delighted with the greeting, that at the end of the interview, he offered Father Matthew a princely gift. This the Father did not accept, nor would he promise to provide his host with one of the triangular glass prisms which he asked for. That was the first and the last time he ever saw the ruling eunuch, and the attitude he assumed at the meeting was highly praised by all the others of that class in the city. Apart from the majordomo of the palace, it was sufficient security that the three leading officials of the city knew that Father Matthew was coming to live there.

At that time there was living in the City of Nankin, a certain distinguished citizen, who had attained to the highest rank among the literary doctors. This in itself is considered by the Chinese to be a very high honor. He had been deprived of the public office he had held and was living as a private citizen, with considerable show, but he was still held in high esteem by the people. This man was widely known as a leader of the three Chinese religious sects we have already mentioned, and his authority among them was great. Living with him at his home there was a well known priest of the idols, who had given up public office, shaved his head, and from being one of the class of the literati he became a minister of the idols, a very unusual thing among the educated Chinese. He was well versed in Chinese affairs, seventy years of age, and a distinguished scientist, with many followers in the sect he had joined. Both of these prominent characters had great respect for Father Matthew, particularly the apostate from the literati, and it caused great wonderment when it was learned that he had been visiting the foreign Father. Some time before, at a congress of the lettered class, when the Christian law was being discussed, this man was the only one to observe continued silence, because he believed that the Christian law was the only true way of life. He gave Father Ricci a folder containing two epigrams which he had composed and these were added to the collection of similar cards that Ricci was making; a common practice among the Chinese. These epigrams written in honor of Father Matthew and his companions would have made a good sized volume, if one had been vain enough to preserve them.

There were two others with whom Father Matthew was also acquainted; two of lesser rank but of no less reputation. One of these claimed to be three hundred years old and, in order to cover his untruth, he said that most of his life had been spent beyond the borders of the realm of China. The question of prolonging life has developed into a craze among the Chinese sages, and this man, with no thought of the truth, had built up a numerous following of disciples who were eager to learn his doctrine of longevity. He was the first of the two to call on Father Matthew and he came, as he said, to build up his own reputation as a mathematician by meeting with the most prominent of mathematicians. He claimed to be able to predict the future, not by observing the heavens, but from the earth, by the precepts of Chinese geology.

The second of these two was a bit more modest, claiming to be only ninety years old, when he appeared to be about sixty. He knew how to cure the so-called incurable diseases, so he claimed, and certain authors did narrate wonders about him in that respect. These two visitors were intimates, and mutual praise did much to build up their reputations; the one for long life and the other for medical science. They were both high in their praise for Father Matthew, to whom they ceded place as a scientist, with the result that some began to suspect that probably Father Matthew himself had been living for a few centuries, but was concealing the fact for a purpose. The uneducated Chinese fall an easy prey to such tales, especially regarding foreigners whose facial contour differs from their own.

Let us here insert a word about Chinese music, an art that is of considerable interest to Europeans. The leaders of the literary class observe a solemn day of sacrifice in honor of Confucius, if sacrifice is the proper word. The Chinese honor the great philosopher as a Master, and not as a deity, and they are accustomed to use the word sacrifice in a broad and indefinite sense. This particular celebration is attended with music, and on the previous day they invite the Chief of Magistrates to attend a rehearsal of the orchestra, to decide whether or not the music will be appropriate for the occasion. Father Ricci was invited to this rehearsal and as there was no question of attending a sacrifice, he accepted the invitation. This orchestral rehearsal was arranged by the priests of the literary class, called Tansu, and it was held in a hall or rather in the Royal Temple, built to honor the Lord of Heaven. Father Matthew was accompanied by the children of the High Magistrate. The priests who composed the orchestra were vested in sumptuous garments, as if they were to attend a sacrifice, and after paying their respects to the Magistrate, they set to playing their various instruments; bronze bells, basin shaped vessels, some made of stone, with skins over them like drums, stringed instruments like a lute, bone flutes and organs played by blowing into them with the mouth rather than with bellows. They had other instruments also shaped like animals, holding reeds in their teeth, through which air was forced from the empty interior. At this rehearsal these curious affairs were all sounded at once, with a result that can be readily imagined, as it was nothing other than a lack of concord, a discord of discords. The Chinese themselves are aware of this. One of their sages said on a certain occasion that the art of music known to their ancestors had evaporated with the centuries, and left only the instruments.

The Royal Temple in which this ceremony was held is well worthy of note. It really is regal both in dimensions and in the majesty of its architecture. It is situated at one end of the city, in a grove, or rather in a pine forest, surrounded by a wall, twelve Italian miles in circumference. The wall structure of the temple is built of brick, all the rest of it is done in wood. It is divided into five sections or naves, each surrounded by two rows of wooden columns. Two men with outstretched arms could scarcely encircle one of these columns, and their height is proportionate to their girth. The roof is highly adorned in relief and gilded over. Despite the fact that this temple was built some two hundred years ago and is no longer used for royal functions, because the King no longer resides in Nankin, it has suffered no deterioration, nor has it lost any of its pristine splendor. In the center of the temple there is an elevated platform, made of beautiful marble, and on the platform two seats or a double throne, each in marble; one is for the King if he is to offer a sacrifice, and the other is left vacant, being intended for the one to whom the King offers the sacrifice, in the event that he might wish to sit there. The peristyle of the outer temple is highly ornamented in fretted design, and the windows are protected from the birds by a metal screen, admitting the light. This is done in all the royal palaces. The doors of the temple are bronze-plated and covered with gold and decorated with specter-like figures of the same material.

Outside of the temple they have erected a series of altars in red colored marble, dedicated to the sun, the moon, the stars, and the mountains of China, and there is a lake representing the sea. They say that the God who is worshipped in the temple is the creator of all that is outside of the temple and that these things are not to be worshipped as deities. It is strictly forbidden, under heavy penalty, to cut down or break the branches of the trees in this grove, hence they have grown to great proportions, which attests their antiquity. Encircling the temple there are a number of caves, in which there were, formerly, warm water baths, used by the King and the temple ministers, before going to the sacrificial ceremonies.

7. Father Ricci Debates with a Minister of the Idols

WE HAVE ALREADY noted that Father Ricci wore the costume of the literary class, and of that particular branch of it known as the Expounders of the Law. It was a modest garb, and the hat that went with it was somewhat like our own biretta, designed in the form of a cross. Not only by his costume but by his preaching also he showed himself to be in truth an expounder of the law, but of the Christian law, and in both respects a confounder of the ministers of the idols. He did not find fault with the literary sect, on the contrary, he praised them and particularly their great philosopher, Confucius, who preferred to observe silence relative to the future life, rather than put forth erroneous ideas about it, and to explain the law by offering precepts for regulating the life of the individual, for the direction of the family, and for the proper government of the kingdom.

Father Matthew's custom of going about in his newly adopted raiment was something unusual for a foreigner, but it had the approval of the literary class. Up to this time, strangers who came to China from the West, dissenting from the doctrines of the literati and from Confucius himself, took to the worship of idols. This subject of Father

Matthew's attire was a common topic of conversation among the most distinguished people, and he was always invited to the meetings of the literary leaders, as a man who adored one God, held to one religion which he believed to be true, and refused to associate with those who sacrificed to misleading deities. This same was true of many of the educated class of that period.

There was a venerable septuagenarian living in Nankin at that time; one of the City Judges, with a reputation for virtue as well as for learning. People came to him from all parts, as to an oracle for instruction, and he must have had a thousand followers. He had abandoned the teachings of the literati and gone over to the worshippers of idols, and to preaching their cult. He did not like the frequent gatherings of people who came from different quarters to consult him, and so he designated certain days of the month on which he could be called, and apart from these days he refused to answer for anyone. He had expressed his desire to see Father Ricci, and Ricci, thinking that with God's help he could perhaps win over the sage to the true faith, arranged through their mutual friend Chiutaiso to pay him a visit.

Their conversation opened on the subject of religion and in their first argument Father Matthew brought him around to admit that the cult of idols was like an apple that was partly good and partly bad, and that one might accept what was good of it and reject the rest. Some of his disciples who were present were horrified to hear their Master make such a concession and he himself seemed to be mentally befuddled, at the realization that he had met someone who argued so pointedly against idol worshipping.

The literary doctors at that time were more active than usual, organizing in different groups that convened for the discussion of moral questions and the pursuit of virtue. At one of these meetings, the master we have just mentioned was holding forth very learnedly, as was his custom, in favor of idol worship and against the doctrines of Confucius, the master mind of the literati. At that particular meeting there happened to be present the Commissioner of Public Works, an officer of high rank and prominent among the literati. Listening to this praise of the idols, which was all in disparagement of Confucius, he became so excited that he broke in on the speaker. He protested in a loud voice that the orator was out of order and out of place, coming to a meeting, where they were all literati and all Chinese, and arriving at such a state of madness as to belie Confucius and to praise idol worship, a cult that was introduced into China from the outside world.

Then he added that the foreigner Matthew Ricci, a member of the literati, was much to be admired because he understood Confucius and rejected the madness of the idols, which the foreigners themselves had long since wiped out in their own home lands. The speaker had never met or seen Father Matthew, and so it was unusual that he should speak so frankly about him. The interruption embarrassed the minister of the Temple, but he covered up his confusion by saying that he had already met this Matthew Ricci and that as yet he did not seem to be particularly learned in Chinese affairs. "It may take some time," he asserted, "but little by little we shall probably educate him to the better things." That put an end to the conference.

Not long after, and before Father Matthew learned what had taken place in the meeting, he received an urgent invitation from the same minister of the idols, to come to his house for dinner. We have mentioned that it is customary with the Chinese to argue over their differences at the dinner table. In order not to jeopardize the development of his Mission, Father Matthew said he was very busy at the time and offered several other excuses for refusing the invitation, but the one inviting would not accept these excuses. Instead, he sent several messengers, at Chiutaiso's advice, who were so insistent upon his going, that the Father decided that he could no longer decline, without appearing to be impolite. So he went, all prepared for a debate. His host, still aware of his former experience, and somewhat diffident about this meeting, had invited a celebrated minister of the temple idols, who was said to have had a great following of disciples and of the laity of both sexes, who called him Master. This sage was one of the Sanhoi and was quite different from the regular cenobites whose supine ignorance renders them infamous. He was an ardent scholar, a philosopher, an orator and a poet, and well versed in the doctrines of the other sects from which he differed. He was at the house when Father Matthew arrived, and surrounded by a coterie of his admirers, twenty or more in number, who had paid their respects to the host and were seated, waiting for the rest of the company.

The invited solon seated himself beside the Father and concealing a supercilious attitude behind a thread worn cloak, he assumed a pose of invitation to an argument. The invitation was accepted and Father Matthew opened the discussion by saying: "Before we descend into the arena for debate, I would like to know what you think of the first principle of heaven and earth and the Creator of all things else, whom we call the God of Heaven." To this, his adversary excitedly replied that he did not deny the existence of a moderator of heaven and earth, but at the same time he did not believe him to be a god or endowed with any particular majesty. "I think," he added, "that I and the others here are his equals and I see no reason why we should cede to him in any respect." He said this in a tone of disdain and with a furrowed brow, as though he himself wished to be looked upon as even superior to that supreme moderator whom he had mentioned. Father Matthew then asked him if he could do what evidently had been done by the creator of heaven and earth, as it seemed to follow from his doctrine that he could. He then admitted that he could create heaven and earth. Now, there happened to be a fireplace in the room, filled with smoldering ashes, and Father Matthew said, "Pray, let us see you create a fireplace like this one here." At this the idol worshipper became excited and in a high voice said that it was quite unbecoming that the Father should ask him to do such a thing. To which Father Matthew, also lifting his voice, retorted that it was also very unbecoming to pretend to be able to do something which one is not able to do. Then the others all joined in at once and a clamor ensued, with everyone demanding to know what they were really talking about. Finally, Chiutaiso allayed the tumult and said that it seemed to him that Father Matthew's question was not at all out of place.

With quiet restored, the profane mystic began, with a long circumlocution, to present the principles of his chimerical doctrine. First, he asked Father Matthew if he were versed in mathematics, saying that he had heard that he had a reputation as an eminent astrologer. To this the Father replied that he had had some training in that science. "Good," said the temple minister, "now when you look upon the sun or the moon, do you go up to the sky, or do the planets come down to you?" "Neither one nor the other," Father Matthew replied. "When we see a thing, we form an image of it in our minds, and when we want to talk about the thing we have seen, or think about it, we draw out the image of the thing, which is stored in our memory." With that the templer stood up at his place, as the victor in the argument. "That's just it," he exclaimed. "In other words, you have created a new sun, a new moon, and in the same way anything else can be created." Whereupon, he looked about proudly and sat down again, relaxing in repose, as one who had clearly proven his point.

It was now Father Matthew's turn, and he explained that the image formed in one's mind was a mental picture of the sun or the moon, and not the actual thing itself. "How great a difference there is between a thing and its image," he continued, "should be evident to anyone; so much so indeed that if one had never seen the sun or the moon, he could not even form a mental picture of either one or the other, to say nothing of actually creating them. If I can see an image of the sun or the moon in a mirror," he said, "shall I be simple enough to say that the mirror created the moon or the sun?" The rest of the company seemed to be more satisfied with this explanation than the disputatious templer, who endeavored to conceal his ignorance by instigating another clamor and committing the worth of his argument to the din that followed. Finally, the host, fearing that something might be said which would injure one side or the other, put an end to the debate, took his templer friend apart from the company and advised him to refrain from debating in the future.

In the meantime, other guests were arriving for the banquet and being placed at the numerous tables. The first place at table was assigned to Father Matthew, because he was a stranger, and during the dinner, they opened a discussion on a question frequently introduced at their gatherings, namely, What are we to think of human nature? Is it essentially good, or bad, or neither? If good, whence the evil it begets? If bad, whence the good it often produces? If neither, how does it happen that it produces both good and evil? Since these men lacked the rules of logic and knew of no distinction between natural and moral goodness, they confounded what is innate in human nature with what is acquired by it. Concerning the fall of human nature in original sin, and likewise concerning divine grace and its operation, of course, they knew absolutely nothing, because they had never even dreamed of such things. Up to this day their philosophers continue to argue about human nature, without ever being able to come to any definite conclusion concerning it. On this occasion they talked and argued about it for a whole hour, and as Father Matthew sat there quietly listening, some of them concluded that perhaps their arguments on the subject were too subtle for him to comprehend. Others, however, were eager to hear what he had to say in solution of so intricate a problem, and as he was about to speak, they all became quiet and settled back to listen with attention.

He began by making a detailed summary, from memory, of all that had been said on the question, which caused them all to open their eyes in wonder, after which he said, "There is no room for doubt that the God of heaven and earth must be considered as infinitely good. Now, if human nature is so weak that we doubt whether it is good or bad in itself, and if man as well as God is the creator of heaven and earth, as the master Sanhoi asserted he was, only a few minutes ago, then we must admit that it is open to doubt as to whether God also is good or bad." Sitting next to Father Ricci there was one of the literati of the class of Licentiates, who was so pleased with this argument, that fearing lest it might not be understood by the company, he stood up and gave a fuller and an excellent explanation of what it meant. At the end of his discourse he turned to the temple cenobite, with a smile, and said, "How will you answer that?" And the only answer to his question was a supercilious grin. At this, Father Matthew and several others insisted upon a verbal answer, rather than a nod or a gesture. To this the minister of the idols retorted with a narrative of peculiar hallucinations from the doctrine of his sect, which Father Matthew interrupted, saying: "Our arguments must be drawn from reason, not from authority. Since we disagree in doctrine and neither of us admits the validity of the books of the other, and since I could quote any number of examples from my books, our argument now is to be settled by reason which is common to us both." The minister of the idols, however, did not appear to be vanquished. Instead of taking up the argument, he rambled on slyly with a flow of nicely formed and sonorous sentences from the idiom of the Chinese language, pretending to prove that he who was good could also be bad. Then Father Matthew continued, just as cleverly as his opponent, saying that the sun was so bright that it could never be anything but bright, because of its natural, innate brightness. This was a new idea to them which had great force, for the simple reason that they knew of no distinction between substance and accident.

There were other subjects discussed at this dinner and when it was over, the temple minister was the only one who would not admit that he was vanquished, though all the others agreed that he was. They were so pleased with Father Matthew's presentation of his side of the question, that they carried on the discussion of the same subjects at their meetings for months afterwards.

Their great error, fatal to the idea of divinity, namely, that God and all things material are one and the same substance, taken from the doctrine of the idol worshippers, has gradually crept into the schools of the literary class, who imagine that God is the soul of the material universe; the one mind, as it were, of a great body.

After the debate at the banquet, some of the disciples of the host became frequent callers on Father Ricci and soon put aside their pantheistic ideas. In order to help others to correct this fallacy, he wrote a treatise on that particular question, and inserted it as a separate chapter in his catechism. When this commentary was read by one of the disciples of the banquet host, he remarked that anyone denying its truth would deny that the sun was bright. The story of the debate at the banquet came to the President of the Magistrates and he congratulated the Father, as did others also, who had concluded that what they had formerly considered to be a barbarous law was not so barbarous as they had imagined. Father Ricci, himself, thanked God that the foundations of the Christian law were finally being laid in the kingdom of China.

8. The Mission House at Nankin

THE ROYAL TREASURY of China was so depleted by the Korean war that the King decided to replenish it. It was rumored through the kingdom that there were many gold and silver mines in various parts of the realm, but that the lure of gold to human avarice had been so great, that thieves and robbers had despoiled the mines of their hordes of wealth. This practice, it was said, had become so common that the ancient kings had closed the mines, with strict orders that they should not be reopened. The present King, however, in his necessity, disregarding the orders of his ancestors, commanded that the mines be reopened and worked, and then levied a new tax of two percent, to be paid into the royal treasury, from all merchandise sold in every province. This tax would have been bearable if the King had appointed the Magistrates to collect it. Instead, he entrusted the collection to the eunuchs and sent two of three of the chiefs among them into every province, to enforce the new levy. Each of these took others of his class with him, of lesser rank but of equal avarice. The chief eunuchs were exempted from the laws and from the jurisdiction of the Magistrates who always administer the laws with moderation.

The eunuchs, as a class, are unlettered and barbarous, lacking shame and piety, utterly arrogant and very monsters of vice. What with these semimen in command, and with their greed developing them into savages, the whole kingdom was in a turmoil within a few months, and in a worse state than it was during the Korean war. The war was external. This evil was from within, and greater, because of the fear it developed. Pilfering, cheating and robbery were everywhere common. The tax and customs bureaus were veritable dens of thieves, and the royal treasury, entrusted by the King to the eunuchs, was thoroughly despoiled. The tax collectors found gold mines, not in the mountains, but in the rich cities. If they were told that a rich man lived here or there, they said he had a silver mine in his house, and immediately decided to ransack and undermine his home. This method of collection resulted in the payment of large sums of money by unfortunate victims before the collectors appeared, in order to save their properties. Sometimes, in order to secure an exemption from being robbed, the cities and even the provinces bartered with the eunuchs, and paid them a large sum of silver, which they said was taken from the mines for the royal treasury. The result of this unusual spoliation was an increase in the prices of all commodities, with a corresponding growth in the general spread of poverty.

Unlike the King's degraded servants, the Magistrates remained loyal to him and to the public charge they administered. They sent frequent notices warning the King that the people were being treated unjustly, that there was danger of a public uprising, and not only danger but that serious outbreaks had already happened in several places. When the King paid no attention to their warnings, they wrote to him, reprehending his conduct in no uncertain terms, and some of them, outside of the royal city, openly opposed the ravages of the eunuchs. But His Majesty was growing fat on the daily provender brought to his palace by his henchmen, and he resolved, not only to pursue his policy, but to punish with heavy penalties the critics and the censors of royalty, and all those who dared to interfere with the work of the eunuchs. As a result, some of the judges were deposed from their high offices, and others were sent to prison in Pekin to serve long terms in chains. With the King's authority renewed, the robbers became more insolent in their attitude and more daring in their depredations.

All of Nankin was frightened by the news of what was happening throughout the country. Father Matthew and his friend the President of the Magistrates, were fearful lest the Fathers, who remained for the winter in Lincin, should fall into the claws of these harpies. To the President it seemed impossible that the eunuchs could miss their valuable luggage, but Father Matthew, concealing his fear, assured him that God would give evidence of how careful He was to protect His own.

On the arrival of the Fathers, after several months of winter and of travel, the President was surprised to learn that they had suffered no molestation and that they had not even realized the presence of any danger. He considered that to be nothing short of a miracle. It increased his interest in divine Providence and in the faith, so much so, indeed, that from that time on he was always pleased to hear it further explained. It was one thing, however, to have him realize the truth of the faith but quite another to have him accept its sacred obligations, when that meant the removal of a domestic impediment of concubines.

Saint Joseph

l at Nankin and heard that a
nd their fondest hopes, they
d rejoiced in the Lord. What
thew was being honored by
in a city from which he was
r occasion, he had had to go
em with more than usual joy
ed over several other houses,
nd none that would serve his
at a loss as to how he could
istrates, permitting him to buy
He had learned from sad ex-
was in itself a guarantee of a
l take the liberty of sponsoring
fact, he was deliberating as to
ner to remain in Nankin, when
d a solution to his doubts.

o highly at the congress of the
him, came to pay him a visit,
r missionaries. After paying the
esy, he said he had heard that
se in which he could establish
red him that he had heard cor-
d a really surprising story. "A
ace, at public expense, for my
oon as it was finished and given
ssession of it, and no one could
d to sell it at a very low price

but no one could be found to move in on the ghosts. Now with your reputation for sanctity," he continued, "if you are not afraid of ghosts, it is yours to purchase and there will be no wrangling about the price, because you may determine that yourself, as you see fit." In all this Father Matthew thought he saw the hand of God and he said, "I adore the One God, who regulates both heaven and earth, and to whom devils and all things are subordinate." He then explained that his confidence in the divine goodness assured him that even devils could not trouble him unless God permitted it to be so. He also said that he had an image of Jesus Christ, the Saviour, at sight of which the devils take flight, and that if this palace suited his needs, he had no fear whatsoever of the evil spirits that might be haunting it.

With the fear of ghosts allayed, his visitor, Leuteu, took him to see the place and, contrary to his expectations, Father Matthew found it more suitable for his purposes than any house he had thus far inspected. It was located in the highest part of the city, safe from any overflow of the river, and situated on the principal street of Nankin, which at that spot was about a stone's throw in width. From the circle of its outlook, one could see the palace of the King and the court buildings of the different tribunals. The halls and the living rooms afforded accommodations for about ten of the missionaries. It was a new house and built to last for years. It could be entered from two sides, and the road in front of it led into another main highway. Fortunately this house was being sold by the Chief of the Bureau of Public Works, and so there was no difficulty in securing the permission of the Magistrates to purchase it; the one thing that had caused so much trouble in the past. It really did seem as if it had been prepared for the Fathers by the hand of God.

Father Cattaneo and his companions arrived as negotiations were being completed for the purchase of the house, and their general opinion was that they should not neglect such a golden opportunity for a permanent settlement. The price of the house was left to them to decide upon. The owner, who wished to keep their friendship, offered it to them for half of what it had cost to build it, and when he learned that the Mission was not possessed of that amount of money, he deferred the payment of half the sum for a whole year. The bargain was closed and within three days the Fathers were settled in their new home.

The Commissioner sent them a document, recording the sale and purchase, and placed a notice over the entrance, prohibiting anyone from interfering with their possession of the property. Both the document and the notice were stamped with his official seal, by the authority of which the Fathers established their permanent center, firmly and quietly, thanks to the grace of God. One result of this transaction was the acquisition of the friendship of the Commissioner, who was satisfied to recover half the price of his house, when he had abandoned hope of getting anything at all for it. Just before he closed the deal for the purchase of the house, Father Ricci showed the official document for its purchase to his friend the Chief of Magistrates, who was somewhat surprised to learn that the whole business had been so quickly and so quietly terminated. He was not too pleased that it had been accomplished without his assistance, but afterwards, when he heard that the evil spirits had taken flight on the arrival of the servants of God, he was loud in his praise of the divine power and protection.

The first night they occupied the house, the Fathers recited appropriate prayers at an altar erected in the main aula, and went through the whole building, carrying a crucifix and sprinkling holy water, and from that time on, with God's grace favoring the spread of the faith in China, the evil spirits made no further appearance. He to whom all beings are subject had permitted the evil spirits to inhabit this house in order to prepare it for the coming of His servants, and when they came the spirits were driven out of it. This story was spread through the whole city and afterwards throughout the kingdom, with the result that respect for the faith was greatly increased. It was generally known that the Magistrates belonging to the Bureau of Public Works had actually tried to live in this house, and that the ministers of the idols had resorted to every means at their disposal to expel the evil spirits from it, but with no success. Even now there are cuts and scratches on the walls and pillars, left there by the exorcising ministers in their useless fury to purify the place, and there is ample testimony of those who experienced the ordeal that nobody could live there unmolested. When it was learned that the evil spirits took flight at the first approach of the Fathers, it was looked upon by the Chinese as a miracle, wrought by God, under whose protection the Missionaries claimed to be laboring.

One day, as the Commissioner was talking, in the presence of Father Matthew, and telling what had happened in his house, he said that when he was building it, they had omitted none of the religious ceremonies practiced by the Chinese during the construction of a new building. "Now," he said, "I can understand why the demons took possession of it. It was because Father Matthew's God commanded them to let no one live there, other than Father Matthew himself."

No sooner had they settled down and forgotten the worries of house hunting, than another vexatious problem presented itself for solution. Father Matthew had promised some of the high officials that he would show them the presents that were to be presented to the King, but he was doubtful lest suspicion might arise, or a tumult be caused by the great number of curious visitors who would come to the house to see them. After due consideration and consultation with the others, it was decided that the promise would be fulfilled, if they were to set aside several successive days on which the people were free to come to view the presents, and then to judge from results as to what course should be followed in the future.

Once it was known that the King's presents were on exhibition, visitors came in crowds to see them. The novelty of the gifts surpassed their expectations to such an extent that astonishment robbed many of their power to praise them, and they seemed never to tire of examining them and of talking about them. Those who came told others and they in turn told others, until the visiting became unbearable and the Fathers had to close the doors. But the spectators would not be denied. They even prepared to force an entrance, after first protesting that their insistence was due, not to any incivility, but rather to their admiration. They gave various other reasons for their importunity, asked pardon for the trouble they were causing, and despite the commotion they were making, they were loud in their praise of Europe, of its art and of its religion.

9. The First Nankin Neophytes Are Baptized

WITH THE SETTLEMENT completed in Nankin, they could not rest contented until they should attempt at Pekin what God had brought to pass at Nankin, but they decided to defer the effort until the following year. Despite the unhappy outcome of the previous journey to Pekin, they were encouraged by the following facts. Experience had taught them how to correct the errors of the year before and times had changed with the coming of peace. They had developed friendship with the Magistrates and now they were thoroughly convinced that unless they could curry favor with the King the developments at Nankin and elsewhere would eventually disappear.

Talk about the gifts for the King had spread far and wide, and it seemed quite possible that it would sooner or later reach the ears of the sovereign himself by means of one or other of the eunuchs, who were continually passing between Nankin and Pekin. It was also just as possible that the novelty of the gifts might stir the curiosity of the King and move him to rashly appropriate them without consulting the owners, and with no benefit to the Mission. With that idea in mind, the Fathers thought it would be better to anticipate the King's interest and in some way to render him beholden to them. It was, therefore, decided to send Father Cattaneo to Macao to acquaint the brethren with what was going on, and to get their counsel on how to proceed in so important a matter. He was also to bring back money for the support of the house, presents to increase the collection for the King, and funds sufficient to pay off the debt on the house.

Since they could see no cessation of the stream of visitors, about which we were just speaking, it seemed advisable for Father Cattaneo to take the clock to Nancian, on his way to Macao, and to place the crucifix and the statues and the triangular glass prisms in safe keeping with one of the admonitors of the King, a friend of theirs, named Scioscelin. At first, their friend was somewhat hesitant about taking these things, because of the reverence due to the images, but he finally accepted them, when they insisted that they were destined for the King, and that it was his duty to be interested in their safety. With that decided upon, it was made known to the public that the presents were to be removed from the residence, and they were carried through the streets of the city in solemn procession and carefully deposited in Scioscelin's palace. He, himself, received the images with great respect, as holy things, and placed incense lamps before them, which he kept continually burning, after the Chinese custom. He permitted some of his friends to see the gifts, but not the common people, who seldom if ever gained entrance into the palace of a Magistrate. With the presents removed, there was no fear of further excitement at the house, and so Father Cattaneo set out with one of the Lay Brothers, who was to accompany him as far as Nancian and wait there for him until he returned from Macao.

The news of what had happened at Nankin had already reached Macao and was received with great rejoicing by the Fathers there, and also by the Portuguese inhabitants. With the arrival of Father Cattaneo, the story was renewed and the rejoicing increased. The news of how the house had been acquired and of how friendly the Magistrates had become was something they would have found difficult to believe, had they not heard it from an eye witness of all that had happened.

But there was a deep note of sadness sounded in the midst of the joy of Macao. A ship that had left Japan for that port was long overdue. Father Egidio di Matta, the treasurer of the vice-province, was known to have sailed in it, and it had just been announced that the ship had been wrecked, with the loss of all on board. The whole city was dependent upon the trade and commerce supplied by this ship. The three Mission settlements were also dependent upon it, as well as the payment for the house purchased in Nankin and the expenses for the journey to Pekin. In these dire straits, it was Father Emanuele Dias, the Rector of the College of Macao, who came to the rescue by opening up his great heart, and, as one might say, revealing its magnanimous charity in favor of the China Mission. He scraped and stinted on all sides, until he finally gathered together enough for everyone to carry through. Then he added still more, to be given to his friends. He sent along another clock, to be added to the gifts for the King. It was smaller than the one they had, but it looked large because of the lavish decorations with which it was adorned. He also gave them a picture of the Blessed Virgin, which he had received from Rome, a life size copy of the one that is said to have been painted by Saint Luke. To these he added a few triangular glass prisms, mirrors, some beautiful vestments, linen cloth, small hour-glasses and many glass vases; things that were necessary to make acquaintances and, as it were, to oil the wheels of social progress. Finally, he went to the trouble of having several organs made, but, as they were late in being completed, they were saved for the Nankin Mission. He appointed Father Didaco Pantoia as a co-worker, to return with Father Cattaneo, either to remain at Nankin or to accompany Father Matthew to Pekin. Father Pantoia belonged to the Province of Toledo. He was destined for the Mission of Japan, but was detained at Macao for lack of transportation. In addition to the gifts he received from the Rector of the College, Father Cattaneo collected many other very useful items, such as two chalices, many books and other things needed at the Mission House.

During the lull in activities, those at Nancian were busy studying Chinese literature. Father Soeiro kept in contact with the friends they had made there, and developed new friendships with other notables. Through the influence of Ciengan, the quasi-king we have already mentioned, Father Soeiro was introduced to one of the chief eunuchs, in charge of collecting the new taxes for the royal treasury. The tax collector said he could arrange for Father Matthew to present his gifts to the King. The kinglet thought this was a perfectly safe approach and he sent a document to Father Soeiro, arranging an appointment for him with the tax collector, at Nancian, and asking him to bring along the gifts, so the Chief Collector could see them and make out a document accordingly, which he would send to the King. Under the guidance of Divine Providence, the notice sent by the so-called king to Father Soeiro never arrived. The messenger to whom it was entrusted never put in an appearance. Other letters were sent to the Father but they were not delivered until the same Divine Providence had settled everything otherwise. The Fathers were beginning to understand the tactics of the eunuchs, and they decided that such important business should not be entrusted to that particular race of disloyal subjects. Father Ricci thanked the king-in-name and through him notified the chief of the tax collectors that he had already opened negotiations along another line, which were not as yet complete.

Father Cattaneo could not get away from Macao as soon as he had planned, and lest his delay might cause a default in payment for the house on the appointed day, he sent on a letter of credit, made payable through a certain Chinese merchant. This was the second experience the Fathers had had in this kind of business, and again it taught them that this was a dangerous risk. The name of the Nankin merchant, the place of payment, and everything connected with the transaction was falsified, and this, for the second time, taught them that they should cease sending letters of credit. The money was recovered, but Father Matthew defaulted in his payment to the owner, which proved to be an unfortunate incident. It was not difficult for him to borrow a small sum for running the house, but the rate of interest to the money lenders for the large amount needed was prohibitive. Somehow or other, the Commissioner, from whom they bought the house, heard of Father Matthew's financial difficulties and sent him word not to worry about the payment due, because he and his colleagues would be glad to defer the payment until Father Cattaneo arrived, and with that worry off his mind, Father Matthew turned his attention to something more pleasant.

By this time it had become generally known that the Missionaries had come into China to propagate the Christian faith, and some of the more courageous of the Chinese notables made no hesitation in searching out the truth of the doctrine of the foreigners.

The first Chinese convert in Nankin, and the most distinguished, was a prominent native, seventy years of age, named Cin. He was one of the nobility and held a military post, which was hereditary in his family, something rare among the Chinese. He had a son with a wide reputation for learning, who had, three times, gained first honors in the triennial examination for military degrees, conducted in all the provinces, and thus he attained to the highest military rank among the Licentiates. At this time, the son was Military Prefect of Nankin. The conversion of the father was remarkable. He was well versed in Catholic doctrine and very devout, and in baptism he took the name of Paul. Not long after his reception, the son followed his father's example and selected Martin as a Christian name. Later on, the whole family, men and women, and some of their relatives were received into the Church. These were the first Christians of Nankin and up to this day they remain a pious and devout Catholic family.

Father Matthew gave the old gentleman a statue which he placed in a domestic chapel, decorated with costly tapestries, in his home. The Fathers came here to celebrate Mass and to instruct the women of the family, whom the Chinese protect very carefully. Next to the chapel there was a furnished room for the use of the Fathers, after their long hours of teaching and instructing the many domestic servants. During the time that this family were idol worshippers, they were quite attentive to their wooden gods, and when they replaced them with a crucifix, they sent a large case of highly decorated graven images to the Mission House. Father Matthew sent the whole collection to Macao, as the first spoils gained from the Tyrant of Nankin, namely, the Devil. Their reception was an occasion of rejoicing and of thanksgiving to God.

Here it seems to be quite opportune to relate how Father Ricci preached the faith at Nankin and afterwards at Pekin, how gentle and at the same time how authoritative he was in explaining it, and how docile his listeners were in receiving it. At the various meetings of their educated class, at which Father Matthew was always present, they usually introduced questions about Europe, and he told them all about the habits and the religious customs of the European Christian world. He explained to them the purpose and the management of the hospitals, of homes for orphans, of pious trusts for the poor, and of charitable societies that cared for destitute widows and for prisoners. At times he would talk about the religious orders of men and women, founded to assure their own eternal salvation and to secure the salvation of others. He told them that certain days of the year were given to God, as holy days, set aside for worship and prayer, so that Christians would not become lax in the practice of their faith. He emphasized the virtue of Christian charity, and the various ways it is practiced, such as the giving of money by way of alms for the support of the poor. In addition, he explained some of the many duties of bishops and priests in cities and towns, who, in order to preserve the faith whole and entire, censored published books, lest anything harmful to faith or morals should be propagated. He also explained the restitution of things stolen or found. One thing which they seemed to approve, but which they were averse to accepting, was the law forbidding concubines, and also the marriage laws, binding kings as well as people, permitting only one wife and forbidding divorce, even where there were no children. Relating to this subject also, he explained the law forbidding the marriage contract for children, and of deferring it to an age of competency.

The Chinese were greatly interested in learning that the Catholic Church recognized an authority higher even than that of the king, and final in religious matters. They wondered that this authority was not inherited by any individual, but invested in one who was elected by a congress of learned, prudent and pious prelates, dedicated to God from early life and bound by a vow of chastity, and that this man governed the Church with great prudence and integrity. The missionaries always invested the exalted position of the Pope with a great deal of dignity, and left no room for suspicion that it was a mere dignity of royalty.

In this way the minds of the Chinese were gradually disposed to considering the advisability of future diplomatic relations, and to understanding that it would mean great progress for the Church in China, if the Emperor were to send a delegation to Rome. The effect produced upon the Chinese converts and also upon many of the pagans by Father Ricci's teaching and writings, was, that they thought of the Pope as of one to whom great respect and reverence were due, being elected, as he was, to that highest dignity from a number of prelates that was world-wide. His explanations of the geographical maps showing the City of Rome also offered him frequent occasion for the introduction of religious instruction.

Another method of building up a friendly attitude toward the Christian world, was the custom of adding short moral precepts to everything the Fathers wrote. Sometimes these were written in their own language and then explained in Chinese. The Chinese like this custom, and frequently make a collection of such sentences, writing them on their fans, or copying them on papers so that they can fix them to the wall and read them.

10. They Set out for Pekin Again

THE ARRIVAL of Father Cattaneo and his companions at Nankin convinced Father Matthew that he could put an end to any doubt about undertaking the journey to Pekin, and the baggage they brought with them was such as to encourage the effort. He presented a few of the Magistrates with some of the novelties that Father Cattaneo brought, in return for which he hoped to obtain letters and recommendations. Chiutaiso had left Nankin some time before, but had lately returned on business, and was living with the Fathers. So Father Matthew took him into counsel, together with their mutual friend, already mentioned, to whom Chiutaiso had introduced him. They were both of the opinion that the only way to go about this adventure was to interest one of the Supreme Magistrates. All three agreed on this, and they went directly to Scioscelin, the King's Adviser, to get his counsel. He told them that by all means the presents should be offered to the King, because talk about them had already become widespread. He assured them also that they need not worry about getting official papers of any kind as a guarantee for their security, as he himself, gladly and officially, would provide whatever was necessary in that regard, as soon as the ice disappeared from the Pekin River. Nothing more opportune could have happened for the advancement of their plans, because such documents would be issued by the particular tribunal to which such affairs pertained. Before that time Father Matthew wanted to petition this tribunal for documents, but he had not dared to do so because he felt that a refusal at that time might cast some sinister reflection on his friend Scioscelin.

Rejoicing in this promise, the Fathers gathered together the presents to put a few decorative finishing touches on them. First, they thought they should put the larger clock, they had just received, in a suitable case. They had already found one at Nancian, done in carved relief and gilded, for the smaller clock. With respect to decorations, however, they were not to be outdone by Nancian. This clock was set in its enclosure with four columns. The case was built with folding doors, opening to either side. The hours were marked on the face of the clock in Chinese capital letters, with an eagle dominating, which pointed to the hour with its beak. The top of the clock formed a beautiful arch, decorated with fluted work in various designs of flowers and leaves, and with beautifully carved dragons. The dragon is the Chinese symbol of royalty, and no one, apart from the royal family, is permitted to use it as an emblem. In the royal palaces all the furniture is covered with dragons, carved in bas relief, or embroidered, or painted. The clock was finished with suitable decorations of gold and of Chinese sandarac, or vermillion. It was an ornament that might well have been placed on exhibition in Europe.

Our friend the President of the Magistrates was returning to his native town. With permission of the King, he had resigned from his high position because some of his rival Magistrates had prevented his promotion to honors which he felt were due to him. Before leaving, he sent letters to his friends in Pekin, recommending the Fathers and their work in the capital city. It was at this time that the King's Adviser showed his real character by holding fast to his promise. He supplied the favorable documents, as he said he would, and he was also one of the many who donated gifts to defray the expenses of the journey. In addition to all this, he also sent letters of recommendation to a certain important Magistrate in Pekin.

In the meantime Father Cattaneo was appointed to remain at Nankin, because he knew the contacts already made there, and was best suited to develop that center. Father Didaco Pantoia and the two Lay Brothers, Sebastian and Emanuele, were to go to Pekin with Father Ricci. Father Giovanni Aroccia was called from Nancian to Nankin as assistant to Father Cattaneo because the settlement there needed more than one man. This left Father Soeiro alone at Nancian until someone should be sent there from Macao.

Just at that time, one of the high stationed eunuchs was leaving for

Pekin, with a cargo of silk, in command of six of the fast sailing boats called cavaliers. Father Ricci and his companions were assigned commodious quarters on one of these boats and given ample space, not only for their personal baggage but for storage of enough furniture for a new house and for a fully equipped chapel. This flotilla was being sent to Pekin by the King's Adviser who had signed the official document for Father Matthew's journey. He personally recommended the Fathers to the eunuch in charge and ordered him to introduce them to the most influential of his kind in Pekin. This he promised to do, but he did more than he promised. During the voyage he was most courteous and obliging and he could never be persuaded to accept money as fare for the passage. In gratitude to the King's Adviser he had taken the Fathers aboard his boat as guests, rather than as passengers, with no charge for anything, but at the same time he was losing nothing by doing so. Before leaving, Father Matthew had spoken to the Adviser, Scioscelin, who gave the eunuch a generous stipend as a reward for his kindness, which he was not averse to accepting. The favors done by the King's Adviser were in some degree returns for various European gifts received from the Fathers. What the King's Adviser prized most of all was the triangular glass prism, which they had left in his custody. He too thought this was a rare gem of considerable value. He sent the Fathers a liberal gift as they were leaving and some of the newly converted Christians, particularly Paul and his son Martin, were especially generous in their charity.

The expedition left Nankin on May eighteenth in the year 1600, and on this journey the Fathers were free to move about as they pleased. At various stopping places they called on the Magistrates, who were always pleased with their visits and the eunuch increased their activities by inviting his friends to come aboard the boat to see the presents for the King. Others also came, prompted by curiosity on hearing of the novelty of the things from Europe. This visiting continued, despite the fact that the Fathers made no secret of their ultimate purpose in trying to win the favor of the King, and in wishing to open a residence in Pekin. In fact, they were also continually and openly discussing the Christian faith whenever an opportunity was presented.

The one in charge of the expedition became more and more obliging every day, not only because of what he had received in Nankin, but because of the advantage he gained by the company of the Fathers. It was because of their presence that his boats were given an immediate passage through the various locks on the canals, where much time can be lost because of the great number of boats waiting to go through. Provision boats and the boats of Magistrates are given preference, but at times there are so many of these, that some of them are delayed for four days or more. True, it was the eunuch who secured the permit for prior passage for himself, but he got it by inviting the captains of other ships to come aboard and view the royal gifts, so as to let his boat through, which they granted as a compliment to the Fathers. This never failed to amuse the eunuch, but he always remained polite and courteous.

There is a Viceroy in the Province of Sciantum, who has jurisdiction over all river boats, even over those that may be conveying provisions to the Royal City. He outranks the judges whose office is to see that the Royal City is never wanting for anything. At that time, this Viceroy was a man from the Province of Sciansi, a devotee of the idols, but deeply interested in the future life. He had already heard much about the Christian faith from his son, who had been introduced to Father Matthew by a friend named Liciu. It so happened that this Liciu and the Viceroy were both living in the City of Zinim. The boats stopped there, and Father Matthew sent a messenger to his friend Liciu, saying he would like to call on him, to talk over his trip to Pekin.

His friend had a reputation as a diplomat in court affairs and also as a prudent counselor. He was an intimate friend of the Viceroy, so intimate indeed that the Viceroy had made a gate in the wall between their properties, which were contiguous, so they could visit one another every day. When Liciu heard that Father Matthew was coming, he immediately informed his neighbor who was so pleased, that he sent the Father a formal invitation and dispatched a palanquin and carriers to bring him to the palace. They gave him a hearty welcome and afterwards listened to him for some time discoursing on Europe and on what the Viceroy was so anxious to hear about, namely, the life to come. Later on, as he was leaving, the Viceroy said to him, "Matthew," giving him the honorable surname of Sithai, "I too want to go to heaven," indicating that he was interested in something other than riches and worldly honors, namely, in his eternal salvation.

Scarcely had Father Matthew arrived aboard the boat, when an unusual noise, as of a tumult, was heard in the town. It was caused by the convoy of the Viceroy, who was traveling with a great retinue, and who was impatient because of the long delay, as he was hastening to reach Father Matthew's boat. The eunuch in command was surprised at the unusual commotion, as were all those on the other boats in the port. The Viceroy finally came aboard and after going through the customary ceremonies observed on official visits, he viewed the King's presents with no end of admiration, as did his retinue of courtiers who could not be denied the spectacle. Following him there came other dignitaries of the city.

The next day Father Matthew returned the official visit, and as an exchange gift he gave the Viceroy some European trinkets, which made up in novelty what they lacked in price. He spent the whole day at the palace and took dinner with Liciu and the children of the Viceroy. He found this visit so entertaining and pleasant that he might well have imagined himself at home in Europe or with his friends in a house of his religious order, rather than on the other side of the world in the midst of pagans.

The Viceroy asked to see the document written at Nankin which was to be offered for an audience with the King. There were some things in it which he did not like; so he carefully wrote another one, which was afterwards elegantly recopied by his domestic librarian. In addition to this he also gave the Fathers many letters to people in Pekin that would be more helpful for their purpose than those they had received at Nankin.

One day the wife of the Viceroy told him that she had had a dream, in which she saw a certain god, in the company of two little children. During the Viceroy's visit to the boat, he had seen a picture of the Blessed Virgin holding the child Jesus, who was being admired by the child John, the Precursor. He told his wife about this picture and she said it was quite significant of her dream, and asked her husband to send an artist to the boat to make an exact copy of it. Chinese artists are not at all adept at such work, and Father Matthew, fearing that an ugly copy would result, sent her an excellent replica of the picture, done by a young man at the Mission House in Nankin. The Viceroy was very grateful for it and promised that he and his whole family would be devoted servants of God's Mother and of her Divine Son.

When Father Matthew was leaving, the Viceroy sent along with him one of his subordinate Magistrates, who, with the authority of his superior, had the Father's boat passed in advance of the others through several narrow straits, along a distance of several miles, which shortened their journey considerably. Arriving at the dock, he discovered that Ricci's boat was some distance outside of the port, where it had been taken by the eunuch in charge of it, who could not tolerate the curious crowd of sightseers whose insolence had almost caused a tumult. Later on, he gave orders to have Father Matthew taken out to his boat.

The Fathers were fully decided upon returning the favors they had received here, at the first possible opportunity. They were also interested in instructing both the Viceroy and his friend Liciu in the mysteries of the Christian faith. This they could not do at that time because of the brevity of their visit, and because of the haste of the one in charge of the voyage to get to Pekin. Within three years of that time both the Viceroy and Liciu were dead. The Viceroy died before retiring from the Magistrature and Liciu committed suicide in Pekin by cutting his throat. Some unknown Magistrate had sent a letter of complaint against Liciu to the King, and in condemnation of the books he had written. Whereupon the King ordered that all his books be burned and that he be cast into prison in chains. Liciu could not endure being publicly degraded and thus having his name become a byword among his enemies. A rare example among the Chinese, he wanted to prove to his disciples, as he had often told them, that he was utterly undisturbed by the fear of death, and in this way he sought to disappoint his enemies, who wanted to see him die in disgrace.

11. Imprisoned in Tiensin

ONE OF THE EUNUCHS whom the King had sent out to plunder, rather than to collect taxes, was named Mathan, and he lived here in Lincin, a very well known port. The people and the garrison of the place rose up against him, burned his house and killed all his servants, and he himself would have met a similar fate, if he had not escaped in disguise and thus eluded their fury. But his fear did not put an end to his avarice, because they say he was worse after the catastrophe than before it.

The eunuch in charge of the fleet of cavaliers stopped at Lincin and went to visit the Collector Mathan, armed with presents, rather than with weapons. Two or three times he was refused admission to Mathan's new residence, and he came to the conclusion that this was due to the fact that the presents were not what Mathan wanted.

The exact time for the arrival of the fleet at Pekin was drawing near, and if the one in charge of it were late, he would run the risk of a heavy fine or perhaps pay with his life. To solve this difficulty, disregarding the friendship he had contracted with the Fathers, and according to the usual infidelity of the eunuchs, he decided to hand over his guests to the avarice of Mathan, the despoiler. In order to proceed on his journey, all unknown to the Fathers, he arranged a plan with some of the Collector's eunuchs. He told them that there were foreigners on one of the boats, who were taking presents to the King, gifts that were absolutely new and very valuable. He assured them that these presents would serve to place Mathan in the good graces of the sovereign, and to prove what he said, with much dissimulation, he brought them aboard the boat and showed them the statues and the clocks. The Fathers had no suspicion whatsover as to the real purpose of their visit. The delighted messengers went posthaste to their master and convinced him that the foreigners undoubtedly had more in their possession than they themselves had seen, and things of even greater value. Few words will sometimes kindle the flame of avarice. He immediately sent word that he was coming to see the King's presents.

Realizing the danger that was at hand, Father Matthew went straightway to see a certain Cantonese, whom he had known at Sciauquin and visited later on at Nankin. He was in search of counsel and of help, and this man held a position of authority in the neighboring cities as a local Magistrate. He had heard that Father Matthew was on his way to Lincin, and for several days past he had someone watching for his arrival. When the servant saw the Father approaching the house, he ran to inform his master that the stranger was coming; the one he had been expecting. The first thing his host did was to assign his visitor a room, as if he were going to stay for some time, but when the eunuch Mathan entered the story, he became very sad and said, "Don't expect to escape his grip without a loss. His class is in favor now with the throne and they are the only people the King calls into counsel. Even the most powerful Magistrates fall prey to them, and so, what chance has a foreigner of escaping their injustice." He cautioned Father Matthew to show everything willingly, and to thank the eunuch for the favor of his visit. "At least," he said, "there may be some hope in that method of procedure," and then he added, "It would be useless to look for someone who can hold him off, and the effort would be fraught with danger." To Father Matthew this sounded like good counsel from a prudent friend.

Before the Father had left the house, a messenger arrived in haste, from Mathan, saying that he was on his way to the Father's boat, and asking him to return to the boat as soon as possible. The Magistrate told the messenger to go back to his master and tell him that Father Matthew was at his house, and that he would not permit him to leave unless he received a direct command. By this he wanted to show that his guest was not wholly destitute of assistance, and that he was protected by the friendship of the Magistrates. It was a blessing from heaven that the eunuch learned that Father Matthew was a friend of this particular Magistrate, because, of all the judges, this was the one he had learned to respect. He had saved others from the clutches of Mathan, and had done it in such a way as to make Mathan look less guilty than he really was. The result of this was that his honesty was being praised on all sides, and in recognition of it, the city afterwards built a temple in his honor and placed his statue in it, with an appropriate inscription, extolling his civic virtues.

Besides the various mansions and temples which Mathan, the Collector, had constructed, he had also built a large and very elegant boat, suitable even for the King to travel in, with salons, rooms and numerous cabins, all very wonderful and commodious. The galleries and the window casings were made of an incorruptible wood, carved in various designs, shining with a coat of varnish in Chinese sandarac and resplendent with gold. He was accustomed to cruise about the river, and it was in this boat that he came to visit the Fathers. Father Matthew greeted him with respect and courtesy. In a lengthy introduction he offered to assist the Fathers in making their presentations to the King and then, in order to examine the presents more thoroughly he ordered that they be transferred to his boat. He was greatly pleased at sight of the presents and said they were gifts worth offering to a king, even to the King of China. He went down on his knees, in reverence to the statues, and promised the Virgin Mary that he would find a place for her in the Palace of the King. He also promised the Fathers that he would forward their request to Pekin as soon as possible. He was promising too much, in order to cover up his deceit from those who knew eunuchs in general and this one in particular, who had a reputation for being exceeding arrogant. Father Ricci thanked him gracefully for the proffered favor, and said he did not wish to cause him so much trouble, because there were several high Magistrates in Pekin, who had agreed to take over his project. He laughed at this and boasted that there were no Magistrates as influential with the King as he was. "Why," he said, "my requests are taken care of by the King, the day after they are presented. Those of others are answered late or not at all." Father Matthew thanked him again and promised him good fortune, on the part of the one whose image he had just honored, if he would assist in promoting the project.

The eunuch in charge of the expedition was dismissed and permitted to pass out of the port without paying the toll, evidently a payment for his treason in betraying those entrusted to his care. One month later, Mathan was to go to the fort of Tiensin, to forward from there the tribute due to the King for the last six months. He wanted to transfer the Fathers to this same place, but he first gave orders to have all their baggage transported to the best of his boats on which, he said, the Fathers were to live until the end of the month. The eunuch who had been in charge of the expedition, sailed away joyfully, and as a present to the Fathers he left them a boy, whom he had bought at Nankin. He said he was giving them this boy because he spoke so distinctly, and he could teach Father Didaco the purity of the Nanchinese tongue.

Mathan wanted to take all the royal gifts to his palace, but Father Matthew opposed this very modestly, saying that the clocks deteriorated very easily when there was no one present to take care of them, and that they wanted to keep the statues because they prayed before them, asking the God of Heaven to bless the work they were doing. The Collector was not insistent. On the contrary, he sent food and other necessities for their journey out to the boat where they were living. Their friend the Magistrate made frequent visits to the craft, and brought other friends with him. In this and in other ways, on almost every visit, he assured them of the good will of the highest Magistrates, and in so doing he was putting a bridle on the avarice, not to say on the cruelty, of the eunuch, who had it in his power to rob the Fathers, not only of their baggage but of their lives as well. The visits of the Magistrates prompted Mathan to increase his attention to the Fathers. One day he invited Father Matthew to a feast and a spectacle, held at his house in the city. He had also invited several of the chief eunuchs of the district. The display of grandeur was worthy of the greatest potentate that one could imagine.

During the feast they presented various comedies; tight-rope walkers, sleight of hand artists, jugglers of goblets, and other such parasites, of whom he had a house full, and whom he supported for his entertainment. It was thus that he passed his days and spent his life, without ever a thought that it would come to an end. Father Matthew had never before seen such an extraordinary spectacle, neither in Europe, nor in India where they have a reputation for such things. One of the jugglers was tossing three big knives, two palms long, one after the other into the air and catching them by the handles, without ever failing. Another one, stretched on his back on the floor, was tossing about a huge earthen pot, with his feet. At times he would throw it into the air, revolving it to one side and then to the other, in a way that would have been difficult to imitate with the hands. Then he did the same thing with a large drum, and again with a big table that was four feet square. Their pantomime play of masked giants, all richly dressed, was unique; with a dialogue for the figures, carried on by someone in the theatre. Perhaps the most amusing act was played by a boy who first danced very gracefully, and then as though falling on the floor, but holding himself off it with his hands, produced a plaster figure, dressed as he was, which crawled out between his feet, and gracefully using its hands instead of its feet, imitated the boy's dancing steps with remarkable skill. Then the figure fell on the floor, and the two began to wrestle and roll about so naturally, that it looked like a match between two living boys.

With the show over, as Father Matthew was leaving, Mathan wrote out the request to be sent to Pekin and handed it to his guest to read. In brief, it mentioned that on one of the boats passing by Lincin there was a foreigner named Matthew Ricci, who was reported to be bringing certain gifts to the King. Since this European seemed to be well disposed, he, Mathan, wanted to help him, and for fear that the boat he was traveling in might meet with some misfortune, there being so many boats in the harbor, he was transferring the stranger to one of his own boats and sending him, well protected, to the fort at Tiensin to await a reply which, it was hoped, would not be long delayed. This request was sent with the same formalities that Magistrates are accustomed to observe in similar cases, as has been described in our first book. This and other letters were carried by one of Mathan's servants, as a messenger, with whom the Fathers went along as far as the fort of Tiensin. There were four soldiers on the boat, acting as wardens during the night. Such is the customary procedure when a message is being forwarded to the King. These guards were placed to prevent the messenger from taking to flight, and to hold the party making the request under continual observation. This messenger had to take an oath that he would not try to escape, and he was held in chains aboard the boat during the voyage.

Mathan arrived at the fort shortly after the Fathers. The reply from Pekin was long in coming. The King wanted to refer this matter to the bureau in charge of ceremonies, according to regular procedure, but that would not help Mathan to curry favor with the King, so his partisans at the court endeavored to have the decision referred back to Mathan for final settlement, and they succeeded in their effort. No sooner was an answer received from Pekin, than Mathan called together the Magistrates local to the citadel, and they all came dressed in damask and purple, and decorated with all the ornaments of their various offices, to hear the answer of the King. In order to dignify the courtroom, with legalistic pomp and grandeur, the eunuch called for a reading of the request sent to the King, and then of the reply received. In his answer, the King called for a description of the presents, which the foreigner was bringing to him. The request forwarded to Pekin made it appear that Mathan knew nothing about the presents, but this was a ruse on the part of the eunuch, so that the King would not suspect that he had tampered with something destined for the sovereign, without his authority. After the readings, Father Matthew was called before the seat of judgment. He was dressed in the cotton robe which criminals wear, and wore the round hat of the man in the street. First, he was ordered to kneel down, as was the usual custom when receiving a command from the King. Next, he was ordered to write out, in presence of the assembly, a full list of all the gifts he was carrying to Pekin. With that done, Mathan immediately took possession of the gifts and had them transported to his residence. Afterwards Father Matthew was asked if he had anything else in his possession. Whereupon, in addition to the statues and the clocks, and the triangular glass prisms, he had to give up his nicely bound Roman Breviary, the clavichord, and a copy of "The World Theatre" by Ortelius.

After this general spoliation, the eunuch sent a second request to the King, but the answer returned was not what he had expected, and from that time on he began to fear that he had made trouble for himself, and to regret that he had interfered in this affair. Although Father Matthew went to see Mathan when they first became acquainted, and always came when he was called for, after this day he saw little of him and wanted to have nothing more to do with him.

Winter was approaching and, to anticipate the ice on the river, the

tax collector was getting ready to leave the fort. Before leaving, he had
the Fathers move into a temple of the idols, with all their belongings,
and placed a guard of four soldiers over them to watch their every
movement night and day, both in the house and when they went outside. They were living in the temple, when one day all unexpectedly,
the eunuch arrived, accompanied by a prominent Magistrate, a friend
of Father Matthew, and a member of the Military Senate, known as
the Pimpithau. The eunuch was surrounded by a band of nearly two
hundred fellow robbers, and glaring at Father Ricci with a look of
anger, he said he had received word from Pekin stating that he, Ricci,
was hiding a collection of precious stones, so he would not have to
present them to the King, and more than that, they claimed he had a
number of associates hidden in his house. Father Matthew stared
back at him and made a flat denial of the whole charge. Then the
eunuch gave orders to have all their baggage brought out into the
adjoining court, where he opened all the boxes and cases, examining
everything very carefully, adding injury to insult by the fury with
which he tossed things about.

In the meantime, the Magistrate stood by with an evident expression
of compassion for his friend. Each time the eunuch came across something he had not seen before, he complained bitterly, charging that it
had been hidden from him, and selecting what he liked, he placed it
apart from the rest of the baggage. Finally, when he failed to find what
he pretended to be looking for, he turned aside, on fire more with
shame than with anger, and took occasion from his disappointment to
increase his injustice, rather than diminish it. Of all the things he saw,
nothing aroused his ire more than the suspended figure of Christ on
the cross. He accused them of carrying this charm for the purpose of
killing the King by enchantment. "Undoubtedly," he said, "this thing
was made, as anyone can see, for no other purpose than to bewitch
one with poisonous sorcery." Father Matthew thought it would be only
a waste of time to talk about a divine mystery to a man who was almost
beside himself with anger. What could be expected from one who increased his accusations with every proof of innocence, and yet consented to things that were utterly incredible. However, when he was
urged to speak, Father Ricci said that the form on the cross was the
image of the holiest of men, according to Christian belief, who chose
that kind of terrible death for the salvation of souls, and in memory of
whom the Christians show him, as he died, in painting and in sculpture.
Here the Senator of the Pimpithau broke in with the remark that he

thought it was quite unbecoming to honor the memory of any man by representing him in such a miserable death. The explanation had no effect whatsoever on the eunuch, who loudly asserted that the Fathers should be punished for their deceitful wiles. When they found several holy pictures, both Mathan and the Magistrate began to think that perhaps these things were in some way connected with religion, rather than with sorcery, and with the rummage and the ransacking at an end, they both sat down, and told the Fathers to do likewise.

Among other things which Mathan took there were two ebony reliquaries, one in the form of a cross, the other shaped like a book. He also took a silver chalice which the Fathers had used in the celebration of Mass. In the re-examination of the spoils he had set apart, he found a small bag containing two hundred gold coins, their expense money for the voyage. He gave this back to Father Matthew, with a remark, as if he were presenting him with a gift. True robber that he was, he thought he was donating to his victims whatever he did not steal from them. Despite the manner of return, the Fathers thanked him for the money, realizing that it had come back, after they had abandoned hope of ever seeing it again. Several demands were made for the return of the reliquaries, but to no avail. With the chalice it was different. Father Matthew insisted upon having it. He told Mathan that it was used in offering sacrifice to the God of Heaven and of earth, and that Christians considered it to be so sacred, that no one could even touch it, except those who were consecrated by special ceremonies to offer the sacrifice. His answer to that was to pick up the chalice and turn it around in his hands, remarking, "What do you mean by saying that no one can touch it. Don't you see me touching it now?" With the wicked and the ignorant, power is permission. Such impudence was too much even for the patience of Father Matthew, who, indignantly and almost in tears, took the money purse and cast it on the floor at the feet of the eunuch. "Take out the weight of the cup, in gold, please, or take all you want of it, but give me back the chalice." This evidently touched the Magistrate of the Pimpithau, who looked at Mathan and said, "You see, he is interested in the cup, not because of its value, but because he considers it to be something sacred. He is offering you double the price for it. I would advise you to give it back to him." At which the eunuch changed his mind and gave back both the chalice and the purse, and then began to assemble the larger presents and the rest of the loot he had set aside, amounting in all to about forty articles. He had selected a flowing robe, some cotton cloth from India, several glass vases, sundials, hour-glasses and other novelties. All this he ordered transported to his house for safe keeping. The larger clock and the statue of the Blessed Virgin were left with the Fathers, and they placed the statue on the altar, on which they celebrated Mass every day.

Mathan returned to Lincin and left the Fathers in the fort, with a guard of soldiers, who were not too particular as to what their prisoners did or where they went. After his departure it was discovered that certain things were missing. Some of the robbers had taken money from the purse, and the big robber had also extracted some and given it to the Magistrate to hold for him. What was stolen, however, was far less than what they had suspected and feared.

This whole dubious episode at the fort gave rise to doubt and to fear, not only that the Pekin project had fallen through but also that the whole expedition and all they had accomplished up to that time, might be ruined in a single day. Human assistance was evidently exhausted. There was nothing left to support them but the grace of God, and this they sought in daily Mass, in constant prayer and in continual bodily mortification and penance. They asked God to come to the assistance of the many souls, possibly dependent upon their labor in this vineyard.

The end of the year was drawing nigh and yet there was no answer from Pekin. Father Matthew wrote two letters to Lincin, one to Mathan and one to the Pimpithau Magistrate and sent them by a servant, overland, because the river was frozen tight. The servant was to wait for answers and bring them back to the fort. Both letters were petitions, requesting that some action be taken relative to a reply from Pekin, and stating that the long delay was causing the Fathers great inconvenience, because of the cold and the poor living quarters. That at least was the burden of the letter sent to the eunuch. In the one to their friend, he asked him either to make another effort to hasten the answer from Pekin, or to advise them what to do in their present plight.

The servant presented the letter to Mathan in his court, where he was received with a burst of abusive language directed against the Fathers. Not only that, but he was chased out of the building with a shower of kicks and of blows, but without an answer. Their friend did not dare either to receive the letter in the open court or to send an answer to it. He called the servant to his palace, secretly, and told him that the outlook for the project of the Fathers was about as hopeless as could be imagined. He said the eunuch had decided to present a charge against the Fathers, accusing them of attempting to do away with the King by means of poisoning, that he had spread this story through the city, together with other calumnies, and that he was raving mad against Father Ricci. He was even boasting that he would send them all back to their native land with their feet bound and laden with chains. In his written answer, the Magistrate counseled his friends to protect their lives by taking to flight and returning to the Province of Canton. The loss of their baggage, he assured them, was only the removal of an impediment. He also advised them to reduce to dust, and if possible to annihilate every sample they had in their possession of the man who was nailed to the cross. If they did not wish to follow his advice, the next best thing for them to do, as he asserted, was to send a request to the King, through their friends the Magistrates in Pekin, asking for permission to return to their own country. This answer was more fear inspiring than they had looked forward to. It convinced them that they were in more danger than they had realized. Of the two counsels offered they decided upon the second, and immediately sent Brother Sebastiano to Pekin, unknown to the guards, who were not ever watchful. He was carrying letters and presents from Father Matthew and other letters from friends in Nankin, but this also, another human endeavor, proved to be of no avail. Heaven had evidently decided to take over full charge of so important an affair.

No one could be found to risk the anger of the eunuch. The Fathers were counseled to give up the idea of sending a petition to the King, because he was listening to no one at that time except to the eunuchs. Some thought it might be better to endeavor to placate the eunuch, despite the fact that he had already ruined any hope of recovering their baggage.

The letters, containing a full accout of all that had happened to the Fathers, were taken to Pekin by the Lay Brother, to solicit the help which they themselves could not ask, being prisoners in the fort. The Brother fulfilled his commission, while the Fathers were earnestly praying for the divine favor, that the news of their plight would be spread abroad. The return of the Brother only convinced them that there was no hope left either from other human resources or from their own human efforts, and that therefore no further attempt should be made. Confidently placing their last hope in divine assistance, they turned their thoughts toward God and prepared themselves resolutely and joyfully to meet any difficulty, even death itself, in the cause they had undertaken.

12. From Prison to Pekin by the King's Command.

IT WOULD SEEM as if Heaven had been waiting for the Fathers to give up all hope of human aid, and to surrender their project entirely into the hands of God. No sooner, indeed, had they done this than Divine Providence came to their assistance, most unexpectedly, as it were, in answer to the prayers of the many who were everywhere storming Heaven for the success of this expedition. With no forewarning whatsoever, the King sent word for them to come to Pekin without delay, and to bring along their presents. He was sending along a Magistrate from the High Court of Ceremonies to assure their safety on the road, and this same tribunal, having already made a thorough investigation of their cause, had also made a full report of their findings to the Throne. The Fathers never discovered how it had come about, that this unlooked for summons arrived after a lapse of six months during which time no new petition was made. They believed that God, who holds the hearts of kings in His hand, had wrought this sudden change for the salvation of souls and in His own mysterious way.

They say that one day, the King, of his own prompting, suddenly remembered a certain petition that had been sent in to him and said, "Where is that clock, I say, where is that clock that rings of itself; the one the foreigners were bringing here to me, as they said in their petition?" The eunuch who always accompanies the King replied, "Your Majesty, if you have not as yet sent an answer to the letter of the eunuch Mathan, how could the foreigners have entered the royal city without your permission?" Whereupon the sovereign despatched the summons we have just mentioned. This summons with an appendix in explanation, was sent by fast horse despatch to Mathan, at Lincin, who immediately, but much against his will sent someone to restore the royal presents, which were kept under guard in the fort.

The river was still frozen over and the journey could not be made by boat, so he ordered the Magistrates of the fort to provide horses and carriers, to take the Fathers to Pekin, and all at public expense. After so many trials and tribulations, the Fathers were overcome with joy and breathing more easily. They gave thanks to God, forgot their past worries, too numerous to be recorded, bolstered up their courage and took to the road. When they got back their belongings, they waited until night and removed the relics from the reliquaries. Then they filled the little cavities with small stones from the Holy Land, so it could not be noticed that any change had been made. They thought it would be better not to rip out the document of authenticity contained in each reliquary, and for fear they might fall into the hands of Christians in their changed condition, a note was inserted in each reliquary explaining what had been done.

There was an incident connected with the restoration of their goods, which they considered to be another intervention of Divine Providence. Heaven alone, it seemed, could have turned to their benefit a gross calumny which Mathan had circulated against them, evidently intent upon their ruin. Among other things which Mathan had set apart at the second examination of their baggage, were all the astronomical books which Father Matthew had collected from various parts, and was saving against the time when the King might call upon him to correct the errors in the Chinese calendars. There was an ancient law of the realm, the enforcement of which had been abandoned long before this time, stating that anyone teaching or studying astronomy, was subject to a death penalty, excepting only the King's mathematicians. This law was made because the ancient Chinese thought that anyone who understood the movements of the stars, could figure out the conjunction of stars that indicated his good fortune, and thus easily take over the kingdom. It was because of this obsolete law that the Collector Mathan separated the books from the rest of the presents and hid them away in a box, on which he placed a sign which read, "The eunuch Mathan, Collector of taxes for the crown, found these books in the baggage of a certain foreigner named Matthew Ricci. Since such books are forbidden property, according to the law of the land, he has set them apart, under guard, until such time as the King has been notified by a special document and disposes of them as he sees fit." The Fathers knew nothing about the segregation of the books until the time came for the restoration of their baggage. When they saw that they were missing, they asked the Magistrates in charge of the fort to replace them. They in turn were unaware of Mathan's design, and having no objection to returning the books they sent an officer to get them and bring them back to the owners. Fortunately, the officer did not know how to read, and hence paid no attention to the sign on the box. Six months had passed since the last tribute had been sent to Pekin from Lincin, and when Mathan returned to the fort for that purpose, he sent the Fathers on their way to the royal city, not knowing that they had the books with them. Soon after their departure he missed the books and berated the Magistrates in charge of the fort, saying that the King had made a special demand for them. Then he sent the same officer who had delivered the books, to overtake the Fathers without delay, and take the books away from them. The officer, however, was looking forward to his return and probably to severe punishment; instead of following the Fathers he took to flight in another direction.

Once their affairs had taken a turn for the better, Mathan began to fear lest they should enter a complaint against him in Pekin. If they had done this and explained all that had happened, it was quite probable that he might have fallen into disfavor with the throne. From that time on a very discreet silence was maintained about the books. Moreover the Fathers were relieved from fear and in a position to supply certain Magistrates interested in their cause with information about what had taken place, which they in turn were eager to have. Much of what had happened was afterwards written out for them in Chinese characters.

The Magistrates of the fort provided eight horses and thirty porters or carriers for the journey to Pekin. These were changed each day at the stopping places. On this particular trip the Fathers were lodged in the palaces of various officials along the route. They were treated very respectfully and they were not charged for anything. On the contrary, they were honored by everyone because it was known that they had been summoned by the King. They arrived in Pekin toward the end of the Chinese year, the twenty-fourth of January, in sixteen hundred and one, and on their arrival they stopped at the palace of a eunuch, just below the city. Here they arranged the presents and put them in order for the next day, when they were carried across the town, with considerable show and excitement, to the royal palace.

where they were deposited, together with what Mathan had sent on.

When the King saw the crucifix, he stood in astonishment and said aloud, "Here is the living God." Despite the fact that this is a stock phrase with the Chinese, he spoke the truth without knowing it. This name is applied to the crucifix, even to this day, in China, and from that time on, the Fathers were called, the men who brought the living God to the King. From wonderment the sovereign seemed to pass into fear at sight of the statues, and not being able to meet their gaze, he sent the statue of the Blessed Virgin to his mother. She also, who was devoted to the images of her lifeless gods, was embarrassed at the sight of the image of the living God. She was frightened at the lifelike posture of the images and she gave orders to have them placed in her treasure vault, where they were occasionally shown to some of the Magistrates, by the eunuchs. These same reported to the Fathers that the King himself paid reverence to the statues and had incense and other perfumes burned before them. The Fathers prayed that God might reward him for his reverence and enlighten him with the light of faith. He kept the smallest of the crucifixes for himself, and placed it in his favorite chamber. It was a rare work of art, sent in by the Father General of the Society of Jesus. All this was told by the eunuchs, and the Fathers believed it with only as much credence as one usually places in what the eunuchs say. The first time the King saw the larger clock, it was not adjusted or running, and consequently it neither kept the time nor struck the hours. So he gave orders to summon the Fathers immediately. This was done, and they came posthaste.

The royal palace in Pekin is entirely surrounded by four walls. During the daytime any man is permitted to pass beyond the first two walls, excepting the sacrificers to idols, who shave their heads. Women are excluded at all times. Only the palace eunuchs are allowed to go in beyond the first two walls. At night only soldiers and eunuchs are permitted to remain within the outer walls. The Fathers were permitted to pass beyond the second outer wall but no further. Here in one of the courtyards they met a multitude of people who had gathered to see the clocks, and here the King sent one of his high-ranking eunuchs to receive them, one of those who kept him constant company and for whose prudence he had high regard. His name was Licin, and he received them most graciously in the name of the King. He wanted to know what their purpose was in bringing presents to the King, and they told him they were foreigners from the Great Occident, as the

·Chinese call Europe, that they were God-fearing men who adored the Director of heaven and earth, with no interest in worldly goods, and neither asking nor expecting presents in return, nor awaiting any recompense. He was quite pleased with this answer and gladly accepted the presents. They told him that the clocks were the invention of very clever artisans, for indicating the time, by day and by night, without anyone's assistance, and that they sounded the hours of themselves on bells, and pointed out the divisions of the hours with an indicator. They explained also that these machines had to be regulated by some one, that this was not a difficult operation, and that the servants could readily learn it in two or three days. All this was reported to His Majesty, who appointed four eunuchs from the College of Mathematicians of the palace, with orders to bring these instruments to his reception room, in three days, and to pay strict attention to the duty assigned them.

They say that the palace eunuchs are divided into orders or grades, like the Magistrates of the kingdom, but with only a few in each order. Because those to be taught how to manipulate the clocks were from that particular order, the Fathers were lodged in the quarters of the mathematicians, where they spent day and night teaching these dull and intellectually sluggish beings. However, they were respectful, and those who were protecting Mathan at the palace provided the Fathers with everything they needed for their support. They probably did this so that no report would be made to the King about the quarrels with Mathan. It had already been rumored about that he had forcibly exacted a large tribute from them, which was not at all true, and the poor unfortunate had already spent a large sum of money, but all in vain, to hush up this report.

By dint of hard work, the four mathematicians who were assigned to the clocks finally acquired sufficient knowledge to regulate them and for fear that something might go wrong, they wrote out every detail of the instruction and of the mechanism of the clocks. For a eunuch to make a mistake in the presence of the King is equivalent to placing his life in danger. They say the sovereign is so rigid with them in this respect that even for a slight fault the poor unfortunates are sometimes beaten to death. Their first care was to ask for the names, in Chinese, of all the wheels, springs and accessories, all of which Ricci gave them in Chinese characters, because if any parts were missing, the names of the parts would be readily forgotten.

During the three days of the lessons and for some days following, the King sent messengers to the Fathers inquiring about everything that happened to come into his head relative to Europe; the customs, the fertility of the land, architecture, clothes, precious stones, marriage and funerals, and European kings. The eunuchs asked all sorts of questions about the Fathers themselves, and those who were employed in their living quarters kept the sovereign informed of the most insignificant and ridiculous things that were happening, even to reporting how often they ate and drank and how much food they consumed. It was the curious, reporting to one more curious than themselves. The Fathers asked the eunuchs if they would inform the King that their own great desire was to live and die in Pekin, and that they wanted nothing else of him. With a view to what they had in mind, this seemed to be an excellent opportunity to make their request, because, as we shall see, the Magistrates had already decided to send them away.

The three days assigned for instructions had not passed before the King called for the clocks. They were brought to him at his order and he was so pleased with them that he immediately promoted the eunuchs and raised their wages. This they were delighted to report to the Fathers and particularly so because, from that day on, two of them were permitted to enter the presence of the King, to wind the small clock, which he always kept before him, because he liked to look at it and to listen to it ringing the time. These two became very important figures in the royal palace. In the courts of all nations it is considered a high honor to be continually in the intimate service of the king. This is the desire of all courtiers and a station to which the Chinese, even more than others, are particularly ambitious to attain. The man who can make or break a friend or an enemy with a single word, is respected by everyone.

There was no place in the royal palace where the big clock could be set, to allow the weights to fall low enough to govern the wheels. So, during the following year the King sent it to the Commissioner of Public Works and ordered him to build a suitable wooden tower for it, after a design made by the Fathers. It turned out to be something worthy of royalty, with the value of the decorations surpassing that of the material. It was covered with carved figures and with alcoves, polished with sandarac and gold; a masterpiece, in an art in which the Chinese are in no wise inferior to Europeans. The Commissioner spent a thousand, three hundred ecus in building this tower, which was not a very large structure but considering the cheapness of this kind of work, Europeans would say that he paid too much. By royal order also, the tower was built in an attractive garden, outside of the second wall, where there are many such beautiful things. They say His Majesty came here at times for recreation, as did other high dignitaries, to see the attractions and among them, this monument to Europe.

His Majesty was so taken by the novelty of the clocks that he wanted to see, not only the other presents but also the strangers who had brought them. His curiosity was by no means sated by what the eunuchs had told him. Yet he refused to break a custom which he had instituted several years before, namely, of never appearing in the company of anyone, save in that of the eunuchs and the concubines. Moreover, he did not wish to favor foreigners over his Magistrates, and so he put aside his wish and continued his persistent solitude. Instead of calling the Fathers, he sent two of the best artists he had, to paint full length pictures of both of them, in full detail, and then to bring the pictures to him. The Chinese are not adept at portrait painting, but in this instance they produced fairly good results. At first sight of the pictures, the King said, "Hoei, hoei. It is quite evident that they are Saracens." The foreigners who came into China from Persia, of whom we shall say more later on, bear a much closer resemblance to Europeans than they do to the Chinese, because of their facial contour and also because of their heavy beards. The eunuch, who was standing beside the King, told him that they were not Saracens, because they ate pork. He then wanted to know how the kings in Europe dressed and whether or not the Fathers had brought along any models of royal palaces. The first question was difficult to answer by description, but one of the Mission servants remembered that they had a picture, dedicated to the Holy Name, which showed angels and men and souls in purgatory, calling upon the Holy Name, and in which were represented European kings and also the Pope and a Duke and an Emperor, with their faces and vestments clearly depicted. This also gave the Fathers an opportunity to explain who He was, whose name was being venerated by the Christian princes, that is, the one who governed heaven and earth and the nether regions as well, and whose name the King of China himself should not hesitate to honor.

Father Matthew wrote out a brief explanation of all this, which was sent with the picture to the King, but he could not appreciate the fine traits of a small figure nor the variation in shading, which the Chinese ignore, so he ordered his royal artists to paint a copy of it, larger and with more coloring. They set to work on this immediately and the Fathers were detained in the palace for three days, supervising their efforts. In this way they showed the King and explained to him what the Fathers could not make him understand. They also supplied him with the information he desired relative to the palaces in Europe. Fortunately, they happened to have a picture of a palace in Spain, named after Saint Lawrence, an elegant print, representing several views, but they found out afterwards that the eunuch kept this for himself, because he could not explain it to his Master. He did, however, present the sovereign with a picture of the Church of Saint Mark and the square in Venice, together with some standards of the Venetian Republic. They say the King laughed when he heard that the princes of Europe lived on upper floors. He thought that going up and down stairs was quite inconvenient, if not dangerous. It is strange how people hold to the customs that please them.

After a few days, the Fathers took over a house near the palace. The friends of Mathan accompanied them everywhere. Two of them, protecting his interests, were especially attentive, writing the notes that were to be brought to the King and returning the answers in his name. Later on, four of the eunuchs who played stringed instruments before the throne came, in the King's name, to see the Fathers. Playing on such instruments is considered to be an advanced art among the Chinese, and the palace musicians outrank the mathematicians. They conduct an elaborate school in the royal palace and they came to ask the Fathers to teach them to play on the clavichord, which was included in the royal presents. From being a casual student, Father Didaco had become very proficient on this instrument, and he went to the palace every day to give them a music lesson. It was at the suggestion of Father Ricci, made a long time before, that Father Didaco had taken lessons on the clavichord from Father Cattaneo, who was an accomplished musician, and in making the suggestion, he was looking forward to this very incident. The Chinese knew little or nothing about such an instrument, and Father Didaco had learned not only to play but to harmonize the various chords.

Contrary to the wishes of the Fathers, before beginning their lessons, the music pupils insisted upon going through the ceremonies, which are customary when a teacher meets new pupils, or rather when pupils select a new teacher. They asked Father Didaco to teach them with patience but with diligence, and not to become impatient if he found them slow to learn this art, hitherto unknown to them. Afterwards they went through the same ceremony with the clavichord, for an assurance of progress, as if it had been a living thing. Before long the Europeans were being entertained at meals and visited by some of the eunuchs in high position. Gradually they became known to the whole palace retinue with some of whom they formed permanent friendships.

For some time past, Father Matthew had been waiting for an opportunity to escape from the claws of the harpy, Mathan. The latest plan of this schemer was to have the King grant a sum of money to the Fathers in return for their presents, then, in one way or another, to appropriate a goodly share of it for himself, and have the Fathers transferred to a southern province, which would have put an end to their efforts in Pekin. It was for this reason that Father Matthew wanted to see the Chief Master of Ceremonies of the palace, to whom the King had turned over the affairs of the Fathers. He was prevented from visiting this official by the eunuchs who were acting as his guards, who were friends of Mathan, and who would not permit Father Matthew to visit any of his own friends in the palace. One of their servants was acting as a spy and never left the company of the Fathers, but one day, by a ruse, he did get rid of this particular guard.

Father Matthew had sent Father Didaco to the palace to give a music lesson and with him he sent one of the Lay Brothers. He himself remained in the house and the servant spy went along with the other two. After their departure, he went to see his friends with whom he had made previous arrangement for the visits. He delivered the letters sent to them from Nankin, made a few new acquaintances, and, in view of the difficulty they were to encounter shortly afterwards, these visits and the new friends they produced proved to be very opportune. No one was more helpful to them than the Governing Magistrate of the High Council. This man had been chief executive of a small city which he governed with great integrity. He had reached his present high position by appointment rather than by promotion through the grades, and in it had changed none of his good habits. His chief duty was the appointment and the dismissal of Magistrates, and so it followed naturally that they all looked up to him with great respect. Father Matthew never discovered how this man came to know that he was in Pekin, yet he not only knew it, but he came of his own accord for a most pleasant visit, before Father Matthew went to see him officially. His surprise visit was rather amazing and as he was leaving, Father Ricci asked him how it came about that he should be the first to call upon one so little known as himself. He answered, "Because, I heard from certain sources that you are an exemplary man, preaching a doctrine that teaches men how to live properly." Father Matthew returned the gracious compliment, and from that time on, with future meetings, their friendship continued to grow, and similar instances also happened with others in authority.

Strange to say, that of all those to whom letters were sent from Nankin, scarcely anyone proved to be of any assistance at all. In fact, most of them would have nothing to do with the Fathers, for fear of falling into disfavor for communicating with foreigners. Perhaps God permitted this to show them how unstable human relations can be. Certainly, if they had not run afoul of Mathan, the Exactor, and if he had not sent their petition to the King, it is not only likely but quite certain that no one else would have done so, because of the same fear of foreigners. If that had happened they would have returned from Pekin, as from a fruitless mission, as they did the first time. They were fully aware of all this and gave thanks to God for it, with a fuller realization of how entirely dependent they were on Divine Providence.

Each of the clavichord pupils was content with learning one piece. Two of the younger ones were apt enough at learning, but they waited for the others to complete the course, and so the time allotted for lessons was drawn out for more than a month. They were quite interested in having the pieces they were playing put to Chinese words, and Father Matthew took this occasion to compose eight pieces which he called "Songs for the Clavichord." These were lyrics, touching upon ethical subjects, teaching lessons of good morals and virtues, and aptly illustrated with quotations from Christian authors. These songs became so popular that numerous requests from the literati were received, asking for copies of them, and giving high praise to the lessons they taught. They said that these songs reminded the King that he should govern the realm with the virtues suggested in the songs, and in order to satisfy the demand for copies of them, the Fathers printed them, together with other pieces, as a musical booklet, written in European lettering and also in Chinese characters.

13. They Lose Their Freedom in Pekin

AMONG THE VARIOUS officers of the Court of Cere-
monies which is divided into branches, there is one Judge or Magistrate who has official charge of Ambassadors from foreign kingdoms,
whether they come to offer service as vassals, or to bring tribute or
other presents to the King. He presides over two palaces or detention
homes, where the foreigners are lodged as soon as they arrive at the
royal court. This judge has several assistants, and at this time their
presiding officer was from the Province of Fuchian. Now, this chairman of the assistant board knew that the Fathers had been introduced
by the eunuch Mathan, and had offered their presents to the King,
without reporting to his board. This seeming affront caused him to
take umbrage, and since he could not turn his wrath upon Mathan,
he turned it upon the Fathers, though they were innocent of any trans-
gression of the law. He ordered four officers of the guards to find the
Fathers and to bring them into his court, without delay, and though
he knew well that the presents had already been delivered to the
King, he pretended not to know it, so as to make it appear that they
had sent a request to the King and then taken flight, which would
constitute a more serious fault.

In the meantime, the Fathers, suspecting nothing, were awaiting a
reply to their request to be allowed to establish a residence in Pekin,
and they were hoping that an answer would be forthcoming when they
had finished giving music lessons to the court musicians. To their great
surprise, ten or more officers entered their house, one day, and told
them to make haste and report to their captain, at his residence, that
he had something to talk over with them. At first they thought this
was a veiled scheme of someone who was hoping to exact a payment
from foreigners, and they were somewhat hesitant in following the
command. Whereupon, the officers put ropes around their necks,
giving them to understand that this was an official public order, and
thus they went to see the captain of the guard. He in turn, delivered
the order issued by the Magistrate in charge of Ambassadors, whom

they were not averse to seeing because, with their presents delivered to the King, they were hoping through the Magistrates to escape further annoyance from the eunuchs. The captain then held them as prisoners until the next day, in his own house, under lock and key and with guards stationed to prevent their escape. When the court lobbyist of the eunuch Mathan heard what had happened, he hastened to the captain's house, broke open the locks and so frightened the guards with threats that they took to flight, chiefly in fear of his accusation that they had used force against strangers, and robbed them of some of their belongings. He offered to conduct the Fathers to a place of greater safety, and told them to pay no attention to the Magistrate for Ambassadors. Father Matthew refused to accept this invitation, despite the fact that the eunuch told him that they were being protected by authority of the King and were being called to the royal palace. They then agreed that they should both appear on the following day at the court of the Magistrate for Ambassadors.

The eunuch was first to appear in the court and he warned the presiding judge, in the name of the King, to have nothing to do with this affair, which had been given over to the eunuch Mathan. He also threatened to swear out a warrant for the arrest of the soldiers and of their captain, for having used force in robbing the strangers of much of their baggage. With that, the Judge turned to his colleagues for advice, and then said that no matter what might have happened, he would not release the Fathers, but would follow the law and send them to the house reserved for foreigners, and when the eunuch saw he was making no headway, he decided to leave, and to hand them over to the Magistrates.

The first proceeding of the court, which was sitting in full session, was to order an examination of the Fathers, in presence of the crowded court, among whom there were several visiting foreigners. The examination lasted for a full hour, with the judge questioning and the Fathers answering from where they were kneeling before him. The scope of the examination consisted in a serious inquisition, as to why Father Matthew had violated the law by overstepping the jurisdiction of his court, and employing the eunuchs to present his gifts to the King. The accused was prepared to answer this charge, and said that he was no more to blame than they were. He claimed he had acted under pressure from the eunuch, and said that since even the highest Magistrates could not resist their power, it was not to be wondered at that foreigners could not oppose it. He explained that up to the present

he had been continually occupied in the royal palace, by order of
the King himself, and that he had been trying from the time of his
arrival to present himself before the court, but was prevented from
doing so by the guard of eunuchs. In addition, he explained that a man
who had lived in different provinces for several years, without restraint, and who had formerly visited the royal city, should be treated
as an inhabitant and not as a foreigner, and that he should be
exempted from the law he was accused of violating. After that the
presiding judge became much more considerate. He told the Fathers
to keep up their courage and have no fear, because he himself would
present their request to the King, and let them know, before long, what
His Majesty decided. One thing, however, he insisted upon, and it
was a severe blow to them, namely, that he did not wish to have them
living in Pekin; hence they would have to retire to the house of the
foreigners. He then promised to see to it that during their stay there,
they would lack nothing they desired.

This palace of the foreigners is a spacious building, surrounded by
walls, and closed in by many gates. The Chinese are not permitted to
enter it, except by special order, and foreigners do not leave it except
to return to their own country when their business in China is completed, unless it be to appear in this court, or at the royal palace on
special summons. There are numerous little rooms in this building,
and at times the foreigners who are present to pay tribute to the King
of China, number more than a thousand. These cells are more like
sheep stalls than rooms in which human beings are supposed to live.
They have no doors, nor are they supplied with furniture of any kind;
not even a chair, a bench or a bed, and this because all orientals, excepting the Chinese, sit, eat, and sleep on the floor.

These numerous visitors do not come into China with the equipage
of real ambassadors. They come for profit, bringing presents and looking for rewards from the King, which, in keeping with the dignity of
so great a prince, are far in excess of the value of the gifts he receives.
With the money received they buy Chinese merchandise and then sell
it in their own countries at a great profit, and from the time they set
foot in China, their expenses and support are paid for out of public
funds. The only purpose the Chinese seem to have in favoring these
ambassadors, or rather these merchants, is to restrain the neighboring
nations, and so it seems to make no difference what kind of presents
they bring to the King. Among the gifts to be offered to the King, the
Fathers saw a sword, which was merely a piece of steel, clumsily

forged on an anvil, to which someone in this house had fitted a wooden handle fashioned with a hatchet. In the same class of gifts there were breast pieces, poorly made of thongs tied together. They also brought horses, so poorly fed that when they reached Pekin they died of starvation. And yet these barbarians, bringing such trifles from long distances, cost the country a pretty penny for their expenses en route. It would seem as though the Chinese paid more attention to a display of grandeur on the part of their sovereign, than to the low station of the would-be ambassadors.

Once the Fathers were settled in this so-called palace, they were treated with more respect than the others who were lodging there. They were assigned to the quarters reserved for the Chinese Magistrates, when they have occasion to visit the place. These rooms are furnished with sofas and beds and silk coverlets of double thickness, with chairs and other such necessities. The servants gave them more attention and their respect increased with the days. No sooner was the news spread abroad that the Fathers were sent to this house, than the friendly Magistrates and other sympathetic leaders obtained permission to visit them, and the President of the Council, himself, having learned more about them from their friends, became so interested that he preferred them to all the other foreigners there.

It is customary to speak to the Council President on bended knees but, omitting that ceremony, he usually asked the Fathers to be seated and even invited them to eat with him. He also asked them if they would make certain mathematical instruments for him and in this way he placed himself in their debt. They were also permitted to fit out a little chapel in this house where they said Mass every day for the success of their undertaking. During the time that they were detained in the Ambassadors' lodging house, some Saracens arrived from the west. They had heard, at least by name, of Europe, India, Persia, of the Turkish Moors and the Persian Ormuzi, and even of the Spaniards and the Venetians. As a present for the King they were bringing pieces of very brilliant marble which is prized very highly by the Chinese. They call it *fusce*, or dusky, and the Fathers are still uncertain as to whether it is jasper or lapis lazuli or neither. In addition to these very hard purple stones, they also brought a quantity of rhubarb. They got this at the frontier, within the Chinese boundary, and they were given carts to transfer it, at the expense of the Crown. Then they sold it in Pekin, a pound for two obols, the equivalent of two Italian baiocchi. It was from these Saracens that the Fathers confirmed their belief that the Kingdom of China was known to them as Cathay, and the royal city as Cambalu, and that there was no other country in the world, known to them as Cathay. It was for this reason that the Fathers sent their early letters to India and to Europe, advising their people to revise their geographical maps, which placed Cathay outside of the northern wall of China. If this seems to contradict what Marco Polo says about the innumerable bridges in the city of Cambalu, perhaps the capital city is smaller now than it was in his time, but even now, one can count ten thousand bridges in the capital; some, large and elegantly built over the rivers, others over steams and lakes and over the canals which are hidden among the scattered streets.

The foreigners who are detained at the residence reserved for them, are treated very well and are furnished with provisions, which would be more abundant save that they are often diverted or stolen by the servants appointed to transport them. At their departure they are entertained at banquets, with a public official acting as their host, and his grade depends upon the importance of the country from which the foreigner came. At these banquets, each of the so-called Ambassadors is seated next to the one who is acting as his host in the King's name, and this rite is looked upon by the Chinese as part of the tribute paid to the throne. At these feasts they have music and singing, and comedies are enacted. Besides the dishes that are served, the guests are given various cooked meats which they may take back to their lodgings, but here again, the house servants rob the chambers, as a sort of harpy pastime, so much so, indeed, that the Ambassadors at this particular time went about armed in order to protect their property. Even as resident guests the Fathers were not tendered such a banquet because they had failed to observe the proper order of reporting to the tribunal. Yet some of their friends began to solicit for such a favor, saying that there would be no objection to it, if Father Matthew were to offer presents to those in charge of such affairs. His reply to this suggestion was that he thought the presents would be better employed if given to excuse them from such affairs.

After three days of forced residence in the Ambassadors' palace, the Fathers were summoned to the palace of the King, to pay their respects to the King's throne, as they would have done if it had been occupied by the King in person. The ceremony is held in a stupendous hall, of great width and of much greater length, and seemingly large enough to hold thirty thousand people, a magnificent and a regal structure. At one end of it there was a high-vaulted room, with five great doors, opening into the King's living quarters. The royal throne is beneath this vaulted dome, and it was the custom for his Majesty to appear on the throne, nearly every day, to hear the petition of his subjects, to expedite royal affairs and to receive legates or Magistrates, who came to thank him for honors conferred. From the time that the present King decided to retire into solitude, all these useless ceremonies are carried on before his empty throne, and not a day passes but many come from distances in the great empire, to congratulate the King for some reason or other.

In this great court, which is surrounded with other magnificent buildings, there is a night guard of three thousand soldiers, besides those who are on guard duty in the various groves encircling the place, about a stone's throw apart. At each of the five doors there are elephants, also placed by way of protection. Those who are called to this court of the throne, must be in waiting at the gates before daybreak. At sunrise the soldiers and the elephants come out, and those who are present to offer congratulations to the King, are admitted wearing a special red robe, and carrying an ivory plaque about two hands long and four fingers, or a single palm, in width, which is held before the mouth. Thus they come before the throne and go through a series of bowing and genuflecting, in slow motion, and with a considerable waste of time. These ceremonies are all rehearsed beforehand under direction of the Prefects of the Ceremonies, so as to avoid mistakes. The Prefects assigned to the Fathers were Chinese of Saracen origin, the presumption being that they were from the same country. They also accompanied the Fathers as sponsors. There were prefects present also to exact a punishment for the slightest fault, and a Magistrate who announced in clear tones, when to bow, when to rise, and what order to be followed.

On the day of his visit to the court of the throne, Father Matthew went to call on the Supreme Judge of the Council, after notifying him that he belonged to the class of the literati, and would be dressed accordingly. The Judge and his colleagues received him with ceremonies appropriate to his class, and promised that he would present a request to the King, in the very near future, relative to his petition.

Returning from the palace to the Residence for Ambassadors, they were led to the Prefect in charge, in order to pay their respects to him, in return for which he arose from his seat, made a profound bow and returned their compliments, with the remark that he was never accustomed to so honoring any of the Ambassadors, even those from the most prominent countries. During the rest of that same day they were visited by several notaries who asked them various questions. One of them, inquiring for information for the Supreme Judge, was anxious to know what their principal purpose was, in coming to China. They took this to be an official inquiry, as it really was, and so they decided to make a clear and a bold statement of their design. They asserted, and put into writing, that they had been sent by their Superiors to preach the law of the One God, the ruler of Heaven and of earth, and that they had brought presents to the King to show the loyalty of men who had lived so long in this kingdom. They added also that they neither hoped for nor expected any public reward or return compensation, and that there was only one thing they wished for, namely, since they had been living in China for so long a time, that the King should grant them permission to live in Pekin, or wherever else he thought best. With this answer, the Prefect asked if they would explain the doctrine they wanted to preach. So they sent him a beautiful breviary containing many church prayers and with it whatever script, pertaining to the Christian faith, they had thus far put into Chinese writing. He kept everything, excepting the breviary, which he returned.

With this information in his possession, the Prefect sent a request to the King, explaining the affairs of the Fathers. He had heard that they were favored and supported by the Magistrates and that they were well informed on Chinese affairs, and for this reason he forbade under heavy penalty that any lawyer should give a copy of his request to the Fathers, but they already knew the principal topics it touched upon. First, he complained bitterly against the eunuch Mathan because he meddled in the affairs of foreigners, which was contrary to the law of the realm, as such matters depended directly upon his court. Secondly, he accused the Fathers also of having violated the same law by bringing presents to the King, through the intervention of the eunuchs, because foreigners should not undertake to gain entrance to the royal court without first obtaining letters patent from the Viceroy of the province through which they entered the kingdom. However, he thought that the foreigners might be pardoned because of their ignorance of Chinese customs, and also that they should be reimbursed for their presents. He judged also that Father Matthew should be granted the honor of wearing the ornaments distinctive of the Magistrates, and that each of the Fathers should be given a certain amount of silk cloth over and above the value of the presents. In conclusion he said that they should all be sent back to the Province of Canton, to reside there, wherever the Magistrates should decide, and if not that, then they should be sent back to their own country. Thus it was that the Prefect in charge of the Residence for Foreigners, at the expense of the Fathers, made up a case against Mathan, who was hated by the Magistrates.

It was known beforehand, through reports received from the eunuchs, that the King was not at all pleased with the arrest of the Fathers, nor with the report that they were being held in detention by the Court of Ceremonies, and that he said, "Why was it necessary to put these men in prison? Are they to be classified as robbers? Let us see what the Judge in charge will do with them." When the request just mentioned was given to him, he put it aside, which was equivalent to denying it. In similar cases the King generally makes a reply, which is returned to the Prefect for him to execute according to the ancient laws and customs. One would scarcely believe how all this annoyed the Magistrates of this particular court. It was generally believed that the King had acted in favor of the Fathers, and it seemed certain that it all came about by solicitation on the part of the Fathers with their friends the eunuchs, because the Prefect had complained about them in his request to the King, and had confined them in the Residence for Foreigners. Furthermore, he had shabbily treated Father Matthew, who had lived so long in the country and had been on familiar terms with the leaders of several provinces. The outcome of it was that the Prefect in charge of the Residence for Foreigners, contrary to the laws of the place, granted the Fathers more liberty and freedom to visit their friends or anyone they wished. Father Matthew took advantage of the privilege and went to call on his friends to ask for their advice and assistance. Some of them were glad to do their utmost on his behalf, especially the very generous member of the High Council, whom Father Matthew had previously visited. Much to the surprise of the Prefect, this friend kept Father Matthew for three or four hours in conversation and wanted to hold a banquet for him in his home.

A whole month went by without an answer to the request sent to the King. The Prefect then forwarded a second request quite different from the first, in which nothing was said about the eunuchs, and in which the Fathers were treated very honorably. He said that they had acted very courteously toward the throne, that they had come of their own accord, without being sent by their sovereign, and that they had brought novel and valuable presents. He also increased the recompense requested in the first petition, of which the Fathers had a copy. This second petition was quite acceptable, save for one item which the King did not like, namely, that the Fathers be permanently dismissed from Pekin. He did not want to see them go away, and yet he did not wish to keep them there contrary to the law, unless the Magistrates asked to have them stay.

The eunuchs who were commissioned to take care of the clocks, also tried to retain the Fathers, fearing that if some accident should happen to one of the clocks there would be no one there to repair it. They tell an amusing story of what the King did, so as not to be deprived of his clock. The Queen Mother had heard some one had given the King a clock that sounded of itself. They use that phrase when speaking of it. She asked the King to have the eunuchs bring it to her so she could see it. Thinking that she might like it and then decide to keep it, and at the same time not wishing to refuse her request, he called those who were in charge of the clock and told them to release the wheels that governed the striking, and thus reduce it to silence. The Queen didn't like the clock that didn't ring, and she sent it back to her son.

To return to what is more serious, the Fathers did not hesitate to advise the Magistrates of the Court of Ceremonies to include in their second notice to the King, their permission for the Fathers to reside in Pekin. They said that in their opinion, this omission was the only reason why the King had not replied to the first request. This they obstinately refused to do, asserting that it was contrary to the law of the land. After presenting a third and other notices to the throne, all of which remained unanswered, they began to realize that each message sent served only to improve the position of the foreigners, and that the King refused to answer because that particular request was not included in their notices. Finally, as this effort seemed to be hopeless, Father Matthew began to look around to see if any help could be obtained from his friends, to extricate the Missioners from their present embarrassment, and from the seeming disgrace connected with it. Some of those whom he approached, tried to influence the Magistrates of the Court of Ceremonies, and it was finally the Judge who presided over the High Court of Magistrates, the one we have already mentioned, who brought the matter to a close.

One day he came to the Prefect, or Provost, of the Residence for Foreigners, and berated him because he had not permitted the Fathers to leave this prison and go into the city. The Prefect answered that he had acted so, because Father Matthew had given over to the eunuchs a matter that pertained to the Court of Rites. Whereupon, their friend became incensed and said, "Who is not aware of the truth that this exactor of taxes is guilty of robbery and of murder? Who is there in the whole catalogue of Magistrates that has courage and daring enough to repress this man, Mathan? And you are complaining because one foreigner could not resist his assault?" With this said, he turned on his heel and departed, taking with him his resentment against a man whom he had appointed to the Magistrature, and from whom he could just as easily withdraw the honor. Fearing what might happen, the Prefect of the Residence, whose rank was inferior to many of his class, sent a messenger to Father Matthew advising him to send in a petition as soon as possible, asking for permission for himself and for his companions to live in the city, because of health conditions and the lack of medicines and of other necessities, in the Residence for Ambassadors. The Prefect then wrote out a document granting them ample power to rent a house and to dwell in any section of the city they preferred. He then assigned them four servants who brought them the same allotment of provisions they were accustomed to receive on every fifth day. This consisted of rice, meat, salt, wine, vegetables and also firewood. They were also given a servant who was always ready to obey their orders. Naturally, they were greatly pleased with this solution of their problem and they gave thanks to God for being delivered from such restraining circumstances. Even if their reputation did suffer because of their detention in such a place, it was fully restored by the liberty granted them, despite the existing laws.

14. The Mission Is Confirmed in Pekin by Royal Authority

ONCE THEY BEGAN to appear in public, the first care of the Fathers was to see to it that they should never be forced to leave Pekin, and then to go about acquiring all the liberty possible to preach the Gospel, and to this end they endeavored to enlist the interest of the Magistrates of the Court of Ceremonies. These Magistrates in turn were growing tired of having their requests left unanswered, and were ready, in one way or another, to put an end to the whole affair. The revisor of requests intended for the King, being a friend of Father Matthew, was also enlisted in the cause in the following manner. They sent him a very accurately drawn up document, to be presented to the sovereign, in which they informed him that they had been prompted to come here because of the nobility and of the renown of the Chinese Kingdom, that they had been on the way for years previous, and that they had lived here in a way that had won the friendship of everyone, even of the highest dignitaries. Only last year, as they explained, they had come into the Royal City in order to offer a few small presents they had gotten together for the King, the best of which was an image of Christ the Saviour, presented for the conservation of peace in the kingdom, and for the happiness and prosperity of the royal family. These presents they had offered as an evidence of their affection and as a proof of their loyalty to the King. They gave assurance that they were looking for nothing in return, because they were men dedicated to the service of God, celibates, without children or dependents, and so without need of supporting families. They assured him that the only request they were making was that the King should designate some place, in the city or elsewhere, for them to live. This request was no more successful than the others. No doubt, it was not answered because according to the law it should have been presented to the Court of Ceremonies, which had already made its mind known to the King, namely, that they did not wish to have the Fathers in the Court City. Instead of sending a formal written reply to this request, the King expressed his decision verbally, and it reached the Fathers through some of the chief eunuchs. It informed them that they might live in the Capital City in all security, and that he wanted to hear no further talk about their returning to a southern province or to their own country. The Fathers accepted this as an official reply to their petition, and they rejoiced in the Lord that finally with the help of Divine Providence they had overcome the opposition and triumphed over all obstacles. Not only were they granted permission to remain, they were also allotted a subsidy from public funds, to be paid every four months, and amounting to eight gold ecus a month, which in this country is not so small an income as it might appear to be in Europe.

Verily he spoke the truth, who said "Your friends will be many when you are prosperous." All those who had given up their friendship, were now making much of it, throughout the whole city, and they were so numerous, that it can scarcely be doubted that Heaven opened up what had been a narrow entrance into a more ample field for the propagation of the Gospel. The Prefect for Foreigners invited Father Matthew into his court and told him, in a much more courteous way than was his custom, that he was permitted by authority of this court to dwell in the Royal Capital, as long as he desired to, and to live wherever he wished to. He said that Pekin was a big city and could very well afford to add one more foreigner to its population. As the news of this permission was spread about, the number of visitors and of friends increased with every day. We shall mention only a few of the many friends, to prevent a repetitious recital from becoming tiresome.

First, we should mention one who had attained to the highest dignity among the Magistrates. In Chinese, such a position is called Cholao, and at that time he was the only one holding this office. Father Matthew had been looking forward to a visit with this particular dignitary, and by way of introduction he brought some little European presents, of which the one that particularly pleased his host was a concave sun-dial, set in ebony and very neatly designed. He was received and detained, not only to sit down and converse but to be present at a banquet, where his host listened with pleasure to what the Fathers were doing and, particularly so, to an explanation of Christian customs. When Father Matthew told him that Christian marriage was contracted between two people only, even though they be of the royalty, the Magistrate turned to the other dignitaries present and said, "There seems to be no further need to inquire about a kingdom in which marriage is so sacred. That alone should be proof enough of how properly everything else is regulated." He sent back to the Fathers a return gift far in excess of the value of what they had given him, consisting of silk cloth and of furs, worth more than forty gold pieces. Then they in turn sent back a present to his son, who, because of the close friendship that thereafter developed, preserved the benevolent attitude of his father over a period of more than eight years, during all of which time he was still in high office. This, of course, developed an incredible prestige and gave them assurance of a permanent status, in almost any eventuality.

What happened at that time was decidedly pertinent to what Father Matthew is said to have conjectured, if not predicted, some years before. One day Brother Sebastiano, who was serving as companion to Father Ricci in the Province of Canton, was complaining about the difficulties they were encountering. Not only were they reaping no fruit from their labor, but, to him it seemed that there was no hope of ever reaping any, where they were. Better to set sail for Japan, he thought, or for some place where we could at least entertain hope of making headway. "Brother," Father Matthew replied, "let's not talk about the difficulties. It's quite evident you do not fully appreciate our position. If impediments should arise, even more obstinate than those we encountered in the beginning, I think I would continue to labor on, rather than rush into the uncertainty of a dark forest. As to what you say about hope, well, never give up hope. Why! On some future day you may see us sitting in with the Cholao." Brother Sebastiano, who is still living, at this writing, often tells this story, much to his own delight and to that of his listeners.

At the time in which we are at present engaged, the Assessor of the Criminal Courts arrived from Nankin on official business. Father Matthew knew him well. He was the friend whose ambition it was to be known as a mathematician. Through him, the Fathers contracted a friendship with the presiding officer of the High Tribunal, who afterwards was promoted to the same position in the Military Senate. He also introduced them to the Assessor of the High Tribunal which appoints all Magistrates throughout the country. This man's name was Fon, and when he was appointed Chairman of the Tribunal of Ceremonies, which had jurisdiction over the Fathers, he confirmed their status in the City of Pekin and thus removed any fear of interference. He also gave orders that the royal stipend of money and of rice, allotted to them by the crown, should be paid as directed.

It happened, not infrequently, that part of the provisions assigned to them were disappearing, or that they were delivered at the wrong time, all of which was due to laxity on the part of the overseers. At that time they were receiving about six gold pieces a month, which was a great help toward supporting their house, considering the fact that they were so far distant from any of their own people and from their assistance. Apart from the supplies granted by the throne, the fact that they were being subsidized from public funds made it evident to everyone that they were there with permission of the King. News of this was spread throughout the whole kingdom and it was considerably exaggerated. As usually happens here, the truth was augmented by the common habit of spreading rumors.

Next to the Cholao we must name the President of the High Council; the one we have several times mentioned as the creator of Magistrates for all the courts. He came from the Province of Honan, and he was quite advanced in age. He was the one who frequently invited Father Matthew to his house and liked to talk about things to be feared and things to be hoped for in the next life. The obligations arising from his official position prevented him from holding more frequent discussions on such subjects, and also from finding the truth. Several years later Father Matthew wrote out a summary of their conversations and inserted it as two chapters in one of his books. Afterwards he wrote a further comment on the same material, thus proving that the worth of a discourse is increased by the dignity of the one who pronounces it.

At that time also they became acquainted with two other Assessors of the Court of Ceremonies. One of these often told Father Matthew that he had a brother in the Province of Canton, who was a Christian and who could never be persuaded to eat meat on certain days. It was because of his brother that this man was so well disposed toward Christianity, but he had not as yet followed his brother's example. He also said that a certain writer of renown, of the lettered class, had inserted something in one of his books against the Christian religion and against Father Matthew's Catechism, which by his authority was deleted and replaced by contrary views. The Fathers could never get him to admit this, but they were assured of it from other sources. There were two other presiding officers of different courts in Nankin, who always visited Father Ricci when they came to Pekin, and who kept up a similar friendship with his brethren at Nankin. One can readily judge from the number of leaders in the Chinese Kingdom, listed among their friends, how many other prominent figures such a roster would include.

At just about this time the palace clock failed to function, due perhaps to the lack of interest or to the carelessness of the eunuchs who had charge of it, and the King gave orders to have it brought to the Father's house for adjustment. As soon as it arrived, and during the two or three days it was there, curious crowds assembled about the place. When the King heard of this he issued orders that in the future the clock should not be taken out of the palace, and that if the clock needed attention, the donors should be called to the palace to take care of it. This, of course, spread about a story of the good will of the King toward the Europeans. Moreover, in order to prevent the continual requests from the eunuchs, for permission for the Fathers to come to the palace, a royal order was issued that they should be permitted to come there four times a year, without asking for permission. From that time on, they could enter the royal palace, not four times a year, but as often as they pleased, and they were free also to bring along their fellow missionaries, who had lately arrived. The good will and the friendship of the eunuchs, fostered by visits and conversation, continued to grow with the days.

Many of the royal relatives, both of the King and of the Queen, were also acquainted with the missionaries. These people make much of public show, but they are never permitted to hold public office of any kind and, if one were to make a comparison, they are quite inferior to Europeans of the same class. Many military and civic leaders were also very friendly toward the missionaries. In fact it seemed that no class or order of distinction was missing from their acquaintance.

With this beginning, the common people, apart from the very lowest type, scarcely dared to look at the threshold of the Mission residence. However, when the novelty of their new existence began to wear off, the Fathers began, with more liberty, to make known the Christian religion. In a short time it became evident that their house was open to everyone, even to the most lowly, and it was from among the poorest that many were won over to Christianity. In truth, it was noticed by Ricci's companions that no matter how busy he happened to be, in the midst of his many occupations, Father Matthew never sent away a poor man. Instead, and as though he had planned it beforehand, he would detain him for a long time in pleasant conversation. One may conjecture from this how numerous his visitors were. On the other hand, in no other year of his life in China was he more frequently invited to banquets, which he could not refuse to attend without being discourteous. Nor would anyone find fault with this, save perhaps those who imagine that there is no difference between European and Chinese banquets. These latter, as has been explained more than once, are instituted for the purpose of discussing serious subjects. Little of anything is eaten at these gatherings and those who attend them generally dine just beforehand. Invitations to such gatherings were gradually diminished, until the Fathers attended them only on special occasions, and these were not frequent.

All beginnings are accorded a certain amount of liberty, especially on such missions as this one, where the result of the labor expended was dependent upon conciliating those, in whose power it rested to sanction a dubious undertaking.

15. Two Remarkable Converts

AMONG THE CHINESE notables who had gained a public reputation, for their knowledge of the Christian religion, there were two who were outstanding. One of these was named Fumochan, a distinguished member of the class of the literati, who was born in the town of Fumiam in the Province of Nankin. As a young man, he belonged to the sect of idol worshippers, but as soon as he acquired his first literary degree, he wrote a book in which he cited the testimony of the ancients who asserted that there was only one God, the Ruler of heaven and of earth, and to this he added his own proof and comment. With the acquisition of his doctorate, and after holding several public offices in Pekin, he was ordered to the Province of Uquam, to take over a position known as the Tauli. He filled his post with great integrity, showing no signs of avarice, wholly devoted to the public welfare and to the exercise of strict justice; especially when judging cases in which widows and the poor were concerned. That was just at the time when the eunuchs rushed forth from the Royal Palace, like stygian furies, to exact the taxes and to work the mines for gold and silver, or rather to prey upon the people.

The tax collector assigned to the Province of Uquam had a reputation for being particularly brutal, and with his cruelty he had the added advantage of belonging to the nobility and of possessing a dangerous skill in controversy. Those Magistrates, to whom money and honors meant more than the public good, played up to the eunuchs and opened the gates for the entrance of all kinds of evil. Some of them, however, faithful to their trusts endeavored to stem the torrent with their authority and with letters of open protest to the King. The man we have just mentioned was first among the protesting Magistrates of the Province of Uquam. Realizing that his authority was not sufficient to hold the eunuch in check, he wrote three factual and complaining letters against him. But the eunuch was not slow on defense. He wrote only one document, in which he accused the Magistrate of treason and called him a rebel against the King's commands, as a result of which, the Magistrate was degraded from office and summoned to Pekin, in chains. Here, on order of the throne, this exceptional man was mercilessly flogged and thrown into a narrow cell, where he was permitted no communication with his friends. This fury of the King he bore with the utmost patience, which served to increase his popularity and the veneration of his name. The Province of Uquam did not hesitate, then and there, to do honor to the name of its defender in an unusual way. It published a number of books commemorating all his public benefactions, printed pictures of him, as true a likeness as they could produce, and had them scattered throughout the province, for the people to honor him privately as being worthy of veneration. Several public temples were built in his honor, in which his statue was placed on an altar, with candles and incense perpetually burning before it. And all this was done with a general manifestation of praise and devotion.

Some time previous to these happenings, this man had heard in Uquam that Father Matthew enjoyed a wide reputation in Nancian and in Nankin, and that all his efforts were being directed toward the public good. At that time he sent one of his pupils to Father Matthew for instruction, but it so happened that preparations for the journey to Pekin were under way, and the pupil, with nothing accomplished, returned to his master and told him that the educated foreigner was on his way to the Capital City. Still thinking of the public welfare, as he was about to be sent to prison in chains, he brought his pupil to Pekin to see Father Matthew and, as soon as the Fathers were released from detention in the Residence of Foreigners, the pupil came to them and explained his visit. With the usual ceremonies and presentation of gifts, he then selected Father Matthew as his teacher. Before Fumochan was sent to prison, Father Matthew went to visit him. They were together for an hour and became so well acquainted that many believed that they were friends of long years standing. This friendship continued during the three years that Fumochan was in prison, and it was preserved by a mutual exchange of letters and favors. Without informing his friends, this man of renown had a reprint made of Father Matthew's Commentary on Friendship, to which he added a preface. He also sent them some geographical maps, and he afterwards had as many copies of them made as they desired. And that was not all. Sparing no expense, he reprinted every available writing of the Fathers, together with high praise and laudation for the authors, which was somewhat immoderate and overdone. He was the first one to assign

Father Matthew the title of Classical Doctor, which he did not refuse because of the prestige it added in preaching the Gospel. He also reprinted Ricci's Catechism in a fuller and more ample edition, in which he praised the Christian law with as much enthusiasm as he condemned the idols. Despite the fact that he was well instructed in the precepts of the Christian religion he could not, in his present circumstances, receive the sacrament of baptism. However, he gave full liberty to all his servants to be baptized if they so desired, and all the while he was very devoted to the crucifix he had received from the Fathers.

Before leaving this man, we should not omit a striking example, for that time, of his testimony to the Christian faith. As we have already noted, Father Matthew sent him the draft of his catechism for examination. His purpose in sending them was to change the mind of Fumochan, rather than for him to change the style of the composition. His answer was that he was greatly pleased with the work. He asked for permission to publish it, at once, but Father Matthew thought that he himself should go over it again for further revision. He said it was not as yet quite ripe for picking, and should be left for a while to mature in the sun. Fumochan's answer to this was couched in the form of a clever fable, quite apposite for application to Christianity. Once upon a time, as he said, there was a man who was reduced to extremities by a stubborn chronic ailment, and someone happened along and promised to restore his health with a certain kind of medicine. The friends of the sick man said, "Well, go ahead and restore it, his present danger needs action, not promises." Then the stranger remarked, "Well and good. I shall go home and write out an elegant prescription, in nicely formed characters." To which they replied, "We are interested in your prescription, not in your elegantly formed characters." Thus far the fable, which he proceeded to explain. "The sick man is the Kingdom of China, which has suffered grievously through centuries because of its ignorance of what is contained in your catechism. You have the prescription of life, and you are preferring elegance of expression to a cure for the present danger. Don't you see how the public good is being affected by such a policy?" This was only one of his many compositions on the same subject.

At the end of three long years, during which the narrow confines of his prison cell were forgotten in the amplitude of his mental activity, the King became so weary of the numerous and continual petitions for his release, that he finally sent him home to his province, where he was to live as a private citizen. After his delivery from prison, he was permitted to remain in Pekin for only three days, and he was kept so busy receiving congratulations, that no time was found for him to be baptized. Not wishing to lose such a prize, Father Matthew managed to meet him in a house somewhere in the suburbs where he could receive the sacrament, but one of his companions in chains, and now at liberty, warned him of the danger of giving the suspicious King another cause for complaint against him. He said that the Fathers working at Nankin could take care of the baptism later on, and since Fumochan was in good health at the time, this seemed to be good advice. With nearly every minute of the time allotted to him in the city taken up by visitors, Father Matthew followed him up, giving him instructions in the faith, and finally saw him depart, with no fear or thought whatever of the misfortune that was to follow. The Fathers at Nankin were instructed to lose no time in bringing this man to Christ, but death outran them. He was taken ill and died in a few days, and it is to be hoped that, repentant for his failings, his desire for baptism was sufficient to replace the sacrament.

The second distinguished personage of the class of the literati to be remembered was named Lingotsun. Several years later, he changed that name for Leo, when he was baptized. He came from Hamceu, the metropolitan city of the Province of Cechian. He was holding an important position in the Department of Public Works, when the Fathers arrived in Pekin, and his reputation for genius was equaled by very few. In his younger days, he was ambitious enough to publish an excellent description of the entire kingdom of China, with accurate maps of the fifteen provinces, which to him meant the entire world. He was quite surprised at the limitations of his own work, when he came upon a map of the world, as made by Father Ricci, and being intellectually honest, he gathered from this a good understanding, if not a full comprehension of the truth. So he immediately made friends with Father Matthew and with the other Fathers for the purpose of studying geography, to which he gave all the time he could spare from his public duties. His first big work was to reproduce the world-map on as large a scale as he could, and he made it about six feet square. The Chinese, as we have said before, can do this kind of work very cleverly, by pleating and folding the surface on delicately made wooden hinges. To complete this work, Father Matthew augmented it by adding other kingdoms, more places of note and various observations. He also placed the sun and stars on the margins, with other decorations, in addition to descriptions of Christian customs and explanations of Christian belief. Several of the literati also ornamented this work with elegantly written introductions. When the plates were being cut for these maps, the printers made a duplicate copy of them, unknown to the Fathers, and in this way two editions of the skillful work were published at once. Even that was not enough to supply the demand for it, and another neophyte published a new edition representing the entire world in eight large maps, thus putting three world maps into circulation at once, in Pekin.

Leo was also interested in the other departments of mathematics, and he put all his help to work constructing mathematical instruments. He mastered a great part of the textbook on geometry, written by Father Clavius, learned the use of the astrolabe, and made one for his own use, which operated with great precision. He then wrote out an exact and a clear commentary on these two branches of science. His mathematical figures and drawings were comparable to any produced in Europe. His work on the astrolabe was published in two volumes, and Father Matthew sent a copy of it to the Very Reverend Father General of the Society of Jesus in Rome, as a sample of the first work of its kind done by the Chinese, and another copy to Father Clavius, under whom he himself had once studied. Leo afterwards proved to be a great help to Father Ricci in translating the Practical Mathematics of Father Clavius from Latin into Chinese, in which work, not a single item of the original was omitted. This was only one of many volumes Father Ricci published for the Chinese. It was surprising how the reputation of the Fathers for learning was spread by his writings, how well known the Mission became because of his public discourses, and how many friends he won for the Missionaries from the various classes of people. All of this, however, was not Father Matthew's principal interest, though it did serve as an allurement, as it were, to attract Leo into the fisherman's net.

After this man was sufficiently instructed in Christian Doctrine, and seemed to be even thirsting for the water of baptism, an investigation of his life revealed an impediment of polygamy, and also that he was keeping concubines in another home some distance away. Of this they had heard nothing previously, nor had they even entertained a suspicion of it. It seemed as if the man had more light to recognize the truth than courage to accept it. However, he did recognize the truth of the Christian religion, and continued not only to preach it but to exhort others to embrace it, as earnestly as though he himself were a neophyte. Some of his family had already joined the Church and were counted among the most devout converts. Finally, he returned to his own province, after being degraded to an inferior post in the Magistrature, because of his free and intemperate way of living, which was judged to be unbecoming to a Magistrate. He wrote to the Fathers frequently from his home and published an edition of Father Matthew's Catechism at his own expense, which he gave around to his friends and put on public sale for the people. He continued to promote Christianity but he did not come into the Church at that time. The Lord was probably saving him to be Father Matthew's last convert, as we shall see later on.

16. The Idol Worshippers Defeat Themselves

THE INTIMATE KNOWLEDGE formed with so many of the Magistrates gradually made it evident that Ricci and his companions had come to preach a new law, which claimed to be the one and only true faith, free from the contamination of sects. It was particularly opposed to the sect of idol worshippers in the doctrine it preached, and even more widely, as well as more efficaciously, in its written books, which were admitted to contain a great deal of undeniable truth.

Although the religious beliefs of the lettered class had nothing in common with idol worship, as is proven from their ancient books, yet there were some of this class who had become disgusted with their particular class doctrines, as being lacking in many essentials, and had gone over to the idol worshippers. One of these was a celebrated scholar from the Royal College, called the Hanlin, who went so far in the delirium of idol worshipping as to abandon his wife and to seek perfection as a celibate. By his evil example he drew many others into ruin, who were led on by the allurement of the fables the idol worshippers recount, relative to the future life. This man, with no regard for commonplace doctrine, was not satisfied with the books which Father Ricci had written in Chinese; so he undertook to discredit the doctrine contained in them. He had gotten copies of these books from the Prefect of the Residence for Foreigners, and he wanted to hold a conference with Father Matthew, whose logic he disdained and at whose reasoning he merely laughed. With the assistance of one of the Magistrates of the Military senate, who held a doctor's degree, he wrote out a series of criticisms on Father Matthew's Commentaries. Between them, they filled the margins of the book with their critical notes; one of them writing in ink and the other in red crayon, so they could distinguish their comment. In many places they approved what was written in the Commentaries relative to contempt of the vanities and the pleasures of this passing life, but whenever they came across a reference to the sect of idol worshippers, they were always violently critical of Father Matthew and of educated Europe in general. What particularly displeased them was the assertion that God and man's soul were not one and the same being, a doctrine which is involved in their first erroneous blasphemy, in which they confound the author of nature with nature itself. Apart from other scoffing criticism, they also found fault with the statement that the sun is larger than the earth. Such was the comment of the one from the Royal College, who wrote in black ink. The other who was called upon to collaborate in red crayon, was less negative. He wrote more courteously, approved of much in the Commentaries, and even praised the author. However, in order to please his friend, he failed to reconcile the doctrines of Christianity with those of the idol worshippers.

There was another individual also, considered to be one of the leading intellectual lights of the royal court, who became contaminated by the sordid pagan ideas of the new literary sect and joined the two just mentioned. When he heard the Fathers condemning the cult of idols and offering proofs of what they said, he became enraged and let fall blasphemous threats against the Supreme Deity. He said that if the God of Heaven has power in heaven, then their idols also can do many things on earth, meaning, of course, that the defenders of idol worship would exercise their power against the foreigners. Just when it looked as if a storm were to break over the heads of the Missionaries, God, against whom it is useless to take counsel, looked down upon them serenely and dissipated the gathering storm clouds, repressing in a moment both His enemies and theirs. Here is how it happened.

The critic from the Royal College gave up his position as a Magistrate, shaved his head and became a Minister of the Idols. His ambition then prompted him to acquire a reputation; so he gathered together disciples and wrote books against the leaders of the literati, praising the apologists of the idols. Suddenly he was stayed, as it seems, by the hand of God. As he was entering the City of Pekin, where a crowd was awaiting him, because of the novelty of his apostasy, one of the royal inspectors wrote out a serious charge against him as a deserter, but chiefly attacking the perversity of the doctrine he was promulgating. The Inspector asked the King to have all his writings burned in public, and recommended that he be punished according to the enormity of his crime. The King's answer was, that he should be brought into court in chains and that all his manuscripts be taken away from him. So he entered Pekin in fear and in ignominy, and being too sensitive at the age of seventy, to bear the shame of such a humiliation, he committed suicide in his prison cell by slashing his throat with a knife. His infamous doctrine came to an end with his ignominious death, which he said was the noblest way to die.

In order to protect the sect of the literati, the Magistrates were quick to take advantage of the King's reply. The presiding judge of the Supreme Tribunal, in another written document, accused certain of the Magistrates and of the literati of abandoning the teachings of Confucius, their Prince and Master, to cultivate an heretical doctrine, much to the detriment of the entire kingdom. Again, it seems as if Heaven, for the general good of the realm, permitted that the answer to the charges against the literati should sound as if it had been dictated by a Christian. This happened, too, despite the fact that the idol worshippers had spread a rumor that the King had gone over to their sect and had, with his own hand, as they said, written out a doctrine for them to follow. That, of course, was false, though it was well known that his mother, his queens, the palace eunuchs, and his relatives, all favored the sect of idols. The King's answer to the charge made by the chief officer of the Supreme Tribunal was to this effect: If the Magistrates want to be slaves to the idols, they should feel ashamed when they are putting on their robes of office. Let them go into the desert, if they wish to, where the cenobites of idol worship should abide. This pronouncement of the King caused the presiding judge of the Magistrates to become more audacious, and after consulting with the Senate, he published a general decree for the benefit of the country at large. He made a regulation to the effect that, if anyone taking part in literary contests, or taking an examination for a literary degree, over all of which he had jurisdiction, should make mention of idol worship, except to deprecate it, that one should be excluded from acquiring any literary degree whatsoever. With the publication of this regulation, a change came over the Royal Court and over the country in general. Disappointment and sorrow were evident on the faces of the devotees of idols. Some of them, unable to bear their shame, retired to their homes and remained indoors, and among these were the three who had conspired to accuse the Fathers. Nor was the hand of Heaven stayed with this.

At that time, there were quite a number of the Ministers of the temple idols residing at the Royal Court, where they had become very prominent. They were leading into error, not only the common people but many of the more prominent, and even the queens in the palace, with whom they communicated by messenger. In addition, they were collecting large stipends from the wealthier eunuchs and building temples to the idols, for the multitude of disciples they were attracting. The most illustrious among them was an old man called Thacon, and a second who was about his equal. Some of the queens had chosen one or the other of these two as a director. The reigning queen had developed the practice of paying homage to the vestments worn by Thacon, because she could not leave the palace, and he, as an idol worshipper, was forbidden to enter it. He is said to have remarked that he was hoping that the King also would select him as his Master.

This Thacon was a man of considerable erudition, astute and cunning, with a knowledge of all the religious sects, and a defender of each one, as circumstances demanded. He wanted to meet Father Ricci, if the Father would make the first call and address him on bended knees, as did some of the Magistrates. He sent these directions to Father Matthew by messenger and they were straightway answered. Father Matthew said he had no desire to learn anything from him, but if he, Thacon, wanted to learn something, he was welcome to come and learn it. Ricci was of opinion that it would be better to avoid all contact with this man's degraded class. The pride of this particular impostor was simply unbearable. What else could he have learned in the school of Satan? Honest men could not put up with it. In fact they had developed a bitter hatred for the man and were looking forward to his downfall. Some one of the court spies entered a written charge against him, but when the King returned no answer to it, his arrogance increased, and persuading himself that he had become the court favorite, he felt himself superior and a victor over his enemies.

It was shortly after Thacon's supposed ascendency that a book appeared, with no author's name assigned, defaming the King, the Queen and several others. It accused them of depriving the rightful heir of his succession to the throne, in order to give it to another son, more dear to the King. The book was circulated anonymously, after being printed and published so secretly that, even up to the present time, the author is not known for certain. A copy of it was sent to the King by some unidentified informer, and he became so indignant that he flew into a rage and ordered a searching inquisition to be established to discover the author. With no regard for law or for justice, many were submitted to torture in search of the truth, and everything that looked like evidence, no matter how trifling, was ruthlessly pursued as being an evident truth. When no progress was being made in discovering the culprit, the King berated the Magistrates, accusing them of being remiss in pressing the search.

During those days the whole city was in a sorrowful plight. Many who were innocent were dragged to prison in chains. People were afraid to leave their homes and no one dared to speak of anything touching upon this subject, knowing that the King's spies were everywhere. Suspicion fell heavily upon the Ministers of the idols, and some of the more prominent among them were thrown into chains. An order was issued for the arrest of Thacon. His papers and his manuscripts were ransacked, but nothing was found in relation to the book in question. They say, however, that evidence of other serious crimes was discovered. One of his associates, professing to be a celibate, was found to be supporting more than a dozen concubines. Others of them were found guilty of having secured large sums of public funds, through the influence of their followers, and this was made known to the whole kingdom by the enraged Magistrates. It was also revealed from some of his letters that Thacon had written certain things disparaging to the reputation of the reigning King. In his indiscretion, he found fault with the King in these letters because he did not favor the adoration of idols, and also because he was not sufficiently attentive to his mother, which, among the Chinese, is one of the few infamous crimes. All this was reported to the sovereign and he gave orders for the calumniator to be punished according to the law. The court which held the power of inflicting punishment for such crimes, let loose the whole torrent of its indignation against this poor unfortunate, and he was so terribly flogged that when they went to replace his chains, he died before they could put them on him. After his death, his name became a byword for one who vainly boasted that he paid no attention to bodily suffering, but he forgot about his boasting and cried out like any other mortal while he was being whipped. By order of the Magistrates, his body was not to be buried. They were suspicious that he was only feigning to be dead and that by some deceit or other he might escape. They could hardly believe that he had died so soon in the flogging. The other sacrificers to idols paid the penalties according to the gravity of their crimes. They were all expelled from the Royal City, taking with them part of the shameful reputation of their sect, and leaving part of it behind them.

The other Coryphaeus of the sect, namely, Hancian, was banished from Pekin to the distant Province of Canton, and when it was discovered that he was held in high esteem in the prominent city of Xaucea, he was relegated to the utmost confines of the province. The one who so boldly asserted that God was powerful only in heaven, learned by bitter experience that God also dominated the world. He was degraded from the high position he held in the Magistrature, stripped of all its insignia and deprived of his literary degree, in perpetuum, all because one of his relatives was held in suspicion, in the inquest for the author of the libelous book, though nothing was proven against the suspect.

Finally, and by means of torture, a confession relative to the infamous book, was exacted from one of the class of the literati, who had become a nefarious character. Some time previous, this man had given up his studies and abandoned his position as a Magistrate, which he had filled very honorably, and relaxed into criminal habits. By clever scheming he had sought, rightly or wrongly, to accumulate riches and the rest of material things which mortals crave, with the result that a terrible sentence was passed against him and quickly executed. He was tied to a stake and the flesh was lacerated and cut from his body in a thousand six hundred pieces. In this way his bones and his head were mercilessly left untouched, so that over and above the agony he suffered, he was forced to look upon his own disintegration. Finally, after being slowly torn to shreds, he was decapitated. This, to the Chinese, means the very depth of ignominy, because they utterly abhor the dismemberment of the human body. Someone who was present at the execution ran off with the victim's head, and threw the pursuing soldiers off his trail by scattering pieces of silver money along his path. It is quite probable that he was promised a reward by the relatives of the man who was executed, if he would recover the head, so it could be buried with the body and thus prevent the disgrace that would follow, if it were taken elsewhere and publicly exposed to the view of the curious.

To return to the worship of idols, condemned as it was by increasing prejudice, discredited by so much ignominy, and deprived of so many protectors, it became so weak and lifeless that it failed to overshadow Christianity, as it had hoped to do. On the contrary, having lost the flower of its honor, which it had proudly and luxuriously paraded before the royal court for so long a time, it had to give way to a new and a growing enlightenment.

Not a few of the neophytes and of the pagans also, as well as the Fathers themselves, were of the opinion that all this was brought about by God, lest the tender plant of the Gospel so recently set in China and, not yet able to endure a storm, should be uprooted by the first blast of persecution.

17. The Harvest Begins to Ripen in Xaucea

HAVING PAUSED for a time after our long peregrinations with the Fathers, let us turn our attention to those in the south, beginning with the condition of affairs in Xaucea, in the Province of Canton. Here we left Father Nicolo Longobardo, a Sicilian, and the Lay Brother Francesco Martinez, where they dwelt alone for several years, because no foreigner could join them, and it was probably better that no one tried to. A lone priest and inexperienced as he was, he succeeded in increasing the harvest stored in the spiritual granary of the Church. His work there was helped out not a little by the publicity given to what had been accomplished in the two royal cities which we have already recounted. Prosperity promotes success. It opened the courts of the Magistrates and gained their favor, the one thing after God which protected and assured the promulgation of the Christian faith.

Several prominent men and women were received into the Church, something quite unusual up to that time in the City of Xaucea. Realizing, however, that the Mission had not made much progress in the town after so many years of residence, Father Nicolo decided to try the suburbs, to see if He who had chosen but few from among the learned and the nobles, would call a greater number among the poorer people. He began this apostolate during the year 1599, just after the feast of the world traveling Apostles, Peter and Paul, in a village called Michia, not far distant from the city. From here he made excursions into the nearby settlements and continued doing so for several years running, and in the following manner. First, he would send one of the converts ahead of him to announce his coming and to tell the people to get ready to hear a preacher who had come from the distant west. On his arrival, he sat down at a table before them and explained the purpose of his coming, namely, to convince them to adore the one true God, the ruler of heaven and of earth, assuring them that no hope of salvation was to be found unless that religious belief was accepted as the truth. Then, he would read the ten commandments and give a brief explanation of each. After that, he told them that he had an image of the one who first gave this law to mankind in general, and placed the crucifix on the table, or in some other convenient place for veneration, with candles and incense burning before it. Then he called upon them all to adore the one whom this figure represented, and to promise henceforth to renounce their idols, which were only imitations of gods who did not exist. The people were not at all reluctant to follow his directions, either because of the reputation of the Christian faith for holiness, or because of the innate inclination of this people to adore some kind of a deity. After these instructions he distributed a compendium of Christian Doctrine, copies of which were given only to certain ones because there were not enough for everyone. Once the multitude became interested in these exhortations, the fire of their interest began to spread and broke out in the city, with the result that many became inflamed with a love of the Gospel.

The first solemn step, for those who wished to be received into the Church, was made when they joined the ranks of the catechumens in the following ceremony. A summary of the Christian faith was placed on an altar. The one who wished to learn about the faith came to the altar and with the customary acts of veneration to Christ the Saviour and Master, took the compendium from the altar and brought it to his home. From that time until they were baptized, they were permitted to attend that part of the sacrifice of the Mass, to which catechumens are admitted. Catechism lessons then followed every day for a considerable period and up to the day of baptism. After the reception of the sacrament, the newly baptized were given beads, medals and an Agnus Dei; as arms for the spiritual combat of life. Many of them celebrated the occasion with great public display. After returning to their homes, they were led out by the other converts to the sound of cymbals and trumpets, and even by the neighboring pagans, with the same display they are accustomed to make for a Magistrate who has been promoted to a new dignity. During a period of three years, the Lord saw this harvest grow to three hundred followers, a considerable number, considering the difficulties encountered at the beginning. Let us mention a few noticeable cases, since we can not record them all.

We should not pass by the first among them to stretch out his hands to God, who was calling him. He was a man of seventy who, more than once before that, felt that he was called to the faith, but could not accept it because he had a faltering memory and did not know how to read. By diligent study and application he overcame both of these difficulties, and they afterwards called him "Savior," because he counseled others of his own age and led them into the Church.

Some of the pagans could not put up with these defections from the cult of images, and chiefly because they realized that those who were abandoning the cult were considered to be its leaders. Many of them went to the houses of the new converts and, in almost a menacing manner, demanded an explanation of what the people were saying about them. The answer was that now they adored only one God of heaven and earth, and that henceforth they wanted to have nothing to do with the infernal monsters who dragged down their followers into eternal fires. Their visitors warned them to remember that their names were inscribed in the records of the temple, and that they should not be casting aside all the service they had rendered to the idols, and thus losing a great benefit. But they remained firm and said that so far as they were concerned, both their names and their services could be deleted from the records, and from memory, adding that they were now certain of one thing, namely, that they would adore one God, and repudiate all other cults. The others then warned them that their gods would seek vengeance for this before long. So it was that the new converts came off victorious and dismissed their unfortunate critics. One of them was asked if he retained any ill feeling because of the abuse he had received, and he answered, "Only compassion, because they are in error and they do not realize it."

The converts were always constant in holding to their obligations. One of them, who in this instance was particularly favored by the grace of God, succeeded in changing the mind of a young man who was especially devoted to the idols. As he would listen to neither reason nor counsel, the neophyte asked him at least to read a commentary on the Christian faith and then to make up his mind as he saw fit. This he decided to do, but the Devil evidently decided to frighten him away from making any progress. When he took the book into his hands he began to tremble and was so affected by his shaking that he could not read. In his fright he handed the book back to the neophyte and his trembling ceased. This happened three or four times in the presence of others and of his mother, and each time with the same result. The boy's parent frightened by this unusual happening and fearing that something worse might beset her son, asked the neophyte if he would take the boy to the preacher from the far west, to ask for protection against his enemy who was so persistent. With that, the new Christian thought of bringing the mother to Christ also, and he persuaded her, much against her inclination, to take all the idols out of her home, and to give them to him for transportation to his house, including a small one which she wanted to keep out of love for her son. Then he gave the book of commentaries back to the boy who held it without trembling and with nothing unusual happening. Both the son and the mother became catechumens, were duly instructed in the faith, and came to Christ in the sacrament of baptism.

The effect of divine grace would seem to be no less evident in the following case. Another neophyte had persuaded a friend of his to accept a catechism, but when his friend learned from it that he had to do away with his idols, he could not bring himself to treating them so harshly. So he went back, returned the Catechism to the disappointed neophyte and started home again, feeling sad about the whole affair. On his way, he met a pagan friend with whom he decided to share his sorrow by telling him the whole story. Later on, by the grace of God, who knows his own, he decided to read the catechism, accepted its enlightenment, resolved without further delay to go through with what he had happily begun, and invited the neophyte to come to his house. "Now," he said, "you will see how serious I am about doing what I have decided upon," and removing all the idols from their thrones of majesty on an altar, he put them in a basket and sent them to the Mission House. He did this as a pledge of his faith, which he sent on in advance, until such time as he could come for instruction, after he had concluded a business affair, which would suffer from delay. This man lived about five miles away from the Mission Center.

One day a neophyte came to Father Nicolo, complaining that his wife, who was still a pagan, in order to insure a safe delivery, had saved one of the idols he was burning. The Father told him to replace the idol Choimae with a picture of the Mother of God, and to ask his wife to repeat seven Our Fathers and seven Hail Marys every day, in honor of the seven feasts of our Blessed Mother. The husband's authority prevailed; their son was born with unusual ease on the feast of the Presentation of the Virgin Mary and, no doubt, with her special assistance. This event resulted in the whole family becoming Christian and led to a special devotion to the Blessed Virgin, which consisted in one of the family attending Mass every Saturday in her honor and bringing candles or incense to burn on the altar.

We shall limit the number of examples, lest one grow tired of their similarity. Now a word about the children. A little boy, not yet six years old, had been slapped by pagan children, about his own age. Remembering what he had heard in the recitation of the Lord's Prayer, he said, "I will forgive you as the Lord has forgiven me." Several days later, his sister, even younger than he was, surpassed his own good example. He struck her, in a moment of impatience, and she answered his blow with the same words he had repeated to the pagan children. The very thought that his little sister had taught him a better lesson than he had taught the pagans caused him to blush with shame.

There was another child, named Agnes, about five years old, whose religious devotion seemed to surpass her age. One day the pagans, with all the pomp and ostentation of their idolatry, were parading through the streets with an idol called Yncon, meaning the Prince of Darkness. The purpose in carrying this monster about was to prevent bad weather, and when they came to the house where Agnes lived, they decided to bring the idol into the house, in honor of her father, who was a prominent citizen. Unnoticed by the rest of the family, the little girl ran to the door, protesting their entrance and crying out, "We are Christians, we want nothing to do with the Prince of Darkness. Where God dwells there is no place for evil spirits or for bad weather," and with that they went away. On another occasion, the pagans were urging her father to make a donation toward defraying the expenses for a celebration they were preparing in honor of the idol that protected their street, and he handed them a copy of the first Commandment to read, saying that he was forbidden to make such a donation. They paid no attention to this and were beginning to become boisterous at his refusal, when Agnes ran into their midst, shouting, "Christians who adore God can not give anything to support the worship of idols." Such wisdom from the mouth of a child prevailed, and subdued the clamor of the idolaters. In fact, they said, it really must be true that the Christian law does forbid it, when a child of her age, who knows no deception, is so insistent upon it. From examples of faith such as these, and at such tender ages, one can readily judge how well inclined the Chinese are to accept the Christian faith, as one can also judge the harvest to be hoped for in the future, from the tender blossoms appearing in the springtime of the new born Church in China.

It was at this time that the Fathers turned their attention to the conversion of the women, which up to then seemed to be a hopeless task. Many of them were more pious than the men, as might be proven by numerous examples, which we shall omit here, as there will be occasion later to cite two or three instances of noble matrons, who gave eminent testimony of their religious piety.

After years of almost desperate hoping, the light of the Gospel had begun to shine, not only in the suburbs, but in the city as well. Here many of the common people had opened their eyes to it, and some of the aristocracy also, whether we consider their aristocracy as composed of the lettered class and the acting Magistrates, or from the viewpoint of riches and family prominence. We shall mention only two individuals, as they were outstanding examples. The first was named Cium. After acquiring his literary degree, he was appointed Magistrate but had not as yet taken over his court. He had been on familiar terms with the Fathers for some years, and in the year 1601 he decided to free himself of all delaying impediments and to enjoy the full liberty of Christianity. Under his direction, his mother and his grandmother were baptized, and afterwards, he and one of his brothers received the sacrament. His mother took the name Mary, and the grandmother chose the name Anna. He himself was not long in following the good example of his elders. Toward the beginning of the month of August of the same year he and his ten-year-old son were enrolled under the banner of Christ, to the great joy and exaltation of all the neophytes. The father was called George and the son Vitus, and they both continued to live piously, serving as examples to others by their public profession of Christianity.

It is difficult to realize to what extent the good example of this distinguished family enhanced the reputation of the Christian faith. Nor did this noble neophyte limit his piety to his own family. A few days after his reception, when the son of his deceased brother fell seriously ill, he seemed to be more interested in the boy's eternal salvation than he was in his bodily illness. The young man's mother, an ardent devotee of the idols, would not even listen to the counsel given her for the spiritual benefit of her son. Cium was then told by Father Nicolo to pay no attention to the mother, but to talk to the boy himself, saying that he could be baptized without her knowing it, and that the ceremonies, save what was necessary for the sacrament, could be deferred to another time. The young man was very well disposed to receive instructions from his uncle and when Father Nicolo came, as it were, to pay him a visit, he baptized him, and by the help of God the grace of the sacrament saved him from the threshold of death. From the very hour of his baptism he began to recover and rapidly regained his full strength and vigor. His quick recovery was a surprise to everyone, but particularly to his mother. When she learned about the baptism, by which they believed he was restored to health, she became so interested in a faith that transmitted its effects from the soul to the body, that she was won over to it. She took the name of Paula, and so joined the company of Mary and of Anna. Of these three, Anna was conspicuous for her religious devotion. She built a chapel in her home so that she could attend Mass, because the law of seclusion forbad Chinese women of her class to leave their homes. The way her chapel was decorated was in itself a sign of her piety. Afterwards she thought the chapel should not be situated so close to the kitchen; so she had it removed to another part of the house.

These three women would come together at times to talk over their Catholic religion, and when they heard of a neighbor, who was also a Christian, they invited her to join their company. They were not at all disturbed by the fact that the neighbor belonged to a lower class of people, with whom the Chinese aristocracy was not accustomed to mingle. In fact they considered that even the peasant women from the villages became their equals by the common bond of religion, and that they were no less noble because of their position in life. They invited them to their homes, to their meetings and to meals, nor did anyone criticize them for it. On the contrary, they were admired for their Christian charity. In the solution of their domestic problems they always consulted Father Nicolo. The good example of this family had a salutary effect in other homes, and the change of attitude that suddenly came over the whole city because of their influence was something extraordinary.

The other celebrity we take occasion to mention was more distinguished than the one just cited. His name was Pheu, and because of his education, his family connections and his reputation for wisdom, he was looked upon as a sort of Cato of Xaucea. He was the most prominent citizen in all public undertakings and the one to whom the city owed the most for the building of roads, for the construction of bridges and for the erection and the repair of the temples of the idols. The strong hand of God led him into the Church on the feast of Saint Jerome in the year 1603. He was on familiar terms with the Fathers for a period of eleven years, but in such a way that he seemed to pay no attention to the spiritual side of life. One day, after this long friendship, he said he felt the sparks of divine grace being kindled in his soul; but they died out, and then he fell into a state of indeliberation which lasted for four more long years. His first serious desires were occasioned by a meeting with Father Nicolo. He asked the Father why he was causing himself so much trouble, running around from one to another of the neighboring villages, and Father Nicolo answered, "Can it be that even now you don't know what prompted us to come here as willing exiles from our fatherland? Your fellow citizens here in the city seem to grow more and more obdurate with every day, in closing their ears to the truth. I go about because I want to see if, perchance, there is anyone in the villages who may be concerned about his eternal salvation. This I want you to realize, namely that all men are equal before God, and the differences which men create between men, really have no solid foundation for their existence." These words, by the grace of God, really touched his heart. So much so indeed, that he never forgot them, as he himself asserted. Just at that time he had to undertake a voyage to the court of Pekin, where he was very cordially received by Father Ricci, with whom he was acquainted. Here he noticed how highly the Chief Magistrates esteemed the Fathers, who were all but despised in Xaucea, and he later felt it his duty to address the Magistrates in convention, in favor of the Fathers, in order to do away with the clouds of suspicion that always hung over the name of a foreigner. After he saw the display of Christianity at the royal court in Pekin, he returned home and spread the news all around, as to what he had seen, and his effort did much toward easing the position of the Fathers in Xaucea and conciliating the good will of the people.

On his return, Father Nicolo again endeavored to persuade Pheu to become a Christian, but there were two big impediments in the path of his struggling will. The first was relative to Divine Providence, which, as he thought, either could not or did not promote God's law, if indeed Christianity were the law of God. His second difficulty had its origin in his own haughty character. He could not consent to humble or belittle himself, according to the Chinese custom, when selecting a teacher, if that teacher were a foreigner. He submitted these two restraining difficulties to a Christian friend, named Luke, who untied both knots so cleverly that he finally threw up his hands. Relative to the first difficulty, he explained that even Confucius the Prince of philosophers, could not escape the criticism of his enemies, and he reminded his friend that their own Chinese philosophers teach that God first tries a man by various tests before selecting him to do great things. As to the second impediment, he said that there really was nothing in it to object to. He said the Fathers were not accustomed to comport themselves as masters, nor were they at all interested in the ceremonies accompanying the selection of a teacher. Their only purpose, as he explained it, was to bring their pupils to God, the Master of all mortals. They spent the whole day together and their conversation at their evening meal, which lasted well into the night, was all on this particular religious subject.

On the following day Pheu came with his friend Luke, to visit the Fathers and to make his final declaration, which was all the more happily received because of its long postponement. He went through a course of instruction and at the time of his baptism, he took the name Stephen, which Father Nicolo had promised him, when he became a Christian. His conversion became a matter of general talk in the city, and word was spread about that there could no longer be any doubt about the Christian law, once it had been accepted by the Cato of Xaucea, after he had studied it for so many years. The fruit looked forward to from this particular tree was quite up to the expectations of those by whom it was cultivated.

Just at this time a catastrophe occurred, which proved the salutary effects of the Christian law and showed the charity that existed among the new converts. The house of one of the neophytes took fire. It was situated in the midst of a hostile neighborhood, which had turned against this man because he had given up the worship of idols. The neighbors could very easily have helped to save the house, but by general consent they refused to. "Let those dogs burn," they said, "who have deserted their gods." The house was burned to the ground but the inhabitants all escaped. Some nearby neophytes came running to lend assistance, but they were too late. What they could not save, however, they restored in abundance. They all contributed what they could to the rebuilding of the home. Some gave money, some tiles and others brought lumber. Workmen contributed their labor and would accept no wages because they were working for a fellow Christian. When the house was finished they furnished it so completely that one was tempted to quote the poet who said, "Ah, ha! It looks as if he had burned down his house." The new house was better built and more imposing. What the fire had destroyed, the flame of charity restored.

As in the city, so in the country, zeal for the faith was increasing with the number of converts. It seemed to the hundred Christians in the village of Cin-Cun that they should build a church of their own. They held a conference with Father Nicolo, selected an ample lot of ground, and the church was built in a surprisingly short time. On the twentieth of April in the year above mentioned, Father Nicolo celebrated the first Mass here, with as great a display as he could arrange. After the Mass, he preached a sermon on the difference between a Catholic Church and a temple of the idols, and at the end of the discourse the congregation knelt and prayed in thanksgiving to God for the gift they had received. A committee of four prefects was formed to take care of the church and of Christian interests. A bronze bell was set up to summon the people to services, and a plentiful supply of holy water was furnished for distribution to the congregation, to be used in case of sickness, and as a ready help in other difficulties. A calendar was also displayed, so the people would know the holy days and church feasts. This venture proved of interest to the pagans as well as to the Christians, with the result that some of them were afterwards converted. Everyone present at the solemn opening of the church went away deeply impressed.

The faith was gradually finding its way into various villages. A Christian, named Mario, carried it into one. While he was visiting friends, he spoke about the Christian religion and interested many, especially an old man who was the village leader. This man was infirm and what he could not do himself, he did through his son and one of his cousins. He sent them to invite Father Nicolo to come and see him, and also sent a horse with appropriate trappings to facilitate the Father's travel. Father Nicolo went, with Mario, and as soon as he appeared the old man put several questions to him, that were subtle enough and quite appropriate. Twice during his visit he engaged in debates of a very solemn nature, with others who were interested. The old man and his whole family were baptized and he took the name of Paul. While Father Nicolo was still occupied on this visit, another messenger arrived, saying that there was a sick man living about two miles away, who wanted to be baptized, one who had formerly known him. So the Missionary hastened to his house, for fear this soul might be lost. Here he was surprised to find others who were sufficiently instructed to receive the sacrament, and before leaving he had thirty new converts. One of these was a very old lady, who had lived to that day, as it would seem, by a special grace of God. Time overtook her just after she was baptized, and the sacrament was her introduction to a better and to a much longer life.

18. Darker Days at Xaucea

THE GATE was large and open wide, as the Apostles said, but the enemy were numerous. When Father Ricci left Xaucea to establish a new settlement, the Reverend Official Visitor of the Society of Jesus was of the opinion that when the Fathers were securely established elsewhere, they should close the Mission at Xaucea. He was of this opinion because of the unhealthy climate, because of the continual trouble arising there, and also because of the sparse hope of reaping a spiritual harvest in that vicinity. That decision had already been made but when the fruits of the labors we have just described began to appear, the question was again brought up for consultation and it was unanimously decided that the promising prospects should not be abandoned because of climate, or because of threatening disturbance. And so the Mission was retained, with the results already mentioned. One may gather from the following how crafty the Devil was in scheming to destroy the pioneer work of this mission, and how much more powerful was Almighty God in dissipating the interventions of the impostor.

There was nothing that caused the Fathers more trouble than the implacable war waged by the Christian law against the worship of false gods. Easy as it was to teach the Chinese that they should worship the one God of Heaven as the supreme deity, it was equally difficult to persuade them to take down all their idols from their majestic thrones, as being wholly unworthy of any attention. They could not rid themselves of the idea that the idols could be considered as ministers of the true God and honored with the same veneration as the Christian saints.

Despite the fact that this people had been wrapped in the darkness of paganism for so many centuries, they never became so perverted, as poets have related in their fables, as to look to their gods for support in doing evil. It has been said of this people that the greater part of them pass their lives in a continual and an amazing practice of the moral virtues, which may or may not be true. That makes little difference, but it is true that apart from that, even when they accept the truth and the sanctity of the Christian faith, they still want to retain the memory of their former holy ones, handed down from their ancestors.

Pagan customs also increase the difficulty of conversion. Those who are to become Christians are strictly forbidden to worship in the public temples, which is difficult enough to stop, but the difficulty is only increased in each individual home. Here they have their lares and penates, in whose company they were born and reared and whom they honor as patrons. Now they must be taken down and removed from their oratories and treated, as it seems to this people, very harshly. There are some who can not bear to see the idols go up in fire and smoke, especially in the domestic fireplace, so they throw them into the river, whence they can never be recovered. All of which to the pagan mentality seems to be not only wholly unnecessary, but quite inhuman as well.

Not the least of the other difficulties arises from their custom of parading their idols through the streets and soliciting money from everyone for the support of the one they are exhibiting. The neophytes have done much to overcome this problem but Father Nicolo was particularly bothered by it at that time. The Chinese have an idol called Hoaquan, from the belief that it presides over the protection of man's eyesight. For this reason it has a third eye in the middle of its forehead. One day this monster was being carried through the streets in procession and with considerable noise, in order to collect money to build a temple for it. Arriving in front of the Mission House, they halted, by way of honoring the Master of the house, who would have passed up the honor very willingly. Before they could be stopped, the idol was placed in the front hallway. The noise they caused attracted Father Nicolo, who hurried into their midst and asked them what they wanted. They took it amiss that he didn't even stop to salute their three-eyed Argus, because in other houses to which they were admitted, it was customary to honor the god with lighted candles and incense and numerous ceremonies, as well as with gifts of money. Since they had come to collect the money, they decided to overlook the seeming irreverence, and to make their petition. This Father Nicolo answered by saying that he admired their natural inclination to piety, but that he sincerely regretted that they were mistaken in their choice of a deity. As for himself, he added, since he adored the only one true God, he was forbidden to promote the worship of idols in any way whatsoever. That was enough to arouse their insolence and to rend the quiet of the place with cries insisting upon his giving what they had come for.

This display and clamor attracted one of the literati, who wanted to appear as a friend of Father Nicolo, and advised him to placate the mob by ceding to their request. He reminded the Missionary that he was a stranger living in a foreign land, and as he had to raise his voice to be heard, Father Nicolo raised his also in reply. He told them that whenever he had been called upon for a donation, he had given liberally, for public works in general, for the paving of streets, for the repair of bridges and for other such things, but for the cultivation of idol worship he could not give even a straw, and they could not even hope for that much, because it was contrary to the law of his faith to do so, whether the gift were much or little. The so-called literatus saw that the refusal was not due to any spirit of avarice; so he sought to settle the matter with a spurious distinction, by advising the Father to give something to the people, not to the idol. But Father Nicolo did not approve of that either, and for various reasons. First, because he thought it would have been illicit; again, it would have been an incentive to those who thought it licit; and finally, because a definite attitude at that time would go far toward putting an end to such amazing intrusions. After an exchange of words, not daring to assert themselves by force, they took their blind god-of-the-eyes out of the house and went away feeling ashamed and repulsed, but hurling back a thousand uncomplimentary epithets. One may surmise from this how they plagued the neophytes, who were formerly accustomed to give donations, when they were so exacting with strangers who professed a different faith. Such difficulties as these were universal and continual. Let us now enumerate a few examples, with special circumstances, but not of long duration.

One day Father Nicolo went out into a district to gather in the spiritual harvest of several months' standing, only to find that it had been intersown with cockle. That was done by an enemy with the assistance of two of the rustic literati, members of the local Academy of Country Teachers. When they learned that some of their disciples had gone over to the Christian religion, without consulting them, they became so angry that they gave vent to a lot of injurious chatter about Christianity and about the man who was preaching it, and their anger blazed up anew when they heard he was coming. Father Nicolo sent word ahead, saying that he was on his way and ready to prove what he was preaching, and that in the presence of anyone who wished to hear him. They, however, willing to hear anything but the truth, turned on the people, in an effort to stir up a public demonstration, calling them harsh names and accusing them of being lazy. Their purpose was to induce the people to send a public written complaint, against a foreign enemy of the idols, to the Mayor of the City, whose jurisdiction extended to the suburbs. Here, the Father showed considerable courage in quieting the disturbance. He sent a messenger to the troublemakers advising them to write into their complaint that the doctrine he would explain was the very same doctrine which the Mayor had already seen and approved and praised, and that the rest of the local Magistrates had already read it and given it the seal of their approval. That put an end to the threatened tumult. Having heard what the Magistrates thought, those who were about to enter the dangerous charge, were glad to forgo it. As a result of this episode, not only was Christianity more at ease and at liberty in that district, but its champion ventured upon a successful excursion into another section, from which he always returned by nightfall. The two local literati who were responsible for the commotion lost their influence and quietly retired to their teaching.

Father Nicolo returned from the experience just described only to find that the whole town was in a dither about the Mission. It had been learned, from letters lately received, that Father Ricci and his companions, en route to Pekin, had been arrested and cast into chains by the eunuch Mathan. The excitement was general and the belief was that the Fathers would be condemned to death or to perpetual imprisonment. This lowering cloud, however, was dissipated by the arrival of the noble neophyte, mentioned some time ago. He said he had passed through the village where the Fathers were detained. At that time he was not a convert and he wondered why the Fathers carried around that sad image of a man attached to a cross, which Mathan vainly alleged was his reason for turning against them. It was then also that the neophyte George dispelled their fears, for just at that time he and his brother and a cousin came to the Mission House, making considerable display on their arrival, which started a rumor that he was about to become a Christian. That in itself was enough to frighten the troublemakers and to check the wiser critics, as they would not dare to disturb anyone, with such protectors. From that time on the Fathers preached the Gospel with more liberty.

A short time afterwards, the official Government Inspector of the Province arrived and he appointed as his Assessors, or assistants, men from whom there seemed to be nothing to fear, so far as the Mission was concerned. One of these was the Mayor of the City of Xaucea, an intimate friend of the Fathers. He was the man, who one day received a copy of the ten commandments from Father Nicolo, and was so moved by the holiness of these precepts and by the height of virtue they prescribed, that he remarked, "The man who would keep that law, could never hold the position of Magistrate." That judgment was pronounced in an open court, and as this was well known to those who were opposed to the Mission, it caused them to cease from any scheming against it. Concerning the second assessor, Father Nicolo had heard nothing, and he took it for granted that this man was not familiar with the history of the Mission, but in this he was somewhat mistaken.

This man had seen the Fathers at work in the Royal Court in Pekin and had frequently held familiar conversation with Father Ricci. When he came to Xaucea and learned that a companion of Father Matthew was at work there, he immediately sent him a goodly present of provisions, which the Mayor of the City had just given him, and he had them transported to the Mission House, with considerable show, through the principal streets of the town. They went to call on him and he told them all about what Father Ricci was doing. On his official return visit, he said he had worked with the Fathers in Pekin, and that two things in particular attracted his attention. First, that when they were separately questioned, they gave exactly the same answers, whence it was concluded that they believed in the same truth. Secondly, that whenever they took part in a conference they never forgot to mention their God, whence he judged that they were so filled with the spirit of their God, that they wished to pour out this fullness upon everyone else.

Friendship with the Magistrates put caution into the minds of the troublemakers and deterred them from causing annoyance, lest it redound upon their own heads. But they would not have been themselves if they had kept quiet for long, so those who couldn't bite began to bark. Referring to the Chinese Christian catechism, they boasted that the law of the Great Occident, was all contained in four little pages, which proved that it was something barbarous, whereas the great tomes of idols were elegantly written, with formulas for praying and solemn directions for driving out evil spirits. Who, they asked, would be so silly as to prefer the little book? This was the question they put to the neophytes, whenever they met them, and their general answer was to say that there was a great deal more to Christianity, but because of the small number of Fathers there, and the fact that they were learning a new language, they didn't as yet have time to put it all into Chinese. This, to their critics seemed to be a trumped up and a feeble answer, and the neophytes, growing weary of being insulted, sent a rather extraordinary letter of petition to Father Longobardo asking him to protect the law he was preaching against such opprobrium. Up to that time he had been so occupied with his duties that he could find no time for writing. Now, for fear he might seem to be neglecting what they called opprobrium, and so as not to turn a deaf ear to his children, he set himself to writing several works, which proved to be very helpful to the converts, and a gag to their garrulous tormentors. He was assisted in his writing by a Chinese scholar, who was acting as instructor to the Fathers.

The first tracts appeared in the form of a prayerbook, with prayers for various occasions, including those for a funeral service and for burial, all done in Chinese characters, but without changing the Latin terminology, save where the change in language demanded it. This was a great relief for the converts, even though they did not understand the text, which also happens in Europe at times, with some who read the divine office in Latin with a feeling of piety, though they may not have a full appreciation of the text they are reading. Later on, he added instructions for confession, a formula for the examination of conscience, devotions to the Blessed Virgin, excerpts on the virtues taken from the Lives of the Saints, and the well known story of Barlaam and Josaphat, as told by Saint John Damascene. At the same time some of the other Fathers were producing various written works, among which was the very useful booklet which Father Giovanni Soeiro published in Nancian, for the instruction of those who were aspiring to be Christians. Most of this book he wrote in bed rather than at his desk. Afflicted as he was with a slow consumptive fever, he knew of no repose while the lamp of life was still burning, and it was not long before it was burned out by the fever. We say nothing here about Father Matthew's catechism, or about the calendar of feast days, which appeared very opportunely at that time. These and other such writings served the converts in good stead to offset the charges of their tormentors.

The Devil's envy knows no end. It was at this same time that a slanderous rumor spread through the town, with the usual speed of that kind of gossip. The report was that the Fathers had been chased out of their old home in Sciauquin, and that all the converts to Christianity there had been severely punished, but this false rumor was soon put to rest by the opportune arrival of a convert from Sciauquin. This whole story was probably the product of the wandering imagination of a young man, whose father was a public Magistrate. He was passing through Xaucea and, speaking of the Fathers, he said they were the foreigners who built a tower at Sciauquin, several years ago, with mysterious caverns underneath it, in which they committed horrible crimes, and when they were discovered they saved themselves by flight. It is difficult to realize how anyone could place credence in a silly story of fugitives being in hiding in that province, almost within sight of Sciauquin and under the particular Viceroy who, as everyone knew, had sent the Fathers to Xaucea, with a written permit to build a house there. It was the light of this truth that dispelled the threatening darkness in this particular instance.

The following incident was somewhat more troublesome. Certain stage players came from Macao to Xaucea, and during the days of the market-fair, they painted posters and put on shows ridiculing everything which the Chinese disliked in the Portuguese. Some of the signs they painted were vulgar, and to omit the manner in which they endeavored to provoke the people to laughter by making fun of the short costumes of the Portuguese, we shall mention how they found fault with those who professed Christianity. They pictured men saying the rosary in church, and wearing swords in their belts, and drew awkward caricatures of men adoring God, on only one knee, of men fighting a duel, and of gatherings in which women were present with men, which the Chinese abhor. Such were the themes of their displays and such the tenor of their plays, which said everything and omitted nothing that they thought would ridicule Christianity. However, these abject villains could not undermine the authority of the Christian law, without God, at the same time, making amends for the injury. The City Magistrates, to a man, praised the Christian law, and a few days after the players arrived, much to the surprise of the many who saw it, on the same street and right in front of the place where they were playing their anti-Christian antics, Father Nicolo happened to meet one of the most serious of the Magistrates, who got out of his gestatorial chair and greeted him with all the ceremonial rites of their customary politeness. Another Magistrate did honor to the Father, at the same place, by accompanying him as he walked along the street.

The incidents we have recounted thus far might be considered as trivial. The following was more serious. There was something going on, of which the Fathers were wholly unaware, and which might well have continued unnoticed, save that Heaven was protecting their cause, and repressed it; unless we are to judge that human industry was somewhat accountable for its remedy. The house at Xaucea, as we have noted, was built on a plot of land close to a pagan temple, and its proximity to this had always been a cause of dissatisfaction to the idol worshippers, but they had concealed their discontent because of their fear of the Magistrates. This attitude lasted during that period when the Fathers were not so occupied with the evil of idol worshipping, but when the question became a common topic for argument because of the increasing number of converts, the idol worshippers could no longer restrain their animosity. The burning of idols and the odor arising from them and being wafted toward the temple, had become too much for them. To them this meant the spreading fame of Christianity, which had ceased to be a secret. In conspiracy with many of their followers, they wrote out a charge against the Fathers and presented it to the Lieutenant Governor, a venal politician, who accepted this serious charge for prosecution.

Fortunately, at that time, there arrived in the city a certain high ranking Magistrate, who belonged to the order of the Tauli, as the Chinese called it. It was his custom to call a general convocation of the people, at stated times, and to exhort them to the practice of virtue. At the close of his address, the prosecutor of the charge against the Fathers fell on his knees before him and told him that certain foreign priests had taken over part of the land belonging to their temple, and were accustomed to gather the simple people together in trouble-making crowds. Then he begged him to put an end to this threat to the public safety.

During the time of this meeting, the Fathers, who knew nothing about what was going on in the temple, were busy decorating their domestic chapel, in expectation of a visit from the member of the Tauli, who lost no time in coming to see them. Father Nicolo had met him previously on two occasions. What, do you imagine, was the Magistrate's reply to the prosecutor, and whoever would have dreamed of seeing the Lieutenant Governor, covered with shame and confusion because of a verdict against him, in favor of foreigners? It was nothing short of the protection of Divine Providence. In presence of the assembled multitude, he said he was convinced that the preachers from the distant west were good men, that they had built their house on that particular spot with permission of the Viceroy, and at their own expense, and that they harmed no one and asked nothing, either of the people or of the Magistrates. As to the crowds they had gathered together up to the present, he said no one should be surprised, if honest men, over a course of years, make a host of friends and of intimates. The Lieutenant Governor had no reply to this. With some evident confusion, he offered the customary salutation and withdrew to the side, where he joined the other Magistrates who were present.

The Tauli member, then taking his cue from the incident concerning the Fathers, addressed the other Magistrates, somewhat as follows. Let us remember that we have been specially favored by Heaven; we who take pride in the possession of both literary and honorary degrees. The office we hold has been entrusted to us by the King, for the government of the people and in his name. Do nothing, therefore, unworthy of Heaven or of the King. It behooves us to avoid that cupidity which persecutes the innocent for the sake of gain. What is born in evil will end in evil, without benefit to ourselves or to our posterity. With these and similar pronouncements made, he dismissed the crowd, whose greatest surprise was to see that his patronage went to the foreigners rather than to a Magistrate who held a high public office in the district.

From the temple, their patron of the Tauli went directly to the Fathers' residence, together with the other Magistrates and followed by most of the temple audience. Father Nicolo, wearing the costume of the literati, met him in the vestibule. He was surprised at his visitor's exceptional politeness, and up to that time Father Nicolo knew nothing of what had happened in the temple.

Coming into the sparsely stocked library, the visitor took up a book and pointed to something in it, which he wanted explained. Father Longobardo told him that that was the permit, granted by the Magistrate to whom that faculty pertained, for the publication of the book. This, he informed him, was a European custom, to prevent the spread of error and of statements contrary to good morals. Then turning to the prosecutor of the charge, who had come in with him, the Tauli Magistrate said, "How orderly must everything be conducted in a country that so carefully supervises the publication of books." From the library they went to the chapel, but they could not open the door because someone had locked it and maliciously stolen the key. A servant was sent to open a window, but that too was locked. Seeing this, the member of the Tauli was about to leave, but fearing that the incident might serve as a pretext for spreading a rumor that they were hiding something which they did not want him to see, they asked him to remain a little longer. They said they were particularly anxious to have him see the chapel because they had decorated it, in honor of his coming. Father Longobardo then had someone break the lock on the door and his visitor thanked him for his consideration, entered the chapel and examined everything, asked a number of questions, which we omit for the sake of brevity, and bowing to the various statues, left the chapel and took his departure. Suffice it to say that he did all that so everyone, and particularly the prosecutor, would realize that he was justified in defending the Fathers, in his speech in the temple. He openly expressed his displeasure at the theft of the key, which was later found among the shrubs in the garden, where the thief had evidently thrown it for fear of being apprehended. For some time after he left the house, he was complaining, saying that he was surprised to find that there were some who insisted upon making trouble for those who profess to be virtuous and law abiding, especially when such people are foreigners, and this he said in the hearing of many.

After the crowd had dispersed, some friends came in to congratulate the Fathers on having such an influential patron, and they told them everything that had taken place in the temple, all of which was surprising news to their unsuspecting hosts. This man's friendship was of long duration and the Prosecutor, himself, afterwards endeavored in various ways, to make amends for the harm he had attempted. He went to Pekin, some time later, and while there he visited the Fathers and told Father Ricci about his more recent relations with those at Xaucea. They were both careful not to touch upon the question of the former accusation. It is not good policy to turn away a former malcontent who seems to give evidence of wishing to become a friend.

Despite all that had happened in Xaucea, the Enemy of mankind was not as yet ready to put aside his scheming and his hatred. A long and a severe drought had come upon the land and the crops were in serious danger. Many prayers were being offered up in the city, a fast was ordered, for some days the markets were closed, candles were lighted and incense burned in front of the houses, flattering some one or other of the idols to favor the people with rain. The substitute and assistant to the Mayor of the town marched on foot, in procession with the elders of the people, clad in the dress of the poor, making genuflections and frequently bowing toward certain places in the Heavens and begging a downpour of rain. All this was in vain, and even the sacrifices to the idols, in perpetual chorus, got no response from their deaf gods. So they gave up hope in the city gods, and for the occasion they brought in a celebrated monster from the country. Its name was Locu. They paraded it about, bowed before it and made offerings to it, but like its counterparts it remained deaf to their pleading. It was this occasion that gave rise to the saying, "Locu is growing old." The same unholy piety was burning high in the suburbs, and in one settlement, where there were many converts, the pagans went to consult an old fortune teller. "What is happening," they asked her, "why is it that none of our gods will listen to us?" And she answered, "The goddess Quomyn is angry, because every day she is having her back burned." The reference was to the burning of the statue idols of this goddess by the neophytes. The effect of this oracular reply was that they became as violently incensed against the Christians, as if they were burning the crops with their own hands.

Some of the malcontents conspired to do away with Father Longobardo as the author of the public calamity, if he dared to return to their village, and also with Mario the convert, who was his constant companion. This was reported by one of the converts, and they both hastened to the place, so as not to appear, through a sense of fear, to be abandoning the converts who were in grave danger from the angry mob, and also so as not to miss an opportunity for martyrdom. When they arrived they found their flock being harassed in daily quarrels but returning the enemy's arguments with as much animation as they came. The converts asked the pagans where their gods were going to get water to make it rain, if they couldn't even save their own idols from being burned, and if they could control the rain, why didn't they use it to put out the fires in which the idols were being destroyed? Moreover, they said, "if it does not rain for us, why don't your gods make it rain only for you, or in those places where there are no converts to Christianity burning up the miserable idols?" These verbal battles went on until finally it rained so hard that the fields were literally soaked and the drought came to an end together with the thirst for Christian blood. Gradually the conspirators became more quiet, or at least more soft spoken, saying that everyone should be permitted to practice the religion that appealed to him. This great change was brought about by the exhortation given by the Tauli Magistrate in the temple, and also from the fact that he had taken the Fathers under his patronage.

Such was the authority of the rulers over both parties in dispute, a blessing secured for the Mission by the gentle Providence of God over the infant Church; not permitting it to be tried beyond its powers, but gradually advancing its progress with each successive trial.

19. Progress in Nankin

LET US NOW turn our attention to the residence in the Royal City of Nankin. There were two priests in residence there; Father Lazzaro Cattaneo, who was recalled from Nancian, and Father Giovanni Roccia. Father Cattaneo managed well and increased the harvest. He won the friendship of the Magistrates and made many converts. Among them were Martin, the son of the first convert, Paul, his wife and all the rest of the family. From Nankin Father Lazzaro returned to Macao, because of ill health, and his Father Assistant, who took over the post and was zealous in following the same lines of development, made more than a hundred converts, within the first two years of his sojourn. It was during this time that Paul, the leading convert of Nankin, died at the age of seventy-four; a man whose extraordinary zeal for the spread of Christianity gave promise of a high award in heaven. From the time he became a Christian, due to his intense devotion, he often expressed a wish to live on for a few years more, so that he might teach others, by his example and his authority, to follow in his footsteps. Like the pious matrons in Xaucea, he built a beautiful chapel in his home, so his women folks could attend Mass, and next to it added another room, as a reception room for converts. The chapel was just completed when the Lord called him, overcome as he was by old age, but his sickness could not prevent him from being present at the first Mass celebrated in his chapel. Several times in his last illness he insisted upon making a general confession. Paul was the first one to be baptized in that city, and also the first one to profit by the sacrament of penance, and he died peacefully and contented.

Martin, the son of Paul, was as gallant as his father. He was the first one in this city who dared to omit certain funeral rites, forbidden by the Church, and to conduct a strictly Christian funeral, despite the criticism it evoked, and his example was followed by many others. There was no lack of objectors who found fault with what he did, each in his own way. Before his father's funeral and against the counsel of those advising him to the contrary, he did a very courageous thing, considering the circumstances in which it was done. It has already been noted that after a death, the Chinese sometimes keep the corpse in the house for a long time before burial. Departing from this custom and facing numerous protests, Martin was the first one to make a public declaration of his father's faith and at the same time of his own. He posted a sign in a public place, where everyone could read it, stating that his father had repudiated the worship of idols and embraced the Christian faith, also, that in his last will and testament he forbad the presence at his funeral of all ministers of the idol worshipping sect and of all or any of their rites or ceremonies. This sign, as it stated, was to attest that he belonged to the same faith as his father, and that he was hereby fulfilling his father's last wish and command. The venerable old man was buried from the Mission House, with full Christian burial ceremonies. This was the first time the converts ever saw a Christian funeral and they found in it a great source of consolation. Father Cattaneo returned about this time, somewhat recovered from his illness, and he brought with him a beautiful statue of the Blessed Virgin, which he placed in a new chapel, and which served to increase the devotion of the neophytes. Before the year was over, however, he had a recurrence of his ailment and was forced to return to Macao.

We come now to what we consider to be an extraordinary conversion to an infant Church. There was an old man of seventy-eight, living in the neighborhood of the Mission Residence. He was Chief of the Military Prefects, before his retirement, after which his position and his properties were transferred to his oldest son. His interest in Christianity was awakened by his servants, and it was not long before he became a convert. When the time came to do away with the household idols, his son entered a vehement protest, asserting that the father had constituted him head of the family, and that he wanted to regulate family affairs according to his own way of thinking. The dissension was long drawn out, but the intensity of the faith of the parent and the grace of God finally conquered. With renewed ardor and with his son present, the old gentleman called two of his convert servants, summoned one of the Fathers, and told them to take every one of the miserable household gods over to the Mission House and burn them. This caused the son to become very angry, but he dared not use force, for fear of his father. Instead, he poured out his indignation on the servants, who left the house bearing a double burden of idols and of contumely. The old man accompanied them to the Mission House, where he witnessed the burning of the idols, and was then baptized with an increase of satisfaction, corresponding to the growing desire with which he had sought it. Later on, the son set aside his animosity and was reconciled with the Fathers, but he was not interested in seeking a way to salvation.

There was another man, named Ciu, who fell sick some time after he had been baptized, and realizing that his life was in danger, he asked to confess his post-baptismal faults, and to fortify his departure with the holy Eucharist. He, too, left orders that he should be buried with Christian ceremonies, and his wife, to whom he committed this request, followed his example by adopting his faith and by sharing it with the rest of her family. Such examples as these had a very salutary effect on all the converts.

The number of Christians was also increasing in the nearby villages. A chapel was erected in the home of one of the more distinguished converts, and his wife, who became the sole custodian, kept it in excellent order. At times the Fathers went there to celebrate Mass and to instruct converts, who were so well cared for at this house that there was scarcely ever an absentee. In addition to her care for the neophytes, this lady also extended her charity to the Fathers, as her namesake, Martha, of the Gospel, did to the Lord.

It was during the second year of Father Cattaneo's sojourn here that something of real importance happened. Paul, the most prominent luminary of this Church, whose death we have just recorded, became a disciple of Christ, at the Mission House. He was one of those men from whom great things are to be expected, and Heaven had ordained that he should ornament this infant church. Born in the City of Scian-hai, about eight days journey from Nankin, in the Province of Nankin, he was a distinguished intellectual, admirably endowed, and naturally inclined to good. What he had been especially looking for, as a member of the sect of the literati, was something about which they are particularly reticent, namely, definite knowledge about the next life and about the immortality of the soul. There is no sect whatever, among the Chinese that utterly rejects this immortality. He had heard much about celestial glory and happiness in the weird hallucination of the idol worshippers, but his active mind could repose in nothing but the truth. In 1597 he gained first place in the examinations for the degree of Licentiate at Pekin, an honor which carried the very highest prestige. In his quest for the Doctorate he was not so fortunate and he counted his failure as a special grace of God, asserting that this was the cause of his salvation. He had only one son and his great fear was that with that son the family might come to an end, an eventuality which the Chinese, somewhat unreasonably, look upon as a catastrophe. With the acquisition of the faith came good fortune; two grandsons and success in his examination for the Doctorate. This examination took place four years after he became a licentiate, but in it he was the victim of an unfortunate incident. By an oversight he was admitted to the examination as number three hundred and one, whereas the law limited the number to three hundred, and so his paper was rejected. With that, not wishing to face the humiliation of returning to his own people, he withdrew to the Province of Canton.

It was here at Xaucea that he first became acquainted with the Fathers, in a conversation with Father Cattaneo, who was living at that Mission at the time, and it was here also that he first made a reverence to a crucifix.

Paul met Father Ricci in Nankin in the year 1600, and spoke to him about the Christian religion, of which he had heard something, previously. This was only a transient meeting, as Paul was in a hurry to get back to his home, and at that time he probably heard no more than that the God in whom Christians believe, is the first principle of all things. It seems, however, as if God had reserved this man to himself for enlightenment. The mystery of the Most Holy Trinity was, in a way, represented to him in a dream. He saw three chapels in a temple. In the first he saw the figure of a person, whom someone present called God the Father. In the second he saw another figure, wearing a royal crown, whom he heard called, God the Son, and he heard a voice telling him to bow down in reverence before these forms. In the third chapel he saw nothing and made no obeisance. It may be that God did not wish to represent the Holy Spirit to a pagan, by the form of a dove, to which we are accustomed, in order not to offend one who was still a pagan, because the Chinese, no matter what sect they may belong to, never pay reverence to any deity unless that deity be represented in human form. Later on, when the doctrine of the Church, relative to the Holy Trinity, was being explained to him at Nankin, he remembered this dream, but said nothing about it, because on another occasion he had heard from one of the Fathers that we should not believe in dreams. Again, a long time afterwards in Pekin, he heard Father Matthew say that in the past God revealed many things to his servants, in dreams. Then he asked the Father if it were permitted to place credence in some dreams, and with considerable exaltation, he narrated the dream just mentioned.

To return to his conversion, in the year 1603 he returned to Nankin on a business trip and went to visit Father Giovanni Roccia. He bowed before the statue of the Blessed Virgin, as he entered the house, and on first hearing of some of the principles of Christianity, he immediately decided to embrace the Catholic faith. During that whole day and up to nightfall, he remained in peaceful contemplation of the principal articles of Christian belief. He took home a compendium of Christian Doctrine and also a manuscript copy of Father Ricci's Catechism; the text of an edition which had not as yet been published. He was so pleased with these two books that he stayed up the whole night reading them, and before he returned on the following day, he had memorized the entire Compendium of Christian Doctrine. He asked Father Roccia to explain certain passages to him, as soon as possible, because he had to return home before the end of the year, and he wanted to be baptized before going. In order to find out whether or not he really was serious about this, the Father told him that he would have to come for instruction, once a day and every day for a week, to which he replied, "Not only once, I shall come twice a day," which he did, and always arriving very promptly. If Father happened to be away when he arrived, he took his lesson from one of the Brothers, or from a house student. He was baptized the day he left for home, and from there he sent back two letters, in which he manifested very clearly how deeply he had imbibed the Doctrines of the Christian law.

Several months later, he came back to Nankin, to review the course he had taken, and he went straight to the Mission House, lest it might appear that he had visited someone else first. This time he stayed with the Fathers for two weeks, much to the joy of his hosts and to the benefit of the domestic servants. He attended the sacrifice of the Mass every day and he was continually making inquiries, for fear, as it seemed, that he might miss some point or other of Christian doctrine. He found a great consolation in going to confession whenever he returned to pay a visit, and especially so, on his way back to Pekin, to retake the examination for the Doctorate. Once he came really rejoicing and, as it were, bringing in the sheaves. He had persuaded two of the class of the literati and several friends from his district, to put aside their idol worship. He taught them their prayers, and not long afterwards they became Christians, all being baptized on the same day.

Let us close this chapter with an incident that resembles a miracle. Just beyond the outer wall of Nankin, there was a man who lay sick for six whole years with every member of his body afflicted. Father Giovanni happened to be in the vicinity, visiting some neophytes, and the sick man sent a messenger to him, announcing that he wished to become a Christian. Father hastened to his side and, as he was departing, left him a copy of the Compendium of Christian Doctrine. The sick man studied it, received instructions and was eventually baptized. The saving water of the sacrament cleansed both his soul and his body, and he gradually became well and strong. There was no one in that section of the city who did not consider his recovery to be something miraculous. But the incident gained more fame than it did spiritual results. That whole neighborhood belonged to the sect that shows its devotion to the idols by the practice of long continued fasting, and they above all others are the most tenacious of their creed and the most difficult to convert.

20. The Rector of the College of Macao
Is Assigned to the China Mission

~~~~~~

WHEN FATHER PIETRO GOMEZ died in Japan, that island and the Chinese Mission constituted a single Vice Province of the Society of Jesus. Among the first to join the China Missions, Father Gomez came as Provincial and was afterwards succeeded by Father Pasio. He had been devoted to this Mission for a long time and was intensely interested in its advancement. When the official Visitor of the Society of Jesus appointed Father Valentine Carvalho, Rector of the College at Macao, Father Emanuele Dias, ex-Rector, was left free. The few Fathers laboring in the four houses of the China Mission at that time were insufficient in number for the work to be done. Father Ricci, the Superior of the Mission had to stay at the Royal Court, a considerable distance from the other settlements, and since he could not visit these centers, a number of questions concerning the Mission, necessarily remained undecided. Father Soeiro lay ill at Nancian of a sickness that was gradually overcoming him, and so Father Emanuele Dias was commissioned to visit and to examine the three houses in the south. This visitation was to be made under the jurisdiction of Father Ricci, the Superior of the Mission, without whose permission no decision was to be acted upon. With this visitation completed, Father Dias was to remain with Father Soeiro until further notice. This appointment to visit the Mission centers came to Father Dias as to a protagonist for whom the curtain was rising for a grand performance. He had always longed for the China Mission, and as Rector of the College at Macao he was very partial to it. The rest of the Fathers were delighted with the news that he was coming, and they sent a general letter to the Father Visitor, begging him to leave Father Dias in their midst and not to deprive the Mission of so ardent a worker.

During his visits to the various centers, Father Dias discovered problems which he could not solve to his satisfaction without first consulting with Father Ricci. He called Father Cattaneo for consultation and noted down whatever was to be referred to Father Matthew, and with all the houses visited, he was called to Pekin; a move on the part of Father Ricci, which proved to be of great advantage for the domestic affairs of all branches of the Mission. His journey was made by river and without any mishaps, and as a companion he took along Brother Giacomo Niva, who was born in Japan, of Chinese parents. As a student in the Jesuit Seminary, Giacomo had acquired great skill as an artist. While still in Japan, the Father Visitor appointed him to the China Mission, and after two years noviceship, he was received into the Society of Jesus.

Father Emanuele Dias remained in Pekin for two months, during which time he and Father Ricci drew up a detailed schedule for the entire Mission. From there he returned again to the different residences in the south. Father Cattaneo went from Nankin to Nancian, as he had done several times before, because of his health. This time, he stayed at Xaucea, where he seemed to improve.

In the meantime, Father Pantoia, who was acting as companion to Father Ricci in Pekin, had learned to speak Chinese, also to read Chinese characters and to write them with great exactness. With these two at work, Christianity was advancing in the Capital City. Everyone gave ear to their preaching of the truths of the Catholic faith, and some embraced it. Not only were there converts from the lower classes but from the educated class as well. One of these, named Cho, was married to the sister of the reigning Queen; the number one wife of the reigning King. Although this man did not rank with the corresponding nobility of Europe, he was still a high dignitary in wealthy society. The two sons of the King's attending physician were also converts to the faith, and one of them had already attained to the highest rank among the literati. Among the converts there was also a schoolmaster, a relative of the President of one of the Tribunals, and with him the nephew of this same President, who first obtained permission from his uncle to become a Christian. This boy evidenced an ardent desire for the faith and he seemed to have a presentiment that he would not labor therein, once he had acquired it. He breathed out his pure soul within a month of his conversion and he was a great loss, as the Fathers had placed high hope in his future.

To the examples cited may be added the extraordinary conversion of a nobleman of the class of the literati. He was the son of a ranking Magistrate and Captain of a Chinese regiment during the Korean War. On retirement from the army he was honored by the King with a sizable pension, to be bequeathed to his offspring in perpetuum. The conquest of this warrior was not an easy matter, as he was deeply steeped in pagan error, and particularly so in the superstitious star reading of future births. It was explained to him that the Devil is frequently concerned in such sorcery by deceiving people, and persuading them, when the forecast is not verified, that this ridiculous wizardry is not wholly impractical, though in truth it is. Aroused, as it were, from a profound sleep, and led on to a real knowledge of physics and metaphysics, he opened his eyes to the truth, and being well instructed, he was baptized and became a Christian on the Feast of Saint Matthew the Apostle, in 1602, taking the name of Paul. From now on, we shall add his surname and call him Li Paul, in the frequent reference we shall make to him, so as to distinguish him from Ciu Paul whom we have already mentioned. One would have to look far for a new convert with more devotion and zeal for his faith than Li Paul, or for one who was more eager to have others share it with him. An example or two of his zeal will suffice for those who like to sample fruits that ripen prematurely.

This man had a beautiful and well stocked library and it took him three full days, with the help of the Fathers, to purge it of all books, forbidden by ecclesiastical regulations. For the most part, these were books treating of the art of divination, and many of them in manuscript form, which increased their value, both as to price and as to the labor expended in producing them. This entire collection was burned up; part of it in his own courtyard, and the rest at the Mission House, on his advice, so that everyone would know that he was seriously resolved to change his religious belief to a true and a more perfect faith. This, too, as he decided, would prevent his importunate pagan friends from trying to persuade him to further amuse himself by returning to his former folly. From a new convert he soon became a trumpeting herald of the word of God, as the Chinese frequently do. In a short time he had converted his mother, his wife, their children and the children's teacher, together with all his men and maid servants, in other words, his entire household. One of his domestics, a valet, and a stubborn individual, feeling that he was being forced by his master to follow the example of the others, swore a desperate oath that he would never give in, and sealed the oath with the most unusual sacrilege of chopping off one of his fingers and throwing it into the fire. This stubborn determination of the servant gradually melted away in the charity of the master, who not only favored and pampered him, but actually took to self-mortification and discipline and to bodily flagellation, in his petition to God for the salvation of his servant. With these aids the victory was slowly accomplished, and both the servant and his wife, who was also a servant in the house, were finally won over.

Li Paul's ardent zeal was by no means confined within his domestic walls. He directed it to his friends and to as many more as he could. If at times he was less successful, that perhaps was due to the fact that he was overenthusiastic. This was no great disadvantage, because it left no one in doubt about this great change for the better that had come over him, or about the fact that he taught more by example than by word.

He had learned much in his long study of the sects of idol worshippers, and he was able to give the Fathers no end of information which proved to be of value in aptly confuting their many errors. He was always very respectful, not only to the Fathers, but to the Brothers, to the students and even to the servants, in short, he seemed to hold as sacred everyone and everything connected with the Mission House. He built a private chapel in his home, to which the Fathers came to celebrate Mass and to instruct the household. He also sent his son to the Mission House to learn how to serve Mass, and on the occasion of the boy's first serving Mass in public, in the Mission Church, the family arranged to hold a public reception for him, somewhat after the European custom, when a newly ordained priest celebrates his first public Mass.

There was a custom introduced at the Mission Center of having the neophytes recite a formula of contrition for their sins, before receiving the sacrament of baptism. This was done before the altar and on their knees, with one of the Fathers directing those who needed the instruction. Out of this custom there developed another, practiced chiefly by some of the educated class, namely, of writing out at home, and of their own accord, a solemn detestation of sin, as a profession of faith, and then reading it in public. Many of these would bear repetition here and would, no doubt, effect a feeling of piety in the hearts of

Europeans, as they did in those of the Fathers who heard them. To prevent a repetition of things similar, we shall cite only the one composed by Li Paul, which will afford a good idea of the others. It ran as follows:

"I, the disciple Li Paul, with all my soul and with firm sincerity, desire to accept the law of Christ, wherefore, in all humility, I lift up my soul to heaven, begging God to harken to my pleading. Born in the Court City of Pekin, I confess that in all my past years I had never heard tell of the divine law of Christianity, nor ever encountered the good and holy men who preach it. Hence it was that I wandered in error, in everything I did and said, by day and by night, like one who was blind and demented. Not long ago, through the mercy of God, it was my good fortune to meet two distinguished men from Europe: Matthew Ricci and Diego Pantoia, both of them highly educated and eminent in their profession, from whom I received and by whom I was taught the holy law of Christ, and was permitted to look upon and to venerate his holy image. It was from them that I came to know my heavenly Father and His law, which He promulgated for the salvation of the world.

"Why then should I not accept this law and follow it and observe its precepts, with all my heart and soul? From the time of my birth up to this my forty-third year, I lived in ignorance of this law, hence I was unable to avoid falling into many faults and errors, and so I ask the Heavenly Father to be generous toward me and in His love and mercy to efface and to pardon all the guilt I incurred, for what was dishonestly acquired, for fraud and error, for what was unchaste and sordid, for words ill spoken, for all desires of doing harm to others, and for all other sins both great and small, knowingly or thoughtlessly committed. From this hour on, and once I am baptized, I promise to avoid sin, to make amends for the past, to honor Christ and to keep His law. With full faith in what is taught by that holy law, and with attention centered upon the ten commandments, I desire never for a moment to swerve, even one iota from their strict observance. I do hereby abjure the old and perverse customs I once followed, and the errors of the present age, and I renounce and condemn whatever else is, in any way whatsoever, not in conformity with the Divine Law, and this in perpetuum, and never by any similar pronouncement to be revoked.

"One thing only do I ask of You, O Father most holy, and merciful Creator of all things. Since this is only the beginning of my new and better life, and I am but a listening novice, with but little understanding of what is more perfect and more subtle in the law, I ask You to enlighten and open my intellect for a fuller comprehension of those things to which human wisdom can not attain, that in the future, with Your assisting grace, I may courageously and continuously reduce what I understand to ready action, and so to live and to die, free from all sin and error, that in time I may come into the enjoyment of Your august presence. In the meantime, gifted with this Holy faith, grant me the power to spread it, as do your servants, throughout the universe, together with their faculty of inducing all men to embrace it. I beseech You most humbly, Heavenly Father, to look upon this as my vow, offered to You in words that arise from my soul, and may it please Your Divine Majesty to hear and to accept it." Signed, Li Paul.

The subscript to this document reads—In the dynasty of Tamin, the thirtieth year of the King Vanlie—the sixth day of the eighth moon.

BOOK FIVE

BOOK FIVE

1. China Becomes an Independent Mission Under Father Ricci

THE CHRISTIAN EXPEDITION to China now numbered four residences, so placed as to measure off the entire length of the kingdom, from north to south, but no penetration had been made as yet from east to west. Because of the influence of the settlement in the capital city, the status of the Mission had been so stabilized, within a few years, that the Christian faith was beginning to flourish in all parts. The flame of Christian zeal, once lighted, was spreading with every day. The neophytes were openly receiving the faith without any opposition. They took part in building Mission-posts, were attending instruction classes and Mass and performing other religious devotions in presence of the rest of the world. Some of the pagans, even of the class of the literati, together with Magistrates of high position, were visiting the Mission House to venerate the crucifix.

Realizing the difficulties encountered in the laws and customs of China, the Official Father Visitor and others of the Society of Jesus, were convinced that they saw the hand of God in what had been accomplished in so few years. For this they gave thanks to God, not only because the light of divine grace was beginning to break through the darkness of centuries, but also because there were many studiously vying to take part in the labor of this particular vineyard.

The reputation of the small number of Mission Houses had spread rapidly into the fifteen provinces of China. It grew as it traveled and, going beyond the truth, as is apt to happen, it reached across the bounds of the kingdom and spread abroad reports of things highly desirable, as if they had already been accomplished. It was reported in Europe that the King of China had become a Christian, that he had granted leave for any of his subjects to embrace the faith, and for the Gospel to be preached everywhere in the Kingdom. As a result the members of other Religious Orders were taking passage in Spanish boats, by way of the Philippine Islands, eager to assist in the work that was being done in China, but as yet the gates to the great kingdom were not as wide open as false rumor had reported.

Moved by the proportions to which the Mission was attaining, the Father Visitor returned from Japan to Macao, whence he could readjust operations in China from a closer base and more easily supply the Mission's needs. Hope for success in China seemed to surpass even that in Japan. In fact, this seemed to be the most important expedition undertaken for the promulgation of Christianity since the exodus of the Apostles to evangelize the whole world. The first step, upon the Visitor's arrival, was to call Father Emanuele Dias for consultation. He was also anxious to see Father Ricci, if this busy missionary could absent himself from Pekin. On hearing of the Visitor's arrival, Father Emanuele and Father Cattaneo hastened to Macao. They told him more than he had expected to hear and he immediately decided to further the cause of the Mission in every way possible. In a word, he granted every concession they asked, and even then he thought that their requests were very moderate. Because of the great scarcity of men who could undertake to learn the difficult language, and at the same time to labor on a mission so full of obstacles, he first confirmed Father Emanuele's appointment and then assigned eight men who were living at Macao, and whom he deemed properly equipped, as members of the China Mission. In addition to this, he also promised more help when the ship arrived, on which some of their brethren were sailing from India. The question of man power, however, was not his only problem, one also had to supply their means of support. The subsidy which the King of Portugal had ordered to be paid to the Mission was frequently turned into other channels for the needs of the realm, and following the early example of the Apostles, no financial burden was ever placed on the converts. Moreover, regarding the support of the Mission, if the converts had been asked to contribute, less difficulty would have been expected from them than from the pagans, who were accustomed to spread stories about the missionaries; saying that they were so poor at home in Europe that they came to wealthy China to mulct the people of their money.

After computing the cost of support for each house, it was decided, because of the low scale of market prices, that thirty gold pieces per annum would be sufficient for food and clothing for each separate community. The Father Visitor also decided that henceforth the Procurator, or Mission Treasurer, of the Japanese Mission, then living at Macao, would also be in charge of the finances of the China Mission. Permission was granted for admission into the Society of Jesus of several Chinese students then studying at Macao. The churches of the mission centers were to be improved, the residences better furnished and the customary gifts to friends and to the Magistrates were sanctioned. By way of alms offered for the Mission, Father Emanuele and some of the other Fathers collected numerous donations from the Portuguese merchants, who were always very generous toward the China undertaking. There were also questions to be discussed which seemed to be very difficult of solution and had to be treated with prudence. Finally, in order to insure more liberty of action in the administration of the China Mission, Father Matthew Ricci, who was deemed to be most experienced in Chinese affairs, was placed in charge of it, as a mission independent of the jurisdiction of the Rector of the College of Macao.

With these arrangements completed, those who had been appointed to the Mission were preparing to set out for their posts when something unexpectedly happened which seriously interfered with their plans, though it did not upset them entirely. The packet boat, already loaded and ready to sail for Japan, was seized and thoroughly ransacked by Dutch pirates, who for several years past had infested these waters. This stunning loss was keenly felt in the City of Macao. As we have mentioned before, the hope and the wealth of the city was carried in these vessels. Scarcely anyone in the town was left untouched by this misfortune, and the loss to the Jesuits in the east was something exceptional, as the full store of supplies for the Japanese Mission had already been placed aboard. Being somewhat accustomed to such reverses, this one did not dishearten the Father Visitor, but it did prevent him from sending into China the number of Fathers and the amount of supplies he had decided upon. Father Emanuele Dias and three others went in at that time, and Father Valignano took care of the house in Macao with reference to the shortage of supplies.

Of the new missionaries, Father Bartolomeo Tedeschi was assigned to remain at Xaucea with Father Nicolo Longobardo, and later on they were joined by Father Girolamo Rodrigues, a Portuguese. Father Pietro Ribero went to Nankin, as a companion to Father Roccia and they were later joined by two others; Father Alphonso Vagnoni, from Piedmont, and the Portuguese Father Feliciano da Silva. Father Emanuele Dias, the former Rector, was advised to live at Nancian, as it was centrally located relative to the three houses under his direction. Together with these came Father Gaspare Ferreira who was assigned to join the two at Pekin. Father Cattaneo was held at Macao because of his health. Here he devoted himself to the spiritual care of the Chinese who were carrying on trade with the Portuguese and, in order to facilitate this work, he dressed as the Fathers do in the interior of the Kingdom of China. In this general entrance certain difficulties were experienced with the collectors of the customs, but only for the luggage they were importing, for which the eunuchs were particularly exacting. It was only through the industry of a Jesuit Lay Brother that the Fathers soon found themselves as comfortably settled as they might have been in many parts of Europe.

Father Gaspare Ferreira, on his way to Pekin, encountered more difficulties than the others, especially from the eunuch in charge of the boat on which he was traveling. This fellow was about to cast the Father's luggage onto the bank of the river, half way on the voyage, if he had not been pacified with a few gold pieces, to which he was looking forward when he planned the incident. They were just coming to the end of their journey when they were shipwrecked right in the harbor of the Capital City. The Father's luggage was all dumped into the water and most of it destroyed, with a loss valued at more than two hundred gold pieces, which meant a consequent strict curtailment of his domestic expenses. Among the ecclesiastical ornaments that were lost there was an exceptionally fine casement, done in gold-covered fluted woodwork for framing a statue. This unfortunate wreck was caused by an unusual rising of the river, due to the incessant rains which that year were really extraordinary and which caused tremendous damage in the Royal City. Rising above its banks, the river swept away many houses, and the King very liberally ordered a hundred thousand gold pieces to be set aside from his treasury for rebuilding the houses and for relieving the poor. Father Gaspare came ashore after the wreck and left Brother Sebastiano on the boat with the servants and the baggage which they had pulled out of the water. They would have saved much more, were it not for the fact that the sailors, who were more savage than the river, had thrown overboard much of what they had stolen. It was only by the grace of God that they saved an elegantly bound set of eight volumes of the Holy Bible, from the Plantin Press, which Cardinal Severini had sent, as a gift, to the China Mission. The box containing these books and other pieces of baggage had been floating in the river for some time before it was salvaged by the predatory sailors. When they opened it and found it contained only books which they could not read, they gave them back to the Brother for a small price which he was quite willing to pay. Fortunately the water had not penetrated the box and the books were in perfect condition. Afterwards, on the Feast of the Assumption of the Blessed Virgin, these books were received by the Fathers and the converts with considerable display and with the celebration of a solemn high Mass. As the books were being brought in, the Acolyte carrying them was preceded by a censer bearer. Later they were placed on a table in the church and the people reverently knelt and kissed them, giving thanks to God for preserving them, after passing through a thousand difficulties on many seas and finally being saved from a last minute shipwreck. Many visitors came to the house to see these books and, wondering at the type and the binding, they would say, "No doubt, there must be a wonderful doctrine contained in books which men make with such art and with so much care."

On the advice of the converts, the Fathers decided to try to recover what had been stolen from them, and their friend Fumo Can, who was still detained in chains, took over the burden of the search for the culprits. Through his influence the Master of the ship and some of his crew were finally brought into custody. The Magistrate judging the case was a friend of the Mission and he was set upon punishing the thieves, but the Fathers pitied them and withdrew all charges, for which Fumo Can took occasion from their clemency to praise the charity of the Christian Law. The result of the court action was the recovery of a box containing sacred relics, and of a few other things of minor value; enough to have made it a worth while effort.

2. Father Ricci's Chinese Writings

~~~~~~

HERE IN CHINA, as was mentioned in the first book of the Diary, literary studies are cultivated to such an extent that there are very few people who are not interested in them to some degree. It is also distinctive of the Chinese, that all their religious sects are spread, and their religious doctrine promulgated, by written books, rather than by the spoken word. They have a great dislike to people gathering together in crowds, and so news is spread chiefly by writing. But this did not hamper the work of the Missionaries, because a book-reading people were probably more readily persuaded by something they would read at leisure, than by something said from a pulpit by a preacher who was not thoroughly acquainted with their language. This does not mean that the Fathers did no preaching to their converts on Sundays and on feast days. The reference is rather to the pagans, who are attracted by books, and who spread about the ideas they find in them, in their private conversations. From this common custom it happened at times that someone, while reading a pious book at home, would come across a passage relative to Christianity, which he committed to memory, and then repeated to his relatives and friends. This proved to be of interest to the Fathers and it served as an incentive to their learning to write in Chinese. This is always a long and a tedious task but, with the grace of God, the time and the attention they gave to overcoming the difficulties and the drudgery of it, proved to be very well spent.

Apart from the fact that writing in Chinese is in itself an accomplishment, and not a common one, any book written in Chinese was sure to find its way with profit into the fifteen provinces of the kingdom. Moreover, it would also be understood by the Japanese, the Koreans, the inhabitants of Cochin China, the Leuchians and even by people of other countries, who would be able to read it as well as the Chinese. While the spoken languages of these different races are as unlike as can be imagined, they can understand written Chinese because each individual character in Chinese writing represents an individual thing.

446

If this were universally true, we would be able to transmit our ideas to people of other countries in writing, though we would not be able to speak to them.

Father Ricci was the first one to begin the study of Chinese literature and he was so well versed in what he learned that he became the admiration of the Chinese lettered class who, in their reading, had never before encountered a foreigner from whom they could learn anything. We are purposely treating of this subject here, so that posterity may know what a great advantage was derived from the knowledge of Chinese, and so that Europeans who read this may realize that the interest the Fathers took in the genius of the people was well placed.

Father Ricci began by teaching the first principles of Geography and of Astronomy, and although in the beginning he taught nothing that was not known to an educated European, for those who obstinately defended the errors handed down to them from their ancestors, his teaching was simply astounding and something beyond their imagining. So much so, indeed, that many of them confessed that up to that time, their ignorance of the better things had rendered them stubborn and proud, but that now their eyes, which had been unwittingly closed by an impervious intellectual blindness, were really being opened to the more serious things in life. Omitting here the commentaries on the four elements and also the Treatise on Friendship, already mentioned, Father Ricci wrote twenty-five tracts on diverse moral questions and on control of the evil propensities of the soul. These were pamphlets which the Chinese call Opinions or Sentences. They were read by some of his Chinese friends before they were published and met with their wholehearted approval. In fact, they deemed it to be quite incredible that a foreigner, coming from a people who up to that time were looked upon as barbarians, could treat so aptly of such subtle subjects, and they all wanted to make copies of his pamphlets.

Fumo Can received copies of these tracts and had them published in a single book to which he added a preface in praise of the work, wherein he made a comparison between this book and another one like it, published by the sect of idol worshippers and called The Forty-two Paragraphs. He thought so highly of this work that he counseled the people of the educated class to read it and then judge between the shady virtue, colored by superstition, and virtue drawn from the fountain head of Christianity, and then to decide which was more proper for the good of the individual, and more useful for the public in general. Their friend Paul added another preface and an epilogue, and the prestige of these two names greatly enhanced the authority of the book. This approval by such distinguished figures served also to augment the reputation of the Christian faith. This was particularly true of their friend Paul's approbations, in which he took occasion to praise the principles of Christianity by stating that he not only approved of them but had already embraced them, as a convert.

Just at that time the Fathers encountered a difficulty, that was somewhat more than average. Their first Compendium of Christian Doctrine was written when they were inexperienced, and with the help of interpreters. To their better trained minds and eyes, it now looked to be truncated and inadequate, and so it was revised, augmented and re-edited by Father Ricci, and the former editions were discontinued. This new edition was written as a more ample explanation of Christian Doctrine, but before being published it was so arranged as to be chiefly adapted for use by the pagans. It was thought that the neophytes would receive sufficient religious instruction from the catechism lessons they attended as catechumens, and from the frequent exhortations they attended, after their conversion. And so this new work consisted entirely of arguments drawn from the natural light of reason, rather than such as are based upon the authority of Holy Scripture. In this way the road was leveled and made clear for the acceptance of the mysteries dependent upon faith and upon the knowledge of divine revelation. The book also contained citations serving its purpose and taken from the ancient Chinese writers; passages which were not merely ornamental, but served to promote the acceptance of this work by the inquiring readers of other Chinese books. It also provided a refutation of all the Chinese religious sects, excepting the one founded on the natural law, as developed by their Prince of Philosophers, Confucius, and adopted by the sect of the literati. Their particular philosophy as developed by the ancients, contains but little that is justly reprehensible. Not many errors will be committed by a thoughtful and a careful man, writing on subjects about which he feels that he is not sufficiently informed. The Fathers were accustomed to use the authority of this sect to their own advantage, by commenting only on what had happened since the time of Confucius, who lived some five hundred years before the coming of Christ. The reply made by Doctor Paul, when he was asked, in company, what he considered to be the basis of the Christian law, might be quoted here, as being very timely. He defined the whole subject in four syllables, or rather in four words, when he said, Ciue, Fo, Pu, Giu, meaning, It does away with idols and completes the law of the literati.

The contents of Father Ricci's tract, which we are now considering, may be summed up as follows. First is presented the proof that there is only one God, who created and governs all things, followed by a proof of the immortality of man's soul, and an explanation of punishment for evil and of reward for good deeds done, especially in the life to come. The Pythagorean doctrine of the transmigration of souls, which is a common doctrine among the Chinese, is thoroughly refuted. Toward the end of the work, there is inserted a practical dissertation on God and Man, followed by an exhortation inviting all the Chinese to ask the Fathers for further explanation of the law which is here presented in brief, rather than explained in full.

This book was really necessary, in order to spread the idea of Christianity through the entire kingdom in a brief space of time, and since it could touch only lightly upon many questions that were frequently asked of the Fathers, the author inserted a number of pleasant and lighter touches to whet the curiosity of the reader, with the result that it made very enjoyable reading. For the same reason, it proved to be quite satisfactory to answer those who had merely heard about Christianity, as it were, in passing. These were the people who were repeatedly calling for a book in which they could read at leisure about what they had heard. It also served as a supplement to the shorter interviews with the Magistrates, who always had more time for reading than they had for talking, due perhaps to the fact that their education had been chiefly acquired by voluminous reading.

This book proved to be a thorn in the side of the idol worshippers, because it stripped them of arms to defend their own vain doctrines, but there was no danger of opposition to it on the part of the literati, because they would thus be refuting their own profession. It seemed to be divine direction, that the faith should be defended by those who realized from the very beginning, that there was nothing in the doctrine of the literati that was contrary to the law of Christianity. Otherwise, if they had been forced to combat all the sects at once, they might have been reduced to silence by accumulated authority, and by the sheer weight of numbers. Due in part to assistance from some of the pagans, this book of Father Ricci's went through four printings and was published in different provinces. Fumo Can, who was one of the literati, had many copies of it printed at his own expense, and gave them to the Fathers for distribution to their friends. He wrote to the Fathers and told them that the amount of money he paid for having the books printed, was spent by way of restitution. He explained this by saying that he had once taken a gift for using his official influence in doing a favor, and that he knew of no better way of amending his fault, than by giving wide publicity to a pamphlet explaining the Christian faith. He did this while he was yet a pagan. There is no telling what this man might have done for Christianity, if his life as a Christian had been extended for some years.

Another book of Father Ricci's which he called Paradoxes, had as many critics as the former, because it contained moral precepts hitherto unheard of by the Chinese. For the most part, it was a running commentary, a sort of continued meditation on death, as a means of maintaining proper order in one's life. It treated a variety of topics, such as: Considering life as a continual dying; Reward for good deeds and punishment for evil is not always fully paid in this life but must be in the next; Silence and restraint of speech are both very difficult, but very useful; Each one should examine his actions and discipline himself for his misdeeds. These and many other similar declarations are confirmed by proofs and citations, by numerous apothegms, and by examples, with apt quotations from the philosophers, from the Fathers of the Church, and from Holy Scripture, in such a way as to make pleasant reading. The paradoxes inserted in the different discourses gave the book no little authority, because they had reference to questions which Father Matthew had already discussed at length with some of the most prominent of the Magistrates.

If all the notices written about this book, by distinguished people, were to be collected in one volume, it would take longer to read that volume, than to read the book itself. This work contained several proemia by friendly critics, which not only lauded its publication, but spoke in terms of the highest praise of European genius, of its numberless books, and of the Christian faith. In order to make it better known, the Fathers distributed copies of it on all sides and used it to fulfill their obligations of giving presents at stated times. Some of their friends sent printers to the Mission House to make copies of it for distribution to their acquaintances. The first printing was exhausted in a year, and it was reprinted twice in the following year; once in the Royal City of Nankin and again in Nancian, the metropolitan city of the Province of Chiansi.

One of the highest ranking Magistrates of the Royal Court of Pekin, a member of the Tauli, was so impressed when he read the book we have been discussing, that he came of his own accord to call on the Fathers in the Capital City. What surprised the Fathers about this man was that no one up to that time had seemed to be more friendly, and at the same time more distant, than he, as was once said of Novius. Seating himself beside Father Ricci, he said, "And you are the author of this book," as he produced a copy of the book. Father Matthew agreed that he had spent considerable time on it, and his visitor continued, "The author of such a book must be a holy man. It has never been my custom, nor did I ever wish, to be hostile toward holy men. Hence, I must ask you to pardon my past indifferences, for which I hope to make amends by my future friendship." Then he went on to talk about other things and concluded with the comment, "There are more than a few who frequently assert that they have no fear of foreigners such as you men, because it is impossible for anyone following your doctrine to injure the public welfare."

3. Celebrated Literati Converts and Their Works

IN 1604, OUR FRIEND Ciu Paul, who had already attained to the Licentiate, came to Pekin, to take the public examination for the highest class of Doctorate. Martin also came, from Nankin, eager to try his fortune for the same degree in the Military Senate. These two were the most distinguished, in fact they were very luminaries, among the converts of the Province of Nankin. Naturally, they were both delighted that the Mission Center in the Capital City was well established, and that the outlook for Christianity there was very promising. Their first interest on arriving was to visit the Mission House, to go to confession and to receive the Holy Eucharist. It was said of Paul, that he was so devout, that when he received Holy Communion, he could not restrain his tears, nor could those who saw him at the altar rail. Before they became Christians, neither one of these men was successful in acquiring the high degree he was seeking. This time, trusting in the help of God, they went down to battle, as it were, in the literary arena, and they came away victorious, each with the degree of Doctor, and each destined for membership in the particular Senate of his choice. A few months later, Martin, whose name was Cin, was appointed Military Prefect in the Province of Cechian. In six months more he was raised to a higher post in Nancian, and shortly afterwards to a post near to the very top of his department. He went ahead in leaps and bounds, instead of passing from grade to grade as is customary.

When the results of the examinations were announced, Ciu Paul's name was not included among those of highest rating. Therefore, according to the national custom, he was listed for appointment as a Magistrate, somewhere outside of the Royal City, but not in a lower court. From there he could aspire to higher honors. But it seems as if Divine Providence had selected this man to be a bulwark of Christianity in Pekin, because he was kept there and appointed to a position of dignity, that surpassed his fondest hopes.

There were three hundred and eight Doctor's degrees granted, for the whole kingdom, after the examination just mentioned. Shortly afterwards there followed another examination, for selection of members to the Royal Academy. Successful candidates in this examination were later attached to the College, called Hanlinien. From the total number of those examined, only twenty-four are selected, and, as holds in all degree examinations, these twenty-four must excel in the exact formation of Chinese written characters. Successful candidates in this examination eventually become the highest Magistrates in the country, and if they are called to fill a Government post, they are appointed directly, rather than by promotion, to the very highest positions.

For sheer lack of confidence, Ciu Paul did not wish to attempt this examination but he ceded to the petitions of the Fathers and of the converts, when they reminded him that the acquisition of higher honors would redound to the benefit of Christianity. Good fortune favored him and he was fourth in order when results were announced, thus increasing his own reputation, and the happiness of the Mission Center. But this was not the end of it all. The twenty-four successful candidates from this examination do not immediately become members of the Royal Academy. What they have won is the right, or the privilege, of aggregation, after they have spent some time under the tutelage of the Colao, the Supreme Magistrate. There is, so to speak, another cast of the dice to be made. Only twelve, or at most fifteen of the twenty-four are eventually selected for the Academy, and these are determined by a series of monthly examinations, in which only one candidate can qualify, generally the highest ranking. Since all twenty-four are called for all of these monthly tests, it frequently happens that a first ranking student in one test will absent himself from some of the remaining examinations, so as to give the others a chance for highest honors, and also so as not to appear too covetous. He is free to do this, and in so doing he makes friends without losing either rank or dignity.

Ciu Paul was now certain of his own status and also of the safety of the Fathers in the Capital, and from that time on he devoted all his efforts to the advancement of their interests and to the spread of Christianity. A rare example of devotion and of holiness of life, he was imitated by the converts and admired by the pagans, among whom, some of the more distinguished would frequently remark, "Is there another man as holy as Ciu Paul?" He brought his aged father, a man over seventy, to Pekin, to win him over to Christ before time should overtake him; and after much effort, both on his part and on that of the Fathers, the old man came to know God and to do away with his idols. Finally, and fortunately at his age, the old gentleman was baptized, about a year and a half before he passed away. We shall leave Ciu Paul for the present, to return to him later on.

The Church in Pekin was gradually developing from infancy to childhood, and it was being helped, not only by Ciu Paul but by other converts for whom he was serving as an example, particularly in his frequent approach to the sacrament of Penance. His son, and, what was more unusual, his wife, followed in his footsteps. There was a problem to be solved here relative to the sequestration of women, and this lady was the first one in Pekin to work out its solution. Before long the converts were asking to receive Holy Communion, but the Fathers were inclined to postpone this privilege in order to increase devotion to the sacrament. Those who were acting as confessors to this family urged their penitents to go to confession several times before receiving their first Holy Communion, to impress upon them the fact that the soul must be as pure as possible when God comes to it. In order to shorten the delay and to fulfill the number of confessions, Li Paul, the other famous Paul already mentioned, went to confession every day, including Sundays and feast days. Such ardent desire for the bread of life could not be too long delayed, and he received his first communion on Easter Sunday, with devotion and tears that touched the hearts of the converts who were present. From that time on, he went to the altar-rail on every ecclesiastical feast day, keeping a strict fast the day before, by way of preparation, and continuing the fast for the rest of that day, as an act of thanksgiving.

This man had someone or other in the Mission House informing him of everything the Fathers did by way of religious practice, so that he could imitate their way of religious life. If fast was being observed there, or other ecclesiastical regulations being put into practice, Li Paul did the same in his own home. When he first heard about indulgences, he was continually asking the Fathers how they could be obtained, and when he read somewhere that a plenary indulgence was granted by the Pope to anyone converting a pagan, his ardor to this end was redoubled. This fervent desire for such a spiritual reward was like a spur that kept him continually moving in search of souls. He was so anxious to receive the sacrament of Confirmation, that they could scarcely restrain him from going to visit the Bishop at Macao, a distance of four months' travel from his home. He was, in reality, on the point of departure when the Fathers persuaded him that an absence of eight months would be detrimental to his family, which was quite true, because his family income had diminished with the sacrifice of certain pagan practices, when he became Christian. In the meantime, he had to return to the Province of Uquam, to settle certain family affairs and to take care of his aged mother. While there he was active spreading a knowledge of Christianity and sending souls to Heaven by baptizing dying children, and by giving sufficient instruction to adults in danger of death and then baptizing them. He wrote frequently to the Fathers, always expressing a desire to return, to visit the Church, but the duty and the care which he owed to his declining mother prevented his return. To the Chinese, it would have been a scandal and an infamous crime if he had done otherwise.

Let us insert here a little story about our friend Ligotsun, who was not as yet a convert. Just a year before this time he was appointed to preside over the examinations in the Province of Fuchian, to be held in the Metropolitan City, for the degree of Licentiate. Perhaps the most distinguished literati of the whole country live in this province, and so his appointment here was a mark of considerable honor and dignity. The results of these examinations are published in writing by the presiding official and on this occasion, for no seeming reason, Ligotsun wrote a high encomium of European literary studies. Later on, he was transferred to a high position in the Province of Sciantum, and when he was leaving, he gave the Fathers most of the furniture from his palace. He also wanted to take one of the Fathers with him, but due to the small number present, his invitation had to be declined. In order to give one an idea of the integrity with which the Chinese Magistrature and its courts are administered, it will be of interest to know that this same man was deprived of the right to all high office, and reduced to a lower post for three years, because a complaint was entered against him to the effect that he exhibited too much levity at the banquets he was accustomed to attend, and also that he was too devoted to the game of chess. After three years of this humiliation he was again recalled to a position of high honor.

It was in this year that the Chief Magistrates of the entire country made their triennial visit to Pekin to pay their respects to the King. During the time they were permitted to remain in the Capital City the streets were so crowded that one made his way along them with difficulty. The Fathers there took occasion of this opportunity to contact the Magistrates and the numerous merchants from the other cities where they had residences. This was a method of increasing the prestige of the house in Pekin, which served as a sort of protecting tree in the shade of which the other houses basked by way of security. On this occasion also, there was no lack of those who complained to the more prominent Magistrates that they had read certain things written by the Fathers in disparagement of the idols. They had hit upon this as a pretext relative to the public peace, which the Fathers, as they said, were probably endeavoring to disturb by their preaching. In this way, it was asserted, they could incite the many who were united to them by a common bond, into general rebellion. These critics were said to be men of distinction. The common people could scarcely hope for much success in grumbling against the Fathers. However, by the grace of God and due to the patronage of certain friends, the missionaries succeeded in frustrating this hostile endeavor of their adversaries.

4.Christianity in Nancian

FATHER GIOVANNI SOEIRO labored all alone at the Nancian Mission for three years, burdened as he was with a serious illness which finally developed into tuberculosis. Another obstacle to the development of his mission was the presence there of so many of the royal relatives, a wealthy and a do-nothing class whose insolence was proverbial. Yet, despite these impediments, his holiness and his extraordinary zeal accomplished more than might have been expected. Most of his converts were from the common people; only a few of the more distinguished individuals were received into the Church during those days. One of these was an old man of eighty, one of the high ranking literati, who developed an unusual zeal for the spread of Christianity. He was a skillful writer and he produced many articles on the principles of the faith, which he had learned from the Fathers. In order to attract the attention of the literati he zealously gathered from their own books an amazing amount of testimony in favor of Christianity.

There was a pagan family living next to the Mission House and one day the father of the family brought in their newborn baby to be baptized. Father Giovanni thought it was not altogether safe to baptize the child at the time, considering the fact that the parents had no idea of abandoning their pagan errors, and doubting also whether or not this apparent piety was genuine or fraudulent. So he placed the child on the altar, sprinkled him with holy water and called him Giovanni. A short time afterwards, the parents moved away from that vicinity, believing that the child was a Christian. Seven years later the father appeared at the Mission House with the child, to thank God for the wonderful manner in which the child was unexpectedly returned to health, from a serious illness. The boy had been unconscious and they had given up hope of his life, when, as he afterwards told them, he thought he saw the majestic Mother of God coming toward him, with a child in her arms. When the child called him by name several times, he awoke, as it were from sleep, and from that moment he began to grow well and strong. None of the domestic servants had the slightest doubt that the lady the child had seen was the same one whose picture they themselves had often seen at the Mission House, and the boy confirmed their belief when he was shown two madonna pictures, and pointed to the one, the original of which, they say, was painted by Saint Luke the Evangelist. It was only then that Father Soeiro told the parent that his child had never been baptized, but that he would baptize him, if they promised never to introduce him to the worship of idols. The child's father agreed to this, but he could not be persuaded to give up his idea of selecting a day of good omen from the Chinese calendar for the performance of the ceremony. So he took the child away with him, but he brought him back on the following day, and after the child was baptized, the parent took home a catechism, to begin studying for his own conversion.

The little flock at Nancian was exemplary in the performance of religious duties. They attended Mass regularly, came in for instruction when in doubt, strictly avoided all pagan ceremonies when conducting a funeral and publicly professed their faith in Christ. All of which went far toward the spread of Christianity.

To cite an example of their ardor, one of the converts, on a business trip outside of the city, went into the house of a pagan acquaintance. Entering the reception room he took a seat with his back to a collection of idols which the pagan had arranged at one end of the room. His host informed him that his position was uncomplimentary to the gods and he answered, "I adore only one God and I am in no wise concerned about idols." With that he made the sign of the cross on himself and then over the idols, moved his chair to the middle of the room and sat down again, still facing away from the statues of the gods, and so his friend let the incident pass. The Chinese are not nearly as interested in the honor they believe to be due to their gods as they are in the courtesy they believe to be due to a friend. At lunch time the pagan host was about to place a few small viands before the idols by way of a good omen offering, when the Christian said, "If you do that, I shall not eat what you put on the table." Then the host omitted the superstitious rite rather than offend his visitor, who considered that he had gained a double victory over the lifeless gods. This same convert had a neighbor whose wife had left him and the husband went to a fortune teller to seek information as to her return. She returned as the fortune teller predicted but when the husband saw her he thought she was possessed of a devil. She was so distraught and furious that he realized that he had an enemy on his hands instead of a housewife. Every pagan rite and ceremony was employed to expel the evil spirit, but without any result. Then the convert intervened. First he recited the Rosary of the Blessed Virgin, then with all the faith in him, he scolded the evil spirit for daring to come into a house so close to his own, where the image of the crucified Christ was kept. After that, he made the sign of the cross over the woman and with strong words commanded the spirit to depart. Then the demoniac became quiet, as did the loquacious demon also. There are many instances of the strong faith of the converts performing such amazing wonders with the use of holy water, too many indeed to be recounted.

These prosperous beginnings of Christianity in Nancian were advanced by the coming of Father Emanuele Dias, who supervised the direction of three houses from his own residence in the south. With him came Father Giovanni Soeiro and Brother Pascal, who had only recently been received into the Society of Jesus. With their coming there began a more energetic cultivation of this part of the vineyard, so active in fact that in the following year, 1605, the number of converts was doubled, and there was a congregation of more than two hundred before their arrival. Among the former converts there were some of the literati and also of the King's relatives. From the royalty, as the Chinese call them when they say, Vansu, the first one to become acquainted with the Fathers was introduced by his brother-in-law, Paul, the Baccalaureate convert we have just discussed. After a drawn out course of instructions, he was baptized on the day on which the Spanish Church celebrates the Feast of the Expectatio Partus. He took the name of Joseph and he was the first of the Chinese Royalty to adore Christ, the King of Kings. This relationship with the King must not be confounded with our European terminology. It is far inferior to our idea of royalty and though the so-called relatives of the King have their own privileges, wealth and dignity, they are never permitted to hold a public office of any kind. Joseph's younger brother followed his example and decided to join him in his religion. His baptism was deferred until the Feast of the Epiphany and he was told that it was on this day that the three kings came from faraway countries to adore the newly born King of Heaven. His answer to this was, "If there were three, we shall be four," and he named a younger brother and a cousin and also presented to Father Emanuele for instruction another boy he had brought with him. He asked that this boy be called Emanuele, and so he was and his parents always called him by that name.

The three adults were received into the Church on the day appointed, baptized with solemn ceremonies and named after the three kings: Melchior, Gaspar and Balthasar. A little later on, Joseph's wife and some of their relatives of both sexes were also converted. The elderly mother of these boys was a widow and very devoted to the worship of idols, so devoted, indeed, that she had passed the ten years previous, according to Chinese custom, practicing a strict fast; eating no meat, fish or eggs, and living solely on vegetable herbs, rice and viands prepared with flour. Her sons tried to persuade her to abandon her superstition and they finally succeeded in doing so. She ended her fasting and had all her sorry idols burned in the fireplace, at the Mission House, together with the beads she used in calling the false gods by their names. She also sent the Father a document, a sort of petition, addressed to the King of the Infernal Regions, which the Ministers of the idols had sold to her. The petition begged His Infernal Majesty to receive her kindly when she died and to cancel whatever punishment was due for her faults. The document was called "A Guide to the Infernal Regions." In exchange for the images she had given up she was presented with a crucifix and a Rosary of the Blessed Virgin. Instead of her customary fast, which she found some difficulty in changing, the regular fasts of the Church were suggested. Her Director told her that the Commandments were a certain road to Heaven, not to the lower regions, and to the King of Heaven by whom Christians will be rewarded for their good deeds. This lady received her instructions from Brother Pascal, in her own house, but she never saw him because Chinese women observe a strict seclusion. He spoke to her through a curtained door and all the time he was doing so he thought he was talking to only one person. When the day came for her to be baptized, he discovered that there were six others also to receive the sacrament instead of only one; her daughter, her niece and four of her maid-servants. When these others were questioned on what they had heard, it was quite evident that they were sufficiently instructed for reception. Their devotion was such that, despite the fact that Chinese women abhor being touched, they evidenced no indisposition to any of the ceremonies, even to the anointing.

The number of converts at this mission was increasing so rapidly that the congregation was becoming too numerous for the church. Three week days were appointed for certain groups to attend Mass, but they were all present on Sundays and Holy Days. It was customary to distribute holy pictures and medals, on the day of a baptism, but the Mission supply of such things, that had to be brought in through many countries and over many seas, was not very great and was soon exhausted. In order to meet the demand, the Fathers had native sculptors carve a wooden stamp, from which pictures could be printed; because the Chinese knew nothing about the art of carving on copper. On the pictures there was printed an explanation of the fact that the God of Heaven having no material form, took upon himself the form of a man, by assuming human nature, and brought with Him the holy law from Heaven, when he came to earth. It was quite necessary to add this explanation, because when the Chinese became Christians, they stripped the rooms of their homes of the statuette idols with which they were adorned and, when there was nothing to replace them, their pagan friends said the Christian religion was empty and bare because it had no God.

At the beginning of a new year, the Chinese place statues of the gods over the main entrance to their homes, so the Christians placed tablets bearing the names of Jesus and Mary over theirs, as a profession of faith, and indicating their household patrons. This also pointed out to visitors where their Christian brethren lived, and gave them all the consolation of knowing that they were in no way inferior, in the observance of the national custom. It was also a solace to the Fathers to know that the homes of their people were distinguished, as were the homes of the chosen people in the midst of the Egyptians, when marked with the blood of the Lamb.

5.Lights and Shadows in Xaucea

FATHER NICOLO LONGOBARDO, as we have noted, carried on a courageous advancement of the small beginnings of Christianity, in the city of Xaucea and in the surrounding villages, and the converts he made grew into a well instructed parish. The Sacrament of Penance made a deep impression on many of them, an impression of astonishment and of admiration, though the idea of confessing their most hidden thoughts to a man, in any capacity, seemed at first to surpass the power of human nature. One would scarcely believe with what feeling of piety and devotion they reverenced the crucifix, after one of the Fathers had preached a sermon on the Passion of Our Lord, on Good Friday. The converts of Xaucea were so well instructed, that when they were drawn into arguments by the pagans, they always came off victorious. With the same constancy, they also learned to put up with insults from the envious and, what hurt more, even with injuries.

It seemed as if the Enemy of mankind never ceased disturbing this community. He had a special representative here at that time; the celebrated Minister of the idols, we have already mentioned, who was proscribed in Pekin, and banished to the Province of Canton, by order of the King. He came here, to a popular temple, called Nancua, about twenty miles distant from the city, and being a distinguished person he attracted a numerous following, even as an exile. Each day increased the number of those who went over to his doctrine, and becoming elated by his popularity, as such characters are apt to, he paraded about with great display. He knew more about what the Fathers were doing than they realized, and he also knew that they were looking forward and hoping for the day when the practice of idol worship would totter and fall. So he decided to use his authority to prevent a threatening danger, but first he thought he should meet this Father Nicolo, and find out what kind of a man he was, who could raise the hopes of people to such sublime heights. At the same time, and in keeping with his pride, he could not submit himself to the humiliation of visiting a foreigner, before the foreigner had called upon him. He would have to start scheming in order to reverse the compliment, but his planning went for naught and he received an answer couched in the same silly terms as the invitation he had sent. Here in this kingdom the Fathers considered it unbecoming for preachers of the divine word, to have anything whatsoever to do with men who were known to be unprincipled, as well as lacking in all moral responsibility. In sheer desperation, the Minister of the idols finally decided to make the first call and he arrived, not only concealing his animosity with a smile but laboring under the false impression, so common with the Chinese, that he was about to meet an illiterate barbarian. After hearing Father Nicolo discourse on things natural, and on what was above nature or contrary to it, and fearing that his visit might result in his being refuted by someone more learned than himself, he said that nothing he had heard was greatly at variance with the doctrines of his own sect. The scathing philippics against his false gods, written in the books of the Fathers were, however, too much for him, and for these he threatened vengeance. Here again we may say that a lowering menace was removed by the timely interference of the helping hand of Heaven. Just when he seemed to be secure in his position and wholly occupied in soliciting disciples, in building temples and in supporting his temple Ministers, there came another order of proscription, issued by the King, banishing him to the Island of Hainan, off the extreme southern coast of the Empire.

With one danger passed, the Fathers and the whole Christian cause came face to face with a more serious difficulty. The Mayor of the town had been informed that it was commanded by the Christian law that converts to Christianity must burn the images of their ancestors. This was regarded by the Chinese as an unholy thing, something more serious in their eyes than it seemed to be to Europeans. Now it happened that Father Nicolo, knowing nothing about the report made to the Mayor, had occasion to pay him a visit. When the Mayor spoke to him about this complaint, he was surprised to discover that His Honor, who believed in the calumnious report, had decided not to punish the Fathers but to admonish them. He then advised Father Nicolo to abstain from a practice which could bring great harm to a foreigner who really should be more considerate of his actions, when dwelling in a foreign land. Whereupon, Father Nicolo, in defense of what had been done, and not denying what he himself had done with certain idols, said he thought that the whole class of the literati was in favor of blotting out all the laws pertaining to the protection of idols. There were many members of the City Council present at this meeting and for their benefit Father Nicolo denied doing anything injurious to ancestors, and quoted the Christian commandment relative to the honor due to one's father and mother. The debate that followed between the two was long and serious, and while not wishing to appear as vanquished, the Mayor was at the same time reluctant to being listed as opposing the preaching of the Gospel. The converts felt that this meeting strengthened their position, when they could say that their Doctors were not afraid to argue the truth of Christianity in the public tribunals.

All this happened just at the time of the arrival of the new member of the Tauli, who had jurisdiction over all the Magistrates of the districts of Xaucea and of Nancian. For fear that the City Prefects might call upon the representative of the Tauli to register complaints similar to those already presented, Father Nicolo decided to anticipate their visit. Among the gifts he offered to the Official Inspector, was a copy of the Commentary on the Christian Catechism, recently published by Father Ricci in Pekin. This high official had heard by chance of Father Ricci; of his coming to the Capital City and how he was favorably received by the Magistrates and even by the King. In the presence of the Council he said that Father Ricci had been detained in Pekin by the King, that he was supported by a subsidy from the royal treasury, and that his company was cultivated by the highest officials. Then he added that he sympathized with the lot of Father Ricci because it appeared that he had been forbidden to return to his own country. To this Father Nicolo replied, saying that his companion had remained in Pekin of his own volition, that he was not sighing for his homeland, and that the purpose of his coming, and of the coming of the other Fathers, was explained in the book he had just presented to the visiting member of the Tauli, which was written and published by Father Ricci himself, right in Pekin. The Official Visitor was quite pleased with the meeting and with the attitude of the Father, and the reception he accorded his guest removed all hope of causing trouble which may have been entertained by the City Prefects. On the contrary they thought he was about to take the Fathers into his patronage, and that was what eventually happened. Even this, however, was not enough to frighten the Ministers of the idols of the neighboring temple. The growth of the number of Christians meant that the number of their own followers was diminishing accordingly, and what affected them more seriously, their income was also dropping off. So they decided that their Chief Sacrificer should call upon Father Nicolo with a view to calling a halt to this particular difficulty. His visit to the Mission House was made up, half of entreaties and half of threats, all of which the Father received with a series of smiles and jests, knowing as he did, the attitude of the local Magistrates.

In this same year, Father Emanuele Dias and his three companions returned to Xaucea, and when the converts heard of his coming, they vied with each other to be first into their little boats and down a distance on the river to meet them, with drums and horns to make it a public reception. They also brought along various dishes of food with which to rejoice the travelers, after their long river trip. When they landed, they were conducted to the Mission House, in broad daylight, with a pompous procession, and with a crowd following to witness

the spectacle. The pagans were astounded at this, but it was a source
of so much happiness to the Fathers that they gave thanks to God,
wondering at the same time if they had seen an end to the long centuries during which this kingdom was closed to foreigners, now that
the preachers of the Gospel were admitted and could parade through
the streets without hindrance. But this was liberty that they were to
enjoy for only a few years. The tumult that was stirred up against them
in Canton, reduced their status to such a low level, that up to present
writing it has never regained its former peace and quiet. It may be
that a growing habit of taking too much for granted served to increase
the already numerous restrictions. After a few days of rest at the
Mission House, where the converts came to visit and to bring them
presents, the visitors began to prepare for departure. One of the four
remained as companion to Father Nicolo. The others set out to voyage
by river travel into the interior of the kingdom, and the converts bade
them adieu with a public demonstration similar to the reception.

Now that Father Longobardo had an assistant to care for the
domestic affairs, he could work more freely for the spread of the faith;
visiting the churches in the neighboring villages, strengthening the
faith of the converts and increasing their numbers. He was kept busy
at the house of the aged Paul; instructing catachumens, baptizing converts and solving difficulties which had arisen during his absence, and
which they had written down so as to recall them more accurately when
their Director arrived. The old gentleman, Paul, was so set upon learning all he could about the faith that it was difficult to separate him
from the company of the Fathers, even when they were giving instructions to the novices. Nor was all the activity centered here. Father
Nicolo was called by one of Paul's relatives, who lived about ten miles
away, and since this man was well known in his community, of a
naturally pious disposition, and at the same time a public benefactor,
it was thought that he might be an added prospect for the further
propagation of the faith.

Paul accompanied the Father on this journey, and when they arrived they discovered that a large crowd had gathered to see and to
hear the preacher. Father Nicolo went into the reception room in which
there was an oratorio, or a sort of prayer corner, where, in the midst
of about fifty idols, he was suprised to see a prominent picture of the
Blessed Virgin, holding the child Jesus, with John the Baptist in
adoration. There was no one there who knew anything about the picture, except that it represented the Mother of God and the Queen of

all queens. The sight of this picture was a source of consolation and of joy to the Father, who characterized it as, "The Lily among the thorns," and concluded that it was a copy of the picture, included in the presents that were given to the King. Taking his text from the occasion, he then preached a sermon on the God-Man and the Blessed Sacrament of the altar, and told them the whole story of John the Baptist. This they heard with rapt attention and they were particularly pleased with his story of the Visitation and with the narrative of how the unborn John was affected by the approach of his Saviour.

Later on, the household audience was so moved by a talk on the mysteries of the Christian faith, that all of them, both family and domestics, decided to forswear their idols and to follow Christ. Not only that, but with evident signs of resentment against them, they immediately took down the idols from their place of adoration and burned them in a fire in the courtyard. After that, the oratorio was blessed, with appropriate prayers, the picture of the Madonna and the Precursor was set up, and Father Nicolo arranged an altar with materials he brought along for that purpose. He then told them all to kneel down and ask pardon of God for having paid divine honor to false gods, to whom it did not belong, and to promise that henceforth they would adore only one God, the Creator and the Moderator of all things.

One day while Father was preaching in this same reception room, there were present three Ministers of the Idols, who were attached to a neighboring temple and monastery, both of which Vaigino, the Father's present host, had built. At the conclusion of the sermon, the preacher and the sacrificing Ministers entered into a long disputation, in which their darkness succumbed to his light, and all three agreed to accept the Christian faith, as soon as the King granted them permission to do so, by public decree. This kind of progress delighted the heart of the aged Paul. That day as the Ministers of the Temple were leaving the house, the wife of the host gave them a scolding for arguing so discourteously with a stranger in her home.

After a few days, in the first baptismal ceremony of this excursion, eighteen people were baptized and made their profession of faith. Vaigino, the host, was not received because he was still bound by the chains of polygamy. This man had no children, which among the Chinese is looked upon as a major misfortune, and he could not be persuaded, at first meeting, to put aside his hope of posterity in favor of this eternal salvation.

In another village, where the converts had built their own church, and where they were increasing and holding fast to their faith, there was an old man of ninety, whose case is worthy of mention. Clinging stubbornly to his errors in his old age, during the four years since Father Longobardo had been there, he would never listen to anything about Christianity. He was not given to idol worship, and having no recollection of ever having done anything wrong, he said his length of life had been granted to him as a reward for his innocence. Finally, through the influence of his son and his nephews, he became a Christian, but he insisted upon postponing his baptism for three months, so as to prepare a celebration for the occasion. This idea was evidently prompted by the Devil, to prevent his prey from being snatched from his talons, but constancy overcame stubbornness. Father Nicolo told him that he would not leave the place until he had washed away the sins of his past life in the saving waters of baptism. Finally they came to an agreement. He was baptized and took the name of Anthony, and a few days later died of old age. Evidently God had granted him grace to live on in this life until he was ready to pass on to a better one.

There had been much talk about the wonders wrought by the sprinkling of holy water, when a woman fell sick in a certain village and the priest was called and asked to bless her with holy water, in order to renew her hope of life. What the priest and the woman were hoping for was accomplished. After blessing her, she was restored to health of body and of soul, and then baptized, together with her husband and several others. Then they all burned their idols. Later on, there were thirty baptized, here, at one ceremony, and counting the converts of the village and of the nearby settlements, there were a hundred and forty received into the Church that year at the residence in Xaucea. Such was the progress of the Church in Xaucea, but it was suddenly stopped, and almost for good, by the storm that broke against the Fathers in the Metropolitan City. This we shall treat in its proper place. The progress made was something worthy of being recorded in the annals of the Church, something also in which the working of Divine Providence was more evident than the noonday sun.

6.Chiutaiso Finally Surrenders to Christ

THERE WERE FOUR priests and one Lay Brother at Nankin, and these, together with some students and the servants, made up a community that was more numerous than usual, and Father Giovanni Soeiro, the Superior, had to purchase a nearby house, to provide sufficient living quarters. Three of the Fathers gave all their time to the study of literature, which left only two for mission work. Hence the harvest reaped was not proportionate to the number in the religious community. Apart from domestic affairs which occupied much of the time of the two mission workers, Father Giovanni was giving daily lessons in Chinese to the others and the Lay Brother was teaching catechism to the neophytes of the common class of people. And yet, with all their crowded days, there were not a few converts, and among them was our long awaited friend Chiutaiso, whom we have already introduced, and whom we shall henceforth call Ignatius. All the Fathers and the cause of Christianity in China were greatly indebted to this man, even when he was a pagan, because a great part of what was accomplished, both in the Canton and in the Chiansi Provinces, was due to his co-operation. With God's grace, it was through his effort that the Nankin settlement was established, and it was chiefly due to his interest that the Fathers were enabled to make the second voyage to the Capital City. Hence it is that the Fathers were very solicitous to repay these benefits in every possible way.

The two serious impediments that occasioned the long delay in his coming into the Church, were: first, that he was living with a concubine, by whom he had two sons, and secondly, his cultivation of idol worship, on which he was planning to write a book that would gain him a great reputation. What drew him to Christianity was the fact that he had an appreciation of its truth and of its sanctity, and such an appreciation that he never failed to praise it in public conventions. Then again, there was the sincere affection for him which the Fathers showed, in words and in deeds. With all these contrary influences drawing him hither and thither, he continued to fluctuate and was never able to settle his mind upon anything definite.

On one of his visits to Nankin, he brought his oldest son with him, a boy of fourteen, whom he placed with the Fathers, to have him educated as a Christian. He had often said that he was convinced that there was no other way of getting to Heaven, except by becoming a Christian. But that alone was not enough where the boy was concerned. He wanted to place him with the other students at the Mission House, where he would be thoroughly instructed in his new faith. This, of course, was very acceptable to the Fathers because of their friendship with the parent and also for the future benefit of the boy. Due to his father's devotion to Father Ricci, the boy was called Matthew, and he took readily to the study of Chinese literature and of European culture. Because of the advantages derived by this boy, resulting from his labor and industry at the Mission House, his father and their relatives and many of the nobles besides, felt that they were indebted to the Fathers for a great benefit received.

It was during this visit of Ignatius to Nankin that Brother Martinez was sent thither on some business or other. These two became acquainted while Ignatius, then known as Chiutaiso, was living with the Fathers in the province of Canton, and since that time they continued to be intimate friends. Discovering on this occasion that his friend was still a pagan, after so many years of indecision, the Brother took the liberty of his friendship to give Chiutaiso a scolding for not abandoning his vagabond way of life, and for still holding to his stubborn method of resisting the grace of God. Evidently the internal working of this same grace of God was operating during the reproving exhortation of Brother Martinez, to such an extent, indeed, that his friend resolved then and there to hearken to the voice of God. Without looking around for further excuse, he set himself to reading and rereading the Treatise of Christian Doctrine, to analyzing and to studying it, and with that done, he finally asked to be baptized. His first step was to marry his concubine. Next he sent to the Mission House all his domestic idols, together with the plates for printing, and his whole library of books on the dogma of the sects, with a request to have them all cast into a fire. He fulfilled to the letter whatever he had promised, and one day he gave such an eloquent refutation of idolatry to an audience of converts, that their utter surprise was surpassed only by their pleasure in hearing him. His baptism took place on the Feast of the Annunciation, which in that year fell on a Friday in Lent, and the Gospel of that day was the story of the raising of Lazarus from the dead. Brother Martinez preached on that occasion and touched upon the three lessons of the day; on God becoming man, on the sufferings of our Lord on the first Good Friday, and on the resurrection of Lazarus. Ignatius was present and he applied the story of Lazarus to his own history with such devotional feeling that those present were deeply and evidently affected. As he was approaching to receive the sacrament of Baptism, he prostrated himself and struck the floor with his forehead four times; a custom well known to the Chinese, as practiced by those who are begging pardon for their faults. After that he read aloud his written declaration of faith, a copy of which he gave to the Fathers as a pledge of his sincerity. We shall offer a translation of this extraordinary document, though realizing that no presentation of it in the garb of another language could hope to preserve the grace and elegance of the original.

"I, Chiu Ignatius, born on the sixth day of the second moon, in the year of Cieu [March 1549] in the City of Ciancieu, district of Suceu, in the Province of Nankin, in the reign of Tamin: I, with all reverence, and wholly repentant of all my sins, do most humbly ask pardon for them, of Almighty God. May He grant that they be washed away in the saving water of baptism and thus render me worthy of acceptance. Being a man of fifty-seven years, I do now realize that for a long time having eyes, I did not see God's holy law and having ears I would not listen to His holy name. On the contrary, I preferred to follow the sect of Scechia [the chief idol of China], though I was fully aware of the fact that it was repugnant to reason and to truth. This doctrine I spread far and wide. This was my major fault, and indeed a heinous sin, which might well have merited the deepest dungeon of the infernal regions.

"Some years ago, it was my good fortune to meet the Masters of the truth who came from the Great West, Matthew Ricci and Lazzaro Cattaneo and the Coadjutor Brother Sebastiano Fernandez. They were the first to inform me of the mysteries of the divinity. Of late I came to know Giovanni Roccia and his companion Francesco Martinez who confirmed my belief in the doctrine I had already learned. These Doctors of the law taught me that God made heaven and earth and mankind and all things else, and that all these must be subject to His law, that no sect or law contrary to His can ever be true, that through His priests God pardons the sins of those who are truly repentant, and that for this repentance He alone grants the reward of eternal happiness in Heaven. Now, believing as I do that by these means man can obtain the grace and blessing of Almighty God, I beseech The Heavenly Father to so imbue my mind with this truth that I may fully live up to it, by honoring the Divine Majesty with constant stability of heart and soul.

"I do hereby promise that from the day on which I receive the holy sacrament of baptism which cleanses the soul of every stain, I shall wholly eradicate from my mind every vestige of belief in false gods, and in the unreasonable doctrine that centers about them. I do promise also that my thoughts and wishes shall in no wise be deliberately and basely directed toward the desire for undue personal aggrandizement, nor toward secular vanity, nor toward any other false and dangerous allurement. Obedient to my heavenly Father, I shall walk in the straight path of His commandments, and by means of new and proper custody over my senses, I shall endeavor manfully to rekindle the light of reason which God has given me, so that it may shine with its originally intended splendor in my own soul and help me to share with others whatever good it may enable me to accomplish.

"As to what pertains to the articles of the Christian faith, though I cannot appreciate the grandeur of each sublime mystery, I do with all my heart humbly submit to what these articles ordain and do firmly believe all that they contain, at the same time begging the Holy Spirit to grant me the light of a better understanding. Now that I am only beginning to believe, my heart is opening to the light of grace like the tender bud of a fragile flower opening to the sun. Wherefore, I pray the Mother of God to intercede with her Divine Son, to grant me strength and vigor of soul, that my resolution may remain firm and constant rather than weak and vacillating. May God open wide the faculties of my soul, that truth may enter in and reason be sustained and my heart remain clean. Would that my mouth might be opened to preach the Divine Law to this whole kingdom, so that all my people would know this law and humbly submit to it."

Such was the courageous conversion of this man, and everyone rejoiced at it. The pagans too expressed great admiration for Christianity when they saw that Ignatius had rejected the worship of the idols, after defending it for so many years.

This shining example does not subtract from the praise due to the other converts, whose zeal became manifest whenever occasion called for it. Examples of their loyalty were of daily occurrence, but they may be omitted here, as having been related to the chronicles of the other centers. There was, however, one unusual conversion, quite worthy of our attention. It was that of a young boy, just entering his studies. He was the son of one of the King's advisers; a position of the very highest dignity. When he was brought from Pekin to Nankin and took up the study of Christianity with Li Paul, in preparation for baptism, he actually memorized the entire catechism.

Here at Nankin, Father Giovanni not only maintained, he even augmented the friendship of the local Magistrates. This served him well on various occasions and chiefly against the nagging of the district leaders, where he lived. At one time, these officials tried to influence the Magistrates to oblige the Fathers to take their regular turns on guard, as night watchmen of the city streets, and this was only one of their many interferences, relative to things which were contrary to their profession. In this particular instance, Father Soeiro was notified beforehand, and anticipated their action by visiting a friendly Magistrate, who took full charge of the matter. He immediately took the case to a higher Magistrate, who settled it, according to the law, and decided in favor of the Fathers. In the decision that was passed down they were exempted in perpetuum from all such demands, because they belonged to the Lettered Class, and because they were foreigners. And so it all ended very much to their liking, and because of the interference of their enemies they were granted a privilege which they themselves would have been very slow in requesting.

7. The First Chinese Edition of Euclid

THE FATHERS IN PEKIN were cautious, and therefore deliberately slow, in beginning to spread Christianity, for fear that the novelty of it might arouse suspicion and impede their immediate purpose of establishing a residence. Once this was accomplished and they were securely settled, there was no further cause for delay, and their every effort was put into the development of the ultimate purpose for which they had come. Here too, at this particular center, they were careful, at first, that the converts should be distinguished by their zeal rather than by their number, and in this respect the converted schoolmaster, Ignatius, whom we have already mentioned, served as an able assistant. The students who came to him were trained in Christian Doctrine as well as in letters. They were all taught to honor the crucifix which he placed in his classroom, and though they did not all become believers, at least they received an explanation of the principal truths of Christianity. There was one boy in his class afterwards called Michael, who was notably slow in learning, and whom he would not admit into his course of Christian Doctrine. He was deferring his admission, either to promote his desire, or because the boy was not as yet ready because of his age, to take up the study of religion. One day, as this boy was on his way home from school, he was either struck by or so terribly frightened by a thunderbolt, that he fell on the road, unconscious. When he came to, he said that while he was lying there, he saw God surrounded by a great number of angels, and that he heard God say, "Now I shall spare his life." He was taken home and after resting for a little while, he called for the schoolmaster, who went to the boy's home and while he was reciting one Our Father and one Hail Mary the boy recovered his full strength and returned to his normal self. Then he told the teacher what we have just narrated. The boy's mother was so pleased with his restoration to health that she offered him to God and asked to have him converted because he wished it. Later on she herself became a regularly practicing Christian and still is today.

Let us cite here an unusual incident that attracted a number of converts to the faith. One of the converts was unjustly accused of a homicide and of several other crimes. It was said that the judge in the case had been bribed with money and presents, by the accusers. The relatives of the accused were surprised by the manner in which the other Christians came to the assistance of their fellow convert. The bribe had more weight with the judge than the man's innocence. A sentence was passed and he was declared guilty. With all hope of restoring justice apparently abandoned, it would seem as if the Lord decided to come to the aid of His faithful converts. The sentence was passed in an inferior court and had to be referred to a higher court for confirmation. The day it was presented to the judge of the higher court, he said that on the very night before, in his sleep, he had seen a man whose face and whose garments were exactly the same as those of a man in a picture that was highly honored at the house of the foreign literati. This man knew the Fathers. He had been at their house and had seen the pictures there, and he said that the figure he had seen in his sleep spoke to him saying, "Why do you not come to the assistance of one of my children who is sadly oppressed?" He read and examined the case presented against the convert, reversed the verdict and declared him innocent. The plaintiff was convicted of perjury and sentenced to a severe whipping.

There was another convert, so overcome by depression that he fell into a dangerous illness. He asked one of the Fathers to come and hear his confession, and he told him that he had seen a majestic lady all in white, with an infant in her arms. There was no picture at the Mission House that would answer to his vision, but he said he believed it was the Blessed Mother and her child Jesus, and that the lady said, "This man can be cured by perspiration treatment, and I wish to have him cured." He was submitted to the treatment, removed from death's door almost immediately, and quickly recovered. In order to make certain of the disposition of the patient, the Father asked him if he had any doubts about the faith and the man said, "Why should I not believe when God himself came to bring me back to life?" When he felt that he had regained his full strength, he came to the church, without advice from anyone, and made a general confession of his whole life, from the time he had become a Christian.

The Fathers were probably more pleased with the reception of one particular convert, at that time, than with any other individual addition to their flock. This was the case of a wealthy dealer in bronze and other metals. He was eighty-two years old, and when he decided to become a Christian, he gave the Fathers his entire collection of gold plated bronze statues of the gods, and his valuable collection of books on pagan doctrine. He was instructed, baptized, and given the name of Fabian. During the three more years that he lived he was an outstanding example of patience under the financial ruin he suffered because of his business competitors, and during that time, though he lived about three miles from the church and was always very busy, he never missed attendance at Mass, on a Sunday or a feast day. Finally, he contracted a mortal illness, more dangerous than his advanced age, and having made his confession, he asked to receive the Blessed Sacrament of the Eucharist, by way of viaticum. There were no conveniences at his home for the celebration of Mass, and at that time it was not customary for the Fathers to carry the Blessed Sacrament through the streets. So they tried to console him by telling him that since he was prevented from receiving the Holy Eucharist, his confession was sufficient to bring him to heaven. As his illness increased, his desire to receive his Lord in the Blessed Sacrament became so great that he had himself carried to the Mission House, where he cried out, "Give me the Body of my Divine Master." Astounded at what he had done, they placed the dying old man on a bed in a nearby room, where he could rest while they were preparing to bring him the Holy Eucharist with proper ceremonies. The path which the priest had to follow from the church to the sickroom was strewn with carpets. The converts present, holding lighted candles, stood in prayerful attitude, forming a long aisle of passage. When Fabian realized that his Lord was approaching, he seemed to gain new life, and lifting up his voice, he said he forgave his competitors, from the bottom of his heart, for the misfortune they had brought upon him. Then he asked pardon of God for all his own sins. A few days later, fortified with the sacraments of Holy Eucharist and Extreme Unction, he went to meet his Lord. His wife, who was a catechumen at the time, had him buried with a Christian funeral, and she too became a Christian, a little later on.

In Pekin, the Fathers lived in rented houses for six years, and this had its disadvantages. The price of moving about was costly and they were unable to find a place that was convenient for erecting a church. The financial losses suffered at Macao were so great and so frequent that the Father Visitor of the Society of Jesus, much as he desired to, was never able to put this center on a sound financial basis, although it was evident that the whole mission was dependent upon it. Five hundred gold pieces would have been sufficient to buy a house large enough for the needs of their community, which at that time consisted of three priests, two Chinese novices, who were born in Macao, and two students, who were being supported by the others. These, plus the domestic servants were too many for the living quarters at their disposal, but there were no funds on hand to buy a larger place and property came high in the Capital City.

While the Fathers were looking about for quarters that would suit their needs, they heard that there was a house for sale, in a very desirable location, almost in the center of the city court district, of ample proportions and at a reasonable price. The low amount being asked for it was due to the fact that it was somewhat old, and was said to be haunted by spirits that were immune to the ceremonies of Chinese exorcism. Several friends were called in for consultation, among them Ciu Paul, and they not only provided good advice but found sufficient money to go ahead with the purchase. With this assistance, the deal was closed in three days, and the Fathers moved into their new residence on the twenty-seventh of August, sixteen hundred and five. The first thing they did was to build in a large and beautiful chapel and with that done, the Pekin center was permanently established and they felt much more at ease. The novices were assigned a section of the house away from domestic activities, and the whole project met with the approval, not only of the Fathers present but of the Father Visitor also, who forwarded money to pay off the debt and to buy the necessary added furniture. Later on, three rooms were added as a top story and three more on the ground floor, allowing them more space and more air. This house was entirely surrounded by a wall, and like so many other Chinese dwellings, when they bought it, it was only one story high, so that all it offered by way of a view, was the open sky above.

The new house became very popular and the Fathers had a host of visitors from every class and rank of the people. The hope of a harvest and the fruit already gathered was consolation for the labor expended. One of the Fathers had to be in the reception room all day long to receive visitors, and it was scarcely necessary to go abroad to preach the Gospel. Many came of their own accord and when asked why they had come they answered in two syllables: Linchiau, I came to accept the doctrine. Some came, prompted by curiosity, but their purpose in coming made little difference, so long as their visit served to make Christ better known. It was encouraging also to know that the visitors were from the higher as well as from the lower classes of the people, counting many from the nobility, the lettered class and the Magistrates. The more widespread the truth becomes in a nation like this, the more divine it is considered to be.

As soon as the house was purchased the Fathers sent the written contract of the sale to the Chief Magistrate of the civil bureau in charge of such affairs, to have him stamp it with his official seal, as proof of the fact that they had purchased a house in the Royal City with full consent of the governing Magistrates. There was one thing, however, that caused them some worry. For five years past they had never been notified about property taxes and had never inquired about them; and now they were being summoned to explain the tax arrears. Father Ricci's fear was that over and above what was due they might also have to pay a sizable fine for the long delay. So he wrote a petition to a Magistrate friend of his who was well acquainted with the tax collector of his district, asking him to consult with the collector, relative to exemptions from ordinary tax burdens, for foreigners who belonged to the class of literati. As a result of the petition, not only did the collector refrain from asking any questions about the past, he also issued a written document exempting the Fathers from taxes, in perpetuum, and removed the name of their residence from the register of places from which tribute was due to the Crown. This written document had more than one advantage attached to it; not only did it exempt them from the burden of taxes, it also served as a public affidavit, attesting that they, as foreigners, enjoyed the right of living in the Royal City. It seemed to the Fathers that, after a fashion, their church had already attained to ecclesiastical liberty in the Capital of the Kingdom.

Shortly after they were settled down in the new residence, they went on an excursion through the villages of the Pantinfu region, of the Pekin Province, about three days' travel from the Capital. Their purpose in making this journey was to find out if the faith was spreading through the country, and they were not at all disappointed with what they discovered. Within the first years of their coming to Pekin, more than a hundred and fifty converts had come into the Church in this district and the numbers continued to increase with the years.

It was during this time that the Fathers undertook a work which at first sight might not seem to be wholly in keeping with the purpose of their mission, but once put into practice proved to be quite beneficial. Doctor Ciu Paul had this one idea in mind: since volumes on faith and morals had already been printed, they should now print something on European sciences, as an introduction to further study, in which novelty should vie with proof. And so, this was done, but nothing pleased the Chinese as much as the volume on the Elements of Euclid. This perhaps was due to the fact that no people esteem mathematics as highly as the Chinese, despite their method of teaching, in which they propose all kinds of propositions but without demonstrations. The result of such a system is that anyone is free to exercise his wildest imagination relative to mathematics, without offering a definite proof of anything. In Euclid, on the contrary, they recognized something different, namely, propositions presented in order and so definitely proven that even the most obstinate could not deny them.

A friend of Paul's who had attained to the licentiate at the same time that he had, but who could not legally aspire to a higher grade, was assigned to collaborate with Father Ricci in preparing this Chinese edition of Euclid. He was the professor from whom Father Didaco was taking daily lessons in Chinese, and who lived at the Mission House to be in closer touch with the Fathers for continual conversation in Chinese. This combination of editors was not so fortunate. Some time previous, Father Ricci had told Paul that no one, unless he were a scholar of exceptional genius, could undertake this task and see it through to the end proposed. Paul, then, set himself to work. By labor and study, and by listening to Father Matthew for long hours, day after day, Ciu Paul made such progress that he wrote out in fine Chinese characters everything he had learned, and within the space of a year they published a very presentable edition of the first six books of the Elements in clear and elegant Chinese style. Here too, it may be noted that the Chinese language is in no wise deficient in idiom or in vocabulary for the proper expression of all of our scientific terminology. Ciu Paul wanted to do the rest of Euclid but Father Ricci thought they had done enough to suit their purpose. Paul then published the six divisions of Euclid in one volume, for which he wrote two preludes. The first one, written in the name of Father Ricci, dealt with the ancient author of the original work, giving credit to Father Clavius, Ricci's former teacher, for his commentary on the original, and whose explanations and principal annotations, Ricci had put into Chinese. This preface also contained an explanation of the application of the various problems and theorems, together with other mathematical data. In the second prelude Ciu Paul wrote a really excellent encomium of European science and letters. This book was greatly admired by the Chinese and it had considerable effect upon the rearrangement of their calendar. For a better understanding of it, many came to Father Ricci to enroll as his pupils, and many also to Ciu Paul, and with a teacher to direct them, they took to European scientific methods as readily as the Europeans themselves, showing a certain keenness of mind for the more subtle demonstrations.

Just after the publication of this book, Ciu Paul's elderly father died, and Paul had to leave Pekin and return to his home to live as a private citizen, for a period of three years of mourning, according to the Chinese custom. During his long absence, one of the Fathers was called from Nankin, on his request, to remain with him to care for the spiritual needs of his family and of his fellow citizens. His father's funeral was conducted with considerable pomp, but with no sign of pagan ceremonies of any kind. He spent more than a hundred and twenty gold pieces to have a special coffin constructed of incorruptible cedar. As part of the funeral service, the Fathers erected a catafalque in the church and covered it over with a black silk tapestry. The Chinese mourning color is white, but they preferred to follow the European ecclesiastical custom. Candles were kept lighted and incense burned around the catafalque, for all of which Paul insisted upon paying, in memory of his father. The converts came in solemn procession to recite the office of the dead, and Paul was present wearing a rough garment of heavy cotton, according to mourning custom. The Mass for the dead was then celebrated and the whole service was rather startling for the converts who had never witnessed it before, and who probably had no idea of how the Church honors men of distinction at their last rites. Doctor Paul took the body of his father to his native village for burial, but before leaving he gave the Fathers all the furniture from his palace, to use and to keep for him, until he should return, to take up his duties again at the expiration of his period of mourning.

8. The Founder of the Chinese Mission Dies at Macao

FATHER ALEXANDER VALIGNANO, the official Visitor of the Society of Jesus, realizing that his years were accumulating, wanted to see the Chinese Mission established on as firm a basis as possible before his work came to an end. During his long years of experience he had developed an extraordinary faculty for the establishment and for the management of missions among the pagans. His present plan was to make an excursion into the Kingdom of China, to visit the Mission Centers and to see at first hand what he had been reading about in letters received. Here, as elsewhere, he thought, our eyes are apt to fail us when we judge things at too great a distance.

Father Cattaneo had been busy among the Chinese at Macao, with not too much success, and Father Valignano decided to take him with him as a companion on the inland journey. On second thought, however, he feared that his decision to enter China might result in trouble for the whole China Mission. He considered it to be quite improbable that a man as well known as he was would not be recognized as one who had spent many years among the Japanese, between whom and the Chinese there was an undying hatred and a mortal enmity, like unto the hatred of Vatinian. So he wrote to each of the Fathers in China to get his opinion and his counsel on this particular matter, only to learn that for very different reasons their ideas were at variance. Father Ricci and some others, considering that the benefit to be derived by the Mission from such a visit far outweighed the possible danger, if there were any danger at all, strongly advised him to undertake the journey. Wherefore, in order to make assurance doubly sure, they asked for letters patent from different Magistrates, and these were obtained through the very ready assistance of Ciu Paul. The letters were issued for Father Cattaneo, who was very well known, to make a return trip into China with his companions, and the whole itinerary was so well arranged by their friends that they were to travel at the expense of the state. A public barge was to be at their disposal when they traveled by water, and three horses and six carriers when they journeyed by land. These letters were first used by Brother Francesco Martinez, who went into the Province of Canton to bring back some of the Fathers, and by means of these letters he not only traveled free, but his meals were supplied, at no charge, wherever he showed them.

Father Valignano had planned to bring in a variety of things that would be useful to the missions, and to give to each center at least a thousand gold pieces, with which they were to buy land, to be cultivated, and in this way to begin a project that would make them, at least partly, self-supporting. It was an inconvenience and a decided risk to have the security of the Mission in China dependent upon a yearly supply of provisions sent in from Macao. Most of the Fathers were dependent upon that supply for support, whereas the purchase of farm land would mean permanent tenure and would disabuse the Chinese of the idea that the Fathers eventually intended to return to their own country to wage war on China. If the amount of money allowed for the security of a mission center seems to be small, foreigners should know that commodities are so abundant and so cheap in China that twice that same amount would serve for the perpetual support of the center, if it were invested in productive soil. Because he could not do more, this was Father Valignano's idea for making the various houses self-supporting.

While all these preparations were being made, and as the Fathers on the various missions were getting ready to give the Father Visitor a pleasant reception, he fell sick of an illness that put an end to his life and to their hopes, in a very short time. He died toward the end of January, sixteen hundred and six. After sixty-nine years of a holy and a laborious life, he went to receive his reward. His death at that time was a blow to both the Japanese and the Chinese Missions. He was the promoter of the first and the founder of the second. He was so solicitous for both of these undertakings, and labored so strenuously for both of them over a long period of years, that the Mission Fathers felt as if they had been left unprotected in the midst of their numerous trials and troubles. Two great and holy men, Francis Xavier and Alexander Valignano, died just as they were about to enter the great Kingdom of China, to begin the work of their desire. After the days of Father Ricci, this same thing happened again, when another official visitor, Father Francesco Pasio, passed away in sixteen hundred and twelve, as he also was getting ready to visit the China Mission.

All this, no doubt, God permitted to happen, not because of the shortcomings of a pagan people, but that these great souls might serve as intercessors before His throne in heaven, where they would be no less interested in the spread of Christianity and far more powerful to promote it.

Father Valignano's interest in the China Mission was evident up to the very end. As he was dying, he commissioned three very capable Fathers to carry out what he had planned, and to provide the mission houses with what he had promised. The only plan of his that met with difficulties and was not fully accomplished, was his design for their annual supply of provisions by planting their own crops.

Among the things received by the different houses, from what he had collected for the Mission, were the ecclesiastical vestments which he had used, some statues and pictures and a few other holy ornaments which he was about to bring with him, all of which have been carefully preserved by the Fathers for those to come, in future memory of this great man.

9. Brother Martinez a Victim of Alleged Rebellion in Canton

DURING THE COURSE of several years of the period of our narrative, the Oriental waters were infested by Dutch pirates. For some years they met with success because the Portuguese ships of that time, though sufficiently armed to repel an attack by eastern or native craft, were not strong enough to resist European guns. At times the East Indians went in for piracy with their smaller boats, but they would not risk an attack on the larger Portuguese traders. In fact, with the coming of the Portuguese the India countries lost the domination of the seas and nearly everywhere in the east were accustomed to get clearance from a foreign Viceroy or from one of the subalterns, before sailing. If their trading ships, which were practically unarmed, fell in with Dutch or English pirates, they were easily taken over and stripped. Later on when they armed their ships with European guns and ammunition, it was a different story, and they frequently scattered or destroyed their enemies.

At this time, the Dutch pirates were so elated with their success that they decided to take over the Portuguese settlements of Malucca and Malacca and of Mozambique. How they fared in this is a matter of history which does not belong to our narrative. Their effort to invade China, though unsuccessful, is somewhat more pertinent. Evidently they were unmindful of their own weakness, or perhaps of the saying, common enough among them, that he who takes too much does not hold it safely. They tried to make a landing in the maritime province of Fuchian, on the southeast coast, making all sorts of promises to the people there, namely: that they would enrich them with merchandise, and that they would drive the Japanese and the Portuguese out of Macao, and the Spaniards out of the Philippines, as if the might of the Chinese Empire needed the help of the Dutch and their ships. When they saw that the Chinese paid no attention to their promises, they turned to threats and tried to frighten them, as though they were children, by firing off their cannon, but their threats had no more effect than their promises. When they realized that they could hope for nothing from a pretended show of power, they turned toward Malacca, to the royal port of Patana, abandoned the idea of warlike expeditions and the conquest of China, and went back to their old trade of piracy. Their chief spot for ambush was in the straits, off Singapore, where they would wait for Portuguese ships returning from China to India, laden with cargoes of Chinese exports.

These same pirates had formerly threatened to attack Macao, believing it to be a rich prize. Since the city was without protection the people were, just at this time, beginning to build a wall to serve as a fort. This fort, or wall, was being erected on a hill, close to the Jesuit College, and at the same time the Jesuit church, which had been accidentally destroyed by fire, was being rebuilt. The Chinese element of the population was bent upon preventing the building of both the church and the wall. The church was completed, despite their protest, but work on the wall was discontinued when fear of the pirates subsided.

Across from the site of the College there was what should be called a rock rather than an island, about a mile and a half in circumference. No one in the memory of the Fathers had ever lived there, and they occupied the place as a recreation center for the students, and erected a small building there. Whereupon, the Chinese thought the Portuguese were fortifying the rock as a stronghold against them. For the time being, they put aside their discontent, awaiting an opportune moment to strike, and one day when the Portuguese were all in their churches, the Magistrates presiding over the soldiers in Macao, with a mob from the lower class of the people, went out to the island, drove out the Brother and the servants by armed force, and burned down their little house. They found a picture of Saint Michael in the chapel and slashed it. The Brother could possibly have withstood the attack, but the Japanese servants would not permit him to risk the danger, and he did not wish to cause an uprising because of a small loss.

The victorious Chinese mob returned to the city, and when the Portuguese saw the smoke arising from the island and realized what had happened, they decided to burn down the house of the Magistrates. However, the Fathers calmed them down and sent them back to their homes. One of the offending Magistrates was a Saracen by birth and by religious profession. There were still many Tartars left in China, and now in their fourth generation they were considered to be natives, and were not excluded from holding public office or from aspiring to the literary class. This man was an inciter to evil, and it was he who broke up the picture, out of sheer hatred for Christianity. The Portuguese had hardly reached their homes when the Brother secretly appeared with the broken picture, to show his Superior what had happened. When the Portuguese servants saw the picture, it was too much for their tempers. They rushed over to the house of the Magistrates, dragged out the Saracen and brought him to the College, his hair all disheveled and his face marked with bruises. The Fathers sent him to the Mayor of the City, who consulted with some Portuguese citizens, and then sent him to his home. The whole affair was taken up in consultation with the Mayor of the neighboring City of Ansan, and the disturbance came to an end. The Fathers retained possession of the little island, but since it was part of the Chinese Empire, they had to put up a sign on it, exposed to public view, and bearing the King's name in Chinese characters, written in gold.

The attitude of mind of the Chinese toward the people of Macao, brought on another and a more dangerous incident, which threatened not only Macao and the Chinese trade, but even the existence of the Christian Mission in China. In the negotiation of some ecclesiastical business, a difference arose which occasioned some discord between one of the diocesan priests and a certain religious. The religious priest, who thought he had been wronged, brought the matter to the attention of the Rector of the College in Macao for adjustment. It happened that the episcopal see was vacant at the time, and the Administrator, who was directing diocesan affairs, openly favored the case of the diocesan priest. The people of the city were divided on the question, two factions arose, and the town became a sorry spectacle, with both secular factions contending almost with arms over an ecclesiastical issue. The party favoring the Administrator was not strong enough to hope for victory, either by force or before the law, and so, some of the lower element among them, who were unreasonably devoted to the Administrator, decided, without consulting him, to adopt a method which might well have ruined themselves as well as their adversaries, and perhaps the whole settlement. They would, as it were, scuttle the ship that had brought them to the island.

They persuaded the gullible Chinese that the trouble in the city was due to the fact that Father Lazzaro Cattaneo, who was still living there and going about in Chinese dress, was planning to take over the Chinese kingdom, and to establish himself as a tyrant. The Portuguese, they said, had chosen him as a leader because he knew all the roads in China and had visited both capital cities. It was reported that they were expecting the arrival of a fleet, in the near future, not only from India but from Japan as well, and that the companions of Father Lazzaro who were spread out in the various parts of China, had rounded up a host of followers and were ready and waiting for the revolution. From Macao, someone sent a book into Canton, containing the details of these rumors. It seems strange, that the ill will and envy of men should go so far at times as to risk their own safety, in order to ruin that of others.

The spread of these stories in Macao caused the Chinese inhabitants to flee to the metropolitan city, or to their own home districts, where they spread fear among the people and caused considerable disturbance. The stories were readily accepted as true, because of the fort that had been built on the rock, and because the Jesuit church had been called another fort. Moreover, the trouble over the little rocky island that had lately disturbed the city, gave a coloring of truth to what was being said. It took but little to terrify a whole people so naturally suspicious.

On hearing what was going on at Macao, the Viceroy of the Province of Canton issued an order for the conscription of the entire military and naval forces of the province. He then had all the houses, outside of the city walls of Canton, destroyed, more than a thousand as reported, causing no end of hardships to the poor. All commerce with the Portuguese was forbidden. No one was allowed to bring food into Macao. The gates in the walls of Canton, on the side facing Macao, were sealed up with stone and mortar, and the day and night watches on the walls were increased in number. An edict printed in large letters was posted, forbidding everyone under heavy penalty to receive anyone from Macao into their homes. This edict forbade especially the reception of foreign priests, who shaved a circle on the top of their heads and let the rest of the hair grow around it, but only one was named, because he was the leader of the conspiracy against the throne. The one named was Father Cattaneo, who was designated in the edict as Cotienieu. He was generally known by this name, which he had chosen, because it is the Chinese interpretation of his first name, Lazzaro, meaning divine assistance. There were many who thought that the citation in the edict referred to Father Ricci, because he was the most widely known priest on the whole mission. The metropolitan city of Canton was boiling over with war-talk, and the King was informed of the trouble by letters, accusing those who had given permission for the building of the wall and the fort. The whole affair developed a troublesome and a dangerous situation for the Fathers in Pekin.

The possible results of what had happened were painfully evident to those in charge of the government of the Portuguese settlement at Macao; so they sent representatives to Canton, who cleared their people of all charges. Then they asked that Macao be no longer deprived of its food supply, particularly as the pirates might take advantage of its unprotected condition to launch an attack. They said it was unbelievable that anyone should accuse them of inciting a conspiracy, after living there for so many years in peace, and just at a time when the city was reduced to poverty and almost depopulated, because no provision ship had arrived from India in more than three years. The result of their visit was that Chinese traders were permitted to return to Macao, but chiefly to gather information relative to the tumult. The truth finally appeared when the whole affair was thoroughly thrashed out, and not a scrap of evidence was revealed to prove that the people of Macao even dreamed of starting a revolution. The people who lost their houses complained very bitterly of the wrong they had suffered, and the High Admiral of the district, called Haitao, who had carried out the project of destruction, tried to persuade them that it was a necessary undertaking. He was fully aware of the fact that there would be a stiff penalty awaiting, if the truth were ever to reach Pekin.

It was during all this tumult that the Father Visitor was getting ready to go into the kingdom. We have mentioned that he called Brother Francesco Martinez from Nancian, to accompany him as a guide. Despite the fact that he was ill with a fever, Brother Martinez got as far as Canton, where everything was in a turmoil. While there he received a letter informing him of the death of Father Valignano, and being in doubt as to whether he should go on to Macao, as directed by Father Nicolo, the Superior at Xaucea, or return whence he had come, he wrote to the Superior of the College at Macao for advice. In the meantime, he informed the Fathers at Xaucea that what was going on in Canton made it evident that a great storm was about to break over the entire mission field in China. He was giving advice to others but refused to accept it himself. Several times he was told by friends to retire to a hiding place, because it was well known there that he was born in Macao. In his innocence, he thought the letters patent he was carrying would serve as sufficient protection, and though still suffering from a fever, he went into the church with the other converts to attend the Holy Week services. Later on, a former Canton convert, who had become an apostate, came to see the Brother and threatened to expose him if he did not pay a sum of money. When he was repulsed, he related the Brother's story to one of the marine guards, telling him that this man was a spy of Cattaneo, the ringleader of the insurrection against the crown.

The guard was looking forward to a big reward from the Magistrates for making such an important arrest; so he made sure of the spy and of the house in which he lived, and then carried the case to the Deputy Mayor in the absence of the chief official. The Deputy was told of a spy from Macao, hiding in a certain place with several companions. He was delighted with the news, because in it he thought he saw a way of protecting the Admiral and the others who were involved, including some Magistrates, from the accusation of the people, who said they had destroyed their houses without sufficient reason. Two sergeants were immediately dispatched to arrest the Brother and the others in the house with him, and to bring them in on horses and surrounded by soldiers, so it would all look very serious. The brother was sick in bed with a fever, but he was ordered to get up, and he and all the others were put in chains. There was an uncle of another Lay Brother present, with two boys, also relatives of the Brother, and two servants whom Francesco Martinez had brought with him. The soldiers made an inventory of everything in the house, then locked it and placed a seal on the lock so that no one could remove anything. Rumor spread quickly through the town that a foreign priest was arrested as a spy, and such a crowd gathered that one could hardly pass along the streets. The fact that this all took place at night made it really frightening; with torches burning to light up the road, and soldiers calling out and pushing their way through the crowd.

Arriving at the palace of the Deputy Mayor, they were immediately subjected to a cross examination without any previous questioning. During this examination, their feet were fastened tightly and painfully to two wooden bars and when the guards hit the bars with a heavy hammer they also hit the victims' feet. All during this torment Brother Martinez never uttered a single word. The guards were astounded at this, because they were accustomed to hearing prisoners weep and groan under this ordeal. The Brother exhorted his companions to remember that the Christian faith prohibited lying and told them not to permit themselves to be overcome either by promises or by torment.

The judge asked Brother Francesco who he was and why he had come into this city. He replied that he had come from Xaucea and not from Macao, and that he had letters patent from Magistrates in highest station, attesting why he was there. The judge demanded to see the letters and when he had read them he was in doubt as to what he should do. After questioning the others separately, he found that what the Brother had said was true, and fearing the indignation of the Magistrates who had written the letters, he was almost ready to free the prisoner.

The plaintiff was present, and when he was called upon to prove his accusation, he turned, with diabolic invention, to one of the boys standing by and asked him, "Do you know that this Francesco, here, bought some powder?" In Chinese the word for powder, to be used for a medical purpose, is the same as the word for gun-powder, provided a small syllable be added, and that small syllable means explosion. The word for powder to explode is ciunhio. Brother Francesco had been sick, and when he admitted that he had bought powder to use for medicine, the plaintiff yelled out, "You see he admits that he bought powder," but he added on the extra syllable, changing his sentence to, "he bought powder to explode." When the Brother heard this, he and several others warned the boy not to lie. The judge realized that the mention of gun-powder had its effect upon the people present, and this seemed to revivify a suspicion that had practically died away. So, he persuaded himself that the case was genuine. He called the boy over to him and asked him what kind of powder the Brother had bought and the boy said, "Powder for medicine." Whereupon, the judge became angry, and changing his mind, as it were, at a sign from others, he began twisting a twig between his fingers, indicating torment, at which the boy became frightened and said it was gun-powder the Brother had bought. With that to work on, as the boy had expected, the judge promised him a full pardon if he would tell all he knew. Whereupon, the boy, as if to make doubly sure of escaping the torment, told a mixture of truth and of lies, much to the liking of those who were questioning him. He said that the Brother was a religious from Macao, and that he had sent to Macao from Canton a quantity of guns and ammunition and other warlike supplies. On hearing this, the judge told someone to take off the Brother's cap to see if he was wearing the clerical tonsure, which he was, because the Brother had already been admitted to minor orders. That seemed to leave no room for further doubt in the mind of the Deputy Mayor, who laughed at the Brother and said, "If this was your purpose in coming here, what are you doing with those documents, signed by the high Magistrates?" Brother Francesco was about to explain, when the judge said, "It will all be made clear in the light of tomorrow," and ordered that they be led off to prison, separately, and in chains.

The next morning, the judge ordered the Brother's traveling bags to be brought to him and opened, and when he found letters written in European characters, books printed in the same, and clothes made in Portuguese style, he needed nothing more to confirm his doubts. Convinced that Brother Martinez had come from Macao, he concluded that the letters patent he was carrying were all counterfeit. The plaintiff, taking advantage of the fact that the judge was in a mood to believe almost anything, told him that Francesco Martinez was a celebrated magician, who could make himself disappear from the sight of everyone if they brought him some water. Hence, he said, they must be very careful not to give him or even to show him any water. As a consequence of this diabolic fiction, Brother Francesco spent many days in chains, suffering from an ever increasing thirst until, a few days before his death, some merciful soul had pity on him and secretly brought him a little water to drink.

The Deputy informed the High Admiral of all that had taken place, and he ordered that the culprits be brought before him. They appeared in the morning and they were kept standing in a public street until evening, waiting for the arrival of a Magistrate Judge. A big crowd had gathered to see the spy. Brother Francesco was recognized by some of his friends, but the guards would not permit anyone to talk to a prisoner. Scarcely had the Admiral come into court when he ordered an unheard of proceeding, namely, that all the accused be cruelly whipped, one by one. The children were spared, as they would have died under such torment. The pitiable sight of Brother Martinez moved the spectators to compassion. His long illness and the torment already suffered made him look more dead than alive.

What the Admiral sought for from this trial, was a reason or an excuse that would free him from the public charge being made against him by the people whose homes had been destroyed. To this end, he was quick in accepting the investigation, as made by the Deputy Mayor, and immediately condemned Brother Martinez to death, and two others with him; the uncle of the two boys and Ignatius, the oldest of the domestic servants. Ignatius was condemned as a companion to the spy, on the charge of treason to the Throne, and the uncle on the same charge for housing those who were plotting against the Throne. With the sentence pronounced, they were remanded to their prison cells, in chains, where Brother Martinez passed a dolorous night, suffering from his wounds and covered with blood. His hands and feet were so tightly bound in iron chains that he was helplessly unable to make the slightest movement to secure a more comfortable position. All this he endured with a marvelous display of patience.

On the following day he was again brought before the Deputy Mayor for the execution of the sentence. He was advised to make an open confession of everything, now that he had been found guilty, and he was warned that if he refused to do so, he would be beaten on the leg that was spared the day before, and on one arm also, leaving the other arm for the Viceroy to apply his punishment. Brother Francesco replied by saying that he was a Christian by profession, that he adored but one God from the time of his childhood, that he was a member of the Society of Jesus and a disciple of Father Matthew Ricci, who was in Pekin. He was very careful to make no mention of the Fathers at Xaucea, fearing that since they were in the same province, they might be summoned to give testimony. He said he had received the letters of the Magistrates on the request of his Master, and that he had concealed nothing and falsified nothing. This confession so angered the Deputy that he ordered the Brother to be beaten again, as he was the day before. But the Brother was not equal to it. It was adding one wound to another, and after the first few cruel blows, he fell unconscious. Whereupon, the Deputy put an end to the flogging, knowing that he would be accountable to the Magistrates if a man died in the process of whipping. So he had the victim placed on a table, still bound in chains with orders to carry him out quickly.

Brother Francesco Martinez died as he was being carried back to prison. Bereft of all human aid at his passing, he very probably was abundantly supplied with God's grace and the divine assistance for his journey to heaven. His death took place on the last day of March, sixteen hundred and six at the same hour of the day that Christ expired on the cross. Brother Martinez was thirty-three years old when he died, fifteen of which he spent serving God in the Society of Jesus, during which time he gave ample proof of his worth to the Fathers and to the converts. He was greatly missed by everyone. He was a man who had developed a habit of continual prayer, and one can readily believe that he passed from the terrific purge of punishment that caused his death, into the immediate enjoyment of the beatific vision.

On hearing of his death, the Magistrates sent orders to the Prefect of the Prison to have him buried where his grave would be easily distinguished from the others, in case the Viceroy should want to make further investigation about him, as the leader of the spies. And so his body was committed to the earth beyond the walls in the clothes he was wearing when he died, the hands still bound in handcuffs, and the heavy chains still dangling from the feet. This probably was permitted by God, so that His servant, being readily identified, would not miss the divine office and burial in consecrated ground, all of which was accorded him with due honor and display, when his body was recovered, as will be related hereinafter.

10.Mythical Rebellion Subsides— Missionaries Cleared of Charges

WHEN THE VICEROY was informed of the rebellion at Macao, he ordered the General of the garrison of Canton, called the Sompin, to muster the full military force of the Province and to set out posthaste and capture the City of Macao. The General, however, very wisely considered the tremendous expense of such an undertaking, and also the probability of an uncertain rebellion followed by a very certain war. So he sent some spies into Macao, who reported that the spirit of rebellion had calmed down, but the City itself had broken up into two factions, which seemed to be evidence enough that the city was not hatching a plot of sedition. These reports were sufficient also to prove that the people held the Lieutenant Governor and the Admiral in high hatred, as being the cause of the tumult.

The Lieutenant Governor, fearing the consequences of the death of Francesco Martinez, tried to attach a capital crime of treason to Ignatius, the servant of the Fathers, a crime which, in fact, had been attempted by the Ministers of the Idols at Xaucea, and with which Ignatius had no connection whatsoever. When he failed in that attempt, he ordered the jailer to cut off all supply of food from Ignatius who was still a prisoner. He hoped in this way to destroy all true evidence of his cruelty and of the wrong he had done to Brother Francesco. Some of his fellow prisoners, however, secretly supplied Ignatius with food enough to keep him alive until the Fathers came to his assistance from Xaucea.

The Lieutenant Governor wrote to the Mayor of the City of Xaucea and ordered him to see if the Fathers were concealing arms or other war apparatus. They searched the house and found nothing, but they placed guards around the property at night, much to the surprise of the Mission community who, as yet, had not heard about Brother Martinez being a prisoner, much less about his death. But it was not long before messengers from Macao told the whole story of the supposed uprising, and how one of the foreign priests had been taken as a spy. Father Cattaneo, who had lived so long at Xaucea, was announced as the ring-leader of the conspiracy. This news shook the town to its foundations, and the converts, as well as the pagan friends of the Mission, ceased coming to visit, for fear of being accused of treason.

When Father Nicolo Longobardo heard the whole story, he decided to make a personal call on the Viceroy, in order to clear up the whole affair and to liberate Brother Francesco. Some of his friends advised him to send a letter by one who could represent him, a formal document covering the case, as was customary. This he did, and his letter arrived at the same time with the Admiral who had come to talk over the same matter with the Viceroy. It was already known to the Viceroy that Brother Martinez had died from the punishment he received, and also that the threat of a tumult at Macao had subsided; but he pretended to know nothing about the whole affair and left the letter unanswered. This was a gesture on his part, which served his purpose of indicating the innocence of the accused. When the Admiral returned to Canton, it was said that he was harshly reprimanded for going ahead in so serious a matter without consultation, and for causing the death by flogging of a man from Macao who was not a spy, but was plainly proven to be a disciple of the European priests who had been invited to live at Xaucea by several Viceroys. After the messengers had delivered their letters they set out for Canton to deliver another to certain Magistrates, who were acquainted with all that had happened. On hearing of the death of Brother Martinez, these messengers went straightway to the prison to comfort the other prisoners, to bring them much needed food and to promise help for the near future. The very thought of a ray of hope appearing through the darkness of such a desperate outlook, was enough to rekindle their fading sparks of life.

The condition of affairs in the Province of Canton at that time was such, that the status of the entire expedition into China was never in more serious danger, but Divine Assistance was not long lacking. It came with the return from Pekin of one of the High Magistrates of the Order of the Tauli, who restored universal order to such an extent that Father Nicolo, who had borne the brunt of it all, was accustomed to style him an angel sent from heaven to re-establish the standing of Christianity. It all came about as follows. The Ciau Tauli returned from Pekin, bearing new honors and confirmed in those already acquired. He was sent to the Metropolitan City of Canton to take over the affairs of the Admiral who had resigned his position, fearing that he would be expelled as the author of the trumped-up rebellion. The new incumbent of his office had contracted an intimate friendship with the Fathers in Pekin, and especially with Father Matthew Ricci. On his arrival at Xaucea, Father Longobardo, a friend of long standing, went to see him and was most cordially received. Speaking publicly and in the open court, he told them a great deal about Father Ricci, and about the other Fathers in Pekin, and said he had received a sundial from them as a gift, and he added that he would like to learn how to regulate it.

In the meantime, Father Nicolo gave him detailed information about the false rebellion, about the unjust death of Brother Martinez and the imprisonment of the others in Canton, and asked him to do what he could for their cause. In order not to miss any point of importance he copied out everything at length in a notebook. He said he would do everything in his power to reveal their innocence, but he did not wish to take Father Nicolo back to Canton with him. He was eager to assist their cause but he wanted everything conducted on a strictly legal basis. Father Nicolo, however, did go to Canton shortly after the Tauli left Xaucea. His purpose in going at that time was to bring back the body of Brother Francesco, but it was too soon to negotiate for that; so he returned to Xaucea, bringing with him the annual allowance of provisions furnished by the Portuguese who had just arrived for trading.

When the new Admiral arrived in the Metropolitan City, he found the place in a turmoil. The over-suspicious people had not put aside their fear of an outbreak. Although he had become fully acquainted with the entire procedure of this affair, he pretended to retain certain doubts relative to the Macao disturbance in order to close the whole case in a strictly legal way. First, he sent a letter to the Mayor of Xaucea, requesting information concerning the identity of Longobardo, Cattaneo, Brother Francesco Martinez and Ignatius. The Mayor, who was aware of the friendship of the Admiral for the Fathers, instituted a hasty investigation and returned a report that would insure the innocence of those concerned. The new Admiral, or Commissioner of Marine Affairs, sent an experienced Military Prefect to investigate conditions at Macao. As he approached the City, he sent word ahead to notify Father Cattaneo of his coming, and to ask his permission to disembark, saying that he wanted to talk over certain matters with him at the college. The Military Prefect thought that Father Cattaneo was not only Director of the College but of the entire city as well. Father Cattaneo answered, saying that the Chinese were not accustomed to ask for permission to disembark at Macao, and that if permission were necessary, he was not the one to grant it. After giving his answer, he went back with the messenger, met the Prefect and brought him to the College, where he was received with all possible respect and courtesy. They showed him every department of the entire institution, and when they entered the library, Father Cattaneo said, pointing to the array of books, "Here are the arms with which I was aspiring to overthrow the Kingdom of China," and when they went into the first classroom, he said, indicating the students, "Here are the soldiers I am training to conquer your Empire." Then he explained that the Fathers were members of a religious order, laboring for their own salvation and for the eternal salvation of others. After his visit to the College, they took him on a survey of the entire city, during which he made an inspection of every religious house, every hostelry and every hospital in the settlement. On his return to Canton, his report was quite contrary to what rumor had spread abroad, and he was especially high in his praise of Father Cattaneo and his companions.

With this information at hand, the new Admiral transferred the entire case from the jurisdiction of the Deputy Mayor to that of the Fourth City Assessor, who was publicly known to have been wholly dissatisfied with what had been going on. After examining the process of the case, he made a report of the harm and of the injustice done and still being done to the Fathers, and also of the confused and inept manner in which the first Admiral and the Deputy Mayor had conducted the whole matter. The new Admiral then summoned the accuser, a Captain of the Marine Guards in Canton, to appear in his court, together with those who were still being held as prisoners. First, addressing the accuser he said, "Approach the bench, you most despicable of mortal men, you who treasonably brought about the death of Francesco Martinez and most unjustly detained the others in prison, after putting them through a long and horrible torment. The vengeance of heaven is now about to fall upon your own head. Where is the gun-powder? Where are the arms and the other paraphernalia of war? Is it thus that three youths are going to make the conquest of the Kingdom? You were prompted to all this by your spirit of avarice, and your thirst for money, and now I will give you full payment for your treachery. I am now sending you to the Viceroy, and if he does not whip you enough for your misdeeds, I shall be waiting here, to see that you receive the full payment for your horrible crime." Whereupon, the accuser, dumbfounded from fear, fell down and struck the floor three times with his forehead, in the Chinese fashion of begging for pardon. Then he was sent to the Assessor, who had taken over his case and from whom he heard a less consoling condemnation. When asked why he had trumped up this calumny, he said he did it to please the Deputy Mayor, who made use of every artifice to prove to the people that the fear of a Portuguese uprising was very well grounded. After that, they were all sent to appear before the Viceroy, but the other prisoners, Ignatius and the uncle and the two boys, were first set at liberty. The purpose in having them appear before the Viceroy was to see that justice was done for what they had suffered at the hands of the accuser. There seemed to be no doubt about the fact that the Viceroy, with a full knowledge of all the facts in the case, would have passed a death sentence upon the guilty accuser, were it not for the fact that the culprit had paid off a relative of the Viceroy to intercede for his life. He escaped a sentence, but he did not dare to return to Canton. He and all his relations went into voluntary exile, after spreading a rumor that he had died; and there may have been some truth in the rumor, because from that time on no one ever saw him again or even heard of him.

During the following year, according to Chinese custom, there took place the general investigation of all Magistrates and Judges, as a result of which the first Admiral and the Deputy Mayor were discharged from office, and declared unsuitable for public office for the rest of their lives. They were both found guilty of malfeasance in handling the supposed Portuguese uprising, and on other added charges.

On learning that all was progressing so favorably, Father Cattaneo, who was at Macao at the time, decided to take advantage of the occasion by sending a brochure to the court in Canton, replying to the calumnious charges that had been made against him. He also mentioned that he was in possession of letters patent, issued by the presiding judge of a court of Nankin, permitting him to return to that city; and he concluded by stating that if it were agreeable to the Tauli, he would like to clear himself of the aforesaid charges in the court of the Tauli in Canton. The new Admiral was quite pleased to receive this request and answered as follows: "Relative to the charges you mention, your innocence is as evident as the sunshine. Of this I have been fully convinced from the beginning. Do not put yourself to the inconvenience of coming to Canton, to answer the charges that have already been judged as utterly false. Rest assured that no one will cause you any further trouble in this respect." He then wrote out a public edict, containing the charges which Father Cattaneo had enumerated and his own reply to the Father's request, informing the people that they could rest at ease, because everything that had been said about the Portuguese and about Father Cattaneo, relative to an attempted rebellion, was utterly untrue. This edict, according to his order, was to be posted in all public places and left exposed for a period of two months.

Just before his death, Father Valignano arranged to have Father Cattaneo return to his post and to take another Father with him. Father Sabatino de Ursis, an Italian, was selected to accompany him; and now that the disturbance had abated, it seemed an opportune time for them to enter the Kingdom. They got as far as Xaucea, in a hired boat, and without any mishap. Father Cattaneo brought along his request to the Admiral and the answer he received to it. The next step in their journey was to Nankin, by boat, to pass on from there through the other provinces. Here Father Cattaneo was recognized by the Commissary of the Government Lodge, who would not permit him to pass over the famous mountain already described. He said that the edicts formerly published against him had not as yet been revoked, and that none of the Magistrates, from there on, would believe him or trust him, because they had not heard of the latest edict published by the new Admiral. This forced them to return to Xaucea where the Admiral who had judged the case was living, and from whom Father Cattaneo asked for a written document proving his innocence of the charges made against him.

Hearing that he was there, the Admiral asked him to appear in his court on the following day; an order which did not seem to be wholly free of danger. Why should the Admiral send him a formal summons to appear in court, with the remark that he himself would dispose of the Cattaneo case on the following day? However, despite the dubious outcome, the Father went to the court, prepared for anything that might happen. As he made his appearance, the Admiral, in order to set him at ease, asked him with a smiling countenance, if he had completed his conquest of the Chinese Empire. Next, he asked him about the Japanese who had landed at Macao, and about the Ethiopian servants of the Portuguese. The Father answered that the Japanese had been driven in there by a storm, that they were received in their distress, as an act of piety, but immediately sent away again on their journey to Japan. As to the Ethiopian servants, he explained that if they had done any harm to the Chinese, they did it unknown to and against the wishes of their masters. The Admiral was in full accord with the decision of Father Cattaneo to quit the City of Macao, where he had calumniators who had formulated the false charges against him. The Fathers found out, later on, that the Admiral had already written to the Viceroy saying that he had seen Cattaneo and declared him absolutely innocent of the charges, and that the whole Macao affair had been peacefully concluded. The Viceroy in turn sent a full and detailed account of the whole affair to the King, exposing the false rumors and demonstrating, with abundant proofs, that the Portuguese at Macao did not wish to, nor were they able to plot a rebellion against the Kingdom. This letter was read by the Fathers, and a copy of it, translated into Portuguese, was sent to their companions in Macao.

Fortified with this document, the two continued their journey peacefully and at Nancian they found letters from Father Ricci, their Superior, in which Father Cattaneo was directed to remain in Nankin, and Father Sabatino to continue the journey to Pekin. The Admiral had given Father Nicolo permission to transport the body of Brother Francesco Martinez; so he went to Canton and recovered the body which was readily identified by the clothes and the chains still on it. These were badges of honor, rather than of disgrace, with which he had been buried. The body was brought to Xaucea, where Brother Francesco was honored with full Christian funeral rites, and wept for by both Christians and pagans alike. All this was very timely, proving his innocence and purging his name and the names of those who were associated with him, of a false and calumnious charge. Later on, his remains were taken to Macao to be buried in the community cemetery. And so ended the great disturbance at Canton, in such a way that the Mission would seem to have profited by it all, rather than suffered any damage to its future prospects. But this was not the end of their troubles. At that very time the Fathers at Xaucea found themselves facing a double danger.

The Mayor of the town, or the sub-President as he was called, was an avaricious fellow, with a reputation for scheming, and for gathering in money from every possible source. They said that by his direction, or at least with his connivance, someone had secretly cast a pamphlet into his courtyard at night, containing a false accusation against Father Nicolo. The names of the four Prefects of Public Order of the district in which the Mission House was situated, were mentioned in this pamphlet, as entering a charge against the Father for misconduct with a woman of that district. The Father was notified that he would have to answer the charge in court. Whereupon, he anticipated their action by calling for an immediate and thorough investigation of the matter, and a public pronouncement of the truth. The four Prefects were called to attest that they were making the accusation. It was reported that this whole affair was the scheme of a certain avaricious man who had to get money to escape an impending danger. He was now seeking to blackmail the Fathers, as he had done only recently to one of the Ministers of the idols, who had to pay dearly to escape a charge and the punishment attached. The four Prefects flatly denied that they had written the accusation, and no amount of whipping or blows could force them to depose otherwise. One of them, in the midst of the punishment being administered, declared that if ever he were to accuse an innocent man of such a heinous crime, neither he nor his posterity could hope to escape the vengeance of heaven. The woman involved broke down under threatened punishment, confessed that she was guilty of misconduct with other men, but persistently denied that she had ever known or seen the foreign priest.

In the meantime the blackmailer approached Father Nicolo several times, and asked for money to declare his innocence, but the Father refused either to give or to promise a single obol, realizing that such a concession could serve as a pretext for future extortions that would be still more difficult to avoid. Both the converts and the pagans showed great admiration for his determination in this matter. Once he realized that there was no further hope of bribe money, the venal Mayor closed the case with a somewhat unusual judgment; the four Prefects were each fined a certain sum, for denying that they had written the accusation. Father Nicolo was declared innocent of this calumny and of all crimes from any other source, and pronounced to be a man who had always enjoyed a high reputation for honesty and integrity. The Fathers felt particularly thankful to God for the part of that judgment pertaining to Father Nicolo, because they realized that a preacher of the Gospel had been freed of a charge that might have been damaging to the whole cause of Christianity.

With that case closed, another followed close upon its heels. With the subsiding of the tumult at Canton, one of the Military Prefects came to Xaucea from the metropolitan city. Because of his talk, the whole neighborhood became persuaded that the section of the city on the other side of the river was in evident danger because of the presence of the Fathers. This offered an occasion for starting trouble and the people sent in a written complaint to the Admiral at Canton; the one who had judged the case of the so-called Macao rebellion. They requested him to expel the Missionaries from the city, because of the trouble they were so frequently causing, across the river, saying that they themselves had more than once been punished by the Magistrates because of them. Although the Admiral Judge was fully aware of the injustice of this petition, and that, according to the law, they should have been punished for making such an accusation, yet he issued an edict, ordering them to be on guard against another of the Fathers arriving there from Macao. If another did arrive, they were not to permit him to pass from there into the other provinces, and he assured them that if this were attempted, all the Fathers would be expelled from the residence. This edict was sufficient to quiet them for the time being, but this disturbing announcement was enough to cause the Fathers to decide upon giving up the residence at Xaucea and transferring their activities to other parts.

The tumult at Canton had turned many against them, it had chilled the ardor of many of the converts, and there was reason to doubt that this district would long remain in repose. However, they decided also not to move hastily, lest it might appear that they had been expelled.

11. Cathay and China

The Extraordinary Odyssey of a Jesuit Lay Brother

LETTERS FROM the Fathers who were living at the Royal Court of Mogor, to their brethren in India, made mention of the famous Empire, which the Saracens called Cathay. This name was formerly known in Europe from the writings of Marco Polo, the Venetian, but through several centuries it was forgotten to such an extent that scarcely anyone now believed in the existence of such a place. The Fathers said in their letters that this kingdom of Cathay was to the east, and a little to the north of the kingdom of Mogor. They also reported that there were many Christians living there, and that they had churches and priests and observed the Christian ceremonies. The Portuguese Father Nicolo Pimenta, the official Visitor of the Society of Jesus in Eastern India, was greatly concerned about holding these people of Cathay in the true faith, through the efforts of the Fathers of the Society. It was not difficult to believe that a people so far distant from the center of Christianity might easily have fallen into various errors. He therefore decided to take up this question with the Pope and with the Catholic King. Orders were sent by the King to his Viceroy, Arias Saldagna, commanding him to co-operate in the undertaking, suggested by the Father Visitor, with money and with his influence. This he did, and very generously, because of his desire for the propagation of the faith and also because of his devotion to the Society. For the accomplishment of a proposed expedition of investigation, the Father Visitor selected the Portuguese Lay Brother Bento de Goës, a prudent man and an exemplary religious. Because of his long residence in the Mogor country, Brother Goës had an excellent knowledge of the Persian language, as well as a keen insight into Saracen customs, both of which seemed to be necessary requirements for the one about to undertake this journey.

In letters sent by Father Matthew Ricci from the Capital of China, the Fathers had read that Cathay was only another name for the King-

dom of China. This had been confirmed by various proofs already offered, but the letters from the Fathers at the Court of Mogor held a
contrary opinion. At first, the Father Visitor was in doubt about which
opinion he should accept, but afterwards he favored that of his brethren
in Mogor. It had been asserted that there were a great number of
Christians in Cathay, and yet at the same time it was generally believed
that this strange sect had never drifted into China. It had also been
denied that there had ever been any sign of Christianity in China,
while the eyewitness testimony of the Saracens seemed to establish the
fact that they had seen such signs in Cathay. Another conjecture was,
that the name of a kingdom contiguous to China was being applied
to the Kingdom of China. In order to put an end to these conflicting
doubts, and also to find out whether or not there was a shorter route
for carrying on commerce with the Chinese people, they finally settled
upon this expedition of investigation.

Relative to the number of Christians who were so definitely said to
be in Cathay, meaning in China as we shall see, the Saracen witnesses
were either grossly exaggerating, as is common with them, or they
were misled by external appearances and reported as true what they
only imagined. They themselves never pay homage to an image of any
kind, and when they saw the numerous idols in the Chinese temples,
which may at times resemble our statues of the Blessed Mother or of
the saints, they may have concluded that Christianity and the religion
of China were one and the same. Probably they also saw lamps and
wax candles on the altars, and pagan ministers wearing vestments
which resemble the pluvials or long robes mentioned in our books of
ceremonies, and so mistook the outward display of the worshippers. It
could be also, that they heard chanting in the temples which sounded
like the Gregorian chant in our churches. All this they could have seen
and heard and other imitations also introduced into heathen rites by
the Devil, an awkward imitator of holy things, trying to usurp the
honor that belongs to God. An accumulation of such evidence could
very easily mislead a number of merchants, especially if they were
Saracen, to believe that the people professed the Christian religion.

When our Brother Bento was ready to begin his journey, he adopted
the dress of a Christian Armenian merchant and, according to Armenian
custom, called himself Abdula, meaning Servant of the Lord, to which
he added the word Isai, or Christian. Achabar, the King of Mogor,
who was a friend of the Jesuit Fathers, and especially of Brother
Bento, gave him various letters patent for different rulers in the

countries that were tributary or friendly to him. Traveling as an Armenian, he would be allowed to pass freely; as a Spaniard, he would most certainly have run into difficulties. His baggage consisted of various wares, to be sold for his own support and also to give him the appearance of a trading merchant. He had an ample supply of goods from India and also from the Mogor country, which were supplied by the Viceroy of India and added to by King Achabar, himself.

Father Jerome Xavier, who had been Director of the Mogor Mission for many years, named two Greeks to accompany Goës on the journey, believing that they were acquainted with the country through which he was to pass. One of these was a priest named Leo Grimano, who went along as company to Bento, the other was a trader named Demetrius. He also took along four servants, Saracens by birth, who had been converted to Christianity. When he came to Laor, the second capital city of the Mogor kingdom, he let the servants go, since they were of no assistance, and instead of them he hired an Armenian named Isaac, who lived in Laor with his wife and family. Isaac was the most devoted of his whole company and remained with him, like a faithful Achates, during the entire journey. Brother Bento bade adieu to his Superior and started on his famous Odyssey, as shown in his letters patent, on the sixth of January, 1603.

Each year a caravan of merchants gathers at Laor to journey to the capital of Cascar, a country with its own king. They travel in groups for company and as protection against bandits. In this caravan there were about five hundred persons, with numerous mules and camels and wagons. It was thus that Bento set out from Laor, in Lent of the year above mentioned, and after a month on the road they arrived at the town of Athec and were not as yet beyond the boundary of the district of Laor. Here they remained for about two weeks before crossing a river, a bow shot in width, in boats supplied for ferrying merchants. They stopped for five days on the opposite side of the river because they heard that there was a numerous band of robbers in the vicinity. Two months later they came to the City of Passaur, where they decided to rest for twenty days.

Later on during the journey, as they were approaching a small town, they came upon a hermit on pilgrimage. He told them that after thirty days of travel they would come into the town of Capherstram, into which no Saracen was permitted to enter under pain of death. Pagan merchants could enter but they could not go into the temples. He said that the people themselves always dressed in black when they went into their temples, and he also remarked that the country was very fertile and produced an abundance of grapes. When Bento arrived there he proved that their wine was about the same as his own. Such a thing is so extraordinary among the Saracens of those regions, that it gave rise to the suspicion that the country might have been inhabited by Christians. After meeting the pilgrim, they made another halt of twenty days, and as that country was also said to be full of bandits, they secured a military escort of four hundred soldiers from the ruler of the district. From here they traveled twenty-five days to a settlement called Ghideli. During this part of the journey, the baggage and the pack animals were sent along the foot of the hills, while the armed merchants kept the robbers off the upper slopes, to prevent them from rolling down boulders on the passing caravan. The merchants pay toll at Ghideli and it was here that they were set upon by the bandits. Many of the party were mortally wounded and it was only with great difficulty that both lives and baggage were saved. Bento and some others fled into the woods but they returned at night and made their escape from the attackers. Twenty days later they arrived at Cabul, a busy trading center within the Mogor territory. Here the whole convoy waited for eight full months, some of them declining to continue the journey and others fearing to proceed in so small a company.

At Cabul the caravan was met by the sister of the King of Cascar, through whose country they had to pass en route to Cathay. The King was Mafamet Can. His sister was the mother of the Lord of Cotan, who was also a king, and she was called Agehanem. The title Age is given by the Saracens to pilgrims who visit the tomb of the prophet at Mecca. This lady was now on her return journey from the long trip to Mecca, where she had gone on pilgrimage out of devotion to her erroneous creed. Being short of money, she came to ask help from the merchants, promising to repay any loan they would make with good interest, when they reached their country. Brother Bento realized that the influence of the letters given to him by the King of Mogor would be at an end when they passed into another country, and in the lady's request he thought he saw an opportunity of gaining the good will of the king of the country into which he would presently enter. With this in mind he made her a loan of six hundred gold pieces, which he had from the sale of his wares, but on condition that there would be no question of interest on the loan. The lady was not to be outdone in generosity. She afterwards repaid him abundantly with pieces of a particular kind of marble which is very highly prized by the Chinese and the most valuable commodity that one could bring to Cathay.

The priest Leo Grimano left the party at Cabul to return to Laor. He was exhausted from travel, and Bento's comrade Demetrius remained there for business reasons. So Brother Goës set out again with the caravan, with the Armenian as his only personal companion. Others had joined the group and they thought they were numerous enough to continue the journey with security. The next town they came to was Ciarica, where there was an abundance of iron, and here Bento met with considerable trouble. They were now at the extremity of the Mogor country and the letters patent which he had from the king, exempting him from tolls and impost, were of no further benefit to him. Ten days later they came to a small settlement called Paruam, the last stop within Mogor territory. After five days' rest they set out on a twenty day trek, over a lofty range of mountains, to a place called Aingharan, and after fifteen days more they came to Calcia, a district where the people have blond hair and beards, like the Belgians, and who live in numerous small settlements scattered about the country. Again, ten days later they were in Gialalabath, where the Bracmans collect tolls, on a grant made in their favor by the King of Bruart. After two weeks more of travel they arrived at Talhan, where they were delayed for a month because of the civil war that was in progress. With the people of Calcia in rebellion, all roads were held to be dangerous. Their next stop was at Cheman which is under the jurisdiction of Abdula Chan, King of Samarhan, Burgavia, Bacharat and other bordering countries.

Cheman is a small town and the Prefect or Mayor of the place advised the merchants to come within the city walls, as protection from attack by the Calcia rebels. The merchants replied that they would prefer to pay the tax and then continue on their way by night. In answer to this, the Mayor ordered them not to proceed, saying that the rebels had no horses but might get them by attacking the caravan and then be able to ravage the country and to do serious harm to the town. He advised them that it would be for their own benefit to join his forces and help beat off the invaders. They were just coming to the town walls when a cry arose that the Calcia rebels were coming. With this, the Mayor and his brave troop took to flight. The merchants quickly built a barricade and behind it piled up a heap of stones to use as weapons in case their arrows gave out. When the Calcians saw this they sent over messengers to say that there was no cause for alarm because they were quite willing to protect and to escort the caravan. The merchants put no trust in this; instead, they held quick counsel and decided to take to flight. Someone reported their design to the rebels and they immediately rushed forward, demolished the baggage ramparts and then took to plundering. Then the robbers called the merchants out of the woods and allowed them to withdraw behind the walls of the empty city, with what little baggage they had left them. Brother Bento lost only one of his horses, which he afterwards recovered in exchange for a quantity of cotton cloth. They stayed in the town, but in constant fear that the rebels might attack the place and kill them all. It happened very timely that one of the high chieftains named Olobet Ebadescan, of Buchara, dispatched his brother to the rebels and he persuaded them by threats to allow the merchants to continue their journey unmolested. During the rest of the journey, however, the rear of the caravan was constantly being harassed by robber bands. On one occasion, while Brother Bento was bringing up the rear, he was caught in a surprise attack by four bandits who were lying in hiding, but he escaped by quick thinking and by the following clever ruse. He snatched off his Persian hat and flung it at them and while they were kicking it around like a football, he put spurs to his horse, got the safe distance of an arrow's flight away from them, and safely joined the caravan.

After eight days of travel over the worst roads imaginable they came to the Tengi-Badascian. Tengi means a rough road, and this one was so very narrow that only one person at a time could pass along it, and it was high up above a river bed. Here the people of a nearby town, assisted by a band of soldiers, made a foray against the travelers and Brother Bento lost three of his horses, which he afterwards bought back by giving sundry presents in exchange for them. They remained here for ten days, after which, in a single day's journey they reached Ciarciunar, where they were forced to halt for five days in the open country because of the heavy rains. Here also, they suffered not only from the weather but from another attack by bandits. From there, in ten days, they reached Serpanil, an absolutely desolate place, with no signs of human habitation; and leaving here they began a laborious climb over the high mountain called Sacrithma. Only the strongest of the horses could make this ascent; the others followed a longer but an easier road around it. Here two of Brother Bento's pack mules went lame with sore feet. The servants, who were themselves exhausted, wanted to turn them loose, but somehow they managed to lead them along in the rear.

Twenty days later they reached the province of Sarcil, where they found a number of villages clustered together. They waited here for two days to rest the horses and two days later they were on the opposite side and at the foot of the mountain named Sacrithma. This mountain was covered with snow, and during the passage over it many of the company were frozen to death. Brother Bento just escaped the same fate when they were snowed in for six whole days. Finally they arrived at Tanghetar, which belonged to the King of Cascar. It was here that Isaac the Armenian fell off the bank of a big river and was unconscious for about eight hours until he was revived by Brother Bento.

Two weeks more of hard travel and they came into the town of Iaconich. The roads during this part of their march were so rough that six of the Brother's horses died of exhaustion. From here Bento went on ahead and alone. It took him five days to reach the capital, Hiarchan, and from there he sent back horses for the caravan and provisions for his companions. Not long afterwards they arrived safely at the capital with all their luggage and merchandise. That was in November of the same year, 1603.

12. Cathay and China Proved to Be Identical

HIARCHAN is the capital of the Kingdom of Cascar and a great trading center, because of the frequent gathering of merchants and the great variety of wares they have to offer. Here the cavaran of Cabul merchants disbands and a new one is formed to set out for Cathay. The leadership of the Cathay caravan is sold to the King, and the chieftain who makes the purchase is granted a sort of royal authority over the travelers during the whole journey. A year went by before a new Cathay expedition was formed. The undertaking is long and dangerous and this particular caravan is formed, not every year, but when sufficient in number can be gathered together, and then only when it is known for certain that they will be allowed to enter Cathay.

The most valuable article for trading, and the best adapted as an investment for the journey, consists of pieces of a kind of translucent marble which, for want of a better name is called jasper. These pieces of jasper, or jade, are intended for the Emperor of Cathay, and they are valuable because of the high price which he feels he must pay for them in keeping with his dignity as Emperor. The specimens which he rejects may be disposed of in private trading. The profit made by the selling of jade is considered to be quite sufficient to make up for all the trouble and expense of the hazardous journey.

This kind of marble is used for making a great variety of articles such as vases, clasps for mantles and belts, and other such ornaments; and when these are artistically designed and carved in flowers and foliage, they make very attractive decorations. This marble, of which there seems to be plenty in the kingdom of Cascar at present, is called tusce by the Chinese. There are two different kinds; the first and the better sort is procured from the river Cotan, not far distant from the capital, in somewhat the same manner as divers go down for pearls, and it is brought up in pieces about the size of thick flints. The second and inferior kind is quarried from mountains and the larger pieces are split into slabs about two ells, or four feet, square. These are then cut into sizes more adaptable for transportation. The mountain from which this marble is procured is almost twenty days' journey from the capital and is called Cansangui-Cascio meaning, "stone mountain." It is probably the mountain mentioned under the same name in some of our geographical accounts of this country. Because of the hardness of this stone, and also because of the distant and forsaken location where it lies, the quarrying of it is a task involving tremendous labor. It is said that the marble is sometimes rendered softer by lighting a huge fire on the surface above it. The right to quarry jade is sold by the King to the highest bidding merchant, and during the period of his lease other prospectors are not permitted to work there. When a group of miners goes to this mountain they bring along provisions for a whole year, knowing that they will not get back to any inhabited settlement for that length of time.

Brother Bento went to pay a visit of courtesy to the King, Mahamethin, by whom he was very graciously received because of the presents he brought. He gave him a watch to be worn on a chain around the neck, a looking glass and other European trinkets with which the king was so pleased and charmed that he took the donor into his friendship and under his patronage. At first, Bento did not make known his desire to go to Cathay. He spoke only of the kingdom of Cialis, east of Cascar, and asked for a royal document for that part of the country. His request was favorably supported by the son of the queen to whom he had given the six hundred pieces of gold. Here too he came into the good graces of several of the courtiers.

Six months had passed when Demetrius, who had set out with him on the journey and then remained behind at Cabul, unexpectedly appeared at Hiarchan. Bento and Isaac the Armenian were delighted at his arrival, but their joy was of short duration; for, not long after his coming, Demetrius was the cause of considerable trouble. It was a custom, with permission of the King, for the merchants to elect one of their number as a so-called emperor, to whom all the others paid honor and gave presents. Demetrius, desiring to save what he had, refused to offer a present, and barely escaped being thrown into prison and flogged, as the so-called emperor had the power of inflicting such punishment upon those who refused to recognize his authority. With the help of a small donation and by the exercise of his tact and intercession, Brother Bento arranged the whole matter with them and secured a pardon for Demetrius. A more serious danger followed when thieves broke into their house, seized the Armenian, bound him up, and then put a knife to his throat to prevent him from calling for help. The noise they made brought Bento and Demetrius and the robbers fled away.

At another time, Brother Bento went away to get the payment for the loan he had made to the mother of the King of Quotan. The capital city where she lived was distant a journey of ten days and he had not returned after a whole month had passed. When the Saracens heard this they spread a false report that Bento was dead. They said he had been put to death by their priests for refusing to call on the name of the prophet. These cunning priests, whom they call Cacisces, then tried to steal his property, claiming he had died without making a will and leaving no heirs. This was a cause of no little trouble to Isaac and Demetrius, who wept daily because of the death of their friend and were in constant fear for their own lives. However, their sorrow was turned into exulting joy, when Bento returned safe and sound. His debt had been generously repaid in pieces of the valuable marble we have described. As an offering of thanksgiving for his safe return he distributed a large sum in alms to the poor, a practice which he followed throughout the entire length of his travels.

One day, as he was seated with a party of Saracens who had invited him to dinner, a raving idiot broke into the company, wielding a sword which he pointed at Bento's heart and ordered him to invoke the name Mahomet. To this he answered that they made no invocation to such a name in the religion which he professed, and so he must definitely refuse to do so. The others came to his assistance and the fanatic was expelled. It was said that this same threat of death, unless he called upon Mahomet, was frequently made to him during his journey, but the grace of God saved him and carried him through to the end.

On another occasion, the King of Cascar sent for him when the priests and the literati of their abominable faith were present. They call their learned class Mullahs. When they asked him what faith he professed, that of Moses or of David or of Mahomet, and in what direction he faced when he prayed, the Brother replied that he professed the faith of Jesus, whom they call Isai, and that it made no difference how they faced to pray because God was everywhere. The last part of his answer gave rise to a discussion among them, because when they pray they always face toward the west. Finally, they concluded that Christianity also might possibly have some good in it.

By this time a native, named Agiasi, was elected chieftain of the proposed caravan of merchants. He had heard that Brother Bento was a virtuous man as well as an outstanding merchant, and so he invited him to a sumptuous banquet at his house, where they had their own kind of music while they were eating. When the meal was over, the chieftain invited Bento to accompany the caravan to Cathay. This was just what he had been waiting for; but his experience with the Saracens had taught him how to deal with them, and so he waited for the invitation to come from them, so that, according to good manners, he would appear to be granting a favor rather than accepting one. Whereupon, the chieftain asked the King to make the request, and it was the King who asked Bento to accompany the Caruan Basa, as the head of the caravan is called. This, Bento agreed to do provided the king would give him letters patent for the entire length of the journey.

Some of his fellow travelers who had come in the caravan from Cabul, were opposed to his setting out in advance, saying that such parties should be made up of larger numbers. They cautioned him against placing any trust in the natives, insisting that this was a plot by which they were planning to do away with his fortune, if not with his life. Bento assured them that he was following the King's desire, and told them that he had made a promise to the leader of the caravan, which, as an honest man, he could not revoke. The concern of his merchant friends was not altogether an idle fear, as many of the natives of the place said that those three Armenians, whom they identified by their common faith, would be murdered as soon as they passed beyond the city walls. Demetrius became frightened and for the second time refused to continue the journey. Not only that, he also tried to persuade Bento to return home from that place. But Goës refused, saying that he had never as yet turned away from the performance of the duty of obedience, because of the fear of death, nor would he at present, on a mission from which the glory of God could be so greatly increased. In addition to this, he insisted that it would be wholly unbecoming to destroy the hope of many, because of the fear of death, and to dissipate the expense entered into by the Archbishop of Goa and the Viceroy. With the help of God who had preserved him in prosperity, he still had hope of completing the expedition. At any rate, he would rather risk his life in this great undertaking than withdraw from what he had set out to do. So he girded himself for the excursion, and in addition to the one he had for himself, he bought ten more horses for his companions to use as pack animals.

In the meantime, the leader of the caravan went to his home, five days' journey from the capital, in order to prepare for the long and hazardous trek. On his arrival there, he sent a message to Bento to get under way as soon as possible and thus to set an example for the other merchants. This he was only too glad to do, and he was on the road by the middle of November, 1604, making for a place called Iolci, where duties were to be paid and the King's papers examined. In the following twenty-five days they passed through Hancialix, Alceghet, Egriar, Mesetelec, Thalec, Horma, Thoantac, Mingieda, Capetal col Zilan, Sarc Guebedal, Aconsersec, Canbasci and Ciacor, finally reaching Acsu. They had passed over extremely difficult roads, heaped with stones in some places, and in others consisting of long dry tracts of sand.

Acsu is a city in the kingdom of Cascar. The ruler there is a nephew of the King, and only twelve years old. Twice he asked to see Brother Bento and each time the Brother was very graciously received. On both occasions he brought the boy some very tasty morsels, such as would please any child. During the performance of a particular dance which was shown for the entertainment of the company, the prince asked Brother Goës how the people danced in his country. Whereupon, Bento, not wishing to be backward with a prince in such a trifling matter, arose from his place and danced about to show him how his people danced at home. He also called upon the prince's mother and showed her the letters he had from the King, which she examined with great interest. Before leaving he gave her some presents, things which women generally admire; a looking glass, muslin from India, and a few lesser trinkets. He was later invited to call on the boy's guardian, who was the administrator of public affairs.

It was during the course of this part of the journey that one of the pack animals fell into a fast flowing river. For some reason or other, the animal's feet had been tied but it broke the rope and swam to the opposite bank of the river. Goës, realizing that the loss of his horse would be very serious, called upon the name of Jesus and straightway the horse turned and swam back to join the caravan. Saved from what looked like a dire misfortune, Bento gave fervent thanks to God for the favor received. It was on this stretch of the journey also that they crossed over the desert called Caracathai, meaning the Black Land of the Cathayans, because it was commonly believed that the Cathayans had lived there for a long time.

Here they waited for fifteen days until the rest of the caravan arrived. Finally they all started out together, passing through Oito-grach, Gazo, Casciani, Dellai, Saregabedal and Ugan, after which they came to Cucia, a little settlement where they remained for a month to rest the pack animals. The poor beasts were almost at the point of exhaustion from the rough roads, from the weight of the marble with which they were burdened and also from the lack of grain. Here Bento was asked by the priests why he did not observe the fast during the period when their people were accustomed to fast. They asked him this question hoping to get him to pay a bribe for exemption, or in order to mulct him of a fine; and they almost compelled him by force to enter their temple. From here, after twenty-five days of travel they reached the City of Cialis, a small town that was well fortified. This district was ruled over by an illegitimate son of the King of Cascar. When this man learned that Bento and his companions professed a faith different from his own, he uttered threats against them and said it was a bold undertaking for any man professing an alien faith to enter that country, and that he would be justified in taking their property and their lives. After he read the letters which Bento had from the King, he calmed down; after he received a few presents, he became rather friendly.

One night, when this ruler had been engaged for some time with his priests and learned advisers in discussing their religion and its laws, he suddenly got the idea of sending for Bento Goës. So he despatched a messenger, with a horse for Bento and a written request for him to come to the royal palace. The odd hour at which this invitation came, and the uncivil treatment they had received at the hands of this prince when they first arrived, made them suspicious that Bento had been summoned to be put to death. He had to tear himself away from his friend Isaac, whom he left in tears, as he begged him to see to it that if Isaac himself escaped alive, he would make every effort to carry to the Jesuit Fathers the news of the death of their Brother Goës.

On his arrival at the palace, he was asked to engage in a discussion with the Doctors of the Mohammedan law and, inspired as he was by Him who said, "It shall be given to you in that hour what you shall say," he defended the truth of Christianity with such cogent reasoning that the Doctors were shamefully silenced. During the discussion, the prince kept his gaze upon the Brother, nodding approval of everything he said, and after expressing his opinion that Christians really were Misermans, meaning true believers, he concluded by saying that his own ancestors had once professed that same faith. When the disputation concluded, Bento was entertained at a lavish meal and asked to stay overnight at the palace. He could not get away until late the next day and by that time Isaac had almost despaired of his return. When he did come back, he found his friend weeping bitterly and firmly convinced by the long delay that Brother Goës had been put to death.

They stayed in Cialis for three months because the chieftain of the caravan did not wish to set out again until a larger group had been enrolled; the larger it was, the more profitable it would be for him. It was for this same reason also that he would not permit others of the company to go on ahead of him. Bento was growing tired of the long delay and of the great expense it was costing him. He was eager to take to the road and by means of more presents to the prince he finally persuaded him to arrange for his departure. This was done despite the chieftain of the caravan and his company, and it put an end to the friendly relations that had formerly existed between them and Brother Bento.

Just as he was getting ready to leave the city of Cialis, the merchants of a former caravan arrived there on their return from Cathay. Following the common custom of pretending to be a foreign embassy, they had reached the capital of the so-called Cathay.

There, in Pekin, they had lived in the same House of Ambassadors with the Fathers of the Society of Jesus, and so they were able to give Brother Goës first-hand information about Father Matthew Ricci and his companions. It was in this way that Bento first learned, and to his great delight, that China was, in truth, the Cathay for which he was headed. These were the very same Saracens, as has been related in a previous book, who lived for a space of nearly three months in the same guest house with the Fathers. They told how the Fathers had made presents to the Emperor of clocks, of a clavichord, of pictures and of other things from Europe, and they also reported that the Fathers were treated with great respect by the leading officials at the capital. But they were mixing the false with the true when they said that the Fathers had often conversed with the Emperor. They gave a good description of the appearances of the Fathers but they did not know their names, due to the fact that they had taken an added name, as was customary with foreigners in China. As positive evidence of their story, they showed a piece of paper on which something had been written in Portuguese by one of the Fathers. The servants had found this among the sweepings from the house, and the Saracens had saved it to show it to their people when they returned home, as a proof that the people who used that kind of writing had gotten into China. Bento and his companions were overjoyed with this news. They no longer entertained any doubt that Cathay was only another name for the kingdom of China, and that the capital, which the Saracens called Cambalu, was the City of Pekin. Before leaving India, Bento knew from letters received from his brethren in China that this was quite in accord with their contention.

On the eve of their departure, the Cialis prince gave Goës several letters of security; and when the question arose as to what name he wished to have written into these letters, and whether or not he wished to be designated as a Christian, he said, "Yes, I most certainly do. I have made the journey thus far bearing the name of Christian, and so I shall end it." This remark was overheard by a venerable old Saracen priest, who immediately pulled off his hat, cast it on the ground and exclaimed, "In very truth this man is a faithful observer of his religion; for here in the presence of the prince and before the rest of us who profess a different faith, he boldly confesses his belief in Jesus. This indeed is not always the way with our own people, who are said to change their religion according to the country in which they are living." Then he turned to Bento and paid him his respects; an unusual honor for a stranger among the Saracens. Thus it is that virtue, like a light in the dark, demands attention even from an unwilling enemy.

From Cialis he took the road again with some of his former companions and a few new ones, and in twenty days they arrived at Pucian within the same kingdom. Here they were received in a friendly manner by the presiding Prefect who provided them with provisions from his own larder. From here they advanced to the fortified town of Turfan where they stayed for a month. Their next stop was at Aramuth and after that Camul, which was also fortified. Again they halted here for another month to rest themselves and their beasts of burden. This town was within the limits and just within the jurisdiction of the Kingdom of Cialis, where they had always been treated with great kindness. Nine days out of Camul, they came to the famous northern wall of China, arriving at a place called Chiaicuon. Here they had to wait twenty-five days for an answer from the Viceroy of the province, to their request to enter. Once within the wall, it took another day of travel to reach the city of Soceu, where they heard talk about Pekin and other places they had heard of. It was here that Brother Bento put aside whatever doubt he may still have retained relative to the identity of Cathay and China in everything except in name.

The district lying between Cialis and the Chinese borderlands is dangerous country, being wide open to the raiding Tartars, and this part of the journey is made by the merchants in fear and in trepidation. They send exploring parties into the neighboring hills to see if the Tartars are moving; and if the roads are clear, they travel at night and quietly. Bento's party came across the bodies of several Saracens who had been bold enough to travel alone and were cruelly murdered. The Tartars seldom slay the natives. They call them their slaves and their shepherds, and they keep themselves supplied from their flocks and their herds. These Tartars never eat wheat or rice or any kind of vegetable. They say, all that is food for beasts, not for men. They eat nothing but flesh meat, including that of horses and camels, and they are said to be a long lived people, some of them surviving to more than a hundred years. The Saracens on the Chinese frontier in this district are not a war-like people. They could very easily be conquered by the Chinese, if the Chinese were interested in subjugating other nations.

It was during this part of the expedition and at night, that Bento was thrown from his horse and lay semiconscious, while the rest of the party, who were out ahead of him, went on without knowing what had happened to him. It was not until they arrived at a stopping place that they missed him, and his companion Isaac went back to look for him. Isaac was searching in the dark and to no avail when he heard a voice calling on the name of Jesus. He followed the sound of the voice and found Bento, who had given up all hope of being able to follow the caravan. His first words were: "What angel has led you to this spot to rescue me from such imminent danger?" With the help of the Armenian he was able to get to the halting place, where he recovered from the effects of his fall.

13. Brother Bento Goës Dies in China

TOWARD THE NORTHERN limits of the western frontier of China the famous wall comes to an end. Here there is a stretch of open country of about two hundred square miles over which the Tartars, who were held back by the wall below, were accustomed to make forays into China. They do this even now, but not with as much success as formerly. Two strongly fortified cities, provided with chosen troops, have been built, in order to prevent these attacks. There is a special Viceroy governing these cities, and other officials besides who receive their orders directly from the Capital.

The Viceroy and the other higher officials live in the City of Canceu, in the Province of Scensi, and there is a special Mayor of the other city, Soceu, which is divided into two sections. The Chinese, whom the Saracens call Cathayans, live in one part of Soceu, and the Saracens, who have come here to trade, from the Kingdom of Cascar and other western countries, inhabit the other section. Many of these merchants have taken wives here and brought up families; hence they are looked upon as natives who will never return to their own lands. They are like the Portuguese who have settled Macao in the Province of Canton, save that the Portuguese make their own laws and have their own judges, while these Saracens are governed by the Chinese. Every night they are shut in behind the walls of their part of the city, but otherwise they are treated as natives and are subject in all things to the Chinese Magistrates. According to law, anyone who lives here for nine years is not allowed to return to his own country.

Under an ancient agreement between the Kingdom of China and seven or eight kingdoms to the west, these countries have permission for seventy-two merchants to enter the Kingdom of China, every sixth year. These merchants travel under the pretext of being ambassadors who are coming to offer tribute to the Emperor. For the most part, the tribute consists of jade, small diamonds, purple colored stone and other such gems from different sources. These quasi-ambassadors travel to the royal court and return, all at public expense. The term tribute is more of a name than a reality, because no one pays more for the jade than the Emperor, who would consider it to be below his dignity to accept a present from a foreigner without paying handsomely for it. They are so sumptuously entertained by the Emperor that, on the average, everyone of them gains at least one gold piece every day, over and above his expenses. It is for this reason that the merchants enter into such keen competition for a place in these embassies, and give such costly presents for these places to the Chief of the caravan, who has the disposal of them. When the time arrives, the so-called ambassadors forge letters in the names of the various kings who are supposed to be sending them, and the letters are filled with the highest praise of the Emperor of China. The Chinese admit other legations of this kind from many other countries, from Cochin China, Siam, Leuchieu, Coria, and from some of the Tartar Chiefs, all of which places a heavy burden on the public treasury. The Chinese people realize that the whole thing is an imposture, but they make nothing of the deception. Rather, by way of adulation to their king, they permit him to believe that the whole world is paying tribute to the Chinese Kingdom, whereas, in fact, China is really paying tribute to the other countries.

Brother Bento arrived in Soceu toward the end of the year 1605. A good proof of the evident protection of Divine Providence was, that he should come to the end of this extraordinary journey with such abundant supplies. He had thirteen horses, five paid servants, two boys whom he bought out of slavery, and an ample supply of the precious marble. His entire holdings were estimated at two thousand five hundred gold pieces, and, what was even more valuable, both he and his friend Isaac were in perfect physical condition.   ·

Here at Soceu he met another group of Saracens who had just returned from Pekin, and they not only confirmed all that had been said about the Fathers at the Capital, but added on considerable that sounded extravagant and unbelievable. They said, for instance, that the Fathers were given a daily allowance of silver by the Emperor, and that this was not counted out to them, but weighed out in bulk. From here Bento wrote to Father Ricci to inform him of his arrival. His letter was sent by Chinese messengers; but Bento did not know the Chinese names of the Fathers nor the part of the city in which they lived, and moreover, the letter was addressed in European writing. The result was, that the messengers were unable to locate the Fathers in Pekin. He wrote again, at Easter time, and this time his letter was entrusted to a Saracen who had escaped from the city; the Saracens being prevented from going or coming without permission of the Magistrates. In this letter besides making known the purpose and the origin of his journey, he asked the Fathers to plan some way of saving him from detention at Soceu, and of returning him to the pleasure of living with his religious brethren, instead of having to live continually with the Saracens. In his letter also, he expressed his desire to return to India by sea, as the Portuguese generally do.

Long before this, the Fathers in China had been notified in letters from the Superior in India, that Brother Goës had started out on his expedition. As each year passed, they had been expecting his arrival and making diligent inquiry about him, of every caravan of merchants that arrived in Pekin on the so-called embassies. Up to this time, however, they could never find out anything about him, either because they did not know the name under which he was traveling, or because the merchants who had previously arrived had never heard of him.

The arrival of this second letter was therefore a source of great joy to the Fathers in Pekin. It was delivered late in the year, toward the middle of November, and they immediately set about arranging to dispatch one of the Society, who was in some way or other to bring him to Pekin. On second thought, however, they gave up this idea, because it seemed to them that it might do more harm than good to bring in another foreigner. Finally, they sent one of the students who had been accepted to enter the Society of Jesus but had not as

yet entered the novitiate. This was Giovanni Fernandes, a young man
of singular prudence and virtue, to whom it seemed perfectly safe
to entrust a commission of so very great importance. As a companion,
he was given one of the converts who was acquainted with that part
of the country.

Fernandes was instructed to do everything in his power to bring
Bento and his companions back to Pekin. If he found it impossible to
evade the vigilance of the Magistrates or to secure their permission, he
was to remain with Bento and send back a letter to the Fathers in
Pekin. If that were to result, they thought they might be able to
bring him in through the influence of their friends at the royal court.

Now, the town in which Bento was being delayed was a four months'
journey from Pekin, and a trip of this kind might seem out of the
question at that time of the year when winter was raging at its worst
in those regions. Yet, Father Matthew would brook no further delay,
for fear that after so long a time on the road Bento might be doubting
whether or not there really were any of the Society in Pekin. And,
indeed, his judgment was well founded; for if they had postponed
their setting out for only a few days, they would never have found
our Bento among the living. They were bringing him a letter from
Father Ricci, concerning the safest way to make the journey, and two
other members of the Society also sent him letters with full details
about everything that was being done in Pekin; news which he had
been most anxiously awaiting.

During the time he was detained in this city, Brother Goës had to
put up with more annoyance from the Saracens than he had experienced on the whole previous course of the expedition. Because of the
high price of provisions here, he was forced to sell his large piece of jade
for about half of its real value. He let it go for twelve hundred pieces
of gold, and much of this had to be used to repay money he had
borrowed. With what remained, he supported his group for a whole
year.

While he was waiting there, the caravan and its Chieftain arrived.
In the meantime, Bento had been forced to spend so much on the
entertainment of visitors, that he was reduced to financial straits, and
had to borrow money to live. In addition to this, he was chosen as
one of the seventy-two ambassadors to go to the capital, and so he
had to buy some more fragments of jade. Without this, he would have
been excluded from taking part in the journey to Pekin; so he hid a

hundred pounds of it in the earth to prevent it from being stolen by the Saracens.

Fernandes set out from Pekin on the eleventh of December, of that year, and he too met with considerable misfortune. At Singhan, the capital city of the Province of Sciansi, his servant deserted him, after robbing him of half of his supplies for the journey. After two months more of difficult travel and of continual trials, he finally arrived at Soceu toward the end of March in 1607.

Fernandes found Bento sick in bed, with a mortal illness. Only the night before, in a dream or in a vision, he had learned that on the following day a member of the Society would arrive from Pekin. With this in mind he ordered his companion, the Armenian, to go to the market-place and to buy some things for distribution among the poor; and at the same time he prayed devoutly that God would not permit the hope that had come to him in his dream to go unfulfilled. Isaac was in the market-place when someone told him about the arrival of a Jesuit from Pekin, and pointed out Giovanni Fernandes. The stranger went along with Isaac and as they entered the house he saluted Bento in Portuguese. When the sick man realized what had happened he took the letters that were offered to him, lifted them up toward heaven and, with tears in his eyes and his soul overflowing with joy, he broke forth into the hymn, Nunc dimittis. He felt that his orders were fulfilled and his pilgrimage at an end. After reading the letters he kept them near his heart all that night. What was said, and the questions that were asked in the conversations of Bento and Fernandes, may be more easily conjectured than narrated at length. Giovanni did his utmost to nurse Bento back to health, in hope that he would become strong enough to undertake the journey to Pekin. But his strength never returned. There was no doctor available, nor proper medicines, nor was there any means of alleviating his illness, save some European dishes which Fernandes prepared for him. Eleven days after Giovanni's arrival, Brother Bento Goës died, not without some suspicion that he had been poisoned by the Saracens.

These Saracens had kept spies on a continual watch to seize upon whatever property the dead man might leave, and this they did most brutally. No part of the loss was felt so keenly as the destruction of Bento's diary of his travels, which he had kept in minute detail. It was this book which the Saracens were so greedily waiting to devour, because it contained a list of the names of his debtors and might have been used to force them to repay the sums of money of which they had defrauded him. They even wanted to have him buried with Saracen rites, but Fernandes excluded their importunate priests and buried him in a respectable place where it would be possible to find the body afterwards. His two companions, the Armenian and Giovanni, had no ritual containing the prayers for burial service; so they piously recited the rosary as they followed Bento to his grave.

Here it would seem only proper to add a short eulogy of a man who was endowed with so great a soul and with such subtle and penetrating sagacity.

Bento Goës, Portuguese by birth, volunteered for the Mogor Mission and was sent thither shortly after he entered the Society of Jesus. Here he labored for many years as an invaluable assistant to the Fathers, instructing Saracens, pagans and neophytes, according to the rules of his grade in the Society of Jesus. Although he was not a priest, he was generally beloved by everyone because of his rare prudence and of his other many and estimable qualities, both natural and acquired. He became an intimate friend of the Mogor King, and when this sovereign sent an embassy to Goa, he sent Goës along with his personal envoy and in the same capacity. The king at that time was formulating a plan for the conquest of Portuguese India, and it may be attributed to the wisdom and the prudence of Bento Goës that a war was averted with so powerful a potentate. Shortly before he died, he wrote to the Fathers in Pekin, advising them never to trust the Saracens and telling them that it would be both dangerous and useless to endeavor to cover the route which he had followed. There is one thing, well known to the members of his Society, which will bear witness to his holiness. Considering the number of years he had been without an opportunity of receiving absolution in sacramental confession, during his last moments, he said, "I am dying without this consolation, and yet, so great is the goodness of God, that my conscience does not bother me in the slightest about anything that may have happened in the years that have passed."

The merchants who traveled in the caravans followed a diabolical custom of dividing up among them the property of any of their number who happened to die on the road. After Bento died, they seized Isaac, bound him and threatened to kill him if he did not call upon the name of Mahomet. Fernandes sent a notice of this to the Viceroy at Canceu and asked to have Isaac set free. The Viceroy answered the petition and ordered the Mayor of Soceu to settle the case justly and to have the boy's uncle returned to him, together with the property of the deceased. At first, the Mayor was favorable to Fernandes, but forty of the Saracens got together and gave him a sum of money as a bribe; then he threatened to have Fernandes flogged and put in prison for three days. But Giovanni was not a man to be frightened away from what he had undertaken. When he ran out of money to prosecute his case, he sold whatever clothes he could spare to raise more. He spent five months trying to terminate his case and always at a great disadvantage, because he could not communicate with Isaac; he himself not knowing the Persian language, and Isaac knowing neither Portuguese nor Latin. Once when they were summoned into court, Fernandes recited the Lord's Prayer and Isaac repeated the name of Bento Goës and said a few words in Portuguese. Apart from themselves, nobody present understood a single word of what they were saying. The judge thought they were talking in the Canton dialect and that they understood each other without any difficulty. Later on, after about two months, Fernandes learned enough of the Persian tongue to be able to converse with the Armenian.

When the Saracens entered an objection and said that their facial contours showed that one was Saracen and the other Chinese, Fernandes answered that his mother was Chinese and that he inherited the character of his features from her. Nothing had more effect upon the judge than what happened one day in the open court. As a protest to their charges, Fernandes said that Isaac was an avowed enemy of the Saracen religion and that, if he did profess that faith, he would not eat pork. Then he took a piece of pork out of his sleeve and, despite the custom of the bystanders, both he and Isaac started to eat it, to the great disgust of all the Saracens present. With that, they gave up the case as hopeless and left the court, spitting at Isaac as they went and saying that he had been deluded by the Chinese impostor. During the whole journey neither Bento nor Issac had eaten any pork, for fear of giving offense to the Saracens, or if they did eat it, they did so in private. What happened in the court induced the judge to favor Giovanni's demand, and he ordered the return of all of Bento's property, of which nothing could be found, except some pieces of the buried jade, which were used to pay a few debts and to supply money for the return to Pekin. Even then, there was not enough to cover the expenses for the long delay, so they had to borrow twenty pieces of gold on a loan for some jade they still retained.

After many trials and much delay they reached Pekin and found the Fathers who had been living in great anxiety. Then there was cause for both grief and happiness; sorrow for the death of Brother Goës, joy for the escape of his companion, the Armenian. Isaac was received as if he were a member of their Society, because Bento had informed them by letter of the great help he had most faithfully rendered during the entire course of his journey. Fernandes brought them a cross, beautifully painted on gold paper, the only one that Bento carried with him while he lived among the Saracens, and also the three documents, given to him by the three kings of Cascar, Quotan and Cialis, all of which are now kept as memorials in the house of the Society in Pekin. Here, too, are the letters patent of Father Jerome Xavier, with other letters of his received during the time of the Goës journey. With these there are more letters from Alexius Menesius, Archbishop of Goa, and from the same Father Xavier to the Fathers of Pekin, in which they say that they are quite certain that Cathay is not far distant from Pekin and that perhaps the two kingdoms are contiguous.

Isaac the Armenian remained a month in Pekin and during that time he related to Father Matthew, with the help of some papers that belonged to Bento, all that he could recall to memory concerning the journey. It is from his narrative that we have taken the story of our last three chapters. From Pekin Isaac went to Macao, over the route which the Fathers generally followed, and there he was received very kindly by the Jesuit community and their friends. On his return voyage to India, the ship on which he was sailing was captured by Dutch pirates in the Straits of Singapore, where he was robbed of his meager possessions and reduced to a state of miserable slavery. He was afterwards ransomed by the Portuguese of Malacca and continued on to India. There he learned of the death of his wife, so he did not return to the Mogor country; instead, he settled down in an East India town called Ciaul, where he is still living at the time of this present writing.

14. Persecution at Nancian— Father Soeiro Dies

DURING 1606 and the year following, the progress of Christianity in Nancian was in no wise retarded, either by the increasing illness of Father Soeiro, or by Father Emanuele's lack of knowledge of the Chinese language. These disadvantages were more than made up for by the constant labor of the other Fathers and in great part also by the industry of Brother Pascal. Within these two years, this Brother increased the number of neophytes by more than two hundred, all of whom manifested an extraordinary piety in their religious devotions. As a result, the reputation of the Christian religion became known throughout the length and breadth of this metropolitan city.

When there seemed to be no further hope of improvement for Father Soeiro, it was thought best to send him to Macao, for a change of climate and possibly for his restoration to health, but all that proved to be in vain. He went to his eternal rest in August of that same year, at the age of forty-one and after twenty-three years of very valuable service in the Society of Jesus. He made his noviceship at Coimbra, in Portugal, and had scarcely finished it, before he applied for the India Mission, whence he was later assigned to the China expedition. He was stationed at the residence in Nancian for more than ten years, where he applied all his energy to the promulgation of Christianity. An exemplary religious, he was generally considered to be a very holy man. He accomplished much and put up with much for a number of years during which he labored all alone among the pagans. At times his mission house was reduced to dire necessity by ill disposed neighbors, and he himself to pitiable straits, but he bore it all with patience and never asked for more than was sent to him as a yearly allowance. His loss was keenly felt by the neophytes, and many of them voluntarily went into mourning when he died.

Through the efforts of Father Emanuele Dias another and a larger house was purchased, in August of 1607, at a price of a thousand gold pieces. This change was necessary, because the house he had was too small for his needs and was situated in a flood area. Just as the community was about to change from one house to the other, a sudden uprising broke out against them. It happened that some of the pedants among the lettered Bachelors, had become dissatisfied with the growing popularity of the Christian faith. So they wrote out a complaint against the Fathers and took it to the governing Pimpithau, the Mayor, who had charge of all city affairs. They were neither well received nor patiently listened to, and he answered them saying, "If this Christian law, against which you are complaining, does not seem good to you, then do not accept it. I have not as yet heard that anyone has been forced into it. If the house which they have bought happens to be large, you are not the ones who are paying for it, and they will never interfere with your property." This answer only aroused their anger, and they went to the Governor of the metropolitan district. It happened that this man, whose name was Lu, was a friend of Father Ricci, with whom he had become acquainted, some years before, in Pekin. He accepted their complaint and then disregarded it, and the lawyers who presented it could not persuade him to give them an answer. This second rebuff also had its effect on their impatience.

At the beginning of each month, the Magistrates hold a public assembly, together with the Bachelors in Philosophy, in the temple of their great Philosopher. When the rites of the new-moon were completed in the temple, and these are civil rather than religious rites, one of those present took advantage of the occasion to speak on behalf of the others, and to address the highest Magistrate present, the Pucinsu. "We wish to warn you," he said, "that there are certain foreign priests in this royal city, who are preaching a law, hitherto unheard of in this kingdom, and who are holding large gatherings of people in their house." Having said this, he referred them to their local Magistrate, called Ticho, who was also head of the school to which the speaker was attached, and he in turn ordered the plaintiffs to present their case in writing, assuring them that he would support it with all his authority, in an effort to have the foreign priests expelled. The complaint was written out that same day and signed with twenty-seven signatures. They gave one copy to the Director of the school and one to the Supreme Magistrate. The content of the document was somewhat as follows.

"Matthew Ricci, Giovanni Soeiro, Emanuele Dias, and certain other foreigners from western kingdoms, men who are guilty of high treason against the throne, are scattered amongst us, in five different provinces. They are continually communicating with each other and are here and there practicing brigandage on the rivers, collecting money, and then distributing it to the people, in order to curry favor with the multitudes. They are frequently visited by the Magistrates, by the high nobility and by the Military Prefects, with whom they have entered into a secret pact, binding unto death.

"These men teach that we should pay no respect to the images of our ancestors, a doctrine which is destined to extinguish the love of future generations for their forebears. Some of them break up the idols, leaving the temples empty and the gods to be pitied, without any patronage. In the beginning they lived in small houses, but by this time they have bought up large and magnificent residences. The doctrine they teach is something infernal. It attracts the ignorant into its fraudulent meshes, and great crowds of this class are continually assembled at their houses. Their doctrine gets beyond the city walls and spreads itself through the neighboring towns and villages and into the open country, and the people become so wrapt up in its falsity, that students are not following their courses, laborers are neglecting their work, farmers are not cultivating their acres, and even the women have no interest in their housework. The whole city has become disturbed, and, whereas in the beginning there were only a hundred or so professing their faith, now there are more than twenty thousand. These priests distribute pictures of some Tartar or Saracen, who they say is God, who came down from heaven to redeem and to instruct all of humanity, and who alone according to their doctrine, can give wealth and happiness; a doctrine by which the simple people are very easily deceived. These men are an abomination on the face of the earth, and there is just ground for fear that once they have erected their own temples, they will start a rebellion, as they did in recent years, according to report, in the provinces of Fuchian and Nankin. Wherefore, moved by their interest in the maintenance of the public good, in the conservation of the realm, and in the preservation, whole and entire, of their ancient laws, the petitioners are presenting this complaint and demanding, in the name of the entire province, that a rescript of it be forwarded to the King, asking that these foreigners be sentenced to death, or banished from the realm, to some deserted island in the sea."

Such, in brief, was the content of the complaint, eloquently worded, with alleged proofs and testimony, and couched in a persuasive style, at which the quasi-literati are very adept. Each of the Magistrates to whom the indictment was presented asserted that the spread of Christianity should be prohibited, and that the foreign priests should be expelled from the city, if the Mayor saw fit, after hearing the case, and notifying the foreigners. All those who knew nothing about the method of conducting affairs in the Chinese kingdom, were fairly well persuaded that the Fathers would at least be chased out of the metropolitan city, and as a result their many friends hesitated to come to their assistance, in what looked like a hopeless case. But the Fathers, themselves, were not too greatly disturbed, placing their confidence in Divine Providence, which had always been present to assist them on other such dangerous occasions. Their first problem was to decide upon the initial step to be taken in a matter of so grave importance.

Many of their friends thought they should seek out an intercessor, who might be induced for a consideration to have the sentence of the Magistrates revoked, as a favor to him. Instead, Father Emanuele, in his own defense, wrote out a request for justice, which he began with an instant petition to the Magistrates to make an exact inquiry into the crimes of which they had been accused, and if they were found guilty, to punish them to the full extent of the law. The Mayor and the same Magistrate, Director of the Schools, received copies of this document, and after the Chief Justice had heard the Fathers and kept them a long time on their knees, clad as criminals, he broke forth with the following questions: "Why is it that you have not left the city, after arousing the hatred of the Baccalaureates? What is this law that you are promulgating? What is this crime you have committed? Why do you forbid the people to honor their ancestors? What infernal image is this that you honor? Where did you get the money to buy these houses?" These and more questions were hurled at them, with little show of civility. Father Emanuele undertook to answer these questions with one of his Lay Brothers acting as an interpreter. First he gave a brief outline of the Christian doctrine. Then he showed that according to the divine law, the first to be honored, after God, were a man's parents. But the judge had no mind to hear or to accept any of this and he made it known that he thought it was all false. After that repulse, with things going from bad to worse, it looked as if they were on the verge of desperation, so much so, indeed, that they increased their prayers, their sacrifices and their bodily penances, in petition for a favorable solution of their difficulty. Their adversaries appeared to be triumphantly victorious. They were already wrangling about the division of the furniture of the Mission residences, and to make results doubly certain, they stirred up the flames anew with added accusations and indictments. They persuaded the civil leaders to urge on the Magistrates. One of the minor Magistrates to whom a copy of the new indictment was given, in order to flatter their zeal, said there was no need to inquire, as to whether or not the Christian law was true. The fact that it was being preached by foreigners was sufficient reason for suppressing it, adding that he himself would exterminate such men, if the complaint had not been handed on to the higher court.

The Mayor, who was somewhat friendly with the Fathers, realizing that there was much in the accusation that was patently false, asked the Magistrate Director of the Schools, if he knew whether or not this man Emanuele was a companion of Matthew Ricci, who was so highly respected at the royal court, and who was granted a subsidy from the royal treasury, because of the gifts he had presented to the King. Did he realize that the Fathers had lived in Nankin for twelve years, and that no true complaint had ever been entered against them for having violated the laws. Then he asked him if he had really given full consideration as to what was to be proven in the present indictment. To this the Director of the Schools replied that he wished the Mayor to make a detailed investigation of the case and then to confer with him. The Chief Justice then ordered the same thing to be done. Fortunately, it was this same Justice who was in charge of city affairs when Father Ricci first arrived in Nancian. It was he who first gave the Fathers permission, with the authority of the Viceroy, to open a house there. After that, through a series of promotions he returned to Nancian, to occupy the highest position in this metropolis. He exercised great prudence in handling the public rebuff the Fathers had received, being careful not to favor either side in the case. He was set on making the truth appear, and yet he did not wish to throw out the case of the quasi-literati because he himself was at one time the Director of their schools.

At that time, some of the accusing element, feeling certain that they had gained a victory, went into the houses of the neophytes looking for pictures of the Saviour, two or three of which they tore to pieces. Father Emanuele then advised the new Christians to hide the pictures from these bandits and, for the time being, not to hang them in their living rooms. He told them that in so doing they were not denying their faith but just preventing further sacrilege. He told them also that they could carry their rosaries in public if they wished to, but that there was no obligation to do so.

After the Mayor had examined the charges of the plaintiffs and the reply of the defendants, he subjected the quasi-literati to an examination in open court, and taking the Fathers under his patronage, he took it upon himself to refute the calumnies of their accusers. He said he was fully convinced that these strangers were honest men, and that he knew that there were only two of them in their local residence and not twenty, as had been asserted. To this they replied that the Chinese were becoming their disciples. To which the Justice in turn replied: "What of it? Why should we be afraid of our own people? Perhaps you are unaware of the fact that Matthew Ricci's company is cultivated by everyone in Pekin, and that he is being subsidized by the royal treasury. How dare the Magistrates who are living outside of the royal city, expel men who have permission to live at the royal court? These men here have lived peacefully in Nankin for twelve years. I command," he added, "that they buy no more large houses, and that the people are not to follow their law." Then in the presence of the court he addressed the Fathers, very kindly, saying that there were some in the city who were angry because they had bought the larger house, when the smaller one would have served their needs.

Relative to the Christian law, he told Father Emanuele that he had no objection whatsoever to its observance by him and by his own people, but that he should not teach it to the people of this country, because in this respect they are not trustworthy. He warned him, that even if the people did accept his religion, in the beginning, they would afterwards turn against it. All this he told them, calmly, and more of a similar nature, and what he said was accepted by all as being quite favorable. Afterwards, while speaking with one of his associates, in open court, he told them that the law which this man professed was quite in keeping with right reason, and that Father Emanuele was a good example of a man who lived according to what he preached. He explained that the Baccalaureates were bold enough to enter charges against Father Emanuele because he was a foreigner and, as they thought, unprotected by any patronage. The Chief Justice then told the Director of the Schools not to make any trouble for the Father, because it was evident that the general charges made by the Baccalaureates were fictitious and trumped up for the purpose of securing bribe money. He said the people of Nancian were a hard lot to please, and that he would give Father Emanuele permission to buy the house because, formerly, when he was Mayor, he gave Father Ricci permission to buy whatever house he wished.

When the court session was over, one of the royal relatives, a class who become even more insolent after they have squandered their wealth, waited for Father Emanuele, for the sole purpose of insulting him, as he was coming out. Afterwards the same individual went to the Mission House to strip it of its furniture, but the late judgment of the Magistrate Mayor deterred him and he was satisfied with making a few threats.

A few days later, the court decision was pronounced and written out, over the seals of the Chief Justice and the leader of the Bachelors, the Director of the Schools. It was then posted at the city gates as a public edict. The following is a summary of their declaration. Having examined the cause of Father Emanuele and his companions, it was found that these men had come here from the West because they had heard so much about the fame of the great Chinese Empire, and that they had already been living in the realm for some years, without any display of ill-will. Father Emanuele should be permitted to practice his own religion, but it was not considered to be the right thing for the common people, who are attracted by novelties, to adore the God of Heaven. For them to go over to the religion of foreigners, would indeed be most unbecoming. Judging from the authority of the poet, it would seem that this foreign doctrine was something that had come down from the light above the highest trees, into the shadow of the lowly valley. It would therefore seem to be against the best interests of the Kingdom, to refrain from warning everyone in a public edict not to abandon the sacrifices of their ancient religion by accepting the cult of foreigners. Such a movement might, indeed, result in calling together certain gatherings, detrimental to the public welfare, and harmful also to the foreigner, himself, Wherefore, the Governor of this district, by order of the high Magistrates, admonishes the said Father Emanuele to refrain from perverting the people, by inducing them to accept a foreign religion. The man who sold him the larger house is to restore his money and Emanuele is to buy a smaller place, sufficient for his needs, and to live there peaceably, as he has done, up to the present. Emanuele, himself, has agreed to these terms and the Military Prefects of the district have been ordered to make a search of the houses there and to confiscate the pictures of the God they speak of, wherever they find them. It is not permitted for any of the native people to go over to the religion of the foreigners, nor is it permitted to gather together for prayer meetings. Whoever does contrary to these prescriptions will be severely punished, and if the Military Prefects are remiss in enforcing them, they will be held to be guilty of the same crimes. To his part of the edict, the Director of the Schools added, that the common people were forbidden to accept the law of the foreigners, and that a sign should be posted above the door of the Fathers' residence, notifying the public that these men were forbidden to have frequent contact with the people.

The Fathers were not too disturbed by this pronouncement, because they were afraid that it was going to be much worse. In fact, everyone thought it was rather favorable, and that the injunction launched against the spread of the faith was a perfunctory order to make it appear that the literati were not wholly overlooked, since the Fathers were not banished from the city, as the literati had demanded. Moreover it was not considered a grave misdemeanor for the Chinese to change their religion, and it was not customary to inflict a serious punishment on those violating such an order. The neophytes, themselves, proved this when they continued, as formerly, to attend Mass with the same devotion, and even with added interest when they brought the catechumens along with them. At first, in order to prevent the appearance of defying the edict, the Fathers divided the new Christians into groups and had the groups attend Mass on three different days in the week, instead of having them all come on Sunday, but the result of that was that they all came on the other days and on Sundays also. It was useless to tell them to stay away because they thought that would be a manifestation of fear. When the Military Prefects of the district made an effort to frighten some of them, so as to collect money from them, they fearlessly said they were Christians and wrote out their names for the Prefects to take to the Magistrates, but not one of them was ever arrested.

It is to be noted that what happened during other persecutions of the Church, happened on this China expedition, and especially so at this particular station. As to persecutions in general, which are permitted by Divine Providence, once the tumult has been allayed, they serve more for the spread of Christianity, than an unending period of unbroken peace. The enemies of the Church sought to banish the Fathers from Nancian, with the result that they became more firmly established there than they were formerly. When Father Ricci first came to this city, the written permission of the Governor to buy a house could not be secured, even with the authority of the Viceroy supporting it. As a result of the persecution just described, the Mayor and two other high Magistrates of this metropolitan seat permitted the Fathers to remain here and also to purchase a home. And this was done in a public edict which made it evident that in the future no one would dare to call the matter into doubt or even to murmur about it.

It was, indeed, all for the greater glory of God, that many remarked that the preachers of the divine law were living under the protection of the Lord, and also in the protecting shadow of the Magistrates, who are, as it were, the Lord's lieutenants. It seems to be evident that the Magistrates had a better knowledge of the Fathers than their pedant adversaries imagined. Formerly, the people here were quite ignorant of the relations existing between the Fathers in Pekin and the high officials of the royal court. Now it is a matter of common talk. It is, in truth, no small proof of the protection of Divine Providence, that the calumnies spread in the Province of Canton had not as yet reached this city. Had it been known that one of the Fathers, namely Father Cattaneo, had been named as leader of the rebellion in Macao, the boldness of the malcontents here would undoubtedly have been increased, and the loyalty of the Mission's friends decreased accordingly. It served a good purpose also, that certain things mentioned in the indictment against the Fathers were manifestly false, because that made people slow to believe other charges, even when they were true or probable. What was said about the Fathers being visited by the Magistrates and the nobles, did not seem to fit in with charges of rebellion and robbery, and the teaching of false doctrine.

In the trial just mentioned, the accusers had named both Father Ricci and Father Soeiro. The Magistrates knew that Father Ricci was living in Pekin, and many had already heard that Father Soeiro was dead. This particular persecution seemed to spread the name of Christianity far and wide, and it was also generally known that the Fathers intended to spread the knowledge of the persecution. Shortly after it, there were many who became curious to learn about this new religion, and who came to hear it explained, and although they did not all accept it, most of them gave it their approval. All this helped wonderfully to increase the fervor of the new Christians and some of them, unknown to the Fathers, had already prepared a document in answer to the plaintiffs. Despite their protests, Father Emanuele took this document from them, deeming it untimely for them to attempt such a thing, without consultation. Some of them were questioning each other as to what they would do if the Magistrates commanded them to abjure their faith, and others asked to be named to take the places of the Fathers, in case they were expelled, so they could preserve and spread the faith. The Fathers never went to the courts without meeting a crowd of their new Christians at the entrance, and if they were delayed there for any length of time, the neophytes always brought them something to eat and to drink, and they always saw to it, that the door-keepers cleared the way for their entrance. In a word, they omitted nothing that they thought to be the duty of good Christians and devoted children.

After the edict was published, two or three of the clerks of the Magistrates brought a copy of it to the Fathers. It was customary to pay them a fee for this, but instead of the fee they asked for a picture of Christ the Saviour, for their devotions, and this, despite the fact that the edict they had in their hands prohibited the exposition of this picture, under grave penalty. They said they intended to become Christians. The Fathers refused to give them a picture, and as they were talking, an artist came into the house with some copies of the picture, which he had just framed. They took one of them away from him, and went away without asking further remuneration. A few days later, one of them fell sick and asked for baptism, and he died five days after he was baptized.

Shortly after this the Chief Justice was promoted to a high office in the Province of Canton. Father Emanuele went in his own boat to pay him a visit and to offer him a gift, on the occasion of his departure. The Father thanked him for the favorable manner in which he had handled the court case, and among other things, he gave him a copy of Father Ricci's book of Christian Doctrine. He read a few pages of this and then turning to several other Magistrates who were present, he said, "How very false it is to say that these men forbid the people to honor their parents, when the very contrary is written into the precepts of their faith." He told Father Emanuele that he could rest assured that his Mission Station would not be disturbed, that he had convinced the Director of the Schools of his innocence of the charges made, and that he had appointed the Mayor as their protector. He then offered Father Emanuele some pieces of gold in return for his gifts, which the Father refused with insistence. He then forced the interpreter to take the gold, and to return it after that would have been considered a discourtesy.

After all that had happened here, it would seem that the cause of the Fathers was better off following the tumult in the city than it was before it, and this was quite evident to their friends. There were many who came to congratulate them and many who insisted that the value of their victory over the native literati, in winning the favor of the Magistrates, was really beyond computation.

15.Persecution Strengthens the Faith at Nancian

THE RIDICULE WHICH the authors of the indictment had to put up with, because of the rebuff they received, was almost unbelievable. They became a sort of public jest, and people pointed their fingers at the leading quasi-literati, who were beaten in court by a foreigner and who received no bribe money. Others were made fun of because they were not summoned to testify about the purchase of the house and they and all their kin were put to shame, because they had been named in a public edict. The Director of the Schools of the literati, becoming incensed with some of his own followers, threatened to strip them of their literary grades, as calumniators. In order to justify themselves before the public, the literati published a pamphlet containing the entire procedure of the trial; all the charges submitted and all the decisions of the judges. These pamphlets were distributed to all prominent citizens and to some of the Magistrates, and copies were sent to the Fathers. Judging from its style and from the excellence of its written characters it was composed by one of the more distinguished scholars of their class. As this was an effort to justify their action, they omitted, as far as possible, any reference to the effect that the case may have had upon their own reputation.

Their first effort was to prove that they had not been prompted to oppose the foreigners, by personal considerations of any kind, asserting that their motives were based upon the preservation of the integrity of the Kingdom and the defense of the laws of their ancestors. They asked the people to remember what great calamities the Chinese Empire had suffered from the very beginning of its existence, because of communications with foreigners. They said that according to the laws and the statutes of the country, such men were locked up in forts and in the prisons, and not permitted to wander about like natives, and much less, indeed, to stir up ill will, by lording it over the people. They accused the Fathers of boasting that their country surpassed the Chinese Empire in grandeur, and said that unlike other outsiders, they refused to recognize its immensity. They said that in imitation of their own country which is called the Great Light, these foreigners called their Europe, the Great Occident, and because the Chinese Emperor is called the Son of Heaven, these men called their God, the Lord of Heaven, exalting everything pertaining to them above things Chinese, as a father or master is exalted above a son. It was charged that the Europeans counted their years from some unknown time, or from the reign of someone other than the King of China, and that the written characters with which they marked the homes of their converts to protect them against evil spirits, were shaped like bows and arrows and axes, and other warlike instruments, which in itself was undoubtedly a presage of evil. The written characters referred to were the letters in the holy names of Jesus and Mary. And so they concluded that it was a dangerous risk to retain such people in their midst, and that no one should be surprised that they were endeavoring to rid their province of a pest, as the ancient literati had often done. In proof of this they made reference to examples, which they had dug up from their historical annals. They said it was wise to remedy an evil at its very beginning, rather than to cure it later on, when it had acquired sufficient force to resist a remedy. In the epilogue to their pamphlet, they let loose their fury on Father Emanuele, calling him a dog and a wolf and saying that his stomach was full of calamitous evil, and that was only part of the intemperate contumely they hurled at him.

The Fathers thought it would be better to bury all this in silence, rather than kick over a hornet's nest, by offering a written reply. It looked like vindication from above when only shortly after the publication of this pamphlet, two of its authors died sudden deaths. Of the three authors, the two who died, almost at the same time, both preachers of the law of the literati, were really unworthy of the profession they pretended to practice. While they were supposed to

be on familiar terms with the Fathers, they really put the torch to the
indictment that flamed up against them. The affliction of several others
with various ailments and misfortune gave the converts an occasion to
recognize the hand of God in the exercise of justice, which indeed
seemed to launch thunderbolts of vindication against the heads of
these calumniators.

When the Fathers decided to buy the larger house, they sold the
smaller one beforehand, on condition that they should be permitted
to remain there until they could move into a new one. Now it happened
to be one of the King's so-called relatives, that class which nobility
renders insolent, who made the purchase and, before the time agreed
upon, he began to pile his furniture into the Fathers' house and to
make every effort to dislodge them. That was at a time when no one
wanted either to sell or to rent a house to them for fear of their enemy
accusers. Just at that time also, seven of their religious brethren arrived
from other parts, and the Fathers were in such a predicament that
they were considering going to a public lodging-house, when one of
their friends loaned them an empty house, small but sufficient to
accommodate them for the time being. Finally, and after considerable
difficulty, they received the money for the house they sold, and then
went about looking for another one, but they could not find one
suitable to their needs. Living as they were in constant fear of law-
suits, they bought a house, large enough to suit their purpose, but due
to the fact that two people claimed its ownership, they stepped into a
lawsuit that lasted for several years. During this period there were
other factions formed for the purpose of causing trouble for the
Fathers but, by the grace of God, they were put an end to, by the
publication of another edict. That whole year, however, was not to be
counted as unfruitful, as it gave the Mission sixty new converts.

There was a venerable old gentleman in the city who for a long
time had held the office of Supreme Colao. He was known to be a man
of wealth, who made considerable display of it, and the opposition
tried to win him over to their cause in the following manner. The
famous temple we have mentioned before, was partly destroyed by
fire. This man was elected head of a committee to collect funds to
repair the damage and, supported by his prestige, they succeeded in
collecting more than ten thousand gold pieces. During the time that
they were soliciting funds, the new converts exempted themselves from
contributing to what they considered, according to their teaching, to
be an unholy cause. When this became known, some of the pagans

were reported to be enjoying the same exemption, by asserting that they were Christians. Whereupon the collectors, again prompted by the quasi-literati, went to the Colao to enter a complaint and he told them that what was being collected by way of alms must not be exacted by force, and that they were not to cause annoyance to anyone. When they spoke to him about Father Emanuele, and complained about the law he was preaching, he said he thought it was a holy law, being preached by a holy man, and that it contained nothing contrary to the laws of the Chinese literati. "But," they objected, "he is a foreigner." "What of it?" he answered. "What have you to fear from a single foreigner in this city, when there are so many thousand Saracens living, unmolested, in both capital cities, who are regularly admitted to the attainment of literary degrees?" Through an acquaintance with one of the quasi-kings, the Fathers contracted a friendship with this man, and he remained quite interested in the progress of Christianity up to the time of his death, and there were many more of the leading citizens who seemed to be just as interested.

During the whole time of the persecution just described, the doors of the church were kept closed to the public, so that it might not appear that they were making little of the edict of the Magistrates, and also to discover the attitude of the surrounding neighborhood. In the interim they had plenty of time to redecorate both the house and the church, and they erected two altars, one in each chapel; the first dedicated to Christ the Saviour and the other to Our Blessed Mother. The church was reopened with great solemnity, on Christmas Day, in 1609, with a great concourse of converts present, and a greater one of pagans. The decorations were all modeled in European style and proved to be very attractive to the eyes of the Chinese. The lights were kept burning day and night on each altar and the converts vied with each other in keeping them supplied with oil. The new chapel brought new ardor to the converts and was the occasion of an unusual haul in the fisherman's net. The converts were regular and devout in going to confession, and when they received Holy Communion, they felt that they had reached the very height of Christian happiness. The attendance at Mass, not only on Sundays and on feast days but on ordinary workdays as well, was really very edifying.

16. The First Sodality of the Blessed Virgin in China

DURING THE YEARS just passed, the Fathers in Pekin were frequently called to the royal palace, and at times they went there of their own accord to confer with the eunuchs, on palace business. As we have remarked elsewhere, they were always called when the clocks needed attention. One day, as Father Ricci and Father Didaco Pantoia arrived at the court, they found the Rector of the College of Mathematics somewhat disturbed because of a royal order. The King had ordered twelve copies of the world-map designed in silk, and done in six pairs of large panels. This map was the work of Father Ricci, which our friend the Magistrate Ligotsum, had published only a short time previous. The Rector was told to get these copies of the map from Father Ricci, because his name was on the original, as its author. He had only recently given a copy of the map to the eunuchs and when they showed it to the King, he was so pleased with it, that he wanted to present a copy of it to each of his sons, and other relatives residing in the palace, so they could hang them on the walls, by way of pleasant ornamental decoration. Up to this time, the Fathers had been restrained, by an imaginary fear, from offering a copy of their map to the royal court. They were afraid that the courtiers would think that their idea of the amplitude of the Chinese Empire was being held in contempt. Up to this time, also, the Chinese said and believed that the realm of China took in the whole world. The Fathers were at fault in their fear, because the King himself, in keeping with his customary good judgment, had no idea that his kingdom would suffer any disparagement by the revelation of the truth.

We have already mentioned that two different impressions of this map had been made, but there was no copy of either impression at the Fathers' residence. Ligotsum had taken one impression, and the other, which the printers used for making copies, was destroyed, when their house was inundated by a river flood. This caused the royal mathematicians some concern, fearing lest the King, disappointed in his wish, might become angry with the eunuchs. There was some doubt in the minds of the eunuchs about there being no copy of the map at the residence. They became suspicious that for some reason or other, it was being hidden; so they came to the house and the Fathers showed them some pieces of the impression that had been salvaged from the flood. They also showed them a copy of the same map, which had been edited by Li Paul, with more ample descriptions, comprising the entire world and made up in eight separate panels, but they were afraid to bring the King a design in eight panels, when he had asked for one in six.

The Fathers said they would engrave another model within a short time, and they were glad to do this, because it offered them another opportunity, which they were always seeking, for emphasizing Christianity. It would take them about a month to complete this new map. They informed the King by letter of what had happened and of what they intended to do, but he decided to save them both labor and expense. He asked them to come to the palace and to model the new plates on the first edition of the map, which was kept there. This they were glad to do, and just at a time when there were various and diverse opinions being expressed about the map itself. Some had their doubts, relative to what was written and engraved on the map against the silly cult of idols, and others could not put up with what was said about the principles of the Christian faith. The Fathers were hoping that the time might come when the King, or one of his successors, while examining the map and reading the commentary on it, would conceive the idea of making an inquiry into the Christian faith. In the meantime, the presence of the map was diminishing the Chinese idea that their Empire embraced the whole world, whereas in this map it was just another, and not the largest, stretch of earth on the globe.

From the administration of a lesser office, to which he had been assigned, Ligotsum, an intimate friend of the Fathers, was appointed mayor of a city in the Pekin Province. While attending to executive affairs there, and carrying on official business with the royal court by mail, he could never be wholly unmindful of his friends. He had learned a great deal about Christianity, and much about mathematics, especially from his study of Euclid, and he was somewhat amazed to realize that the Chinese had never heard of Euclid, before the coming of Father Ricci. He permitted all of his family and of his retinue to become Christians, and even exhorted them thereto. Two young men who were relatives of his, both holders of literary degrees, became converts of unusual devotion. They were prompted to this by their own intellectual ability, assisted by the grace of God, and no doubt also by the influence of so great a person, who was forever talking about the Christian law, and who insisted that apart from it salvation was nowhere to be found. And yet he was one of those who praise the truth to the skies, but do not embrace it.

One of the young men converts named Michael had been very devoted to the cult of the idols. From the time of his childhood, he had been nourished and instructed in this practice by the impious piety of his parents, by frequent prayers and pagan fasting and other sacrilegious training. It was said of him, that shortly after he was born, he said, "I do not belong to this family, I belong to our relatives who are ministers of the temples." If there is any truth in this, it probably was an artifice of the devil, who was planning to have this child brought up as one thoroughly imbued with idolatry. Later on, he resolved to give over whatever property he had, to his son, and to retire into solitude as a temple minister. When he heard of and read about the Christian faith, he changed his mind, renounced the sect he had been following in ignorance rather than by choice, and turning his like into dislike, set out to refute its absurdity, both in his speech and in his writings. During all the time that he was living in the royal city, he was continually talking and writing about Christianity, and during the absence of his teachers, for fear he might forget what he had learned, he made a copy of the Church calendar, and of what are called movable feasts, and learned how to distinguish them, as they do in Europe.

Not satisfied with being able to recite the entire abridged Catechism from memory, in Chinese, Michael also learned to recite it in Latin, as well as the Chinese can. Their difficulty in this respect is due to the lack of certain corresponding letters. In addition to this he also memorized other formulas of prayer, which had not as yet been translated into Chinese. Both he and his companion Jerome, went to confession before leaving Pekin on a ten day journey, with a relative who had been appointed Magistrate in a country town. We shall have occasion to make mention of this same Michael later on in our Annals, being published with this history. While he was absent from Pekin, his aged father came to Pekin to visit him, from the distant province of Cechian. This visit was very much to the son's liking, as it turned out to be the father's road to salvation, as is fondly hoped. The son's enthusiasm for the Christian faith had such an influence upon his father, that he gave up idol worship, which he had practiced for more than fifty years. At that time, he wrote to his father, saying that he himself had cast off the foolishness of the idol worshippers, as he would throw away an old pair of worn out shoes. When he returned home he set an example for the conversion of all his relatives.

Litgotsum had not as yet left the royal capital when something extraordinary happened in his home that greatly enhanced the influence of Christianity. One of his domestic servants who had been receiving instructions in the faith, without the knowledge of his master, fell sick of a disease of such a nature, that the rest of the servants would not go near him. When the day arrived, on which he was to be baptized, one of the Fathers went to the house and cleaned up the sickroom, after filling the house with an odor of burning incense. This attracted the other domestics and when they saw what had happened, they were amazed to see that the charity of the Christian law surpassed the demands of duty. When the Master heard what had happened, he admired the great act of charity and accused himself of having abandoned his servant in such a crisis. Here they had an occasion for imitating, as well as for praising virtue. The sick man was baptized and died within three days, invoking the names of the Holy Trinity and offering hope to the other servants, of accomplishing their own salvation, in a short space of time. The Master afterwards spoke very highly to his many friends of this act of charity.

Prompted by what had taken place at his home, two of his officials, or rather of his court attendants, who were with him only during the time that he was at the royal court, decided to accept the faith, and their acquisition meant much to the cause of Christianity, which they not only embraced but were eager to promulgate. One of them took the name of Andrew. He was of lower station and not so well off financially, and his Christian influence was more or less confined to his own household. The other, named Luke, who was very wealthy and known to everyone at the royal court, began to change his way of living by making restitution for the fraud and venality by which he had amassed his riches. He was very solicitous for the welfare of his father, who was seventy years old, and realizing that the old gentleman had not many years to live, he did everything he could to interest him in the next life rather than in the present. It was this ardent desire of his to care for his father that practically forced this man out of his own state of hesitation, and landed him, as it were, full force,

within the pale of the church. His father happened to be almost stone
deaf, so he feared, and rightfully, that the old gentleman would not
be able to hear or to understand what the Fathers were teaching him.
To overcome this difficulty, he went to the Mission House himself and
took lessons in Christian doctrine, which he afterwards taught to his
father, partly by word and partly by sign language. In this way they
were both won over, as he concluded that it was not the part of prudence to be laboring for the salvation of another's soul and neglecting
that of his own.

This particular enthusiast had more than a few obstacles to be
cleared away before he could fulfill his desire, but he finally got rid
of them, with the special help of the grace of God. To begin with,
besides his lawful wife, he was keeping a concubine, who, when she
heard that he would see her no more, flew into a terrible rage and
heaped a thousand imprecations on the heads of the Fathers. She
even threatened to commit suicide by hanging herself at her own door.
It is not an uncommon custom here, for those who cannot overcome
a serious disappointment to end their own lives in despair. They do
this to expose the authors of their desperation to the rigor of the law,
it being customary to mete out almost the same punishment to those
who in any way cause the death of another, as to those who are convicted of murder. With the help of Heaven and with the assistance of
the Fathers, he paid no attention to the woman's threats. He was set
upon saving his soul, and he was ready to submit to anything to save
it, and in this instance, he understood that it would be publicly known
that his former conduct was directly contrary to the law of the Church.
The importunate woman was partly placated by half willingly accepting a payment, and on second thought, she decided not to throw away
her life. With that over, he sent home, unharmed, to her mother, a
young girl whom he was supporting to become a future concubine.
Then he converted his lawful wife. Next, he built a big furnace and
burned up an extensive collection of idols, which he replaced in his
home with an imposing picture of Christ the Saviour. This picture was
kept on the same altar where the idols were formerly exhibited, after
the altar had been remodeled, and a devotional light was kept perpetually burning before the picture. Some of this man's relatives were
decidedly set against his conversion, but he paid no attention to their
threats. On the other hand, many of his friends, influenced by the
reasons he offered for changing his way of life, as well as by his good
example, were attracted by his decision and induced to follow his
example.

Before his conversion, he had been president of a society that was founded to promote the cult of the idols. After his conversion, some of the members of this society spread about the rumor that he left the society after defrauding it of a large portion of its funds. When he heard this, he returned to one of their meetings and, after giving them the reason for his resignation, he protested that he had been unjustly accused of stealing, said he wanted to hear from them what he had stolen and how he had in any way injured the society. Then he said he would replace tenfold every coin that they could prove he had taken. There was no one present who was ready to support the rumor that they had sent abroad and they answered very calmly, that every man should be permitted to practice the religion of his own choosing, without interference from others. Relative to the money, they said there was nothing to be paid back and that it was understood by everyone that formerly, he had always been very liberal with his fortune. With that said, he departed; and as the days went by, he gradually withdrew from their company, until he had no further contact with any of them.

This man's idea for attracting the attention of his relatives to Christianity was rather unique. He said he wanted to leave to posterity a memorial of the new law which was first accepted by his parents and afterwards by himself. He had an artist paint a very large picture of Christ, and in the picture, at either side, he inserted the pictures of his relatives who had become Christians. These figures were kneeling, holding a rosary and wearing a small reliquary, with a cross, suspended from a necklace. The figures inserted were perfect likenesses of the persons represented. This picture stirred up the interest of many, who felt that they would not be counted in the number of his relatives unless they identified their relationship by manifesting their faith. A man of universal charity, one could scarcely reckon his liberality to prisoners, his settlement of disputes, and other such pious interests.

This same Luke was really the founder of the Sodality of The Blessed Virgin in China. On the Feast of the Nativity of the Blessed Virgin in 1609, he gathered together the first members of this society, and though he had been prompted by the Fathers to do so, he really should be recorded as the founder of the organization. When he learned how the Sodality was conducted in Europe, he called the members together and wrote out the rules and the by-laws, which he then brought to Father Ricci for approval. Later on, their rule book was duly sanctioned, with the addition of a few directions required by the Roman Sodality of The Blessed Virgin.

The Chinese are always religiously exact about their funeral rites, and one of the functions of the Sodality was to supervise the funerals of the converts. In this pious practice they were helping the poor and making certain that their obsequies were conducted with strictly Christian ceremonies. On special feast days the Sodality members took great pleasure in decorating the church. They held regular meetings in the parish house, on the first Sunday of the month, and at their first meeting Luke was unanimously elected President. At every regular gathering, one of the Fathers gave an exhortation, and then conducted a question period to answer their difficulties. This society was called the Sodality of The Blessed Virgin. It began with forty members, whose influence in the community was accountable for a gradual, and eventually for a great, increase in Christian piety. Within a year of Luke's conversion more than a hundred new Christians were added to the parish, and their coming into the fold was due in no small part to his encouragement and his good example. On Christmas Day, there were forty who received Holy Communion, and the religious piety of this little group, in the beginning, soon developed a noticeable spirit of devotion among the converts.

17.The Church Grows in Nankin

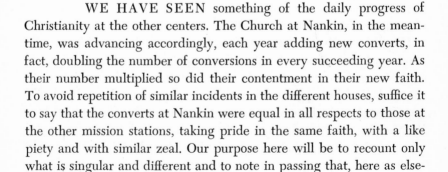

WE HAVE SEEN something of the daily progress of Christianity at the other centers. The Church at Nankin, in the meantime, was advancing accordingly, each year adding new converts, in fact, doubling the number of conversions in every succeeding year. As their number multiplied so did their contentment in their new faith. To avoid repetition of similar incidents in the different houses, suffice it to say that the converts at Nankin were equal in all respects to those at the other mission stations, taking pride in the same faith, with a like piety and with similar zeal. Our purpose here will be to recount only what is singular and different and to note in passing that, here as elsewhere, the spread of false rumors caused more fear than actual harm.

In 1606 the Magistrates arrested one of the citizens and fifteen or sixteen of his accomplices on a charge of treason against the Crown. He was convicted of having assembled about three thousand conspirators, bent upon the destruction of the Magistrates of Nankin. It was said that a book was discovered containing the plan of the rebellion, the names of all the conspirators, an outline of how they were to divide all public offices among them and which one was to occupy the position of this or that official, named to be murdered. As generally happens when too many know a secret, one of them, discontented with the office assigned to him, turned traitor and betrayed the plot. The book in question revealed that they intended to slay the Magistrates, take over the palace of the former kings and seize the treasury, together with its collection of valuable antiques of the centuries past. Certainly, if such an insurrection had not been nipped in the bud, the kingdom would have suffered a universal calamity. The conspirators were put to a horrible death, in the following cruel process of prolonged torment, generally meted out to conspirators. A large metal plate, circular in form, is placed around the neck of the victim and firmly locked. This heavy weight falls on the shoulders and it is so large that the culprit cannot reach his hand to his mouth, and others have to feed him. Under this weight he has to stand day and night until the flesh of his legs putrefies from his bodily excretions, and when the legs collapse, the whole body goes to ruin. Some of these men lived in this torment for fifteen days. At times it happens that their executioners are bribed to give them some respite during the night. The rumors of this rebellion gave the emissaries of the Devil an opportunity to spread the story that the Fathers were the real authors of the uprising. This disturbed the converts and caused a falling off in their number, but when the excitement ceased their enrollment was doubled. The clouds of suspicion were soon dissipated and the sunshine of peace returned.

During the years of retirement, which Father Cattaneo spent in Macao, because of his health, Father Giovanni Roccia was in charge at Nankin. In 1609, by order of Father Ricci, he took over the mission at Nancian and by order of the Father General of the Society, Father Emanuele returned to Macao. Father Alfonso Vagnoni, a Piedmontese, who had spent four years studying the Chinese language and knew it perfectly, remained at Nankin. Father Peter Ribero was left there as his assistant because Father Feliciano da Silva, who could not live in the climate of Nankin, fell seriously ill and returned to the College at Macao for treatment. When he recovered his health, he returned to his station and with his coming the progress of the faith was continued, the number of converts increased and friendly relations with the Magistrates were renewed. The arrival of Ciu Paul in Nankin gave an impetus to this progress.

Ciu Paul had gone to his home district to spend the period of mourning for his father, and during that time he had paid several visits to Macao. Every time this man met his former pagan instructor he was advised to return to the sect of the idols but he only ridiculed his master's counsel. It would be difficult to state what a tremendous asset this man was to the cause of Christianity. He trained Ignatius, a convert of some years, in the ways of piety and he led many others into the fold, although he himself was busily engaged with other affairs. Paul was so well versed in the Spiritual Exercises of Saint Ignatius that he introduced them as a practice among the Chinese. They in turn were religiously inclined, and one might conclude from their effects that these same Spiritual Exercises are capable of working wonders in this kingdom.

When Ciu Paul was returning to Pekin, after his period of mourning, to take over the office he had relinquished, he was detained over Christmas Eve, outside of the city walls, and spent that holy night very sadly in a temple of one of the suburbs. At daybreak on Christmas Day, he notified the Fathers of his coming, and ordered a palanquin to get into the city. The conveyance was so long in coming that he began to worry lest he might be late for Mass; so he made most of the journey on foot, through the heavy winter mud that covered the roads. He lived for a time at the Mission House, so the Fathers could become acquainted with the Magistrates who came to visit him, and he brought about the conversion of one of the highest of them, of whom we shall hear later on. There were about a hundred converts every year at this station of Nankin, and to promote their devotion and piety, in imitation of the center in Pekin, the Fathers instituted, here, a second Sodality of the Blessed Virgin, which accomplished all they had hoped for.

While mortal men were promoting the glory of the Immortal God, the Divine Presence made itself known at times by the accomplishment of the extraordinary. There was a girl here possessed of a devil, who insistently appeared to her in various forms, endeavoring to persuade her to abandon the path of virtue. At times he would appear as a merchant or as a temple minister, now as an old man and again as a youth, but always tempting her to shameful sin, and saying that nothing would satisfy him but the blood of a child. The exorcists were called in from the pagan temple, but the spirit only ridiculed their rites, showing no fear and causing the lights and the candles to fall off the altar of the idols. A certain convert in the neighborhood, an artisan, happened to hear about this, and while speaking with some of the pagans, he explained to them that God had power over spirits, as well as over men. "Then why don't you do something for that girl, who is a neighbor of yours," they said. "Certainly," he explained, "God has power over the Devil, and if He were to use it, the Devil would be chased away." Then they all went over to see the girl's parents and asked them, whether or not they wanted to have her freed from her tormentor, and if they did, then they should begin to adore the true God. This they consented to do, and one of the Lay Brothers brought them a picture of Christ and told them to call upon the name of Jesus. They took all the idols off the domestic altar and the whole family began a series of instructions in Christian doctrine. From that day on, there was no evidence of the evil spirit in the house, although threatening yells were heard in the courtyard, and when the family was baptized, that was the end of their difficulty. This incident became a common topic of conversation, and it caused considerable wonder on the part of many, when they realized that the power of God worked so readily where all the efforts of the Chinese exorcists amounted to nothing.

In this same year, one of the highest ranking Magistrates of the royal court was received into the church. Thus far, he was the most exalted pagan dignitary to become converted. Ciu Paul was superior, but he was appointed to his high office after he became a Christian. This man's title corresponded to what we might call the High Chancellor, the Tuncinsu, in Chinese. Part of his duty was to revise all petitions forwarded to the King, and in addition to other offices he held, he was one of the four High Magistrates of the royal city. He had been friendly with the Fathers for some years, but he had never shown any particular inclination toward Christianity. On the contrary, as he himself said, after he became a Christian, when he first read Father Ricci's Catechism, he didn't like it at all, because it so thoroughly refuted certain inane beliefs to which he, at that time, was very earnestly devoted. Father Alfonso thought he had noticed in him a certain disdain for religion, and a dislike to talk about eternal salvation, and so, he interested him in something much more to his liking, namely, mathematics.

There is no better example to illustrate the fact that Heaven has employed the sciences for converting the solons of China. Father Alfonso had a celestial sphere and a terrestrial globe made for him, which he

decorated with appropriate commentary. This increased their friendship and their mutual esteem, and one day, when the Magistrate was
very seriously lauding the study of the sciences, Father Alfonso said,
"What you have learned from me, Sir, up to the present, is wholly trivial in comparison with the mysteries of faith. The adoration of God is
a more sublime science than the contemplation of the stars, and anyone
would agree that it is more important to establish an eternal home in
heaven than to be merely looking up at it and talking about it." He told
him also that the substantial return he himself would like to make for
his friendship and for the many favors he had received from him, would
be to secure his eternal salvation. One thing he said he would like to
have him do, was to examine the law of Christianity with the same intense interest he put into the study of mathematics, to see whether or
not he thought it worthy of acceptance by those who had direction of
the Chinese kingdom, and then, with the assistance of divine grace, to
make a decision according to what he had learned. These words were
not lost on a man of his genius. He said he would be glad to undertake
a close reading of the Christian precepts. He was then asked to re-read
Father Ricci's catechism attentively and with his new disposition of
mind. Then he was given the four new dissertations that had only
lately been added to the catechism: one on God, another on the immortality of the soul, a third on original sin and the fourth on The God-
Man. The illuminating grace of God was not lacking from the good will
put into his reading, and once he attained the truth, he proved by his
example what we learned by long experience, namely, that the Chinese
are more readily persuaded by books than by verbal argumentation
about the Christian Law.

This man's intellect had been won over and submitted to the truth,
but his will was still enmeshed in certain doubts from which he was
striving to gain its liberty. One of these entanglements was a certain
inept Chinese prepossession, which urged them to seek every possible
means of prolonging the present life. Now it happened that our new
Christian soldier had formerly had certain pagan impostors as teachers,
whose nonsense had so affected him, that he had written and edited
a treatise on the prolongation of life, and as this hope of longevity had
led him into certain superstitious practices, he could not very easily
abandon them, even after he had become a Christian. There was also
another scruple that caused him considerable anxiety. He was terribly
disturbed about the choice of lucky and unlucky days on which to conduct business. He had been accustomed to consult deceiving fortune-

tellers about future events and he found it difficult to break off this habit, to which he had been a slave from his youth. These difficult knots were so aptly untied for him by responses received from the Fathers, that he placed all the blame upon his own credulity in such nonsense and soon conceived a horror for such blind folly.

The first step in this man's notable conversion was to courageously cut away from all pagan superstitions, and the determination of his decision to do so was aptly proven in two different instances. He was told of an artist who had come to the royal court, boasting that he could paint the exact likenesses of the ancestors of any family, even if they had been dead for centuries and there was no memory of them remaining, provided only he was furnished with their true names. This last phrase was added on to bolster up his assertion. Our convert had an urgent desire to replace the portraits of his ancestors which had been lost in a fire when a certain town was destroyed during a Japanese invasion, and he was just about to call in the impostor painter. Then a doubt arose in his mind as to whether or not this would be quite in keeping with Christian ethics. To solve his doubt, he wrote a letter to the Fathers and they answered him with a dilemma, saying that this man was either an impostor, or that he was working with the aid of the Devil. They explained that it is not the part of a prudent man to be taken in by an impostor, nor is it ever permitted for a Christian to partake in the work of the Devil, consequently, such a work must be either useless or illicit. This was enough to persuade him to abandon a hoax to which he was about to fall an innocent victim.

Proof of the second instance will be offered presently. He wanted to send the Fathers a letter of thanks and a magnificent offering for having received him into the faith, but they refused to listen to this for reasons already explained, and also because it is contrary to their rule to accept any remuneration for their spiritual ministrations. Then he asked them to send him a picture of Christ for his own personal devotion. One of the Fathers brought this picture to him and he received it, clad in the full array of his official apparel. Later on, he did honor to his teacher by tendering him a sumptuous banquet, and a few days afterwards he was enrolled in the army of Christ, taking the name John in baptism, publicly announcing that his heart was filled with joy, and that he could actually feel the spiritual force of the saving water of the sacrament. After the ceremony, he augmented his former gift with a liberal supply of silk cloth, as an offering in thanksgiving, but this again was refused. At first he was somewhat amazed at the procedure of refusing his gifts, but he was calm about it, and afterwards he gave approval as well as praise to the reasons behind it.

Shortly after his conversion, his aged mother died, and according to Chinese custom, he gave up all official business and retired to his home for a mourning period of three years. Before his departure, he again presented the gifts, which had been formerly refused, and this time in such a way that they had to be accepted. There was question at the time of building a new church, and he sent in a large donation to begin the work, under such title that it could be accepted without demur, and could not be refused without danger of giving offense. When he was leaving, one of the Fathers accompanied him for half a day's journey, to make certain that he knew the ceremonies to be observed at his mother's Christian burial. Before leaving him, the Father reminded him of the necessity of the strict observance of the Christian precepts, and John said, "You know the spirit in which I embraced the law of Christ, and the difficulty I had in cutting loose from my former errors. Well, I deliberately chose this day on which to set out on my journey, because it is marked in the Chinese calendar as a day on which one is strictly forbidden to start out on a trip of any kind, and I did this to spite the Devil, who had deluded me for so many years." Then they parted with a mutual feeling of contentment. After he had settled down at home, he wrote several compelling letters asking to have one of the Fathers visit him as often as convenient, so that he could use his leisure time in the further study of Christian doctrine. Such a request could not be very easily refused.

The conversion of this extraordinary man and the example of the convert Leo, or Ligotsum, produced a tremendous influence on the rest of the new Christian community. We shall have more to say about Leo in connection with the residence in Pekin. Here were two outstanding examples inciting the other Christians to the imitation of their own Chinese leaders, who had developed into patterns of unusual virtue and piety. This influence was made evident to everyone on the Christmas night that Leo spent with the other converts praying and meditating, pouring out his heart in expiation for his past sins, and wearing no sign or insignia of the dignity of his exalted position.

18. Father Cattaneo and Ciu Paul at Scianhai

THE THREE YEARS that Ciu Paul passed in retirement, in mourning for his father, were spent in improving the material and the spiritual welfare of his family and of his fellow citizens. He asked Father Ricci to send him one of the Fathers to direct this work, and Father Cattaneo, who was less occupied since he returned to Nankin from Macao, was despatched to his assistance.

Paul's home town was Scianhai, in the Nankin Province, a city of lesser importance, called a Haien or a district city. It is about a hundred and forty-four Italian miles from the royal city of Nankin, twenty-nine degrees latitude, not far distant from the Oriental Sea, on the Korean side, and too close to the Japanese Islands to please the inhabitants. When the wind is favorable, the voyage across the strait to Japan can be made in twenty-four hours. Pirates frequent the neighboring waters, hence a strong garrison is maintained for the protection of the city, and a fleet to guard and defend the maritime frontier. The city takes its name from its maritime position, Scianhai meaning by the sea. There are two miles of wall around this town, and there are as many houses in the suburbs as in the city proper, forty thousand families, generally designated as that many fires or hearths. One must not be surprised to learn that there are such large numbers of people in Chinese cities, when even the villages and the hamlets are over-crowded. The whole country surrounding this city is a level plateau, more like a vast city of gardens than a countryside, with an unbroken view of towers and villas and farms. In this outer stretch there are more than twenty thousand families, which, in addition to the population of the city and the suburbs, amount to more than three hundred thousand people under the jurisdiction of this one city. This one jurisdiction pays an annual tax to the royal treasury amounting to a hundred and fifty thousand gold pieces which is paid in silver, weighed out to a corresponding value. The tax in rice is equivalent to that in currency, making a total of three hundred thousand gold pieces in value. One may gather from this what a fabulous amount of tribute is paid to the King each year from the entire country.

This section of the province is especially rich in rice, and in cotton for making different kinds of cloth, and they say there are two hundred thousand weavers here. The cloth is exported from here to the royal court in Pekin and to the other provinces. The people here, especially those in the city, are very active and somewhat unsettled, well endowed intellectually, counting many scholars and literati among them, and consequently many Magistrates who formerly held high positions and now are retired as wealthy men, living in magnificent palaces. The streets of the city are narrow. The climate here is very mild, accounting for the fact that the people here live longer than in other parts of the kingdom. Here a man of sixty is not considered old. Very many of these people live to be eighty or ninety and some of them live beyond a hundred. Ciu Paul was born here.

Rather than have Father Cattaneo travel alone, Paul had planned to go to Nankin to get him, and while there to have a memorial service for his father. He also wanted to secure the necessary permission for Father Cattaneo to preach the Gospel in the Scianhai district, but he did not leave his home town because he was taking care of a sick relative, one of the literati, whom he was instructing for conversion and preparing for baptism. He sent the majordomo of his house to accompany Father Cattaneo on the voyage, and bearing a letter of profuse apology for not being able to come himself, as he had planned. He also sent along a liberal allowance to defray the expenses of the journey. While Father Cattaneo was en route, Paul was instructing his sick relative in Christian Doctrine. He gave him a picture of the Blessed Virgin, for his private devotion, and also a rosary, on which he was continually praying that he would not die before being baptized. He professed a sincere repentance for his sins, and this with his ardent desire for baptism, let us hope, was sufficient for his eternal salvation. Father Cattaneo delayed no longer than it took him to make the trip, but he did not arrive in time to administer the sacrament. Up to that time the Fathers had not translated the form for baptism into Chinese, for use in case of emergency. The Latin formula had been written out in Chinese characters, but very few of the Chinese could use this. Later on this difficulty was remedied.

Father Cattaneo left Nankin toward the end of the year 1608. Paul came part of the way to meet him, in his own boat, and kept him as a house-guest for three days, with every expression of welcome and of friendship. Paul was grieved to think that his relative had died without being baptized, but his grief was assuaged when it was explained to him that his friend's ardent desire for baptism, together with his true repentance for his sins, was equivalent to the reception of the sacrament; something which Paul had not as yet learned.

After going over all the ceremonies together, the funeral of Paul's father was conducted strictly according to Christian rites, and the pagan ministers of the temple were decidedly disappointed, at having lost the generous offering they would have received for conducting the funeral of so prominent a citizen. Whereupon, they spread the story that the Christian Law prevented posterity from honoring their ancestors, but the story soon faded out, because the Chinese knew that it was written into the law that next to God, a Christian honors his parents.

Paul's household spent three days rejoicing, in honor of the Father's arrival. Magistrates and other prominent citizens came to pay their respects. After this, his guest reminded him that it was not the best thing for the advancement of the faith, for him to take up residence at Paul's house, because there he would meet only the distinguished people of the city and Paul's more intimate friends. So his host arranged for him to live at the house of a friend, until such time as he could have suitable quarters prepared, in a separate house. The new house was in one of the suburbs, an appropriate place for the enjoyment of liberty and of mental repose, but Father Cattaneo was to have few, if any, leisure hours. So many people came to see him that he could not give time and attention to each of them, and he was soon showing signs of fatigue. He could scarcely find time for the celebration of Mass, for the reading of his daily office, and for his own personal needs. Often enough, nearly all of his regular duties had to be postponed until late hours. All this, however, was not without its reward. In the first short period of thronging activity he made fifty converts and before two years were up, he made two hundred; something that had not happened at the other stations, in so short a time, during a pioneering period. Because of the increasing number of interested visitors, Ciu Paul bought a house in the city, which was better suited for the Father's work, and here many things happened for the glory of God, which are well worth recording. For the sake of brevity, we shall confine our report to the more striking events.

The frequent visits of the Mayor of the city gave rise to a great deal of gossip. They said he was going to become a Christian. That was not so, but it promoted an interest in Christianity and brought a number of people inquiring about the faith. Extraordinary things were happening here, through the power of the sign of the cross. One of the converts and his son fell sick, at the same time, of an intermittent fever. He asked Father Cattaneo for a crucifix, and when the crucifix was brought into the house, they were immediately cured. Wonders were worked among the pagans, as well as favors wrought for the faithful. A young bride was tormented by the Devil, who prevented her from sleeping and from eating, and caused her to utter all sorts of unbecoming expressions. A neophyte neighbor counseled her to pray to God, and proposed that she become a Christian. She agreed to this and from the moment she learned to make the sign of the cross, there was no more trouble from the evil spirit, nor any further difficulty in eating and sleeping. Later on she was baptized and became the first Christian woman in this part of the country.

Before his baptism, one of the converts had burned all his idols and, God permitting, the Devil avenged the burning in a peculiar way. Whenever he attempted to boil rice, the rice disappeared and there was nothing left but a pot full of water, as black as ink. He came to consult the Father and he was given a crucifix to keep in his home, and that was the end of the evil spirit of the kitchen. When one of Ciu Paul's servants was seized by a sudden illness, Father Cattaneo went to visit him, gave him a course of instructions and he began to recover rapidly, from the moment he was baptized. In a few days he was up and about and perfectly restored to health. In gratitude for his recovery, he asked his master if he could go to live with the Father, as his servant, and help take care of the chapel. The permission was granted, and he proved to be a very exact and helpful worker. Many of the pagans were cured of their bodily ailments by contemplating the crucifix and promising that they would become Christians. One of these, a young man, was cured of his illness and then went back on his promise. One day he went home and discovered a serpent in his house. Every time he tried to kill it, it squirmed away and escaped. That night he had a dream, whether it occurred perchance or was something designed for his salvation, it is difficult to say. He seemed to hear someone saying, "Do you wish to believe in me, or not?" When he repeated that he did not, the same voice said, "If you believe, I shall kill the serpent. If not, I shall let him be." He was terribly frightened at all this, and he thought he bowed his head, as if giving his assent. At any rate, it prompted him to fulfill the promise he had made and then abandoned.

God's clemency was also extended to a certain pagan, whose son was a Christian. The boy could not persuade his father to give up the worship of his idols, so he promised to pray before the crucifix, in his father's name, every time his father venerated the statues of the false gods. The parent fell sick, and one night he thought he saw Him, before whose image the son was accustomed to pray, and he thought he heard Him say, "I would like to come to your assistance." From that time on he began to recover his strength. He hadn't the slightest doubt about the help he had received from God, nor any hesitation in accepting His law and becoming a Christian. Our last unique example of extraordinary devotion, is that of a kindly and pious old man, who went about continually praying on his beads, at times confining his prayers to the five sorrowful mysteries, and again reciting the entire fifteen decades of the rosary. He said, that while he was praying he could scent the sweet odor of perfume that permeated the church during services on feast days. Perhaps this was a reward for the sweet incense of his prayer, ascending to the throne of heaven. These unusual happenings were a great consolation to the converts, who endeavored by their zeal and devotion to render themselves worthy of such graces.

The first celebration of Christmas Eve, in this city, was something out of the ordinary. The converts were all present, including Ciu Paul. Father Cattaneo read the first nocturn of the Matins of the Feast, in Chinese, and preached an appropriate sermon at each Mass. Ciu Paul was always the central figure on such occasions, and he was so attentive to the converts of the lower social classes, that he always invited some of them to come and sit with him; whereas, on state occasions, they had so much respect for the dignity of his high position, that they would scarcely dare to look at him. The funeral service held for his father in Pekin was repeated here, with the same display and ecclesiastical rites; and although there was only one priest here to officiate, the novelty of it and the sacred rites and ceremonies supplied the solemnity which proved to be very pleasing to the converts. They seemed to take a special delight in the fact that the Christian ceremonies were much more impressive than those of the pagans.

Just at this time, four Lay Brothers completed their noviceship, and one of them, Francis Lagea, was sent to share the work of Father Cattaneo, and to lighten his burden. Not long afterwards, this Mission was closed, because the number of Fathers was not sufficient to maintain stations in the smaller cities. Moreover, they were preparing to open a residence in Hancian, the metropolitan city of the Province of Cechian, which was only a three day journey from this mission at Scianhai, and it was thought that this new field could be taken care of from there. It was the opinion of the Fathers that they could accomplish more in the larger cities of the kingdom. And so, with the full consent of Ciu Paul, who had already returned to Pekin, the direction of this mission was transferred to Hancian, and the new converts, agreeing that the larger undertaking was more for the glory of God, had no objection to the departure of the Fathers.

Concerning this particular mission at Hancian, nothing further will be said in this diary, because it was begun after the death of Father Ricci, with which the first volume of Chinese history is closed. However, so that our readers may not be deprived of what was accomplished there, a separate work containing the annals of the two following years will be published, which may be added to the present diary to make a complete history.

19. A Weird Journey from Xaucea to Macao

ALTHOUGH IT MIGHT seem that the good will of the Magistrates and the honesty of the new Admiral, in judging the case of Father Cattaneo, had restored affairs at Xaucea to their former condition, the wound that was inflicted by wagging tongues was not as yet fully healed and probably never could be. The tumult of the so-called rebellion had just ceased, when another incident occurred that proved to be almost as troublesome.

One of the domestic servants was sent with letters from Xaucea to Macao, and on his return journey with the replies, he was apprehended by the military guards. Sending letters to foreigners outside of the realm is nothing less than treason. The servant was ordered to pay a ransom to the guards, who are always bent on making money in this way, and he might easily have bought his freedom at not too large a price. For some unexplainable reason, however, he refused to open his purse, and his resistance cost the Fathers dearly and himself even more, because what might have terminated as a minor incident, eventually stirred up no end of trouble. He was arrested within the limits of the City of Ansan, which is about equidistant from the metropolitan city of Canton and Macao, about a day's journey in either direction. First he was brought to the Mayor of Ansan, who sent him to the Mayor of Canton, and he in turn ordered the case transferred to the Admiral, because it involved a foreigner. At the Admiral's court he was first given a flogging and then thrown into chains, after which his case was passed over to the Governor and his council, to be studied and then adjudicated according to the law.

The Assessors of the Governor's Council sent for interpreters to find out what was written in the letters. There were some Portuguese in the city, who read the letters, by order of the Magistrates, and with the help of their interpreters translated them into Chinese. Then the Librarians put them together, in one binding, and with the originals, placed them in the city archives. Fortunately, and Heaven must be thanked for it, there was nothing in the letters that could in any way offend the ever suspicious Chinese. The letters treated only of domestic affairs, and praised the Chinese public administration. And yet, although this was the published opinion of the interpreters, for fear that leniency in this instance might open the way to future evil, the servant who was carrying the letters was condemned for life, to servitude to the King, and Father Longobardo who sent the letters to Macao, was banished from the Province of Canton to the interior of the kingdom. This sentence, however, was never carried out, because it was never confirmed by the higher Magistrates. What resulted from it, will be revealed later on.

In this same year of 1609, Father Bartholomew Tedeschi died here, after seven years' residence in Xaucea, as co-laborer with Father Longobardo. Father Tedeschi was an Italian, from the Sabine district, and while he was studying in Rome, with the Jesuit Fathers, he always took great delight in listening to, and in reading about, the Fathers who returned to Europe from India. This was the occasion, as he himself said, of his being called by God to go to India. He applied for entrance into the Society of Jesus and was received, and later on, with no less zeal, he obtained permission from his superiors to go on the India

Mission. Father Tedeschi was always a popular member of his religious community. He died of a violent fever that was annually recurrent. When he felt that he was approaching the end, he gave one of his fellow priests a little note book, in which he had written every criticism of himself that he had heard, as coming from others, and every self-accusation that his own conscience revealed, laying bare, as it were, every nook and corner of his soul. When his companion read it all, he marveled at a man who could make such a searching investigation of his own life, and prove to be such a striking example of innocence. Later, this same priest was called to hear his general confession, from the time he entered the Society, and after receiving Holy Communion, as viaticum, he died on the Feast of Saint James, on the ninth day of his sickness. In keeping with the Chinese custom, all the converts and his many other friends came to the Mission House to mourn his departure. The funeral services in the church were celebrated with more than usual display, because Father Emanuele Dias and Father Rodrigues were present. They were on their way to Macao, and were waiting at Xaucea for an opportunity to make the crossing. Foreigners cannot return to Macao, in safety, without permission of the Magistrates, and it was not until two months later that they set out, taking with them the body of Father Tedeschi, for burial in the cemetery that belonged to the Fathers, in Macao.

Since we have mentioned these two Fathers, in connection with Xaucea, this would seem to be the proper place to record their voyage from here to Macao, a journey replete with danger, from start to finish, and significant of the special protection of Divine Providence. Father Emanuele was on his way to Macao, by order of the General of the Society of Jesus, to become Rector of the college there. Father Rodrigues, who could find no alleviation from his serious illness in China, was being sent there to care for his health. Father Longobardo was to take the place of Father Emanuele, as Superior of the three houses in the southern section of the China Mission, under the jurisdiction of Father Ricci. They thought it would be an assurance of safety en route, if they were to take the body of Father Tedeschi with them, for burial at Macao. The Chinese, either from superstitious fear, or out of reverence for the dead, will not go near a coffin.

They left Xaucea with one of the Lay Brothers and in a few days, with a favorable river current, they arrived at Canton. The big difficulty at Canton at all times is to arrange for a change of boats, to make the two day sailing voyage to Macao. For fear of being recognized as

foreigners, by some of the numerous military guards, they came to an-
chor in a less frequented harbor, about half a league from the city.
Here the Lay Brother went ashore and arranged with a boat owner, for
the transportation of the coffin to Macao, with instructions to notify the
Rector of the College that the Fathers were coming, so that he could
arrange the safest method for their approach to the College, once they
had landed. Necessity dictated this plan of action, because they failed
to find any Portuguese merchants in the market place to convey this
information. The body of Father Tedeschi arrived and was buried in
the church cemetery. Forty days passed and they could not find a
sailor who would risk the danger of transporting foreigners, which
was against the law. After that lapse of time, it was only to be expected
that they had been arrested.

They were still aboard their boat, and one day, just before daybreak,
several military guards paid them an unexpected and a noisy visit,
crying out that they were searching for women who had been kid-
napped. It was a cold morning and the Fathers were wrapped up in
blankets, in their beds, and the fact that they were, is what saved
them from arrest. When the guards approached, they put out their
feet from underneath the blankets, and this was evidence enough for
the guards, that their quarry was not there. Chinese women have
very small feet, which are kept, at all times, night and day, tightly
wrapt in bandages, to prevent them from enlarging. This visit, however, caused them considerable worry. It was known by some of the
guards that there were foreigners aboard that boat, and it looked as
if the woman element was only a pretext for the raid. Later on, it
proved to be true that by order of the Magistrates, the police were
looking for certain fugitive women. When they saw that there were
no women aboard the boat, they went away without further search,
but by the grace of God, their eyes were closed to certain other things
during their search. They may not have been looking for such things,
but right before them were several breviaries, other books with
European bindings, and various added evidence of the presence of
foreigners.

A Portuguese trader had stopped his boat on the other side of the
river, on his voyage to Macao, and in their imminent danger they
hastened to inform him to come to their assistance unless he wished
to abandon them to fate. This man, with considerable risk to himself,
sent over his interpreter to bring them across to his boat. And here, in
passing, we should say a word in praise of the Portuguese, for the

many dangers they braved to assist the cause of Christianity. As they were leaving their own boat, they sent the Lay Brother back to Xaucea, fearing that he might not be able to submit to an ordeal, if perchance they encountered some exacting trial. When the Captain of the Portuguese boat saw them and realized from their faces, who they were, he could not be persuaded to take them on his boat, if they had promised to fill it with silver. So they had to remain on the river bank over night, hiding beneath the trees to escape notice, and when that was not safe enough, one of them climbed up in a tree and the other crept under some bushes. Here they spent one of those sleepless nights, in which fear can do more harm than the evil being feared. And yet, the refusal of the Captain to take them aboard his boat, was still another example of the protection of Divine Providence. They had scarcely gotten out of sight, when one of the fast moving customs boats approached the Portuguese craft to inspect it for contraband cargo. Certainly, if the Fathers had been on the boat at that time, their voyage would have come to an abrupt termination. The Portuguese trader had no idea of abandoning them. He sympathized with them as if he were sharing a common danger. He sent the Captain ashore; the one who had kept the Fathers from going aboard, with instructions, to look for a house where they could hide until other boats came along that were bound for Macao. The Captain went off on the errand but he failed to come back, and they began to fear, not without reason, that he had gone to some Magistrate to betray them. They spent that night partly in prayer and partly in keeping out of sight of guards, and it seemed quite certain that they would have surrendered themselves to the Magistrates, if the dawn had not brought better counsel.

It seemed to be a safer plan to present oneself for prison chains, rather than to be cast into them. Their anxiety was increasing with the approaching dawn. They were weighing their desire to suffer for the faith, against the harm that might follow for the Christian Mission in China. With the first shafts of light, their last hope of human help was about to fade away, when they looked down from the bank where they were hiding and saw a fisherman's boat, at the water's edge. The fisherman was on the shore, with his family, an ordinary early morning scene. The Portuguese merchant's interpreter joined the fisherman and bargained with him, either to take the Fathers back to their own boat, or to take them to Macao, if they discovered that the Lay Brother had already departed with their boat. Their growing fear proved to be a reality. The Lay Brother had already departed for Xaucea, in their boat.

From there on, the trip to Macao was a series of hazards and inconveniences. The fishing boat they were on was small and they had to outwit the river police in their fast moving galleys. When they sighted a boat they pretended to be fishermen, and when it disappeared they had to bend to the oars. Most of their progress was made at night. They came to a desert island, where the fisherman decided to put in for a day and to continue the journey during the quiet of the night. Their faithful guide told the Fathers to walk about on the island for relaxation and distraction, which they assuredly needed after the strenuous days they had just passed through. One of them, while walking toward the interior of the island, came upon the body of a man who had been cruelly murdered; his head was split open with a large stone that was lying beside him. They thought this had been done by robbers, and judged the place to be dangerous, but they met with no one during their stay on the shore. That night they put off again and arrived at Macao early the next morning on the feast of Saint Ursula, October the twenty-first.

That same morning a Dutch pirate had been sighted from the shore and the banks were crowded with military guards and with curious spectators. The fisherman was frightened at the sight of the crowd, for fear he might be recognized by the Chinese and reported to the City Magistrates for taking foreigners out of the country by ferrying them across to Macao. So he put the Fathers ashore before coming to the city, but only a short distance away from it. From there they made their way to the top of a hill, close to the city, where there is a chapel dedicated to the Blessed Virgin. This chapel is called the Journey's Guide, because it faces to the open sea, in the direction of the oncoming Japanese trading ships, the argosies that bring in the sustaining fortune of the entire city. Here they gave thanks to the Blessed Mother, Guide of Travelers, for having brought them, under God, through so many perils, into a harbor of safety, and they sent a messenger to the Rector of the College to inform him of their arrival. They had come in Chinese dress, and it would be quite unbecoming, especially in the eyes of the Chinese, if they were to walk through the city to the College in that garb. This was particularly true since the city, which was poorly protected, was trembling with warlike excitement, because of the report that a pirate fleet was hiding among the neighboring islands.

There was great rejoicing at the house when they arrived, which made them forget the hardships they had passed through, until such time as they could recall them all, to tell them to the others, with heartfelt thanks for their delivery. Such trials are frequently encountered by those who volunteer to labor on the missions among the pagans, and they are not cited here as being exceptional to this particular expedition. Witness, too, the ambition of the brave men of Europe, who undergo the hardships of sailing the seas in quest of the wealth and the luxury which mortals crave, but to what end, in comparison to that for which the missionary is laboring.

20. The Death of Father Ricci

THE REPUTATION enjoyed by Father Matthew Ricci, during the period of his residence in the royal city of Pekin, was something with which Heaven favored him, in testimony of the Gospel he was preaching. Living among a people who in many respects were both subtle and sagacious, and who thought of all other nations as barbarous, he was held in so high repute that no other may ever hope to gain such renown, nor will it avail him to aspire to it. During the few years that he was in Pekin he was continually occupied with an almost incessant line of visitors, who came from all directions, and his return visits, which could not be omitted without violating a time-honored Chinese custom, seemed to double his activities. Numerous letters were sent to him, from all parts of the Chinese world, by those whom he knew and by many unknown to him, inquiring about various articles of Christian Doctrine, about the belief of those who sacrificed to idols, and about passages that appeared in his published works, and he considered it no great burden to answer them all.

The educated Chinese are so particularly exacting about literary style in their correspondence, that if Father Ricci had not given as much attention to his style of writing, as he did to the subject he was treating, it would have lessened their opinion of his treatment of the matter and also of the doctrine he professed. Since he was general Superior of the China Mission, he had also to reply to the correspondence of his religious brethren, which he did, at length and very carefully. He had a real deep affection for every one of his fellow missionaries. Continually occupied as he was, he never refrained from receiving and from holding familiar conversation with the most lowly of the converts, and if their visits interrupted more serious business, he smiled on them as he did on the most important people who were accustomed to call on him. In fact, it was his constant practice to give more time and more attention to the lowly among his converts. If we add to all this the time and labor he spent in writing and publishing books, and the lessons given to the other Fathers, which he never omitted up to the very end, no matter how busy he happened to be, it would seem that there was little if any time left over for necessary relaxation. And yet he was so apt in the disposition of his day, that he not only found sufficient time for his regular spiritual exercises, but for others as well, and not satisfied with doing certain things according to schedule, he managed to find enough time for extra things, over and above what was necessary or important. His companions marveled at what he accomplished, so much so, indeed, that they were left in doubt as to which deserved more praise; his tireless mental activity, which stopped at nothing, or his indefatigable physical ability, for which no task was too daring.

Thus far we have been considering his regular routine, but much took place in the year 1610 that was out of the ordinary, enough indeed to overwhelm him, but not enough to make him give up. The Magistrates from every province in the kingdom, some five thousand in number, assembled in Pekin, to pay their respects to the King. At that same time, the examinations for the Chinese Doctorate were being held. These examinations are given only at the royal court, and though there are only three hundred chosen for the degree, there are more than five thousand of the lettered class, who enter for it. All this activity in Pekin greatly increased the work of Father Ricci, and what made it more difficult for him was the fact that it all took place during the season of Lent. He was a strict observer of the ecclesiastical fasts, and his companions could never persuade him to continue a meal that had been interrupted by a visitor, or to take a meal out of the regular time, or to indulge his appetite in the slightest by eating or drinking. At that time also he was building a church, and most of the responsibility and the worry of this undertaking fell upon him, with no good results, especially as he was deprived of the assistance and the counsel of the Literary Doctor, Leo, who was sick at his home.

One day, when Father Ricci returned to the Mission House, thoroughly fatigued from consulting with visitors at the court, he took to his bed to rest. At first the other Fathers thought he was suffering from an attack of migraine, to which he was subject, and which he could usually shake off with a day's rest. When questioned, he said it was something quite different, and told them that he was sick unto death from utter exhaustion, and he seemed to be so unconcerned about it, that when one of them asked how he felt, he said, "Just at present I am wavering in doubt as to which of two things I would prefer; to accept my eternal reward, which is not far away, or to continue the routine of my daily labors, on this Christian Mission."

He fell sick on the third day of May, and on that day the convert, Doctor Leo, sent the medical doctor who was tending him to take care of Father Ricci. After a few days, when his prescriptions resulted in no improvement, the Fathers called in six of the best known medical men in the city. After consultation, in which they came to no common decision, they left three different kinds of medicine, but they also left the Fathers in doubt as to which of the three should be used. Many of the new converts had come to visit the patient, and they knelt before a crucifix and prayed that God would direct the Fathers to use the remedy that would be most helpful. It was a source of great admiration to hear with what earnest devotion some of the converts prayed that God might take some years off their own lives and prolong the life of their common father. Finally, one medicine was tried, but with no effect, save to increase their sorrow. The only one to be satisfied with it was the patient himself, who felt that he was finally coming to the end of his labors. He seemed to be particularly happy about this and his almost joyful disposition served to lighten the grief of both the Fathers and the converts.

On the sixth day of his illness, he made a general confession of his whole life, and the Father who attended him was so overcome by his light-hearted disposition, that he said he had never in his whole life experienced more spiritual joy than that which radiated from the gentility and the innocence of soul of Father Matthew. On the morning of the following day he prepared himself for the reception of the holy viaticum, and though he was so ill that they had not dared to remove him from his bed, when he heard them approaching with the Blessed Sacrament, he summoned all his strength, and without assistance from anyone, got up from his bed and knelt on the floor. This sight so affected everyone present that their eyes filled with tears. On the following afternoon, the height of his fever brought on delirium that caused him to wander in imagination, but his wanderings were, so to speak, from the abundance of his heart, and revealed what was passing through his mind. During the following night and the next day, he frequently talked about the converts, about the church he was building, about the conversion of the Chinese people, and even about the conversion of the King. The delirium left him the next day, and he asked for Extreme Unction, and in full control of his senses he answered all the prayers at the anointing, without any prompting.

The four members of the Society who were present asked him for a last paternal blessing, and he addressed each of them privately, exhorting them to continue the practice of religious virtue. Then turning to one of the Lay Brothers he told him that he would ask God for the blessing of perseverance in the Society of Jesus for him, adding that nothing better or more pleasant could happen than what he himself was experiencing at that moment. One of the Fathers then asked him if he realized the condition in which he was leaving them, when they were so dependent upon his assistance, and he answered, "I am leaving you on the threshold of an open door, that leads to a great reward, but only after labors endured and dangers encountered." Another asked him if he would tell them at this crucial hour, how they could repay the love he had shown them. "By always being very considerate and kind toward the Fathers when they arrive from Europe," he replied, "not only with your ordinary kindness but with increased affection, so that in each of you, they may find as much consolation as they found in the general company of their religious brothers at home."

His great zeal for souls was evident in what were almost his dying words, when he said, "I have great affection in the Lord for Father Peter Cotton, who is now at the court of the King of France. Although he does not know me, I had decided to write to him this year and to congratulate him for having done so much for the glory of God. I also wanted to tell him what we were trying to do in China. Now it is too late for writing, and so I must ask if you will kindly request him to consider me excused." If this last request of our beloved Father has not as yet been fulfilled by those to whom it was recommended, the mention of it made here, we hope, will suffice for its accomplishment.

He spoke in turn, and very gently, with the Fathers and with the converts, and toward evening of the eleventh of May, sitting up in his bed, without a struggle, and without any bodily motion, he half closed his eyes, as if falling asleep, and then he closed them and he was asleep in the Lord. Father Matthew Ricci was dead.

The great gathering of converts that convened when the Father was dying, had to be restrained in their weeping and their lamentations, for fear that their grief might appear to be immoderate, and thus injure the truth of their faith and detract from the glory of their departed Father. So they turned their grief into praise and each one in his own way began to laud his exceptional virtue, calling him a saint, and the Apostle of China. They begged and prayed and finally persuaded one of the Lay Brothers, who was an artist, to paint a picture of Father Matthew, for their common consolation.

The Chinese place their dead in wooden coffins, which are made of incorruptible wood, when that is obtainable, sparing no expense in the making. This was something which the Fathers could not afford, because of their vow of poverty, and also because of their present financial condition. It would seem, however, that the Lord did not wish to deny this exceptional funeral distinction to his faithful servant who was being honored in heaven, and who was yet to be honored on earth during the course of the following year, as we shall see.

When Doctor Leo, who was Father Ricci's last convert, heard of the departure of his beloved spiritual father, he sent messengers to the Mission House to offer his condolence. He was too ill at the time to come, in person, but he told the Fathers not to worry about the casket, that it was his pleasure to take care of funeral expenses for one from whom he had twice received the gift of life, only a few days before. He told them also not to worry about the body, if there happened to be some delay, because the law of nature would not affect the body of so great a man, and what he said was only too true. After more than two days, in the height of the summer heat, the face remained perfectly natural, and the whole countenance held the color of a living person, rather than that of one who was dead, as though reflecting a happier life in which he continued to live. The body was placed in the casket and taken to the church, where a funeral Mass was celebrated and the Office of the Dead chanted by the Fathers and the converts. Afterwards, it was returned to the house and, in keeping with the Chinese custom, placed on a platform for mourning visitors to see.

The Chinese never bury within the city walls, and during the time that they are making funeral arrangements, or waiting to purchase a plot in one of the suburbs, they place the body in a wooden box, and then hermetically seal the box with a glossy bituminous substance. Thus sealed the casket will remain absolutely impenetrable to fetid gases for years.

For some time past, Father Ricci had been looking forward, not only to his own death, but to the purchase of a cemetery plot, in the suburbs. In fact he had actually bought one but, for some reason or other, question arose as to the price to be paid for it, and the vendor withdrew his offer. At that time he told the Fathers it made little difference, because before long they would own another and a better cemetery. Judging from his words, he seemed to have had some foresight of what was to come, and when the time did come, it was the King of China who donated the plot of ground, as a final resting place for Father Ricci and his companions. Not only that, but he seems also to have had a prevision of the time of his death. He prolonged, into his last few months, the completion of the History of Christianity in China, which Claude Aquaviva, the General of the Society of Jesus, asked him to write, burned all his letters, catalogued his writings, and composed two schedules, one for domestic affairs and one for the entire mission. The one for the whole mission was addressed to Father Nicolo Longobardo, as Superior of the China Mission, and signed, Matthew Ricci, former Superior. It is not very probable that he wrote these directions during his illness, because he told the Fathers to open his desk, when he died, to read the schedule pertaining to them, and to send the other one to Father Longobardo.

The news of the death of Father Ricci brought a gathering of his friends, the Magistrates, and others of high station, to mourn his departure, as they are accustomed to, and with tears of sincere sorrow, they showed their admiration for him with expressions such as, O Holy Man! O Very Holy Man. The sorrow and the weeping were not limited to Pekin. In the other Mission Centers, the Fathers, the converts, and his many friends, all bemoaned the departure of their beloved Father. The converts at Nankin were particularly affected. They sent funeral gifts, among which was a striking panegyric in praise of his virtue. Not to be outdone, the converts of Pekin wrote another one, as glowing as the first. These were posted on either side of the catafalque and read with great appreciation by many of the visiting mourners.

Having touched upon the life of Father Ricci at the opening of our history, it is only fitting that we bring it to a close, with his own words, spoken as the course of his life was approaching its end. On several occasions, during his last few months, he said, "My dear Fathers, thinking it all over, in an effort to determine what would be the best thing for me to do, for the advancement of the China Mission, I have come to the conclusion that nothing could be more advantageous to its progress than the arrival of the day on which I shall die." When they objected and said, that for this same end, his life seemed to be necessary for many years to come, he questioned their objection and gave various reasons for his assertion. Certainly if we were to compare all that followed his demise with what went before it, we would have to say, omne tulit punctum, he summed up the whole matter in a single sentence. Nor is it to be wondered at that he should advance the Christian Mission in China from his seat in heaven, where he has even a stronger desire, as well as more power, to do so.

21. Ricci's Tomb: A Gift from the King of China

THE LABORS ENDURED by Father Matthew Ricci had prospered because of the assisting grace of Almighty God, and not wishing to terminate the effects of his efforts with the close of his life, as unto Sampson, God granted him more power in death than he had exercised while living on earth. With the funeral service performed according to the rites of the Church, Father Matthew's body, in the sealed coffin, was kept in the Mission House, according to Chinese custom, until a place beyond the city walls could be purchased for its interment. This caused the Fathers some concern, because of the lack of space in the house and also because of this unusual situation. Up to this time, all of those who had died on the China Mission were buried in the cemetery of the College, at Macao, and it was an order to be followed, that the bodies of those who died elsewhere were to be returned to Macao, for common burial. This order could not be followed in the present instance, and even though it could be, it seemed better not to do so, because it was quite evident that in taking the common father of the Mission, Heaven had ordained that something extraordinary was to result from his death.

On the day of the funeral Mass, one of the converts, who were present in great number, a man of distinction in the lettered class who was well acquainted with proceedings at the royal court, conceived the idea, after returning to his house, that perhaps the King might give a piece of land as a burial plot for Father Ricci. This he thought would serve as a confirmation of the legally valid existence in the kingdom of the Mission and of the faith as well. The idea seemed to be worth while presenting to the Fathers, so he went back to the Mission House, presented his proposition, and easily persuaded them that it would be worth their endeavor to discover what issue would result from their effort in an undertaking of so great importance. In consultation with him they outlined a petition to be sent to the King, and then sent it to Leo, whom Father Ricci had recently baptized, for him to fill it in and polish it off in proper literary style. Leo was a prominent Magistrate and celebrated for his elegant oratorical diction, and he not only completed the petition and approved of the Father's endeavor, but offered to promote it. Later on, he did much for its advancement while he remained at the royal court. The petition was then shown to several of their most influential friends, who were civic leaders, to find out what they thought of it, to discover whether or not they were attempting something too daring, and also, if they favored it, to secure their influential support as its promoters, when the time came to make the presentation. They were unanimous in favoring it, and also in offering their assistance to advance it, and this indeed was extraordinary, because such an undertaking could easily contain an element of danger. Up to that time, no king had ever granted land for the burial of a foreigner, and when this favor was granted by the Crown for a native, great and powerful as he may have been, it was not received without difficulty, nor without exorbitant remuneration.

The petition to the King was presented in the name of Father Diego Pantoia, who was Acting Superior. Father Sebastiano Redus was in charge of domestic affairs. Allowing for the difference in idiom, the translation of the petition runs as follows:

"I, Diego Pantoia, subject of a kingdom of the Great Occident, present a humble request in favor of another subject of a foreign realm, lately deceased. I, relying upon your renowned generosity, am hereby asking for a place of burial for him, so that your royal liberality may be bounteously extended to include all men, even strangers who come from the most distant regions. I, Diego Pantoia, a stranger from a very distant kingdom, moved by the fame and the glory of your most exalted country, traveled the seas for three full years, covering more than six thousand leagues, amid endless trials and troubles, finally arriving at the court of your Royal Majesty, together with Matthew Ricci and three other companions, in the twenty-eighth year of Vanlie, the twelfth moon. At that time, we presented Your Royal Majesty with some small gifts brought from our native land, and since then we have been receiving a subsidy from the Crown for our maintenance. This indeed was a particularly gracious benefit, for which our hearts can scarcely contain their profound feeling of appreciation, and which we could never repay, even with the spilling of our blood. In the nineteenth year of Vanlie, the first moon, we petitioned your Exalted Majesty to assign us a place to live, so that the splendor of your royal clemency and kindness might illumine the lives of newly arrived strangers. We waited for years to learn the expression of your will, and yet in all that time, through no merit of our own, but due rather to your kingly generosity, we never lacked provision for our sustenance.

"On the eighteenth of the third moon, of the thirty-eighth year of Vanlie, the aging Father Ricci died of a malady, leaving me, as it were, an orphan, the subject of a distant realm, in such a state as to elicit universal compassion and pity in my many trials. To return to my native land with his body would mean to undertake a very long voyage, and sailors fear to take a corpse aboard their ships. Hence it is impossible for me to bring his body back to his native soil. Considering that we have already lived for years in Your Majesty's protecting shadow, is it not possible to number us among your subjects, as belonging to the people who follow your royal car, so that your clemency, like unto that of Yao, may not be bound by the limits of your empire but extended to foreign kingdoms.

"As in life we were nourished by your royal bounty, so in death we trust that you will grant us a clod of earth for a shroud. This we ask, in view of the fact that my companion, Matthew Ricci, from the time of his arrival in this great kingdom, sedulously applied himself to the study of Chinese letters, and practiced those virtues which are set forth in your books. Moreover, with purity of intention and with external devotion, he burned holy incense, night and day, on the altar of The God of Heaven, and prayed for the well-being of Your Majesty, in return for your many benefits. Everyone, great and small, at the royal court, knew him as a true and a faithful soul. I, indeed, would never dare to feign what is not so; and hence they called him, One who longs to learn, an upright man. The many books he wrote sustain this title, and in the kingdoms overseas he was renowned as a celebrated scientist. Here too, from the time of his arrival, his company was sought for by the Magistrates.

"Coming from a foreign realm, how can I and my companions hope for more than pertains to our humble station? We are deeply grieved to think that we do not possess a plot of ground in which to bury our companion, and we beseech you, with tears, to kindly grant us the benevolent favor of assigning a piece of land, or a place in a temple, to entomb the body of one who has come here from a far distant province. We who survive him, I and my companions, promise to be like him, in life and in death. Carefully following the example set by our brother deceased, and praying to the God of Heaven, we shall ask for a thousand years of life for your mother and for you, so that we may rejoice in the peace and the quiet of Your Majesty's great Empire, to our own consolation and contentment. If granted so great and so signal a favor, insignificant and small as little ants, as we may be, yet we shall show ourselves to be most grateful for it, and henceforth we shall stand with souls burdened with desire to show our appreciation. We shall await the decision of Your Royal Majesty."

Such was the content of the petition. If we seem to have adhered closely to the Chinese style in our version of it, we have done so expressly, in the belief that it will thus be more acceptable. It must be evident to everyone that every language has a grace and a beauty distinctive of its own particular idiom.

Before continuing our narrative, we must explain, in brief, a few points, which, if not clarified, might obscure the proper understanding of what is to follow. To begin with, one may, perhaps, entertain a doubt as to why it was written in the petition that the Fathers were prompted to come to China by the fame and the glory of the Chinese Empire, when their real motive for coming was to spread the Gospel. It must be understood that the Kingdom of China is closed to all foreigners, save to the three classes of people to whom the law grants an entrance. First, there are those who come annually, and of their own accord, from neighboring kingdoms, to offer tribute to the King of China. This causes no worry or concern to the Chinese, because China is not bent upon conquest. Secondly, there are those who do not wish to be looked upon as paying tribute but, moved by the vast extent of the Chinese Kingdom, come to honor the King, as being the leader and the greatest of all kings. These people come in search of wealth and fortune, under the lying pretext that they were sent in by the kings of their own native countries. Such are the Saracen merchants who appear from time to time from the west, and in whose company, some few years past, one of our Lay Brothers set out from the kingdom of the Mogors in search of China, and proved to the world that it was identical with Cathay. The third class is made up of those who are moved by the fame of the great empire, and come here to establish a permanent residence, attracted, as the Chinese think, by their reputation for virtue. Formerly there were many such, but now the Chinese are not as attractive as they imagine. The Missionary Fathers work in China as belonging to this third class, so as to be within the law, and also because those belonging to the two former classes are inevitably sent back to their own countries. Moreover, while here, those of the second class are treated more like cattle than like legates, because Imperial China has no desire whatsoever to contract alliances with other kingdoms. It is under the third title, which is perhaps less real than assumed or appropriated, that the Fathers are permitted to remain in China and their brethren allowed to come in, and yet is it not to be thought that they conceal the purpose for which they came, namely, to preach the Gospel. Everyone who has anything to do with them is aware of this, and their Magistrate friends protect themselves with this same legal pretext, in order to retain them in the kingdom.

Another thing that needs explanation here is the Chinese system of administration. China is a monarchy, in which everything depends upon the fiat of the King, and his decision on any question may be had only after the submission of written documents. Such documents as are not approved are merely put aside. Such as are approved for further consideration, he sends once, and then a second time, to the highest Magistrates in the kingdom, for them to advise him of the most becoming thing to do. They are then returned for his approbation, and he seldom differs from their judgment. This system will be more clearly presented in the continuation of our narrative.

Father Pantoia's request was written in the form and style required for the occasion, and was authorized ‑‑ith the proper seals. In such cases one must scrupulously observe a number of such requirements. Before these requests can be presented to the King, they must be identified and approved of by one of the high Magistrates, who is free to send them on or to reject them, as he sees fit. This is true for all reports to the crown, excepting those that come from the Royal Inspectors, who are free at all times to send reports to the King, without anyone's approbation.

Fearing that his effort might meet with some obstacle at the very outset, Father Pantoia, through the influence of the Chief Inspector, arranged with the Chancellor of Documents to have his petition forwarded to the King on the same day on which it was received, in fact, at the very moment of its reception. According to custom, the one making the request must present a copy of it to each of the Magistrates whose duty it is to know the content of the petition. This was done, and a copy was given to each of the two Mandarins, who at that time occupied the exalted position of Colao. One of these was a native of the Province of Fuquian. Before he reached his present high post, he was on very familiar terms with the Fathers, as a judge in Nankin, and since his promotion to his present dignity, he had twice entertained Father Ricci, at his home in Pekin. On reading the petition, he seemed to be deeply affected over the death of Father Ricci, whom he repeatedly recalled, attaching the most laudatory titles to his name. With reference to the petition, he said that this great man deserved more than was being asked for, and that he was worthy of a temple containing a statue. This is the customary tribute to a public benefactor. He then went on to explain that there was no Chinese law, nor any precedent, upon which a foreigner could base a request for a place of burial, but, as he added, he would give the request his immediate attention, to see if he could think up some way of having it granted. He communicated this to the Fathers through one of his subaltern judges, not being able to call upon them in person, because of illness. This was done with a purpose, because he wished to favor their cause. It is a general custom in the royal court, for one who is intent upon promoting the cause of a friend, to sedulously avoid his company, so as to prevent any suspicion of venality.

With the cause thus far advanced, the Fathers devoted their time to prayer, at home, awaiting the decision of the King, which should be announced within three days. Undoubtedly, when the petition was presented to the King, He who holds the hearts of kings in His hand, influenced the heart of this particular sovereign, by recalling to his memory the gifts he had received from the Fathers, and the presence of the portable clock, which he never left out of his sight. He sent their request together with others to the Calao, already mentioned, for him to pass upon it, according to custom. This the Calao did, immediately, and forwarded it to the particular tribunal that had charge of such affairs. Three days later it was returned, as approved, to the Magistrate who first sent it to the King, and whose duty it was to determine the particular council to which such a petition to the throne should be referred.

The governing body of the Kingdom of China is made up of six councils, or royal courts, namely, the Courts of Magistrates, Rites, Finance, Public Works, Military Affairs, and the Court of Criminal Procedure. The Magistrate holding the petition of the Fathers decided that since it concerned a gift to be given by the King, it should be referred to the Court of Finance, so he forwarded it to this court for their consideration. The Fathers were not too pleased with this, because there was no Magistrate or Judge in this court well enough known to them to promote their cause. Father Pantoia spoke about this to the Chief Court Inspector, who said he would endeavor to have the petition transferred from the Court of Finance to the Court of Rites, in which there were several Magistrates who were particularly friendly with the Fathers.

Legally this case could be handled by the Court of Rites, because this court had jurisdiction over whatever pertained to foreigners. The Chief Inspector was successful in his endeavor and the case was accordingly transferred. Apart from the help of Heaven, it was beginning to look as though they might also be favored with some human assistance. To this end, Father Pantoia called upon two of the judges to whom the petition had been forwarded, by the Chief Magistrate of the Court of Rites, and brought them a little gift of some books which the Fathers had just published, in Chinese, and also a copy of the world map. They were both unknown to the Fathers, and yet, they approved of the petition and liberally promised to promote it. One of them, when he came to return the visit, as was usually done, said that his response to the King would be in keeping with what they desired, and that, not only because of his esteem for them, but because their petition was strongly recommended to him by the Calao, who was his cousin. This, of course, greatly increased their feeling of assurance, for a successful issue for their undertaking.

The convert Leo went to call upon the Chief Magistrate of the Court of Rites, a very earnest man, of considerable distinction because of the dignity of his high office and of his literary fame, and one who was highly respected for his honest and upright way of life. Leo talked with him at length about the position of the Fathers, as he might have talked to his former teacher, knowing that the outcome of the case was now wholly dependent upon his decision, with the result that he was liberal in promising, and afterwards carried out his promise in full.

In the meantime, while they were quietly awaiting the decision of the Court of Rites, there was one member of the court who was endeavoring to persuade his colleagues, that it would be sufficient for the Fathers if they were assigned part of one of the pagan temples, wherein they could live, together with the pagan ministers. Doctor Leo informed the Fathers of this, while he was en route from the royal court to take over his duties elsewhere. He also enclosed letters addressed to the judge who had made the suggestion, in which he asked him to have no scruple about promoting the cause of the Fathers, and not to think for a minute that they could have anything in common with the ministers of the pagan temples, whose life and education and doctrine and learning, were so vastly different from that of the Fathers. This caused the petitioners no little concern. It looked like a decided setback that would not only be wholly out of keeping with their way of life, if it ever came to pass, but most unbecoming with respect to Christian practice. It was not long before they learned that their fear was unfounded and that something quite in keeping with their hope was under way, which would enable them to breathe more easily.

The petition and the reply to it were returned to the King within a month, and considering the customary delays in Chinese negotiations, this may be considered as being unusually prompt. It was returned from the Tribunal of Rites and written as follows. The first part of the document was a word-for-word copy of the original petition, and the rest of it, as given here, was the court's evaluation of the request it contained.

"According to Your Majesty's command, this matter has been adjudicated by the Tribunal to which it pertains. When it was brought to my attention, I searched the constitutions and discovered a law to the following effect: If one of the foreigners who are accustomed to visit this country should die in the course of the journey, if he is a foreign subject, for foreign kings have also come here, and he has not as yet arrived at the royal court, our representative in the province in which he dies, shall grant him a place of burial, and erect a stone on his grave, properly engraved to indicate who he was, and why he came here. Another section of the law reads to this effect:

That if the deceased had already visited the royal court and had not as yet received the remuneration which is customarily granted by the Crown, the Mayor of the royal city will defray the expenses of his funeral. If he had already received a benefit of the royal munificence, the cost of his interment shall be taken therefrom.

"Now, although Matthew Ricci did not come here as the legate of a foreign king, he did come here, prompted by the renown of this kingdom, from a very remote part of the world, and for some years, up to his recent death, brought on by premature old age, he was supported by the royal treasury. His body could not possibly be taken back to his far off native land. Are not his mortal remains, still unburied, full worthy of your commiseration? If so, is it not wholly just that I should favor the request of Diego Pantoia, and search the laws just quoted for an interpretation pertinent to his petition? I would therefore urge that he be granted the plot of ground he asked for, to be used as a grave, which if granted, would mean still another benefit added to the accumulated favors already granted by Your Sovereign Majesty.

At first sight of this document, I saw and I fully realized that it is your pre-eminent renown, as well as the fame of your rule that has attracted the attention of the most distant kingdoms and regions. In our day, as has never happened in former years, the subjects of these foreign countries come here, allured and induced as they are by the just laws and the pleasing customs of your administration, as witness the example of this same Matthew Ricci and his companions. These men finally came to the royal court, after completing a journey of immensurable distance. They presented Your Royal Majesty with gifts, in return for which they have been continual recipients of your royal largess for a period of years. This same Matthew Ricci was covetous only of learning, and he accomplished much by constant application, as is evident in the publication of his celebrated books. He died only recently, and who is there who would not be moved to pity by the fact that his body, so remotely distant from his native land, still lies unburied? Now his companion, Diego Pantoia, is asking for a little land for his grave. True he did not come as a legate from his own country, but he lived here for so long a time under the benign patronage of Your Majesty, that he wanted to be considered as one of our own people. Since it was your generosity that supported him while he lived, and his companions as well, who could imagine that his body would be left on the earth without sepulture. Diego Pantoia, and the companions left to him, believe that life and death should be alike in this, namely, that both the living and the dead should be included in kingly clemency.

"Therefore, in full agreement with his other postulates, on behalf of this Tribunal, I most humbly request that Your Majesty issue an order from this Tribunal to the Mayor of the royal city, to find an unoccupied temple, and also a lot of land for the burial of Matthew Ricci, the temple to serve as a habitation for Diego Pantoia and his companions, wherein they may dwell, in the free observance of their professed law, honoring the God of Heaven, and praying to their God for the well-being of Your Royal Majesty. It is indeed worthy of Your greatness to include the dry wood (the dead) in your charity, and to extend your benevolence to the stranger from afar. This, indeed, will stimulate their growing interest to spread the fame of your kingdom far and wide, for all time to come. Though I dare not, nor would I presume, to state anything on my own authority, I do hereby render the enclosed information, so that Your Majesty may decide upon it in such manner as may be most beneficial to the interests of Your Royal Highness. The thirty-eighth year of Vanlie, the twenty-third of the fourth moon. Thus far the petition."

After the King had reviewed this document, he sent it on the following day to the Calao, for his opinion, according to routine procedure. He then sent it back to the King, with his full approval, who, with his own hand signed it, Xi, meaning, let it be done, or, so it is approved. This final reply was made on the third day, and that terminated the whole affair. As was to be expected, the Fathers offered abundant thanks to God, for the accomplishment of a cause, by which the preaching of the Gospel was finally established in the Kingdom of China, and the grace of God was no less evident in the manner in which the King's mandate was expedited than it was in the process of securing it. The difficulties that arose in the execution of the order, disappeared as if the head officials of the entire royal court had been influenced from Heaven to co-operate in patronizing a few poor foreigners.

With this much happily accomplished, the Fathers turned their attention to thanking those who had been instrumental in securing so great a benefit from the King. Father Diego Pantoia, who was expert in this kind of work, made several copies of an exquisite carving of sun, moon, and star dials, together, on single pieces of ivory. Their poverty would not permit him to use more precious material, but the ivory carvings were novel and very pleasing, and the desire on the part of the Magistrates to learn how to read the dials, gave the Fathers an entrance into their homes and into private studies. These visits gave them prestige with the Magistrates and an opportunity for bringing their cause to a timely conclusion.

The Calao, himself, was particularly gracious toward Father Pantoja, even inviting him into his museum. He was so apt in his study of the dials that he soon learned how to regulate the sun-dial, and found great pleasure in experimenting with it. Father Pantoja asked him if he would arrange with the Mayor of Pekin for the selection of a suitable plot of land. He did this and even more, as we shall presently see. The President of the Tribunal of Rites, to whom the final reply of the King was chiefly due, was not forgotten, when thanks and gifts were being considered. This man was so courteous in receiving the visit of Father Pantoja, and so attentive to him at his departure, that no Magistrate before him ever exceeded his benevolence, nor can others aspire to it.

When the Father went to visit this Magistrate, before he returned his decision on the petition to the King, to ask him to change certain things in his reply, which seemed to be somewhat detrimental to the future promulgation of the Gospel, he did not hesitate to take note of it. In fact, he said, "What you refer to is merely a formal and a solemn method of expression used by the Tribunals, which adds nothing to the document, nor subtracts anything from it. What Tribunal is there in the royal court," he added, "that does not know that the law you preach is both true and just? I have taken such interest in your cause, that the very highest favor you hope for may eventually be granted. And not only that, I have also written to the Mayor of the City of Pekin, in whose hands the affair now rests, asking him to find a place that will be to your liking. He and I are more than friends, we are like two brothers." The other judges of the Court of Rites, following the example of their chief, did not hesitate to honor the Fathers and to favor them as well. Not only the judges, but their clerks also, who are frequently more difficult to deal with, placed no obstacles in the way of the proceedings in the hope perhaps of secret remuneration. Thus it happened that this very important undertaking was successfully completed, at very little expense. The converts could scarcely restrain their joy, with the success attained. They were amazed at the attention given to the Fathers by so prominent a man as the Calao, and they said it was now very plain to them, that the whole affair was especially supervised by the good and the almighty God.

Having terminated his visits of obligation with this last event, Father Pantoia turned his attention to conciliating the Mayor of the city. He was unknown to the Fathers and there was some fear that he might not be particularly interested in their affairs. Again, however, He who holds the hearts of all men in His hands, rendered the Mayor, above all others, so favorable to the cause that he did not hesitate to incur the jealousy of the other dignitaries, nor, from that time on, the necessity of having to defend the Fathers against many attacks. He was so favorably affected by Father Pantoia's first visit that he generously promised to do all that was asked of him. It happened very fortunately, too, that while the Father was talking with him, letters arrived from one high Magistrate, and a request from another, asking him to favor the request of the Fathers. From these he learned of the great respect which the high dignitaries of the royal court entertained for the Fathers, with the result that his mind, already well disposed, was won over entirely to their interests. On the following day, and with considerable display of apparel, he sent his messengers to the Mission House, with a very worthwhile present, then he himself arrived shortly afterwards. From the time of that first visit he became so friendly that in subsequent calls, his visiting card, which according to custom was always presented, was signed, Your Servant, a courtesy which is only extended to equals and to intimates.

It happened by mere chance, just at that time, that one of the Magistrates, without whose seal the King's order could not be presented to the Mayor, having been nominated to his position only a few months before, but not as yet confirmed by the King, was still without an official seal. This absence retarded negotiations with the Fathers, and with many others as well. As advised by their Magistrate friends, the Fathers were at that time looking for a suitable place for the grave of Father Ricci, but they could find nothing to their liking. So they decided to leave the choice of a location to the Magistrates, trusting in the Lord that this would serve to free them from any unpopularity, as it actually did, when it became known that they had asked for a place from the King, and received it by order of the Magistrates.

While these activities were going on, and the whole affair seemed to be dragging on to an unnecessary length, much to their surprise, one of their friends in the Tribunal of Rites, wrote to them, saying that it was time to get in touch with the Mayor, because the King's order was to be delivered to him on the following day. They were somewhat astonished at this, and at a loss to understand the sudden and unexpected concession of this favor, when it was commonly known that the above mentioned Magistrate had not as yet been authorized to use his seal. Father Pantoia went to see the Calao, to remind him that their case was still pending, for fear it had happened to slip his memory in the midst of his many affairs, and to ask him to exert his authority with the Mayor. When the Father came into his presence, the Calao anticipated his request with the remark, "I have not forgotten your petition. Being somewhat fearful that it might be unduly delayed, I ordered that document, only, to be brought to me without a seal, and I sent it to the Mayor, with my personal recommendation for immediate action. However, my recommendation was scarcely necessary, because the Mayor is wholly bent upon favoring the cause, and holds the Fathers in very high esteem. Moreover, I have also talked over the case with one of my colleagues in the Tribunal, who must pass on it." He said all this in the presence of many bystanders, who were surprised at hearing it, almost as much as was Father Pantoia himself, upon whom it finally dawned, just where this unexpected favor had come from. May Heaven reward this man's benevolence some day, by granting him the light of faith.

Full and favorable letters recommending the cause to the Mayor, were also forthcoming from the Chief of the Tribunal of Rites, and the Mayor himself was not at all reluctant to receive requests from men of so high station, because their requests rendered them beholden to him, and also because he could fall back on their authority, if critics should arise to censure his action, as actually happened. That same day Father Pantoia went to visit the Mayor and brought him a little gift, which he had some difficulty in persuading him to accept.

On the following day, sitting in with his own tribunal, he ordered two of his subalterns, to whose offices the more intimate affairs of the people pertained, to send out investigators to locate a place that would be suitable for the grave in question, and to return a report to him, without delay. Father Pantoia found these subalterns to the Mayor very well inclined, when he went to visit them. Among the Chinese, inferior officers always think along the same lines as their superiors. The investigators who were sent out were told to go to the Mission House, to find out just what kind of a place the Fathers wanted, and the subalterns had been instructed before hand to follow the advice of the Fathers, as far as that was possible. After three or four days of search they designated four places, and asked the Fathers to come and inspect these sites, while pretending that they were intent upon purchasing a suburban home, to which they could retire for rest and study, as the Chinese frequently do. When they had seen them all, they could select the one they judged to be most suitable for their design.

Among the places selected there was a temple, that was formerly a suburban villa. It belonged to one of the high-stationed eunuchs of the royal palace, who for some crime or other was condemned to death. He was in prison at the time, awaiting the day of his execution, which the King had not as yet assigned. When this man realized that he had not only fallen from the good graces of the King, but was reduced to helpless extremities, in order to save his country home from spoliation, he had it converted into a temple, and gave it the attractive title, Rule of Benevolence. According to general practice in China, when a eunuch is degraded and sent to prison, his property belongs to the first to lay hold of it. It is against the law of the realm to erect a private temple, but many of the more influential eunuchs build such temples, with the connivance of the Magistrates, and these temples, like all others, are under the jurisdiction of the Tribunal of Rites. Thus it happened that the plan designed by the unfortunate eunuch to save his temple turned out to be the cause of his losing it. The Fathers were unaware of the fact that the eunuch was still alive when they selected his property. Had they known this, they would never have chosen it in preference to several other sites, but when they did discover it, they were no longer free to ask for another.

This country residence was wonderfully suited to their purpose. Since it was a temple only in name, but a villa in reality, there was only one temple minister in attendance. Once the Fathers decided upon the place, the investigators informed the subalterns. One of the subalterns then sent out a man to estimate the price of the property and to inquire of the guardians how much it was worth. This subaltern was probably looking forward to a sizable remuneration. His messenger returned, however, only to inform him that there could be no question of a price involved, concerning a gift from the Crown, and that he could not even make an inquiry about a price, because if the owner ever discovered what was being done, he would move heaven and earth to retain his villa. This, he assured him, would happen in the purchase of any temple, none of which were lacking guardians and owners. The subaltern in turn, who was more bent upon money than upon reasoning, told the man to obey his orders.

As the messenger went along, and not too happily, on his second errand, he happened, as it would seem by divine intervention, to see one of Father Pantoia's servants standing at the entrance to the home of a friendly Magistrate, and he stopped to tell him where he was going, for what purpose, and how unwillingly. The Father was calling on the Magistrate to discuss a question connected with the villa property, so the servant asked his friend if he would mind waiting for a few minutes, and then went into the house and told the whole story. Father Pantoia was no less surprised than the Magistrate, and immediately they both became suspicious of someone looking for a recompense. The Magistrate, who was a man of higher authority, ordered the appraiser to put off his errand until he had written to the Assistant Mayor, who had sent him out. He told the appraiser that he was personally interested in the affairs of the Fathers and that he would handle them as he would his own; also to inform his superior that as an Assistant to the Mayor, he should have nothing to say about the price of the property, which the Mayor himself would attend to, and that, as an assistant, he was commissioned by the Mayor to select a place, and for that only. The Assistant Mayor, being an inferior official, replied immediately and modestly saying he would do as directed. He said the same thing to Father Pantoia, who went directly to see him, and then to see the Mayor himself, to inform him of what had happened. As a result of this visit, the Mayor, in session with his council, wrote out the following direction: "It will not be necessary to pay a price for the temple known as, The Rule of Benevolence, because it belonged to a eunuch who has been condemned to death by the King. The Minister of Idols, dwelling there, is to vacate the place, and it is to be handed over immediately to Diego Pantoia and his companions."

Up to this point, the negotiations were supposed to have been carried on in strict secrecy, but before this latest decision of the Mayor was announced, some one or other of the clerks informed the relatives of the prisoner eunuch, that there was question of his temple being given over to the foreigners from the Great Occident, by order of the King. They were loath to believe this report, and hence they did nothing about it until the final decision of the Mayor was expressed. After the Mayor had spoken, the Fathers said a prayer of thanks for his pronouncement, in the belief that there was nothing more to be done for its confirmation, wholly unmindful, as they were, of the difficulties yet to be encountered before the affair was terminated. Father Pantoia thanked the Mayor, asked him to summon the custodian Minister of the temple and to inform him of his release from duty there. This was done without delay, and two sergeants were sent to inform the Minister to appear at the Mayor's office on the following day.

The sergeants set out with a written warrant, inscribed on a tablet, the usual form for such a summons, and on their way they met the Minister on the road, little dreaming of what they had in mind. They took him to the Mayor's palace where he remained until the next day, wondering what it was all about, and of what crime he was going to be accused. When he appeared, on his knees, before the Mayor, he was told to move out of the temple, and to find other living quarters, because the temple had been given over to Diego Pantoia and his companions, by order of the King, with the explanation that their religious belief was entirely different from his, and he would never be able to live a common life with them. He went away without saying a word, happy to escape the flogging he feared would result, if he had been accused of some serious crime. Without losing a moment, he went to the temple, on that same day, packed his belongings and disappeared.

On that same day also, the Fathers with some of their converts for company, took possession of the place. One can easily imagine how all this affected the imprisoned eunuch and his following. Some of them hastened to the villa and the Fathers told them that they had asked the King for a place, for the burial of one of their deceased companions, and that this place had been assigned to them by the Magistrates, of their own initiative, and without any prompting or begging for it. The King and the Magistrates had only to be mentioned, to turn them away, and they departed wondering whither they should turn for counsel in so desperate a situation. They were afraid that if they caused any trouble, it would redound to the extreme misfortune of the eunuch who was in prison, and this became evident when another eunuch came to the Fathers and said, he believed that they had taken over the villa by order of the Magistrates and that they had not seized upon it. He said he thought he was doing only what he had a right to do, by coming to talk with them, and he hoped they would not take it amiss. Father Pantoia told him that they had no reason to be offended, because they had in no way exceeded the bounds of reason. Time and the sense of loss helped to remove all fear from the eunuch's friends.

One day, having timed the occasion, when both of the Fathers were absent from the villa, a number of the lower class eunuchs, in small bands, invaded the place, and when they discovered the Lay Brother and some of the converts, who were left there to guard the house, they fell on their knees as a salutation to the foreign lords of the villa, although the so-called foreign lords were not there at the time. The ceremony of falling on the knees was like their ordinary gesture when honoring or calling upon the name of the King. "What else are the new owners lacking," they said, "other than a kingdom, when they are so powerful that they can take over the property of the eunuchs?" With this and a few other cynical compliments, they said that the temple had been given over by the King and the Magistrates, but not the furniture of the temple. Whereupon, they proceeded to remove much of the furnishings of the place, whether those present liked it or not, including several pieces of precious stone, which the Chinese value highly, because of its beauty. Many of them went away with the furniture they had seized, but some remained to talk with the Brother and the converts. "Tell me," said one of them to the Brother, "what is this mysterious potion possessed by your master, with which he so completely captivates the minds of so many men?" "My Master," the Brother replied, and the Brothers were in the habit of using that title here, when speaking of the Fathers, "My Master has virtue and education and books, and the law of the Most High God, which he preaches on all occasions, and really, there is no more powerful concoction than that for captivating the minds of the great." "Now," said the other, "since you are one of his disciples, why don't you tell him, and insist upon it, too, that he should ask the Magistrates for a bigger and a better temple than this one?" "You had better do the asking yourself," the Brother replied, "because it would not be in keeping with his reserve and his modesty to ask for something larger and more ornate. Whatever is given him by the King and the Magistrates, he considers to be the very best."

With these prudent remarks of the Brother, and with a rather long exhortation on the subject, made by one of the converts, who happened to be present, they seemed to be placated, and they went away without causing further trouble. As they were passing through an outer hallway in which there was an altar to the idols, one of them fell on his knees and began to talk to the principal statue. "Good-bye," he said, "and farewell for the last time. From now on I shall not be free to enter this hall, as I was formerly." Another one, venting his displeasure, spoke to the same idol, in somewhat plainer and probably more truthful terms. "You heap of stuff and mud," he began, and this particular monster was fashioned from clay and gilded over, "if you were not powerful enough to save your temple and to take care of yourself, how can I hope for anything from you? You are worthy of no honor, whatsoever, and so I shall neither thank you nor even recognize you." Some of the others said that this statue was formerly called after another idol, but its name had been changed, and the other idol was now taking vengeance on this one for having stolen its name. With these and smiliar reproaches to the idols, they finally departed from what was once their temple.

The tricks of the eunuchs were not as yet at an end. The condemned one saw that he was so thoroughly blocked, in all directions, from endeavoring to save anything in his own name, without risking the gravest danger, that he made over his villa to one of the high court eunuchs, who was a particular favorite of the queen dowager, on condition that he would make every effort to get it away from the foreigners. This fellow left nothing undone to cause trouble, working at first through the younger eunuchs, and trying by threats and menaces to take over the property, but all in vain. When he heard that the Fathers had reported their troubles to the King, and that they could not be made to give up the villa, except by an imperial edict, his activities became somewhat less troublesome. If this altercation with the eunuch did not remove all controversy relative to the villa, it served at least to prevent future trouble from those who were still disgruntled. The Mayor and the Chief of the Tribunal of Rites, each wrote out a separate edict, to be posted at the entrance of the villa property. The content of the Mayor's edict was somewhat as follows. He told how the King, in his great clemency, which embraced even the remotest of kingdoms, having conferred many benefits upon the Fathers, over a period of years, was now desirous of assuring them of his good will in the past, by a more recent expression of his benevolence. He was, therefore, giving them this property, as to subjects of his realm, to be used as a burial place for Matthew Ricci, and as a perpetual home for his companions, wherein to practice their own religion, and to pray for the life and safety of the King and of his mother, and for the peace and the welfare of the entire kingdom. Fearing, however, that someone might cause further disturbance, the Mayor forbade anyone to enter the property without permission of the Fathers, or to molest them in any way, under penalty of being arrested, bound, and brought into his court, where severe judgment would be administered. The edict of the President of the Tribunal of Rites was couched in similar sentiments.

These edicts sufficed to repress the insolence of some complaining critics, but they were not taken in good part by the petulant eunuchs. They still had two batteries in reserve, with which they hoped to breach the defenses erected against them. The first of these was the influence of the major-domo eunuch of the royal court. At that time when the King saw no one on business of any kind, nearly all negotiations of the realm were carried on by the court eunuchs. One of these was the King's associate and another was almost his substitute in state affairs. The eunuch competitors for the villa influenced this second courtier to send a letter to the Mayor of Pekin, in which he arrogantly and violently accused him, among other things, of robbing the eunuchs of the beautiful villa and giving it over to foreigners. The Mayor paid no attention to this letter, nor would he even honor it with a reply; instead, he returned a copy of the King's grant and of the mandate sent to him by the Tribunal of Rites. When the eunuch saw these, he sent back a letter on the following day asking pardon for his error, and saying that he had not known of the King's grant. The Mayor, himself, told this to the Fathers, and advised them to call on the eunuch and to bring him a copy of all the books they had written in Chinese, on Christianity, on the various virtues, and on the science of mathematics.

These were all collected, the next day, and put aside, together with a beautiful statue of the Blessed Virgin, a sun-dial, done in ivory, and other novelties which the Fathers had brought with them.

On the day of their visit, they were first admitted to an outer chamber and while waiting there, to be introduced, they showed the gifts to the other eunuchs, who were curious to see them, and as they were principally attracted by the statue of the Blessed Mother, the Fathers took occasion to give them an instruction on the Christian faith. After what seemed to be an endless period of waiting, the eunuch sent out a messenger to say that he was too busy to be interrupted at that time, and to ask them to send in their requests in writing, by the messenger, for him to read. But they replied, in return, urging him not to send away foreigners from a distant land, who were making their first call to see him. With that he invited them in, dressed as they were in the garb of the Chinese licentiate. As he was about to receive them, he seated himself in a chair and waited for them to fall on their knees, as others did when they came into his presence. However, they merely stood erect, where they were, because they owed this eunuch no more deference than they did the high Magistrates, and when he saw that his gesture had failed, he stood up and received them with the ceremonies which the Chinese observe when receiving their equals.

The conversation that followed was carried on, as they stood facing each other. The Fathers complained that because of the actions of some of the eunuchs, they were not permitted, up to that time, to enjoy the advantage of the liberality of the King, conferred by the authority of the Magistrates, and they asked him to interpose his influence to correct the situation. First he gave his reason for sending his letter to the Mayor, and then added that he was not aware of the King's desire, when he sent it. He assured them that no one would molest them in the future, and said that there was no question of calling into doubt any statute of a high tribunal, proceeding from the generous liberality of the King. He guaranteed the security of their property, for the burial of their companion, and also as a residence, in which they could make the most of the royal munificence. After thanking him, they were unable to persuade him to accept the gifts they offered. He examined the presents and he was particularly attracted by the statue of the Blessed Virgin, but he refused to take anything as a thank offering, as the Chinese do at times and without any breach of propriety.

The second means of attack upon the possession of the villa property, which the contending eunuchs held in reserve, was bolstered up by having recourse to the King's mother. They had saved this for a last onslaught, when their cause had become desperate. This elderly lady, as has been recorded, was an intense devotee of the idols. The eunuch who was pleading the cause, one of the few who enjoyed her favor, came to her one day and complained that a temple of the gods, worth many thousands in gold, had been taken from him and given over to certain aliens who had no reverence for the idols and actually threw them into the water or burned them up, and he asked her if she would speak to the King about it. To which she is reported to have answered: "Even though the temple was worth much more than you say, what is the value of the place in comparison with the bounty of the King? It really would not be worth while speaking to him about it. Certainly, if the foreigners you mention were to send in a complaint to the King, about the eunuch under sentence, that would mean the end of his life." This was enough to silence the complaining favorite, who dared not go any further, and it also put an end to the hope and to the machinations of the rest of his class.

It still remained, however, for the Enemy of the human race to carry on. It was mentioned, some time previous, that the case of the villa property pertained for judgment to the Tribunal of the Treasury, and that the Fathers had had it transferred to the Tribunal of Rites. It was therefore in order for the Tribunal of Rites to inform the Tribunal of the Treasury that the property was donated by the King, as a gift, and that consequently it should be declared free from future taxation and its title removed from the taxable records. The case was, therefore, returned to the Chief of the Bureau of Finance, from whom it had been taken and he, probably feeling that he was losing some slight personal profit, quite in keeping with his reputation, decided upon the risky procedure of reopening the whole affair. He sent a letter to the Assistant Mayor who had formerly commissioned his men to select a location, demanding an explanation of his reason for assigning such a magnificent property to the Fathers. This letter was sent as a letter patent, bearing the official seal of his office, but it had no effect upon the subaltern Mayor. He merely sent a copy of the document to Father Pantoia, by one of his court clerks, to ask him if he wanted anything included in the reply to it. The Father said he thought it better not to answer it at all, but to assume the attitude that the one who sent the letter would do well to see that it was recalled.

Father Pantoia then went to call on the Chief of the Treasury, and explained to him that the King had given them not only a place for the tomb, but also a residence as a dwelling place, and if it happened to be somewhat imposing, then that was in keeping with the dignity of the imperial largess, and not with the dignity of the Fathers. Then he asked him to recall the document he had issued. His host was no little surprised at the confidence with which this request was made, and he told him that if he had any grievance to present, to hand it in, in writing to the Tribunal, which would be in session on the following day. With that, Father Pantoia left him and went to see another member of the same tribunal, with whom he was on friendly terms. He told him the whole story and, as this man was a friend of the author of the document, the Father asked him to advise the author not to be the only one to oppose the decisions of so many of the Magistrates, because no good could come from it, and if they took offense at his action, it might possibly result in considerable harm. This man did just what the Father had asked him to do, and evidently he did it very thoroughly. On the following day the Chief of the Exchequer, and author of the letter patent, sent a very courteous letter to Father Pantoja, promising to see to it that everything would be settled according to his wishes.

With Father Pantoia's reply there was sent along a little gift from their European novelties, and apparently the whole affair was brought to a close. Within a few days the letter in question was publicly recalled, and the royal treasury declared the property exempt from taxation, in perpetuum. This really signed the finis to a case which, as is fondly hoped, will go far to promote the glory of God, in the future.

Now that the Fathers had entered into the peaceful possession of their inheritance, they went all together to offer thanks to the King, observing the same ceremonies that were practiced when they first came to the royal court to thank the sovereign for his grant of a subsidy, and which need no repetition here. Finally, with all this trouble brought to a satisfactory conclusion, the tenure of the property was further confirmed and secured by three more documents, issued by three other tribunals, which are not named here because they are not known in Europe. Suffice it to say that within the royal court, these three titles strike terror because of their reputation for severity.

Not content with the favors he had already granted of his own accord, the Mayor of the City of Pekin, decided to honor the name of Father Ricci, and through him to honor his companions. In keeping with a Chinese practice already described in the annals of the Nankin Mission, he sent out to the villa, a plaque engraved in large letters, to be placed on the tomb of Father Matthew, and the presentation of it was made with considerable display. A large group of his followers carried it in parade through the principal streets of the city, with drums beating and trumpets sounding. The plaque was very attractive because of its artistic design and of the beauty of its large lettering. It was donated in perpetual memory of his friendship with so distinguished a personage as Father Matthew Ricci. The inscription, as such inscriptions are usually designed, consisted of four letters: Mo, Y, Lie, Yen. These four brief but very significant syllables mean, "To one who attained renown for justice, and wrote illustrious books." Beneath this in smaller letters was written, "To Matthew Ricci, from the Great Occident, erected by Hoam Kie Sci, Mayor of the Royal City of Pekin."

The villa is situated about three-fifths of a mile from one of the city gates, in an open country space, such as the eunuchs of the royal court select for villas or for places of burial. The house is solidly built in brick and of excellent workmanship, the columns being all of wood, after Chinese custom. They do not favor stone pillars, even in the building of palaces for the king or for the magistrates. The residence was built about thirty years ago and promises to last for a long time.

Without going into detail about its construction, one can get an idea of its magnificence from the fact that it cost forty thousand gold pieces to build it, a sum which may not seem large in Europe, but is sufficient to constitute a fortune in China. The place is secluded and wonderfully adapted for retirement and study. In fact it was to this end that the Magistrates, through whom it was obtained, were looking forward, namely: that the Fathers might have a place apart, removed from the noise and the tumult of the city, where they could translate European books into Chinese; something that many had been calling for. This custom of retiring to some quiet Tusculum for study is more common in China than it is in Europe.

To return to the tomb of Father Ricci, the Chinese frequently keep the bodies of their deceased in the home, hermetically sealed in a coffin, and sometimes for years, until they have built or discovered a suitable place for burial. The casket is covered over with a shiny bituminous substance, rendering it absolutely impervious to gases. The casket containing the body of Father Ricci was kept for almost a year from the time of his death, beside the altar of the domestic chapel. When the Fathers came into the peaceful possession of the villa, the body was taken there, to await the preparation of a cemetery, according to ecclesiastical directions, and the installment of a chapel. The transfer to the villa was made without the usual display and pomp exhibited by the Chinese on such occasions, more suited to a triumphal parade than to a funeral procession. Such a demonstration, moreover, would have been out of keeping with the poverty of the Mission, to say nothing of the observance of religious decorum. The transfer of the body from the Mission Center to the new residence took place during the morning hours and was attended by a large following of the converts, carrying lighted candles, in procession behind a large cross, borne beneath a canopy. The coffin was placed in a room adjacent to the house chapel and stationed, after Chinese fashion, to accommodate those who would come to pay their last respects to the departed.

Father Nicolo Longobardo, Superior of the entire Mission, arrived shortly after the transfer, the burial having been deferred to await his coming. Under his direction, the first Christian cemetery in China was designed. At one end of the garden, a brick chapel was built, hexagonal in shape and in vaulted design. From either side of the chapel a semi-circular wall was extended forming an enclosure that was to serve as a burial place for members of the Mission. In the middle of the plot there were four cypress trees, which are emblems of mourn-

ing with the Chinese, as with others, and which were so aptly placed,
that one might think they were planted long ago, to shade the future
tomb of Matthew Ricci. After excavating a section of the earth, a brick
tomb was constructed in the excavation, of convenient size to contain
the casket. Strange to say, as it seemed by the design of Heaven, the
life-long antagonist of the idols who was being buried here, brought
down the idols with him, to their own last resting place. The statue
idol of the chief god of this former temple was broken up and crushed,
and used to make cement for the brick construction of Matthew Ricci's
tomb.

In the meantime, while the tomb was being built, the one-time
temple was being purged of its abominations, in order to transform it
into a church, dedicated to Christ the Saviour. In the main hall there
was a very large altar, made of stone and of brick, with a beautifully
paneled ceiling. As is customary in the temples, the color of the altar
was red. Private homes are forbidden to use this color. Over the middle of the altar there was seated a horrible looking monster in clay, but
gilded all over from head to foot. The Chinese called it Ti cam, and it
was supposed to preside over the earth, and especially over treasures.
It was their Pluto, with a scepter in its hand and a crown on its head,
like an earthly king. On either side of this main figure stood four of its
ministers, made of the same material. At the sides of the hall there
were two spacious tables and on each table statues of the five rulers of
the infernal regions. On the walls above the tables there were gro-
tesque paintings of these same rulers, each seated on his own throne of
judgment, dispensing sentences of condemnation to the lower regions,
to culprits guilty of the particular crimes that pertained to his jurisdiction for judgment. In front of these judges there were many demons, some horrible in appearance, and more terrible for the instruments of torture they used, than those already depicted. They were so
life-like that it would seem as if the demons themselves had taught
others how to paint them. The pitiable victims were being so cruelly
tortured by the punishments administered in the infernal regions, that
it frightened one just to look at them. Some were being roasted on iron
spits, others fried in boiling oil, some torn to pieces, others sawed in
two, some lacerated by mad dogs or pounded with hammers, and still
others writhing under various torments. The first of the five rulers was
the one to discover the various crimes, which they said he did by looking into a mirror, where they were supposed to be hidden. Then he
would dispatch the culprit to the court of another ruler, who sat in

judgment on that particular crime. One of these courts passed sentence upon men who, because of their crimes, had to suffer a transmigration of soul. Cruel men were turned into tigers, the lecherous into swine, and so for the different vices. Some who were less guilty were reduced from higher station to conditions of toil and poverty.

The doctrine of Pythagorean Metempsychosis is surprisingly widespread through the entire kingdom of China. Indeed, it would seem that the Devil had so built up these terror-striking images of Hades, that they actually incite to crime rather than prevent it, because, horrible as the punishments are represented to be, people are taught that they can be easily avoided, if they will devote themselves to the worship of idols, which is equivalent to saying: if they will add the greatest of sins to those of which they are already guilty. Painted on the wall also, there is a large balance scales, in one pan of which there is a man, laden down with every sort of crime, and in the other a prayer book of the idol-worshippers, which outweighs the whole accumulation of crime, indicating that if one reads this book, the punishment due for his crimes, no matter how great they be, will all be remitted. Represented as flowing through the middle of the infernal regions, there is a horribly colored river of torment, sweeping along innumerable victims. There are two bridges passing over the river; one of gold and one of silver. Those who have been particularly devout in worshipping the idols may pass over these bridges, wearing the insignia of the particular idols they cultivated, and they are led on by the ministers of these idols, under whose guidance they pass through the torments, unmolested, into verdant fields and pleasant groves.

On another wall there was a painting, representing infernal caves, full of fire and serpents and horrible demons, with one of the ministers of the idols coming through the bronze gates of a cave, rescuing his mother from the flames, despite all the devils resisting him. This was only one of many such outlandish scenes. And so it happens that the punishments which God has made known to men to prevent them from committing sin, and to withhold them from sin by a sense of fear, are used by the Devil, to destroy the souls of men, because this impostor enemy of the human race makes use of these same punishments to incite men to sin. He presumes to do more, and to permit his ministers to do more, than is done by a just God, the author of the punishment, by permitting sin without any retribution, or by pardoning from punishment for the most trivial reasons. As depicted in this temple, every penalty listed for any kind of sin had an inscription attached to it, reading: "Whoever calls upon the name of one or other idol, a thousand times, will be pardoned from this punishment." In this way, the Devil prompts men to sin, by teaching how simple and easy it is to avoid any penalty for it.

After removing them from their altars in the former temple, the clay idols were reduced to dust and the wooden ones consigned to the flames. The family servants were particularly energetic in this destruction, endeavoring to outdo one another in a contest of demolition, in which they were urged on by the hope of profit to be discovered. The Chinese generally fill the empty stomachs of the idols with medals and semi-precious stones, which the servants, as though contending in a game, were seeking to discover, in dismembering the images. This annihilation of the idols became known to the former owners of the place, but realizing that there was no hope of recovering the property, they decided to do nothing about it. In fact, their alleged interest in the place as a domicile of the idols was only a pretext for recovering the estate, and not a prompting to protect the statue-gods.

The altar of the gods was dismantled and the pictures on the walls were whitewashed. A place was then prepared, above a new altar, for a picture of Christ the Saviour, beautifully painted by one of the Lay Brothers, since he had come to the new residence. In it Christ is sitting on a magnificent throne in the center, with angels hovering above and the apostles standing below, on either side, listening to his teaching.

With this much accomplished, the Feast of All Saints was designated as the day for the burial of Father Ricci and for the consecration of the church. On the eve of the feast the picture of Christ, in a gilded frame, was put in place, where idols formerly stood, and the proper worship of the one true God established, in place of idolatry. On the day appointed, all the converts were present, with lighted candles and incense to add to the solemnity. First, the Mass of the day was celebrated, with an organ and other musical instruments playing, and with as much display as could be arranged. When this Mass was over, the casket was brought into the church, the Office of the Dead was recited, and this was followed by the funeral Mass, at which a eulogy was delivered.

The procession to the tomb was headed by the most distinguished converts, bearing the casket, and the others followed, weeping and praying, in a solemn funeral line. On arrival at the tomb, the casket was placed at the entrance to the hexagonal chapel, in which another painting of Christ the Saviour had been installed. The prayers were read at the grave and the coffin was lowered into place in the tomb. The grief and sorrow of all present was very evident, as though they were mourning the departure of their father. Doctor Paul was especially affected. Over and above his attitude toward the Fathers and toward the Christian religion, which was as natural as if he had been born and brought up in Europe, this man was particularly devoted to Father Ricci. Weeping and in deep grief, a man of high station and dignity, as he was, as a last sad expression of his friendship, he could not refrain from taking hold of the ropes to assist in reposing his friend in his last resting place. Before dispersing, the converts did not forget their devotional compliments of bowing and kneeling, as is their wont, before the picture of Christ and at the tomb, after which the Fathers thanked them for honoring the ceremonies with their presence, and then all retired. For some days following there were gatherings of the pagan friends of the Mission, who came to pay their respects to the departed, so many indeed that it was necessary for one of the Fathers to remain on duty to receive them.

Besides the public church and the funeral chapel, the Fathers erected another altar, dedicated to the Blessed Virgin, in fulfillment of a solemn promise. They had obligated themselves to this at the very beginning of the negotiations, by making this promise of an altar dedicated to the Mother of God, in order to solicit her assistance and her patronage. And it would seem, indeed, that this was not done without direction from above, because every major success accomplished during that time, and following their promise, took place on some feast day of the Blessed Mother. With that promise fulfilled, they had two Chinese written characters inscribed on the architrave of the main entrance to the building, reading, "Royal Munificence," a title held in high esteem by the Chinese, higher in fact than is appreciated by Europeans.

As the news of all that had happened here was gradually spreading about, many became interested in seeing the place. All those who came to visit were delighted with what they saw, and seeing God adored here, they carried away a new idea of their Creator, instilled by the picture of Christ, and enlarged by their conversation with the Fathers. Here ends the story of this all important episode of the Mission annals; a development which we fondly hope will go far toward the future spread of Christianity.

Although the King's permission to teach the Gospel freely, to which the Fathers were looking forward, was not forthcoming, their position will be readily understood by any one who has a knowledge of the many fetters clasped upon this unfortunate people, living under the tyranny of the Enemy of the human race. He will also realize that something important was accomplished in this latest acquisition, and perhaps something more important than anything done during the long and difficult struggle of the thirty years previous. This, indeed, because the honor paid to the founder of the Mission, was not only a firm confirmation of the entire missionary expedition, but the very recognition on the part of the King and the Magistrates, of the purpose of this new residence, and of the profession of Christianity therein, was almost equivalent to their approbation of the Christian law.

Who is not surpised to learn that the King of China donated a home and a place of burial to poor foreigners? This privilege was never before granted to an extern, and it is accorded only rarely to the highest Magistrates, who have been distinguished for public service. Who will not wonder at hearing that these same foreigners demolished pagan idols and tore down their altars, not only under the eyes of the capital city, but in view of the entire realm, with the knowledge of the royal court and of the Queen Mother herself, with the approbation of high tribunals, and of the whole Senate of the Magistrates, and then replaced the idols with pictures of Christ the Saviour and of the Blessed Mother. What could be more amazing than that they prayed at their own altar for the well-being of the King, at the King's own request, and that by his own wish, his name was inscribed upon that altar.

Finally, it must be evident that this whole history was wrought under the guidance of Divine Providence, as appears from the narrative, recounting, as it were, so many miracles in one great miracle. This is something readily realized, not only by the Fathers of the Mission, who understood the psychology of this kingdom, but also by their converts, their friends, the pagans, and even their enemies. When one stops to realize how the high Magistrates held out against their own colleagues, and against their own people, without any remuneration, or any hope of reward, and refused to rest until the Fathers were in secure possession of the property granted to them, he must conclude that all this was accomplished, not through human industry alone but with the assistance of the One who governs human hearts, and all things else, by the mere expression of His will.

Nor should it be forgotten that Father Matthew Ricci, the author and the prime mover of this whole expedition, was first to find a resting place in death within this kingdom, and to secure the same for his companions. Those who had died before in this field of labor were buried in the community cemetery of the College of Macao, within the confines of the kingdom, but on a coastal island. And so, those who still labor in this vineyard, including your narrator, will not only lay down their lives here, but will leave their bodies as well, as a testimony to this people and to the rest of the world.

GENERAL INDEX

Second and subsequent spellings are identifications from D'Elia's Fonti Ricciane.

*=Confer Chinese Index.

A.

Abacus, Chinese, 231
Abdula (assumed name of Goës), 500
Abdula Chan, 503
Academic Bachelors, 34; dress of, 34; honors, 47
Academic degrees, 26
Academies, literary, 47; royal, 37
Accents, in speaking Chinese, 27; marks for, invented by Jesuits, 315
Achabar, 500   King of Mogor
Aconsersec, 509   Aconterzec
Acsu, 509
Acting and actors, 23
Administration, Chinese system of, 41 sq., 570; public, 47 sq.
Administrators, 43 sq.
Admiral, The Grand of Canton, 197
  *Haitu
Affinity and marriage, 76
Age, coming of, year, 76
Agehanem, 502   Hagghanum
Agiasi, 508   Hagiasiz
Aingharan, 503   Aingheran
Albuquerque, Giovanni, Bishop of Goa, 118
Alceghet, 509
Alchemists, 90
Alchemy, 90
Alexander VI, Pope, 172
Almanacs, 83
Almeida, Antonio, S.J., 175 sq., 195, 224, 235; death of, 240
Aloes, 18
Alphabet, Japanese, 29; none in Chinese, 29
Alvarez, Francesco, 120

*Ama, 129
Ambassadors, of foreign countries, how treated, 379, lodgings of, 379
Amidabu, 98
Ancestor worship, 462
Anchorets, Chinese, 267
Annals of the King, 50
Annuities, 46
*Ansam, 140, 141, 172, 239
Ansan, 196, 554; cf. Ansam
Antiques, 79; counterfeiters of, 79
Apostle, Bartholomew, 98
Apostles, 98
Aquaviva, Claudio, S.J., 179, 296
Aramuth, 513
Architecture, 19
*Arequeiram, 12
Aristocracy, Chinese, 41, 45
Arithmetic, 30
Arms, forbidden, 58
Army, Chinese, as bondsmen, 89
Arrocia, Giovanni, de, S.J., 355   de Roccia, de Rocha
Art, of painting in oil, 22
Arts, liberal, 26
Assessors, 48
Astrolabes, 330, 398
Astrologers, 85
Astrology, 31
Astronomers, Chinese, 31; of the royal court of Pekin, 32
Astronomical instruments, 30, 31; Ricci's, 169
Astronomy, 30
Athec, 501
Auguries, 85
Augustinians, 180

H.

I.

CHINESE INDEX

D = D'Elia, "Fonti Ricciane"
Y = Lien-Sheng Yang, "Topics In Chinese History."

Column 1, Manuscript
Column 2, Modern spelling

A.

Ama	A-ma	阿 媽		129
Ansam	Hsiang-shan	香 山		140,141, 172,239
Ansan	cf. Ansam			
Arequeiram	pin-lang	檳 榔	(D.I,p.18)	12

B.

Betre	pin-lang yeh	檳榔葉	(D.I,p.18)	12

C.

Cabacondono	Kampakudono	關白殿		260
Cambaco	Kampaku	關 白		229
Canceu	Kan-chou	甘 州		262,264, 514
Cancian	Kan-hsien	贛 縣		282
Canton	Kuang-tung	廣 東		5,128,254, 262
Cechiam	Chekiang	浙 江		317
Cechian	cf. Cechiam			240,266, 282,305, 397
Cequian	cf. Cechiam		(Y.p.25)	145,176
Ceu	Chou	州		52
Chaifamfu	K'ai-feng-fu	開封府	(Y.p.25)	107,109

F.

Falanci	Fo-lang-chi	佛郎機		128
Fon	Feng (Ch'i)	馮(琦)	(D.II,p.156)	391
Fu	Fu	府	(Y.p.24)	9,52
Fuchian	Fukien	福 建		267,304, 379,571
Fumiam	Feng-yang	鳳 陽	(D.II,p.162)	394
Fumo-Can	Feng Mu-kang	馮慕岡 (馮應京)		447
Fumochan	cf. Fumo-Can			394
Fuquiam	Fukine	福 建		35
Fuquian	cf. Fuquiam			174,136, 268
Fusce	Yü-shih	玉 石		382

G.

Guam	Wang	王	(Y.p.24)	43,285,297
Guam-puon	Wang P'an	王 泮	(D.I,p.198)	145
Guer-Pim	Wei-ping	圍 屏		194

H.

Haien	Hsien	縣		549
Hainam	Hai-nan	海 南	(Y.p.24)	8
Hainan	c. Hainam			254,297
Hai-tao	Hai-tao	海 道		133,139
Haitu	cf. Hai-tao			171
Hamceu	Hang-chou	杭 州		316 sq. 397
Hamcheu	cf. Hamceu		(Y.p.25)	108
Han	Han	漢		6,7
Hancian	Han-shan	憨 山	(D.II,p.187)	404
Hancian	Hang-chou	杭 州		554
Hanlin Academy	Han-lin-yüan	翰林院		328,399
Hanlinien	cf. Hanlin Academy			50

L.

MATTHEW RICCI was born in Macerata, in the Papal States, Oct. 6th, 1552. He entered the Society of Jesus in Rome, Aug. 15th, 1571, where he made his philosophical and theological studies. Here, he also studied under Christopher Clavius, perhaps the most noted mathematician of his day.

Ricci arrived in Goa in September, 1578, and four years later went to Macao, in preparation for the China Mission. During his twenty years in China (1583-1610) by means of his revelations in the sciences, his world map, his corrections of the Chinese calendar and his Chinese writings, he changed the ideas of an entirely secluded nation relative to the outside world. Ricci introduced China to Europe and Europe to China, and founded the first permanent Christian Missions in the Celestial Empire. As a high Mandarin, his work was subsidized by the Emperor of China, who also donated a plot of ground for Ricci's burial and a palace residence as a home for his successors on the China Mission.

LOUIS J. GALLAGHER, S.J. Born in Boston, July 22nd, 1885. Entered the Society of Jesus Aug. 15th, 1905; Ordained 1920; Head Master Xavier High School, N. Y. City, 1921-22; Assistant Director of Papal Relief Mission to Russia, 1922-23; Diplomatic Courier for the Vatican, to transport the relics of Blessed Andrew Bobola from Moscow to Rome, 1923; Dean, College of Arts and Sciences, Georgetown University, 1924-26; Assistant to Provincial, New England Province of the Society of Jesus, 1926-1932; President, Boston College, 1932-37; Co-founder of The Institute of Social Order, 1941-43; Author of, "The Test Heritage" ('38), "The Life of Saint Andrew Bobola" ('39), "The China That Was" ('42), "Episode on Beacon Hill" ('50); Archivist of the New England Province of the Society of Jesus; Lecturer and Writer.